RSF: The Russell Sage Foundation
Journal of the Social Sciences

*A Half Century of Change in the
Lives of American Women*

VOLUME 2 • NUMBER 4 • AUGUST 2016

RSF: The Russell Sage Foundation Journal of the Social Sciences   ISSN 2377-8261

The Russell Sage Foundation

The Russell Sage Foundation, one of the oldest of America's general purpose foundations, was established in 1907 by Mrs. Margaret Olivia Sage for "the improvement of social and living conditions in the United States." The foundation seeks to fulfill this mandate by fostering the development and dissemination of knowledge about the country's political, social, and economic problems. While the foundation endeavors to assure the accuracy and objectivity of each book it publishes, the conclusions and interpretations in Russell Sage Foundation publications are those of the authors and not of the foundation, its trustees, or its staff. Publication by Russell Sage, therefore, does not imply foundation endorsement.

Board of Trustees

Sara S. McLanahan, *Chair*
Larry M. Bartels
Karen S. Cook
W. Bowman Cutter III
Sheldon H. Danziger
Kathryn Edin
Lawrence F. Katz
David Laibson
Nicholas Lemann
Martha Minow
Peter R. Orszag
Claude M. Steele
Shelley E. Taylor
Richard H. Thaler
Hirokazu Yoshikawa

Mission Statement

RSF: The Russell Sage Foundation Journal of the Social Sciences is a peer-reviewed, open-access journal of original empirical research articles by both established and emerging scholars. It is designed to promote cross-disciplinary collaborations on timely issues of interest to academics, policymakers, and the public at large. Each issue is thematic in nature and focuses on a specific research question or area of interest. The introduction to each issue will include an accessible, broad, and synthetic overview of the research question under consideration and the current thinking from the various social sciences.

RSF Journal Editorial Board

Elizabeth O. Ananat, Duke University
Annette Bernhardt, University of California, Berkeley
Karen S. Cook, Stanford University
Sheldon H. Danziger, RSF President
Janet C. Gornick, The CUNY Graduate Center
Jennifer Hochschild, Harvard University
Douglas S. Massey, Princeton University
Mary E. Pattillo, Northwestern University
James Sidanius, Harvard University
Mary C. Waters, Harvard University
Bruce Western, Harvard University

Copyright © 2016 by Russell Sage Foundation. All rights reserved. Printed in the United States of America. No part of this publication may be reproduced, stored in a retrieval system, or transmitted in any form or by any means, electronic, mechanical, photocopying, recording, or otherwise, without the prior written permission of the publisher. Reproduction by the United States Government in whole or in part is permitted for any purpose.

Opinions expressed in this journal are not necessarily those of the editors, editorial board, trustees, or the Russell Sage Foundation.

We invite scholars to submit proposals for potential issues through the *RSF* application portal: https://rsfjournal.onlineapplicationportal.com/. Submissions should be addressed to Suzanne Nichols, Director of Publications.

To view the complete text and additional features online please go to **www.rsfjournal.org**.

Russell Sage Foundation
112 East 64th Street
New York, NY 10065

ISSN (print): 2377-8253
ISSN (electronic): 2377-8261
ISBN: 978-0-87154-047-8

RSF: The Russell Sage Foundation
Journal of the Social Sciences

VOLUME 2 NUMBER 4
AUGUST 2016

A Half Century of Change in the Lives of American Women

ISSUE EDITORS
Martha J. Bailey, University of Michigan
Thomas A. DiPrete, Columbia University

CONTENTS

Five Decades of Remarkable but Slowing Change in U.S. Women's Economic and Social Status and Political Participation **1**
Martha J. Bailey and Thomas A. DiPrete

Part I. Working Hours, Opting Out, and the Gender Wage Gap

The Opt-Out Continuation: Education, Work, and Motherhood from 1984 to 2012 **34**
Tanya Byker

Long Work Hours, Part-Time Work, and Trends in the Gender Gap in Pay, the Motherhood Wage Penalty, and the Fatherhood Wage Premium **71**
Kim A. Weeden, Youngjoo Cha, and Mauricio Bucca

Part II. Motherhood, Work, and the Family Pay Gap

The Family Gap in Pay: New Evidence for 1967 to 2013 **104**
Ipshita Pal and Jane Waldfogel

Motherhood and the Wages of Women in Professional Occupations **128**
Claudia Buchmann and Anne McDaniel

Part III. Women's Work in Nontraditionally Female Occupations and STEM Fields

Gender Differences in the Early Career Outcomes of College Graduates: The Influence of Sex-Type of Degree Field Across Four Cohorts **152**
Kimberlee A. Shauman

Explaining the Gender Wage Gap in STEM: Does Field Sex Composition Matter? **194**
Katherine Michelmore and Sharon Sassler

Part IV. Marriage, Divorce, and Women's Earnings

Trends in Relative Earnings and Marital Dissolution: Are Wives Who Outearn Their Husbands Still More Likely to Divorce? **218**
Christine R. Schwartz and Pilar Gonalons-Pons

Selection and Specialization in the Evolution of Marriage Earnings Gaps **237**
Chinhui Juhn and Kristin McCue

Part V. Education, Work, and Political Participation

Advances and Ambivalence: The Consequences of Women's Educational and Workforce Changes for Women's Political Participation in the United States, 1952 to 2012 **272**
Ashley Jardina and Nancy Burns

Five Decades of Remarkable but Slowing Change in U.S. Women's Economic and Social Status and Political Participation

MARTHA J. BAILEY AND THOMAS A. DiPRETE

The last fifty years of women's social and economic progress have been lauded as the "grand gender convergence," the "second demographic transition," and the "rise of women"—terms pointing to the remarkable transformation in women's social and economic roles since the 1960s. Many metrics document these changes.

Women made up less than one-third of all U.S. employees in 1950 (Toossi 2002), but today make up almost half (BLS 2014). In the 1960s, they earned around 60 percent of what men did, but this figure has risen today to about 80 percent (Blau and Kahn, forthcoming). Currently, more women than men enroll in and complete college (Goldin, Katz, and Kuziemko 2006; DiPrete and Buchmann 2013), and changes in women's roles as mothers and partners have redefined the "typical" American family (Lundberg and Pollak 2007).

U.S. women hold some of the most influential jobs in the country and are contenders for others. In 2007, Nancy Pelosi became the first female Speaker of the U.S. House of Representatives. In 2015, Janet Yellen was sworn in as the first chairwoman of the Federal Reserve Board of Governors. In 2016, two women were U.S. presidential candidates (Hillary Clinton and Carly Fiorina).

Despite these advances, other evidence suggests that women's progress has slowed or stalled. Pay gaps at the top of the income distribution are large (Bertrand and Hallock 2001; Bertrand, Goldin, and Katz 2010; Guvenen, Kaplan, and Song 2014). Women make up less than 10 percent of corporate boards and less than 2 percent of CEOs (Matsa and Miller 2011). The integration of women into the so-called STEM fields has been slow since 1990 (Jacobs 1995; Bradley 2000; Xie and Shauman 2003).[1] The odds that a woman earns a physical science, engineering, or economics major have hardly changed in the past twenty years (Goldin and Rouse 2000; England and Li 2006; Goldin, Katz, and Kuziemko 2006; Mann and DiPrete 2013; Goldin 2015).

U.S. women's health and happiness also

Martha J. Bailey is associate professor of economics and research associate professor at the Population Studies Center at the University of Michigan. She is also faculty research affiliate at the National Bureau of Economic Research. **Thomas A. DiPrete** is Giddings Professor of Sociology at Columbia University and member of the faculty of the Columbia Population Research Center. He is also co-director of the Institute for Social and Economic Research and Policy at Columbia and co-director of the Center for the Study of Wealth and Inequality at Columbia.

We are grateful to two anonymous referees and Lawrence Kahn for their comments. We also thank Francine Blau and Lawrence Kahn for generously sharing their data relating to the gender gap in wages. Direct correspondence to: Martha J. Bailey at baileymj@umich.edu, Department of Economics, University of Michigan, 611 Tappan St., Ann Arbor, MI 48109; and Thomas A. DiPrete at tad61@columbia.edu, Columbia University, 601B Knox Hall, MC 9649, 606 W. 122nd St., New York, NY 10027.

1. STEM is an acronym for science, technology, engineering, and mathematics. Economics is not a STEM field but shares STEM tendencies in these trends.

seem to be lagging. Betsey Stevenson and Justin Wolfers (2009) found that women in recent years report being less happy than they did more than fifty years ago, both absolutely and relative to men (Stevenson and Wolfers 2009), though it is also true that women generally report greater happiness than men from 1974 to the present even as the gender gap in favor of women has been shrinking over time (Hout 2016).[2] American women's longevity has stopped increasing at the rate of women in other developed countries (Crimmins, Preston, and Cohen 2011), and American women continue to have higher morbidity rates than American men (Ross, Masters, and Hummer 2012). Some commentators argue that the groundswell of support for women's equality is ebbing (England 2010; Cotter, Hermsen, and Vanneman 2011; Fortin 2015b).

Whether and how to address gender inequality is more contentious. A common theme in the media, epitomized by Anne-Marie Slaughter's 2012 *Atlantic* article ("Why women still can't have it all") is that institutions have been slow to accommodate work-life balance (Glass and Estes 1997; Glass and Finley 2002; Gornick and Meyers 2005; Goldin and Katz 2011; Goldin 2014). Indeed, the United States lags behind all other advanced countries in providing basic workplace accommodations for parenthood and paid leave (Council of Economic Advisors 2014). Other commentators argue that women themselves need to change. Sheryl Sandberg's best-selling book encouraged women to *Lean In* to achieve more in their careers (2013).

This special issue of the Russell Sage Foundation's *Interdisciplinary Journal in Social Science* focuses on these changes in the United States, beginning around 1960 and ending around 2010. This introduction aims to provide an overview of the very large literature on this topic, and provide a quantitative history documenting this remarkable half century. This issue's articles are authored by economists, political scientists, and sociologists; each quantifies and discusses the changes in women's social, familial, and economic roles and highlights their implications for the evolution of U.S. society, family, and economy. We conclude with summaries of each of the volume's nine articles, which delve into specific issues in greater detail.

THE GENDER GAP IN WAGES

Our overview of women's progress begins with one of the most easily observed metrics of women's social and economic progress: the difference in wage earnings between men and women. This gap in wages can be defined in a variety of ways, but economists typically focus on the ratio of women's to men's wage earnings.

Figure 1 reproduces the wage earnings ratio from 1955 to 2014 from Francine Blau and Lawrence Kahn's survey of the literature (forthcoming).[3] The printed data values report the gender ratio in 1955, in each decade (1960, 1970, 1980, 1990, 2000), and then in 2013 for annual and in 2014 for weekly wage earnings series. The story is one of long-term, continuous progress, and slowing progress after 1990. After an increase in the pay gap between 1955 and the 1970s, the gap closed from around 60 percent to around 80 percent today. Blau and Kahn report that, by 2013, women earned about 78 per-

---

2. Michael Hout (2016) shows most of the happiness decline occurred among the poor; the affluent are roughly as happy currently as they were in the 1970s.

3. Estimating wage earnings per unit of work is complicated by the fact that many sources ask individuals about earnings and wages in the previous year, not per hour. Moreover, many workers may not know exactly what they earn per hour if they are paid on a salary basis. To adjust for these differences, the literature typically focuses on full-time civilian men and women who should have completed their educations, are unlikely to have retired (ages twenty-five to sixty-four), and are not working on farms or self-employed. To transform annual wage earnings into weekly wage earnings, the literature divides information on annual wage earnings by an estimate of hours worked last year or usual hours worked. To adjust for top-coding in the Current Population Surveys (CPS), much of the literature multiplies top-coded values by 1.45. Finally, extreme outliers are excluded: Blau and Kahn, for instance, exclude those earning less than $2 per hour in 2010 dollars. Earnings are adjusted into 2010 dollars using the Personal Consumption Expenditures deflator.

Figure 1. Gender Earnings Ratios of Full-Time Workers, 1955–2014

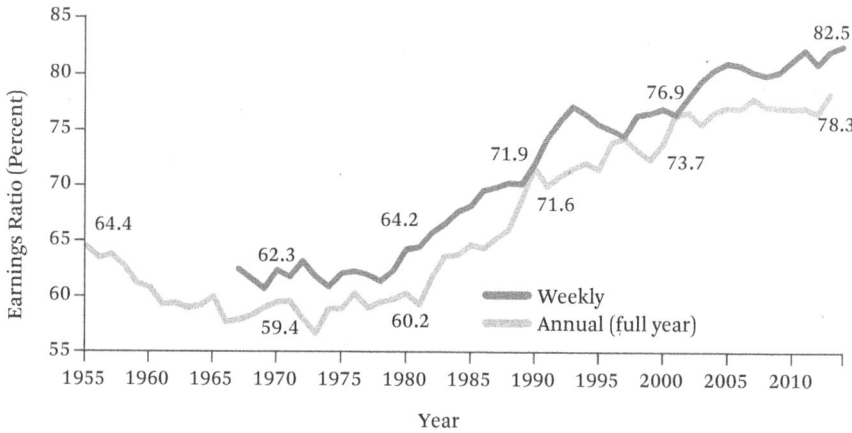

Source: Authors' compilation based on CPS (Blau and Kahn, forthcoming).

cent of what men did on an annual basis and about 83 percent on a weekly basis. The annual ratio is slightly lower than the weekly ratio, in large part because women work fewer weeks per year than men on average. The fastest decade of convergence in the wage compensation of men and women was the 1980s, a phenomenon reflecting increases in women's labor-force participation and their experience working for pay. In 1990, full-time women earned 72 percent as much as men. But convergence in the gender gap has been slower since 1990. By 2000, this ratio had only nudged up to 77 percent and, by 2010, to 83 percent.

Progress at the average masks differences in the pace of this progress across skill groups (observed in datasets such as the Current Population Surveys, CPS, and Panel Study of Income Dynamics, PSID). In 1980 women at the 10th percentile earned 69 percent of what men at the 10th percentile did, whereas women at the 90th percentile earned only 64 percent of what men at the 90th percentile did. The differences in the pay gaps at the highest and lowest percentiles have also been widening. In 2010 women at the 10th percentile earned 88 percent of what men at the 10th percentile did, whereas women at the 90th percentile earned 77 percent of what men at the 90th percentile did (Blau and Kahn, forthcoming). In short, higher gaps in wages have been more persistent for women in the upper part of the wage distribution than in the lower part of the wage distribution (Blau and Kahn 1997; Fortin and Lemieux 1998).

PRE-MARKET FACTORS: EDUCATION AND OCCUPATION

Much of the change in the pay gap reflects changing conditions and choices that take place before labor market entry. These "pre-market" factors include family background, educational and occupational aspirations, K–12 school quality and curriculum, ability and effort in school, where and how much postsecondary education to pursue, as well as major, degree, and field choices. These choices and outcomes, in turn, facilitate entry into some occupations and hamper entry into others. Labor market and broader societal changes, meanwhile, combined with changing patterns of women's academic preparation and aspirations. This produced a gradual reduction in occupational segregation by gender, though the rate of integration has diminished in recent years (Jacobs 1989; Cotter, Hermsen, and Vanneman 2004; Stainback and Tomaskovic-Devey 2012).

A decomposition of data from the PSID attributes a large and growing amount of the gender gap in wage earnings to pre-market and occupational factors (Blau and Kahn, forthcoming, table 4B). In 1980, around 3 percent of the gender gap could be attributed to differences in education and nearly 11 percent to occupational differences.[4] The role of occupational differences has grown. In 2010, the representation of men and women in different occupations explained almost one-third of the gender gap in pay. But, because women today attain more education than men, the gender gap would have been at least 6 percent larger had men achieved as much education as women.

Choices and constraints after entering the labor market also play a role. The time spent working and learning on the job increases know-how and experience, and women's historical rise in compensation reflects the gradual improvement in their labor-force experience and quantity of skills learned on the job. Women with more experience and expertise may be more likely to be promoted, resulting in higher pay, more leadership responsibilities, and higher status. One recent study uses the American Time Use Surveys (ATUS) to show that, between 1965 and 2003, women's work in paid employment grew by 6.2 hours per week (Aguiar and Hurst 2007). The resulting increase in women's work experience has played an important role in the narrowing of pay gaps (O'Neill and Polachek 1993; Blau and Kahn 1997). In 1980, differences in labor-force experience accounted for approximately 21 percent of the gender gap but only 14 percent in 2010 (Blau and Kahn, forthcoming, table 4B).

The differences in the role of labor-force experience play much larger roles in determining the gender gap in the wages in different segments of the economy. Marianne Bertrand, Claudia Goldin, and Lawrence Katz (2010) show that, although women and men MBAs have similar earnings at the beginning of their careers, the gender gap grows to almost 60 log points within roughly fifteen years of graduation—a difference partly driven by career interruptions around the time of a birth as well as shorter hours worked after childbirth.

Differences in industry or occupation of employment have also impacted women's compensation and status, both absolutely and relative to men. For instance, women have historically been much more heavily concentrated in lower earning industries and those with lower union coverage (that is, childcare and services) (Charles and Grusky 2004). Occupational segregation by gender has decreased, but the gains have been slower in the past two decades than before (Stainback and Tomaskovic-Devey 2012). The explanatory power of industry of work remains an important determinant of the gender gap in wages today. In 1980, differences in industry of work and unionization accounted for around 15.8 percent of the wage gap. By 2010, this figure had barely risen to 16.3 percent, but the share explained by unionization had fallen to essentially zero.[5] This means that the share explained by differences in industry of employment rose from around 10 to 18 percent over these thirty years (Blau and Kahn, forthcoming).

Another reason why industry and occupation of employment matter relates to the effects of broad economic trends on specific industries and occupations that—due to the different distributions of men and women in these occupations and industries—affected men and women differently. Some scholars have surmised that the computerization of the workplace reduced the demand for labor in sectors of the economy where more men were concentrated (like manufacturing) and raised demand for jobs (like office work) where more women worked (Weinberg 2000; Welch 2000). Although this is true in some sectors, broader economic trends appear to have had the reverse effect. Blau and Kahn estimate that the convergence in the gender gap would have been 5 to 6 percentage points larger if the overall distribution of wages had remained stable (2007). They argue that women in the 1990s were "swimming upstream" against an economy pushing their pay in the other direction.

The erosion of the minimum wage also worked against a declining gender gap (Lee 1999; Card and DiNardo 2002). John DiNardo,

---

4. Note that this section's attribution in words like *explained by* or *accounted for* is not intended as a causal statement but as a statistical one.

5. The decline in unionization in the American workforce has been more extensive for males than for females and has had a larger effect on the male wage distribution than on the female wage distribution (Western and Rosenfeld 2011).

Figure 2. U.S. Women's Labor-Force Participation, 1910–2010

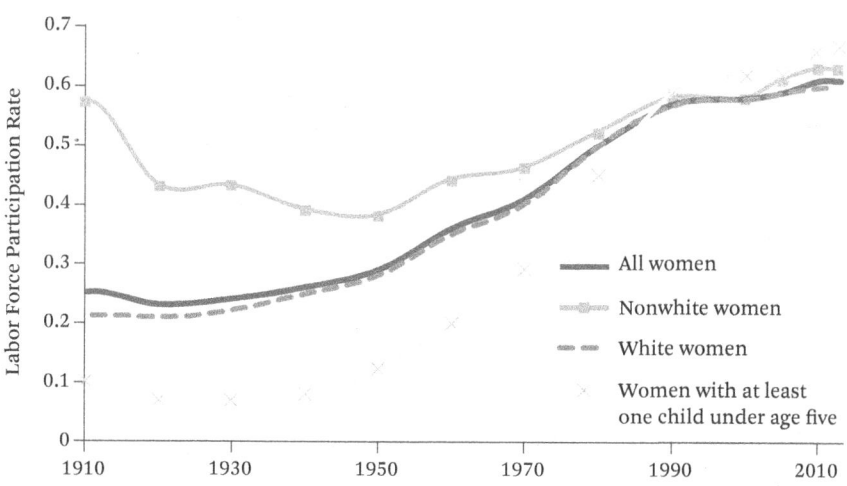

Sources: Authors' calculations based on decennial censuses and ACS (Ruggles et al. 2010).
Notes: Decennial censuses from 1910 to 2000 decennial censuses and ACS from 2005, 2010, and 2013. Samples are restricted to women ages sixteen and older who do not reside in group quarters. Allocated values are omitted. Historical comparisons necessitate that race categories are very crude and do not account for changes in how individuals self-identify by race or ethnicity over time.

Nicole Fortin, and Thomas Lemieux (1996) note that, in 1979, the modal wage for a woman with a high school diploma was identical to the federal minimum wage. As the value of the federal minimum wage plummeted by 30 percent over the next decade, wages at the bottom end of the distribution would have fallen by more had women not continued to increase their relative positions in the wage distribution. Despite considerable consensus that economic changes over this period tended to work against women, the magnitude of these effects depends largely on the reference group (Fortin and Lemieux 1998).

THE ROLE OF SELECTION

Other more difficult to measure factors have contributed to the decline in the gender gap in wages. One such factor is *selection*, a term that refers to changes in the distribution of characteristics among working women (relative to nonworking women) that are compensated (or penalized) in the labor market. Many of these characteristics are observed. As women increased their labor-force participation rates over the twentieth century, from around 20 percent in 1900 to 59 percent in 2010 (as shown in figure 2), the share of married women workers and working mothers changed dramatically. For instance, roughly 32 percent of married women ages sixteen to sixty-four were in the labor force in 1960, but today their labor-force participation rates have doubled to exceed that of the overall working-age, female population (59 percent). Similarly, the growing representation of mothers with young children is yet another important change in U.S. labor markets. Historically, very few women with children ages five and under worked for pay. In 2010, the labor-force participation rates of mothers with young children had risen to more than 60 percent.

These transformations have been accompanied by changes in the racial composition of working women. Historically, nonwhite women were significantly more likely to be labor-market participants, in large part because their husbands tended to earn less (Costa 2000).[6] In

---

6. Unfortunately, historical comparisons with the 1960s cannot be meaningfully broken down into smaller race or ethnicity groups, because census and survey questions about race or ethnicity in 1960 and 1970 were crude by today's standards.

1960, nonwhite women were almost 30 percent more likely to work than white women. By 2010, however, these race gaps in women's labor-force participation had almost completely evaporated (for more detailed reviews of these changes over the last hundred years, see Goldin 1990; Juhn and Potter 2006).

Alongside these compositional changes in the labor force, unmeasured characteristics of working women have also likely changed. If researchers could observe wage offers by firms to workers who chose not to work, researchers could directly calculate the effects of changes in selection on the gender gap in wages. But because wage offers and characteristics that determine wage offers are not observed in most labor-market surveys, the quantitative importance of selection for explaining women's wage gains is difficult to pin down.

Researchers have used various methodologies to estimate the importance of selection, but these calculations depend on assumptions that are almost impossible to test. Blau and Kahn (2006) estimate that selection on unobservable labor-market relevant skills changed from very positive to less positive between the 1980s and 1990s, meaning that the advantage in terms of unmeasured skills of new entrants had fallen for the average working woman between the 1980s and 1990s. It follows that convergence in the gender wage gap would have been slower in the 1980s but faster in the 1990s without these changes in selection. Casey Mulligan and Yona Rubinstein (2008), however, reach different conclusions using different methods. After accounting for compositional changes using a Heckman two-step procedure and an alternative procedure of identification at infinity, they argue that the convergence in the gender gap between the late 1970s and early 1990s is due almost entirely to selection on unobservable characteristics.

CULTURE AND SOCIAL-PSYCHOLOGICAL FORCES

The extent to which gender differences reflect environmental conditions (*nurture*), biology (*nature*), or the interaction of the two is the subject of a long-standing academic debate. Some recent work suggests a role for nature,[7] but many studies provide strong evidence that conditions in the family and the broader environment play important roles.

It is clear that cultural and institutional constraints play important roles from birth. Parents' treatment of children is related to their perceptions and expectations about their children's abilities and future opportunities, both of which are linked to gender. Choice of college major, first job, and when to have a family are not independent of labor-market realities such as gender discrimination, rigid work schedules, shift work, and required long hours. Women who expect their spouses not to support them or employers to discriminate against them—by paying them less for comparable work or by hiring or promoting them less—may opt out of certain jobs. They may avoid industries in which they fear unfriendly work environments, sexual harassment, and overt discrimination that may take the form of hostile or sarcastic comments, inappropriate humor or physical contact, and intentional or de facto exclusion from professional clubs or extracurricular activities (Lopez, Hodson, and Roscigno 2009).

---

7. For instance, some studies link testosterone levels with willingness to take financial risks (Apicella et al. 2008). The difficulty with this literature is that it is unclear whether testosterone levels are the cause or the consequences of other biological differences, and testosterone levels can be influenced by the environment as well as by behavior that has environmental rather than biological causes (Freese, Li, and Wade 2003). Other work links fluctuations in women's hormones associated with menstrual cycles with outcomes. Arndt Broder and Natalia Hohmann (2003) link these hormone fluctuations to women's willingness to take risks. Andrea Ichino and Enrico Moretti (2009) show that menstruating women working at banks in Italy are more likely to be absent from work, thus implying that nature increases the gender gap. Work by Jonah Rockoff and Mariesa Herrmann (2012) in the United States, however, fails to find such associations among New York City public school teachers. The latter finding, therefore, suggests that responses to biological differences are mediated by institutions, industry, or culture. These examples fit within a broader literature that finds genetic effects on outcomes such as measured intelligence to be strongly conditioned by the environment (Nisbett et al. 2012). In short, this literature supports the conclusion that forces other than biological ones play a large role in the expression of nature.

Similarly, employers who expect women to leave the labor force when they have children may invest differently in their female employees (Coate and Loury 1993; Thomas 2014). The perception of discrimination and "chilly climates" in certain industries and occupations may in turn affect women's pre-market investment in education and skills. These perceptions of discrimination also encourage men to specialize in the more time-flexible tasks in the domestic division of labor (Charles 2011), which can exacerbate gender gaps in home and market production. The resiliency of these cultural and institutional barriers (or their rapid deterioration) may hasten or slow the speed of change (Fernandez 2013).

Other factors such as gender differences in risk aversion, competitiveness, and willingness to negotiate predict certain types of career choices and outcomes. We provide a brief review of these studies here but refer interested readers to more comprehensive reviews by Bertrand (2010) and Muriel Niederle and Lise Vesterlund (2010).

Differences in men and women's willingness to compete has been highlighted as an important potential impediment to women's career progress (Ridgeway 2001; Ridgeway and Correll 2004). For instance, differences in competitiveness may matter if promotions to more lucrative positions or assignments in the workplace are often very competitive. If women shy away from competition, they would be less likely to win these promotions. Indeed, recent work shows that, holding ability constant, women are less likely to choose to compete (Niederle and Vesterlund 2010). Differences in competitiveness translated into striking differences in selection into more prestigious math- and science-intensive tracks (Buser, Niederle, and Oosterbeek 2014).

More interesting, however, is that gender differences in perceptions of own task competence, own aspirations to pursue careers related to task activities, and competitiveness related to these tasks are mediated by the environment. Shelley Correll (2001, 2004) uses both experimental and nonexperimental evidence to demonstrate how gender differences in perceptions about task competence and about aspirations for career-relevant activities emerge from culturally gendered differences in beliefs about tasks. She finds that experimental dissociation of gender from task beliefs eliminates gender gaps in perceptions of task competence and also in aspirations for career-relevant activities requiring competence with the task.[8] Alison Booth and Patrick Nolen (2012) examine gender differences in willingness to compete in a laboratory setting where students are assigned to mixed-sex groups and single-sex groups. Moreover, they examine how students respond based on whether their school is a single-sex or mixed-sex school. They find that the gender gap in choosing to compete was similar in magnitude to comparable studies (Niederle and Vesterlund 2007, 2010), but that girls who attended a single-sex school were *42 percentage points* more likely to choose to enter the tournament than girls from a coed school—even after controlling for ability, learning, family-background, and age. It remains unclear to what extent competitiveness is correlated with unobserved determinants of where parents choose to send their children (that is, parents send their more risk-loving daughters to private girls' schools).

International evidence also suggests that environments help determine competitiveness. In one case study, Uri Gneezy, Kenneth Leonard, and John List (2009) show that gender differences in competitiveness are reversed in the Khasi, a matrilineal society in India. Similar studies indicate that both gender differences in performance and gender differences in attitudes toward STEM careers appear to be influenced by the local school environment (Legewie and DiPrete 2012, 2014; Mann, Legewie, and DiPrete 2015). Measured gender differences in competitiveness and their effects may also be manipulated by the structure of laboratory experiments. By repeating a math competition up to five times in primary classrooms (as well as a number of other experiment characteristics), Christopher Cotton, Frank McIntyre, and Joseph Price (2013) show that boys' advantage in competition does not persist beyond the first round and may also be elimi-

---

8. For a comprehensive review of the related literature on experimental and nonexperimental studies of self-affirmation and its effects on performance, see Cohen and Sherman 2014.

nated by altering time pressure or the assigned competitive task.

Outside of the lab, cultural and social-psychological forces may play even larger roles. Even in the absence of explicit, overt discrimination, stereotypes and stigma can socialize gender segregation and inequality.[9] Social-psychological factors may influence educational and occupational choices and reinforce the continuing occupational segregation in the American labor market. Maria Charles (2011) notes that behaving in accordance with stereotypes is a strategy for affirming one's gender identity. Behaving contrary to stereotypes concerning, for example, math, science, or the pursuit of elite corporate positions imposes greater costs to women than to men among those who value a strong and culturally coherent gender identity. As with overt discrimination, these cultural factors can influence pre-market choices, decisions to promote or remain in a position, and, in turn, the gender wage gap.

A growing number of studies find that stereotypes not only affect the process by which people evaluate others. They also affect performance and self-evaluation of performance in tasks that are coded as either especially suitable or especially unsuitable for that person's gender (Correll 2004; Ridgeway 2006; Correll, Benard, and Paik 2007; Cohen et al. 2009; Charles 2011; Sherman et al. 2013; Cohen and Sherman 2014). For example, reminding subjects that they are women (given negative stereotypes about women's negotiation abilities) has led women to perform substantially worse in negotiations in laboratory experiments (Kray, Thompson, and Galinsky 2001; Kray, Galinsky, and Thompson 2002). This is not unique to women: gender priming also affects men's level of altruism when they are assigned to mixed gender groups (Boschini, Muren, and Persson 2012).

A related finding concerns professor gender. In a compelling study of U.S. Air Force Academy students, the random assignment of students to STEM courses taught by women had a large effect on female students' performance in these classes but little on men's performance. Higher-performing women randomly assigned to take math and science from female professors were also much more likely to enroll in more STEM classes and graduate with a STEM degree (Carrell, Page, and West 2010). Although the reason for this effect is unclear, these results may be related to how having a professor who challenges gender stereotypes alters women's perceptions of their own abilities.

Another potential explanation is that bias is operating at the professorial level which could affect students more directly. Women professors in STEM may better recognize female students' abilities by, for example, calling on them in class or acknowledging their achievements. Some evidence for this later phenomenon comes from studies of corporate leadership. Greater representation of women on U.S. corporate boards is strongly associated with the likelihood of employing women in top management positions (Matsa and Miller 2011). Similarly, Lisa Cohen and Joseph Broschak (2013) find that the proportion of newly created jobs first filled by women in 153 New York City advertising agencies over thirteen years was positively affected by the proportion of female managers in the agency. Moreover, Matt Huffman, Phillip Cohen, and Jessica Pearlman analyze thirty years of administrative data from the Equal Employment Opportunity Commission and find that the presence of women in managerial positions in an establishment was positively associated with occupational gender integration in the establishment, with the strongest desegregating effects of female managers occurring in larger and growing establishments (2010). The evidence does not all favor effects in one direction. Another study demonstrates that a higher share of female mangers in an industry does not invariably reduce gender gaps in pay or promotions (Penner, Toro-Tulla, and Huffman 2012).

Subjective bias in evaluators is yet another way stereotypes cloud evaluations of men and women, a bias persisting among even the most elite and educated evaluators. A recent working paper of women's promotions in economics

---

9. For an overview of economic models of discrimination, see Altonji and Blank 1999; for a recent overview of sociological and psychological models of how discrimination emerges from social norms and implicit and explicit prejudicial attitudes, see Quillian 2006.

suggests that the field gives women less credit for their academic publications if they coauthor with men, presumably because the field attributes more of the intellectual work to their male coauthors (Sarsons 2015). This systematic bias bears directly on the large gender tenure gap in economics. Among economists with initial placements in the top thirty economics programs, only 32 percent of women, versus 49 percent of men, received tenure. For the PhD cohort of the early 1990s initially placed at other PhD-granting institutions, only 29 percent of women received tenure, versus 43 percent of men (Hilmer and Hilmer 2010). These biases operate in the press as well, with even top female economists being relegated to the second author by journalists. A recent analysis of gender differences in retention and promotion across the social sciences in nineteen American research universities suggests that the gender gap in tenure rates in sociology departments may be similar to that found in economics (Box-Steffensmeier et al. 2015).

PREPARATION FOR CAREERS: THE ROLE OF EDUCATION AND OCCUPATIONAL CHOICE

Fifty years ago, women lagged behind men in their educational attainment. In the United States and most industrialized societies, however, the days when gender inequality in education meant economic disadvantages for women have long passed. In fact, women have made substantial gains in all realms of education and now outperform men on many key educational benchmarks. In 1970, 58 percent of college students were men, but by the 1980s (cohorts born in the 1960s), the gender gap in college enrollment had reversed. In 2010, 57 percent of all college students were women. Women are also more likely than men to persist in college, to graduate, and to enroll in graduate school (DiPrete and Buchmann 2013). As of 2013, women earned 57 percent of bachelor's degrees and 61 percent of associate's degrees.

Figure 3, which displays college completion rates of twenty-six- to twenty-eight-year-olds by birth year from the U.S. census, shows that men led women beginning with the birth cohorts of 1910, the ratio peaking in cohorts born

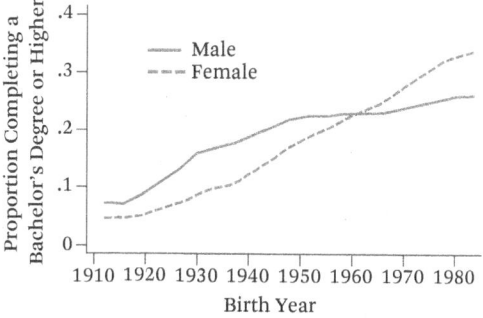

Figure 3. Bachelor's Degree or More

Source: DiPrete and Buchmann 2013.

in the 1920s and 1930s (see also DiPrete and Buchmann 2006; Goldin, Katz, and Kuziemko 2006). Women born in the 1940s began closing the gap, and their gains accelerated to the extent that women born in the late 1950s and early 1960s (who were of college age during the 1980s) overtook men in their rates of college completion.

Women have continued to increase their educational attainment at roughly the same rate since the 1960s. On a cohort by cohort basis, the male college graduation rate peaked around the birth cohort of 1950 and then remained essentially flat for the next fifteen years of cohort or so (DiPrete and Buchmann 2006). Thereafter, male cohorts gradually increased their rate of college completion, but these gains lagged behind the contemporaneous gains for women and the gains for male cohorts born before 1950. By 2010, women ages twenty-six to twenty-eight had more than an 8 percentage point lead in college degree receipt over their male counterparts. This constitutes an enormous change in the relative position of men and women in a very short time.

Women's now-sizable lead in college completion has occurred despite the scientific consensus that girls and boys have similar aptitude. Girls generally outperform boys on verbal tests and lag behind boys on math tests, especially in the population at the lower end of the test score distribution, but gender differences in cognitive ability, as measured by test scores, appear too small to account for the current gender gap in college completion. These small differences in test score performance have re-

Figure 4. Women's Share of Advanced Degrees

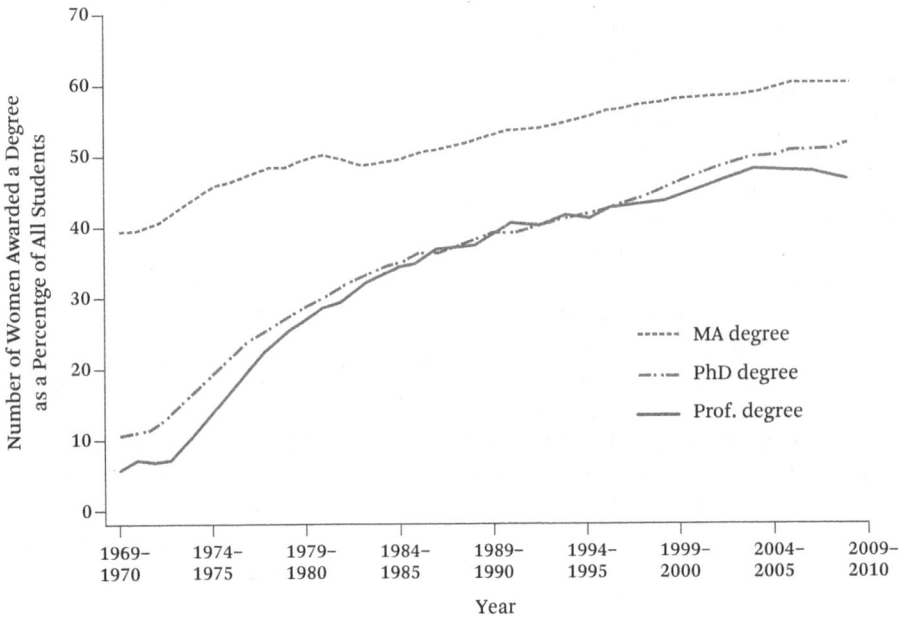

Source: DiPrete and Buchmann 2013.

mained fairly stable, whereas the gender gap in educational attainment has reversed from a male advantage to a female advantage that continues to grow. From grade school on, girls outperform boys on teacher assessments of classroom performance and in social and behavioral "noncognitive" skills that have been linked both to academic success and to the growing gender gap in academic performance and educational attainment (for a comprehensive review, see Buchmann, DiPrete, and McDaniel 2008).

Women have also made impressive gains in completing advanced degrees relative to men. Today, women have achieved equality or surpassed men in the number of degrees earned at every level of education. From 1969 to 1970, as figure 4 shows, women made up almost 40 percent of master's degrees, 11 percent of doctoral degrees, and 6 percent of professional degrees. The share of master's degrees earned by women has grown over the last three decades, and women currently earn 60 percent of the total.

The number of professional degrees awarded to women has increased dramatically since 1970, including degrees in business, medicine, dentistry, and law. Women now earn 47 percent of all professional degrees (DiPrete and Buchmann 2013; Blau, Ferber, and Winkler 2014). Figure 5 presents this remarkable takeoff. In 1970, men completed sixteen times more professional degrees than women. Since 1982, however, that number has declined slightly—from 40,229 in 1982 to 34,661 in 2010. Over the same period, the number of women's professional degrees has increased by almost twenty times—from 1,534 in 1970 to 30,289 in 2010. But since 1990, the pattern has changed to one of smaller, uneven gains. With the exception of a continued gradual rise in the proportion of advanced degrees in business conferred to women, the share of advanced degrees for women has remained fairly stable.

The gendered pattern for doctoral degrees conferred is similar to that of professional degrees. Men completed almost eight times as many doctoral degrees as women in the 1969–1970 school year (58,137 versus 6,861 for women). However, by 2009–2010, more doctoral degrees were awarded to women than men, 81,953 versus 76,605, and women now earn 52 percent of all doctoral degrees (DiPrete and Buchmann 2013; Blau, Ferber, and Winkler 2014). If these

Figure 5. Advanced Degrees Awarded to Women

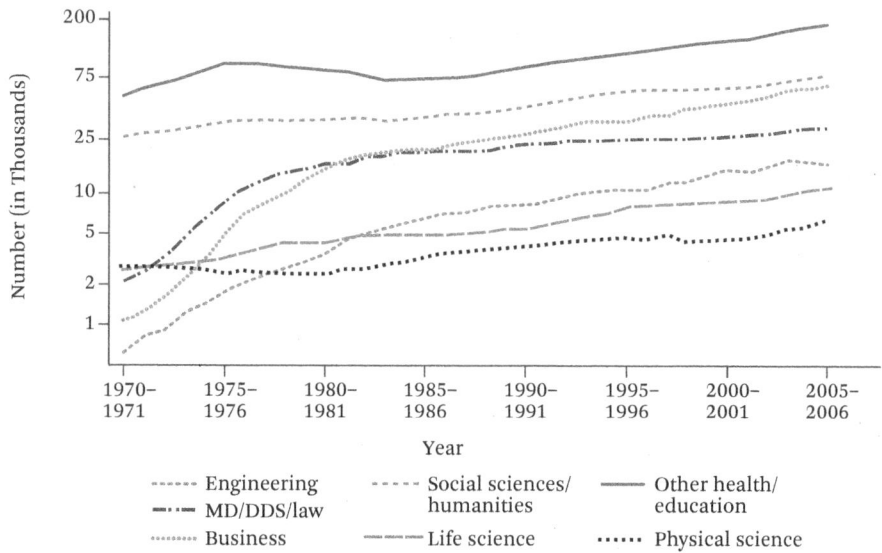

Source: DiPrete and Buchmann 2013.
Note: The y-axis is on a log scale.

trends follow the gender gap in bachelor's and master's degrees, we should expect a gap to emerge favoring women in the coming years.

Despite parity in the rate of degree completion, convergence has not carried over to all fields of study, especially the "STEM" fields. During the 1970s and 1980s, women made rapid advances into bachelor-level fields that were formerly male dominated, but change has been smaller and more uneven since around 1990 (England and Li 2006; Goldin, Katz, and Kuziemko 2006; Bronson 2013; Hegewisch and Liepmann 2013). Although women have continued to increase their share of undergraduate majors in biological and biomedical sciences, the odds that a physical science or engineering major is female have hardly changed in the past twenty years (Mann and DiPrete 2013; Ceci et al. 2014). The same is true for the field of economics (Goldin 2015).

Because girls have begun to outperform boys in many STEM subjects in high school, the persistence of these degree gaps is especially surprising. Data collected by the National Center for Education Statistics (NCES) show that high school girls have earned higher grades, on average, than boys since at least the senior class of 1972 and have had a clear advantage over boys since 1992 in the completion of Algebra II and Chemistry, which are gateways to more advanced math and science courses in high school (DiPrete and Buchmann 2013). By 2004, girls opened up a clear lead over boys in the taking of precalculus or calculus. Likewise, their lead in taking at least chemistry or Physics I has widened since 2004, though boys retain slight leads over girls in the taking of calculus and at least one of Chemistry II, Physics II, or advanced biology (Dalton et al. 2007).

Women's educational gains ensuing from these positive performance shifts and increased STEM enrollments affected their ultimate occupations. Unsurprisingly, occupational segregation by sex has evolved similarly to major and degree choices (Jacobs 2003). A period of rapid change in the 1970s and 1980s was followed by slower change and then stagnation. Francine Blau, Peter Brummund, and Albert Liu (2013) document the declining pace of change in occupational gender segregation, with the index of dissimilarity falling by 6.1 percentage points in the 1970s, 4.3 percentage points in the 1980s, 2.1 percentage points in the 1990s, and 1.1 percentage points in the 2000s. Given this slowing rate of change, 50

Figure 6. U.S. General Fertility Rate and Completed Childbearing

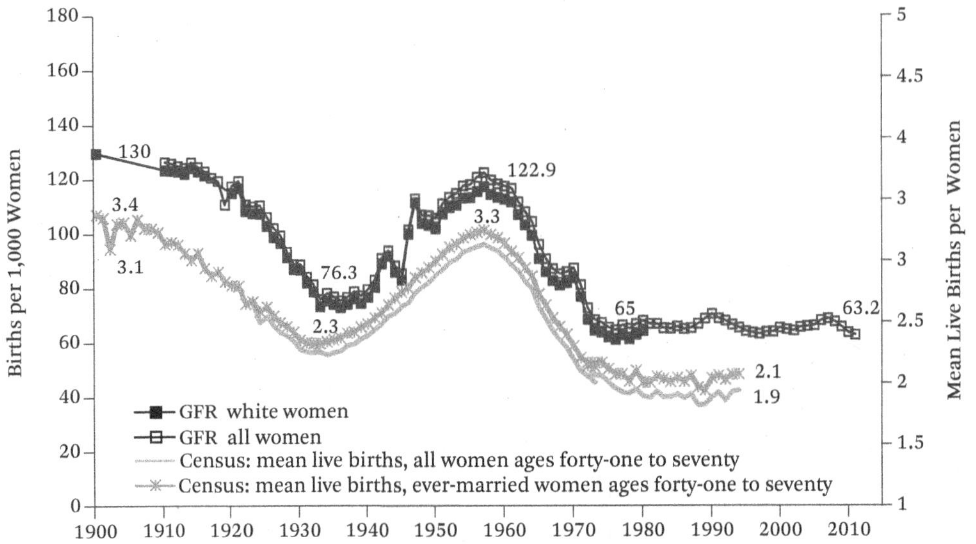

Sources: Authors' compilation (CDC 2000; Ruggles et al. 2010).
Notes: Fertility rates are from the CDC's historical 1909 to 2000 statistics (CDC 2000). Mean live births are computed using the 1940 to 1990 decennial census IPUMS samples (Ruggles et al. 2010) and the 1995 to 2010 June CPS. The general fertility rate (right vertical axis) is the number of births per thousand women (all or white women only) ages fifteen to forty-four in the population from Vital Statistics.

percent of women would have to change occupations in order to have the same distribution across occupations as do men.

This slow change can be partially attributed to the relatively strong growth of occupations that are more intensely segregated by gender, such as nursing (Hegewisch and Liepmann 2013). However, even after taking differential growth rates into account, the rate of integration of occupations has slowed, and some occupations—such as kindergarten teacher, secretary, or carpenter—remain overwhelmingly male or overwhelmingly female. If a *nontraditional occupation* is defined as one that is less than 25 percent male or less than 25 percent female, only 6 percent of women, versus 44 percent of men, work in nontraditional female occupations (Hegewisch and Matite 2013). At the same time, nontraditional male occupations employ only 5 percent of all men, but 40 percent of all women. Today, around 60 percent of American workers work in occupations that employ both men and women, and about 40 percent of both genders work in occupations that employ very few members of the opposite sex.

Although the rate of change is slowing, the gender gap in education and occupation is still narrowing. Because education and occupation are correlated with other measures of well-being, changes in women's health statuses have been evident. Although less-educated women generally report worse health than do less-educated men (unless the comparison is between older individuals), the self-reported health of college-educated women is nearly as good as that of college-educated men (Ross, Masters, and Hummer 2012). If part of this relationship is causal, rising levels of education for women may be closing the gender gap in self-reported health. Equally important, women's educational gains extend far beyond the realm of personal health and have significant implications for marriage, childbearing, and family structure, which we discuss next.

CHANGES IN CHILDBEARING, MARRIAGE, AND FAMILY STRUCTURE

Accompanying the dramatic changes in women's career preparation and labor-market outcomes have been changes in their roles as

Figure 7. Mean Age at First Marriage-Cohabitation and First Birth and Share Ever Marrying

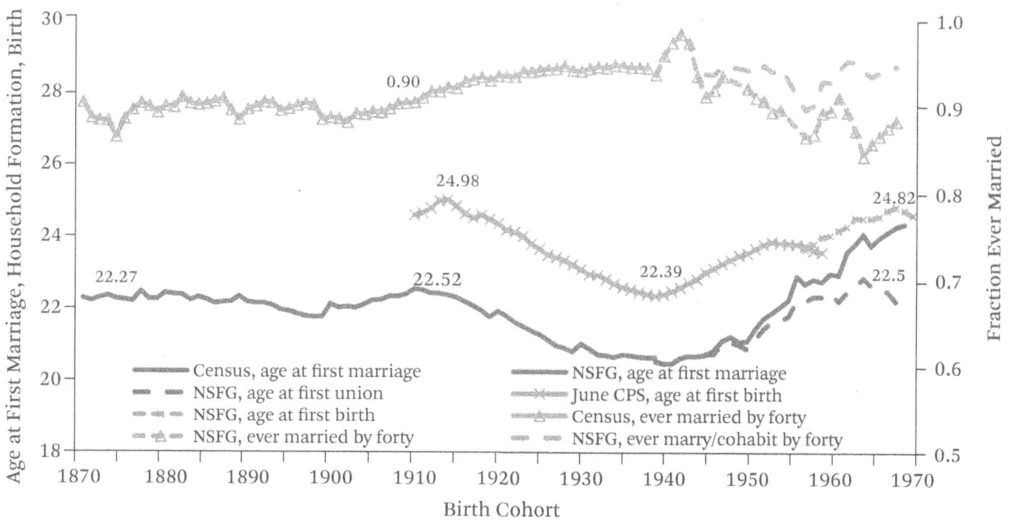

Sources: Authors' compilation based on IPUMS samples (Ruggles et al. 2010), CPS, and National Survey of Family Growth (Smock et al. 2013).

Notes: Decennial census figures from 1940 through 1980; CPS figures from 1979 to 1995; NSFG figures from 1982 through 2010. The figure plots the mean age at first marriage (conditional on ever married by age thirty-nine), first household formation or union (the younger of first marriage or first nonmarital cohabitation), first birth (left vertical axis), and share ever married (right vertical axis) against single year-of-birth cohort. The NSFG and CPS trends are based on three-year cohort moving averages.

mothers and partners. Figure 6 shows that U.S fertility rates have declined over the last fifty years, from around 122.9 births per thousand women ages fifteen to forty-four, and have stabilized at around half of that figure. Similarly, completed childbearing by age forty-one has declined from a high of 3.3 children for women born in the mid-1930s to around two children for women born around 1970 (Bailey, Guldi, and Hershbein 2014).[10]

These changes in the number of children correspond to another important shift in American family structure since 1960: the disassociation of childbearing and marriage. In 1970, only 11 percent of American children were born to unmarried parents; by 2009, the figure had risen to 41 percent (Martinez, Daniels, and Chandra 2012). In the last fifty years, the share of children living with unmarried parents has risen from just over 5 percent to over four times that rate today (Ellwood and Jencks 2004), with a considerably higher fraction expected to experience parental cohabitation at some point in their childhood (Graefe and Lichter 1999). These changes signal important shifts in the relationships between children, parents, and other adult relatives such as grandparents (Selzer and Bianchi 2013). They have affected other dimensions of partnership as well. Figure 7 shows that, although the share of women marrying by age thirty-five has fallen, the same share of American women form unions (through marriage or cohabitation) by the age of thirty-five as did fifty years ago. First union by age thirty-five is roughly as high as at any other time in the past hundred

10. Mean live births (on the left vertical axis) is the mean self-reported number of children ever born for each birth cohort as measured between the ages of forty-one and seventy (indexed to year by adding twenty-five years to mother's year of birth; for example, mean children ever born to the birth cohort of 1870 corresponds to the year 1895 on the graph's horizontal axis). In addition, we include rates for never married women as measured in the 1970 through 1990 censuses. Computations use population weights.

years, and the average woman today first forms a union at just over age twenty-two—the same age as she did before the baby boom (Bailey, Guldi, and Hershbein 2014). In short, the terms of unions have changed. Even though the age at first union, including cohabitation, has changed very little, women tend to marry about 3.7 years later than they did around 1960 (birth cohorts around 1940; for men this number is 2.7 years).

Another important change relates to "who" marries. Marriage is increasingly becoming an institution of the elite. More-educated women are more likely than less-educated women to marry by age forty-five and, conditional on marriage, they divorce at substantially lower rates. Marriage rates have diverged sharply by race since the 1960s, nonwhites being substantially less likely to ever be married (Stevenson and Wolfers 2006; McLanahan and Watson 2011). Trends in age at first marriage have also diverged, with the most-educated women now marrying much later than their least-educated counterparts (Bailey, Guldi, and Hershbein 2014). This final pattern may be, at least in part, related to increases in women's education and occupational investments which leads them to delay family formation.

THE ROLES OF TECHNOLOGY AND POLICIES

The labor market and family changes described have both stimulated and been affected by important developments in the technologies of preventing childbearing and of enabling childbearing for women seeking to get pregnant at older ages. This literature is large, so this section describes only some of its key findings.

Modern Contraception and Abortion

A growing literature in economics suggests many of the longer-term changes in family formation and childbearing—as well as the previously described changes in women's education and labor-force outcomes—are related to the introduction of modern contraception and abortion.

In 1957, the Food and Drug Administration's approval of "the Pill" for the regulation of menses, and later, in 1960, as an oral contraceptive, decreased women's uncertainty related to the timing and circumstances of conception.[11] The Pill was wildly popular. In 1965, 25 percent of white married women and 15 percent of nonwhite married women reported having ever used the Pill. By 1970, these figures reached 50 percent and 60 percent (Bailey 2010). By 1973, nearly 65 percent of married women age fifteen to twenty-four using any contraception chose the Pill (Westoff 1976).

Beginning in 1969, the legalization of abortion, first in a subset of states and then in the remaining states in 1973 with *Roe v. Wade*, provided additional insurance against unintended pregnancy and unanticipated circumstances after conception (Levine and Staiger 2002). According to the Guttmacher Institute, nearly 20 percent of pregnancies ended in abortion during the first year of *Roe v. Wade*, and this share rose to 30 percent over the next decade, before decreasing through today (Henshaw and Kost 2008).

Recent studies suggest that access to abortion had important implications for women's childbearing. Using the staggered legalization, Phillip Levine and his colleagues (1996, 1999) show that the early legalization of abortion in five states around 1970 led to a 5 percent reduction in the birth rate of women of childbearing age relative to the decline in the rest of the United States. The effects are larger for teens, women over age thirty-five, and nonwhites, and they also vary systematically by distance to early repeal states (Levine et al. 1996, 1999; Angrist and Evans 1996). Once Levine and his colleagues (1996) account for cross-state travel to early repeal states, they estimate that the legalization of abortion reduced birth rates by almost 8 percent.[12] Evidence is more limited,

---

11. The first modern intrauterine device (IUD) made from plastic, the Margulies Spiral, was introduced in 1960, but IUDs with copper were not brought to market until the 1970s (Hutchings et al. 1985).

12. Other recent changes in funding, regulations, and program interventions allow the evaluation of more recent policy changes. In contrast to estimates using variation in the 1960s and early 1970s, subsequent restrictions on abortion, like parental involvement or mandatory waiting periods, have been found to have minimal effects on fertility rates, with some evidence showing a slight reduction in abortion rates (and increased contraceptive

however, that changes in abortion access translated into changes in women's labor-force outcomes. More specifically, Joshua Angrist and William Evans (1996) show that abortion reform appears to have affected schooling and labor-market outcomes among African American women, although the statistical strength of these results tempers their conclusions.

The technology of the Pill complemented the insurance conferred by legal abortion. For the first time in history, both women and men could plan their childbearing with virtual certainty around their personal circumstances and human capital investments. Unintended pregnancies could be prevented, and women had options if unforeseen circumstances arose after conception (for example, if a partner chose not to support the child). This greater control allowed childbirth to be timed to benefit both children and their parents. Women and men could pursue more education, find better jobs and mates, and provide better financial and other support for their children. Figure 6 shows why, despite these outcomes, estimating the effects of the Pill or abortion is challenging: their introduction corresponded to the peak of the baby boom (in the case of the Pill) and occurred in the midst of dramatic declines in childbearing (in the case of abortion).

Recent research uses "natural" or "quasi-" experimental methods to isolate the impacts of these technological innovations, for example, using variation in state-level restrictions on the sale of the Pill before *Griswold v. Connecticut* and *Griswold*'s weakening of these restrictions. As much as 40 percent of the decline in the marital fertility rate from 1955 to 1965 might be attributable to the Pill (Bailey 2010). Another study showed that the county-level expansion of federally funded family planning programs reduced fertility rates by roughly 2 percent within five years (Bailey 2012). Finally, state-level restrictions on contraceptive access for unmarried, younger women show how these restrictions affected women's career investments (Goldin and Katz 2002). Recent studies also show that legal access to the Pill affected marital and birth timing and had broad effects on women's and men's education, career investments, and lifetime wage earnings (Goldin and Katz 2002; Bailey 2006, 2009; Guldi 2008; Hock 2008; Bailey, Hershbein, and Miller 2012).[13] Women and men were more likely to enroll and complete college. Women were more likely to work for pay, invest in on-the-job training, and pursue nontraditional professional occupations.

As women aged, these investments paid off. Thirty percent of the convergence of the gender wage gap in the 1990s can be attributed to these changing investments made possible by the Pill (Bailey, Hershbein, and Miller 2012). Moreover, women who gained access to oral contraception before age twenty were significantly less likely to live in poverty (Browne and LaLumia 2014). They also appear more likely to cohabit before marriage, which in turn may have directly and indirectly altered the gendered division of labor in the household (Christensen 2011).

Greater cohabitation rates imply important changes in matching between men and women, as well as changes in women's bargaining power. A rising age at first marriage among more educated women indicates that they gained more time to search for a mate, increasing both the quality of their matches and, potentially, the earnings of their households. The rise in cohabitation may also imply substantial

---

use) among teens (Bitler and Zavodny 2001; Levine 2003). Similarly, limiting the use of Medicaid funding for abortion does not appreciably affect birth rates and lowers abortion rates only slightly, as many women are induced to travel to nearby states for an abortion (Blank, George, and London 1996) or, for teens, are less likely to get pregnant (Kane and Staiger 1996). A recent study also shows that increased Medicaid eligibility for family planning services for the near poor leads to reduced birth rates for teens and older women, and these effects appear to be driven by increased contraceptive use (Kearney and Levine 2009).

13. In a recent working paper, Caitlin Myers (2012) argues that her estimates of the effects of changes in legal access to the Pill for younger women differ from those of Goldin and Katz (2002) and Bailey (2006). Although smaller, the magnitudes of her updated estimates are not statistically different from published estimates (Bailey, Guldi, and Hershbein 2013).

changes in matching between men and women as well as further changes in the gendered division of labor. It also implies a shift in the meaning and implications of marriage. Marriage may have increasingly become a status symbol (McLanahan and Watson 2011), or it may be motivated by consumption (rather than production) complementarities (Stevenson and Wolfers 2007).

Antidiscrimination Policies

The long view makes clear that the extent and intensity of sex-based discrimination has decreased markedly over the last fifty years. Explicit mentions of sex in job ads, the dismissal of women from positions when they marry ("marriage bars," Goldin 1991), or requirements that flight attendants be age twenty-five, size four, and single have been largely relegated to the past (for some lively accounts of the reality of being a working woman fifty years ago, see Collins 2009).

Part of this transition may be attributable to antidiscrimination policies. The 1963 Equal Pay Act mandates equal pay for men and women who are performing the same jobs.[14] Title VII of the 1964 Civil Rights Act prohibits sex-based discrimination in either the terms or conditions of employment. Title IX of the 1972 Educational Amendments to the Civil Rights Act banned discrimination in educational institutions receiving federal assistance, which covered the exclusion of pregnant teens from public high schools as well as gender-based discrimination in colleges and universities. The 1978 Pregnancy Discrimination Act requires employers to treat pregnant women the same as other similarly capable employees (for detailed reviews, see Leonard 1990; Albiston 2007).

Yet isolating the effects of these policies in a context of the shifting labor markets, families, and culture is challenging, because these policies tended to be applied at a national level. This means that researchers face considerable difficulties in separating employees into sensible "treatment" and "control" groups to infer policy effects. Consequently, direct empirical evidence that federal labor-market antidiscrimination policies mattered is scant. The time series evidence alone provides few obvious clues. Even as the legal basis for sex discrimination ended in the 1960s, the gender gap in pay changed little (see figure 1). The ambiguous and arguably limited impact of the courts certainly lies in part in the fact that an organization paying women and men different salaries in the same job was a smaller component of the gender pay gap than differences in pay by the same organization for jobs that are arguably comparable but where one job is more female dominated than the other. Courts have been reluctant to issue judgments in favor of plaintiffs in cases involving what some have called "values discrimination"; this fact has limited the impact of antidiscrimination laws on the gender pay gap (Nelson and Bridges 1999).

One way that antidiscrimination policies may have mattered, however, is in contributing to the broader social and cultural movement that altered women's expectations about their work lives and pay. The redefinition of gender identity and the corresponding legitimation of women's career ambitions that was in part facilitated by the passage of legal barriers to gender employment discrimination may have inspired a younger generation of women to invest more in labor-market careers. Consistent with this hypothesis, Claudia Goldin (2006, figure 2) shows that the proportion of teenage women who expected to be in the labor force at age thirty-five increased from around 33 percent for those interviewed in the late 1960s to around twice that by the mid-1970s. By the late 1970s, this figure had risen to above 80 percent.

Antidiscrimination laws, regulations, and enforcement practices may well have contributed to this trend, partly by improving the effectiveness of organizational personnel reforms aimed to promoting equity, such as official promotion of equity, constraints on managerial discretion, increases in transparency, and internal or external monitoring to promote accountability (Dobbin, Schrage, and Ka-

---

14. "Equal work" is defined narrowly. If the pay inequality is due to something other than the sex of the employee, then unequal pay is still permitted.

lev 2015). Other, less well-known policies also appear to have had labor-market effects. Title IX, for instance, increased women's participation in high school athletics, which may have increased women's ability to navigate competitive, male-dominated careers (Stevenson 2010). On the other hand, the enactment of the 1978 Pregnancy Discrimination Act slowed the wage growth of married women of childbearing age, largely because employers shifted the costs of the increase in the cost of insurance for these groups to these employees (Gruber 1994).

Smaller-scale industry- and firm-level policy changes also increased women's integration in labor markets. Kevin Stainback and Donald Tomaskovic-Devey (2012) show that just over half of the decline in occupational segregation between white men and either white or black women occurred from internal desegregation of existing firms, with the rest coming from the closing of relatively more segregated establishments and the opening of relatively less segregated establishments. One of the most compelling studies of localized antidiscrimination policies is Claudia Goldin and Cecilia Rouse's (2000) examination of orchestras' shift to "blind auditions". A unique feature of orchestras is that candidates only need to play an instrument and not speak during their audition. Goldin and Rouse's natural experiment uses a change in orchestras' auditions to use screens to conceal the identity of candidates. They then examine whether this policy increased the representation of women in orchestras and find that sex-blind auditions increased the probability that a woman would advance out of the preliminary trials by 50 percent. Sex-blind auditions furthermore increase by several times the probability that a woman will be the winner of the position in the final round. Their estimated magnitudes imply that blind auditions explain between 25 to 46 percent of the increase in women's representation in orchestras since 1970.

Whether restricting managerial discretion is the optimal strategy for reducing gender discrimination across the labor market as a whole, however, has been cast in doubt by recent research. Frank Dobbin and his colleagues conclude after their study of 816 establishments over a thirty-year period that organizational reforms that "engage managers in recruiting and training women and minorities for management posts" (2015, 1034) had more positive effects than policies intended to restrict the discretion of managers to discriminate against women and minorities. Evidence is considerable that discrimination emerges out of what Barbara Reskin (2000, 320) calls "normal cognitive processes . . . that occur regardless of people's motives" and that produces unequal outcomes through evaluation and attribution biases. How best to create to reduce the strength of cognitive biases is still an open and important research question.

PARENTAL LEAVE, HOURS REQUIREMENTS, AND CHILDCARE POLICIES

More recent work has focused on the impact of labor-market policies relating to parental leave. The increase in married mothers' labor-force participation and dual-earner families has created substantial demand for workplace policies that are "flexible" or "family friendly." Issues of balancing work and family life have been amplified by the rise in work hours (Jacobs and Gerson 2004) and women's entry into more demanding (and highly compensated) occupations. For historical or institutional reasons, many of these occupations do not allow for part-time work and many informally require more than standard forty-hour work weeks for continued employment or promotion.

In practice, many working parents are forced to choose either full-time or no employment. For a variety of cultural and economic reasons (including that women often earn less than men), the pattern of parental leave-taking has remained strongly gendered. Over the past two decades, around 20 percent of women have taken some time off of work for the birth of a child. The rate is lower among men, though it increased from 13 to 16 percent between 1995 and 2012 (Klerman, Daley, and Pozniak 2012). The larger gender gap is in the duration of leave. In 2012, 70 percent of men who took parental leave were away from work for ten days or less. In contrast, 78 percent of women taking parental leave were away from work for more than ten days; 40 percent of women who took parental leave were away for sixty days or more (Klerman, Daley, and Pozniak 2012). Survey evidence also shows that many working mothers prefer to work less. In survey data, 44 percent of mothers who currently work full time report that they would prefer to work part time (Wang, Parker, and Taylor 2013).

Parental leave provides one approach to mitigating the potentially negative effects of childbearing on women's careers and also for increasing men's ability to remain at home with new children. In other countries that make up the Organization for Economic Cooperation and Development (OECD), paid leave is considerably more generous. The OECD average is eighty weeks of leave, which includes thirty-three weeks of full-time equivalent paid leave (Byker 2016). Advocates argue that parental leave allows parents to preserve their attachment to the labor force and to their employers, which many argue should increase women's earnings and help close the gender gap. Opposing arguments suggest that more generous leave policies cause employers to discriminate against women by promoting them less or assigning them to tasks where other employees can easily replace them (when they take leave, for instance). The jury is still out on whether these policies reduce women's wage growth or promote women's career advancement (Ruhm 1998; Lalive and Zweimuller 2009; Blau and Kahn 2013).

Only recently have U.S. policies responded to the growing demand for reduced work requirements for parents. The 1993 Family and Medical Leave Act (FMLA) requires employers to provide up to twelve weeks of unpaid leave for a variety of issues, including childbirth. Some states have changed their policies to go further than the FMLA. More recently, California and New Jersey have passed laws to mandate paid leave for parents. California's policy provides for up to six weeks of paid leave at up to 55 percent of salary for a maximum of $1,075 per week.

The earliest research on FMLA found no measurable effect on women and men's leave taking (Han and Waldfogel 2003) or on women's employment outcomes (Han, Ruhm, and Waldfogel 2009). A recent working paper, however, provides a theoretical argument for how mandated maternity leave could affect firms' investments in their female employees and, ultimately, women's promotions. Using the PSID and the Multi-City Study of Urban Inequality, Mallika Thomas (2014) finds evidence suggesting that FMLA reduced the likelihood that women are promoted.

Paid leave laws do appear to have increased the use of parental leave (Espinola-Arredondo and Mondal 2010; Rossin-Slater, Ruhm, and Waldfogel 2013), though they find limited evidence that women's labor-force attachment responded. Tanya Byker (2016) uses detailed monthly information on women's employment to show that paid leave laws reduce short-term separations of women from their employers by 5 to 10 percentage points. Consistent with the structure of the policy, the largest effects of paid leave were among women with less than a college degree. More time is needed before the longer-term effects of these policies can be evaluated.

Some of the most interesting emerging evidence relating to family friendly policies is that they may shift how women select into occupations or firms in ways that benefit employers. This is similar to the finding that, in lab environments, introducing a gender quota has the effect of increasing the entry of high-performing women into more competitive environments (Niederle, Segal, and Vesterlund 2013). Similarly, capping the maximum work requirements in medical residencies altered the women who chose these specialties but did not affect men's choices (Wasserman 2015). Women's responses to these policies may help explain why some of the most profitable companies in Silicon Valley are adopting extremely generous family leave policies (Garcia 2015; Greenberg 2015).

Recent studies—based on imperfect data—suggest that the fraction of firms offering family-friendly work policies has been increasing. The Council of Economic Advisors' 2014 report notes that more than 75 percent of employers say they allow at least some workers to change their starting and ending times. At the same time, only 49 percent of all workers and 47 percent of full-time workers reported in 2011 that they have flexible work hours. Moreover, flexibility was reported to be more frequent for higher skilled workers. Employers cite costs as the reason why they do not further expand the use of flexible working hours; additionally, provision of such benefits is biased in favor of the incumbents of high-status jobs requiring high levels of education.

According to the Council of Economic Advisors, 74 percent of employers allowed some workers to gradually increase work hours after the birth or adoption of a child, but only 47 percent allowed most of their workers this flexibility. Only 37 percent of employers allowed most employees a few days off without having to use vacation days to care for sick children. Fifty-eight percent reported that they provided paid maternity leave for female employees. However, only 39 percent of workers in the American Time Use Surveys reported that they had access to paid family leave. As evidenced here, work-family balance is still a rarity for many employed mothers in the United States.

CULTURAL CHANGE

Changes in culture either caused by or resulting from these factors are difficult to quantify. Yet the increasing prevalence of more egalitarian sex-role attitudes in American society is an important and relatively recent development. Several studies document large changes since the 1960s. In a panel study of white mothers in metropolitan Detroit, only about 33 percent in 1962 disagreed that most important decisions in the life of the family should be made by "the man of the house." By the early 1990s, the proportion of these women disagreeing had risen to 84 percent for the mothers, and 78 percent of their adult sons also disagreed (Thornton and Young-DeMarco 2001). In 1977, only 33 percent of women over eighteen in the General Social Survey disagreed that "it is much better for everyone involved if the man is the achiever outside the home and the woman takes care of the home and family." By the mid-1990s, the proportion of women disagreeing with this statement had risen to nearly 66 percent, as had the proportion of men (Thornton and Young-DeMarco 2001).

However, David Cotter, Joan Hermsen, and Reeve Vanneman (2011) show that, since the mid-1990s, the fraction of men and women who support gender egalitarianism has stopped its upward trend. Many scholars explain the "stalled" gender revolution as an outcome of three conditions: persisting beliefs in "gender essentialism" (that is, women and men are "innately and fundamentally different" in interests and skills), a failure to achieve greater egalitarianism in domestic work and childrearing, and an adjustment by even strongly career-oriented women to the reality of dual pressures from work and family by making career compromises even if they have not actually adopted an ideology of "opting out" (Charles and Bradley 2002; Stone 2007; England 2010).

Changes in culture surrounding gender, in large part, are the consequences of the considerable changes in childbearing, parenting, educational attainment, and career investments that have occurred over the past fifty years. Arland Thornton, Duane Alwin, and Donald Camburn (1983) argue that the growth in egalitarian attitudes was a consequence of growing educational attainment on the part of both men and women, growing labor market experience on the part of married women, and the transmission of more gender egalitarian attitudes from mothers to daughters. Changes in access to modern contraception documented in previous sections may also encourage more egalitarian attitudes surrounding women's careers, motherhood, and domestic division of labor.

This shift toward more egalitarian attitudes has been accompanied by growing heterogeneity in the nature of the marital "exchange."[15] Historically, because men often specialized in market work (the output of which can be saved or accrued as an asset) and women in home production (the output of which is often more ephemeral, for example, clean laundry and

---

15. The Becker production model of marriage treats marriage as a contract in which the two parties follow their "natural" comparative advantages to split domestic and market work in order to create a "marital surplus." This surplus is divided between parties and provides an economic rationale for the union. The Becker method of calculating the value of marital surplus has been extensively criticized as ignoring the gains to marriage that can result even when both wives and husbands invest in their careers (Oppenheimer 1997).

meals), marital dissolution often meant that "men gained" financially and that "women lost." Men often took the income and assets with them and women bore the loss of the male income and gained sole responsibility for supporting dependents. But, over time, the rise in women's work and the growing economic interdependency of men and women has meant that by 1990 the typical divorcing male suffered a net loss in household-size-adjusted income following union dissolution as a consequence of losing the wife's income (McManus and DiPrete 2001), even though the financial consequences were typically worse for the woman than for her ex-partner. Meanwhile, recent estimates of the marriage premium find that women and men's wages grow following marriage (Budig and England 2001; Glauber 2007; Killewald and Gough 2013). Changes in women's labor-market participation and the change in the risk (and the laws surrounding divorce) have affected how households save and how women invest in their careers (Voena 2015)—all of which has changed the culture of marriage, family, and division of labor.

On the other hand, changes in culture are also a catalyzing force for change. The disaffection with domesticity at the height of the baby boom (as captured in Betty Friedan's 1963 bestseller, *The Feminine Mystique*), and the rise of second wave feminism likely played important roles (Mason, Czajka, and Arber 1976). At the same time, it is also likely that more recent developments are the continuation of an evolution that extends back in time to the first wave of feminism of the late nineteenth and early twentieth centuries, as well as women's empowerment during World War II. For instance, Raquel Fernandez, Alessandra Fogli, and Claudia Olivetti (2004) show that boys raised in families with working mothers during World War II were more likely to have wives who worked outside the home. Nicole Fortin (2015a) shows that beliefs about gender roles have a great deal of power in explaining both the evolution of women's labor-force participation during the last fifty years and the leveling off of these changes in the mid-1990s (for a more detailed cross-country summary of trends in happiness and well-being by gender, see Fortin 2015b).

Although much has changed, features of an older culture remain imprinted in today's economy and society. Even as changes in the age at first marriage and motherhood—in conjunction with changes in women's human capital and wages—have altered women's bargaining power within unions, the household division of labor has persisted. In a study of trends in time use by women and their male partners from the middle 1960s to the early 2000s, Suzanne Bianchi, John Robinson, and Melissa Milkie (2006) and Bianchi (2011) show a decline in the average housework of U.S. mothers from thirty-two hours in 1965 to eighteen in the middle 2000s, with most of this decline being in the "core" housework tasks of meal preparation, laundry, and housecleaning. Offsetting the decline was an upward trend in time spent at primary childcare time by U.S. mothers. After dropping from an average of ten hours a week in 1965 to 8.5 hours in 1975, primary childcare began rising after 1985 to almost fourteen hours a week by 2003 to 2008. Fathers, in contrast, doubled their hours spent on housework from 1965 to 1985 from an average of four to an average of ten hours per week, and they nearly tripled the amount of time devoted to primary childcare (from 2.5 hours between 1965 and 1985 to seven hours a week between 2003 and 2008).

Mark Aguiar and Erik Hurst (2007) show that total hours of childcare done by both sexes has increased by equal amounts, but the share of childcare done by men has risen from around 20 to 30 percent of the weekly hours. The bulk of nonmarket work (such as shopping and conducting household chores) also continues to be done by women and the share performed by men has fallen. In 1965, women spent around thirty-three hours per week on these tasks and men fewer than ten. By 2003, women had reduced their nonmarket work to 22.6 hours, and men had increased to thirteen. This implies that the share of nonmarket work done by men increased from 24 percent to around 36 percent between 1965 and 2003. Even though much has changed in labor markets and in homes, the division of nonmarket work in households has remained strongly gendered.

Many scholars have explored the persistence of culture through the lens of the norm about women earning less than their husbands (Brines 1994; Killewald and Gough 2010; Schwartz and Gonalons-Pons, this volume). In a recent and provocative study, Marianne Bertrand, Emir Kamenica, and Jessica Pan (2015) document in administrative and census data the persistence of a large discontinuity of wives' share of household income at 50 percent. Between 1970 and 1990, it appears that the discontinuity at 50 percent grew slightly, even as women's wages and career investments rose, though it has shrunk since 2000. In addition, recent internet and speed dating studies show that both men and women continue to prefer relationships in which men have higher status than their female partners (Fisman et al. 2006; Hitsch, Hortacsu, and Ariely 2010).

Scholars have argued about the cultural explanations for these patterns. In her analysis of PSID data, Jule Brines (1994) finds that women whose share of household income was more than 50 percent actually did more housework than women making slightly less, a pattern she refers to as a "gender display," which, she argues, offset the gender deviance of their making more money than their husband. Bertrand, Kamenica, and Pan (2015) use the PSID and fixed-effects models to estimate the woman's housework response to relative earnings, confirming Brines. Alexandra Killewald and Margaret Gough (2010) generate different estimates using more flexible linear splines. This reanalysis argues that the relationship between a woman's relative earnings and housework is actually a nonlinear relationship between the woman's absolute earnings and housework. Housework reductions are four times larger for women in the second to lowest quartile of the earnings distribution than above the median, and they are eight times larger for women in the lowest quartile than above the median. More work remains to be done to understand these findings. Where these studies agree, however, is that women generally do more housework than their husbands, even if they make as much or more money. In short, culture is slowly changing, but long-standing norms and perceptions about gender persist and can continue to impede convergence in women's and men's economic and social status.

VOLUME SUMMARY

The papers in this volume address several important aspects of career and family and find evidence of continued but uneven change in the status and behavior of both women and men. The questions in these papers range from the size of the family pay gap (sometimes called the "motherhood penalty") to the impact of persistent gender differences in fields of study.

The volume begins with two papers providing novel descriptions of recent changes in women's labor supply. The first, by Tanya Byker, engages the recent debate over whether highly educated women are increasingly likely to drop out of the labor force to care for children—a phenomenon called the opt-out revolution. This paper uses rich monthly information from the 1984 to 2008 Surveys of Income and Program Participation (SIPP) to quantify changes in labor-force participation and hours of work for mothers for two years before and after childbirth. Consistent with recent claims that labor-force participation rates drop around the time of childbirth, Byker documents a large (at least 18 percentage points) and persistent drop in women's participation after births for all education groups.

However, Byker's intertemporal comparisons reject recent claims of an "opt-out revolution." Byker finds surprisingly little change in opting out trends across the last thirty years. Before and after the enactment of the Family and Medical Leave Act of 1993 (FMLA), the drop in women's labor-force participation eight months after the birth compared with the year before the birth is remarkably similar and not statistically distinguishable. She does, however, find considerable heterogeneity by race, with black mothers less likely than white or Hispanic mothers to opt-out following the birth of a child.

Kim Weeden, Youngjoo Cha, and Mauricio Bucca address another interesting dimension of women's labor supply that affects the gender wage gap: women's representation in jobs demanding more than fifty hours per week. Both the rising returns to working these longer hours between 1969 and 2014 and the continued disproportionate representation of men in these positions play an increasingly important role in the gender gap in wages. Using the CPS Merged Outgoing Rotation Groups from 1984 to 2014, Weeden and her colleagues document how the hourly wages associated with long hours have risen relatively rapidly, both in absolute terms and after adjusting for education and demographic characteristics of employees in those jobs. This trend has been accompanied by a growing wage gap since 2000 in the wages of full-time and part-time workers. They estimate that the wage gap between fathers and mothers would be 15 percent lower if the observed growth in the wage premium for long hours had not occurred.

The articles that follow describe the evolution of the so-called motherhood gap, or family gap over the last forty-five years. The first, by Ipshita Pal and Jane Waldfogel, analyzes differences in pay between mothers and women without children in the 1967 to 2013 CPS. They document that, at the start of the period, the family pay gap was a fairly sizable 5 to 6 percent on average and rose to around 8 to 10 percent during the 1970s and early 1980s, producing findings that go against the conventional wisdom. Unlike the stalled convergence in other areas of the gender gap, the family gap fell quickly after 1990 to under 2 percent by the 2011 to 2013 period. Interestingly, these raw figures are fairly unaffected by controls for occupation, part-time work, or industry controls. They are also similar for mothers who have at least completed high school. Another fascinating finding is that the pay gap has disappeared or even reversed for married mothers, white mothers, and highly educated women. In contrast, the gap has persisted for unmarried mothers, mothers with less than high school completion, and non-Hispanic black mothers. The trend has also differed by age of youngest child, with the gap disappearing for mothers with children under six, but remaining at around 6 percent for mothers whose youngest child is over six.

Claudia Buchmann and Anne McDaniel shift the focus to the changing situation of women in professional and managerial positions. Using 1980 to 2010 censuses and ACS data, they document declines in the pay gap across a myriad of professional occupational groups; however, the magnitude of these declines varied by occupation in often surprising ways. In the traditionally male-dominated occupations of medicine, law, and STEM fields, mothers have completely erased the negative family pay gap and now even show a small positive premium, making them similar in this respect to fathers in these occupations. Interestingly, a motherhood gap persists (even though smaller in size) for mothers who work in professions that are dominated by women. They conclude with several possible explanations for why the sign of the family pay gap has reversed for women in the most elite occupations, thus setting an agenda for future research on this important issue.

The next set of papers explores the implications of women's increasing entry into nontraditionally female and STEM fields. Kimberlee Shauman's paper explores the changing influence of the sex-composition of degree field in the early outcomes of college graduates. Using data from the National Longitudinal Study of the Class of 1972 and more recent data from the Baccalaureate and Beyond Studies, she studies men and women who major in subjects that are nontraditional for their gender and graduated between 1976 and 1978, in 1993, in 2000, and in 2008. Consistent with other research, Shauman finds that the entry of women into more male-dominated fields has slowed for cohorts graduating since the early 1990s. In contrast, men's distribution across fields according to their gender composition changed very little across the last four decades. Field integration, in other words, has occurred through shifts in the behavior of women much more so than of men. Shauman finds a small but persistent tendency for men and women to be less likely to work in a job that is closely related to their field of study when the field is atypical for their gender. Another fascinating finding is that of a persistent negative relationship between the share of women in a field and starting salaries for full-time employed graduates from that field, and that the relationship became more negative over time. Women generally earned less than men in their first year, even controlling for hours worked, and the gap was especially large for graduates of male-dominated fields. At the same time, the relative advantage to women of majoring in male-dominated fields increased across the period studied.

Katherine Michelmore and Sharon Sassler examine trends in the size of the gender gap in wages in STEM fields. Their analysis uses the 1995 to 2008 National Science Foundation's Scientists and Engineers Statistical Data System and includes STEM majors who graduated from college between 1970 and 2004 and who work at least thirty-five hours per week. They find a wage gap of about 20 percentage points between women and men in these fields. Most of this difference, they argue, is due to differences in work experience. Consequently, this gap has been falling across cohorts as more women move into STEM fields and as the work experience gap between male and female STEM workers has fallen. Similar to that of Buchmann and McDaniel, Michelmore and Sassler's analysis finds that the gender wage gap in STEM fields is generally smaller than it is in other occupations, which suggests that the gender gap in wages would decrease if a greater proportion of women college graduates entered STEM fields. The authors also identify two forces that work to maintain a gender wage gap in STEM fields: a tendency for women to work in lower paid STEM occupations and a continuing gender wage gap among computer scientists that has not changed across cohorts. This latter force, they argue, suggests that women are not getting the same returns to experience in computer science as are their male coworkers.

The next set of papers focuses on the relationship between women's work and their marriage outcomes. Although women generally earn less than men, the growth in the wages and hours of female workers has—along with assortative matching—increased the share of marriages in which the wife earns more than her male partner. Using the 1968 to 2009 PSID, Christine Schwartz and Pilar Gonalons-Pons investigate whether marriages in which women outearn their partners are more likely to dissolve. True to conventional wisdom, they find that such marriages were, indeed, more vulnerable to divorce during the 1970s and 1980s. Over time, however, this heightened divorce risk has essentially disappeared. Average real household earnings have increased by more than 30 percent for couples where wives earn more than husbands, whereas the real earnings of couples in which wives earn no more than their husbands has barely changed. Schwartz and Gonalons-Pons hypothesize that the growing economic advantage of having a high-earning wife may have facilitated the adaptation of this cultural norm to more egalitarian marriages.

Chinhui Juhn and Kristin McCue examine the reverse relationship, running from marriage to earnings. Of particular interest is the standard cross-sectional finding that married men earn from 10 percent to 40 percent more than single men but that married women earn significantly less than unmarried women with similar human capital characteristics. The two primary explanations relate to selection, the process by which the characteristics related to earnings differ between those who marry and those who do not, and specialization, the process by which spouses increase the total family output when one spouse invests more heavily in the labor market and the other invests more in home production. Using data from the SIPP that has been matched to Social Security Administration earnings records from 1954 to 2011, Juhn and McCue find a decline in the marriage earnings gap associated with specialization for women, particularly when children are not present. They also find an increasing selection of more educated women into marriage between cohorts born from 1936 to 1945 (who entered labor markets between 1954 and 1963) and 1966 to 1975 (who entered labor markets between 1984 and 1993) that further reduced the difference between earnings of married and single women. When these selection effects are not taken into account, a positive marriage gap is evident even among women with children. Their analysis suggests a growing marriage premium for men, even when they use a fixed-effects specification as an attempt to control for selection. Taken literally, this finding implies an increase in specialization or selection into marriage based on predicted earnings trajectories—a puzzle they leave for future research.

The volume's final paper, by Ashley Jardina and Nancy Burns, examines how political participation by sex has changed in recent decades as women's social and economic roles have changed. A long history of research on political participation has made it clear that resources such as educational attainment and the civic skills individuals acquired in the workforce are important predictors of political participation. Not surprisingly, then, in the middle of the twentieth century, when most American women did not attend college and did work at home as caretakers, women's levels of political participation were relatively low. Women voted, donated to campaigns, expressed interest in elections, and participated in campaign activities at much lower rates than men. Jardina and Burns posit, however, that the impressive economic and educational gains women made over the course of the next five decades ought to have had similarly profound consequences for women's levels of political participation. They note that while women's levels of participation have certainly increased in recent decades, their engagement with the political world is perhaps more tepid than we might expect to see given the magnitude of the social and economic changes women have experienced. Jardina and Burns argue that men's and women's attitudes about gender roles explain why greater increases in women's political participation have not occurred. Even though both sexes have become more egalitarian in their views over time, this shift has been slow, and a persistent and sizeable minority of both men and women continue to endorse traditional gender roles. As a final part of their paper, the authors address the level of support for governmental policies that would reduce the conflict between work and family: federally supported childcare, parental leave, equal pay for equal work, and federal efforts to prevent job discrimination against women. In each case, they show that the level of support for such policies is relatively low among those who have more traditional views about women's role in employment and in the home.

REFERENCES

Aguiar, Mark, and Erik Hurst. 2007. "Measuring Trends in Leisure: The Allocation of Time over Five Decades." *Quarterly Journal of Economics* 122(3): 969–1006.

Albiston, Catherine. 2007. "Institutional Perspectives on Law, Work, and Family." *Annual Review of Law and Social Science* 3(1): 397–426.

Altonji, Joseph, and Rebecca M. Blank. 1999. "Race and Gender in the Labor Market." In *Handbook of Labor Economics*, vol. 3, edited by Orley Ashenfelter and David Card. Philadelphia, Pa. Elsevier.

Angrist, Joshua D., and William N. Evans. 1996. "Schooling and Labor Market Consequences of the 1970 State Abortion Reforms." NBER working paper 5406. Cambridge, Mass.: National Bureau of Economic Research.

Apicella, Coren, Anna Dreber, Benjamin Campbell, Peter Gray, Moshe Hoffman, and Anthony Little. 2008. "Testosterone and Financial Risk Preferences." *Evolution and Human Behavior* 29(6): 384–90.

Bailey, Martha J. 2006. "More Power to the Pill: The Impact of Contraceptive Freedom on Women's Lifecycle Labor Supply." *Quarterly Journal of Economics* 121(1): 289–320.

———. 2009. "Erratum and Addendum." Accessed September 2, 2015. http://www-personal.umich.edu/~baileymj/Bailey_Erratum.pdf.

———. 2010. "'Momma's Got the Pill': How Anthony Comstock and Griswold v. Connecticut Shaped U.S. Childbearing." *American Economic Review* 100(1): 98–129.

———. 2012. "Reexamining the Impact of U.S. Family Planning Programs on Fertility: Evidence from the War on Poverty and the Early Years of Title X." *American Economic Journal: Applied Economics* 4(2): 62–97.

Bailey, Martha J., Melanie Guldi, and Brad J. Hershbein. 2013. "Further Evidence on the Internal Validity of the Early Legal Access Research Design." *Journal of Policy Analysis and Management* 32(4): 899–904.

———. 2014. "Is There a Case for a 'Second Demographic Transition': Three Distinctive Features of the Post-1960 U.S. Fertility Decline." In *Human Capital and History: The American Record*, edited by Leah P. Boustan, Carola Frydman and Robert A. Margo. Cambridge, Mass.: National Bureau of Economics Research.

Bailey, Martha J., Brad J. Hershbein, and Amalia R.

Miller. 2012. "The Opt-In Revolution? Contraception and the Gender Gap in Wages." *American Economic Journal: Applied Economics* 4(3): 225–54.

Bertrand, Marianne. 2010. "New Perspectives on Gender." In *Handbook of Labor Economics*, vol. 4B, edited by Orley Ashenfelter and David Card. Philadelphia, Pa.: Elsevier.

Bertrand, Marianne, Claudia Goldin, and Lawrence F. Katz. 2010. "Dynamics of the Gender Gap for Young Professionals in the Financial and Corporate Sectors." *American Economic Journal: Applied Economics* 2(3): 228–55.

Bertrand, Marianne, and Kevin Hallock. 2001. "The Gender Gap in Top Corporate Jobs." *Industrial and Labor Relations Review* 55: 3–21. Accessed March 31, 2016. http://digitalcommons.ilr.cornell.edu/hrpubs/14/.

Bertrand, Marianne, Emir Kamenica, and Jessica Pan. 2015. "Gender Identity and Relative Income within Households." *Quarterly Journal of Economics* 130(3): 571–614.

Bianchi, Susan M. 2011. "Changing Families, Changing Workplaces." *The Future of Children* 21(2): 15–36.

Bianchi, Susan M., John P. Robinson, and Melissa A. Milkie. 2006. *Changing Rhythms of American Family Life*. New York: Russell Sage Foundation.

Bitler, Marianne P., and Madeline Zavodny. 2001. "The Effect of Abortion Restrictions on the Timing of Abortions." *Journal of Health Economics* 20(6): 1011–32.

Blank, Rebecca M., Christine George, and Rebecca London. 1996. "State Abortion Rates: The Impact of Policies, Providers, Politics, Demographics, and Economic Environment." *Journal of Health Economics* 15(5): 513–53.

Blau, Francine D., Peter Brummund, and Albert Yung-Hsu Liu. 2013. "Trends in Occupational Segregation by Gender 1970–2009: Adjusting for the Impact of Changes in the Occupational Coding System." *Demography* 50(2): 471–92.

Blau, Francine D., Marianne A. Ferber, and Anne W. Winkler. 2014. *The Economics of Women, Men, and Work*, 7th ed. Upper Saddle River, N.J.: Prentice Hall/Pearson.

Blau, Francine D., and Lawrence M. Kahn. 1997. "Swimming Upstream: Trends in the Gender Wage Differential in the 1980s." *Journal of Labor Economics* 15(1): 1–42.

———. 2006. "The U.S. Gender Pay Gap in the 1990s: Slowing Convergence." *Industrial & Labor Relations Review* 60(1): 45–66.

———. 2007. "Changes in the Labor Supply Behavior of Married Women: 1980–2000." *Journal of Labor Economics* 25(3): 393–438.

———. 2013. "Female Labor Supply: Why Is the US Falling Behind?" *American Economic Review* 103(3): 251–56.

———. Forthcoming. "The Gender Wage Gap: Extent, Trends, and Sources." *Journal of Economic Literature*.

Booth, Alison L., and Patrick J. Nolen. 2012. "Choosing to Compete: How Different Are Girls and Boys?" *Journal of Economic Behavior & Organization* 81(2): 542–55.

Boschini, Anne, Astri Muren, and Mats Persson. 2012. "Constructing Gender Differences in the Economics Lab." *Journal of Economic Behavior & Organization* 84(3): 741–52.

Box-Steffensmeier, Janet, Raphael Cunha, Rouman Varbanov, Yee Shaw Hoh, Margaret A. Knisley, and Mary Alice Holmes. 2015. "Survival Analysis of Faculty Retention and Promotion in the Social Sciences by Gender." *PloS One* 10(11): e0143093.

Bradley, Karen. 2000. "The Incorporation of Women into Higher Education: Paradoxical Outcomes?" *Sociology of Education* 73(1): 1–18.

Brines, Julie. 1994. "Economic Dependency, Gender, and the Division of Labor at Home." *American Journal of Sociology* 100(3): 652–88.

Broder, Arndt, and Natalia Hohmann. 2003. "Variations in Risk Taking Behavior over the Menstrual Cycle: An Improved Replication." *Evolution and Human Behavior* 24(6): 391–98.

Bronson, Mary Ann. 2013. "Degrees Are Forever: Marriage, Educational Investment, and Lifecycle Labor Decisions of Men and Women." Unpublished manuscript, University of California, Los Angeles.

Browne, Stephanie P., and Sara LaLumia. 2014. "The Effects of Contraception on Female Poverty." *Journal of Policy Analysis and Management* 33(3): 602–22.

Buchmann, Claudia, Thomas A. DiPrete, and Anne McDaniel. 2008. "Gender Inequalities in Education." *Annual Review of Sociology* 34(1): 319–37.

Budig, Michelle, and Paula England. 2001. "The Wage Penalty for Motherhood." *American Sociological Review* 66(2): 204–25.

Bureau of Labor Statistics (BLS). 2014. "Women in

the Labor Force: A Databook." Report no. 1052. Washington: U.S. Department of Labor.

Buser, Thomas, Muriel Niederle, and Hessel Oosterbeek. 2014. "Gender, Competitiveness, and Career Choices." *Quarterly Journal of Economics* 129(3): 1409–47.

Byker, Tanya. 2016. "Paid Parental Leave Laws in the United States: Does Short-Duration Leave Affect Women's Labor-Force Attachment?" *American Economic Review, Papers and Proceedings* (May).

Card, David, and John E. DiNardo. 2002. "Skill-Biased Technological Change and Rising Wage Inequality: Some Problems and Puzzles." *Journal of Labor Economics* 20(4): 733–83.

Carrell, Scott E., Marianne E. Page, and James T. West. 2010. "Sex and Science: How Professor Gender Perpetuates the Gender Gap." *Quarterly Journal of Economics* 125(3): 1101–44.

Ceci, Stephen J., Donna K. Ginther, Shulamit Kahn, and Wendy M. Williams. 2014. "Women in Academic Science: A Changing Landscape." *Psychological Science* 15(3): 75–141.

Centers for Disease Control and Prevention (CDC). 2000. "Historical Statistics: Table 1-1. Live Births, Birth Rates, and Fertility Rates, by Race: United States, 1909–2000." Accessed March 31, 2016. http://www.cdc.gov/nchs/data/statab/t001x01.pdf.

Charles, Maria. 2011. "A World of Difference: International Trends in Women's Economic Status." *Annual Review of Sociology* 37(1): 355–71.

Charles, Maria, and Karen Bradley. 2002. "Equal but Separate? A Cross-National Study of Sex Segregation in Higher Education." *American Sociological Review* 67(4): 573–99.

Charles, Maria, and David B. Grusky. 2004. *Occupational Ghettos: The Worldwide Segregation of Women and Men*. Palo Alto, Calif.: Stanford University Press.

Christensen, Finn. 2011. "The Pill and Partnerships: The Impact of the Birth Control Pill on Cohabitation." *Journal of Population Economics* 25(1): 29–52.

Coate, Stephanie, and Glenn Loury. 1993. "Will Affirmative-Action Policies Eliminate Negative Stereotypes?" *American Economic Review* 83(2): 92–98.

Cohen, Geoffrey L., Julio Garcia, Valerie Purdue-Vaughns, Nancy Apfel, and Patricia Brzustoski. 2009. "Recursive Processes of Self-Affirmation: Intervening to Close the Minority Achievement Gap." *Science* 324(5925): 400–3.

Cohen, Geoffrey L., and David K. Sherman. 2014. "The Psychology of Change: Self-Affirmation and Social Psychological Intervention." *Annual Review of Psychology* 65: 333–71.

Cohen, Lisa E., and Joseph P. Broschak. 2013. "Whose Jobs Are These? The Impact of the Proportion of Female Managers on the Number of New Management Jobs Filled by Women Versus Men." *Administrative Science Quarterly* 58(4): 509–41.

Collins, Gail. 2009. *When Everything Changed: The Amazing Journey of American Women from 1960 to the Present*. New York: Little, Brown.

Correll, Shelley J. 2001. "Gender and the Career Choice Process: The Role of Biased Self-Assessments." *American Journal of Sociology* 106(6): 1691–730.

———. 2004. "Constraints into Preferences: Gender, Status, and Emerging Career Aspirations." *American Sociological Review* 69(1): 93–113.

Correll, Shelley J., Stephen Benard, and In Paik. 2007. "Getting a Job: Is There a Motherhood Penalty?" *American Journal of Sociology* 112(5): 1297–339.

Costa, Dora L. 2000. "From Mill Town to Board Room: The Rise of Women's Paid Labor." *Journal of Economic Perspectives* 14(4): 101–22.

Cotter, David A., Joan M. Hermsen, and Reeve Vanneman. 2004. *RSF Census Series. Year 2000. Gender Inequality at Work*. New York: Russell Sage Foundation.

———. 2011. "The End of the Gender Revolution? Gender Role Attitudes from 1977 to 2008." *American Journal of Sociology* 117(1): 259–89.

Cotton, Christopher, Frank McIntyre, and Joseph Price. 2013. "Gender Differences in Repeated Competition: Evidence from School Math Contests." *Journal of Economic Behavior & Organization* 86(February): 52–66.

Council of Economic Advisors. 2014. "The Economics of Paid and Unpaid Leave." Accessed September 5, 2015. https://www.whitehouse.gov/sites/default/files/docs/leave_report_final.pdf.

Crimmins, Eileen M., Samuel H. Preston, and Barney Cohen, eds. 2011. *Explaining Divergent Levels of Longevity in High-Income Countries*. Washington, D.C.: National Academies Press.

Dalton, Ben, Steven J. Ingels, Jane Downing, and

Robert Bozick. 2007. *Advanced Mathematics and Science Coursetaking in the Spring High School Senior Classes of 1982, 1992, and 2004*. Washington: U.S. Department of Education.

DiNardo, John, Nicole M. Fortin, and Thomas Lemieux. 1996. "Labor Market Institutions and the Distribution of Wages, 1973–1992: A Semiparametric Approach." *Econometrica* 64(5): 1001–44.

DiPrete, Thomas A., and Claudia Buchmann. 2006. "Gender-Specific Trends in the Value of Education and the Emerging Gender Gap in College Completion." *Demography* 43(1): 1–24.

———. 2013. *The Rise of Women: The Growing Gender Gap in Education and What It Means for American Schools*. New York: Russell Sage Foundation.

Dobbin, Frank, Daniel Schrage, and Alexandra Kalev. 2015. "Rage Against the Iron Cage: The Varied Effects of Bureaucratic Personnel Reforms on Diversity." *American Sociological Review* 80(5): 1014–44. Accessed April 1, 2016. http://scholar.harvard.edu/files/dobbin/files/asr2015.pdf?m=1450808944.

Ellwood, David T., and Christopher Jencks. 2004. "The Uneven Spread of Single Parent Families: What Do We Know? Where Do We Look for Answers?" In *Social Inequality*, edited by Kathryn Neckerman. Cambridge, Mass: Harvard University Press.

England, Paula. 2010. "The Gender Revolution: Uneven and Stalled." *Gender & Society* 24(2): 149–66.

England, Paula, and Su Li. 2006. "Desegregation Stalled: The Changing Gender Composition of College Majors, 1971–2002." *Gender & Society* 20(5): 657–77.

Espinola-Arredondo, Ana, and Sunita Mondal. 2010. "The Effect of Parental Leave on Female Employment: Evidence from State Policies." *School of Economic Sciences* working paper no. 2008–15. Pullman: Washington State University.

Fernandez, Raquel. 2013. "Cultural Change as Learning: The Evolution of Female Labor-Force Participation over a Century." *American Economic Review* 103(1): 472–550.

Fernandez, Raquel, Alessandra Fogli, and Claudia Olivetti. 2004. "Mothers and Sons: Preference Formation and Female Labor Force Dynamics." *Quarterly Journal of Economics* 119(4): 1249–99.

Fisman, Raymond, Sheena S. Iyengar, Emir Kamenica, and Itamar Simonson. 2006. "Gender Differences in Mate Selection: Evidence from a Speed Dating Experiment." *Quarterly Journal of Economics* 121(May): 673–97.

Fortin, Nicole M. 2015a. "How Does Subjective Well-Being Vary Around the World by Gender and Age." In *World Happiness Report*, edited by John F. Helliwell, Richard Layard, and Jeffrey Sachs. New York: Columbia University Press.

———. 2015b. "Gender Role Attitudes and Women's Labor Market Participation: Opting Out, AIDS, and the Persistent Appeal of Housewifery." *Annals of Economics and Statistics* 117–118, Special Issue on the Economics of Gender (June 2015): 379–401.

Fortin, Nicole M., and Thomas Lemieux. 1998. "Rank Regressions, Wage Distributions, and the Gender Gap." *Journal of Human Resources* 33(3): 610–43.

Freese, Jeremy, Jui-Chung Allen Li, and Lisa D. Wade. 2003. "The Potential Relevances of Biology to Social Inquiry." *Annual Review of Sociology* 29: 233–56.

Friedan, Betty. 1963. *The Feminine Mystique*. New York: W. W. Norton.

Garcia, Patricia. 2015. "Why Silicon Valley's Paid Leave Policies Need to Go Viral." *Vogue*, August 6. Accessed March 31, 2016. http://www.vogue.com/13291620/paid-parental-leave-netflix-silicon-valley/.

Glass, Jennifer L., and Sarah Beth Estes. 1997. "The Family Responsive Workplace." *Annual Review of Sociology* 23: 289–313.

Glass, Jennifer L., and Ashley Finley. 2002. "Coverage and Effectiveness of Family-Responsive Workplace Policies." *Human Resource Management Review* 12(3): 313–37.

Glauber, Rebecca. 2007. "Race and Gender in Families and at Work: The Fatherhood Wage Premium." *Gender & Society* 22(1): 8–30.

Gneezy, Uri, Kenneth L. Leonard, and John A. List. 2009. "Gender Differences in Competition: Evidence from a Matrilineal and a Patriarchal Society." *Econometrica* 77(5): 1637–64.

Goldin, Claudia. 1990. *Understanding the Gender Gap: An Economic History of American Women*. New York: Oxford University Press.

———. 1991. "Marriage Bars: Discrimination Against Married Women Workers, 1920's to 1950's." In *Favorites of Fortune: Technology, Growth and*

Economic Development Since the Industrial Revolution, edited by Henry Rosovsky, David Landes, and Patrice Higgonet. Cambridge, Mass.: Harvard University Press.

——. 2006. "The Quiet Revolution That Transformed Women's Employment, Education, and Family." *American Economic Review* 96(2): 1–21.

——. 2014. "A Grand Gender Convergence: Its Last Chapter." *American Economic Review* 104(4): 1091–19.

——. 2015. "Undergraduate Women in Economics: Background Facts." Harvard University. Accessed September 2, 2015. http://scholar.harvard.edu/goldin/background-facts.

Goldin, Claudia, and Lawrence F. Katz. 2002. "The Power of the Pill: Oral Contraceptives and Women's Career and Marriage Decisions." *Journal of Political Economy* 110(4): 730–70.

——. 2011. "The Cost of Workplace Flexibility for High-Powered Professionals." *Annals of the American Academy of Political and Social Science* 638(1): 45–67.

Goldin, Claudia, Lawrence Katz, and Ilyana Kuziemko. 2006. "The Homecoming of American College Women: The Reversal of the College Gender Gap." *Journal of Economic Perspectives* 20(4): 133–56.

Goldin, Claudia, and Cecilia Rouse. 2000. "Orchestrating Impartiality: The Impact Of 'Blind' Auditions on Female Musicians." *American Economic Review* 90(4): 715–41.

Gornick, Janet, and Marcia Meyers. 2005. *Families that Work: Policies for Reconciling Parenthood and Employment.* New York: Russell Sage Foundation.

Graefe, Deborah, and Daniel Lichter. 1999. "Life Course Transitions of American Children: Parental Cohabitation, Marriage, and Single Motherhood." *Demography* 36(2): 205–17.

Greenberg, Julia. 2015. "Tech's Selfish Reasons for Offering More Parental Leave." *Wired,* August 13. Accessed March 31, 2016. http://www.wired.com/2015/08/techs-selfish-reasons-offering-parental-leave/.

Gruber, Jonathan. 1994. "The Incidence of Mandated Maternity Benefits." *American Economic Review* 84(3): 622–41.

Guldi, Melanie. 2008. "Fertility Effects of Abortion and Pill Access for Minors." *Demography* 45(4): 817–27.

Guvenen, Fatih, Greg Kaplan, and Jae Song. 2014. "The Glass Ceiling and The Paper Floor: Gender Differences Among Top Earners, 1981–2012." NBER working paper no. 20560. Cambridge, Mass.: National Bureau of Economic Research.

Han, Wen Jui, Christopher J. Ruhm, and Jane Waldfogel. 2009. "Parental Leave Policies and Parents' Employment and Leave-Taking." *Journal of Policy Analysis and Management* 28(1): 29–54.

Han, Wen Jui, and Jane Waldfogel. 2003. "Parental Leave: The Impact of Recent Legislation on Parents' Leave Taking." *Demography* 40(1): 191–200.

Hegewisch, Ariane, and Hannah Liepmann. 2013. "Occupational Segregation and the Gender Wage Gap in the US." In *Handbook of Research on Gender and Economic Life*, edited by Deborah M. Figart and Tonia L. Warnecke. Gloucester, UK: Edward Elgar Publishing.

Hegewisch, Ariane, and Max Matite. 2013. "The Gender Wage Gap by Occupation." *ICWPR* Fact Sheet no. C431. Washington, D.C.: Institute for Women's Policy Research.

Henshaw, Stanley K., and Kathryn Kost. 2008. *Trends in the Characteristics of Women Obtaining Abortions, 1974 to 2004.* New York: Guttmacher Institute.

Hilmer, Christiana, and Michael Hilmer. 2010. "Are There Gender Differences in the Job Mobility Patterns of Academic Economists?" *American Economic Review* 100(2): 353–57.

Hitsch, Gunter J., Ali Hortacsu, and Dan Ariely. 2010. "Matching and Sorting in Online Dating." *American Economic Review* 100(1): 130–63.

Hock, Heinrich. 2008. "The Pill and the College Attainment of American Women and Men." Department of Economics working paper no. 2007-10-1. Tallahassee: University of Florida.

Hout, Michael. 2016. "Money and Morale: Growing Inequality Affects How Americans View Themselves and Others." *Annals of the American Academy of Political and Social Sciences* 663(1): 204–28.

Huffman, Matt L., Phillip N. Cohen, and Jessica Pearlman. 2010. "Engendering Change: Organizational Dynamics and Workplace Gender Desegregation, 1975–2005." *Administrative Science Quarterly* 55(2): 255–77.

Hutchings, Jane E., Patti J. Benson, Gordon W. Perkin, and Richard M. Soderstrom. 1985. "The IUD after 20 Years." *Family Planning Perspectives* 17(6): 250–55.

Ichino, Andrea, and Enrico Moretti. 2009. "Biological Gender Differences, Absenteeism, and the Earnings Gap." *American Economic Journal: Applied Economics* 1(1): 183-218.

Jacobs, Jerry A. 1989. "Long-Term Trends in Occupational Segregation by Sex." *American Journal of Sociology* 95(1): 160-73.

———. 1995. "Gender and Academic Specialties: Trends among Recipients of College Degrees in the 1980s." *Sociology of Education* 68(2): 81-98.

———. 2003. "Detours on the Road to Equality: Women, Work and Higher Education." *Contexts* 2(1): 32-41.

Jacobs, Jerry A., and Kathleen Gerson. 2004. *The Time Divide*. Cambridge, Mass.: Harvard University Press.

Juhn, Chinhui, and Simon Potter. 2006. "Changes in Labor Force Participation in the United States." *Journal of Economic Perspectives* 20(3): 27-46.

National Bureau of Economic Research (NBER). "June Current Population Surveys: 1979-2010." Accessed March 31, 2016. http://www.nber.org/data/current-population-survey-data.html.

Kane, Thomas, and Douglas Staiger. 1996. "Teen Motherhood and Abortion Access." *Quarterly Journal of Economics* 111(2): 467-506.

Kearney, Melissa S., and Phillip Levine. 2009. "Subsidized Contraception, Fertility, and Sexual Behavior." *Review of Economics and Statistics* 91(1): 137-51.

Killewald, Alexandra, and Margaret Gough. 2010. "Money Isn't Everything: Wives' Earnings and Housework Time." *Social Science Research* 39(6): 987-1003.

———. 2013. "Does Specialization Explain Marriage Penalties and Premiums?" *American Sociological Review* 78(3): 477-502.

Klerman, Jacob Alex, Kelly Daley, and Alyssa Pozniak. 2012. *Family and Medical Leave in 2012: Technical Report*. Cambridge, Mass.: Abt Associates. Accessed March 31, 2016. http://www.dol.gov/asp/evaluation/fmla/FMLA-2012-Technical-Report.pdf.

Kray, Laura J., Adam D. Galinsky and Leigh Thompson. 2002. "Reversing the Gender Gap in Negotiations: An Exploration of Stereotype Regeneration." *Organizational Behavior and Human Decision Processes* 87(2): 386-410.

Kray, Laura J., Leigh Thompson, and Adam D. Galinsky. 2001. "Battle of the Sexes: Gender Stereotype Confirmation and Reactance in Negotiations." *Journal of Personality and Social Psychology* 80(6): 942-58.

Lalive, Rafael, and Joseph Zweimuller. 2009. "How Does Parental Leave Affect Fertility and Return to Work? Evidence from Two Natural Experiments." *Quarterly Journal of Economics* 124(3): 1363-402.

Lee, David S. 1999. "Wage Inequality in the United States during the 1980s: Rising Dispersion or Falling Minimum Wage?" *Quarterly Journal of Economics* 114(3): 977-1023.

Legewie, Joscha, and Thomas A. DiPrete. 2012. "School Context and the Gender Gap in Educational Achievement." *American Sociological Review* 77(3): 463-85.

———. 2014. "The High School Environment and the Gender Gap in Science and Engineering." *Sociology of Education* 87(4): 259-80.

Leonard, Jonathon. 1990. "The Impact of Affirmative Action Regulation and Equal Opportunity Law on Employment." *Journal of Economic Perspectives* 4(4): 47-63.

Levine, Phillip. 2003. "Parental Involvement Laws and Fertility Behavior " *Journal of Health Economics* 22: 861-78.

Levine, Phillip, and Douglas Staiger. 2002. "Abortion as Insurance." *NBER* working paper no. 8813. Cambridge, Mass.: National Bureau of Economic Research.

Levine, Phillip, Douglas Staiger, Thomas Kane, and David Zimmerman. 1996. "Roe v. Wade and American Fertility." *NBER* working paper no. 5615. Cambridge, Mass.: National Bureau of Economic Research.

———. 1999. "Roe v. Wade and American Fertility." *American Journal of Public Health* 89(2): 199-204.

Lopez, Steven, Randy Hodson, and Vincent Roscigno. 2009. "Power, Status, and Abuse at Work: General and Sexual Harassment Compared." *Sociological Quarterly* 50(1): 3-27.

Lundberg, Shelly, and Robert A. Pollak. 2007. "The American Family and Family Economics." *Journal of Economic Perspectives* 21(2): 3-26.

Mann, Allison, and Thomas A. DiPrete. 2013. "Trends in Gender Segregation in the Choice of Science and Engineering Majors." *Social Science Research* 42(6): 1519-41.

Mann, Allison, Joscha Legewie, and Thomas A. DiPrete. 2015. "The Role of School Performance in Narrowing Gender Gaps in the Formation of

STEM Aspirations: A Cross-National Study." *Frontiers in Psychology* 6 (February): 1–11.

Martinez, Gladys, Kimberly Daniels, and Anjani Chandra. 2012. "Fertility of Men and Women Aged 15–44 Years in the United States: National Survey of Family Growth." National Health Statistics Reports 1–28. April 12, 2012.

Mason, Karen Oppenheim, John L. Czajka, and Sara Arber. 1976. "Changes in U.S. Women's Sex-Role Attitudes, 1964–1974." *American Sociological Review* 41: 573–96.

Matsa, David A., and Amalia R. Miller. 2011. "Chipping Away at the Glass Ceiling: Gender Spillovers in Corporate Leadership." *American Economic Review* 101(3): 635.

McLanahan, Sara, and Tara Watson. 2011. "Marriage Meets the Joneses: Relative Income, Identity, and Marital Status." *Journal of Human Resources* 46(3): 482–517.

McManus, Patricia A., and Thomas A. DiPrete. 2001. "Losers and Winners: The Financial Consequences of Separation and Divorce for Men." *American Sociological Review* 66(2): 246–68.

Mulligan, Casey B., and Yona Rubinstein. 2008. "Selection, Investment, and Women's Relative Wages over Time." *Quarterly Journal of Economics* 123(3): 1061–110.

Myers, Caitlin. 2012. "Power of the Pill or Power of Abortion? Re-Examining the Effects of Young Women's Access to Reproductive Control." *IZA* discussion paper no. 6661. Bonn: Institute for the Study of Labor.

National Center of Health Statistics. 2001. "Live Births, Birth Rates, and Fertility Rates, by Race: United States, 1909–2000." Accessed September 2, 2015. http://www.cdc.gov/nchs/data/statab/t001x01.pdf.

Nelson, Robert, and William Bridges. 1999. *Legalizing Gender Inequality: Courts, Markets, and Unequal Pay for Women in America*. Cambridge: Cambridge University Press.

Niederle, Muriel, Carmit Segal, and Lise Vesterlund. 2013. "How Costly Is Diversity? Affirmative Action in Light of Gender Differences in Competitiveness." *Management Science* 59(1): 1–16.

Niederle, Muriel, and Lise Vesterlund. 2007. "Do Women Shy Away from Competition? Do Men Compete Too Much?" *Quarterly Journal of Economics* 122(3): 1067–101.

———. 2010. "Explaining the Gender Gap in Math Test Scores: The Role of Competition." *Journal of Economic Perspectives* 24(2): 129–44.

Nisbett, Richard E., Joshua Aronson, Clancy Blair, William Dickens, James Flynn, Diane F. Halpern, and Eric Turkheimer. 2012. "Intelligence: New Findings and Theoretical Developments." *American Psychologist* 67(2): 130.

O'Neill, June, and Solomon Polachek. 1993. "Why the Gender Gap in Wages Narrowed in the 1980s." *Journal of Labor Economics* 11(1): 205–28.

Oppenheimer, Valerie K. 1997. "Women's Employment and the Gain to Marriage: The Specialization and Trading Model." *Annual Review of Sociology* 23: 431–53.

Penner, Andrew, Harold Toro-Tulla, and Matt Huffman. 2012. "Do Women Managers Ameliorate Gender Differences in Wages? Evidence from a Large Grocery Retailer." *Sociological Perspectives* 55(2): 365–81.

Quillian, Lincoln. 2006. "New Approaches to Understanding Racial Prejudice and Discrimination." *Annual Review of Sociology* 32: 299–328.

Reskin, Barbara. 2000. "The Proximate Causes of Employment Discrimination." *Contemporary Sociology* 29(2): 319–28.

Ridgeway, Cecilia L. 2001. "Gender, Status, and Leadership." *Journal of Social Issues* 57(4): 637–55.

———. 2006. "Gender as an Organizing Force in Social Relations: Implications for the Future of Inequality." In *The Declining Significance of Gender*, edited by Francine D. Blau, Mary C. Brinton, and David B. Grusky. New York: Russell Sage Foundation.

Ridgeway, Cecilia L., and Shelley J. Correll. 2004. "Unpacking the Gender System." *Gender & Society* 18(4): 510.

Rockoff, Jonah, and Mariesa Herrmann. 2012. "Worker Absence and Productivity: Evidence from Teaching." *Journal of Labor Economics* 30(4): 749–82.

Ross, Catherine E., Ryan K. Masters, and Robert A. Hummer. 2012. "Education and the Gender Gaps in Health and Mortality." *Demography* 49(4): 1157–83.

Rossin-Slater, Maya, Christopher Ruhm, and Jane Waldfogel. 2013. "The Effects of California's Paid Family Leave Program on Mothers' Leave-Taking and Subsequent Labor Market Outcomes." *Journal of Policy Analysis and Management* 32(2): 224–45.

Ruggles, Steven, J. Trent Alexander, Ron Goeken, Matthew B. Schroeder, and Matthew Sobek. 2010. Integrated Public Use Microdata Series, Version 5.0 [Machine-readable database]. Minneapolis: University of Minnesota.

Ruhm, Christopher J. 1998. "The Economic Consequences of Parental Leave Mandates: Lessons from Europe." *Quarterly Journal of Economics* 113(1): 285–317.

Sandberg, Sheryl. 2013. *Lean In: Women, Work, and the Will to Lead*. New York: Random House.

Sarsons, Heather. 2015. "Gender Differences in Recognition for Group Work." Harvard University working paper. Cambridge, Mass.: Harvard University.

Schwartz, Christine R., and Pilar Gonalons-Pons. 2016. "Trends in Relative Earnings and Marital Dissolution: Are Wives Who Outearn Their Husbands More Likely to Divorce?" *RSF: The Russell Sage Journal of the Social Sciences* 2(4). doi: 10.7758/RSF.2016.2.4.08.

Selzer, Judith A., and Susan M. Bianchi. 2013. "Demographic Change and Parent-Child Relationships in Adulthood." *Annual Review of Sociology* 39: 275–90.

Sherman, David K., Kimberly A. Hartson, Kevin R. Binning, Valerie Purdie-Vaughns, Julio Garcia, Suzanne Taborsky-Barba, Sarah Tomassetti, A. David Nussbaum, and Geoffrey L. Cohen. 2013. "Deflecting the Trajectory and Changing the Narrative: How Self-Affirmation Affects Academic Performance and Motivation Under Identity Threat." *Journal of Personality and Social Psychology* 104(4): 591–618.

Slaughter, Anne-Marie. 2012. "Why Women Still Can't Have It All." *The Atlantic* (July/August). Accessed March 31, 2016. http://www.theatlantic.com/magazine/archive/2012/07/why-women-still-cant-have-it-all/309020/.

Smock, Pamela J., Peter Granda, and Lynette Hoelter. 2013. Integrated Fertility Survey Series, Release 7, 1955–2002 [United States]. ICPSR26344-v7. Ann Arbor, Mich.: Inter-university Consortium for Political and Social Research, [distributor]. Accessed May 14, 2015. http://doi.org/10.3886/ICPSR26344.v7.

Stainback, Kevin, and Donald Tomaskovic-Devey. 2012. *Documenting Desegregation: Racial and Gender Segregation in Private-Sector Employment Since the Civil Rights Act*. New York: Russell Sage Foundation.

Stevenson, Betsey. 2010. "Beyond the Classroom: Using Title IX to Measure the Return to High School Sports." *Review of Economics and Statistics* 92(2): 284–301.

Stevenson, Betsey, and Justin Wolfers. 2006. "Bargaining in the Shadow of the Law: Divorce Laws and Family Distress." *Quarterly Journal of Economics* 121(1): 267–88.

———. 2007. "Marriage and Divorce: Changes and Their Driving Forces." *Journal of Economic Perspectives* 21(2): 27–52.

———. 2009. "The Paradox of Declining Female Happiness." *American Economic Journal: Economic Policy* 1(2): 190–225.

Stone, Pamela. 2007. "Opting Out: Why Women Really Quit Careers and Head Home." *Journal of Family and Economic Issues* 29(1): 185–87.

Thomas, Mallika. 2014. "The Impact of Mandated Maternity Benefits on the Gender Differential in Promotions: Examining the Role of Adverse Selection." *Department of Economics* working paper. Chicago: University of Chicago.

Thornton, Arland, Duane F. Alwin, and Donald Camburn. 1983. "Causes and Consequences of Sex-Role Attitudes and Attitude Change." *American Sociological Review* 48(2): 211–27.

Thornton, Arland, and L. Young-DeMarco. 2001. "Four Decades of Trends in Attitudes Toward Family Issues in the United States: The 1960s Through the 1990s." *Journal of Marriage and the Family* 63(4): 1009–37.

Toossi, Mitra. 2002. "A Century of Change: The U.S. Labor Force, 1950–2050." *Monthly Labor Review* 125(5)(May): 15–28.

Voena, Alessandra. 2015. "Yours, Mine, and Ours: Do Divorce Laws Affect the Intertemporal Behavior of Married Couples." *American Economic Review* 105(8): 2295–332.

Wang, Wendy, Kim Parker, and Paul Taylor. 2013. "Breadwinner Moms: Mothers are the Sole or Primary Provider in Four-in-Ten Households with Children; Public Conflicted about the Growing Trend." Washington, D.C.: Pew Research Center. Accessed March 31, 2016. http://www.pewsocialtrends.org/files/2013/05/Breadwinner_moms_final.pdf.

Wasserman, Melanie. 2015. "Hours Constraints, Occupational Choice and Fertility: Evidence from Medical Residents." *MIT* working paper. Cambridge: Massachusetts Institute of Technology. Accessed March 31, 2016. http://economics.mit.edu/files/10943.

Weinberg, Bruce. 2000. "Computer Use and the Demand for Female Workers." *Industrial & Labor Relations Review* 53(2): 290–308.

Welch, Finis. 2000. "Growth in Women's Relative Wages and in Inequality Among Men: One Phenomenon or Two?" *American Economic Review* 90(2): 444–49.

Western, Bruce, and Jake Rosenfeld. 2011. "Unions, Norms, and the Rise in U.S. Wage Inequality." *American Sociological Review* 76(4): 513–37.

Westoff, Charles F. 1976. "Trends in Contraceptive Practice: 1965–1973." *Family Planning Perspectives* 8(1): 54–57.

Xie, Yue, and Kimberlee Shauman. 2003. *Women in Science: Career Processes and Outcomes*. Cambridge, Mass.: Harvard University Press.

PART I

Working Hours, Opting Out, and the Gender Wage Gap

The Opt-Out Continuation: Education, Work, and Motherhood from 1984 to 2012

TANYA BYKER

Debate about an increasing trend in highly educated women dropping out of the labor force to care for children—an opt-out revolution—has been considerable. I use unique features of the of Survey of Income and Program Participation—a large nationally representative sample, longitudinal structure, monthly labor-force outcomes, and repeated panels—to study trends in women's birth-related career interruptions over time and across the education spectrum. Methodologically, I use event studies to compare women's monthly labor-force outcomes on the extensive and intensive margins from twenty-four months before to twenty-four months after births in the 1980s, 1990s, and 2000s. Rather than an abrupt change in opting out, I find that the pattern of birth-related interruptions has changed surprisingly little over the past thirty years—substantial and sustained interruptions remain common for mothers in all education categories. Rather than a revolution, I find an opt-out continuation.

Keywords: opting out, maternal labor supply, labor-force participation, gender gap

It is well known that women's labor-force participation increased substantially over the last sixty years—nearly doubling from around 30 percent in 1950 to just under 60 percent in 1990 before leveling off. It is less well known, however, that the labor-force participation of mothers of young children rose even more sharply—increasing sixfold, from less than 10 percent in 1950 to over 60 percent by 2000 among women with children under the age of two (see figures 1 through 3). By returning to the labor force more quickly after births, women accumulated more years of work experience than previous generations and this increased experience was a key driver in the narrowing of the gender gap in earnings (Blau and Kahn 1997, 2004).

Yet at the beginning of the twenty-first century, a gender gap in both labor-force participation and earnings persists despite the elimination and reversal of the gender gap in career-focused educational investments (Goldin 2006; Goldin, Katz, and Kuziemko 2006). Lisa Belkin's 2003 claim in the *New York Times* of a revolutionary exodus of professional women from the workplace to care for their children offered a potential explanation for this persistence. Her claim of an "opt-out revolution," however, was based on selected interviews with highly educated women and sparked debate both in the popular media and academic literature.

In their early work on the intermittency of

Tanya Byker is assistant professor of economics at Middlebury College.

The author is grateful to Martha Bailey, Charlie Brown, Mary Corcoran, Robert Garlick, Andrew Goodman-Bacon, Brad Hershbein, David Lam, Matt Rutledge, Jeff Smith, and Pamela Smock for helpful comments and guidance. This research was supported in part by an NICHD training grant to the Population Studies Center at the University of Michigan (T32 HD007339). Direct correspondence to: Tanya Byker at tbyker@middlebury.edu, Department of Economics, Middlebury College, Warner Hall, 303 College St., Middlebury, VT 05753.

Figure 1. Labor-Force Participation of Women, All Education Groups

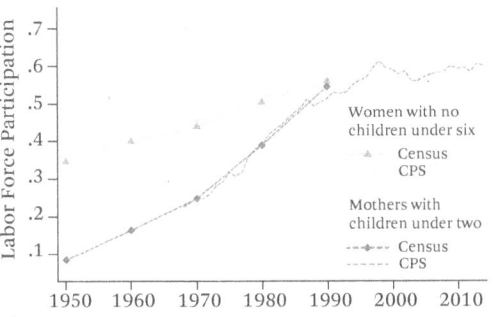

Source: Author's compilation based on U.S. Censuses 1950–1990 (Ruggles et al. 2010), Current Population Survey 1968–2014 (King et al. 2010).
Notes: Sample includes women over fifteen years old. "Women with no children under six" includes women with older children as well as women with no children.

Figure 2. Labor-Force Participation of Women, Less than Bachelor's

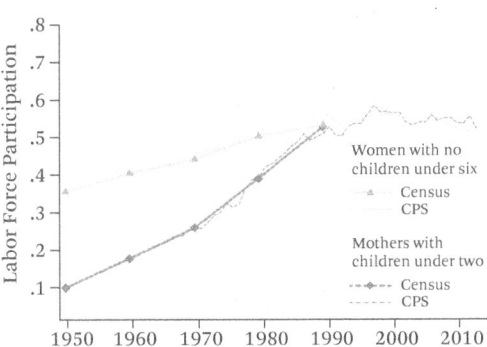

Source: Author's compilation based on U.S. Censuses 1950–1990 (Ruggles et al. 2010), Current Population Survey 1968–2014 (King et al. 2010).
Notes: See notes to figure 1.

Figure 3. Labor-Force Participation of Women, at Least Bachelor's

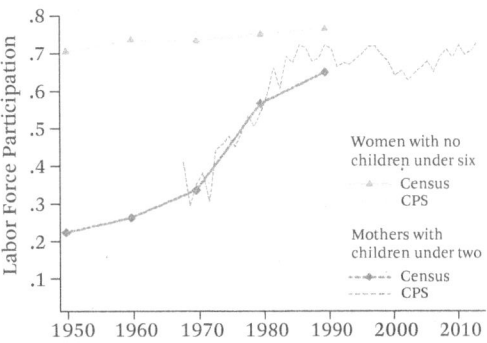

Source: Author's compilation based on U.S. Censuses 1950–1990 (Ruggles et al. 2010), Current Population Survey 1968–2014 (King et al. 2010).
Notes: See notes to figure 1.

women's work, Jacob Mincer and Solomon Polachek estimated that in the mid-1960s women spent on average eight years out of the labor force during their childbearing years, and that many in fact never returned to work after having a child (1974). The trends shown in figures 1 through 3 make it clear this type of permanent exit is no longer the typical trajectory. However, women need not exit the labor force permanently when they become mothers for Belkin's claims to lead to a persistent gender gap. Even brief absences from the labor force result in significant and persistent wage penalties (Hotchkiss and Pitts 2003). The opting out described by Belkin's subjects amounted to career interruptions—extended periods out of the labor force. Currently, the literature has no measure of career interruptions around childbirth across the education spectrum or by race, and no measure of how trends in interruptions have changed over time.

Quantifying career interruptions requires the ability to follow women over time to establish a baseline prior to birth from which a disruption occurs. The Survey of Income and Program Participation (SIPP) provides monthly outcomes for large nationally representative panels of women who gave birth in the 1980s, 1990s, and 2000s. Using an event study methodology in the SIPP, I study the pattern of women's work in terms of labor-force participation and hours from the two years prior to two years following a birth. Because the SIPP's sample size is large, I am able to show how career interruptions vary across the education spectrum and between first and subsequent births. Furthermore, figures 4 through 6 show that the

Figure 4. Labor-Force Participation, with and Without Infant Children, Whites

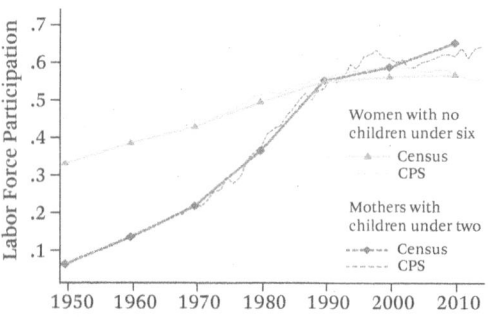

Source: Author's compilation based on U.S. Censuses 1950–1990 (Ruggles et al. 2010), Current Population Survey 1968–2014 (King et al. 2010).
Notes: Sample includes women over fifteen years old. White women includes individuals who identify as white, but not Hispanic. Similarly, black women includes women who identify as black, but not Hispanic.

Figure 5. Labor-Force Participation, with and Without Infant Children, Blacks

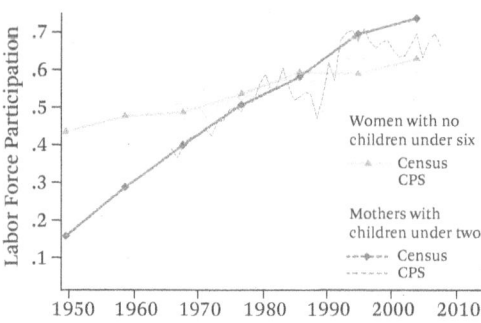

Source: Author's compilation based on U.S. Censuses 1950–1990 (Ruggles et al. 2010), Current Population Survey 1968–2014 (King et al. 2010).
Notes: See notes to figure 4.

Figure 6. Labor-Force Participation, with and Without Infant Children, Hispanics

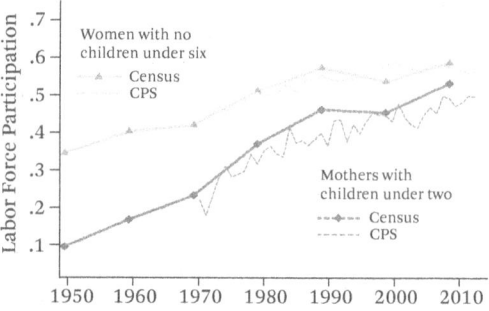

Source: Author's compilation based on U.S. Censuses 1950–1990 (Ruggles et al. 2010), Current Population Survey 1968–2014 (King et al. 2010).
Notes: See notes to figure 4.

levels and historical trends in labor-force participation among African American and Hispanic mothers differ substantially from each other and from white mothers—the SIPP's large sample also allows me to investigate these differences.

I find that women who gave birth in the 2000s show a 26 percent drop in labor-force participation from a year before first births to two years after subsequent births. The patterns and timing of opting out vary substantially by education and race. Women with less than a bachelor's degree start to exit the labor force as early as a year before birth, earlier than more-educated women whose participation rates do not fall until around three months before they have first births. Less-educated women also exhibit a steeper labor-force exit-and-return pattern in the months directly around birth that is not seen among more-educated mothers, indicating that many less-educated women exit the labor force briefly around giving birth. The overall levels of participation increase monotonically in education, but rates of opting out are highest among women with only a bachelor's degree—a 30 percent drop in labor-force participation from 92 percent participation a year before first births to 64 percent two years after subsequent births. The comparable drop for women with less than a bachelor's degree is 26 percent—from 82 percent to 61 percent. For women with at least a master's, the drop is 19 percent from 95 percent participation before first births to 77 percent after subsequent births.

Because SIPP panels were fielded repeatedly over time, I am able to study how opting out has changed, or failed to change, over time. I find that despite notable differences from the 1980s to the 2000s, the patterns of career interruption in the two years after birth have changed surprisingly little over the past thirty years. When I compare these patterns of opting out across decades, I find that the abrupt exit-and-return pattern in the six months right around birth was more pronounced before the 2000s across the education spectrum, particularly in the 1980s. So although this short-term exit pattern has disappeared for women with at least a bachelor's degree, it lingers for less-educated women. Tanya Byker (2016) hypothesizes that this is caused by increasing access to paid leave among more-educated women, which allows them to maintain attachment with their employer while taking leave to care for a newborn child.[1] Looking beyond the six-month window around birth, however, the rates of opting out are not statistically distinguishable between the 2000s and the 1980s, except for most-educated mothers, who have at least a master's degree and have become somewhat more attached to the labor force on average. Overall, I find substantial and sustained career interruptions for mothers in all education categories over the past three decades. Rather than a revolution, the data point to an opt-out *continuation* at all levels of education.

For those women who stay in the labor force after a birth, opting for fewer hours may allow them to balance work and motherhood. I find that, on average, women work fewer hours after giving birth in all three decades. However, the proportion of women, particularly the more educated, opting for part-time work (less than thirty-five hours a week) has fallen since the 1980s. Only around 22 percent of college-educated women and 33 percent of those with less than a bachelor's degree are working part-time two years after a birth in the 2000s. This is surprising given recent opinion polls, which indicate that the majority of working mothers believe that it would be ideal for themselves and their children if they worked part time (Wang, Parker, and Taylor 2013). This, combined with the finding that 40 percent of *nonworking* mothers also think working part time would be their ideal situation, suggests that a lack of good part-time options may be a driver of the opt-out continuation.

The patterns of opting out for black and Hispanic mothers show stark differences from the overall averages. Black women with less than a bachelor's degree actually opt *in* on average—labor-force participation of less-educated black women increases from around 60 percent a year prior to first births to 72 percent two years after subsequent births, an 18 percent increase. Black women with at least a bachelor's degree participate at rates similar to white women with bachelor's degrees prior to first births—over 90 percent—but, in contrast to white women, they opt out substantially less—only an 11 percent drop in participation from before first births to after subsequent births. Hispanic mothers with less than a bachelor's degree participate at much lower levels overall and opt out at rates close to the average for less-educated women—from 64 percent a year before first births to 46 percent two years after subsequent births, a 28 percent drop. College-educated Hispanic mothers participate around 90 percent before first births, but at only 63 percent two years after subsequent births, a 32 percent drop.

A DYNAMIC MEASURE ADDRESSES OPEN QUESTIONS ABOUT OPTING OUT

The literature on opting has proceeded along two lines—one using nationally representative cross-sectional data to test Belkin's claims of an opt-out revolution and another using proprietary data sets to follow the career paths of graduates of elite institutions. For instance, Heather Antecol's (2011) careful analysis using the census and Current Population Survey has the advantage of looking across decades and evaluating trends by education and occupation groups, but her measures of opting out are limited to static point-in-time averages of labor-force attachment for women with children under six compared with women without children. On the other hand, Marianne Bertrand, Claudia Goldin, and Lawrence Katz (2010) conduct a detailed analysis of the work histories of elite business school graduates, but examine only recent cohorts and cannot comment on opting out in the broader population (see also

---

1. Women who are on leave maintain attachment to their employers and are considered in the labor force.

Wood, Corcoran, and Courant 1993; Herr and Wolfram 2012; Buchmann and McDaniel, this issue; Pal and Waldfogel, this issue).

Cross-sectional measures of opting out, called the child penalty or the child effect, proxy for mothers' pre-birth levels of labor-force attachment with the work behavior of childless women. Antecol (2011), Heather Boushey (2005), and Christine Percheski (2008) use this type of measure to describe trends in opting out. These three papers define the populations of women they are studying differently and examine different margins of labor-force attachment, but all find that the penalty in labor-force participation fell substantially from the 1980s to the 1990s and remained essentially flat from the 1990s into the 2000s. Depending on the specification, they find that the penalty has been stable in a range of 19 to 22 percent since the 1990s.[2]

However, using childless women as the reference group is problematic. The group of all childless women combines those who may never have children and those who will eventually have them. This is unlikely to be a stable comparison group if marriage patterns or fertility change over time. The child-penalty comparison—all women with children under five or six versus all women without children—conflates important similarities and differences in trends over the last thirty years. For example, it could be that women in the 1980s stayed out of work longer or had more children (or both). But if they had similar opting-out behavior on a per-child basis in the child's first and second years, then the existing measures of opting out would simply show a decrease over time. These measures would fail to distinguish differences in marriage or fertility behavior from differences in work behavior.

The detailed proprietary datasets that Jane Herr and Catherine Wolfram (2012), Bertrand and her colleagues (2010), and Robert Wood, Mary Corcoran, and Paul Courant (1993) use allow them to observe individuals at multiple points in their careers, often before and after they have children. Bertrand and her colleagues study University of Chicago MBAs, and Wood and his colleagues study University of Michigan JDs. Both studies find that most of the large gender gap in earnings between male and female graduates ten to fifteen years after graduation (despite nearly identical average earnings after graduation) can be explained by the deficit in women's work experience due to time spent out of work to care for children. Herr and Wolfram examine the work trajectories of Harvard undergraduates, focusing on those who went on to graduate school, to estimate a causal impact of the family friendliness of jobs (as measured by the flexibility of work hours) on women's rates of opting out. These studies provide detailed results for women with advanced degrees from elite institutions but do not comment on opting out for the rest of the education distribution or make comparisons over time.

If the goal is to understand why there are so few female CEOs or members of Congress, focusing on highly educated women is key to understanding what drives the gender gap in these realms. But if we think about education as a human capital investment in pursuing a career, then even in this context it is relevant to consider how the labor supply behavior of women who get advanced degrees differs from their counterparts. More broadly, I am concerned that the opting-out debate has been considered resolved or even debunked as something that relates only to elite women with high-earning husbands. Understanding how childbearing affects the work outcomes of women across the socioeconomic spectrum is important to understanding the gender gap in earnings that persists across skill levels.

EVENT STUDY METHODOLOGY TO MEASURE OPTING OUT IN LONGITUDINAL DATA, 1984–2012

The Survey of Income and Program Participation allows comparison of the monthly dynamic labor-force outcomes of a nationally representative sample of mothers across multiple decades. Sample sizes range from twenty thou-

---

2. Antecol and Boushey measure the child penalty in each calendar year (or decade) for all women in addition to conducting separate analysis by education category. Percheski focuses exclusively on women who identify as being in managerial or professional occupations and measures the penalty by birth cohort.

sand households for the 1984 panel to forty-five thousand households for the 1996 and 2004 panels. These large sample sizes contain high enough numbers of births for women born from the 1950s to the 1980s to document statistically significant trends over time by detailed education categories and by first births versus subsequent births within these categories.

I use the 2008, 2004, 1996, and pooled 1984 to 1986 SIPP panels.[3] My sample consists of all women ages eighteen to forty-five who gave birth during one of the panels.[4] Although the SIPP core waves do not provide direct information on when a woman gives birth, I construct this date by matching own children to mothers using family relationship variables and the month and date of birth of each member of the household. I determine that a birth occurs when a newborn child identified as the mother's own appears in the household record. If no other own children are in the household when a woman gives birth, I code it as a first birth; otherwise, I code it as a subsequent birth.[5] In some cases, a woman will give birth more than once during a SIPP panel. Given that the panels are up to four years long, especially for women who give birth early in the panel, this is not unusual. In the results that follow, I use the first recorded birth as the reference event for my analysis. That a woman has another child may naturally affect her outcomes, but the choice to have another child may be jointly determined with other labor-force outcomes.

I define three education categories: less than bachelor's, bachelor's, and master's plus. When categorizing women by time-varying characteristics such as age or educational attainment, I use the month of birth as the reference period. Table 1 gives details of the time frame of each SIPP panel and summary statistics for my sample of women who give birth. More detailed information on the birth sample by education category is provided in table 2 and table 3, which provide information for the black and Hispanic portions of the sample.

The primary outcome variables of interest are labor-force participation and weekly hours worked in a given month. A woman is considered to be in the labor force in a month if she is "with a job" at least one week of the month, including months when she is absent from work without pay; on layoff; or "not with a job" all month but on layoff or looking for work. She is only coded out of the labor force if she had "no job all month, no time on layoff, and no time looking for work." Note that women who are "on leave" are coded as labor-force participants, for example under the Family and Medical Leave Act (FMLA).[6] I test the robustness of my findings to using employment—defined as being with a job at least one week of the month—as the outcome of interest rather

---

3. The first SIPP panel ran from 1984 to 1986. The Census Bureau initially fielded smaller, shorter, overlapping panels starting each year. The schedule was changed in 1996, and larger, longer, non-overlapping panels are now fielded approximately every four years.

4. I exclude women giving birth before age eighteen because my focus is not on young teen mothers who are unlikely to have prior labor market experience. Boushey (2005) and Antecol (2010) present results for women ages twenty-five to forty-four. Because I focus on birth events for women by educational attainment, extending the population to include women eighteen to twenty-five makes my results more representative for women with less than a college degree given that they tend to be younger when they have children. For example, looking at outcomes around first birth for women age twenty-five to forty-five with only a high school diploma will give a distorted picture of the high school graduate population because most women in this education category have first births before the age of twenty-five. Adding mothers under age twenty-five, however has almost no effect on the sample of college-educated women giving birth and should not affect comparability with previous work on opting out among women with at least a college degree.

5. If a mother has a child (children) who lives outside of the household when she gives birth, she will be mischaracterized as a first-time mother, but this is likely to be a rare occurrence. The SIPP core waves do not ask number of own children ever born.

6. The FMLA went into effect in August 1993. The act requires businesses with fifty or more employees to provide up to twelve weeks of unpaid job-protected leave per year to employees who have worked for at least twelve

Table 1. Summary of SIPP Panels and Birth Sample

	2004–2008 Panels		1996 Panel		1984–1986 Panels	
A: Summary information on 1984–1986, 1996, 2004–2008 SIPP panels						
Waves	12		12			
Dates	February 2004–August 2012		April 1996–March 2000		October 1983–April 1988	
Households[a]	43540		36730		45105	
Women (eighteen to forty-five)	25317		24102		31316	
Births (eighteen to forty-five)	6,284		3,395		3,670	
First	2,621	42.8%	1,486	43.9%	1,987	53.9%
Subsequent	3,663	57.2	1,909	56.1	1,683	46.1
B: Summary characteristics of birth sample (mothers age eighteen to forty-five) (Unweighted numbers of observations, weighted percentages)						
Race						
White	3,964	59.5%	2,222	63.0%	2,874	77.2%
Black	760	13.1	449	14.5	480	14.8
Hispanic	1,043	19.4	564	17.8	178	4.4
Other	517	8.0	160	4.6	138	3.6
Marital status						
Married spouse present	4,218	69.4	2,440	73.8	2,944	80.5
Separated, divorced, widowed	426	5.8	255	6.5	249	6.6
Never married	1,640	24.8	700	19.8	477	13.0
Education[b]						
Less than bachelor's	4,377	68.9	2,577	75.3	3,054	83.1
High school or less	2,363	37.0	1,601	46.2	1,809	49.2
Some college[c]	2,014	31.9	976	29.1	1,245	33.9
Bachelor's only	1,305	21.2	663	20.2	386	10.5
Master's plus	602	9.9	155	4.5	230	6.4
Master's	450	7.4	114	3.3		
Professional	89	1.4	25	0.7		
PhD	63	1.0	16	0.5		
At least bachelor's	1907	31.1	818	24.7	616	16.9

Source: Author's calculations based on the Survey of Income and Program Participation (1984, 1985, 1986, 1996, 2004, and 2008 panels).

Notes: The sample includes all women ages eighteen to forty-five who give birth during one of the SIPP panels. For time-varying characteristics like education, the reference level is the level in the month that a woman gives birth.

[a]The number of households and number of women in the full panel based on the total number that appear in the survey as opposed to the number appearing in wave 1.

[b]Ambiguity in 1980s coding of education variables makes it impossible to make an exact distinction between some college, bachelors, and graduate degree.

[c]Includes associates and vocational degrees.

Table 2. Characteristics by Education

	2000s	1990s	1980s
Less than bachelor's			
Married, spouse present			
First births	0.48	0.59	0.75
Subsequent births	0.65	0.72	0.80
Education relative to spouse			
Wife's education ≥ husband's	0.71	0.69	0.65
Age at first birth	24.4	24.5	24.6
	(5.3)	(5.4)	(4.7)
Parity of subsequent births	2.7	2.7	2.7
	(1.0)	(1.0)	(1.0)
Bachelor's only			
Married, spouse present			
First births	0.91	0.93	0.92
Subsequent births	0.95	0.96	0.97
Education relative to spouse			
Wife's education ≥ husband's	0.81	0.82	0.75
Age at first birth	30.0	29.4	28.4
	(4.4)	(4.1)	(3.7)
Parity of subsequent births	2.5	2.5	2.4
	(0.8)	(0.7)	(0.6)
Master's plus			
Married, spouse present			
First births	0.95	0.95	0.98
Subsequent births	0.98	0.95	0.98
Education relative to spouse			
Wife's education ≥ husband's	0.57	0.57	0.51
Age at first birth	32.2	32.4	30.5
	(4.1)	(4.6)	(3.8)
Parity of subsequent births	2.4	2.4	2.4
	(0.7)	(0.7)	(0.6)

Source: Author's calculations based on the Survey of Income and Program Participation (1984, 1985, 1986, 1996, 2004, and 2008 panels).
Notes: The birth sample includes women ages eighteen to forty-five who gave birth during one of the SIPP panels. Standard deviations in parentheses when relevant.

than labor-force participation, which includes layoff and job search, and find that the overall trends are quite similar. These results are available on request. To measure whether women opt for fewer hours, I use a categorical variable for whether a respondent worked more or less than thirty-five hours in a typical week conditional on working.[7]

---

months and at least 1,250 hours who need leave for covered reasons, including the birth of a child (Waldfogel 2001). The states of California, New Jersey, and Rhode Island mandate paid family leave (Byker 2016). Washington state signed a paid leave law in 2007, but it is not yet in effect due to lack of a funding mechanism. New York state enacted a law in 2016 effective January 2018.

7. This is *monthly* in the 1996 and 2004 SIPP panels, but only for a four-month reference period in the 1984 to 1986 panels.

Table 3. Characteristics by Race

	2000s	1990s	1980s
A: Black			
Less than bachelor's			
Married, spouse present			
First births	0.21	0.24	0.39
Subsequent births	0.30	0.34	0.43
Education relative to spouse			
Wife's education ≥ husband's	0.70	0.70	0.67
Age at first birth	23.5	23.3	23.7
	(5.2)	(5.7)	(4.5)
Parity of subsequent births	2.8	2.7	2.9
	(1.1)	(.9)	(1.1)
Sample size	651	399	442
At least bachelor's			
Married, spouse present			
First births	0.69	0.76	0.61
Subsequent births	0.77	0.68	0.82
Education relative to spouse			
Wife's education ≥ husband's	0.85	0.89	0.95
Age at first birth	30.6	31.3	28.1
	(2.5)	(2.4)	(2.5)
Sample size	109	50	38
B: Hispanic			
Less than bachelor's			
Married, spouse present			
First births	0.49	0.59	0.71
Subsequent births	0.73	0.73	0.75
Education relative to spouse			
Wife's education ≥ husband's	0.78	0.76	0.82
Age at first birth	23.6	23.0	24.3
	(4.9)	(4.6)	(4.8)
Sample size	949	522	171
At least bachelor's			
Married, spouse present			
First births	0.82	0.79	0.72
Subsequent births	0.91	0.92	1.00
Education relative to spouse			
Wife's education ≥ husband's	0.89	0.93	1.00
Age at first birth	29.2	28.8	28.2
	(2.5)	(2.4)	(2.5)
Sample size	94	42	7

Source: Author's calculations based on the Survey of Income and Program Participation (1984, 1985, 1986, 1996, 2004, and 2008 panels).
Notes: The birth sample includes women ages eighteen to forty-five who gave birth during one of the SIPP panels. Standard deviations in parentheses when relevant.

Methodology—Event Study

To estimate how labor-force outcomes change around the event of birth, I pool information on all women who give birth during a given SIPP panel. Then, following Louis Jacobson, Robert LaLonde, and Daniel Sullivan's 1993 study, I estimate the following regression model by least squares:

$$Y_{it} = \alpha_i + \Sigma_{j=-25}^{25} D_{it}^j \delta_j + \gamma_t + \varepsilon_{it},$$

where Y_{it} is the work outcome of interest for woman i in month t, α_i are individual fixed effects and γ_t are year fixed effects. Defining b_i as the month a woman gives birth, then

$$D_{it}^j = \begin{cases} \mathbf{1}(t < b_i - 24) \text{ for } j \leq -25 \\ \mathbf{1}(t = b_i + j) \text{ for } -24 \leq j \leq -13 \text{ and} \\ \quad -11 \leq j \leq 24 \\ \text{omitted for } j = -12 \\ \mathbf{1}(t > b_i + 24) \text{ for } j \geq 25 \end{cases}$$

The D_{it}^j are thus a set of dummy variables, one for each month from twenty-four months before to twenty-four months after a woman gives birth, omitting the dummy for twelve months before birth.[8] For example, $D_{it}^j = 1$ if in period t, woman i gave birth j months earlier (or if j is negative, j months later.) The dummies jointly represent a time line indexed to the date a woman gives birth and make it possible to estimate average outcomes for women who are j months before (or after) birth even if these women gave birth in different calendar months. Because I omit D_{it}^{-12}, the δ_j coefficients map out the time path of changes in outcomes relative to outcomes a year before the birth. The δ_j's provide a detailed monthly measure of opting out for the two years after a woman gives birth.[9] Including the twenty-four months before birth makes it possible to see whether women experience changes in outcomes in the months leading up to birth.

The SIPP panels are three to four years in duration. As a result, using all of the births that occur in each panel will mean that not all women in my sample have information for the full twenty-four lead and twenty-four lag months of the event study window because women give birth at different points over the course of the panel. The individual fixed-effects specification in equation (1), however, gives consistent estimates of opting out for an unbalanced panel as long as the reason why a woman has missing information is uncorrelated with the ε_{it}'s. Aside from attrition, whether I have data for a woman in any month j depends only on when during the panel she gave birth. In other words, all I require for consistency is that, conditional on giving birth during the panel, and any time invariant characteristics, when over the course of the panel that birth falls, is random. It seems very unlikely that women would time their births relative to the Census Bureau's schedule for fielding SIPP panels. Although we may be worried that over time, age at first birth for different cohorts has shifted and that a one- or two-year difference in time of birth is relevant, by using fixed effects, we control for mothers' birth cohort. Another concern is that women may time births relative to the business cycle. This may be a legitimate concern and for this reason I include year fixed effects in some specifications. Panel attrition remains a legitimate concern, therefore I reproduce the main results of the paper on a sample that excludes all women who left the panel or were absent from the panel for more than three straight months. The results are essentially the same. These results are available on request.[10]

I estimate equation (1) separately by education group, parity, and decade to make comparisons across these three dimensions. To claim that the pattern of opting out for a series

---

8. I also include a single dummy for all months more than twenty-four months before birth, and a dummy for all months more than twenty-four months after birth.

9. In the case of the binary labor-force participation outcome, I estimate a linear probability model. I calculate variance using a Huber-White heteroscedasticity-robust estimator clustered at the individual mother level. This allows for arbitrary covariance over time within units, and allows for heteroscedasticity across units, which is essential given that the linear probability model inherently has heteroskedastic errors.

10. Note that in 2004, the Census Bureau randomly dropped half of the sample for budget reasons. I do not count these women as having attrited from the sample in my robustness checks. Also, some women enter the panel

of months is not statistically significantly different across decades, I test whether I can reject that the difference between coefficients for each decade for that series of months are jointly equal to zero. I operationalize this test by pooling the data from all panels and interacting dummies for each panel with each month-relative-to-birth dummy and testing if the series of relevant interaction terms are jointly equal to zero. The results of these tests are given in table A1. I also investigate how opting out differs by race by estimating models separately for black and Hispanic mothers by education and parity.

RESULTS: THE OPT-OUT CONTINUATION

The event study methodology lends itself well to a graphical presentation of results so that the time path of outcomes from the two years before to two years after birth is easily visualized. By plotting the δ_j coefficients estimated in equation (1) I can show dynamic changes in monthly outcomes relative to one year before birth. The changing contour of levels of outcomes—such as labor-force participation—over the time line is also interesting and relevant particularly when comparing trends across decades or between education categories. These level plots are easily constructed by adding the δ_j's to the constant, which in the individual fixed-effects regression is an average of the estimated individual fixed effects.[11] In a specification that does not use year fixed effects, the constant is an estimate of average labor-force participation for all women in the left-out time period—one year prior to giving birth.

Estimates of Opting Out in the 2000s

Figures 7 through 10 plot estimates of the level of labor-force participation in the four years around birth by parity and education for women ages eighteen to forty-five who gave birth from 2004 to 2012 using the 2004 and 2008 SIPP panels.[12] Figure 7 presents labor-force participation for first and subsequent births of all women who gave birth during the panel. It shows substantial and sustained opting out of the labor force starting as early as one year before birth and lasting at least two years after both first and subsequent births; and that the estimates of these drops are highly statistically significant. For first births, labor-force participation fell from 82 percent one year before birth to around 68 percent in the year after birth—a drop of 14 percentage points—and hovered around 70 percent two years after birth. Labor-force participation two years prior to subsequent births was around 10 percentage points lower than participation in the two years prior to first births, but the relative rates of opting out were quite similar for the first and subsequent births, at least at this aggregate level of all women in the birth sample. Comparing rates a year before first births with those two years after subsequent births, figure 7 shows a 21 percentage point drop in labor-force participation. Figures A1 and A2 extend the event study window to its maximum width from around four years before to four years after births. Given that sample sizes more than two years away from birth become small, the estimates outside the window presented in the paper are less precise, but these figures provide suggestive evidence that participation rates remain below pre-birth levels for at least four years.

Figures 8 through 10, which present estimates of opting out behavior for women in three education groups, reveal substantial variation in labor-force participation around birth. Three main differences across groups—less than a bachelor's, only a bachelor's, and at least a master's degree—are evident. First, the

---

after the beginning of the panel because they enter a household that is in the panel. These women are also not excluded in the robustness check.

11. For this reason, when results are displayed in levels, I show results from models that do not include year fixed effects, but I could alternatively plot levels relative to a reference year. The results are not substantively different.

12. Heteroscedasticity-robust standard errors clustered at the mother level are used to construct 95-percent point-wise confidence intervals that account for the standard errors of the estimates of the constant and the δ_j coefficients (and their covariance).

overall level of labor-force participation is rising in education—a year before first births 76 percent of women with less than a bachelor's degree are in the labor force, versus 90 percent of women with a bachelor's and 95 percent of women with at least a master's. Second, less-educated women exit the labor force earlier in the months leading up to a birth than more-educated women—participation begins to drop as early at twelve months before birth among women with less than a bachelor's but remains relatively stable until about two to five months before birth for women with bachelor's and graduate degrees. Third, the trajectory of average participation for less-educated women shows a steeper fall in participation around birth followed by a steeper rebound in the year after birth, compared with a smoother drop and leveling off among more-educated women. The smoother profile implies that the majority of more-educated women who leave the labor force take an extended time away from it. Although the dip and return pattern indicates that some less-educated women exit briefly around a birth and return to work relatively quickly within the first six months after a birth.

Despite these differences in level and pattern of labor-force participation, all education groups experience a statistically significant, substantial, and sustained drop in labor-force participation around childbearing. As a summary measure, comparing participation a year prior to a first birth and two years after a subsequent birth, the drop for women with less than a bachelor's degree is 18 percentage points, for those with only a bachelor's is 28 percentage points, and for those with at least a master's is 18 percentage points.[13] The following paragraphs discuss the trends by education in more detail, including differences by parity.

Figure 8 presents estimates for women who had less than a bachelor's degree when they gave birth. The trend in labor-force participation for this group is upward from two years prior to one year prior to first births. Given that a quarter of this group was twenty years old or younger at first birth, and that 45 percent had some college education, this trend is largely explained by transitions from school enrollment to work.[14] Labor-force participation reaches a peak around 76 percent one year before first births and immediately starts to fall from that time through the second month after birth, reaching its lowest point of 55 percent two months afterward. By the seventh month, participation has returned to 62 percent and remains relatively stable for at least two years. Two years before subsequent births, the participation rate for women without a bachelor's degree is 6 percentage points lower than a year before first births, but the pattern of opting out is quite similar to that around first births for less-educated women.

Figures 9 and 10 show results for women with bachelor's and advanced degrees. For women with a bachelor's degree, labor-force participation is stable at around 90 percent from two years to around six months before first births, and at about 75 percent from two years to a year before subsequent births. The estimates for women with at least a master's degree are noisier given the substantially smaller sample size; however, we see participation rates around 95 percent up to two months before first births and 80 percent up to a year before subsequent births. Among women with only a bachelor's degree experiencing first births, labor-force participation falls from 92 percent in twelve to six months before birth to around to 77 percent in the six to twelve months after. By twenty-four months after, participation rates for this group remained around 77 percent—16 percent lower than a year before. The extended event study in figures A1 and A2

---

13. The y-axis for the figures in the paper are in the units of percentage points so I state changes as percentage point changes. However, given that different groups of women experience changes starting from different base levels, it is useful to convert these to percentage changes. In this case, the drop for women with less than a bachelor's degree is 24 percent, for women with only a bachelor's is 30 percent, and for women with at least a master's nearly 20 percent.

14. I am able to track school enrollment in the SIPP. Figures A3 through A6 confirm this explanation for the rising trend in labor-force participation prior to first births for mothers with less than a bachelor's degree as full-time school enrollment falls from 35 percent to 20 percent in the penultimate year before birth.

Figure 7. Labor-Force Participation, All Mothers

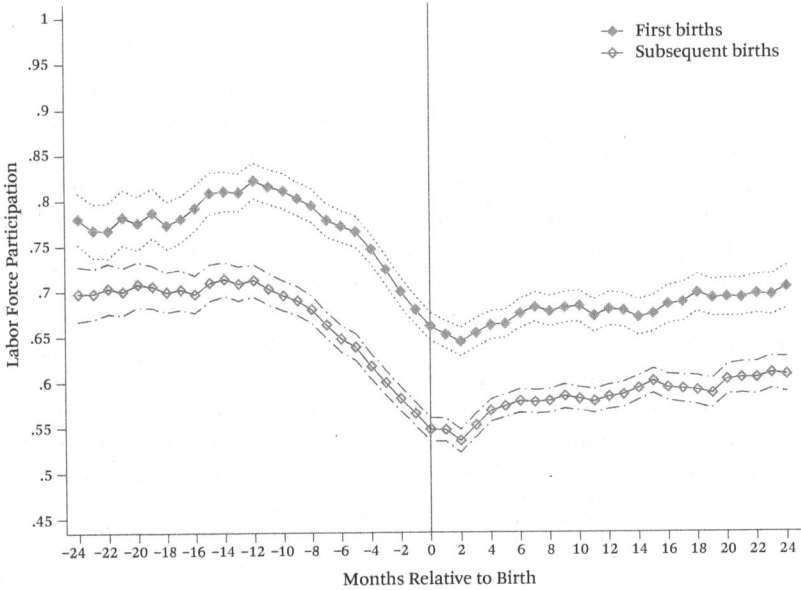

Source: Author's calculations based on the 2004 and 2008 Survey of Income and Program Participation panels.
Notes: Women age eighteen to forty-five who give birth during the panels. Plots show labor force participation from twenty-four months before to twenty-four months after birth (plotting the coefficients from equation (1) added to the constant with dependent variable an indicator for being in the labor force estimated separately by education and parity). Dashed lines are 95 percent point-wise confidence intervals.

Figure 8. Labor-Force Participation, Less than Bachelor's

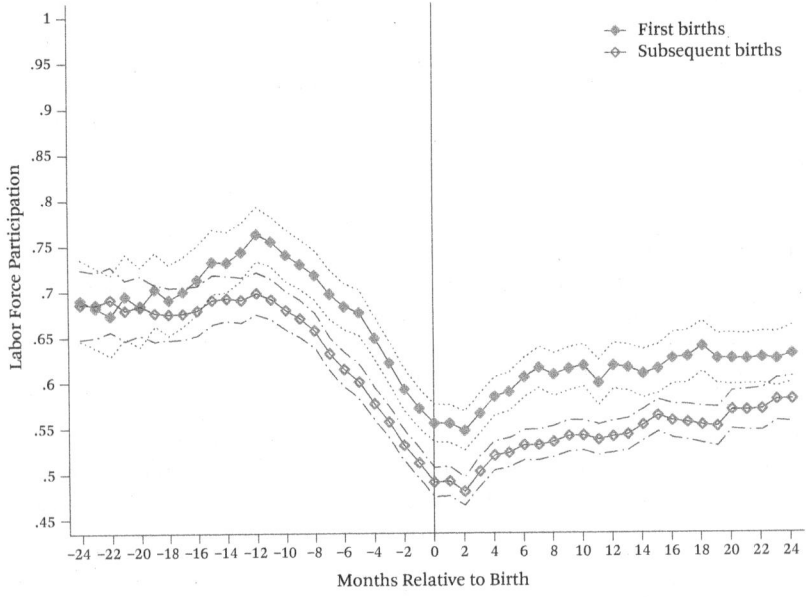

Source: Author's calculations based on the 2004 and 2008 Survey of Income and Program Participation panels.
Notes: See notes to figure 7.

Figure 9. Labor-Force Participation, Bachelor's Only

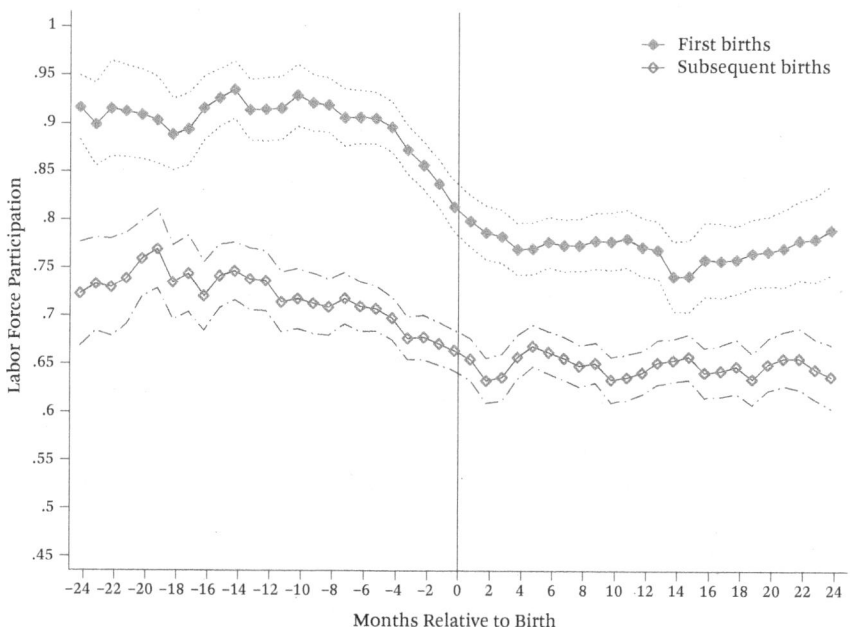

Source: Author's calculations based on the 2004 and 2008 Survey of Income and Program Participation panels.
Notes: See notes to figure 7.

Figure 10. Labor-Force Participation, Master's Degree Plus

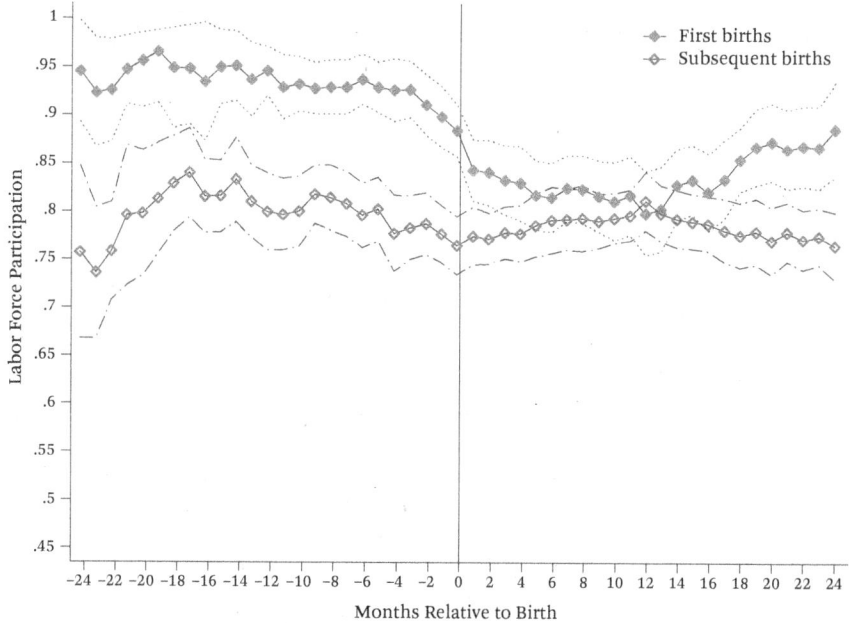

Source: Author's calculations based on the 2004 and 2008 Survey of Income and Program Participation panels.
Notes: See notes to figure 7.

shows that this lower participation persists into the fourth year after birth. Although estimates this long after birth are not as precise, they are statistically significantly lower than participation rates before birth. The master's-plus women opt out at lower, but still substantial, rates, participation falling for first-time mothers from above 90 percent to around 80 percent during the year after first births, returning close to pre-birth levels only by the end of the second year afterward. The declines in labor-force participation start earlier for subsequent births than for first births for both the bachelor's and at-least-master's women. The rates of decline are less steep after subsequent births, particularly for women with at least a master's degree, but importantly, occur from base levels of participation that are about 15 percentage points lower than a year before first births.

Has Opting Out Changed?

Belkin's opt-out revolution implies that women's behavior changed dramatically over time. I test this claim by comparing women's opting-out behavior across the 1980s, 1990s, and 2000s in terms of both labor-force participation and hours worked. I find that, despite notable changes in participation around birth over the past twenty-five years, the similarities are more striking than the differences. The rate of women opting into part-time work, meanwhile, has decreased for more-educated mothers.

Comparing Rates

I estimate equation (1) separately by education, parity and decade using the birth samples from the 1984–1986, 1996, 2004, and 2008 SIPP panels. Figures 11 through 18 compare the δ_j coefficients across the three decades for each education and parity, thus showing the monthly changes (rather than levels) in labor-force participation relative to participation one year before birth.[15]

Both differences and surprising similarities in opting-out behavior across the three decades are notable. The main difference is the much steeper drop and return pattern immediately following a birth in the 1980s compared with the later decades, indicating a lower incidence of short-term labor-force exits around birth over time. The shift from the 1980s to the 2000s is particularly large for college-educated mothers; the least-educated mothers still show some evidence of short-term intermittency around birth in the 2000s (as discussed earlier). One explanation for the less dramatic fall in labor-force participation in the months directly around birth in the later decades is the increase in family-friendly policies that allow women to take leave rather than exit the labor force right around birth that have largely benefited more-educated workers.[16]

Looking beyond six to eight months after birth, however, the similarities in opting out are striking. As figure 11 shows, in each decade women's participation rate in the one to two years after a first birth was 15 to 17 percentage points lower than one year before the birth, and the differences are not statistically significant. Contrary to Belkin's claim, the size of the reduction in the participation rate of college-educated mothers did not grow between the 1980s and 2000s—the drop was roughly 14 percentage points after first births in both decades. To the extent that behavior changed at all beyond the early months around birth, evidence indicates a reduction in opting out among women with at least a master's degree.

As seen in figures 13 through 16, sharper drops followed by steeper recoveries in the 1980s, compared with those in the 1990s and 2000s, are echoed in the experiences of both women with less than a college education and those with bachelor's degrees, though the magnitudes and base levels of participation before birth differ across the two groups. For

---

15. The legend for each subsection gives the reference level of participation at twelve months before birth for each respective group. Confidence intervals are omitted to make the figures legible, but figures with confidence intervals are available on request.

16. Family-friendly policies include Family Medical Leave Act in 1993 or paid leave policies, which were mandated in California, Rhode Island, and New Jersey in the 2000s and are offered voluntarily by some firms. Byker (2016) examines the impact of paid leave laws on opting-out behavior and concludes that paid leave is instrumental in reducing short-term departures from the labor force around birth, particularly for less-educated women.

women without a college degree at subsequent births, opting-out behavior changes from the 1980s to the 2000s. All three decades show an initial 25 percentage point drop in labor-force participation more than a year before birth, but in the 1980s women returned at a significantly faster rate than in the 1990s and 2000s. In results not shown here, I separate women with some college from women with a high school diploma or less and find that the divergence is driven by the less-educated mothers who stay out of the labor force after subsequent births at higher rates in the later decades. This result is surprising in light of welfare reform in the 1990s that encouraged women, including those with young children, to return to work.[17]

Figure 15 presents estimates of opting out around first births for women with only a bachelor's degree. From twelve to four months before birth, the pattern of opting out is almost identical across the decades. From around four months before to six months after birth, we again find that women in the 1980s opt out at significantly higher rates, falling to 32 percentage points below pre-birth levels versus only 25 percentage points in the 1990s and 15 points in the 2000s. This steeper fall of the 1980s, however, is followed by a steeper rise, and by eight months after birth the relative change in labor-force participation is almost identical across the three decades. The patterns of opting out from six to twenty-four months after birth are not statistically significantly different comparing the 1980s and the 2000s.[18] The fourth column of table A1 provides the results of statistical tests of an opt-out continuation for various intervals around birth. For women with bachelor's degrees experiencing subsequent births, the opting-out patterns and level of pre-birth participation are quite similar over the three decades; the only notable differences are a delay in leaving the labor force before birth in the 1990s and higher initial rates of opting out in the 1980s.

The estimates for women with at least a master's degree are less precise because sample sizes are smaller, but it is at this education level that we see the biggest changes in behavior over time. Figure 17 shows that following an almost identical absence of opting out from twelve to two months before first births, women in the 1980s opted out around 10 percentage points more than in the later decades, though labor-force participation did fall in the in the 1990s and 2000s, bouncing around 7 to 15 percentage points below the year before birth. Figure 18 shows that estimates of opting out after subsequent births were greater in the 1990s than in the 1980s and 2000s, though these estimates are not precise. No opting out around subsequent births occurring during the 2004 panel was statistically significant. However, labor-force participation a year before these births was 16 percentage points lower than for similarly educated women in the 2000s birth sample—81 versus 95 percent.

Opting for Fewer Hours

Opting out usually refers to women exiting the labor force. However, to balance work and family, women may choose instead to reduce their work hours rather than leave altogether after they have children. Figures 19 through 22 compare the proportion of women who were working fewer than thirty-five hours a week—part time, around first births, conditional on working, by education across the 1980s, 1990s, and 2000s.[19] Across the education spectrum, the proportion of women working part time increases substantially after first births in all three decades. The transition to part-time work

---

17. Breaking this high-school-or-less group down further, I find that the increased opting out in the 2000s is partially driven by unmarried women with less than a high school diploma, the population likely to be affected by welfare reform. However, opting out is also more prevalent in the 2000s than in earlier decades among married mothers with a high school diploma or less.

18. As described, this claim is based on a test that fails to reject that the full set of δ_6 to δ_{24} coefficients are jointly different in the 2000s from the 1980s.

19. The proportion of women working part time before subsequent births is quite similar to the proportion two years after first births and does not change substantially after subsequent births, so these results are excluded.

Figure 11. Changes in Labor-Force Participation, All, First Births

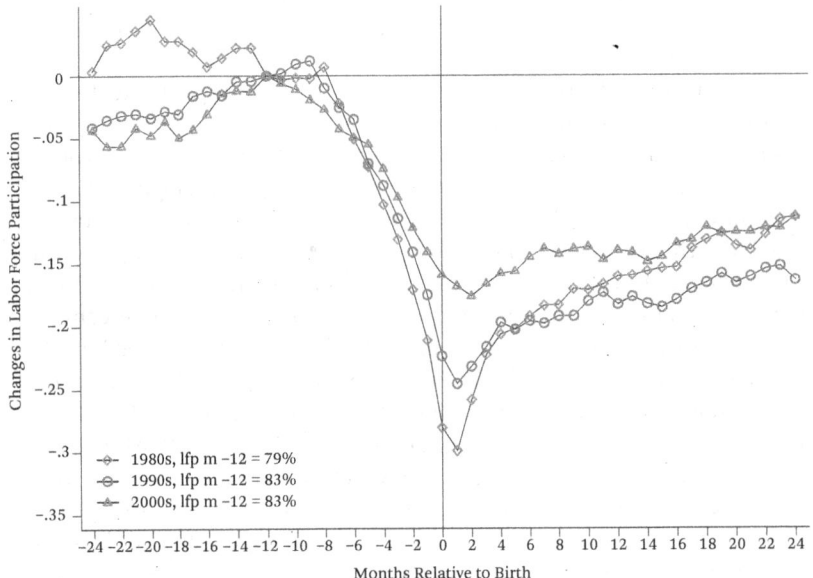

Source: Author's calculations based on the 1984–1986, 1996, 2004, and 2008 Survey of Income and Program Participation panels.
Notes: Women age eighteen to forty-five who give birth during one of the panels. Plots show *changes* in labor force participation from twenty-four months before to twenty-four months after birth (plotting the coefficients from equation (1) with dependent variable an indicator for being in the labor force estimated separately by education and parity).

Figure 12. Changes in Labor-Force Participation, All, Subsequent Births

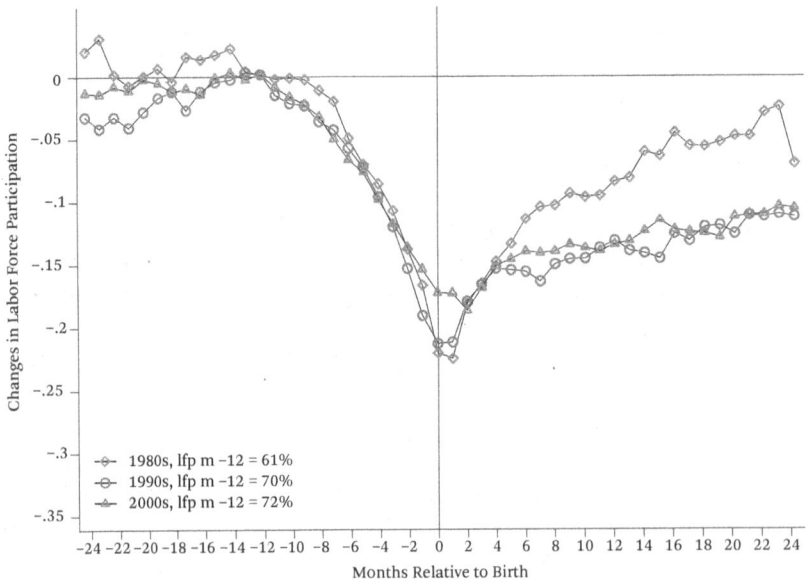

Source: Author's calculations based on the 1984–1986, 1996, 2004, and 2008 Survey of Income and Program Participation panels.
Notes: See notes to figure 11.

Figure 13. Changes in Labor-Force Participation, Less than Bachelor's, First Births

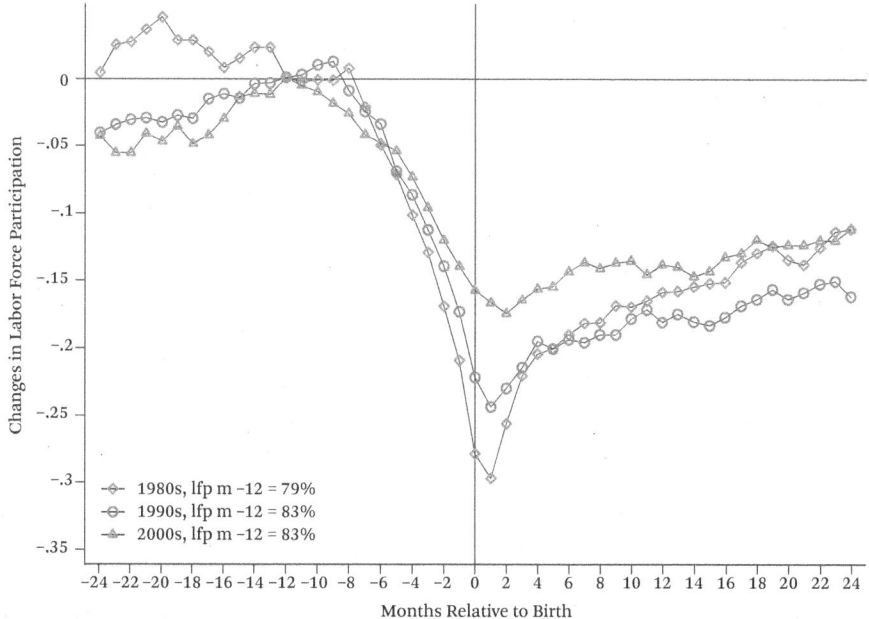

Source: Author's calculations based on the 1984–1986, 1996, 2004, and 2008 Survey of Income and Program Participation panels.
Notes: See notes to figure 11.

Figure 14. Changes in Labor-Force Participation, Less than Bachelor's, Subsequent Births

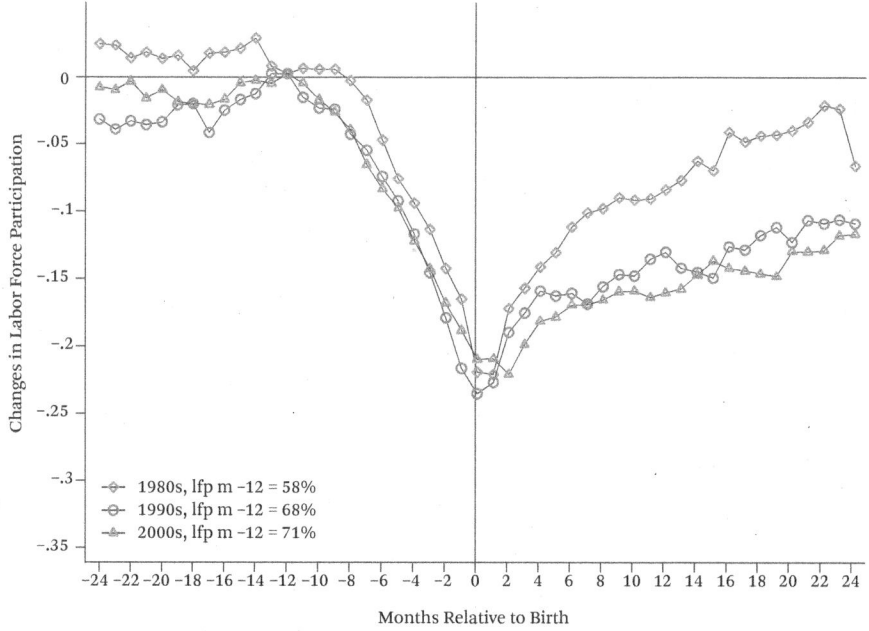

Source: Author's calculations based on the 1984–1986, 1996, 2004, and 2008 Survey of Income and Program Participation panels.
Notes: See notes to figure 11.

Figure 15. Changes in Labor-Force Participation, at Least Bachelor's, First Births

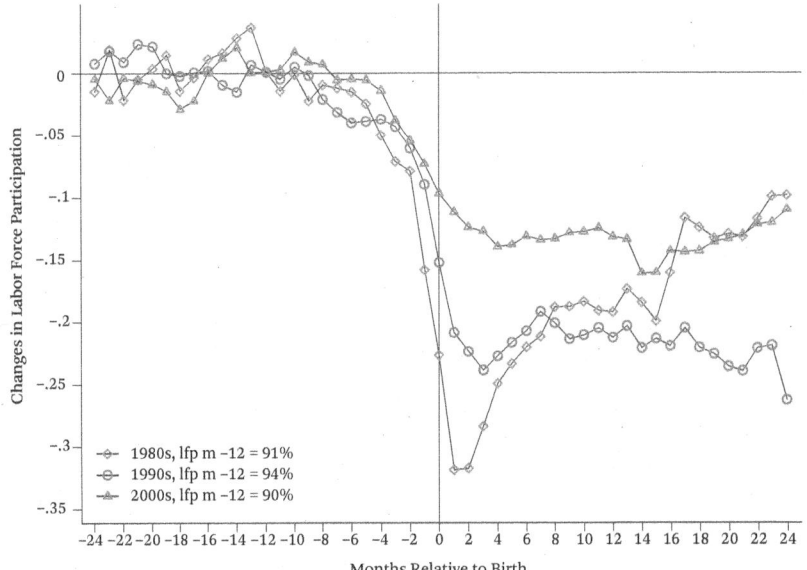

Source: Author's calculations based on the 1984–1986, 1996, 2004, and 2008 Survey of Income and Program Participation panels.
Notes: Women age eighteen to forty-five who give birth during one of the panels. Plots show *changes* in labor-force participation from twenty-four months before to twenty-four months after birth (plotting the coefficients from equation (1) with dependent variable an indicator for being in the labor force estimated separately by education and parity).

Figure 16. Changes in Labor-Force Participation, at Least Bachelor's, Subsequent Births

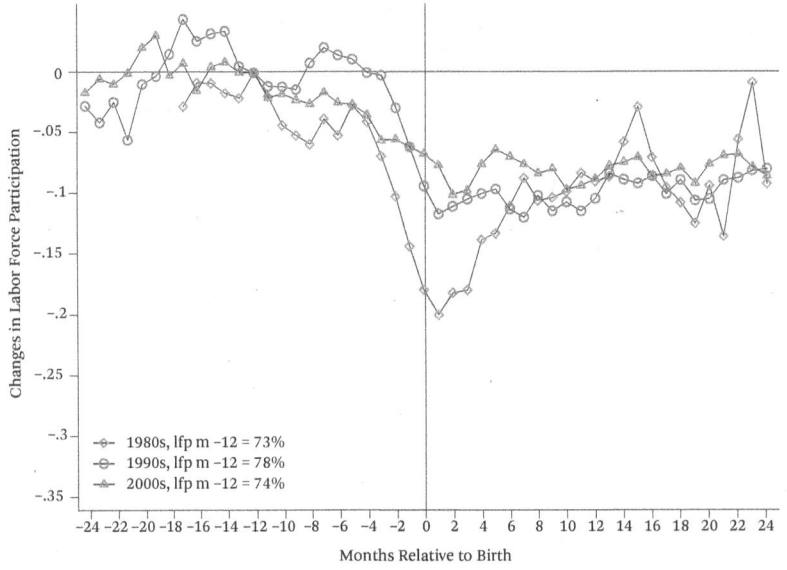

Source: Author's calculations based on the 1984–1986, 1996, 2004, and 2008 Survey of Income and Program Participation panels.
Notes: See notes to figure 15.

Figure 17. Changes in Labor-Force Participation, Master's Plus, First Births

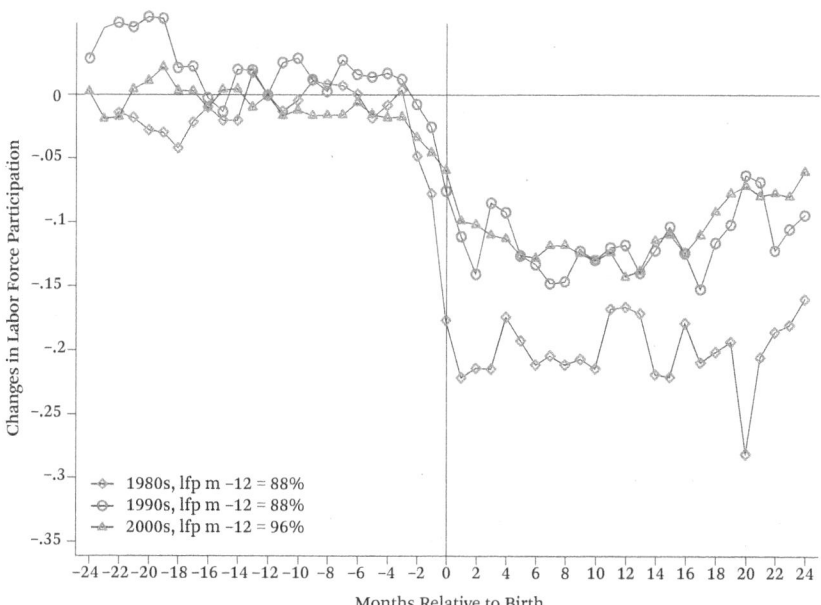

Source: Author's calculations based on the 1984–1986, 1996, 2004, and 2008 Survey of Income and Program Participation panels.
Notes: See notes to figure 15.

Figure 18. Changes in Labor-Force Participation, Master's Plus, Subsequent Births

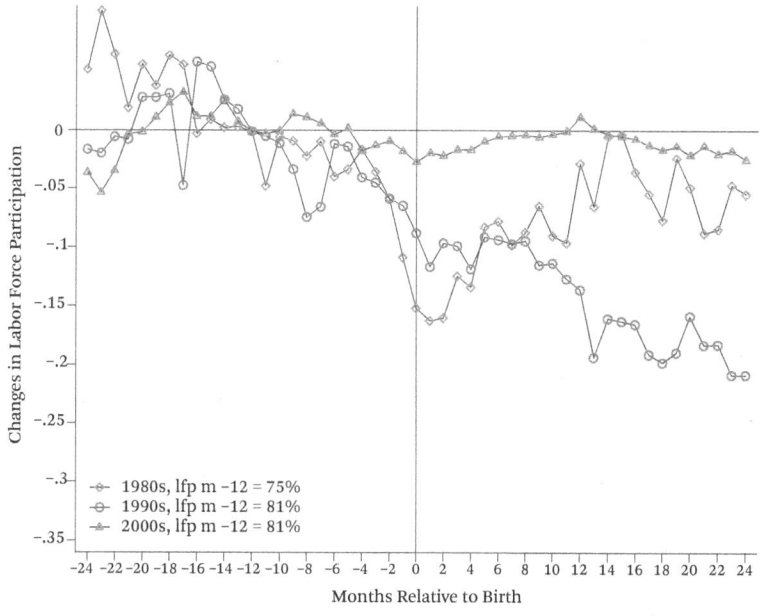

Source: Author's calculations based on the 1984–1986, 1996, 2004, and 2008 Survey of Income and Program Participation panels.
Notes: See notes to figure 15.

Figure 19. Part-Time Work, All, First Births

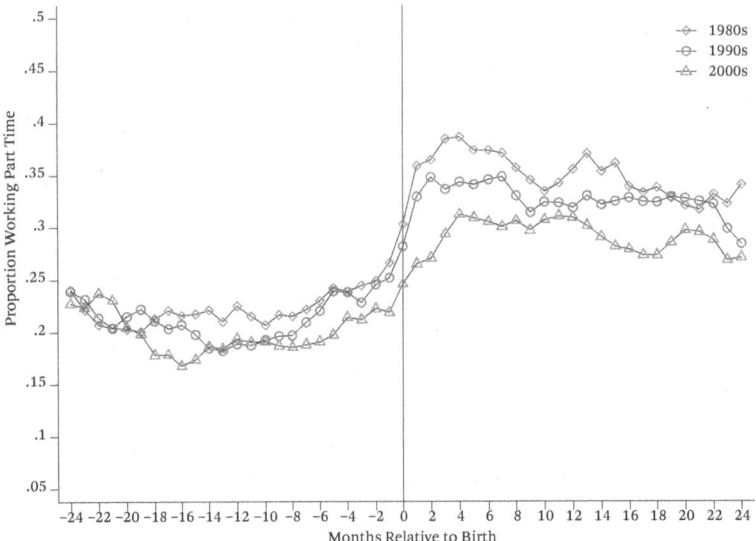

Source: Author's calculations based on on the 1984–1986, 1996, 2004, and 2008 Survey of Income and Program Participation panels.
Notes: Women age eighteen to forty-five who give birth during the panels. Plots show proportion working part time (less than thirty-five hours a week) conditional on working from twenty-four months before to twenty-four months after birth (plotting the coefficients from equation (1) with the dependent variable an indicator for working part-time estimated separately by education and parity).

Figure 20. Part-Time Work, Less than Bachelor's, First Births

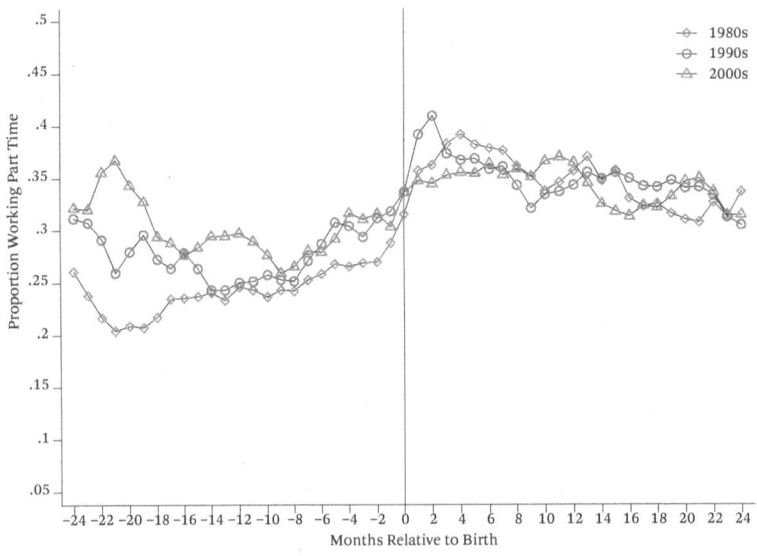

Source: Author's calculations based on on the 1984–1986, 1996, 2004, and 2008 Survey of Income and Program Participation panels.
Notes: See notes to figure 19.

Figure 21. Part-Time Work, at Least Bachelor's, First Births

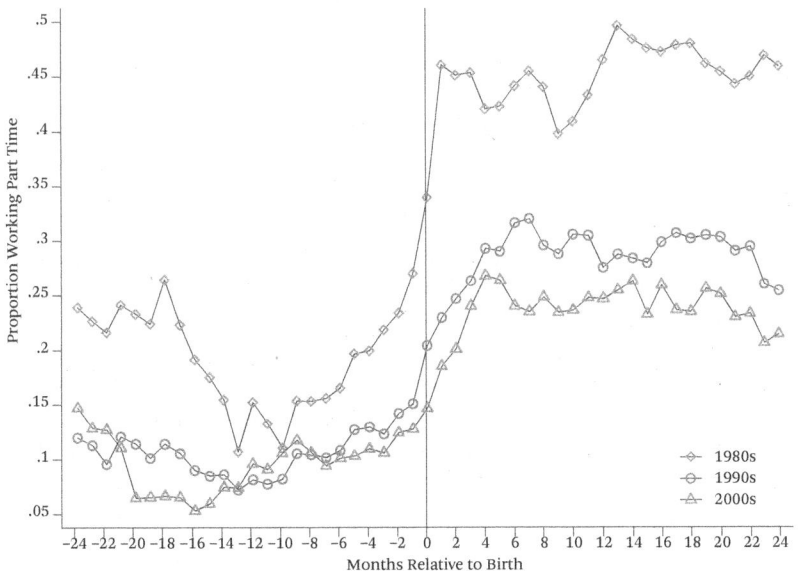

Source: Author's calculations based on on the 1984–1986, 1996, 2004, and 2008 Survey of Income and Program Participation panels.
Notes: See notes to figure 19.

Figure 22. Part-Time Work, Master's Plus, First Births

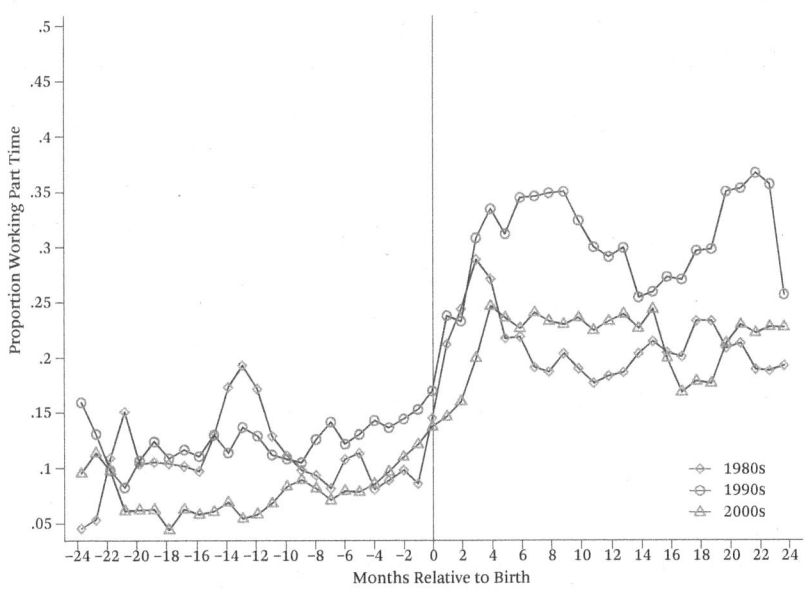

Source: Author's calculations based on on the 1984–1986, 1996, 2004, and 2008 Survey of Income and Program Participation panels.
Notes: See notes to figure 19.

has diminished over time for more-educated women, however.

Figure 20 shows that the proportion of women with less than a bachelor's degree who shift into part-time work after first births has remained relatively stable since the 1980s—a five to 10 percentage point increase from a base around 27 percent a year earlier. Figures 21 and 22 show that, for women with bachelor's degrees and those with at least a master's, both the shifts into part-time work after birth and the changes over time in these shifts are more substantial. The 1980s saw a relatively large increase in part-time work after first births—from 15 percent a year before to 45 percent a year after among women with bachelor's degrees, and from 10 percent to around 32 percent for those with at least master's degrees. In the 1990s and 2000s, from pre-birth levels of part-time work around 10 percent, the increase was substantially less—to about 29 in the 1990 and 24 percent in the 2000s in the two years after birth for women with bachelor's degrees and to 20 percent for those with at least a master's. This is surprising given recent opinion polls, which indicate that the majority of working mothers believe it would be ideal for themselves and their children if they worked part-time (Wang, Parker, and Taylor 2013). This, combined with the finding that 40 percent of nonworking mothers also think that working part time would be their ideal situation, suggests that a lack of good part-time options may be a driver of the opt-out continuation.[20]

Opting Out by Race and Marital Status

Figures 4 through 6 show that, historically, black mothers participated in the labor force at substantially higher rates than white mothers and that their participation increased more steeply through the 1970s, though the participation rates of black and white mothers have started to converge since the 1990s. In contrast, Hispanic mothers historically participated at lower levels, similar to white mothers through the 1970s, but their participation did not rise as steeply in the 1980s and 1990s. In 2010, only around 50 percent of Hispanic mothers with children under two were in the labor force, versus 72 percent of black mothers and 68 percent of white mothers.

Motivated by these differences in historical trends, I examine labor-force participation around birth by education and parity for black and Hispanic women. Figures 23 through 26 reveal that opting-out patterns for black and Hispanic mothers are distinctly different from the profiles for the full sample presented in figures 7 through 10. Black women with at least a bachelor's opt out substantially less than the overall average, and less-educated black women actually opt in to the labor force after first births. Meanwhile, Hispanic mothers with bachelor's degrees opt out at rates well above the average.

Figures 23 and 24 show opting-out patterns by parity for black mothers giving birth in the 2000s with less than a bachelor's degree and at least a bachelor's degree respectively. In contrast to all of the patterns in figures 4 through 6, figure 23 shows that labor-force participation is lowest before first births and that black women actually opt in on average after having children. Participation reaches a peak around 60 to 64 percent in the year before a first birth and then takes a 15 percentage point drop in the eight months centered around birth before rebounding to 65 percent a year after birth. A year before higher-order births, black mothers with less than a bachelor's degree are participating at a much higher level, around 80 percent, before falling to 65 percent at the month of birth and to about 72 percent a year to two years after birth—a 17 percent increase comparing a year before first births to two years after subsequent ones.

Figure 24 shows noisier estimates because the sample of black college-educated women is smaller. We see, though, that black women with at least a bachelor's degree participate at rates similar to white women with bachelor's degrees before first births—over 90 percent. In contrast to white women, however, they opt out substantially less—only 10 percentage points.

Figures 25 and 26 show opting out for Hispanic mothers. Among Hispanic women with

---

20. The proportion of working women with at least a bachelor's degree who claim that working part time would be ideal is over 60 percent as seen in table A2, which gives results of the Pew study by education and race.

less than a bachelor's degree, labor-force participation is stable at around 60 percent before first births and at 50 percent from six months to two years after first births, taking a brief steeper dip in the four to six months around birth. The pattern for higher-order births is almost identical, but participation rates level off at around 40 to 45 percent two years after subsequent births—overall a 28 percent drop in labor-force participation. Figure 26 shows that college-educated Hispanic mothers participate around 90 percent before first births but at only 63 percent two years after subsequent births, a 32 percent drop.

Opting Out by Marital Status

Because I can link fathers to births in the SIPP if they are present as a spouse at the time of birth, I also briefly address married fathers' (lack of) opting out behavior. Figures 27 through 30 offer two primary takeaways. First, married women are less likely to reenter the labor force than unmarried women. Second, because fathers do not opt out of the labor force after a birth, by two years after subsequent births, the gap between mothers' and fathers' labor-force participation is 30 to 45 percentage points on average. Figures A7 through A10 indicate that this pattern of diverging participation within married couples along traditional gender lines has held remarkably stable over the past thirty years.

Figures 27 and 28 show that among women with less than a bachelor's degree, married women reduce their participation after births substantially more than unmarried women after higher-order births—two years after birth only 52 percent of married women are in the labor force compared with 70 percent of unmarried women.[21] Table 2 and table 3 indicate that marital status at birth varies substantially by education: only 48 percent of women with less than a bachelor's degree married at first birth in the 2000s versus 91 percent of those with bachelor's and 95 percent of those with master's degrees or more. Because the vast majority of highly educated women are married at the time of birth, I do not show opting out for unmarried women with at least a bachelor's degree in figures 29 and 30. Instead, I use this as an opportunity to compare the work behavior of wives and husbands around the time of birth. Figures 27 through 30 each tell the same story regarding married father's labor-force participation around birth: about 95 percent and does not waver at any point during the event study window from two years before to two years after first or subsequent births for either education group. Meanwhile, the gap between the participation of husbands and wives grows to 42 percentage points for households in which the woman has less than a bachelor's degree and to 32 percentage points in households with more-educated mothers. This is despite nearly identical participation rates among husbands and college-educated wives a year before first births.

CONCLUSION

I have implemented a new dynamic measure of opting out across the education distribution in the 1980s, 1990s, and 2000s. I do not find an abrupt increase in opting out over the past three decades among highly educated women. In this, I concur with other recent findings rejecting an opt-out revolution. However, in the 2000s, a substantial and statistically significant percentage of women leave the labor force when they give birth. The rate of labor-force participation remains low for at least two years after first and subsequent births for women in all education categories—a pattern surprisingly similar to opting out for mothers in the 1990s and 1980s.

Although the opting-out profile is broadly similar across education, race, and marital status, investigating the differences in magnitude and timing provides motivation for future research. For example, women who are married are more likely to opt out (or at least to stay out longer) perhaps because they have more household resources. The vast majority of highly educated mothers are married and, as a result, have more resources. However, highly educated women also give up more in terms of future or current earnings when they exit the labor force. So why do they opt out at such high a rate?

---

21. Marital status is defined by status during the month of birth. Marital status may change after birth.

Figure 23. Opting Out in the 2000s, Blacks, Less than Bachelor's

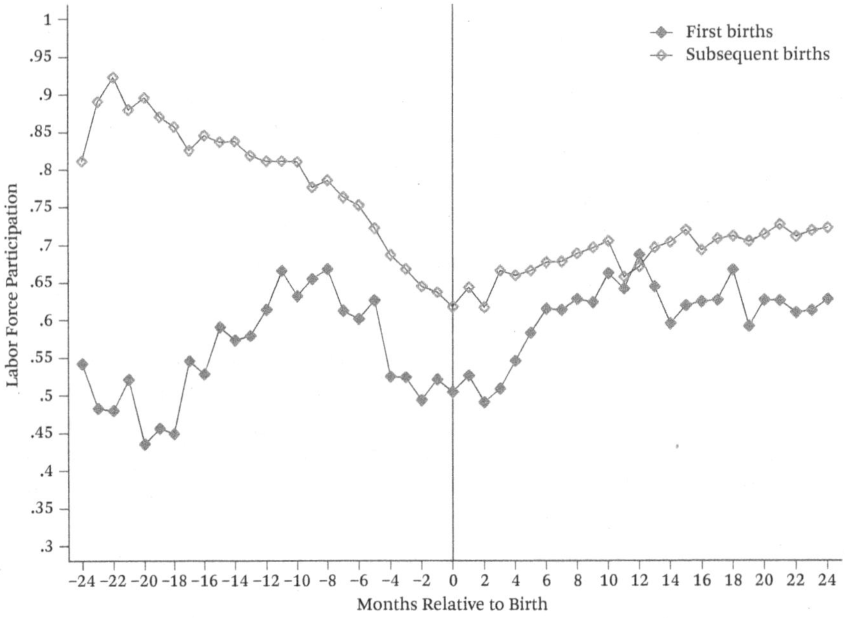

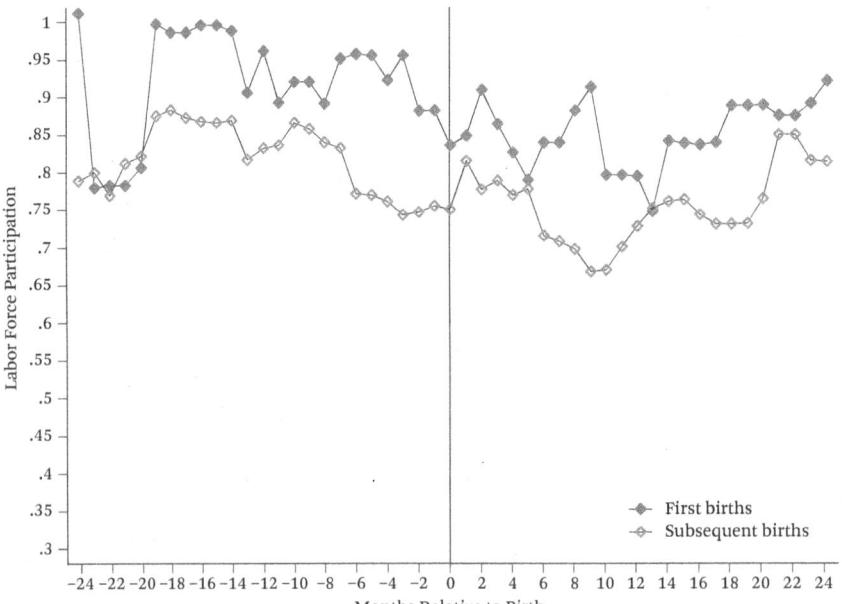

Source: Author's calculations based on the 2004 and 2008 Survey of Income and Program Participation panels.
Notes: Women age eighteen to forty-five who give birth during the panels. Plots show labor-force participation from twenty-four months before to twenty-four months after birth (plotting the coefficients from equation (1) added to the constant with dependent variable an indicator for being in the labor force estimated separately by race, education, and parity).

Figure 24. Opting Out in the 2000s, Blacks, at Least Bachelor's

Source: Author's calculations based on the 2004 and 2008 Survey of Income and Program Participation panels.
Notes: See notes to figure 23.

Figure 25. Opting Out in the 2000s, Hispanic, Less than Bachelor's

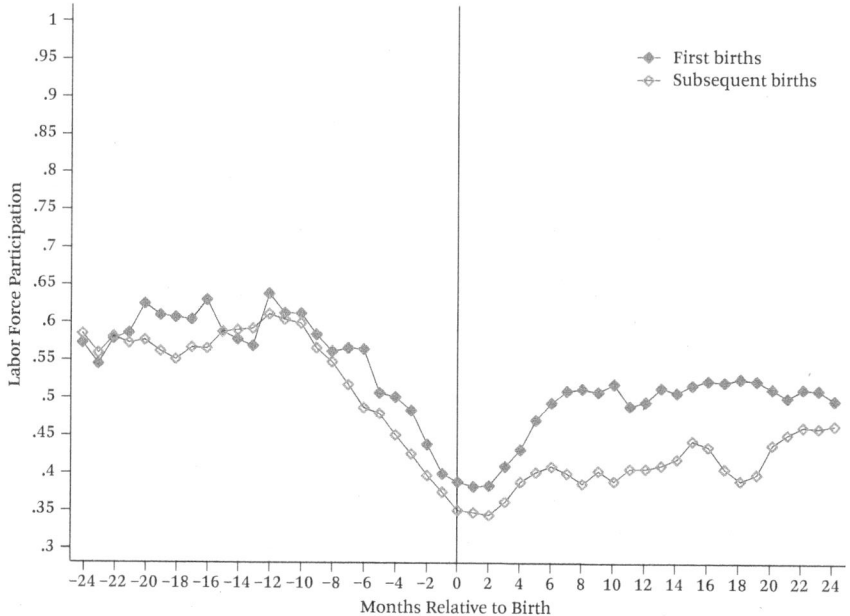

Source: Author's calculations based on the 2004 and 2008 Survey of Income and Program Participation panels.
Notes: See notes to figure 23.

Figure 26. Opting Out in the 2000s, Hispanics, at Least Bachelor's

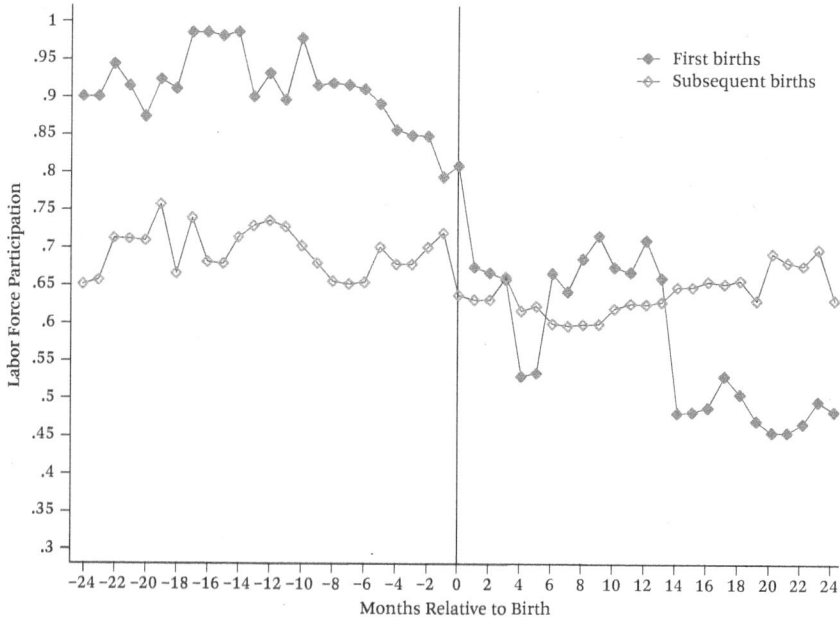

Source: Author's calculations based on the 2004 and 2008 Survey of Income and Program Participation panels.
Notes: See notes to figure 23.

Figure 27. Fathers' and Mothers' Labor-Force Participation, Less than Bachelor's, First Births

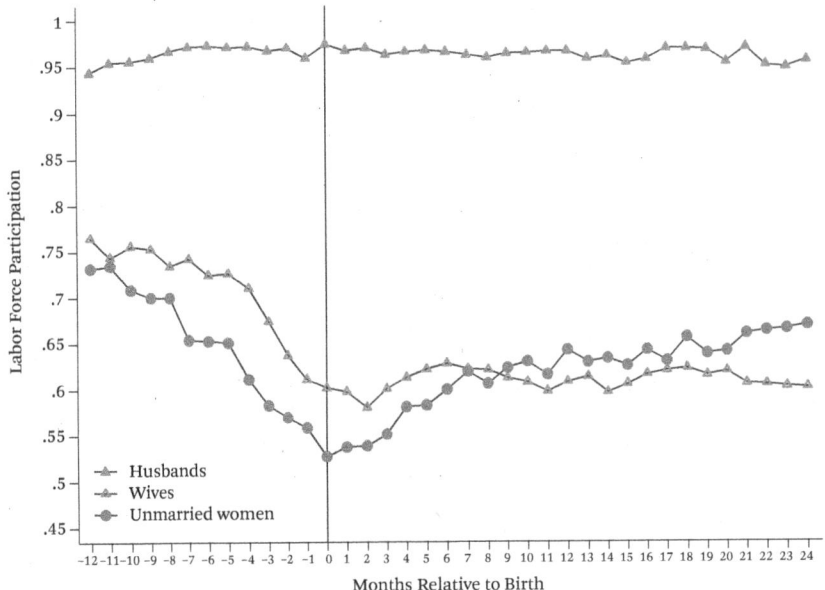

Source: Author's calculations based on the 2004 and 2008 Survey of Income and Program Participation panels.
Notes: Women age eighteen to forty-five who give birth during the panels and their spouses where relevant. Wives are women who were married with spouse present in the month they gave birth. Plots show labor-force participation from twenty-four months before to twenty-four months after birth (plotting the coefficients from equation (1) added to the constant with dependent variable an indicator for being in the labor force estimated separately by marital status, education, and parity).

Figure 28. Fathers' and Mothers' Labor-Force Participation, Less than Bachelor's, Subsequent Births

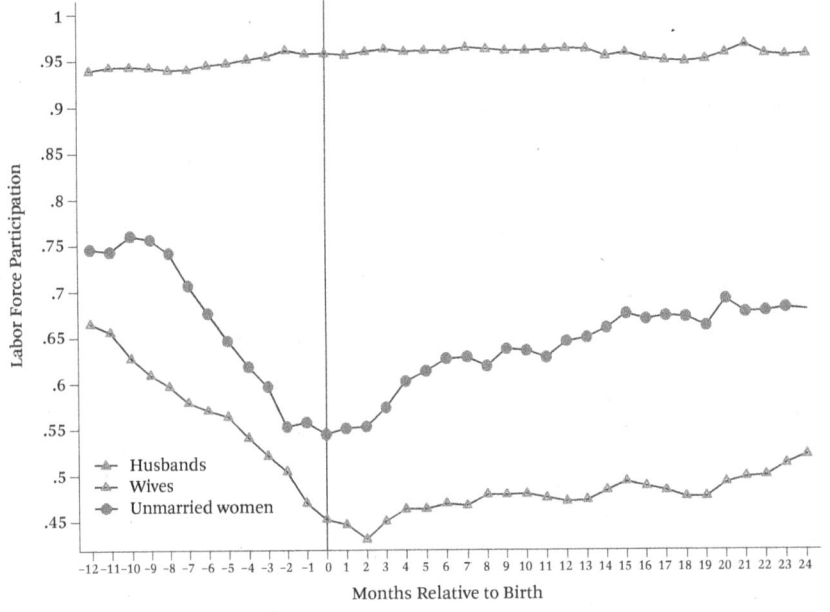

Source: Author's calculations based on the 2004 and 2008 Survey of Income and Program Participation panels.
Notes: See notes to figure 27.

Figure 29. Fathers' and Mothers' Labor Force Participation, at Least Bachelor's, First Births

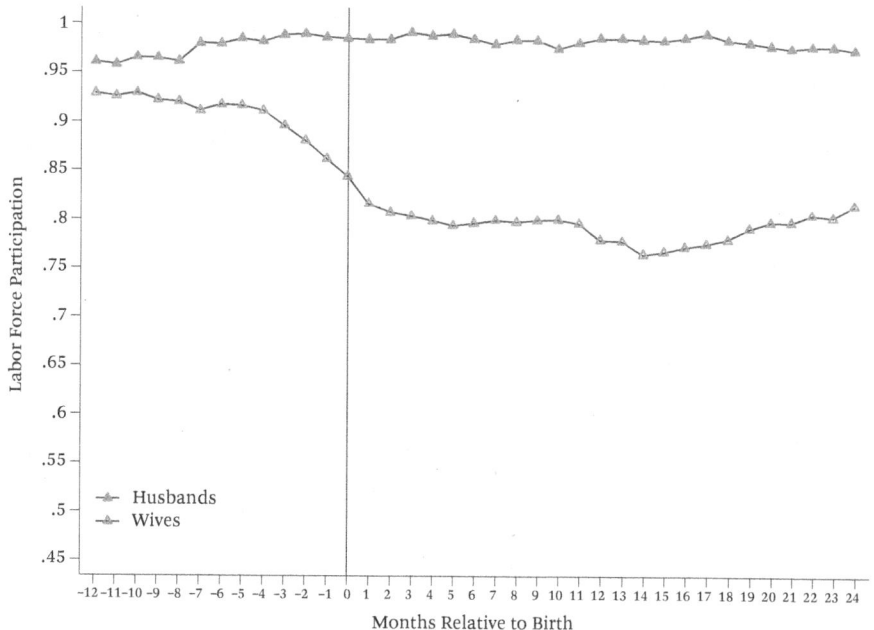

Source: Author's calculations based on the 2004 and 2008 Survey of Income and Program Participation panels.
Notes: See notes to figure 27.

Figure 30. Fathers' and Mothers' Labor-Force Participation, at Least Bachelor's, Subsequent Births

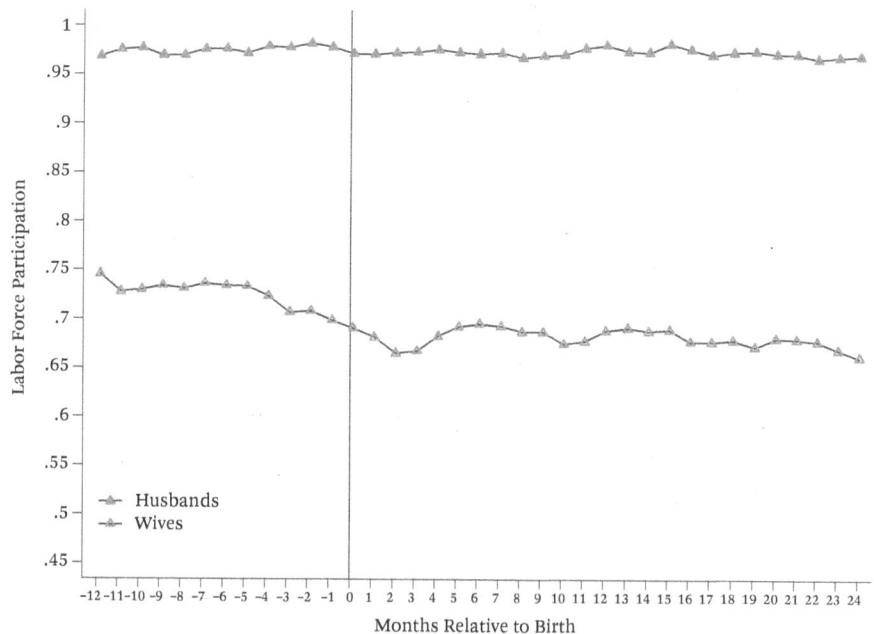

Source: Author's calculations based on the 2004 and 2008 Survey of Income and Program Participation panels.
Notes: See notes to figure 27.

Part-time or flexible work could provide an alternative to opting out. The Pew survey finds that half of working women would prefer to work part time when their children are young, yet I find that far fewer than half do so. The percentage preferring part-time work rises to 62 percent among college-educated working mothers, yet I find that the rate of part-time work among these women has fallen to around 25 percent since the 1980s. This inconsistency may be explained by a lack of desirable part-time alternatives, making labor-force exit the best among less than ideal alternatives for many women. One of the women in Belkin's story states that she quit her job when her son was young because she was denied a part-time option. The Pew finding that 41 percent of nonworking mothers also claim part-time work would be ideal is suggestive evidence to corroborate this hypothesis. Resolving this puzzle may involve investigating nuances by occupation. As Claudia Goldin points out in her 2014 presidential address, occupations vary in the wage penalty to both time away and reduced hours, and that many of the occupations that highly skilled women have shifted into in recent decades like business and law exhibit this nonlinearity in rewards to long hours and uninterrupted attachment (Goldin 2014; see also Weeden, Cha, and Bucca, this issue).

Because the opting-out profile has remained relatively stable since the 1980s—any changes actually increasing rather than decreasing participation (such as in the months immediately around birth among women with at least a master's)—opting out does not offer an explanation for the plateau in the growth of women's labor-force participation. But an opt-out continuation, combined with a relative shift into occupations that penalize time away from work and reward long hours, may explain the persistence of the gender gap in earnings.

APPENDIX

Figure A1. 2004 and 2008 SIPP Panels: Maximum Event Study Window, First Births

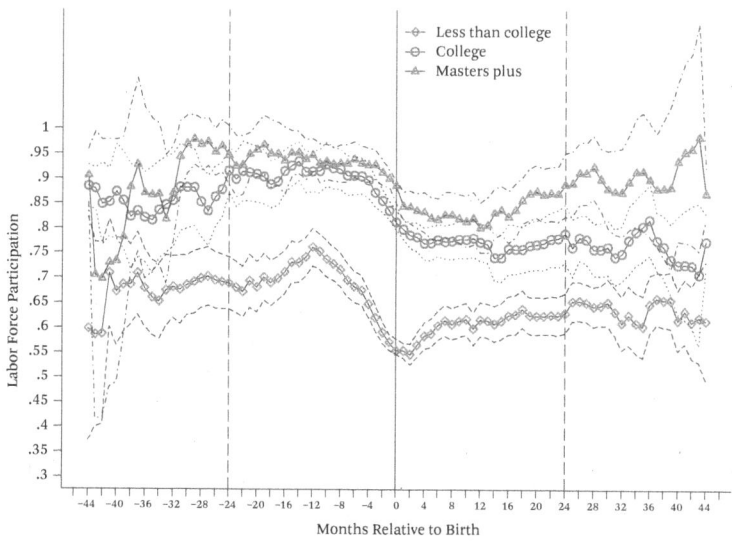

Source: Author's calculations based on the 2004 and 2008 Survey of Income and Program Participation panels.
Notes: Women age eighteen to forty-five who give birth during the panels. Plots show labor-force participation from forty-eight months before to forty-eight months after birth (plotting the coefficients from equation (1) added to the constant with dependent variable an indicator for being in the labor force estimated separately by education and parity). Dashed lines are 95 percent point-wise confidence intervals.

Figure A2. 2004 and 2008 SIPP Panels: Maximum Event Study Window, Subsequent Births

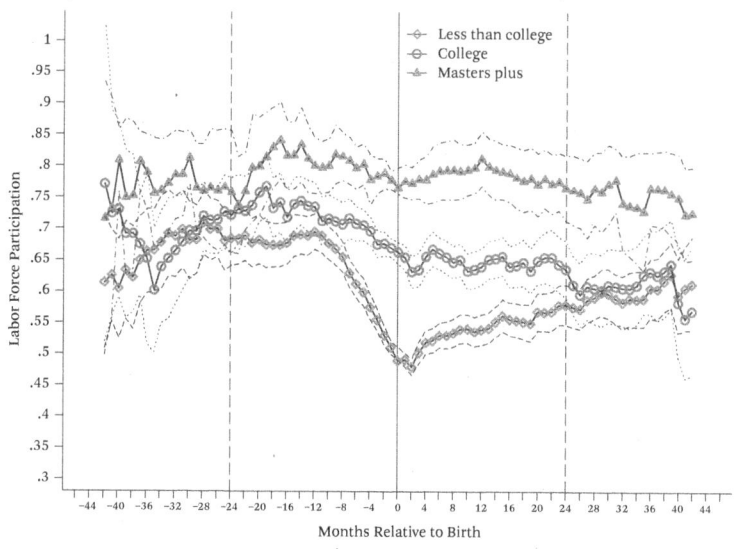

Source: Author's calculations based on the 2004 and 2008 Survey of Income and Program Participation panels.
Notes: See notes to figure A1.

Figure A3. School Enrollment Around Birth, Less than Bachelor's, Full Time

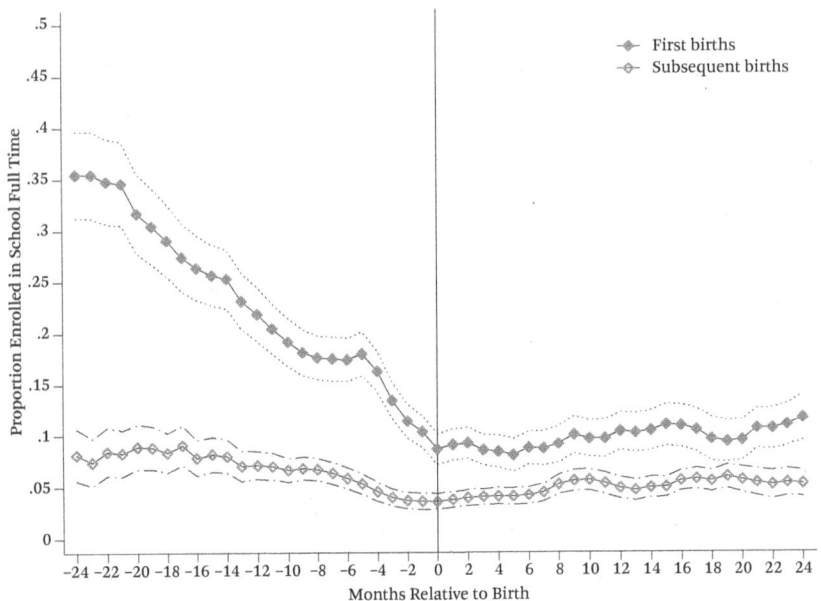

Source: Author's calculations based on the 2004 and 2008 Survey of Income and Program Participation panels.
Notes: Women age eighteen to forty-five who give birth during the panels. Plots show proportion enrolled in school from twenty-four months before to twenty-four months after birth (plotting the coefficients from equation (1) added to the constant estimated separately by education and parity). Dashed lines are 95 percent point-wise confidence intervals.

Figure A4. School Enrollment Around Birth, Less than Bachelor's, Enrolled

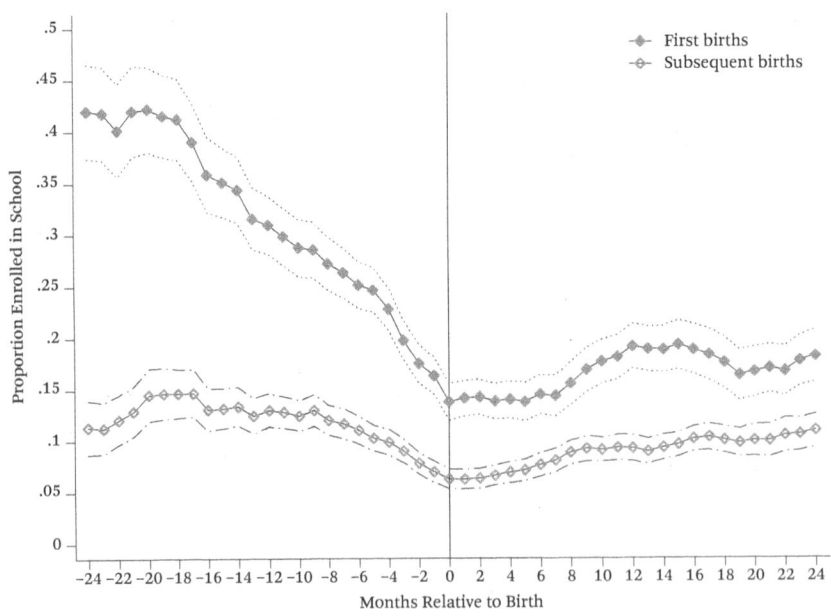

Source: Author's calculations based on the 2004 and 2008 Survey of Income and Program Participation panels.
Notes: See notes to figure A3.

Figure A5. School Enrollment Around Birth, at Least Bachelor's, Full Time

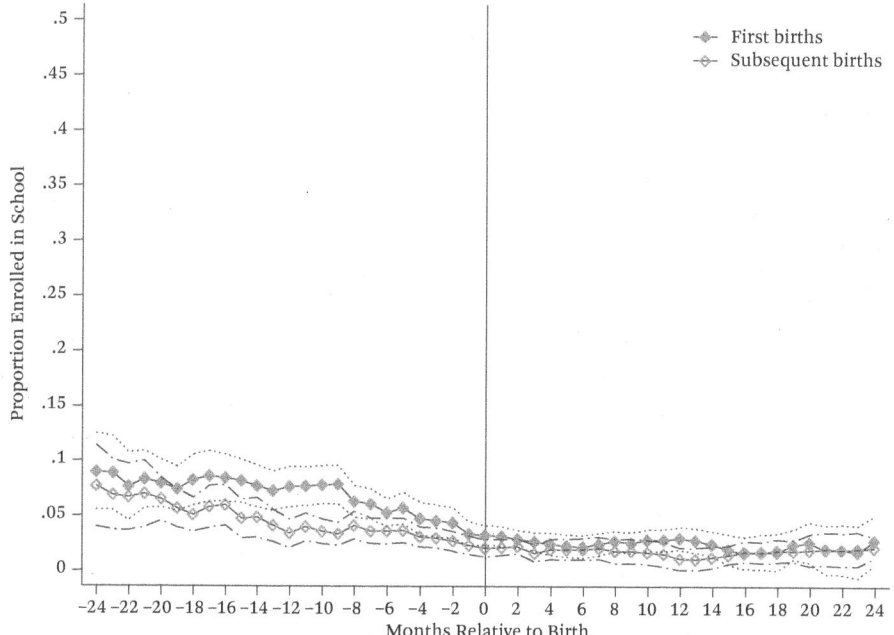

Source: Author's calculations based on the 2004 and 2008 Survey of Income and Program Participation panels.
Notes: See notes to figure A3.

Figure A6. School Enrollment Around Birth, at Least Bachelor's, Enrolled

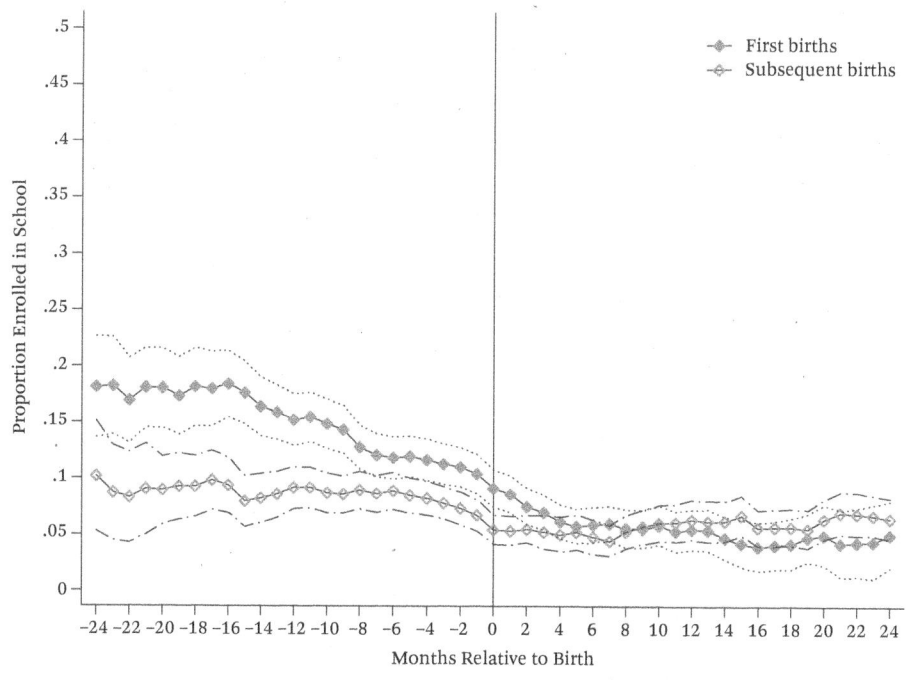

Source: Author's calculations based on the 2004 and 2008 Survey of Income and Program Participation panels.
Notes: See notes to figure A3.

Figure A7. Husbands and Wives Participation, Less than Bachelor's, First Births

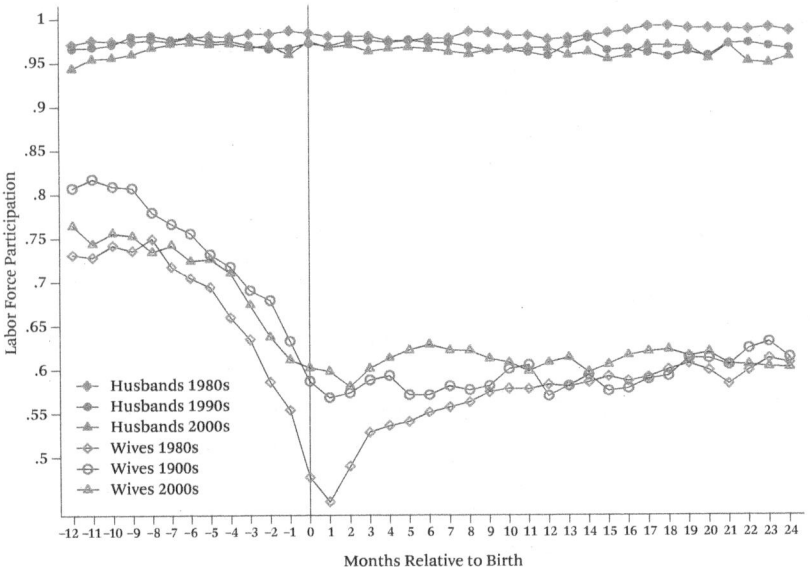

Source: Author's calculations based on the 1984–1986, 1996, 2004, and 2008 Survey of Income and Program Participation panels.
Notes: Women age eighteen to forty-five who give birth during the panels and their spouse. Wives are women who were married with spouse present in the month they gave birth. Plots show labor-force participation from twelve months before to twenty-four months after birth (plotting the coefficients added to the constant from equation (1) with the dependent variable an indicator for being in the labor force estimated separately by marital status, education, and parity).

Figure A8. Husbands and Wives Participation, Less than Bachelor's, Subsequent Births

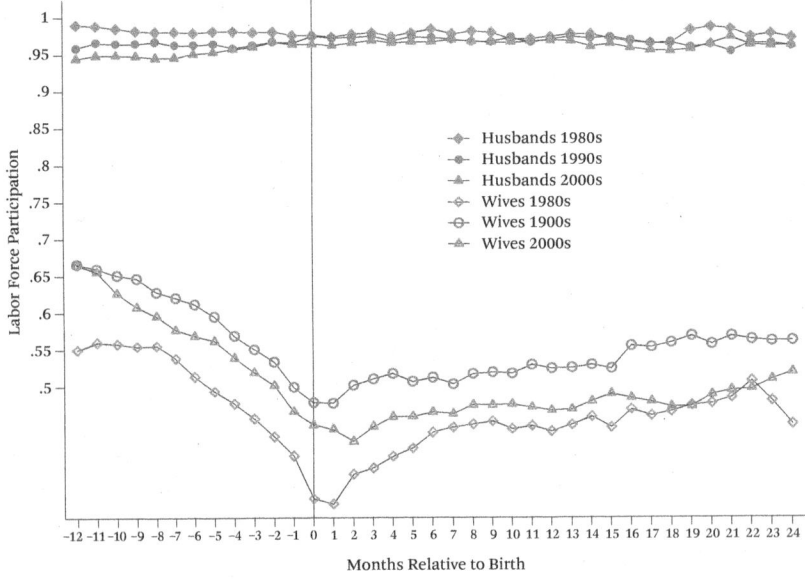

Source: Author's calculations based on the 1984–1986, 1996, 2004, and 2008 Survey of Income and Program Participation panels.
Notes: See notes to figure A7.

Figure A9. Husbands and Wives Participation, at Least Bachelor's, First Births

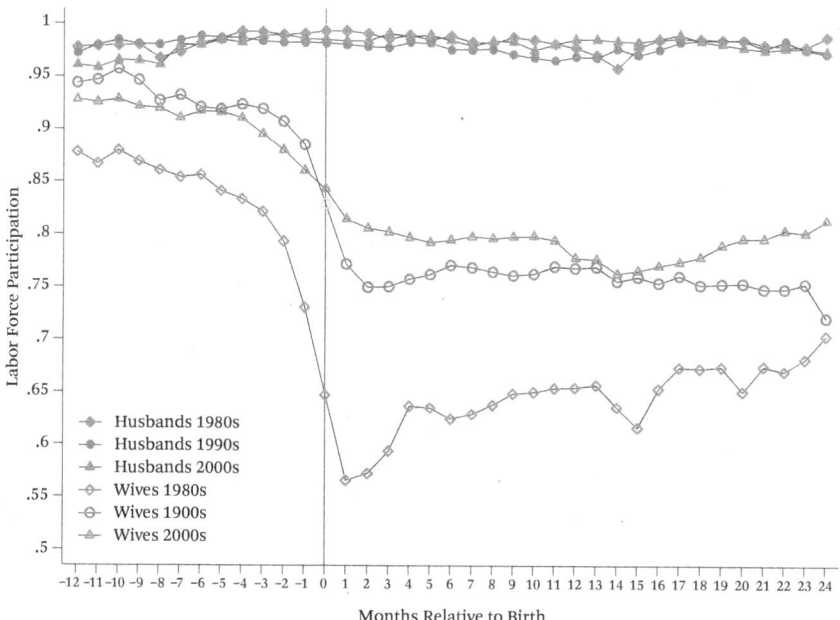

Source: Author's calculations based on the 1984–1986, 1996, 2004, and 2008 Survey of Income and Program Participation panels.
Notes: See notes to figure A7.

Figure A10. Husbands and Wives Participation, at Least Bachelor's, Subsequent Births

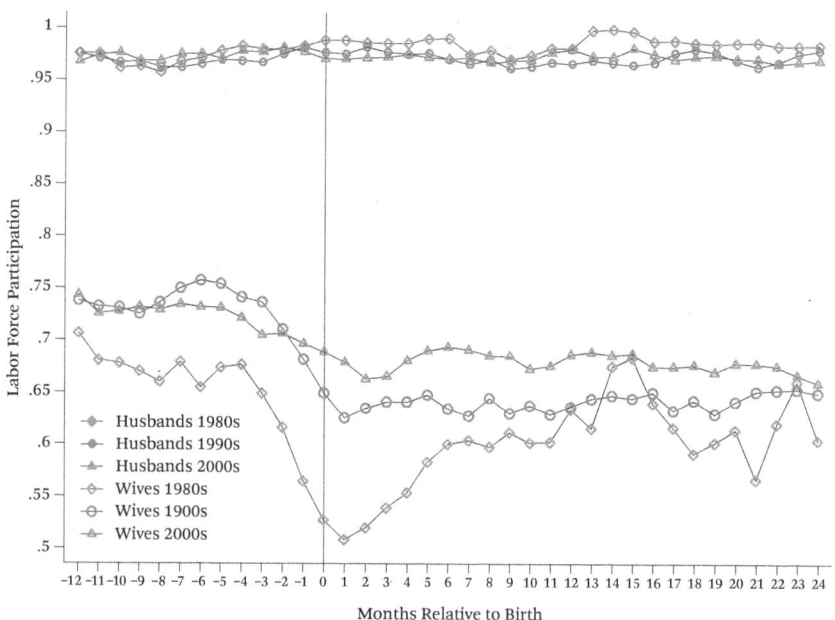

Source: Author's calculations based on the 1984–1986, 1996, 2004, and 2008 Survey of Income and Program Participation panels.
Notes: See notes to figure A7.

Table A1. Opting-Out Rates over Time and Statistical Test of Opt-Out Continuation

Average change in lfp compared with a year prior to birth:	(1) 2000s	(2) 1990s	(3) 1980s	(1) vs (3) Test of difference in opt-out profiles between 1980s and 2000s (p-values)[a]
Less than bachelor's				
First births				
–Six to birth	−0.141	−0.141	−0.159	0.000
Birth to six months	−0.190	−0.215	−0.234	0.000
Six to twelve months	−0.151	−0.172	−0.168	0.502
Six to twenty-four months	−0.143	−0.148	−0.144	0.600
Subsequent births				
–Six to birth	−0.143	−0.142	−0.131	0.028
Birth to six months	−0.192	−0.172	−0.178	0.000
Six to twelve months	−0.160	−0.130	−0.117	0.349
Six to twenty-four months	−0.145	−0.108	−0.095	0.217
Rate of opt out after subsequent births compared with women prior to first births[b]				
Six months	−0.230	−0.246	−0.303	
Twelve months	−0.221	−0.211	−0.283	
Twenty-four months	−0.181	−0.178	−0.280	
Bachelor's only				
First births				
–Six to birth	−0.045	−0.058	−0.115	0.144
Birth to six months	−0.129	−0.194	−0.303	0.001
Six to twelve months	−0.138	−0.180	−0.250	0.696
Six to twenty-four months	−0.145	−0.187	−0.230	0.638
Subsequent births				
–Six to birth	−0.050	−0.019	−0.093	0.070
Birth to six months	−0.082	−0.097	−0.166	0.021
Six to twelve months	−0.089	−0.100	−0.109	0.630
Six to twenty-four months	−0.089	−0.084	−0.103	0.414
Rate of opt out after subsequent births compared with women prior to first births[b]				
Six months	−0.253	−0.300	−0.272	
Twelve months	−0.274	−0.289	−0.259	
Twenty-four months	−0.278	−0.259	−0.266	
Master's plus				
First births				
–Six to birth	−0.030	−0.023	−0.043	0.091
Birth to six months	−0.108	−0.134	−0.192	0.344
Six to twelve months	−0.130	−0.167	−0.180	0.317
Six to twenty-four months	−0.108	−0.165	−0.178	0.211
Subsequent births				
–Six to birth	−0.016	−0.037	−0.065	0.027
Birth to six months	−0.022	−0.093	−0.137	0.433
Six to twelve months	−0.004	−0.093	−0.068	0.448
Six to twenty-four months	−0.014	−0.137	−0.037	0.271

Table A1. (*continued*)

Average change in lfp compared with a year prior to birth:	(1) 2000s	(2) 1990s	(3) 1980s	(1) vs (3) Test of difference in opt-out profiles between 1980s and 2000s (p-values)[a]
Rate of opt out after subsequent births compared with women prior to first births[b]				
Six months	−0.153	−0.224	−0.254	
Twelve months	−0.133	−0.264	−0.185	
Twenty-four months	−0.180	−0.332	−0.197	

Source: Author's calculations based on the Survey of Income and Program Participation (2000s: 2004 and 2008 panels, 1990s: 1996 panel, 1980s: 1984, 1985, and 1986 panels).
[a]Test that the difference between the full set of δ coefficients from the relevant interval are jointly different in the 2000s from the 1980s. Based on pooling the data from the 1980s and 2000s panels and estimating equation (1) interacting dummies for each panel with each month-relative-to-birth dummy and testing if the series of relevant interaction terms are jointly equal to zero.
[b]This is an approximate measure, since first-birth mothers are different from subsequent-birth mothers.

Table A2. Mothers' Opinions About Their Ideal Work Situation

A. By Education

Percent who answer ...	Not Working	Working	Less than Bachelor's Not Working	Less than Bachelor's Working	At Least Bachelor's Not Working	At Least Bachelor's Working
Considering everything, what would be the ideal situation for YOU—working:						
Full-time	22	37	26	43	13	29
Part-time	41	50	43	43	34	62
Not at all	35	11	29	13	53	8
Sample size	124	229	86	119	38	110

B. By Race

Percent who answer ...	White Not Working	White Working	Black Not Working	Black Working	Hispanic Not Working	Hispanic Working
Considering everything, what would be the ideal situation for YOU—working:						
Full-time	11	28	49	63	29	47
Part-time	39	58	21	27	52	43
Not at all	48	12	30	10	19	11
Sample size	68	136	19	34	32	39

Source: Pew Research Center "Gender and Generations" dataset. Survey conducted November to December 2012. Respondents were over the age of eighteen and reported having at least one child under the age of eighteen. The Pew Research Center bears no responsibility for the analyses or interpretations of the data presented here.

REFERENCES

Antecol, Heather. 2011. "The Opt-Out Revolution: Recent Trends in Female Labor Supply." *Research in Labor Economics* 33(1): 45–83.

Belkin, Lisa. 2003. "The Opt-Out Revolution." *New York Times Magazine*, October 26, pp. 23–32.

Bertrand, Marianne, Claudia Goldin, and Lawrence Katz. 2010. "Dynamics of the Gender Gap for Young Professionals in the Corporate and Financial Sectors." *American Economic Journal: Applied Economics* 2(3): 228–55.

Blau, Francine D., and Lawrence M. Kahn. 1997. "Swimming Upstream: Trends in the Gender Wage Differential in the 1980s." *Journal of Labor Economics* 15(1): 1–42.

———. 2004. "The US Gender Pay Gap in the 1990s: Slowing Convergence." *NBER* working paper no. 10853. Cambridge, Mass. National Bureau of Economic Research.

Boushey, Heather. 2005. "Are Women Opting Out? Debunking the Myth." Briefing Paper no. 2005-111-2. Washington, D.C.: Center for Economic and Policy Research. Accessed April 4, 2016. http://www.cepr.net/documents/publications/opt_out_2005_11_2.pdf.

Buchmann, Claudia, and Anne McDaniel. 2016. "Motherhood and the Wages of Women in Professional Occupations." *RSF: The Russell Sage Journal of the Social Sciences* 2(4). doi: 10.7758/RSF.2016.2.4.05.

Byker, Tanya. 2016. "Paid Parental Leave Laws in the United States: Does Short-Duration Leave Affect Women's Labor-Force Attachment?" *American Economic Review* 106(5): 242–46.

Goldin, Claudia. 2006. "The Quiet Revolution that Transformed Women's Employment, Education and Family." *American Economic Review* 96(2): 1–21.

———. 2014. "A Grand Gender Convergence: Its Last Chapter." *American Economic Review* 104(4): 1091–119.

Goldin, Claudia, Lawrence F. Katz, and Ilyana Kuziemko. 2006. "The Homecoming of American College Women: The Reversal of the College Gender Gap." *Journal of Economic Perspectives* 20(4): 133–56.

Herr, Jane Leber, and Catherine Wolfram. 2012. "Opt-Out Rates at Motherhood Across High-Education Career Paths." *Industrial and Labor Relations Review* 65(4): 928–50.

Hotchkiss, Julie, and M. Melinda Pitts. 2003. "At What Level of Labor-Market Intermittency Are Women Penalized?" *American Economic Review* 93(2): 233–37.

Jacobson, Louis S., Robert LaLonde, and Daniel G. Sullivan. 1993. "Earnings Losses of Displaced Workers." *American Economic Review* 83(4): 685–709.

King, Miriam, Steven Ruggles, J. Trent Alexander, Sarah Flood, Katie Genadek, Matthew B. Schroeder, Brandon Trampe, and Rebecca Vick. 2010. *Integrated Public Use Microdata Series, Current Population Survey: Version 3.0*. [Machine-readable database]. Minneapolis: University of Minnesota.

Mincer, Jacob, and Solomon Polachek. 1974. "Family Investments in Human Capital: Earnings of Women." *Journal of Political Economy* 82(2): S76-S108.

Pal, Ipshita, and Jane Waldfogel. 2016. "The Family Gap in Pay: New Evidence for 1967 to 2013." *RSF: The Russell Sage Journal of the Social Sciences* 2(4). doi: 10.7758/RSF.2016.2.4.04.

Percheski, Christine. 2008. "Opting Out? Cohort Differences in Professional Women's Employment Rates from 1960 to 2005." *American Sociological Review* 73(3): 497–517.

Ruggles, Steven J., Trent Alexander, Katie Genadek, Ronald Goeken, Matthew B. Schroeder, and Matthew Sobek. 2010. *Integrated Public Use Microdata Series: Version 5.0* [Machine-readable database]. Minneapolis: University of Minnesota.

Waldfogel, Jane. 2001. "Family Medical Leave: Evidence from the 2000 Surveys." *Monthly Labor Review* 124(9): 17–23.

Wang, Wendy, Kim Parker, and Paul Taylor. 2013. "Breadwinner Moms." Washington, D.C.: Pew Research Center.

Weeden, Kim A., Youngjoo Cha, and Mauricio Bucca. 2016. "Long Work Hours, Part-Time Work, and Trends in the Gender Gap in Pay, the Motherhood Wage Penalty, and the Fatherhood Wage Premium." *RSF: The Russell Sage Journal of the Social Sciences* 2(4). doi: 10.7758/RSF.2016.2.4.03.

Wood, Robert G., Mary Corcoran, and Paul Courant. 1993. "Pay Differences Among the Highly Paid: The Male-Female Earnings Gap in Lawyers' Salaries." *Journal of Labor Economics* 11(3): 417–41.

Long Work Hours, Part-Time Work, and Trends in the Gender Gap in Pay, the Motherhood Wage Penalty, and the Fatherhood Wage Premium

KIM A. WEEDEN, YOUNGJOO CHA, AND MAURICIO BUCCA

We assess how changes in the social organization and compensation of work hours over the last three decades are associated with changes in wage differentials among mothers, fathers, childless women, and childless men. We find that large differences between gender and parental status groups in long work hours (fifty or more per week), coupled with sharply rising hourly wages for long work hours, contributed to rising gender gaps in wages (especially among parents), motherhood wage penalties, and fatherhood wage premiums. Changes in the representation of these groups in part-time work, by contrast, is associated with a decline in the gender gap in wages among parents and in the motherhood wage penalty, but an increase in the fatherhood wage premium. These findings offer important clues into why gender and family wage differentials still persist.

Keywords: gender inequality, family wage gap, gender wage gap, motherhood wage penalty, fatherhood wage premium, work hours, long work hours, overwork

After converging relatively rapidly in the 1970s and 1980s, the gender gap in hourly wages shrank only modestly over the next thirty-five years. Today, median weekly wages of full-time women are 83 percent of the median weekly wages of men, an increase of just three percentage points since 2004 (BLS 2015). This stalled convergence in the gender gap in wages has led to a large and vibrant research literature that seeks to understand why change has been so slow (England 2010).

One of the key empirical insights of this literature is that the gender gap in wages at the aggregate level is perpetuated by persistent gender differences in individual labor market behaviors: whether men and women work for pay, the occupations and industries in which they work, and the number of hours per week they work. These gender differences emerge in the context of structural changes in the distribution of jobs with particular attributes (such as expected work hours) and in the wages associated with these attributes, resulting in complex and offsetting effects on the gender

---

Kim A. Weeden is Jan Rock Zubrow '77 Professor of Sociology and director of the Center for the Study of Inequality at Cornell University. **Youngjoo Cha** is associate professor of sociology at Indiana University. **Mauricio Bucca** is a doctoral candidate in the Department of Sociology at Cornell University.

We thank Martha Bailey, Sheldon Danziger, Tom DiPrete, and the anonymous reviewers for their helpful comments on an earlier version of this paper. Direct correspondence to: Kim Weeden at kw74@cornell.edu, 323 Uris Hall, Ithaca, NY 14853; Youngjoo Cha at cha5@indiana.edu; and Mauricio Bucca at mebucca@gmail.com. A one-click Stata replication package for the analyses in this paper is available at www.kimweeden.com/manuscripts.

gap in wages.[1] For example, Youngjoo Cha and Kim Weeden (2014) show that the diffusion of long work hours in the United States in the 1990s and 2000s, coupled with the persistent gender gap in long work hours and rising hourly compensation for long work hours, was associated with an increase in the gender gap in wages after adjusting for other wage-relevant attributes. These trends largely offset wage-equalizing shifts in women's educational attainment.

A second empirical insight is that much of what appears to be a gender wage gap is better understood as a gender-specific family gap in pay or, as they are known in the economic and sociological literatures, the *motherhood wage penalty* and *fatherhood wage premium*: mothers earn less than observationally similar childless women (Pal and Waldfogel, this volume; Waldfogel 1998; Budig and England 2001; Avellar and Smock 2003; Gangl and Ziefle 2009; Staff and Mortimer 2012; Cooke 2014; Kahn, Garcia-Manglano, and Bianchi 2014), and fathers earn more than observationally similar childless men (Pal and Waldfogel, this volume; Waldfogel 1998; Lundberg and Rose 2000; Glauber 2008; Killewald 2012). As in the broader gender literature, the research on family wage differentials emphasizes wage-relevant labor market behaviors, including work hours, of parents compared with childless adults. Curiously, however, explicit efforts to tie trends in the distribution of work hours between mothers and childless women, or between fathers and childless men, to trends in family wage gaps are relatively few and far between. Those that do typically emphasize shifts in the distribution of parents and childless adults across part-time and full-time work but ignore long work hours (see, for example, Waldfogel 1998; Pal and Waldfogel, this volume; Buchmann and McDaniel, this volume).

We bring together these two streams of research by describing the empirical relationship between trends in work hours in the United States, the gender wage gap among parents and among childless adults, and the family wage gap among women and among men. The first set of comparisons is motivated by our expectation that changes in work hours and in the hourly pay of different work hours had a stronger association with the gender gap in wages among parents than among childless adults. The second set is motivated by our expectation that growth or decline in family wage gaps result from the interplay of changes in the distribution of work hours among parents and childless adults and structural changes in the hourly pay associated with part-time work, full-time work, and long work hours.

We assess these expectations using nationally representative labor force data from the Current Population Survey (CPS). First, we briefly situate our analyses in the broader literatures on the sources of the stagnation in the gender and family gap in wages.

WORK HOURS AND THE GENDER WAGE GAP

In accounting for the slow convergence in the gender gap in wages over the last two decades, gender scholars point to widespread cultural beliefs about the existence of deeply rooted and often biologically based differences in men's and women's traits and skills (Charles and Grusky 2004; Ridgeway 2011; Cotter, Hermsen, and Vanneman 2011). These cultural beliefs affect men's and women's labor market decisions, employers' hiring decisions, and institutional configurations such as the availability of policies that would support workers who wish to combine paid and unpaid labor. Because the underlying cultural beliefs are slow to change, so the argument goes, gender differences in the labor market behaviors that generate a gender gap in wages are also slow to change.

One implication of this argument is that the proximate sources of the gender wage gap, and of stagnation in the gender wage gap, are likely

---

1. We realize that one cannot safely interpret the results of wage equation models based on observational data as causal, except under the implausible assumption that the observed covariates capture all wage-relevant differences between mothers and fathers, for example, or between mothers and childless women. We use the term *effect* sparingly. The exception is in our discussion of our decomposition models, where *price change effect* and *quantity change effect* are standard terminology (see data and methods).

to be especially pronounced among parents. After all, a core feature of gender essentialism is the belief that women naturally excel at nurturance, personal service, and childrearing (Charles and Grusky 2004, 19; Ridgeway and Correll 2004). This stereotype makes it likely that more mothers than fathers or childless adults will devote a greater share of their time to childrearing, more difficult for mothers to avoid social sanctions if they do not curtail their paid work hours during their childrearing years, and less likely that employers will hire mothers for jobs that require stereotypically male-typed skills or work hours (Ridgeway and Correll 2004).

This prediction is supported, albeit indirectly, by the empirical literature on the proximate sources of the gender gap in wages. Take, for example, housework, which affects the time and energy that is available for paid labor. The housework time gaps between mothers and fathers are larger than the gaps among all adults (Bianchi et al. 2012), and though a growing percentage of Americans state a preference for egalitarian divisions of household labor (Gerson 2009; Pedulla and Thébaud 2015), parental gaps in housework have stalled. Or, consider discrimination, which affects wage gaps directly but also creates unequal opportunities for workers to enter jobs with different levels of pay and work hours. Although several audit or other quasi-experimental studies show evidence of gender discrimination in high status occupations, others show that such discrimination is limited to mothers (Correll, Benard, and Paik 2007).

The conflict between work and nonwork roles may also be greater for mothers than it is for fathers or childless adults. This is especially true in workplaces and occupations where employers expect workers to put in long hours, and where workers derive social status from working long work hours (Jacobs and Gerson 2004; Sharone 2004; Reid 2015). In these settings, the ideal worker is someone who is available to clients and supervisors at all hours of the day or night, is able to travel or relocate for work, and prioritizes career success over family or leisure (Williams 2000). This image of an ideal worker is hard to reconcile with the stereotype of the ideal mother, a mother who is available to her family at all hours of the day or night, is able to travel or relocate to support her children's enrichment activities, and prioritizes family over career success. To be sure, fathers, childless men, and childless women in "greedy organizations" (Coser 1967) or occupations may also experience work-life conflicts, but they are often more able to "pass" as ideal workers, in part because employers interpret their behavior more favorably than identical behavior by mothers (Reid 2015; Correll, Benard, and Paik 2007; Williams 2003). As a result, the gender gap in long work hours among parents is likely to be greater among parents than childless adults and, given its roots in gender essentialist beliefs, also more resistant to change.

Organizational scholars have also noted that a growing share of jobs are organized as part-time work, contingent work, temporary work, contract work, and other "nonstandard employment relations" that weaken any expectation, tacit or otherwise, that employees will work a regular, forty-hour work week (Kalleberg 2011). The growth of these nonstandard employment relations, like the emergent culture of overwork, has different implications for gender gaps in work hours among parents than among childless adults. Historically, the gender gap in part-time work has been much greater for parents than for childless adults: mothers have long been more likely to work part-time than childless women, presumably because part-time work is easier to combine with the time demands of childrearing; fathers, by contrast, have been much less likely to work part time than childless men, perhaps because of cultural expectations surrounding male breadwinning (Townsend 2002). However, the growth in part-time work has largely been in involuntary part-time work (Kalleberg 2000), and it has been accompanied by a decline in the gender gap in part-time work, especially among parents.

Gender gaps in work hours, and changes in them, are only relevant to the gender gap in hourly pay if different work hours are associated with different levels of hourly pay. In this regard, part-time work often pays lower hourly wages than full-time work that is comparable in terms of tasks and skill requirements (Kalleberg 2000, 2011). Claudia Goldin (2014) argues that pay is nonlinear with respect to hours in many occupations, because hours are worth more if they are worked continuously in long blocks and if they are timed to overlap with the hours of colleagues. Moreover, the relative pay of different work hours is changing: for example, Cha and Weeden find that the hourly pay of workers who put in fifty or more hours per week has increased dramatically relative to full-time workers with similar observed attributes (2014; see also Kuhn and Lozano 2008).

These wage disparities for different work hours, when coupled with gender gaps in work hours and trends in those hours that vary by parental status, have potentially important implications for gender gaps in wages. First, in a world in which mothers are more likely to work part time and less likely to work long hours than other groups, and in which fathers are more likely to work long hours and less likely to work part time, gender gaps in wages will be greater among parents than among childless adults merely because of differences in the relative pay of different work hours. Second, and related, changes in the relative pay for part time and long work hours will have stronger associations with trends in the gender gap in wages among parents than among childless adults.

WORK HOURS AND THE FAMILY WAGE GAP

As we noted in our introductory comments, we also wish to flip our comparisons around to assess how trends in within-gender family wage differentials—the motherhood wage penalty and the fatherhood wage premium—are associated with trends in work hours and in the relative pay of different work hours. Research estimates that the motherhood wage penalty is between 6 percent and 15 percent per child, the higher estimates coming from models that correct for differential selection of mothers and childless women into paid labor (Gangl and Ziefle 2009). Approximately one-third of the education-adjusted motherhood wage penalty disappears in models that also adjust for work experience; much of the rest is associated with the employment situation of mothers after childbirth, especially their greater likelihood of entering part-time work. Similarly, much of the fatherhood wage premium is associated with work hour behaviors: when men become fathers, they increase their paid work hours by an estimated forty hours per child per year, and their hourly pay increases by about 4 percent per child (Lundberg and Rose 2000; Glauber 2008).[2]

Unlike the literature on the gender gap in wages, the literature on family wage gaps has been less concerned with trends. Indeed, much of it relies on longitudinal data from a single cohort, using within-person variation in parental status to estimate the "causal" effect of having a child on wages. There are important exceptions. For example, Markus Gangl and Andrea Zeifle show that the motherhood wage penalty was smaller for a cohort of women born in the late 1950s than for a cohort born in the early 1960s (2009). Sarah Avellar and Pamela Smock find no change in the motherhood wage penalty between a cohort of women born between 1944 and 1954 and another born between 1980 and 1984 (2003). However, Pal and Waldfogel show a decline in the motherhood wage penalty, from 6 to 1 percent, between 1993 and 2013 (this volume). Similarly, Shelly Lundberg and Elina Rose find a decline in the fatherhood wage premium between men born between 1943 and 1950 and those born between 1951 and 1974 (2000).

Our goal is not to replicate these studies' focus on identifying, to the extent possible with observational data, the causal effect of parental status on wages. Rather, it is to describe the empirical relationship between trends in family wage gaps, changes in the distribution of work hours between mothers and childless women and between fathers and childless

---

2. Shelly Lundberg and Elina Rose (2000) report a nonlinear association between children and men's work hours and wages: the first child is associated with a large increase in hours and wages; the second, a smaller increase; and subsequent children, no increase. Evidence of nonlinearities in the motherhood wage penalty is mixed (see, for example, Gangl and Ziefle 2009). We focus on the average family wage differential for parents and childless adults.

men, and changes in the wage returns to different work hours. We also take a more encompassing view of work hours than much of the family wage gap literature, focusing on long work hours as well as part-time hours.

DATA, VARIABLES, AND METHODS

We first describe, for each of our four gender and parental status groups, trends in: wage and salary employment; work hours, conditional on employment; and the hourly wages associated with different levels of work hours, providing both unadjusted mean wages and mean wages after adjusting for education, experience, and other standard wage predictors. We then use a technique developed by Chinhui Juhn, Kevin Murphy, and Brooks Pierce (1991) to decompose trends in the gender gap in wages within parental groups, and trends in the family gap in wages within genders, into changes that are generated by shifts in the share of the relevant groups who work part time, full time, or long work hours (the *quantity effect*), and changes that are generated by shifts in the relative wages of different work hours (the *price effect*).

Data

The data for these analyses come from the May (1969–1984) and Merged Outgoing Rotation Groups, or MORG (1979–2014) of the Current Population Survey files compiled and distributed by the National Bureau of Economic Research.[3] Our base analytic sample is limited to noninstitutionalized civilian workers ages eighteen to sixty-four years. Except for our analysis of trends in wage and salary employment as a share of the total population, we restrict the sample to currently employed wage and salary workers with nonmissing values on the parental status questions (see following section). The multivariate analyses of wages further restrict the sample to workers with nonmissing and nonzero hours with valid wage information. Finally, the Juhn, Murphy, and Pierce (JMP) decomposition analyses are further restricted to CPS years 1984 and 2014 or, for the period-specific decompositions, 1984, 1993, 2004, and 2014. The sample sizes differ across analyses, and we present them in the notes to the tables and figures. All analyses use the BLS-provided sampling weights.

Variables

The outcome variable in our analyses is hourly wages. We estimate the hourly wages of workers who are not typically paid by the hour by dividing weekly wages by the number of hours usually worked per week. We exclude workers whose hourly wages fall below $1 per hour or more than $100 per hour in 1979 U.S. dollars, and we multiply wages that are top-coded by the BLS to ensure confidentiality by 1.4 (Card and DiNardo 2002). We adjust nominal wages for inflation using the Bureau of Economic Analysis's Personal Consumption Expenditures Deflator, and express all wages in 2014 dollars. In the multivariate and decomposition analyses, we take the natural log of hourly wages (measured in pennies); in the bivariate analyses, we keep wages in the natural metric to ease interpretation.

We measure parental status with a binary variable that we constructed from a CPS variable that indicates the number of children under the age of eighteen who are related to the household head (up through the 1988 CPS) or in the primary family (the 1989–2014 CPS) and who reside in the sampled household.[4] The CPS files are constructed so that all members of the household (May) or primary family (MORG), including children, receive the same value on the parental status variable. We identify parents and childless adults by limiting the May and 1984–1988 MORG sample to heads of households, including heads of single-person households, and their spouses. In the 1989 through 2014 surveys, data on children were

---

3. We prefer the May-MORG to the March series because the latter has far fewer cases, reports annual income (which, for job changers, may not have been earned from the occupation or work hours in the reference week), and does not report usual hours at the main job.

4. For ninety-six cases in the 2010 through 2014 surveys, the CPS variable indicating the number of children was logically inconsistent with a variable indicating the ages of the children. We exclude these cases from our analysis.

collected for primary families rather than households. For these surveys, we limit the sample to adult heads of primary families, their spouses, and respondents who are not in primary families, where the latter includes childless adults who live alone or in nonfamily groups (such as roommates or boarders).

Two other complexities with the parental status measure need to be kept in mind when interpreting the results. First, the variables necessary to identify parents are missing from the 1982 and 1983 surveys (May and MORG), the 1994 through 1998 MORG surveys, and the 1999 MORG surveys collected before November. Second, we cannot identify parents of children who do not reside in the household or who are over the age of eighteen.[5] In supplementary analyses, we reestimate our models on a sample of men and women of childrearing years (age eighteen to forty-five). We found similar patterns as in the full sample, but with greater differences between childless adults and parents in the association between long work hours and wage differentials.

Our measure of work hours is based on a CPS variable that asks respondents how many hours they usually work, referring to the main job or, in the May surveys, "this job." In the MORG series, usual hours are edited and missing cases imputed by the BLS. Beginning with the 2000 survey, the BLS added a category for "hours vary," which constitutes about 3 percent of wage and salary workers. Rather than exclude these cases, we assume that their hours worked last week are a reasonable proxy for usual work hours. This proxy will overstate usual hours at the main job for workers with more than one job, but understate usual hours for workers who are not working in the reference week because of illness, vacation, holidays, strikes, or temporary layoffs.[6] In the May supplements, the usual hours variable is not available until 1973, so we begin our descriptive analysis of trends with this year. If usual hours are missing, we assume hours worked at the main job, a variable available only for the 5 percent of the sample who are dual job holders and only prior to 1981, are a valid proxy. If this variable is also missing, we exclude the case. Of the many specifications we tested, this provides the closest match to distribution of work hours in the MORG data for the years between 1979 and 1984, when both May and MORG files are available. Even so, we recommend caution in comparing across the May and MORG series.

We convert work hours into a set of five dummy variables using standard cut points in the work-family literature and in administrative publications: one to twenty hours, twenty-one to thirty-four hours, thirty-five to forty hours, forty-one to forty-nine hours, and fifty hours or more. We use this five-category measure in our bivariate analyses, but for ease of presentation aggregate to a three-category measure—part time (one to thirty-four hours), full time (thirty-five to forty-nine hours), and long work hours (fifty hours or more)—in our multivariate analyses.[7] Sensitivity checks fit to data pooled across parental status show that other cut points generate very similar results (see Cha and Weeden 2014).

Our multivariate wage equations adjust for standard predictors of wages: race (non-Hispanic white, non-Hispanic African American, Hispanic, other race), age and its square, education (less than high school, high school, some college, college graduate, advanced degree), marital status (currently married, unmarried), potential years of work experience (age in years minus schooling in years minus 6) and its square, region, metropolitan residence, and public-sector employment. The JMP decompositions of the family wage gap include an identical set of covariates, but the

---

5. Alexandra Killewald (2012) shows that fathers of nonresident and nonbiological children, unlike other fathers, do not experience a wage premium. One might anticipate an attenuated motherhood wage penalty for nonresident and nonbiological mothers.

6. We also imputed usual hours for the hours-vary cases using multivariate imputation, but because the results using this measure were nearly identical, we fall back on the simpler proxy.

7. We do not differentiate between voluntary and involuntary part-time hours. Our prior work showed that the two forms of part-time work have similar associations with wages (Cha and Weeden 2014).

decompositions of the gender wage gap exclude marital status because the assumption that the association of marital status with wages is equal for men and women is unsustainable. Tables A1 and A2 present descriptive statistics for the covariates in our multivariate analyses by gender and parental status for 1984 and 2014.

Our wage equations do not adjust for occupation, union membership, employer tenure, or actual work experience. Employer tenure and actual work experience are not available in the CPS, and union membership is not consistently available. However, analyses comparing CPS with other data sources show that including union membership, employer tenure, and actual work experience does not appreciably alter the relationship between work hours and wages (Cha and Weeden 2014). Occupation is available in the CPS, but adjusting for it may understate the true associations between work hours and wages, and hence the magnitude of family wage differentials, if one assumes that occupation is partly endogenous to parental status (Gangl and Ziefle 2009). As a sensitivity check, we reestimated our multivariate and decomposition models using data from which we first purged all possible association between wages and occupations by fitting fixed effects of occupations. Where these results differ from our main results, we report them. Finally, we also tested models that exclude potential work experience, on the argument that experience, too, is endogenous to parental status; this specification yielded nearly identical work hour coefficients as those that we present here.

Methods

Most of our analysis rests on simple bivariate trends or on standard ordinary least squares (OLS) regression, which we assume is familiar to most readers. The JMP decomposition method, however, warrants some explanation. It begins with a standard wage equation fit to data from one demographic group (for example, men or childless adults), and assumes that the observed associations between the covariates and wages for this group also hold for the other demographic group (such as women or parents) in the absence of discrimination.[8] Formally,

$$y_{it} = x_{it}b_t + \sigma_t\theta_t, \quad (1)$$

where y_{it} is the log of wages for individual i in year t; x is a vector of independent variables; b is a vector of regression coefficients; σ is the residual standard deviation of the baseline group's wages for year t; and θ is a standardized residual with a mean of zero and variance of 1 for each year. We provide these regression coefficients in tables A3 and A4.

The change in the between-group wage gap between two time points, denoted by 0 and 1, can be decomposed into four components:

$$\text{Observed x effect} = (\Delta x_1 - \Delta x_0)b_1 \quad (2)$$
$$\text{Observed price effect} = \Delta x_0(b_1 - b_0) \quad (3)$$
$$\text{Unobserved quantity effect} = (\Delta\theta_1 - \Delta\theta_0)\sigma_1 \quad (4)$$
$$\text{Unobserved price effect} = \Delta\theta_0(\sigma_1 - \sigma_0) \quad (5)$$

In these equations, Δ denotes the average male-female (or parent-childless adult) difference in the variable it precedes. The *observed x effect*, equation (2), also known as the quantity change effect, is the portion of the change in the gender (or family) wage gap between the two time points that is associated with changes in the quantity of each of the observed predictors (such as experience or education) in x. The *observed price effect*, equation (3), is the portion of the change in the gender (or family) wage gap that is associated with changes in the net wage returns to each observed predictor. Equations (4) and (5) estimate the contribution of price and quantity changes in unobserved variables on the changes in the gender or family wage gaps and are not central to our discussion.

---

8. We begin with a wage equation for men (in the analysis of gender wage gaps) and childless adults (in the analyses of family wage gaps). Results from analyses that use wage equations for women and parents, respectively, have a similar pattern. We report key results from this specification in the footnotes; full results are available from the first author.

Figure 1. Trends in Percentage of Men and Women in Wage and Salary Employment

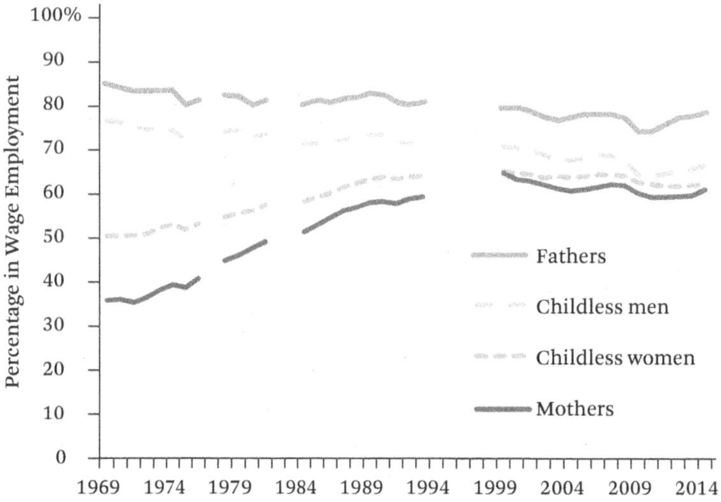

Source: Authors' calculations based on MORG-CPS (BLS).
Notes: May (1969–1981; n=812,614) and MORG (1984–2014; n=5,522,133) CPS. Breaks in data indicate years in which parental status is unavailable. Samples are restricted to workers age eighteen to sixty-five.

RESULTS

Trends in Wage and Salary Employment

Changes in work hours, conditional on being employed, take place against the backdrop of changes in participation in paid and unpaid labor. In figure 1, we graph trends in the percentage of each of the four parental status and gender groups (relative to the total population) who are employed as wage and salary workers as of the reference week. Figures A1 and A2 provide analogous trends by race.

Trends in wage employment show the now-familiar story of partial convergence across parental status and gender groups, a convergence driven both by the declining share of fathers and childless men who are employed for pay and by the rising share of mothers and childless women who are employed for pay. The decline in men's wage employment is evident throughout the forty-five years in the CPS: childless men, for example, decreased their wage employment from 76 percent in 1969 to 66 percent in 2014. The growth of women's wage employment was concentrated in the 1970s and 1980s, when it increased from 36 to 59 percent (mothers) and from 50 to 64 percent (childless women). For both groups of women, the share in wage employment declined slightly between 1999 and 2014 (see also Byker, this volume).

Trends in Work Hours

Figures 2 through 5 present, for each gender and parental status group, the percentage of wage earners in each work hour category: at least fifty hours per week (the top and darkest shaded area); the two full-time categories (the next two areas from the top, corresponding to forty-one to forty-nine hours and thirty-five to forty hours, respectively); and the two part-time categories (the two lightest shaded areas, corresponding to twenty-one to thirty-four hours and, at the very bottom, one to twenty hours). Figures A3 through A6 provide analogous trends by race.

The gender gap in long work hours between childless men and childless women (figures 2 and 3, respectively), and between fathers and mothers (figures 4 and 5), is both substantial and persistent. In the early 1970s, when the CPS began collecting information on usual work hours, 15 percent of childless men and 4 percent of childless women worked fifty or more hours per week. By 1999, the peak of long work hours in the United States, 21 percent of

Figure 2. Percentage of Workers in Work Hour Categories, Childless Men

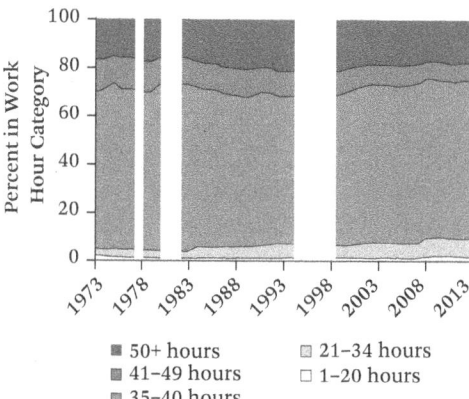

Source: Authors' calculations based on CPS-MORG (BLS).
Notes: Estimates from 1973 to 1978 are from the May CPS (N =59,054), those from 1979 to 2014 are from the MORG files (N =1,055,418).

Figure 4. Percentage of Workers in Work Hour Categories, Fathers

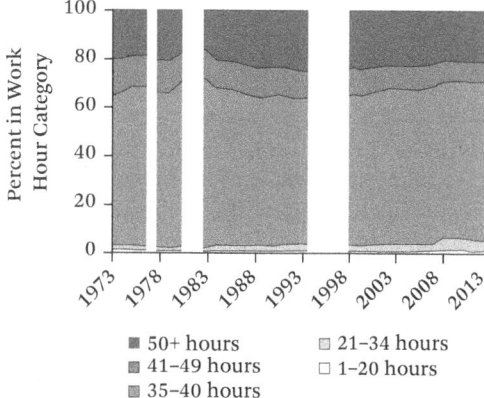

Source: Authors' calculations based on CPS-MORG (BLS).
Notes: Estimates from 1973 to 1978 are from the May CPS (N =79,372), those from 1979 to 2014 are from the MORG files (N =820,451).

Figure 3. Percentage of Workers in Work Hour Categories, Childless Women

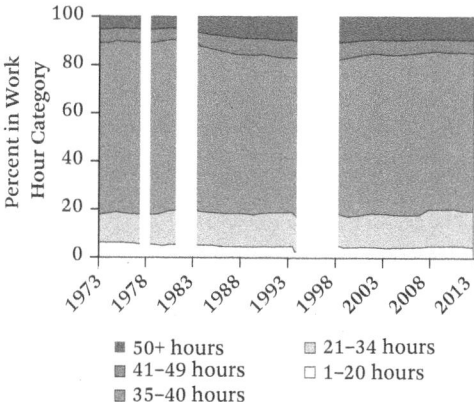

Source: Authors' calculations based on CPS-MORG (BLS).
Notes: Estimates from 1973 to 1978 are from the May CPS (N=45,256), those from 1979 to 2014 are from the MORG files (N =1,017,123).

Figure 5. Percentage of Workers in Work Hour Categories, Mothers

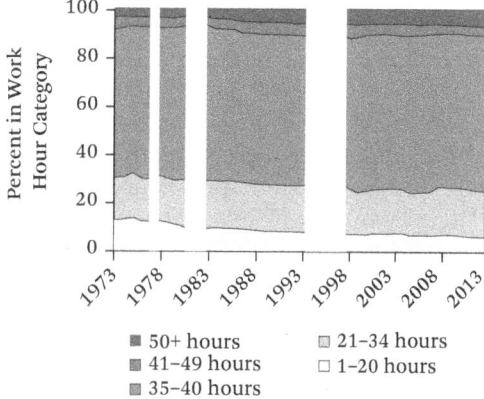

Source: Authors' calculations based on CPS-MORG (BLS).
Notes: Estimates from 1973 to 1978 are from the May CPS (N =45,085), those from 1979 to 2014 are from the MORG files (N=787,998).

childless men and 10 percent of childless women worked them. The share of these groups declined slightly through the 2000s, dropped precipitously in the aftermath of the Great Recession, and began to rise again during the economic recovery. As of 2014, 18 percent of childless men and 9 percent of childless women worked at least fifty hours per week, still below peak levels but up 1 to 2 percentage points since the recession. Figures 2 and 3 show that childless men and childless women's share of long work hours moved in tandem, meaning that the gender gap in long work hours among childless adults remains essentially unchanged.

Among parents, the gender gap in long work hours was just as persistent (compare figures 4 and 5). In 1973, 20 percent of fathers worked at least fifty hours per week, versus only 3 percent of mothers. These percentages rose to a late-1990s peak of 24 percent of fathers and 6 percent of mothers. The recent recession had less of an impact on long work hours among parents than it did among childless adults: the percentage of fathers declined by only 2 percentage points between 2007 and 2009, and the percentage of mothers by less than 1 point. By 2014, the percentage of mothers rebounded to its prerecession peak of 6 percent, and the percentage of fathers rose to 20 percent. Despite these fluctuations, the gap between fathers and mothers was nearly the same in 2014 as it was in 1984, though it expanded slightly in the middle years.

We also note that the gender gap in long work hours among parents greatly exceeds the gap among childless adults. In 2014, for example, the ratio of fathers to mothers who work long hours was more than three to one, compared to a two to one ratio among childless adults. This comparatively large gender gap in long work hours among parents is driven both by the smaller percentage of mothers than childless women who work long hours, and by the larger percentage of fathers than childless men who work long hours. This implies, of course, that the within-gender gaps in long work hours between parents and childless adults have a different "sign" for men and women. Moreover, within-gender gaps in long work hours widened between the beginning of the 1980s and the late 1990s, and although they narrowed in the subsequent years, they did not return to earlier levels. As we will discuss below, this opens the door for a quantity change effect of long work hours on the family wage gaps.

Trends in part-time work are indicated by changes in the bottom area (one to twenty hours per week) and the second area from the bottom (twenty-one to thirty-four hours per week) in figures 2 though 5. With the exception of the sharp decline in very low work hours among mothers in the late 1970s, the trends in the two categories of part-time work are consistent; for the sake of brevity, we discuss them as one category.

Like the gender gap in long work hours, the gender gap in part-time work is greater among parents than among childless adults. As shown in figures 2 through 5, the percentage of part-time workers is the highest among mothers, who are followed in turn by childless women, childless men, and fathers. This pattern is evident in all years, but strongest in 1970s and 1980s, in large part because the percentages of men and women who work part time converged in more recent years. This recent convergence was driven by the well-known decline in the percentage of mothers who work part time (from 30 percent in 1973 to 25 percent in 2014), as well as by an increase in the percentage of part-time fathers (from 3 percent in 1973 to 5 percent in 2014) and especially of part-time childless men (from 5 percent in the early 1970s to 10 percent in 2014). All groups show an uptick in part-time work during the Great Recession, but their postrecession experiences differed: childless women quickly returned to prerecession levels and held steady, mothers returned to prerecession levels and continued to decline, but neither childless men nor fathers had returned to prerecession levels of part-time work by 2014.

Trend in Mean Wages by Work Hours, Parental Status, and Gender

The association between trends in work hours and trends in gender and family wage gaps depends, of course, on the wages associated with different work hours. Figures 6 through 8 present the mean unadjusted wages associated with long work hours (figure 6), full-time work thirty-five to forty-nine hours per week, figure 7), and part-time work (one to thirty-four hours per week, figure 8). Figures 6 through 8, as well as subsequent figures that include wage information, begin with 1984, the first year of the MORG series in which the measures of parental status is available.

The first noteworthy result of figures 6, 7, and 8 is that the unadjusted hourly wages for men and women who work long hours rose faster than the hourly wages of full-time work-

Figure 6. Unadjusted Mean Hourly Wages, Long Hours

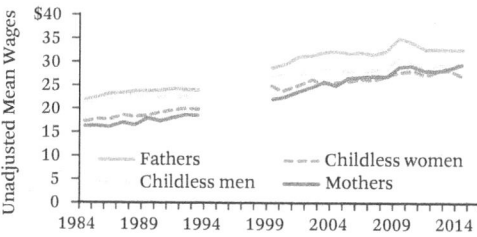

Source: Authors' calculations based on MORG-CPS (BLS).
Note: Fifty or more hours per week. N=458,355.

Figure 7. Unadjusted Mean Hourly Wages, Full-Time

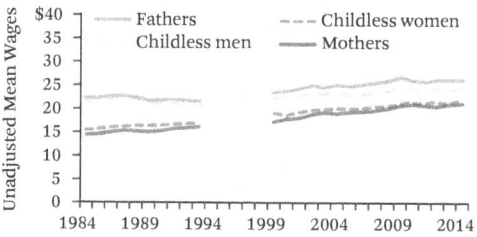

Source: Authors' calculations based on MORG-CPS (BLS).
Note: Thirty-five to forty-nine hours per week. N = 2,578,837.

Figure 8. Unadjusted Mean Hourly Wages, Part-Time

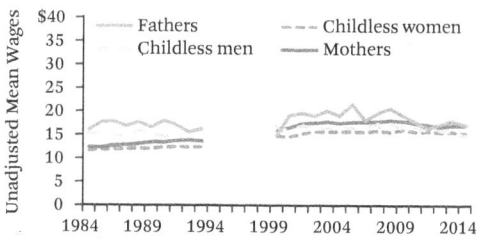

Source: Authors' calculations based on MORG-CPS (BLS).
Note: One to thirty-four hours per week. N=495,950.

ers of the same gender and parental status. For example, fathers who worked long hours earned, on average, $22 per hour (in 2014 dollars) in 1984 and $33 per hour in 2014, a 50 percent increase (figure 6). By comparison, full-time fathers also earned $22 per hour in 1984, but their mean hourly wages had increased to only $26 per hour by 2014 (figure 7). The mean wages of mothers and childless women who worked long hours also increase more rapidly than those of full-time women: mothers who worked long hours saw their mean hourly wages nearly double (from $16 in 1984 to $30 in 2014), compared with a 50 percent increase (from $14 to $21) for full-time mothers (compare figures 6 and 7). By the early 2010s, the hourly wage gaps between mothers and childless women who worked long hours, on one hand, and childless men, on the other, had largely disappeared.

The hourly wage growth for part-time work was much less substantial, and though gender and parental status groups varied somewhat, for no group did growth match that of workers who worked full time or long hours (figure 8). A trend in the wages of part-time men is hard to discern, in part because so few fathers work part time. Part-time mothers and childless women saw their mean wages rise, but only modestly in absolute and percentage terms. Specifically, part-time mothers' mean wages grew by $5 per hour, from $12 to $17, between 1984 and 2014, an increase of 42 percent. Part-time, childless women's mean wages grew by only $3 per hour, from $12 to $15, or 25 percent.

The overall story of unadjusted wage growth, then, is some convergence across gender and parental status groups, driven by the comparatively weaker wage growth for childless men than for mothers or childless women. Even so, the trend lines across gender and parental status groups are by and large parallel, and gender and family gaps in mean unadjusted wages remain substantial in 2014.

These cross-group differences in unadjusted wages graphed in figures 6 through 8 could, of course, merely reflect compositional changes if, for example, the proportion of workers with a college degree grew faster among workers who put in long hours than among those who work full time. We can gain some leverage on this by regressing (logged) hourly wages on work hours and predictors of wages (see also tables A1 and A2). The coefficients pertaining to long work hours are presented in figure 9,

Figure 9. Adjusted Mean Hourly Wages, Long Hours

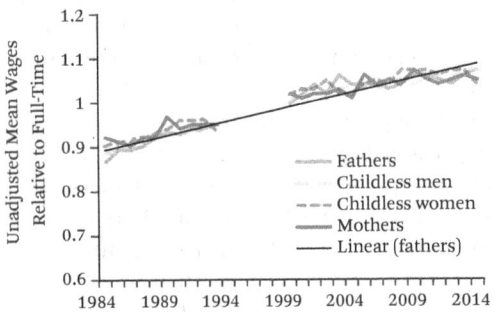

Source: Authors' calculations based on MORG-CPS (BLS).
Notes: Fifty or more hours per week. Estimates are from a regression of logged hourly wages on work hours, age and its square, education, potential experience and its square, race, region, metropolitan status, and public-private sector. N=3,533,142.

Figure 10. Adjusted Mean Hourly Wages, Part-Time

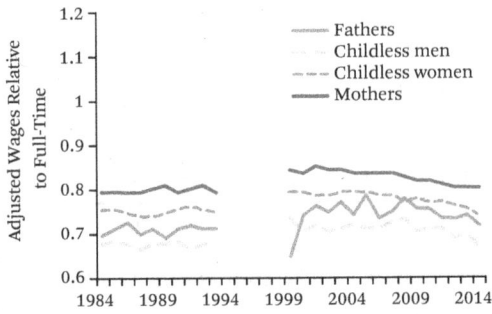

Source: Authors' calculations based on MORG-CPS (BLS).
Notes: One to thirty-four hours per week. Estimates are from a regression of logged hourly wages on work hours, age and its square, education, potential experience and its square, race, region, metropolitan status, and public-private sector. N=3,533,142.

and those pertaining to part-time work hours in figure 10; all work hour coefficients are large enough multiples of their standard errors to be significant at conventional levels ($\alpha = 0.05$). These coefficients are interpreted as the proportional wage increase (values greater than unity) or decrease (values less than unity) associated with long work hours relative to full-time workers, after adjusting for other predictors.

For the most part, work hour differences in trends in adjusted wages show a similar pattern as trends in unadjusted wages (compare figures 9 and 10 with figures 6 through 8). The adjusted hourly wages of workers who work fifty or more hours per week rose more dramatically than those of full-time workers of the same gender and parental status. Notably, however, figure 9 shows that the mean adjusted wages of workers who put in long hours fell well short of those of full-time workers in the first half of our data series, implying a "wage penalty" for long work hours. The magnitude of this wage penalty declined steadily between 1984 and the early 1990s, and by 2000 it had become a wage premium (coefficients exceeded unity). The wage premium grew until the early 2010s, after which it leveled off somewhat (see the trend line for fathers). Even so, by 2014,

workers who worked fifty or more hours per week earned between 4 and 7 percent more than their full-time counterparts, even adjusting for education and other wage-relevant characteristics.

The second key result in figure 9 is that the trend in the group-specific wage premium for long work hours did not differ substantially by gender or parental status: among mothers, for example, it was comparable to the long-hour wage premium among fathers. Note that this does not imply that mothers and fathers receive identical wages for long work hours (see figures 6, 7, and 8), because the relevant comparison is within groups.

Figure 10, the analogous graph for part-time wages, shows that the adjusted mean wages of part-time workers fell short of those of full-time workers in all years and for all gender and parental status groups. The size of this part-time wage penalty varies by gender and parental status. It is largest among childless men, such that part-time childless men earn approximately 67 percent of the wages of full-time childless men adjusting for other attributes, and smallest among mothers, such that part-time mothers earn about 80 percent of the wages of full-time mothers.

Between 1984 and the mid-2000s, the negative wage differential between part-time work and full-time work did not change appreciably for any parental status or gender group, but afterward it declined sharply. The wage gap between part-time and full-time mothers, for example, grew by about 4 percentage points between 2007 (0.84) and 2014 (0.80). Taken together, figures 9 and 10 imply that up until the late 2000s, growth in the relative wages associated with long work hours was the dominant trend. In the last decade, the decline in the relative wages associated with part-time work was also pronounced. The JMP decompositions, which we turn to next, tease out these relationships between changes in the relative wages of work hours and changes in gender and parental status wage gaps.

Decomposition of Trends in Gender Wage Gaps

The JMP decompositions relevant to trends in the gender wage gaps within parental status groups are presented in table 1. Between 1984 and 2014, the gender gap in wages among parents decreased by 0.19 log points, and the gender gap in wages among childless adults decreased by 0.20 log points (see table 1 entries for total change in gender wage gap). Changes in observed factors account for about 25 percent of the change in the gender wage gap for childless adults (that is, 0.049/0.193 = 0.25) and 17 percent of the change for parents (0.033/0.197 = 0.17).

For both groups, changes in long work hours are associated with widening the gender wage gap, adjusting for other observed factors, but this association is stronger among parents than childless adults. Among childless adults, rising wage returns to long work hours are associated with an increase in the gender gap in wages by 0.016 log points, about 9 percent of the size of the total change in the gender wage gap. Among parents, this price effect of long work hours is nearly twice as large: 0.029 log points, comparable to 15 percent of the total change in the gender wage gap.[9] Put differently, in a hypothetical world in which the hourly wages associated with long work hours remained at 1984 levels, the gender wage gap among childless adults would be about 9 percent lower than we observe today, and the gender wage gap among parents would be 15 percent lower. To put this in context, the effect of changes in the wage returns to different educational degrees is about 10 percent of the total change for childless adults, and 5 percent of the total change for parents (for all decomposition coefficients, see tables A5 and A6).[10]

By contrast, the quantity change effect of long work hours is quite small for both parents and nonparents. For childless adults, changes in the gender gap in long work hours are associated with increase in the gender wage differential by a trivial 1 percent of the total change. For parents, the estimated quantity change is essentially null (0.2 percent). This is anticipated by figures 2 through 5, which show no difference between 1984 and 2014 in the gender gap in long work hours.

By taking 1984 and 2014 as the starting and ending points, the preceding decomposition results may gloss over differences in the timing of price and quantity effects of long work hours. Columns 2 through 4 of table 1 present results from three JMP decompositions that use data from 1984, 1993, 2004, and 2014 to estimate wage trends across three time periods. These period-specific results show that the contribution of rising prices for long work hours to the expansion of the gender gap in wages is particularly pronounced in the first two decades of our data. This finding is consistent with figures 9 and 10, which show that the steeper wage growth of long work hours relative to full-time work leveled off around 2010. Very little of the change in the gender gap

---

9. If we use the wage equation for women as the base for the Juhn, Murphy, and Pierce decomposition, we find a price change effect of long work hours 0.019 log points (10 percent) among parents and 0.011 log points (6 percent) among childless adults. If we purge the data of all occupation-wage associations, we find a smaller price change effect: 7 percent for parents versus 14 percent in the main results; 6 percent for childless adults versus 8 percent in the main results.

10. The education price effects are calculated by summing the price change coefficients of the education categories and dividing by the total change (x100).

Table 1. Selected Coefficients from JMP Decomposition of Gender Wage Gap

	1984-2014	1984-1993	1994-2004	2004-2014
Panel A: Childless adults				
Total change in gender wage gap	-0.193	-0.133	-0.048	-0.012
From observed factors	-0.049	-0.037	-0.015	0.004
From unobserved factors	-0.144	-0.095	-0.032	-0.016
Long work hours				
Change from long work hours	0.018	0.007	0.008	0.003
Quantity change	0.002	-0.001	0.001	0.000
Price change	0.016	0.008	0.007	0.003
Quantity as % of total change	0.9	0.5	1.9	0.2
Price as % of total change	8.3	5.9	14.3	25.2
Part-time work hours				
Change from part-time work	-0.012	-0.011	-0.008	0.007
Quantity change	-0.013	-0.010	-0.003	0.001
Price change	0.001	-0.001	-0.005	0.007
Quantity as % of total change	6.6	7.6	6.7	5.1
Price as % of total change	0.3	1.0	10.1	56.3
N	152,266	148,959	159,615	162,922
Panel B: Parents				
Total change in gender wage gap	-0.197	-0.122	-0.023	-0.051
From observed factors	-0.033	-0.015	-0.001	-0.017
From unobserved factors	-0.164	-0.107	-0.022	-0.034
Long work hours				
Change from long work hours	0.029	0.012	0.015	0.003
Quantity change	0.000	-0.003	0.000	-0.001
Price change	0.029	0.015	0.014	0.004
Quantity as % of total change	0.2	2.8	1.8	1.6
Price as % of total change	14.8	12.4	63.2	7.2
Part-time work hours				
Change from part-time work	-0.029	-0.014	-0.014	0.000
Quantity change	-0.024	-0.009	-0.006	-0.007
Price change	-0.005	-0.005	-0.008	0.007
Quantity as % of total change	12.2	7.0	27.4	14.3
Price as % of total change	2.3	4.5	34.4	13.3
N	120,380	130,161	125,240	115,459

Source: Authors' compilation based on 1984-2014 CPS-MORG (BLS).
Note: See text for sample restrictions. Models adjust for age, age squared, race, education, potential experience and its square, region, metropolitan status, and public-private sector. See A5 and A6 for all price and quantity change effects, and tables A3 and A4 for the underlying regression coefficients.

in wages is associated with changes in the shares of the parents relative to childless adults who work long hours (the quantity change effect) in any of the time periods.

In contrast to long work hours, changes in part-time work were associated with declines in the gender gaps in wages for parents and childless adults, primarily through nontrivial changes in the shares of these groups who work part time (see table 1). Between 1984 and 2014, the reduction of the part-time work hour gap between childless men and childless women was associated with an estimated 0.013 log point reduction in the gender gap in wages, or

7 percent of the total decline. Among parents, the decline in the gender gap in part-time work was associated with a 0.024 log point decline in the gender gap in wages, or 12 percent of the total change.[11] The quantity effects of part-time work in the metric of log points are relatively unaffected by eliminating all occupation-wage association from the data. However, in terms of percentage of the total change in the wage gap, purging the occupation-wage association reduces the quantity changes by more than half, to 3 percent for childless adults and 5 percent for parents.

Changes in the adjusted hourly wages of part-time work, by contrast, had very little impact on gender wage gaps for either parents or childless adults across the 1984 to 2014 period. The period from 2004 to 2014 is a possible exception: in these ten years, the declining hourly wages of part-time work relative to full-time work was associated with an expansion of the gender wage gap among parents, and among childless adults, that largely offset the contraction of the wage gap attributable to convergence in the shares of men and women who worked part time. However, the price change effect in this period is greatly attenuated after we purge all occupation-wage associations from the data. The more robust story is that convergence in the shares of part-time workers among fathers and childless men, and mothers and childless women, contributed to convergence in the within-group gender wage gaps.

Decomposition of Trends in Family Wage Gaps

Our final set of results quantifies the association between changes in work hours and within-gender wage differentials between parents and childless adults. Table 2 provides the relevant estimates for wage differentials among women and men.[12] In both cases, the within-gender wage gap is calculated by subtracting parents' wages from childless adults' wages: it is positive for women (because childless women earn more, on average, than mothers) and negative for men (because childless men earn less, on average, than fathers). A positive coefficient for women means that the covariate is associated with an increase in the motherhood wage penalty; a positive coefficient for men means that the listed covariate is associated with a decline in the fatherhood wage premium.

The first rows in each panel of table 2 provide estimates of the total changes in the family wage gaps for women and men, respectively. The wage gap between mothers and childless women declined by 0.041 log points, about 4 percentage points, between 1984 and 2014. By contrast, the wage gap between fathers and childless men increased: in 1984, fathers earned 6 percent higher wages than observationally similar childless men, but by 2014 they earned 11 percent higher wages. The increase in the fatherhood wage premium is 0.037 log points, again about 4 percentage points.

The growth in the hourly pay of those who work long hours was associated with an increase in the family wage gaps for both men and women. Between 1984 and 2014, rising hourly wages for long work hours was associated with an expansion of the motherhood wage penalty by an estimated 0.004 log points, about 9 percent of the total change in motherhood wage penalty. In percentage terms, this price change effect appears to be larger in 1993 and 2004 than in either of the two flanking decades (see columns 2–4, table 2). Rising pay for long work hours also increased the wage gap between fathers and childless men, but by an even greater magnitude: 0.006 log points, or 18 percent of the total change, between 1984 and 2014. Changes in the relative share of mothers and childless women, and of fathers and childless men, who work long hours were not associated with changes in the motherhood wage penalty or fatherhood wage premium, respectively, perhaps because these quantity changes were so modest (see also figures 2 through 5).

Just as in the gender wage decompositions, the association between trends in part-time work and trends in family wage gaps is driven primarily by changing shares of each group in

---

11. In decompositions that use the women's wage equation as the base, these percentages are 5 percent (childless adults) and 8 percent (parents).

12. Tables A7 and A8 present the full set of coefficients for the JMP decompositions of the family wage gap.

Table 2. Selected Coefficients from JMP Decomposition of Family Wage Gap

	1984–2014	1984–1993	1993–2004	2004–2014
Panel A: Women				
Total change in family wage gap	−0.041	−0.008	−0.002	−0.030
From observed factors	0.012	0.009	0.012	−0.010
From unobserved factors	−0.053	−0.018	−0.015	−0.021
Long work hours				
Change from long work hours	0.003	0.000	0.003	0.000
Quantity change	0.000	−0.001	0.000	0.000
Price change	0.004	0.001	0.003	0.001
Quantity as % of total change	1.0	13.5	1.4	0.5
Price as % of total change	9.0	15.7	121.0	1.8
Part-time work hours				
Change from part-time work	−0.012	−0.002	−0.008	−0.002
Quantity change	−0.013	−0.002	−0.004	−0.006
Price change	0.001	0.000	−0.004	0.003
Quantity as % of total change	31.0	28.5	165.9	18.6
Price as % of total change	2.0	6.0	175.7	10.4
N	131,721	134,404	142,285	139,602
Panel B: Men				
Total change in family wage gap	−0.037	−0.018	−0.027	−0.009
From observed factors	−0.019	−0.005	−0.003	−0.011
From unobserved factors	−0.018	−0.013	−0.024	0.020
Long work hours				
Change from long work hours	−0.005	−0.001	−0.003	−0.001
Quantity change	0.001	0.001	0.001	0.000
Price change	−0.006	−0.002	−0.004	−0.001
Quantity as % of total change	2.7	5.1	2.2	5.0
Price as % of total change	17.5	13.2	13.8	13.4
Part-time work hours				
Change from part-time work	−0.004	−0.003	0.001	−0.002
Quantity change	−0.004	−0.004	−0.001	0.001
Price change	0.000	0.001	0.002	−0.003
Quantity as % of total change	11.1	21.1	3.4	7.5
Price as % of total change	1.1	3.4	7.9	34.6
N	140,925	144,716	142,570	138,779

Source: Authors' compilation based on 1984–2014 CPS-MORG (BLS).
Note: See text for sample restrictions. Models adjust for age, age squared, race, marital status, education, potential experience and its square, region, metropolitan status, and public-private sector. See tables A8 and A9 for all price and quantity change effects.

part-time work (quantity change effects), not by changing hourly wages for part-time work (price change effects). The comparatively rapid decline in the share of mothers who work part-time compressed the motherhood wage penalty by 0.012 log points, or 31 percent of the total change between 1984 and 2014. During the same period, the comparatively rapid increase in part-time work among childless men increased the fatherhood wage premium by about 0.004 log points, or 11 percent of the total change (see table 2, column 1, panel B).[13]

---

13. If we use the women's wage equation as the base for the decomposition, the quantity effect of part-time work decreases to 25 percent of the total for women, 10 percent for men.

For both genders, price change effects of part-time work were modest in the 1984 to 2014 period. Column 4 in table 2 shows some indication of price change effects in the 2004 to 2014 period, as indicated by the positive price change coefficient for women (0.003 log points) and negative price change coefficient for men (–0.003 log points). The within-gender comparisons thus show that price changes in long work hours were more influential for changes in the fatherhood wage premium than the motherhood wage penalty, whereas quantity changes in part-time work were more influential for changes in the motherhood wage penalty than in the fatherhood wage premium.

CONCLUSION

One of the puzzles of contemporary gender scholarship is why gender and family wage gaps have been so persistent. In this article, we have focused on one proximate source of between-group wage inequalities, namely work hours. Our analysis is inspired by the argument that cultural beliefs about men and women's "natural" traits lead to persistent gender and parental status gaps in wage-relevant behaviors and outcomes. In this context, it is unsurprising that even though the share of workers in all gender and parental status groups who worked fifty or more hours per week rose in the 1990s through the mid-2000s, the gap in long work hours between "mothers and others" remained the most extreme. Gender and parental status gaps in part-time work hours have been less resistant to change, although a far greater share of mothers still work part time than childless women, fathers, or childless men.

"Sticky" gender and parental status gaps in work hours, coupled with changes in how different levels of work hours are compensated, have a strong association with trends in the gender gap in wages, in the motherhood wage penalty, and in the fatherhood wage premium. We have shown, first, that the rise (and later, partial retreat) in the share of Americans who work long hours had the net effect of increasing the gender wage gap (especially among parents) the motherhood wage penalty, and the fatherhood wage premium. Second, the association between trends in work hours and trends in wage gaps emerges because the mean hourly wages of workers who work long hours grew markedly compared to the wages of other, observationally similar workers who "only" work full time. This wage growth was gender and parental-status neutral in the sense that all long-hour workers saw their relative wages grow. It was not neutral in its consequences for aggregate levels of inequality. Because of the distributions of long work hours, as a group mothers benefited the least, and fathers the most, from the steep increase in the wage premium for working fifty or more hours per week. Our results suggest that the gender gap in human-capital adjusted wages among parents would be 15 percent lower if the hourly wages of long work hours had not increased. Similarly, the gender gap in wages among childless adults would be 8 percent lower, the motherhood wage penalty would be 9 percent lower, and the fatherhood wage premium would be 18 percent lower than what we in fact observe between 1984 and 2014.

We have also shown that changes in the part-time work were associated with declining gender gaps in wages for parents and for childless adults, a decline in the motherhood wage penalty, and an increase in the fatherhood wage premium. However, these associations are driven by changes in composition, not in the relative wages of part-time work: specifically, a growing share of childless men and a declining share of women, particularly mothers, who work part time. These shifts in the composition of part-time work were associated with a decline of 12 percent in the wage gap between mothers and fathers, 6 percent between childless women and men, and 30 percent between mothers and childless women. They were associated with an 11 percent increase in the wage gap between fathers and childless men over the thirty years of our study, albeit off a lower baseline gap than the other comparisons.

Across the entire labor force, changes in the shares of part-time workers from each demographic group and changes in the relative wages of different work hours had offsetting effects on between-group inequalities in human-capital adjusted wages. The convergence in part-time work hours across parental status and gender groups over the thirty years of the CPS data suggest that greater equality in work hours is possible, and with it a further reduction in the gender gap in wages. However, much of this convergence may be at the expense of men and women who would prefer full-time work but cannot find it.

Convergence in long work hours, too, would go far to reduce wage gaps. Such convergence could, logically, occur by reducing the share of fathers and childless men who work long hours or by increasing the share of mothers and childless women who do. Given evidence that many workers put in long work hours less out of preference than out of the fear that they will incur career penalties if they do not (Clarkberg and Moen 2001; see also Reid 2015), and given the association between long work hours and productivity may be more illusory than real, the preferred solution (from the standpoint of maximizing happiness) would seem to be to reduce the career sanctions for workers who avoid long hours. Our results also suggest, however, that gender and family wage gaps are affected by changes in the workplace and in workplace policies that affect disparities in the wages associated with different work hours. To the extent that part-time work is disproportionately minimum wage work, raising the minimum wage is likely to decrease the motherhood wage penalty. At the same time, policy changes that benefit workers who put in long hours, such as raising the salary threshold for overtime pay, may have the unanticipated consequence of exacerbating gender and family wage gaps.

APPENDIX

Table A1. Means and Standard Deviations for Variables in Regression and Decomposition Analyses, 1984

	Childless Adults				Parents			
	Men		Women		Men		Women	
	Mean	SD	Mean	SD	Mean	SD	Mean	SD
Natural log of hourly wages, in 2014 pennies	7.51	0.55	7.18	0.48	7.57	0.50	7.12	0.47
Hourly wages, in 2014 dollars	21.23	13.08	14.80	8.33	22.12	12.19	13.89	8.09
Full-time (reference category)	0.79		0.76		0.80		0.68	
Part-time	0.06		0.19		0.03		0.29	
Long work hours	0.15		0.05		0.18		0.03	
Age	40.34	13.56	40.34	13.73	36.89	8.47	35.16	7.61
Married	0.74		0.77		1.00		0.97	
Non-Hispanic white (reference category)	0.84		0.84		0.81		0.77	
Non-Hispanic black	0.09		0.09		0.09		0.14	
Hispanic	0.05		0.04		0.07		0.06	
Other race	0.02		0.02		0.03		0.03	
Less than high school (reference category)	0.18		0.13		0.16		0.13	
High school graduate	0.34		0.39		0.36		0.45	
Some college	0.22		0.23		0.22		0.24	
College graduate	0.18		0.17		0.16		0.13	
Advanced degree	0.09		0.07		0.09		0.05	
Potential work experience	21.33	14.37	21.28	14.62	17.90	8.94	16.33	7.91
East (reference category)	0.21		0.22		0.20		0.19	
Midwest	0.24		0.24		0.26		0.26	
South	0.33		0.33		0.34		0.36	
West	0.21		0.21		0.19		0.19	
Metropolitan residence	0.75		0.75		0.69		0.70	
Public sector	0.17		0.21		0.17		0.21	
N	37,372		34,941		36,482		29,829	

Source: Authors' calculations based on 1984 CPS-MORG (BLS).

Table A2. Means and Standard Deviations for Variables in Regression and Decomposition Analyses, 2014

	Childless Adults				Parents			
	Men		Women		Men		Women	
	Mean	SD	Mean	SD	Mean	SD	Mean	SD
Natural log of hourly wages, in 2014 pennies	7.60	0.60	7.46	0.57	7.70	0.62	7.44	0.59
Hourly wages in 2014 dollars	24.21	17.19	20.82	14.70	27.08	19.24	20.75	15.56
Full-time (reference category)	0.74		0.72		0.75		0.70	
Part-time	0.09		0.19		0.05		0.24	
Long work hours	0.17		0.09		0.20		0.06	
Age	43.32	13.24	44.84	13.27	40.30	8.65	38.09	8.46
Married	0.65		0.71		0.93		0.83	
Non-Hispanic white (reference category)	0.18		0.18		0.18		0.18	
Non-Hispanic black	0.11		0.12		0.09		0.14	
Hispanic	0.15		0.11		0.22		0.19	
Other race	0.07		0.07		0.09		0.08	
Less than high school (reference category)	0.07		0.04		0.09		0.06	
High school graduate	0.31		0.26		0.29		0.25	
Some college	0.28		0.31		0.25		0.31	
College graduate	0.23		0.26		0.23		0.25	
Advanced degree	0.11		0.14		0.14		0.15	
Potential work experience	23.54	13.54	24.65	13.78	20.49	8.74	17.93	8.45
East (reference category)	0.18		0.18		0.18		0.18	
Midwest	0.22		0.23		0.22		0.23	
South	0.37		0.36		0.37		0.38	
West	0.23		0.22		0.24		0.22	
Metropolitan residence	0.87		0.86		0.87		0.86	
Public sector	0.13		0.19		0.14		0.19	
N	40,457		39,496		26,614		27,455	

Source: Authors' calculations based on 2014 CPS-MORG (BLS).

Table A3. Regression Coefficients in JMP Decompositions of the Gender Gap in Wages, Childless Adults

	1984		1993		2004		2014	
	Men	Women	Men	Women	Men	Women	Men	Women
Part-time hours (hours/wk)	−0.401**	−0.280**	−0.388**	−0.285**	−0.337**	−0.234**	−0.407**	−0.296**
	(0.015)	(0.007)	(0.013)	(0.007)	(0.011)	(0.007)	(0.010)	(0.007)
Long work hours (50+/wk)	−0.119**	−0.097**	−0.044**	−0.059**	0.039**	0.021*	0.076**	0.041**
	(0.008)	(0.014)	(0.008)	(0.011)	(0.008)	(0.010)	(0.008)	(0.011)
Age	0.074**	0.080**	0.071**	0.094**	0.044**	0.078**	0.037**	0.074**
	(0.005)	(0.005)	(0.005)	(0.006)	(0.005)	(0.006)	(0.005)	(0.006)
Age^2	−0.000**	−0.001**	−0.000**	−0.001**	−0.000**	−0.000**	−0.000**	−0.000**
	(0.000)	(0.000)	(0.000)	(0.000)	(0.000)	(0.000)	(0.000)	(0.000)
Non-Hispanic black	−0.190**	−0.083**	−0.186**	−0.071**	−0.166**	−0.089**	−0.181**	−0.092**
	(0.010)	(0.008)	(0.010)	(0.009)	(0.009)	(0.008)	(0.009)	(0.008)
Hispanic	−0.164**	−0.094**	−0.162**	−0.081**	−0.151**	−0.087**	−0.133**	−0.091**
	(0.013)	(0.012)	(0.011)	(0.012)	(0.010)	(0.010)	(0.009)	(0.009)
Other race	−0.151**	−0.067**	−0.084**	−0.094**	−0.062**	−0.042**	−0.055**	−0.027*
	(0.019)	(0.016)	(0.016)	(0.014)	(0.014)	(0.013)	(0.013)	(0.012)
High school graduate	0.051**	0.096**	0.072**	0.090**	0.120**	0.142**	0.181**	0.092**
	(0.011)	(0.011)	(0.013)	(0.014)	(0.013)	(0.014)	(0.015)	(0.018)
Some college	0.087**	0.185**	0.140**	0.211**	0.206**	0.244**	0.266**	0.190**
	(0.014)	(0.014)	(0.016)	(0.018)	(0.016)	(0.018)	(0.019)	(0.022)
College graduate	0.220**	0.278**	0.322**	0.353**	0.442**	0.444**	0.547**	0.417**
	(0.021)	(0.022)	(0.024)	(0.028)	(0.023)	(0.027)	(0.026)	(0.030)
Advanced degree	0.206**	0.370**	0.376**	0.427**	0.554**	0.549**	0.721**	0.496**
	(0.026)	(0.028)	(0.032)	(0.036)	(0.030)	(0.035)	(0.034)	(0.038)

(continued)

Table A3. *(continued)*

	1984		1993		2004		2014	
	Men	Women	Men	Women	Men	Women	Men	Women
Potential work experience	-0.025**	-0.033**	-0.021**	-0.040**	-0.006	-0.031**	-0.002	-0.035**
	(0.004)	(0.004)	(0.004)	(0.005)	(0.003)	(0.004)	(0.004)	(0.005)
Potential work experience^2	-0.000**	0.000	-0.000**	0.000	-0.000**	-0.000	-0.000**	-0.000
	(0.000)	(0.000)	(0.000)	(0.000)	(0.000)	(0.000)	(0.000)	(0.000)
Midwest	0.007	-0.040**	-0.066**	-0.088**	-0.041**	-0.052**	-0.077**	-0.088**
	(0.007)	(0.007)	(0.007)	(0.007)	(0.008)	(0.007)	(0.009)	(0.008)
South	-0.040**	-0.074**	-0.108**	-0.122**	-0.064**	-0.080**	-0.063**	-0.097**
	(0.008)	(0.007)	(0.007)	(0.007)	(0.008)	(0.007)	(0.008)	(0.008)
West	0.059**	0.027**	-0.015	-0.003	0.007	0.012	0.007	-0.001
	(0.008)	(0.007)	(0.008)	(0.008)	(0.009)	(0.008)	(0.009)	(0.009)
Metropolitan residence	0.134**	0.143**	0.137**	0.167**	0.128**	0.141**	0.091**	0.117**
	(0.007)	(0.006)	(0.007)	(0.006)	(0.007)	(0.006)	(0.007)	(0.007)
Public sector	-0.041**	0.065**	0.047**	0.095**	0.004	0.038**	0.016*	0.023**
	(0.007)	(0.006)	(0.007)	(0.006)	(0.008)	(0.006)	(0.008)	(0.007)
Constant	5.656**	5.419**	5.622**	5.114**	6.147**	5.428**	6.261**	5.540**
	(0.077)	(0.083)	(0.080)	(0.095)	(0.071)	(0.088)	(0.083)	(0.095)
N	37,372	34,941	38,311	38,335	41,600	41,369	40,457	39,496
R^2	0.31	0.30	0.35	0.35	0.34	0.34	0.34	0.34

Source: Authors' calculations based on 1984, 1993, 2004, and 2014 CPS-MORG (BLS).

Notes: Robust standard errors in parentheses. Regression models used in the JMP decompositions of parental status wage gaps also include marital status as a predictor of wages; these results are available from the first author on request.

Table A4. Regression Coefficients in JMP Decompositions of the Gender Gap in Wages, Parents

	1984		1993		2004		2014	
	Men	Women	Men	Women	Men	Women	Men	Women
Part-time hours (below 35/wk)	−0.361**	−0.225**	−0.338**	−0.230**	−0.302**	−0.177**	−0.338**	−0.217**
	(0.021)	(0.006)	(0.023)	(0.007)	(0.021)	(0.007)	(0.017)	(0.008)
Long work hours (50+/wk)	−0.138**	−0.082**	−0.048**	−0.047**	0.042**	0.012	0.068**	0.053**
	(0.007)	(0.019)	(0.007)	(0.014)	(0.008)	(0.015)	(0.009)	(0.016)
Age	0.056**	0.110**	0.095**	0.130**	0.063**	0.078**	0.056**	0.083**
	(0.006)	(0.007)	(0.007)	(0.009)	(0.006)	(0.007)	(0.007)	(0.008)
Age^2	−0.000	−0.001**	−0.001**	−0.001**	−0.000**	−0.000**	−0.000**	−0.000**
	(0.000)	(0.000)	(0.000)	(0.000)	(0.000)	(0.000)	(0.000)	(0.000)
Non-Hispanic black	−0.184**	−0.052**	−0.214**	−0.094**	−0.229**	−0.097**	−0.237**	−0.114**
	(0.009)	(0.008)	(0.011)	(0.008)	(0.011)	(0.008)	(0.013)	(0.009)
Hispanic	−0.173**	−0.038**	−0.193**	−0.084**	−0.205**	−0.100**	−0.157**	−0.107**
	(0.011)	(0.011)	(0.012)	(0.011)	(0.010)	(0.009)	(0.010)	(0.009)
Other race	−0.178**	−0.061**	−0.146**	−0.076**	−0.117**	−0.068**	−0.030*	−0.005
	(0.017)	(0.016)	(0.015)	(0.015)	(0.015)	(0.015)	(0.014)	(0.014)
High school graduate	0.076**	0.042**	0.074**	0.044**	0.102**	0.106**	0.119**	0.065**
	(0.011)	(0.011)	(0.012)	(0.014)	(0.015)	(0.015)	(0.017)	(0.016)
Some college	0.128**	0.144**	0.156**	0.158**	0.208**	0.209**	0.226**	0.144**
	(0.015)	(0.015)	(0.016)	(0.019)	(0.019)	(0.019)	(0.021)	(0.021)
College graduate	0.263**	0.204**	0.327**	0.290**	0.458**	0.448**	0.514**	0.416**
	(0.021)	(0.023)	(0.023)	(0.029)	(0.026)	(0.028)	(0.029)	(0.030)
Advanced degree	0.275**	0.329**	0.389**	0.361**	0.601**	0.543**	0.648**	0.533**
	(0.026)	(0.029)	(0.030)	(0.037)	(0.033)	(0.035)	(0.037)	(0.039)

(continued)

Table A4. (continued)

	1984		1993		2004		2014	
	Men	Women	Men	Women	Men	Women	Men	Women
Potential work experience	-0.014**	-0.055**	-0.032**	-0.060**	-0.012**	-0.036**	-0.008	-0.038**
	(0.004)	(0.004)	(0.004)	(0.006)	(0.004)	(0.005)	(0.005)	(0.005)
Potential work experience^2	-0.001**	0.000**	-0.000	0.000**	-0.000**	-0.000	-0.000**	-0.000
	(0.000)	(0.000)	(0.000)	(0.000)	(0.000)	(0.000)	(0.000)	(0.000)
Midwest	0.001	-0.013	-0.061**	-0.092**	-0.029**	-0.051**	-0.070**	-0.069**
	(0.007)	(0.008)	(0.008)	(0.008)	(0.009)	(0.009)	(0.011)	(0.010)
South	-0.052**	-0.053**	-0.097**	-0.145**	-0.066**	-0.086**	-0.082**	-0.081**
	(0.007)	(0.008)	(0.008)	(0.008)	(0.009)	(0.009)	(0.011)	(0.010)
West	0.057**	0.054**	0.008	-0.006	0.005	0.017	-0.016	0.013
	(0.008)	(0.008)	(0.009)	(0.009)	(0.010)	(0.010)	(0.011)	(0.011)
Metropolitan residence	0.142**	0.129**	0.168**	0.173**	0.133**	0.133**	0.099**	0.111**
	(0.006)	(0.006)	(0.006)	(0.006)	(0.007)	(0.007)	(0.009)	(0.008)
Public sector	-0.073**	0.053**	-0.003	0.057**	-0.049**	-0.016*	-0.033**	-0.030**
	(0.006)	(0.007)	(0.007)	(0.007)	(0.009)	(0.008)	(0.010)	(0.008)
Constant	5.973**	5.030**	5.319**	4.664**	5.936**	5.485**	5.965**	5.414**
	(0.085)	(0.100)	(0.101)	(0.131)	(0.097)	(0.110)	(0.114)	(0.117)
N	36,482	29,829	32,551	31,299	30,108	31,282	26,614	27,455
R^2	0.31	0.28	0.36	0.34	0.38	0.35	0.38	0.40

Source: Authors' calculations based on 1984, 1993, 2004, and 2014 CPS-MORG (BLS).

Notes: Robust standard errors in parentheses. The regression models used in the JMP decompositions of parental status wage gaps also include marital status as a predictor of wages; these results are available from the first author on request.

* $p < 0.05$; ** $p < 0.01$

Table A5. Coefficients from JMP Decomposition of Gender Gap in (Logged) Wages, Childless Adults

	1984 to 2014		1984 to 1993		1993 to 2004		2004 to 2014	
Total change in gender wage gap	−0.193		−0.133		−0.048		−0.012	
	Price	Quantity	Price	Quantity	Price	Quantity	Price	Quantity
All observed factors	0.006	−0.054	0.000	−0.038	0.008	−0.024	0.007	−0.003
Part-time hours	0.001	−0.013	−0.001	−0.010	−0.005	−0.003	0.007	0.001
Long work hours	0.016	0.002	0.008	−0.001	0.007	0.001	0.003	0.000
Age	0.056	−0.113	0.003	−0.076	0.047	−0.051	0.010	0.010
Age^2	−0.014	0.038	0.004	0.023	−0.026	0.021	0.003	−0.002
Non-Hispanic black	0.000	0.003	0.000	0.000	0.000	0.002	0.000	0.001
Hispanic	0.001	−0.005	0.000	−0.003	0.001	−0.003	0.001	0.001
Other race	0.000	0.000	0.000	−0.001	0.000	0.000	0.000	0.000
High school graduate	0.006	0.005	0.000	0.002	0.001	0.003	0.003	0.003
Some college	−0.005	−0.001	−0.001	−0.001	−0.002	−0.002	−0.002	0.002
College graduate	−0.009	−0.007	−0.001	−0.003	−0.002	−0.002	−0.003	−0.006
Advanced degree	−0.013	−0.010	0.001	−0.004	−0.002	−0.006	−0.004	−0.007
Experience	−0.025	0.029	−0.003	0.022	−0.021	0.011	−0.004	−0.002
Experience^2	−0.005	0.016	−0.004	0.011	0.009	0.005	−0.007	−0.004
Midwest	0.001	0.000	0.000	0.000	0.000	0.000	0.000	0.000
South	0.000	0.000	0.000	0.000	0.000	0.000	0.000	0.000
West	−0.001	0.000	−0.001	0.000	0.000	0.000	0.000	0.000
Metropolitan	0.000	0.001	0.000	0.000	0.000	0.001	0.000	0.000
Public sector	−0.003	0.001	−0.004	0.000	0.003	−0.001	−0.001	0.000
Total unobserved effects	−0.144		−0.095		−0.032		−0.016	
N	152,266		148,959		159,615		162,922	

Source: Authors' compilation based on 1984 and 2014 CPS-MORG (BLS).
Notes: Omitted categories are white (race), less than high school diploma (education), and East (region). See tables A3 and A4 for underlying regression coefficients and their robust standard errors.

Table A6. Coefficients from JMP Decomposition of Gender Gap in (Logged) Wages, Parents

	1984 to 2014		1984 to 1993		1993 to 2004		2004 to 2014	
Total change in gender wage gap	−0.197		−0.122		−0.023		−0.051	
	Price	Quantity	Price	Quantity	Price	Quantity	Price	Quantity
All observed factors	0.020	−0.053	0.008	−0.023	0.012	−0.012	0.016	−0.033
Part-time hours	−0.005	−0.024	−0.005	−0.009	−0.008	−0.006	0.007	−0.007
Long work hours	0.029	0.000	0.015	−0.003	0.014	0.000	0.004	−0.001
Age	0.000	0.027	0.056	−0.015	−0.056	0.024	−0.013	0.031
Age²	−0.030	−0.004	−0.059	0.002	0.034	−0.011	0.014	−0.015
Non-Hispanic black	0.003	0.001	0.001	0.000	0.001	0.003	0.000	−0.002
Hispanic	0.000	−0.004	−0.001	−0.003	0.000	−0.002	0.001	0.001
Other race	0.001	−0.002	0.000	0.000	0.000	−0.001	0.001	−0.001
High school graduate	0.002	0.010	0.000	0.004	0.000	0.002	0.001	0.004
Some college	−0.006	−0.005	−0.001	−0.004	−0.003	−0.002	−0.001	0.002
College graduate	−0.005	−0.011	0.001	−0.002	0.001	−0.004	−0.001	−0.011
Advanced degree	−0.001	−0.012	0.003	−0.003	0.005	−0.002	0.000	−0.016
Experience	0.016	−0.014	−0.025	0.002	0.037	−0.013	0.009	−0.009
Experience²	0.018	−0.017	0.025	0.006	−0.014	−0.001	−0.005	−0.009
Midwest	0.001	0.000	0.000	0.000	0.000	0.000	0.001	0.000
South	0.000	−0.001	0.001	0.000	0.000	0.000	0.000	0.000
West	−0.002	0.001	−0.001	0.001	0.000	0.000	−0.001	0.000
Metropolitan	0.000	0.001	0.000	0.001	0.000	0.001	0.000	−0.001
Public sector	−0.002	0.001	−0.004	0.001	0.003	0.000	−0.001	0.000
Total unobserved effects	−0.164		−0.107		−0.022		−0.034	
N	120,380		130,161		125,240		115,459	

Source: Authors' compilation based on 1984 and 2014 CPS-MORG (BLS).

Notes: Omitted categories are white (race), less than high school diploma (education), and East (region). See tables A3 and A4 for underlying regression coefficients and their robust standard errors.

Table A7. Coefficients from JMP Decomposition of Family Gap in (Logged) Wages, Women

	1984 to 2014		1984 to 1993		1993 to 2004		2004 to 2014	
Total change in parental status wage gap	−0.041		−0.008		−0.002		−0.030	
	Price	Quantity	Price	Quantity	Price	Quantity	Price	Quantity
All observed factors	0.047	−0.035	0.010	−0.001	0.013	0.000	0.027	−0.037
Part-time hours	0.001	−0.013	0.000	−0.002	−0.004	−0.004	0.003	−0.006
Long work hours	0.004	0.000	0.001	−0.001	0.003	0.000	0.001	0.000
Age	−0.049	0.126	0.073	0.012	−0.095	0.074	−0.036	0.050
Age^2	0.139	−0.075	−0.042	0.001	0.089	−0.043	0.093	−0.033
Non-Hispanic black	0.000	−0.002	−0.001	−0.001	0.001	0.000	0.000	−0.001
Hispanic	0.000	0.005	0.000	0.001	0.000	0.003	0.000	0.001
Other race	0.000	0.000	0.000	0.000	0.000	0.000	0.000	0.000
Married	−0.003	0.000	−0.004	0.000	0.001	0.001	−0.001	0.000
High school graduate	0.000	0.006	0.000	0.003	−0.001	0.001	−0.001	0.003
Some college	0.000	0.002	−0.001	−0.003	0.000	0.002	0.000	0.004
College graduate	0.002	−0.006	0.002	−0.001	0.002	−0.003	0.000	−0.004
Advanced degree	−0.001	−0.011	0.001	0.000	0.003	0.002	0.001	−0.019
Experience	−0.017	−0.058	−0.036	−0.005	0.048	−0.029	−0.026	−0.028
Experience^2	−0.028	0.001	0.012	0.000	−0.032	0.002	−0.006	−0.002
Midwest	0.000	−0.001	0.001	0.000	0.000	−0.001	0.000	0.000
South	0.000	−0.002	0.001	−0.001	0.000	−0.002	0.000	0.001
West	0.000	−0.001	0.000	0.000	0.000	0.000	0.000	0.000
Metropolitan	0.000	−0.008	0.001	−0.002	0.000	−0.005	0.000	−0.002
Public sector	0.000	0.000	0.000	0.000	−0.001	0.002	0.000	−0.001
Total unobserved effects	−0.053		−0.107		−0.015		−0.021	
N	131,721		134,404		142,285		139,602	

Source: Authors' compilation based on CPS-MORG (BLS).
Notes: Omitted categories are white (race), less than high school diploma (education), and East (region). See tables A3 and A4 for underlying regression coefficients and their robust standard errors

Table A8. Coefficients from JMP Decomposition of Family Gap in (Logged) Wages, Men

	1984 to 2014		1984 to 1993		1993 to 2004		2004 to 2014	
Total change in parental status wage gap	−0.037		−0.018		−0.027		0.009	
	Price	Quantity	Price	Quantity	Price	Quantity	Price	Quantity
All observed factors	0.004	−0.023	0.006	−0.012	0.004	−0.007	−0.002	−0.008
Part-time hours	0.000	−0.004	0.001	−0.004	0.002	−0.001	−0.003	0.001
Long work hours	−0.006	0.001	−0.002	0.001	−0.004	0.001	−0.001	0.000
Age	−0.108	−0.030	−0.007	−0.042	−0.067	−0.012	−0.023	0.015
Age^2	0.034	0.006	−0.018	0.015	0.052	0.003	−0.005	−0.006
Non-Hispanic black	0.000	−0.003	0.000	−0.001	0.000	−0.001	0.000	0.000
Hispanic	−0.002	0.007	0.000	0.001	−0.001	0.004	−0.001	0.001
Other race	−0.002	0.002	0.000	0.000	0.000	0.000	0.000	0.001
Married	0.008	−0.003	0.004	−0.003	0.009	−0.001	−0.005	0.001
High school graduate	0.003	0.002	0.000	0.001	0.001	0.002	0.001	0.001
Some college	0.006	0.004	0.000	0.001	0.001	0.001	0.002	0.004
College graduate	0.002	−0.003	0.001	−0.002	0.000	−0.001	0.001	0.000
Advanced degree	−0.016	−0.007	−0.001	−0.002	−0.002	−0.002	−0.005	−0.011
Experience	0.070	0.010	0.013	0.015	0.038	0.005	0.011	−0.003
Experience^2	0.016	0.005	0.016	0.012	−0.026	0.002	0.028	−0.012
Midwest	−0.001	0.000	0.000	0.000	0.000	−0.001	0.000	0.000
South	0.000	0.000	0.000	0.000	0.000	−0.002	0.000	0.001
West	0.001	−0.002	0.000	−0.001	0.000	0.000	0.000	0.000
Metropolitan	0.000	−0.008	0.000	−0.003	0.000	−0.004	0.000	−0.001
Public sector	0.000	0.000	0.000	0.000	0.000	0.000	0.000	0.000
Total unobserved effects	−0.018		−0.013		−0.024		0.020	
N	140,925		144,716		142,570		138,779	

Source: Authors' compilation based on CPS-MORG (BLS).

Notes: Omitted categories are white (race), less than high school diploma (education), and East (region). See tables A3 and A4 for underlying regression coefficients and their robust standard errors

Figure A1. Participation in Wage and Salary Employment, Men

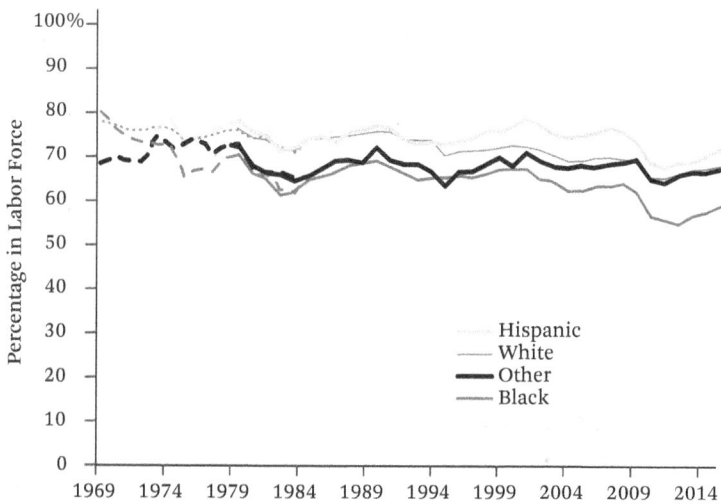

Source: Authors' calculations based on MORG-CPS (BLS).
Notes: May-CPS: dotted lines, N=645,984; MORG: solid lines, N=4,423,990. Race categories are mutually exclusive after 1972. Before 1973, Hispanic ethnicity is not available.

Figure A2. Participation in Wage and Salary Employment, Women

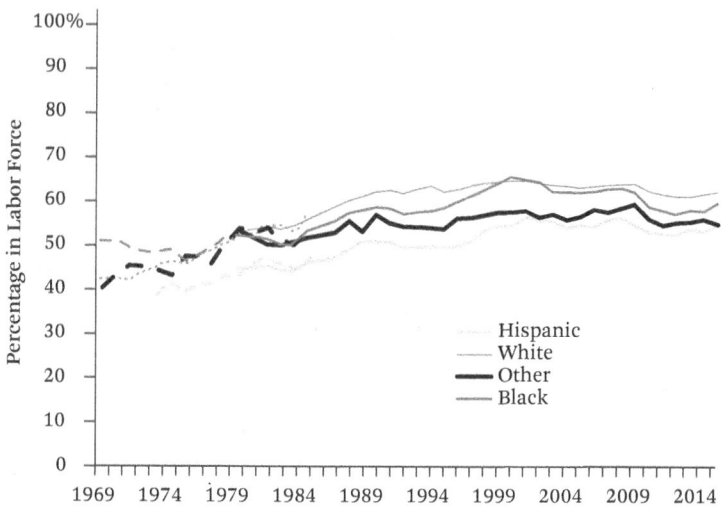

Source: Authors' calculations based on MORG-CPS (BLS).
Notes: May-CPS: dotted lines, N=714,725; MORG: solid lines, N=4,790,476. Race categories are mutually exclusive after 1972. Before 1973, Hispanic ethnicity is not available.

Figure A3. Work Hours Among Wage and Salary Employees, Non-Hispanic White Men

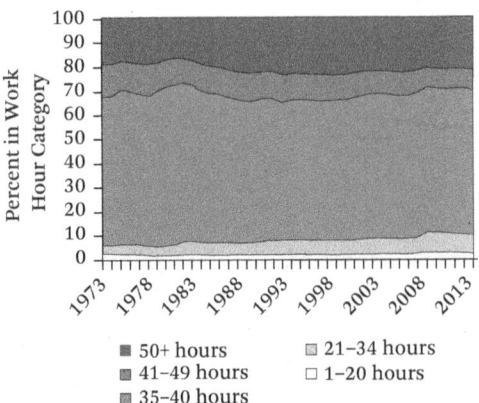

- 50+ hours
- 41–49 hours
- 35–40 hours
- 21–34 hours
- 1–20 hours

Source: Authors' calculations based on CPS-MORG (BLS)
Notes: May-CPS (1973–1984; N=188,676); MORG (1979–2014; Ns: NH=2,433,905).

Figure A5. Work Hours Among Wage and Salary Employees, Non-Hispanic Black Men

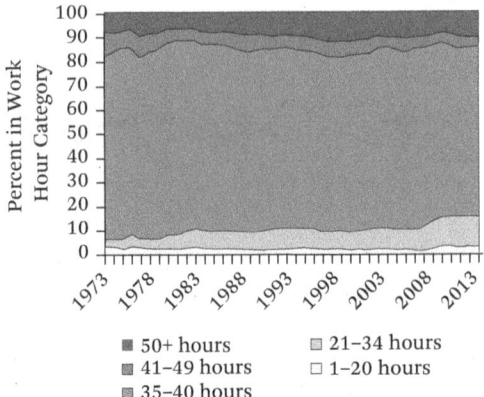

- 50+ hours
- 41–49 hours
- 35–40 hours
- 21–34 hours
- 1–20 hours

Source: Authors' calculations based on MORG-CPS (BLS)
Notes: May-CPS (1973–1984; N=16,161); MORG (1979–2014; N=245,336).

Figure A4. Work Hours Among Wage and Salary Employees, Non-Hispanic White Women

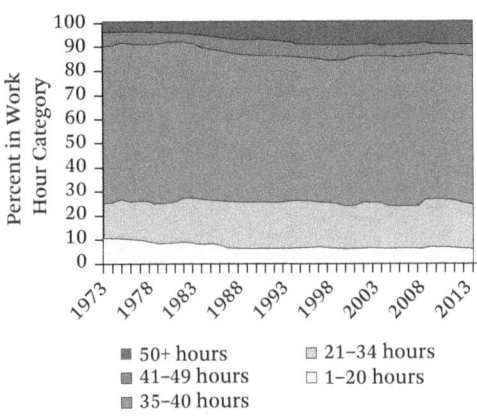

- 50+ hours
- 41–49 hours
- 35–40 hours
- 21–34 hours
- 1–20 hours

Source: Authors' calculations based on MORG-CPS (BLS)
Notes: May-CPS (1973–1984; N=126,931); MORG (1979–2014; N=2,209,279).

Figure A6. Work Hours Among Wage and Salary Employees, Non-Hispanic Black Women

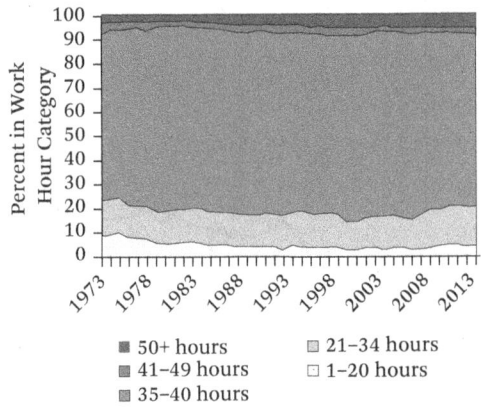

- 50+ hours
- 41–49 hours
- 35–40 hours
- 21–34 hours
- 1–20 hours

Source: Authors' calculations based on MORG-CPS (BLS)
Notes: May-CPS (1973–1984; N=14,242); MORG (1979–2014; N=305,552).

REFERENCES

Avellar, Sarah, and Pamela Smock. 2003. "Has the Price of Motherhood Declined over Time? A Cross-Cohort Comparison of the Motherhood Wage Penalty." *Journal of Marriage and the Family* 65(3): 597–607.

Bianchi, Suzanne M., Liana C. Sayer, Melissa A. Milkie, and John P. Robinson. 2012. "Housework: Who Did, Does or Will Do It, and How Much Does It Matter?" *Social Forces* 91(1): 55–63.

Buchmann, Claudia, and Anne McDaniel. 2016. "Motherhood and the Wages of Women in Professional Occupations." *RSF: The Russell Sage Journal of the Social Sciences* 2(4). doi: 10.7758/RSF.2016.2.4.05.

Budig, Michelle J., and Paula England. 2001. "The Wage Penalty for Motherhood." *American Sociological Review* 66(2): 204–25.

Bureau of Labor Statistics (BLS). 2015. "Highlights of Women's Earnings in 2014." Report no. 1058. Washington: U.S. Department of Labor. Accessed June 27, 2016. http://www.bls.gov/opub/reports/womens-earnings/archive/highlights-of-womens-earnings-in-2014.pdf

Byker, Tanya. 2016. "The Opt-Out Continuation: Education, Work, and Motherhood from 1984 to 2012." *RSF: The Russell Sage Journal of the Social Sciences* 2(4). doi: 10.7758/RSF.2016.2.4.02.

Card, David, and John E. DiNardo. 2002. "Skill-Biased Technological Change and Rising Wage Inequality: Some Problems and Puzzles." *Journal of Labor Economics* 20(4): 733–83.

Cha, Youngjoo, and Kim A. Weeden. 2014. "Overwork and the Slow Convergence in the Gender Gap in Wages." *American Sociological Review* 79(3): 457–84.

Charles, Maria, and David B. Grusky. 2004. *Occupational Ghettos: The Worldwide Segregation of Women and Men*. Stanford, Calif.: Stanford University Press.

Clarkberg, Marin, and Phyllis Moen. 2001. "Understanding the Time-Squeeze: Married Couples' Preferred and Actual Work-Hour Strategies." *American Behavioral Scientist* 44(7): 1115–35.

Cooke, Lynn Prince. 2014. "Gendered Parenthood Penalties and Premiums across the Earnings Distribution in Australia, the United Kingdom, and the United States." *European Sociological Review* 30(3): 360–72.

Correll, Shelley J., Stephen Benard, and In Paik. 2007. "Getting a Job: Is There a Motherhood Wage Penalty?" *American Journal of Sociology* 112(5): 1297–338.

Coser, Lewis A. 1967. "Greedy Organizations." *European Journal of Sociology* 8(2): 196–215.

Cotter, David, Joan M. Hermsen, and Reeve Vanneman. 2011. "The End of the Gender Revolution? Gender Role Attitudes from 1977 to 2008." *American Journal of Sociology* 117(1): 259–89.

England, Paula. 2010. "The Gender Revolution: Uneven and Stalled." *Gender & Society* 24(2): 149–66.

Gangl, Markus, and Andrea Ziefle. 2009. "Motherhood, Labor Force Behavior, and Woman's Careers: An Empirical Assessment of the Wage Penalty for Motherhood in Britain, Germany, and the United States." *Demography* 46(2): 341–69.

Gerson, Kathleen. 2009. *The Unfinished Revolution: How a New Generation Is Reshaping Family, Work, and Gender in America*. Oxford: Oxford University Press.

Glauber, Rebecca. 2008. "Race and Gender in Families and at Work: The Fatherhood Wage Premium." *Gender and Society* 22(1): 8–30.

Goldin, Claudia. 2014. "A Grand Gender Convergence: Its Last Chapter." *American Economic Review*. 104(4): 1091–119.

Jacobs, Jerry A., and Kathleen Gerson. 2004. *The Time Divide: Work, Family, and Gender Inequality*. Cambridge, Mass.: Harvard University Press.

Juhn, Chinhui, Kevin M. Murphy, and Brooks Pierce. 1991. "Accounting for the Slowdown in Black-White Wage Convergence." In *Workers and Their Wages*, edited by Marvin H. Kosters. Washington, D.C.: AEI Press.

Kahn, Joan R., Javier Garcia-Manglano, and Suzanne M. Bianchi. 2014. "The Motherhood Penalty at Midlife: Long-Term Effects of Children on Women's Careers." *Journal of Marriage and the Family* 76(1): 56–72.

Kalleberg, Arne L. 2000. "Nonstandard Employment Relations: Part-Time, Temporary, and Contract Work." *Annual Review of Sociology* 26: 341–65.

———. 2011. *Good Jobs, Bad Jobs: The Rise of Polarized and Precarious Employment Systems in the United States, 1970s to 2000s*. New York: Russell Sage Foundation.

Killewald, Alexandra. 2012. "A Reconsideration of the Fatherhood Wage Premium: Marriage, Coresidence, Biology, and Father's Wages." *American Sociological Review* 78(1): 96–116.

Kuhn, Peter J., and Fernando A. Lozano. 2008. "The Expanding Workweek? Understanding Trends in Long Work Hours Among U.S. Men, 1979–2006." *Journal of Labor Economics* 26(2): 311–43.

Lundberg, Shelly J., and Eliana Rose. 2000. "Parenthood and the Earnings of Married Men and Women." *Journal of Labour Economics* 7(6): 689–710.

National Bureau of Economic Research (NBER). 1969–1984. "CPS May Supplement." Accessed April 11, 2016. http://www.nber.org/data/may.html.

———. 1979–2014. "CPS Merged Outgoing Rotation Groups." Accessed April 11, 2016. http://www.nber.org/data/morg.html.

Pal, Ipshita, and Jane Waldfogel. 2016. "The Family Gap in Pay: New Evidence for 1967 to 2013." *RSF: The Russell Sage Journal of the Social Sciences* 2(4). doi: 10.7758/RSF.2016.2.4.04.

Pedulla, David S., and Sarah J. Thébaud. 2015. "Can We Finish the Revolution? Gender, Work-Family Ideals, and Institutional Constraint." *American Sociological Review* 80(1): 116–39.

Reid, Erin. 2015. "Embracing, Passing, Revealing, and the Ideal Worker Image: How People Navigate Expected and Experienced Professional Identities." *Organization Science* 26(4): 997–1017.

Ridgeway, Cecilia L. 2011. *Framed by Gender: How Gender Inequality Persists in the Modern World.* Oxford: Oxford University Press.

Ridgeway, Cecilia L., and Shelley J. Correll. 2004. "Motherhood as a Status Characteristic." *Journal of Social Issues* 60(4): 683–700.

Sharone, Ofer. 2004. "Engineering Overwork: Bell-Curve Management at a High-Tech Firm." In *Fighting for Time: Shifting Boundaries of Work and Social Life*, edited by Cynthia Fuchs Epstein and Arne L. Kalleberg. New York: Russell Sage Foundation.

Staff, Jeremy, and Jeylan T Mortimer. 2012. "Explaining the Motherhood Wage Penalty During the Occupational Career." *Demography* 49(1): 1–21.

Townsend, Nicholas W. 2002. *The Package Deal: Marriage, Work, and Fatherhood in Men's Lives.* Philadelphia, Pa.: Temple University Press.

Waldfogel, Jane. 1998. "Understanding the 'Family Gap' in Pay for Women with Children." *The Journal of Economic Perspectives* 12(1): 127–56.

Williams, Joan C. 2000. *Unbending Gender: Why Family and Work Conflict and What to Do About It.* New York: Oxford University Press.

———, ed. 2003. "Litigating the Glass Ceiling and the Maternal Wall: Using Stereotyping and Cognitive Bias Evidence to Prove Gender Discrimination." *Employee Rights and Employment Policy Journal* 7(2).

PART II
Motherhood, Work, and the Family Pay Gap

The Family Gap in Pay: New Evidence for 1967 to 2013

IPSHITA PAL AND JANE WALDFOGEL

This paper provides new evidence on the family gap in pay—the differential in hourly wages between women with children and women without children—between 1967 and 2013, five decades that include important changes in women's employment, especially mothers' employment, policy reforms as well as contrasting economic cycles. We use data from the Current Population Survey and adjust for selection into motherhood, by estimating ordinary least square models and (as a robustness check) applying augmented inverse probability of treatment weighting, using the standard doubly robust estimator. For women overall, we find a decline in the family gap over this period from 6 percent in 1967 and 1968 to about 1 percent in 2011 through 2013. However, results vary by marital status, education, race-ethnicity, immigration status, temporal flexibility, and occupation. The most striking difference we find is between mothers who are married and those who are not. The family gap declined for married mothers and was replaced by a positive wage differential in the most recent period, whereas for unmarried mothers, a wage gap persisted throughout the two decades, rising to a notable high of 10 percent in 1996 through 1998.

Keywords: family gap, gender gap

The family gap in pay—the differential in hourly wages between women with children and women without children—has drawn considerable attention from economists and sociologists. Increasingly rigorous studies have examined the magnitude of the gap at particular points in time, across groups, and across countries. Yet we know surprisingly little about long-term or recent trends in the family gap in pay. Our previous work analyzing data from 1977, 1987, 1997, and 2007 suggests that the motherhood wage gap has fallen in recent decades for some groups, non-Hispanic whites and married women, but increased for others,

Hispanics and never-married women (Pal and Waldfogel 2014). In this paper, we focus on a longer period, from 1967 to 2013, five decades that included dramatic changes in family structures, increases in women's and especially mothers' labor-force participation, gradual changes in men's role in the household, a declining gender wage gap, important welfare reforms that primarily affected low-income and single-mother families and finally, relative stagnation of work-family reconciliation policies as well as contrasting economic cycles.

We extend our previous work in three main ways. First, we include several earlier as well as

Jane Waldfogel is Compton Foundation Centennial Professor at Columbia University School of Social Work and visiting professor at the Centre for Analysis of Social Exclusion at the London School of Economics. **Ipshita Pal** is a recent PhD graduate of Columbia University School of Social Work and fellow of the Columbia Population Research Center.

Direct correspondence to: Jane Waldfogel at j.waldfogel@columbia.edu, Columbia University School of Social Work, 1255 Amsterdam Ave., New York, NY 10027; and Ipshita Pal at i.pal@columbia.edu, Columbia University School of Social Work, 1255 Amsterdam Ave., New York, NY 10027.

several more recent years of data, our prior analyses having ended in 2007, before the Great Recession. We also include all the years of data between 1967 and 2013 rather than selected time points so that we can describe trends in the family gap more precisely. Second, we examine the trends by age of children and again by number of children. Finally, we analyze more specific subgroups (such as immigrant versus nonimmigrant women, splitting the nonmarried subgroup into cohabiting with partner and no partner), taking advantage of the more detailed data for the later periods. Two other subgroup analyses—by occupation and by temporal flexibility—merit attention, but these issues are analyzed elsewhere (see, in this volume, both Buchmann and McDaniel, and Weeden, Cha, and Bucca; for the importance of work hours and temporal flexibility, see Goldin 2014). To our knowledge, no existing research examines trends in the motherhood wage gap in the United States over these five decades, and only limited research examines the gap for the twenty-first century. Our primary goal is to learn the extent to which the family gap in pay has changed over this period and for which groups. Second, although our analysis is primarily descriptive, we hope our results will also shed light on the role that factors such as policy and labor market changes may have played.

Using data on nationally representative samples of women from the Current Population Survey (CPS), Annual Social and Economic Supplements for March 1968 through March 2014, we estimate ordinary least square models, controlling for various human capital, demographic and family characteristics. We also check the robustness of our results by employing augmented inverse probability of treatment weighting (AIPW), the standard doubly robust estimator (Robins, Rotnitzky, and Zhao 1994; Scharfstein, Rotnitzky, and Robins 1999; Wooldridge 2007; Rotnitzky et al. 2012; Słoczyński and Wooldridge 2014).

To briefly preview our results, we find a decline in the family gap in pay for women overall, from 6 percent in 1967 and 1968 to about 1 percent in 2011 through 2013. However, results vary by marital status, education, race-ethnicity, immigration status, temporal flexibility, and occupation. The most striking difference we find is between mothers who are married and those who are not. Over this period, the wage gap declined for married mothers and was even replaced by a positive differential in the most recent period, whereas it persisted for unmarried mothers, even rising to 10 percent from 1996 through 1998.

PRIOR RESEARCH

Researchers have long argued that at least a portion of the gender wage gap is attributable to the presence of children, pointing to a significant difference in the hourly pay between women with and without children (Hill 1979; Fuchs 1988).[1] The earliest studies directly estimating the associations between children and women's wages find a family wage gap of 10 to 15 percent and evidence of an increasing gap from 1980 to 1990 even as the gender wage gap was declining (Korenman and Neumark 1992; Waldfogel 1997). A robust body of research has developed in the two decades since then with the use of increasingly sophisticated methods to deal with endogeneity and selection bias. Researchers have used pooled ordinary least squares (OLS) and fixed-effects models as well as instrumental variables models to gauge the link between motherhood and wages (Korenman and Neumark 1992; Taniguchi 1999; Budig and England 2001; Anderson, Binder, and Krause 2002; Baum 2002; Avellar and Smock 2003; Amuedo-Dorantes and Kimmel 2008; Winder 2008).

Credible estimates of the wage gap at different periods exist, from both cross-sectional and longitudinal datasets, and for various economic and demographic subgroups of interest.[2] At the same time, however, comparing estimates across studies and gauging changes in the gap over time from these studies has

---

1. Victor Fuchs uses census data from 1960 and CPS data from 1986 and shows that women with children earn 7 to 9 percent less than childless women.

2. Most recently, a cross-national study uses 2004 LIS data for the United States and recentered influence function regressions to find a striking 18 percent wage gap at the 10th percentile, none at the 90th, and 2 to 6

become increasingly challenging. The research on variation by education and skill level, for instance, is inconclusive so far—some researchers have found the wage gap to be smaller or even absent at the highest end of the educational achievement distribution and larger in the middle (Taniguchi 1999; Todd 2001; Anderson, Binder, and Krause 2003; Amuedo-Dorantes and Kimmel 2005). Contrary to these findings, other researchers find no gaps for the least educated mothers and the largest gaps for women with the highest skill levels (Anderson, Binder, and Krause 2002; Wilde, Batchelder, and Ellwood 2010). Estimates of the variation in the wage gap by race and ethnicity is somewhat more consistent. Studies find that Hispanic mothers face no wage gap or smaller differentials than other groups (Budig and England 2001; Glauber 2007; England et al., forthcoming). Black mothers also tend to face smaller differentials (Waldfogel 1997; Glauber 2007; but see Anderson, Binder, and Krause 2003). With regard to variation by marital status, some evidence has linked marriage to a larger motherhood wage gap; other studies, however, have found the opposite.[3] Finally, one study has also looked at the variation by immigration status and found a lower wage gap for immigrant women than for native-born women (Srivastava and Rodgers 2013).

Most of these studies examine the family gap for a specific time or for a short period. Only a few published studies have examined trends over time (Waldfogel 1998a; Avellar and Smock 2003).[4]

DATA AND METHODS

Our data is drawn from the 1968 through 2014 March Current Population Survey, a nationally representative survey of the noninstitutionalized population in the United States, which provides retrospective data on earnings in the prior year as well as comprehensive information on individual characteristics and family demographics.[5]

Our primary analysis sample consists of women ages twenty-five to forty-four who worked in the prior year and reported any income from employment. We include both full-time and part-time workers but in our main analyses exclude the self-employed. As mentioned, employment rates of mothers have increased between the late 1960s and recent times; we see the same in our samples, with mothers of one child, and to some extent mothers of two children, now showing rates

---

percent at different points in between (Cooke 2014). See Gough and Noonan 2013 for a review of the U.S. evidence. Many other studies examine the family gap in other countries and across countries (see Todd 2001; Harkness and Waldfogel 2003; Sigle-Rushton and Waldfogel 2007; Gangl and Ziefle 2009; Cooke 2014). For a detailed review of the current U.S. and international evidence prepared for the International Labour Organization, see Grimshaw and Rubery 2015.

3. For larger family wage gaps for married mothers, see Budig and England 2001; Glauber 2007; Loughran and Zissimopoulos 2009. Michelle Budig and Melissa Hodges (2010) include interactions of marital status with the number of children at different income quantiles and find that never-married women earned lower penalties than both the married and the divorced or separated in the bottom quantiles only, whereas ever-married women at the top earnings quantiles earned a motherhood bonus. For a reanalysis using unconditional quantile regressions and the original researchers' response, see Killewald and Bearak 2014 and Budig and Hodges 2014 respectively. In earlier work, we find that the magnitude of the family gap has decreased over time for married mothers, but increased for never-married mothers (Pal and Waldfogel 2014). Rebecca Glauber (2013) finds similar trend differences by marital status for the period from 1980 to 2010.

4. In our prior work, we estimate the change in the family gap over 1977 to 2007 using data from the 1978, 1988, 1998, and 2008 March CPS and adjust for selection using ordinary least squares and simple inverse probability of treatment weighted regressions. We find that the wage gap in 2007 is not significantly different to that in 1977, at about 5 to 6 percent. Glauber (2013) examines long-term trends by marital status for the period between 1980 and 2010.

5. Data used in this research is from Miriam King and her colleagues (2010) and available at the Minnesota Population Center's Integrated Public Use Microdata Series website (https://cps.ipums.org).

very close to that of childless women. The percentage of mothers who are employed, however, is relatively stable when we look more closely at our later samples, from 74 percent between 1993 and 1995 to 72 percent in between 2011 and 2013, with a high of 79 percent between 1999 and 2001. The proportion of non-mothers who are employed is stable, at around 86 percent over the 1990s and at 81 percent to 83 percent over the 2000s, with a low of 79 percent between 2011 and 2013 (see figures A1 and A2).

To create larger and more stable samples, we have pooled the data for three-year periods: wages for 2011 through 2013 (data from March 2012 to 2014 CPS), 2008 through 2010, and so on back to 1967 (though the earliest period has only two years of data, 1967 and 1968). We did not pool the entire forty-five years because we are interested in addressing selection into motherhood and we cannot reasonably assume that to be stable over time. A further argument against pooling the forty-five years is that the coefficients on characteristics in the model may have changed over time. To eliminate extreme values, we dropped observations for which the hourly wage was less than 45 percent of the federal minimum wage for the year, and for which the hourly wage was more than $200.[6]

Our focal outcome variable is the natural log of hourly wages. From 1976 forward, we calculate the wage in each year by first creating a variable to denote the *total hours worked last year* (product of *weeks worked last year* and *usual hours worked per week last year*) and then dividing the *annual wage and salary income from last year* by this variable to arrive at the *hourly wage*. We define hourly wages pre-1976 as similarly as possible given the more limited data available in those years.[7] We adjust wages for inflation using the annual average CPI-U (Consumer Price Index, all Urban Consumers, provided by the Bureau of Labor Statistics) and express all income in 2014 dollars. Our key independent variable is a dummy variable for *mother*, which we define based on the presence of own children under the age of eighteen in the household. We also estimated some models allowing the associations between motherhood and wages to vary by number of children and by age of children (see figures A1 and A2).

Estimating the links between children and women's wages is complicated by selection into motherhood. Women who have children (or have more children) may differ from other women in ways that also affect their wages; if so, the failure to control for those differences will lead to biased estimates of the effect of children on women's pay. The standard approach to addressing such selection in the family gap literature is to estimate multivariate OLS regression models that include controls for the types of characteristics thought to affect both motherhood and wages—characteristics such as age, education, race-ethnicity, and so on. We adopt this approach in our first set of models.

$$Ln(Wage)_i = \beta_0 + \beta_1 Mother_i + \Sigma \beta_j X_{ji} + \varepsilon_i \quad (1)$$

where *Ln(Wage)* is the natural log of hourly wage (in 2014 dollars) for the i-th respondent; *Mother* is a dummy variable denoting whether a woman is a mother or not (as defined); *X* is the covariate vector and includes j demographic, family, and human capital variables (*age* and *age squared*, and dummies denoting

---

6. Prior estimates find the maximum hourly wages in the United States for 2011 to be $175 (Mishel and Shierholz 2011). In our sample, we find 62 percent of the greater than two hundred hourly wage observations in the 2013 survey year, and 83 percent in the 2014 survey year, to include improbable hours or weeks of work reported, so they likely involve errors (see also Schmitt 2003; Larrimore et al. 2008).

7. Specifically, we take three decisions regarding variables to ensure as much consistency as possible. First, usual hours of work last year variable is only available from 1976 survey year. So, for the 1968 to 1975 samples, we use the hours of work last week. Second, because hours worked last week can be zero, we ran an unadjusted regression of "usual hours worked last year" on "hours worked last week" and replaced the zero hours with the predicted values for last year's hours from this regression. This affects only 2.4 percent of the sample. Three, weeks worked last year is available in intervals for the period before 1976, so we use the midpoints of each interval.

educational attainment, family status, and race and ethnicity) as well as dummy variables for year. We use four categories for educational attainment: less than high school, high school only, some college, or college degree or more. We use two categories for family status: married or unmarried.[8] We use three categories for race-ethnicity: white, black, and others.[9] Our coefficient of interest in equation (1), β_1, provides an estimate of the percentage difference in wages between mothers and nonmothers in the given period. All models also include a control for year because each sample pools data for a three-year period.

A more refined approach to addressing selection, now quite common though until recently not on this topic, is the estimation of propensity score matching or weighting models (Rosenbaum and Rubin 1983, 1984, 1985; Austin 2011). These models take the same kinds of observed characteristics into account and adjust estimates for the likelihood of being in the treatment group (in this case, mothers). A major assumption underlying these approaches is the ignorability of treatment assignment or conditional independence; that is, conditional on a set of observed covariates, the outcome is independent of treatment assignment. The propensity score of each woman is the probability of being a mother, conditional on observed pretreatment covariates.

$$Mother_i = \beta_0 + \Sigma\beta_j X_{ji} + u_i \qquad (2)$$

where Mother is the binary treatment (mother or nonmother) and Xj represents a vector of covariates that determine selection into motherhood and includes but is not limited to all covariates in the corresponding regression equation. The predicted probability from this probit model is the propensity score. The adjusted regression, equation (1), using the re-weighted sample allows us to place more weight on those nonmothers who had a higher propensity score.

Specifically, drawing from a growing body of literature on doubly robust causal estimation techniques, we use augmented inverse probability of treatment weighting (Robins and Rotnitzky 1995; Robins, Rotnitzky, and Zhao 1994; Bang and Robins 2005; Tsiatis 2006; Wooldridge 2007, 2010; Glynn and Quinn 2010; Tan 2010; Funk et al. 2011; most recently summarized in Słoczyński and Woolridge 2014).[10] We assume that our treatment model could be misspecified but that our outcome model is correctly specified and therefore apply the augmented inverse probability of treatment weighting.[11] The AIPW estimator thus offers us a theoretical advantage over simple inverse probability weighting (IPW) because it remains unbiased even if the treatment model is misspecified. It is an IPW estimator but includes an augmentation term that corrects the estimator when the treatment model is misspecified. If the treatment specification is correct, the augmentation term disappears as the sam-

8. The way that cohabitors are identified is not completely consistent over the period. So in our main models we distinguish only between married and unmarried women. The married category includes women who report being married, spouse present. The unmarried category includes all others (married spouse absent, divorced, separated, widowed, and single). In supplemental models, we further divide unmarried women into those who are likely cohabiting and those who are not cohabiting.

9. Race and ethnic origin are not consistently defined in the CPS over the period of our study. In our main models, we therefore only use the three race categories of white, black, and others, but in subgroup analyses, we also include Hispanic and separate the race categories into non-Hispanic white and non-Hispanic black. We do not show the others category in subgroup analysis because the residual group changes too much between these two categorizations to be meaningful.

10. The advantage of this method is summarized in a 2011 article published in the American Journal of Epidemiology: "Doubly robust estimation combines a form of outcome regression with a model for the exposure (i.e., the propensity score) to estimate the causal effect of an exposure on an outcome. When used individually to estimate a causal effect, both outcome regression and propensity score methods are unbiased only if the statistical model is correctly specified. The doubly robust estimator combines these 2 approaches such that only 1 of the 2 models need be correctly specified to obtain an unbiased effect estimator" (Funk et al 2011).

11. AIPW and other doubly robust causal estimation techniques have been used in statistics, biostatistics and epidemiology but to our knowledge, have not previously been applied in the family gap literature.

Figure 1. Mean Hourly Wages for Mothers and Nonmothers

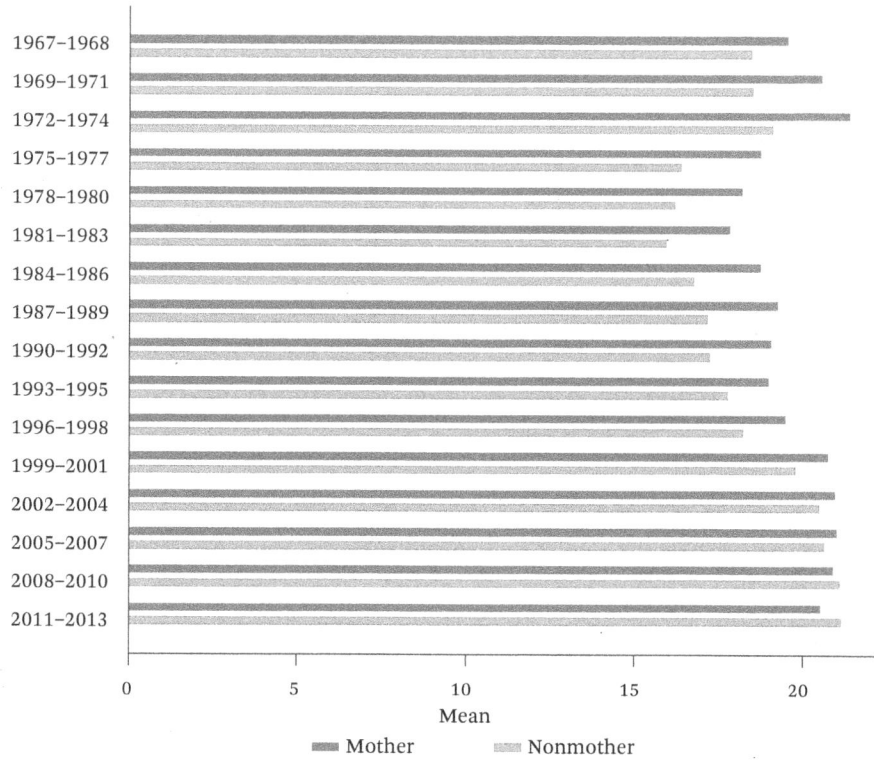

Source: Authors' calculations based on CPS data (sourced from King et al. 2010).
Notes: Wages in 2014 dollars. Sample is restricted to prime working age, twenty-five to forty-four years; motherhood status is defined by the presence of children under age eighteen in the household. Sample means, unweighted.

ple size becomes large (Słoczyński and Wooldridge 2014). The estimator requires the overlap assumption to be satisfied—that is, each individual should have a positive probability of receiving each treatment level.

A common limitation of both the OLS and the AIPW models is that they adjust only for observable differences between groups. Unobservable differences may still remain between women who become mothers and those who do not. For example, the former group may be less career oriented. If so, even estimates from fully controlled or weighted regression models could still be biased.

The methods to be used to correct for selection into motherhood have certain limitations.[12] Our estimates could still be biased by selection on unobservable variables. Nevertheless, we hope they will help shed light both on recent trends in the family gap in pay and possible factors that might help explain them. We are especially interested in the role of welfare reforms and changes in the labor market. In particular, we would like to know whether the timing of changes in the family gap for unmarried mothers coincide with welfare reforms, and how the family gap changes, both for women overall and for different groups, during different portions of the economic cycle.

RESULTS

Figure 1 shows the unadjusted mean wages of mothers and nonmothers over the sixteen periods in our study. In the earliest years, moth-

---

12. Another challenge to causal estimation is selection into employment. Women, and particularly those with children, do not always participate in the labor market, and thus at any single point in time, the wage sample will contain a selected group of wage-earners. If that selection is correlated with wages (for example, if the

Figure 2. Distribution of Hourly Wages of Mothers and Nonmothers

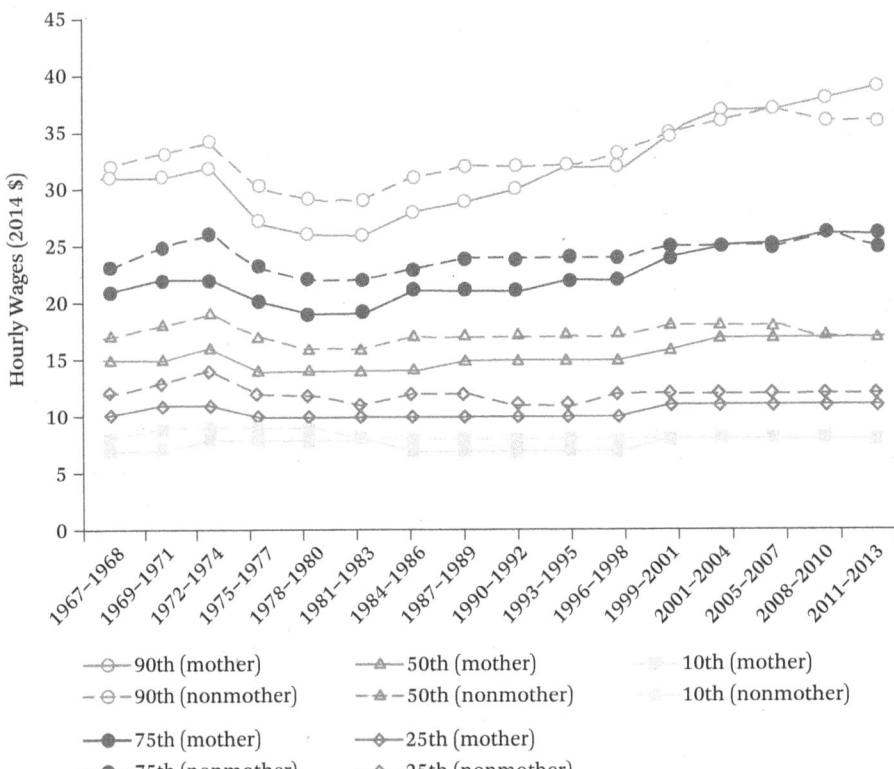

Source: Authors' calculations based on CPS data (sourced from King et al. 2010).
Notes: Wages in 2014 dollars. Sample is restricted to prime working age, twenty-five to forty-four years; motherhood status is defined by the presence of children under age eighteen in the household. Sample statistics, unweighted.

ers' hourly wages on average are below those of nonmothers, but over time the gap closes, mothers' hourly wages on average exceeding those of nonmothers in the last two periods, from 2008 to 2010 and from 2011 to 2013. Figure 2 displays a more detailed picture of the gaps between mothers' and nonmothers' hourly wages at the 10th, 25th, 50th, 75th, and 90th percentiles. For women at each of these points in the distribution, mothers' hourly wages trail nonmothers' until about the end of the 1990s. For each of these percentiles, it appears that the gap is decreasing over time. However, over time, the trends also appear to diverge, mothers in the 10th and 25th percentile almost catching up to nonmothers at the end of the period, but with a small gap remaining. In contrast, comparison of median wages shows the gap disappearing by the end of the period. Finally, for the 75th and 90th percentiles, moth-

---

mothers who work are those who face the smallest wage penalties), estimates that do not take it into account will be biased. The standard method in the family gap literature to address such bias is the use of a selection correction model (Heckman 1979). However, such models have important limitations. They may not address all the factors associated with selection into employment and in particular those that are not observable. In addition, they rely on assumptions about the exogeneity of the predictors used in the selection regression (most commonly other household income), and their results may be sensitive to which predictors are included. For this reason, we do not estimate such models.

Figure 3. Family Wage Gap

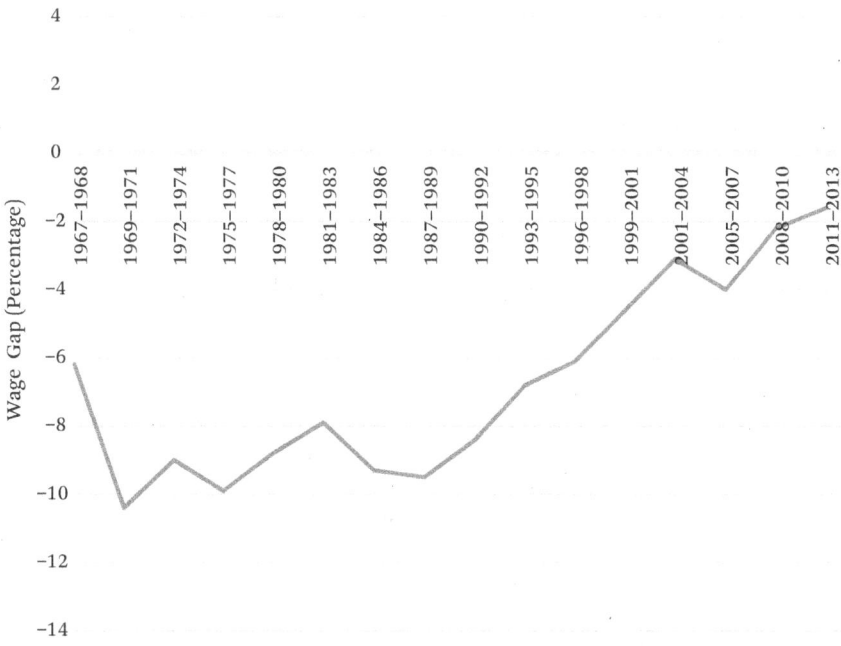

Source: Authors' calculations based on CPS data (sourced from King et al. 2010).
Notes: Results from OLS regression of ln hourly wages (in 2014 dollars) on *mother* dummy variable. Sample is restricted to prime working age, twenty-five to forty-four years; Motherhood status is defined by the presence of children under age eighteen in the household. All models include controls for age, age_squared, and dummies for education, race, married, as well as year. All coefficients on mother are significant at $p < 0.001$, except for 2012 through 2014, where it is significant at $p < 0.01$. Please see figure A3 for a graph showing estimated coefficients on mother and confidence intervals and figures A4 for supplemental results comparing OLS with AIPW models.

ers appear to overtake nonmothers over time, the positive wage differential being more distinct in the 90th percentile.

Although they provide a glimpse of the trends in the family gap in pay, these descriptive results do not tell us how wages compare holding constant differences in characteristics between mothers and nonmothers (for full descriptive statistics of these characteristics for mothers and nonmothers for each period, see tables A2 through A4).

Accordingly, figure 3 shows results from our regression models. The OLS results indicate a significant wage gap for mothers in each period that declines in magnitude over time, from 6.2 percent in 1967 and 1968 to 1 percent in 2011 through 2013. As a robustness check, we also provide AIPW estimates in figure A4; these models show a similar trend (though with slightly smaller magnitudes and only a marginally significant less than 1 percent wage gap in the most recent period).

We also examine trends in the motherhood wage differential by number and age of children in figures 4 and 5. Figure 4 shows that, over time, the family wage gaps for mothers whose youngest child is less than six years old and those whose youngest child is more than six years old, have diverged substantially. Both groups were facing a 6 percent negative wage differential in 1967 and 1968. Over time, however, the gap decreased for the former group, who started facing a positive wage differential toward the end of the period under study. For the latter group, the wage gap increased over the 1970s and 1980s, and then decreased to 6

Figure 4. Family Wage Gap, Age of Youngest Child

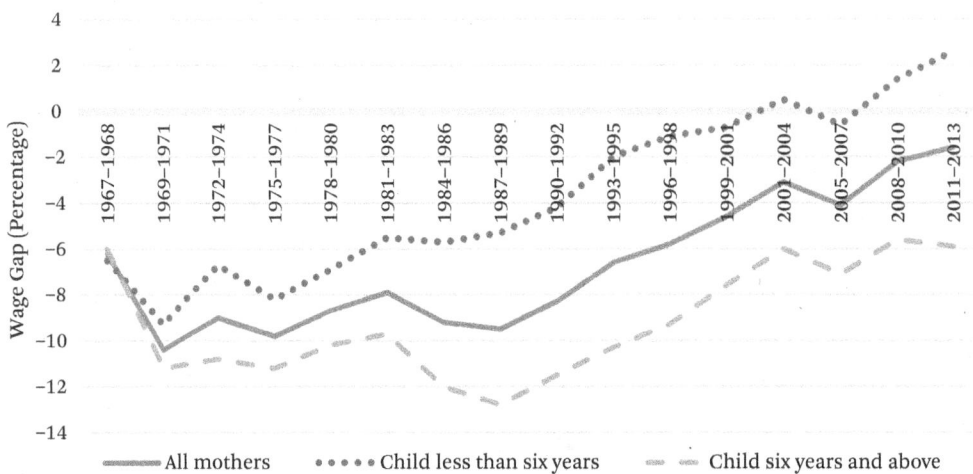

Source: Authors' calculations based on CPS data (sourced from King et al. 2010).
Notes: Results from OLS regression of ln hourly wages (in 2014 dollars) on *mother* dummy variable. Sample is restricted to prime working age, twenty-five to forty-four years; Motherhood status is defined by the presence of children under age eighteen in the household. All models include controls for age, age_squared, and dummies for education, race, married, as well as year.

Figure 5. Family Wage Gap, Number of Children

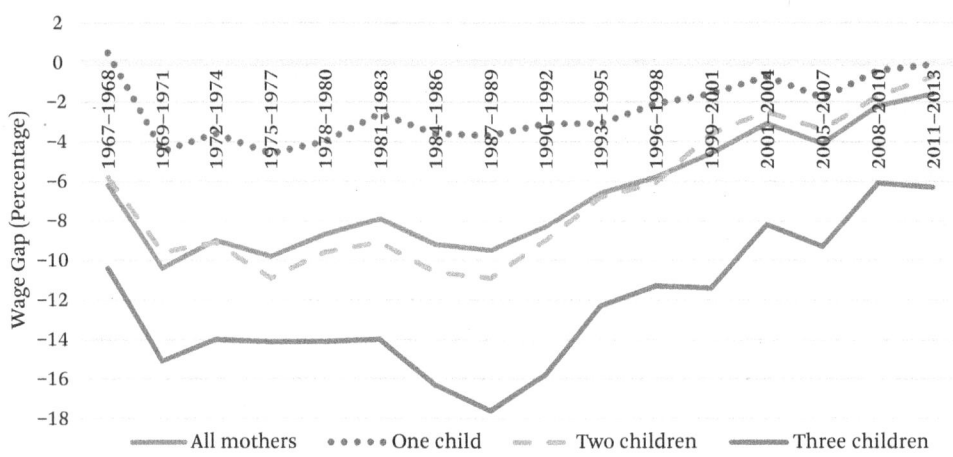

Source: Authors' calculations based on CPS data (sourced from King et al. 2010).
Notes: See notes to figure 4.

percent in 2011 to 2013. Figure 5 shows the wage differential by number of children. As expected, mothers with three or more children face the largest negative differentials in each period, though the gap itself appears to decrease over time. Trends for mothers with two children closely mirror the main model. Mothers with only one child, though, face a wage gap lower than the average for all mothers in each period, and no significant gaps in the most recent periods.

In figure 6, we successively add controls for part-time work, occupation, and industry. We find, as expected, that the differential associ-

Figure 6. Family Wage Gap, Controlling for Part Time, Occupation, and Industry

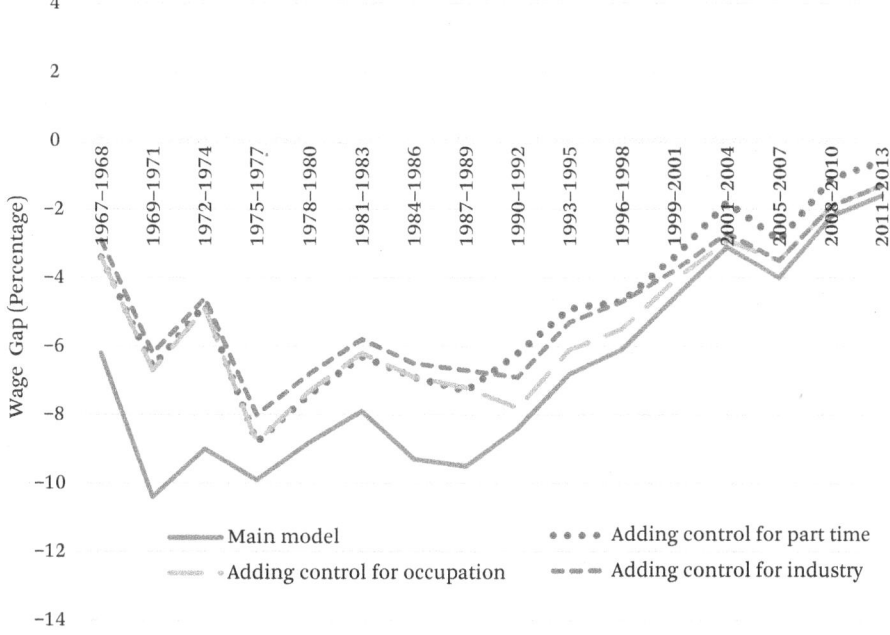

Source: Authors' calculations based on CPS data (sourced from King et al. 2010).
Notes: Results from OLS regression of ln hourly wages (in 2014 dollars) on *mother* dummy variable. Sample is restricted to prime working age, twenty-five to forty-four years; motherhood status is defined by the presence of children under age eighteen in the household. All models include controls for age, age_squared, and dummies for education, race, married, as well as year. Main model (figure 3) is included for comparison. Controls for part time, occupation, and industry are added successively. Coefficients on mother from all three models are significant at $p < 0.001$, except in the last two years, where it is significant at $p < 0.01$ or $p < 0.05$. Coefficient on mother for 2011 to 2013 in the model including control for part time only, is not significant. Graphs showing estimated coefficients on *mother* and confidence intervals available on request.

ated with motherhood is smaller when we control for part-time work (because a portion of mothers' lower average wages is accounted for by their higher propensity to work in lower-paid part-time jobs). In the most recent period, the wage gap is no longer significant. Controlling for occupation and for industry does not make much of a difference to the results.

Trends by Subgroup

We next examine the extent to which the family gap varies across groups and whether that variation has changed over time. We therefore repeat our main models (OLS) for subgroups defined by marital status, education, race-ethnicity, and immigration status (figures 7, 8, 9, and A5).[13] The most striking difference is between mothers who are married and those who are not. As shown in figure 6, for married mothers, the family gap in pay declined and was replaced by a positive wage differential in the most recent period; for unmarried mothers, however, the negative wage differential persisted throughout the period (with the exception of 1967 to 1968 when it was essentially zero), even rising to 10 percent over the 1996 to

---

13. We do not include controls for part-time work, occupation, or industry in our subgroup analyses. For analyses by occupation and work hours, see—in this volume—Buchmann and McDaniel and Weeden, Cha, and Bucca.

Figure 7. Family Wage Gap, Relationship Status

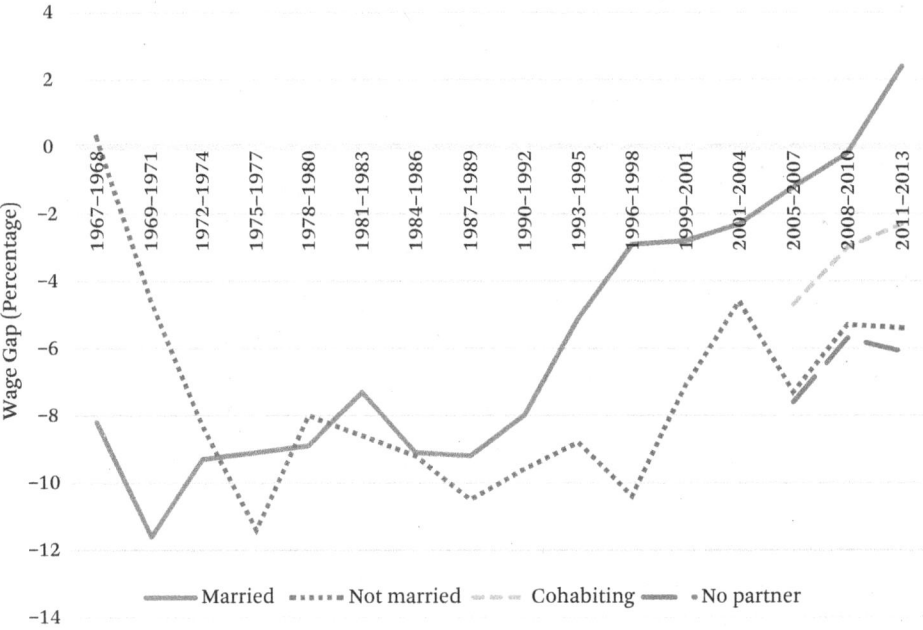

Source: Authors' calculations based on CPS data (sourced from King et al. 2010).
Notes: Results from OLS regression of ln hourly wages (in 2014 dollars) on *mother* dummy variable. Sample is restricted to prime working age, twenty-five to forty-four years; motherhood status is defined by the presence of children under age eighteen in the household. All models include controls for age, age_squared, and dummies for education, race, as well as year. Coefficients on mother from all three models are significant at $p < 0.001$, except in the last two years, where it is significant at $p < 0.01$ or $p < 0.05$. Coefficient on mother for 2011–2013 in the model including control for part time only is not significant. Graphs showing estimated coefficients on *mother* and confidence intervals available on request.

1998 period.[14] These results are consistent with Buchmann and MacDaniel in this volume.

Examining the trends by race and ethnicity (figure 8), we again find considerable differences across subgroups. Comparing non-Hispanic white mothers with non-Hispanic black mothers presents some interesting trends. Until the beginning of the 1990s, black mothers faced smaller percentage gaps than their white counterparts, but this pattern reverses between 1996 and 2001 as the family gap narrows for white mothers and increases for black mothers to reach 8 to 10 percent. After this, the declining trend continues for white mothers such that between 2011 and 2013, they face a marginally significant 1.6 percent wage gap; the gap for black mothers, on the other hand, seems to fluctuate between 3 and 5 percent over the same period. For Hispanic mothers, the insignificant wage gap in the early years was followed by a significant 3 to 5 percent gap from 1975 to 1986, but no significant gaps after that, except from 1996 to 1998 and from 2005 to 2007, which each had a 4 percent gap. These results are consistent with the expectation from prior studies that examine the

---

14. For the last three periods, we are able to split the nonmarried mothers into two groups, cohabiting mothers and single mothers, and find that trends in the wage gap for nonmarried mothers are driven by single mothers, who face persistent negative wage penalties that reach a maximum of 10 to 11 percent from 1996 to 1998. Cohabiting mothers appear to face about a 7 percent wage gap in the earliest two periods, but no significant penalties thereafter, except from 2008 to 2010.

Figure 8. Family Wage Gap, Race-Ethnicity

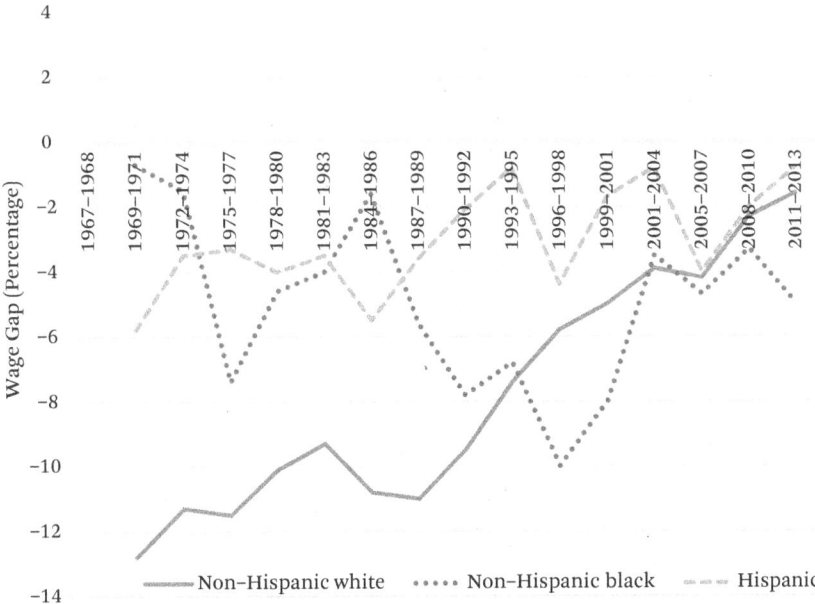

Source: Authors' calculations based on CPS data (sourced from King et al. 2010).
Notes: Results from OLS regression of ln hourly wages (in 2014 dollars) on *mother* dummy variable. Sample is restricted to prime working age, twenty-five to forty-four years; motherhood status is defined by the presence of children under age eighteen in the household. All models include controls for age, age_squared, and dummies for education, married, as well as year.
Information on Hispanic identity is not available prior to 1970.
The wage gap is not significant or only marginally significant ($p < 0.10$) for Hispanic mothers throughout the time period, except in 1996–1998, 2006–2008, and in the decade 1975–1986. Coefficients are also not significant for models showing the gap for non-Hispanic black mothers in the first two periods. All other coefficients are significant. Graphs showing estimated coefficients on *mother* and confidence intervals available on request.

family wage gap for shorter periods or at specific times and find that Hispanic mothers tend to face no wage gap or smaller differentials than other groups, and that black mothers tend to face smaller differentials than their white counterparts (Waldfogel 1997; Budig and England 2001; Glauber 2007; but see Anderson, Binder, and Krause 2003). Turning to education subgroups (in figure 9), we find little evidence of a significant motherhood wage gap among those with less than a high school education throughout the period under study. In contrast, we find significant gaps for the three more-educated groups but that these decline over the period. Women with the highest level of education (college graduates) tend to face the smallest gaps among the three more-educated groups: their wage gap fluctuates between 4 and 12 percent, falling to 2 percent from 2008 to 2010 and finally vanishing in the most recent period. For those with just a high school education and those with some college, we find a gradual decline in the wage gap over time from as much as 13 to 16 percent in the beginning of the period to 2 to 3 percent in the end.

Results by immigration status (figure A5) show the absence of a family wage gap for foreign-born mothers through most of the period during which we can identify them (from 1993 onward), and a 4 percent positive differential in the most recent data, among foreign-born mothers. These results are consistent with the only other study that has looked at the

Figure 9. Family Wage Gap, Education

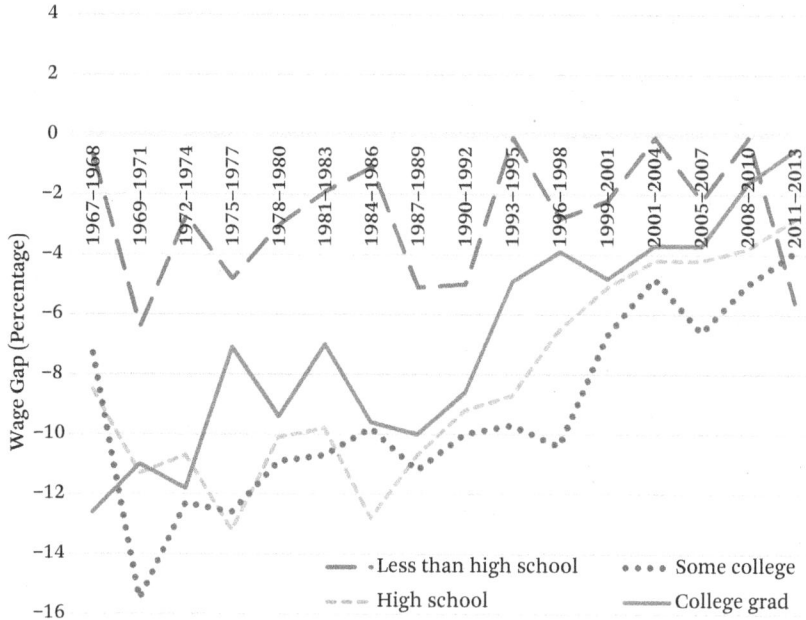

Source: Authors' calculations based on CPS data (sourced from King et al. 2010).
Notes: Results from OLS regression of ln hourly wages (in 2014 dollars) on *mother* dummy variable. Sample is restricted to prime working age, twenty-five to forty-four years; motherhood status is defined by the presence of children under age eighteen in the household. All models include controls for age, age_squared, and dummies for race, married, as well as year.
Coefficients are not significant in models for women with less than a high school diploma. All other coefficients are significant. Graphs showing estimated coefficients on *mother* and confidence intervals available on request.

family wage gap by immigration status (Srivastava and Rodgers 2013).

DISCUSSION

Several explanations for a family wage gap at any given time are plausible. Drawing mainly on the work of Gary Becker (1981, 1985), researchers have emphasized three, which are not mutually exclusive. First, mothers and nonmothers may differ in terms of their human capital. In addition to differences that may precede and be associated with the selection into motherhood, differences may arise subsequent to and as a result of motherhood. Chief among these would be reductions in work experience and job-specific tenure, switches into part-time jobs, and reductions in effort or motivation, which follow directly from Becker's model of household specialization. Theoretically, women's comparative biological advantage in care work might make it more efficient for them to put more resources such as time and effort into the household economy; in turn, this would imply less time and effort available for the market economy, which might be reflected in reduced work hours and lower wages. Second, mothers and nonmothers may work in different types of jobs, mothers being more likely to be concentrated in more family-friendly occupations or industries.[15] Third, employers may discriminate against mothers, assuming or perceiving them to be less dedicated or career focused (Correll, Benard, and Paik 2007; Benard and Correll 2010). Individually and to-

---

15. Budig and England (2001), however, find no evidence of occupational characteristics influencing mothers' pay, once part-time work is accounted for.

gether, each of these ideas may explain the presence of a family wage gap (except in the most recent periods for certain subgroups). These theories provide a useful framework for understanding the family gap in pay but may not fully explain how or why it changed during the period under study because of the role of several potentially contradictory socioeconomic and policy forces.

First, changes in women's labor-force participation over the last several decades have been dramatic. Most notably, mothers are returning to work sooner after childbirth than they did in the 1960s and 1970s. Among women with a first birth, only 10 percent were working three months after birth; slightly more than 10 percent were working twelve months after birth between 1961 and 1965; these proportions increased to 44 percent and 64 percent between 2005 and 2007 (Laughlin 2011). Inasmuch as employment continuity as well as work experience are critical to wages, mothers' increased labor-force attachment could explain the narrowing of the family wage gap, at least for married mothers and those who have at least a high school diploma, and especially those with a college degree.

Second, over the past several decades, men's role in childrearing and home production has changed. Even though parenting has become more intensive, both mothers and fathers spending more time in childrearing than they did in earlier decades, the increase for fathers has been greater, almost tripling between the 1965–1985 and 2003–2008 periods (Bianchi 2011; Parker and Wang 2013). Moreover, mothers' time in household work has declined sharply over time and father's household work time has correspondingly increased (Parker and Wang 2013). These shifts might have helped close the wage gap between mothers and non-mothers by enabling mothers to conserve the effort that they would have earlier expended on nonmarket work. In addition, fathers' greater involvement in childcare and household work may have facilitated mothers' increased attachment to the labor force (Raley, Bianchi, and Wang 2012). These developments would be expected to lead to a decline in the family wage gap over the past forty years. Our results for married mothers are consistent with this expectation.

On the other hand, changes in the composition of the workforce could negatively affect trends in the family gap. In particular, the 1996 federal welfare reform (following earlier federal and state reforms that began in the late 1980s and early 1990s) pushed low-income single mothers into the labor market in large numbers. If those newly entering the labor market had lower human capital (including unobserved factors that might lead to a larger wage differential for mothers) than the women who worked before welfare reform, this change could have led to an increase in the family gap, particularly in the 1990s. We find some evidence of this in our results for black and Hispanic women (who are more likely than non-Hispanic white women to be low income), and further evidence when we estimate our models separately for unmarried women (who are most likely to be affected by welfare policy).[16]

Finally, policies to help mothers reconcile work and family have been fairly stagnant in the United States over the past several decades. Although the enactment of the Family and Medical Leave Act in 1994 was much heralded, the United States remains the only developed country without any national paid leave policy or universal childcare provision. Cross-national research shows that motherhood wage gaps are likely to be relatively lower in countries with stronger work-family reconciliation policies (Gornick and Meyers 2003; Misra, Budig, and Moller 2007; Budig, Misra, and Boeckman 2012). Other research shows that a moderate duration of paid parental leave has a positive effect on women's wages, and that mothers who have leave coverage and use it to take leave and return to work received a wage premium almost large enough to offset the negative differential associated with having a child (Ruhm

---

16. Another possibly relevant change in the composition of the workforce is the increase in highly skilled women opting out of the labor market in the 2000s. However, according to Heather Boushey (2008), this trend has been primarily driven by the weak economy and has affected both nonmothers and mothers, suggesting that it is not likely to explain changes in the wage gap between mothers and nonmothers (see also Byker in this volume).

1998; Waldfogel 1998b). On the other hand, researchers testing the effect of the Family and Medical Leave Act—which provides eligible mothers only an unpaid leave of twelve weeks—have found no such positive effect (Waldfogel 1999; Baum 2003). These results support the idea that childbirth requires reallocation of time, resources, and effort within the family. It therefore follows that in the absence of strong labor-market attachment and employment protection policies, childbirth may become a potential point of temporary or permanent exit for women (Becker 1981, 1985; Blau and Kahn 2013). Leaving the labor market reduces women's cumulative work experience and lowers their chances of advancement within a profession, factors that contribute to lower earnings for women with children. Given the importance of continued labor-force attachment and better job matches for wages, the lack of strong work-family policies is likely to have a negative effect on the wages of women with children. These developments (or lack) thus predict an increasing, or at best, a stagnating family wage gap. We find these ideas helpful in explaining the divergent trends in the family wage gap by number of children.

Although we cannot formally test explanations for what we find in terms of both change and lack of change in the family gap over time, we hope that our results will shed light on the role of these various factors. More immediately, they also provide some information about potential winners and losers as U.S. gender and work roles continue to evolve. The good news is that married women who have children seem to face much smaller gaps than they did in the past—indeed, their wages are now on a par or above those of married women without children. But the bad news is that unmarried mothers seem to face larger family gaps than their married peers and larger gaps than their group faced in the past. Given single women's heavy reliance on their own earnings, it is particularly concerning that they should face lower wages when they have children. Unlike in married families, we cannot look to their spouses to help take up the slack. We can however look to employer and public policies, including in the all important domains of paid leave, childcare, and workplace flexibility.

APPENDIX

Figure A1. Women's Employment Rates (%), Motherhood Status

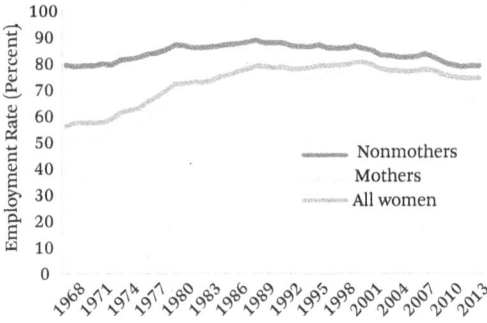

Source: Authors' calculations based on CPS data (sourced from King et al. 2010).
Note: Sample is restricted to prime working age, twenty-five to forty-four years; employment rate = (No. of respondents reporting >0 weeks worked last year / Total no. of respondents) * 100; motherhood status is defined by the presence of children under age eighteen in the household.

Figure A2. Women's Employment Rates (%), Number of Children

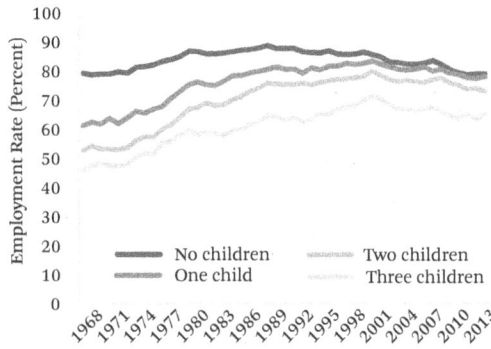

Source: Authors' calculations based on CPS data (sourced from King et al. 2010).
Note: See note to figure A1.

Figure A3. Family Wage Gap, Coefficients on Mother from OLS Regression on ln Hourly Wage with Confidence Intervals

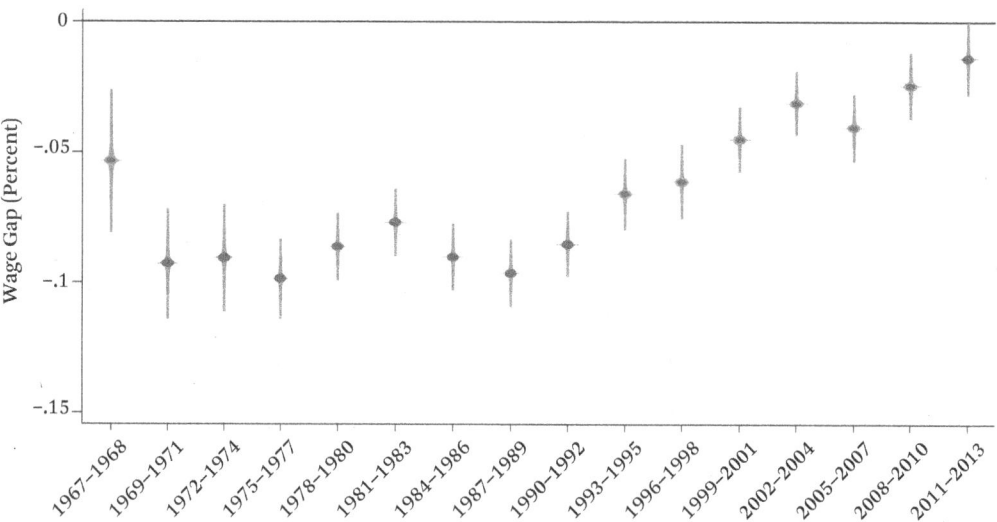

Source: Authors' calculations based on CPS data (sourced from King et al. 2010).
Notes: Results from OLS regression of ln hourly wages (in 2014 dollars) on *mother* dummy variable. Sample is restricted to prime working age, twenty-five to forty-four years; motherhood status is defined by the presence of children under age eighteen in the household. All models (including selection models) include controls for age, age_squared, and dummies for education, married, as well as year.

Figure A4. Family Wage Gap, OLS and AIPW Models

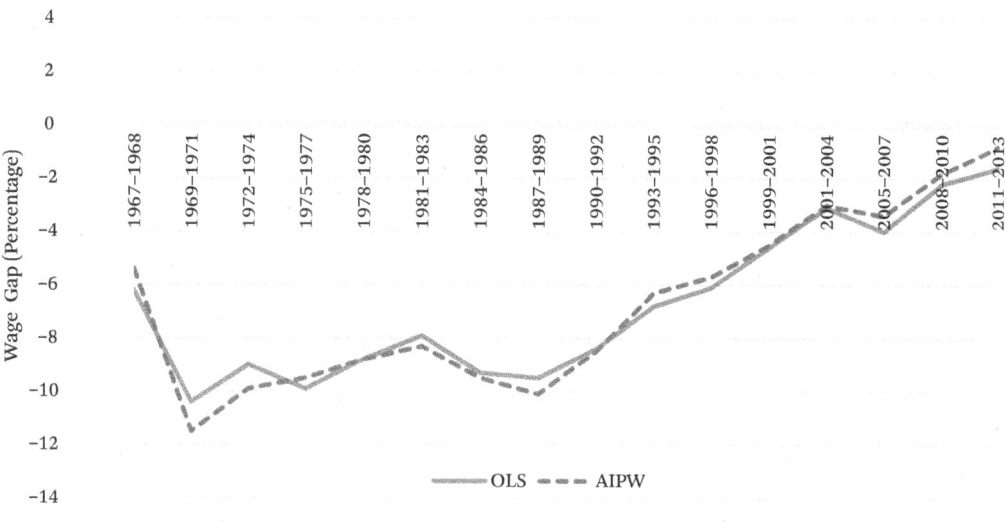

Source: Authors' calculations based on CPS data (sourced from King et al. 2010).
Notes: See notes to figure A3.

Figure A5. Family Wage Gap, Immigration Status

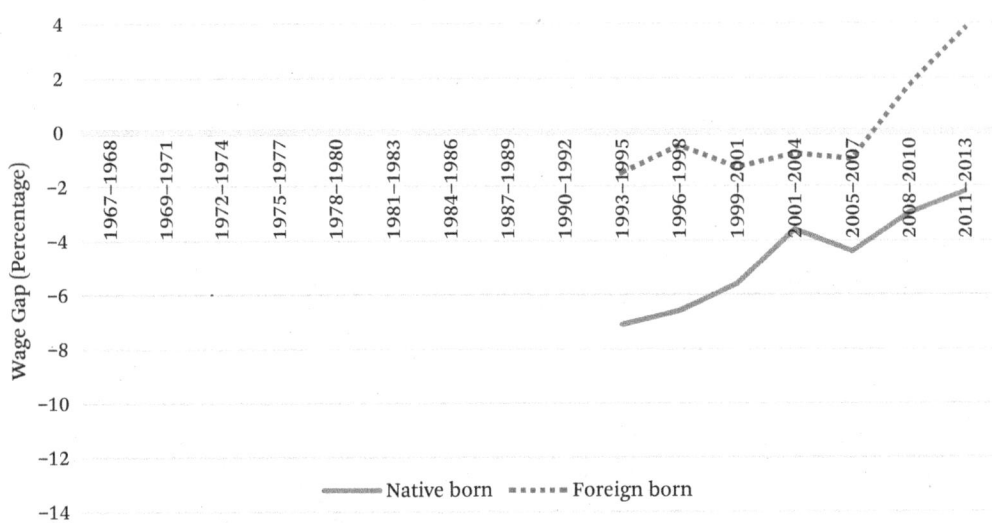

Source: Authors' calculations based on CPS data (sourced from King et al. 2010).
Notes: Results from OLS regression of ln hourly wages (in 2014 dollars) on *mother* dummy variable. Sample is restricted to prime working age, twenty-five to forty-four years; motherhood status is defined by the presence of children under age eighteen in the household. All models include controls for age, age_squared, and dummies for race, married, education as well as year. Coefficients are not significant in models for foreign-born women (except between 2011 and 2013) All other coefficients are significant. Graphs showing estimated coefficients on *mother* and confidence intervals available on request.

Table A1. Descriptive Statistics, 1967–1977

	1967–1968		1969–1971		1972–1974		1975–1977	
	Mother	Nonmother	Mother	Nonmother	Mother	Nonmother	Mother	Nonmother
Age	34.6	34.1	34.5	33.5	34.0	32.4	33.9	31.8
	(0.05)	(0.09)	(0.04)	(0.077)	(0.04)	(0.072)	(0.04)	(0.059)
Hours worked	32.3	37.1	31.9	36.7	32.3	36.9	33.9	38.6
	(0.093)	(0.122)	(0.078)	(0.107)	(0.077)	(0.103)	(0.073)	(0.076)
Weeks worked	37.8	44.9	37.7	44.8	38.3	45.2	38.7	45.5
	(0.147)	(0.165)	(0.121)	(0.140)	(0.119)	(0.130)	(0.107)	(0.117)
Education								
Less than high school	33%	23%	29%	21%	24%	16%	21%	12%
High school	47%	44%	49%	43%	50%	39%	49%	36%
Some college	10%	13%	12%	14%	14%	17%	16%	20%
Graduate	10%	20%	10%	22%	13%	29%	14%	32%
Relationship								
Married	84%	50%	84%	49%	81%	51%	80%	48%
Not married	16%	50%	16%	51%	19%	49%	20%	52%
Race								
White	85%	84%	85%	84%	85%	87%	86%	87%
Black	14%	14%	14%	14%	13%	11%	12%	10%
Full time	73%	91%	71%	91%	72%	90%	68%	88%
Part time	27%	9%	29%	9%	28%	10%	32%	13%
Observation	12,472	5,308	18,496	7,621	18,514	8,311	24,009	11,237

Source: Authors' compilation based on CPS data (sources from King et al. 2010).

Note: Sample is restricted to prime working age, twenty-five to forty-four years; motherhood status is defined by the presence of children under age eighteen in the household.

Table A2. Descriptive Statistics, 1978–1989

	1978–1980		1981–1983		1984–1986		1987–1989	
	Mother	Nonmother	Mother	Nonmother	Mother	Nonmother	Mother	Nonmother
Age	33.8	31.8	33.9	32.2	34.2	32.6	34.4	33.1
	(0.03)	(0.048)	(0.03)	(0.045)	(0.03)	(0.043)	(0.02)	(0.043)
Hours worked	34.2	38.7	34.1	38.5	34.5	39.2	35.0	39.7
	(0.063)	(0.067)	(0.063)	(0.066)	(0.061)	(0.062)	(0.060)	(0.060)
Weeks worked	40.0	45.9	41.3	46.3	42.3	46.9	43.1	47.7
	(0.091)	(0.094)	(0.089)	(0.088)	(0.083)	(0.078)	(0.080)	(0.071)
Education								
Less than high school	17%	10%	14%	8%	12%	8%	11%	7%
High school	48%	36%	47%	36%	46%	36%	46%	35%
Some college	19%	21%	21%	22%	22%	23%	23%	23%
Graduate	16%	33%	18%	34%	20%	34%	20%	35%
Relationship								
Married	79%	45%	78%	43%	78%	43%	77%	43%
Not married	21%	55%	22%	57%	22%	58%	23%	57%
Race								
White	86%	87%	85%	87%	85%	87%	85%	87%
Black	11%	10%	11%	9%	11%	10%	12%	10%
Full time	69%	87%	68%	86%	69%	87%	70%	88%
Part time	31%	13%	32%	14%	31%	13%	30%	12%
Observation	30,957	16,052	30,248	17,659	32,325	20,007	33,110	20,783

Source: Authors' compilation based on CPS data (sources from King et al. 2010).
Note: Sample is restricted to prime working age, twenty-five to forty-four years; motherhood status is defined by the presence of children under age eighteen in the household.

Table A3. Descriptive Statistics, 1990–2001

	1990–1992		1993–1995		1996–1998		1999–2001	
	Mother	Nonmother	Mother	Nonmother	Mother	Nonmother	Mother	Nonmother
Age	34.9	33.6	35.1	33.6	35.3	33.9	35.6	34.1
	(0.029)	(0.042)	(0.030)	(0.045)	(0.032)	(0.048)	(0.025)	(0.043)
Hours worked	35.4	39.7	35.6	39.9	36.1	40.0	36.3	40.2
	(0.058)	(0.060)	(0.062)	(0.068)	(0.063)	(0.071)	(0.050)	(0.063)
Weeks worked	43.8	47.4	44.3	47.6	45.0	47.8	45.7	48.1
	(0.076)	(0.071)	(0.078)	(0.076)	(0.078)	(0.078)	(0.059)	(0.068)
Education								
Less than high school	10%	7%	10%	7%	10%	6%	9%	7%
High school	40%	31%	35%	28%	35%	27%	32%	26%
Some college	28%	27%	33%	29%	32%	29%	33%	29%
Graduate	21%	35%	23%	36%	23%	38%	26%	38%
Relationship								
Married	77%	42%	75%	41%	74%	39%	73%	38%
Not married	24%	58%	25%	59%	27%	61%	27%	63%
Race								
White	84%	86%	83%	84%	84%	84%	83%	78%
Black	11%	10%	11%	10%	12%	11%	12%	14%
Full time	71%	87%	71%	87%	74%	87%	74%	88%
Part time	29%	13%	29%	13%	26%	13%	26%	12%
Observation	33,537	21,693	30,682	18,802	28,002	17,060	44,336	21,287

Source: Authors' compilation based on CPS data (sources from King et al. 2010).
Note: Sample is restricted to prime working age, twenty-five to forty-four years; motherhood status is defined by the presence of children under age eighteen in the household.

Table A4. Descriptive Statistics, 2002–2013

	2002–2004		2005–2007				2008–2010				2011–2013	
	Mother	Nonmother	Mother	Nonmother			Mother	Nonmother			Mother	Nonmother
Age	35.7	34.2	35.6	33.7			35.6	33.3			35.6	33.2
	(0.025)	(0.043)	(0.026)	(0.044)			(0.026)	(0.043)			(0.029)	(0.044)
Hours worked	36.1	39.6	36.6	39.8			36.4	39.3			36.7	39.1
	(0.049)	(0.062)	(0.049)	(0.063)			(0.050)	(0.065)			(0.055)	(0.069)
Weeks worked	46.0	47.9	46.4	48.4			46.3	47.9			46.6	48.1
	(0.056)	(0.070)	(0.057)	(0.067)			(0.059)	(0.071)			(0.063)	(0.073)
Education												
Less than high school	8%	7%	8%	6%			8%	6%			7%	5%
High school	30%	26%	28%	24%			25%	22%			22%	20%
Some college	34%	27%	33%	28%			33%	27%			32%	27%
Graduate	28%	40%	31%	42%			35%	45%			38%	48%
Relationship												
Married	72%	37%	71%	35%			71%	33%			69%	31%
Not married	28%	63%	29%	65%			29%	67%			31%	69%
Race												
White	82%	76%	81%	74%			80%	73%			80%	73%
Black	12%	15%	12%	15%			12%	15%			12%	14%
Full time	74%	87%	76%	87%			75%	85%			75%	84%
Part time	26%	13%	25%	13%			25%	15%			25%	16%
Observation	47,392	21,626	43,892	20,470			41,488	21,065			33,704	18,839

Source: Authors' compilation based on CPS data (sources from King et al. 2010).
Note: Sample is restricted to prime working age, twenty-five to forty-four years; motherhood status is defined by the presence of children under age eighteen in the household.

REFERENCES

Amuedo-Dorantes, Catalina, and Jean Kimmel. 2005. "The Motherhood Wage Gap for Women in the United States: The Importance of College and Fertility Delay." *Review of Economics of the Household* 3(1): 17–48.

———. 2008. "New Evidence on the Motherhood Wage Gap." *IZA* discussion paper no. 3662. Bonn: Institute for the Study of Labor.

Anderson, Deborah J., Melissa Binder, and Kate Krause. 2002. "The Motherhood Wage Penalty: Which Mothers Pay It and Why?" *American Economic Review* 92(2): 354–58.

———. 2003. "Motherhood Wage Penalty Revisited: Experience, Heterogeneity, Work Effort, and Work-Schedule Flexibility." *Industrial and Labor Relations Review* 56(2): 273–94.

Austin, Peter C. 2011. "An Introduction to Propensity Score Methods for Reducing the Effects of Confounding in Observational Studies." *Multivariate Behavioral Research* 46(3): 399–424.

Avellar, Sarah, and Pamela J. Smock. 2003. "Has the Price of Motherhood Declined over Time? A Cross-Cohort Comparison of the Motherhood Wage Penalty." *Journal of Marriage and Family* 65(3): 597–607.

Bang, Heejung, and James M. Robins. 2005. "Doubly Robust Estimation in Missing Data and Causal Inference Models." *Biometrics* 61(4): 962–72.

Baum, Charles L., II. 2002. "The Effect of Work Interruptions on Women's Wages." *Labour* 16(1): 1–37.

———. 2003. "The Effect of State Maternity Leave Legislation and the 1993 Family and Medical Leave Act on Employment and Wages." *Labour Economics* 10(5): 573–96.

Becker, Gary S. 1981. *A Treatise on the Family*. Cambridge, Mass.: Harvard University Press.

———. 1985. "Human Capital, Effort, and the Sexual Division of Labor." *Journal of Labor Economics* 3(1): S33–S58.

Benard, Stephen, and Shelley J. Correll. 2010. "Normative Discrimination and the Motherhood Penalty." *Gender and Society* 24(5): 616–46.

Bianchi, Suzanne M. 2011. "Family Change and Time Allocation in American Families." *Annals of the American Academy of Political and Social Science* 638(1): 21–44.

Blau, Francine D., and Lawrence M. Kahn. 2013. "Female Labor Supply: Why Is the United States Falling Behind?" *The American Economic Review* 103(3): 251–56.

Boushey, Heather. 2008. "Opting Out? The Effect of Children on Women's Employment in the United States." *Feminist Economics* 14(1): 1–36.

Buchmann, Claudia, and Anne McDaniel. 2016. "Motherhood and the Wages of Women in Professional Occupations." *RSF: The Russell Sage Journal of the Social Sciences* 2(4). doi: 10.7758/RSF.2016.2.4.05.

Budig, Michelle J., and Paula England. 2001. "The Wage Penalty for Motherhood." *American Sociological Review* 66(2): 204–25.

Budig, Michelle J., and Melissa J. Hodges. 2010. "Differences in Disadvantage: Variation in the Motherhood Penalty across White Women's Earnings Distribution." *American Sociological Review* 75(5): 705–28.

———. 2014. "Statistical Models and Empirical Evidence for Differences in the Motherhood Penalty Across the Earnings Distribution." *American Sociological Review* 79(2): 358–64.

Budig, Michelle J., Joya Misra, and Irene Boeckmann. 2012. "How Cultural Attitudes and Work-Family Policies Combine to Predict Maternal Earnings Cross-Nationally." Paper presented at the Population Association of America Annual Meeting. San Francisco (May 3–5, 2012).

Cooke, Lynn Prince. 2014. "Gendered Parenthood Penalties and Premiums Across the Earnings Distribution in Australia, the United Kingdom, and the United States." *European Sociological Review* 30(3): 360–72.

Correll, Shelley J., Stephen Benard, and In Paik. 2007. "Getting a Job: Is There a Motherhood Penalty?" *American Journal of Sociology* 112(5): 1297–339.

England, Paula, Jonathan Bearak, Michelle Budig, and Melissa Hodges. Forthcoming. "Do Highly Paid, Highly Skilled Women Experience the Largest Motherhood Penalty?" *American Sociological Review*.

Fuchs, Victor R. 1988. *Women's Quest for Economic Equality*. Cambridge, Mass.: Harvard University Press.

Funk, Michele Jonsson, Daniel Westreich, Chris Wiesen, Til Stürmer, M. Alan Brookhart, and Marie Davidian. 2011. "Doubly Robust Estimation of Causal Effects." *American Journal of Epidemiology* 173(7): 761–67.

Gangl, Markus, and Andrea Ziefle. 2009. "Motherhood, Labor Force Behavior, and Women's Careers: An Empirical Assessment of the Wage Penalty for Motherhood in Britain, Germany, and the United States." *Demography* 46(2): 341–69.

Glauber, Rebecca. 2007. "Marriage and the Motherhood Wage Penalty Among African Americans, Hispanics, and Whites." *Journal of Marriage and Family* 69(4): 951–61.

———. 2013. "Increasing Inequality: Trends in the Motherhood Wage Penalty, 1980–2010." Paper presented at the Population Association of America Annual Meeting. New Orleans (April 12, 2013).

Glynn, Adam N., and Kevin M. Quinn. 2010. "An Introduction to the Augmented Inverse Propensity Weighted Estimator." *Political Analysis* 18(1): 36–56.

Goldin, Claudia. 2014. "A Grand Gender Convergence: Its Last Chapter." *American Economic Review* 104(4): 1091–19.

Gornick, Janet C., and Marcia K. Meyers. 2003. *Families That Work: Policies for Reconciling Parenthood and Employment*. New York: Russell Sage Foundation.

Gough, Margaret, and Mary Noonan. 2013. "A Review of the Motherhood Wage Penalty in the United States." *Sociology Compass* 7(4): 328–42.

Grimshaw, Damian, and Jill Rubery. 2015. "The Motherhood Pay Gap: A Review of the Issues, Theory and International Evidence." *Conditions of Work and Employment Series* no. 57. Geneva: International Labour Office.

Harkness, Susan, and Jane Waldfogel. 2003. "The Family Gap in Pay: Evidence from Seven Industrialized Countries." *Research in Labor Economics* 22: 369–413.

Heckman, James J. 1979. "Sample Selection Bias as a Specification Error." *Econometrica: Journal of the Econometric Society* 47(1): 153–61.

Hill, Martha S. 1979. "The Wage Effects of Marital Status and Children." *Journal of Human Resources* 14(4): 579–94.

Killewald, Alexandra, and Jonathan Bearak. 2014. "Is the Motherhood Penalty Larger for Low-Wage Women? A Comment on Quantile Regression." *American Sociological Review* 79(2): 350–57.

King, Miriam, Steven Ruggles, J. Trent Alexander, Sarah Flood, Katie Genadek, Matthew B. Schroeder, Brandon Trampe, and Rebecca Vick. 2010. Integrated Public Use Microdata Series, Current Population Survey: Version 3.0 [Machine-readable database]. Minneapolis: University of Minnesota.

Korenman, Sanders, and David Neumark. 1992. "Marriage, Motherhood, and Wages." *Journal of Human Resources* 27(2): 233–55.

Larrimore, Jeff, Richard V. Burkhauser, Shuaizhang Feng, and Laura Zayatz. 2008. "Consistent Cell Means for Topcoded Incomes in the Public Use March CPS (1976–2007)." *Journal of Economic and Social Measurement* 33(2/3): 89–128.

Laughlin, Lynda Lvonne. 2011. *Maternity Leave and Employment Patterns of First-Time Mothers: 1961–2008*. Washington: U.S. Census Bureau.

Loughran, David S., and Julie M. Zissimopoulos. 2009. "Why Wait? The Effect of Marriage and Childbearing on the Wages of Men and Women." *Journal of Human Resources* 44(2): 326–49.

Mishel, Lawrence, and Heidi Shierholz. 2011. *State of Working America*. Washington, D.C.: Economic Policy Institute.

Misra, Joya, Michelle J. Budig, and Stephanie Moller. 2007. "Reconciliation Policies and the Effects of Motherhood on Employment, Earnings, and Poverty." *Journal of Comparative Policy Analysis* 9(2): 135–55.

Pal, Ipshita, and Jane Waldfogel. 2014. "Re-Visiting the Family Gap in Pay in the United States." Columbia Population Research Center (CPRC) working paper no. 14-02. New York: Columbia University.

Parker, Kim, and Wendy Wang. 2013. *Modern Parenthood: Roles of Moms and Dads Converge as They Balance Work and Family*. Washington, D.C.: Pew Research Center.

Robins, James M., and Andrea Rotnitzky. 1995. "Semiparametric Efficiency in Multivariate Regression Models with Missing Data." *Journal of American Statistical Association* 90(429): 122–29.

Robins, James M., Andrea Rotnitzky, and Lue Ping Zhao. 1994. "Estimation of Regression Coefficients When Some Regressors Are Not Always Observed." *Journal of the American Statistical Association* 89(427): 846–66.

Rosenbaum, Paul R., and Donald B. Rubin. 1983. "The Central Role of the Propensity Score in Observational Studies for Causal Effects." *Biometrika* 70(1): 41–55.

———. 1984. "Reducing Bias in Observational Studies Using Sub-Classification on the Propensity

Score." *Journal of the American Statistical Association* 79(387): 516–24.

———. 1985. "Constructing a Control Group Using Multivariate Matched Sampling Methods that Incorporate the Propensity Score." *American Statistician* 39(1): 33–38.

Rotnitzky, Andrea, Quanhong Lei, Mariela Sued, and James M. Robins. 2012. "Improved Double-Robust Estimation in Missing Data and Causal Inference Models." *Biometrika* 99(2): 439–56.

Ruhm, Christopher J. 1998. "The Economic Consequences of Parental Leave Mandates: Lessons from Europe." *Quarterly Journal of Economics* 108(1): 285–317.

Scharfstein, D. O., Andrea Rotnitzky, and James M. Robins. 1999. "Rejoinder." *Journal of the American Statistical Association* 94(448): 1135–46.

Schmitt, John. 2003. "Creating a Consistent Hourly Wage Series from the Current Population Survey's Outgoing Rotation Group, 1979–2002." Washington, D.C.: Center for Economic and Policy Research.

Sigle-Rushton, Wendy, and Jane Waldfogel. 2007. "Motherhood and Women's Earnings in Anglo-American, Continental European, and Nordic Countries." *Feminist Economics* 13(2): 55–91.

Srivastava, Anjali, and William M. Rodgers III. 2013. "The Motherhood Wage Gap for U.S. First-Generation Immigrant and Native Women." *National Poverty Center* working paper series no. 13-08. Ann Arbor: University of Michigan. Accessed April 5, 2016. http://www.npc.umich.edu/publications/working_papers/.

Słoczyński, Tymon, and Jeffrey M. Wooldridge. 2014. "A General Double Robustness Result for Estimating Average Treatment Effects." *IZA* discussion paper no. 8084. Bonn: Institute for the Study of Labor.

Tan, Zhiquiang. 2010. "Bounded, Efficient and Doubly Robust Estimation with Inverse Weighting." *Biometrika* 97(3): 661–82.

Taniguchi, Hiromi. 1999. "The Timing of Childbearing and Women's Wages." *Journal of Marriage and the Family* 61(4): 1008–19.

Todd, Erin L. 2001. "Educational Attainment and Family Gaps in Women's Wages: Evidence from Five Industrialized Countries." *LIS* working paper no. 246. Esch-Belval: Luxembourg Income Study.

Tsiatis, Anastasios A. 2006. *Semiparametric Theory and Missing Data*. New York: Springer.

Waldfogel, Jane. 1997. "The Effect of Children on Women's Wages." *American Sociological Review* 62(2): 209–17.

———. 1998a. "Understanding the 'Family Gap' in Pay for Women with Children." *Journal of Economic Perspectives* 12(1): 137–56.

———. 1998b. "The Family Gap for Young Women in the United States and Britain: Can Maternity Leave Make a Difference?" *Journal of Labor Economics* 16(3): 505–45.

Weeden, Kim A., Youngjoo Cha, and Mauricio Bucca. 2016. "Long Work Hours, Part-Time Work, and Trends in the Gender Gap in Pay, the Motherhood Wage Penalty, and the Fatherhood Wage Premium." *RSF: The Russell Sage Journal of the Social Sciences* 2(4). doi: 10.7758/RSF.2016.2.4.03.

Wilde, Elizabeth Ty, Lily Batchelder, and David T. Ellwood. 2010. "The Mommy Track Divides: The Impact of Childbearing on Wages of Women of Differing Skill Levels." *NBER* working paper no. w16582. Cambridge, Mass.: National Bureau of Economic Research.

Winder, Katie L. 2008. "Endogenous Fertility and the Motherhood Wage Penalty." Technical Report. Merced: University of California.

Wooldridge, Jeffrey M. 2007. "Inverse Probability Weighted Estimation for General Missing Data Problems." *Journal of Econometrics* 141(2): 1281–301.

———. 2010. *Econometric Analysis of Cross Section and Panel Data*, 2nd ed. Cambridge, Mass.: MIT Press.

Motherhood and the Wages of Women in Professional Occupations

CLAUDIA BUCHMANN AND ANNE McDANIEL

It is well established that mothers are paid less than childless women and that fathers tend to earn higher wages relative to childless men, but we do not know whether these findings apply to workers in all occupations. Using IPUMS and ACS data from 1980 and 2010, we examine the family wage gap for highly educated professionals, the most advantaged sector of the occupational distribution. Results indicate that the size of the negative wage differential for motherhood has declined over time in all professions. Moreover, in the traditionally male-dominated professions of STEM, medicine, and law, women with children experience a positive wage differential, whereas their counterparts in female-dominated professions continue to experience a negative one. The positive differential for fatherhood has remained stable over time. These findings underscore the growing heterogeneity of women's experiences in combining work and family and raise important questions for further research.

Keywords: work, family, professional women, wages

In 2009, American women reached an important milestone in the world of work. For the first time in history, women were the majority (51.4 percent) of workers in highly paid managerial and professional occupations despite being only 47 percent of the total workforce (Chao and Rones 2007). This milestone is undoubtedly related to widespread societal changes that are well documented elsewhere and include rapid rises in women's educational attainment (DiPrete and Buchmann 2013), declining discrimination against women in the labor market, the expansion of work-family policies in many workplaces (Gornick and Meyers 2003), and a host of other factors.

As women's labor-force participation has increased substantially, they have also made inroads into previously male-dominated occupations. Among college-educated thirty- to forty-four-year-olds, women now make up 51 percent of postsecondary education professionals, 45 percent of business professionals, 41 percent of attorneys, and 45 percent of medical professionals (see figure 1). These tradi-

Claudia Buchmann is professor of sociology at the Ohio State University. **Anne McDaniel** is associate director in the Center for the Study of Student Life at the Ohio State University.

This project was supported by Award Number R01EB010584 from the National Institute of Biomedical Imaging and Bioengineering and a Coca Cola Critical Difference for Women Grant Program at the Ohio State University. The content is solely the responsibility of the authors and does not necessarily represent the official views of the National Institute of Biomedical Imaging and Bioengineering or the National Institutes of Health. Siqi Han provided research assistance. We appreciate helpful comments from Martha Bailey, Tom DiPrete, and anonymous reviewers. Direct correspondence to: Claudia Buchmann at buchmann.4@osu.edu, The Ohio State University Department of Sociology, 238 Townshend Hall 1885 Neil Avenue Mall, Columbus, OH 43210; and Anne McDaniel at mcdaniel.145@osu.edu, The Ohio State University Center for the Study of Student Life, 517 Lincoln Tower, 1800 Cannon Drive, Columbus, OH 43210.

Figure 1. Women's Share of Professional Occupations in 1960, 1980, and 2010

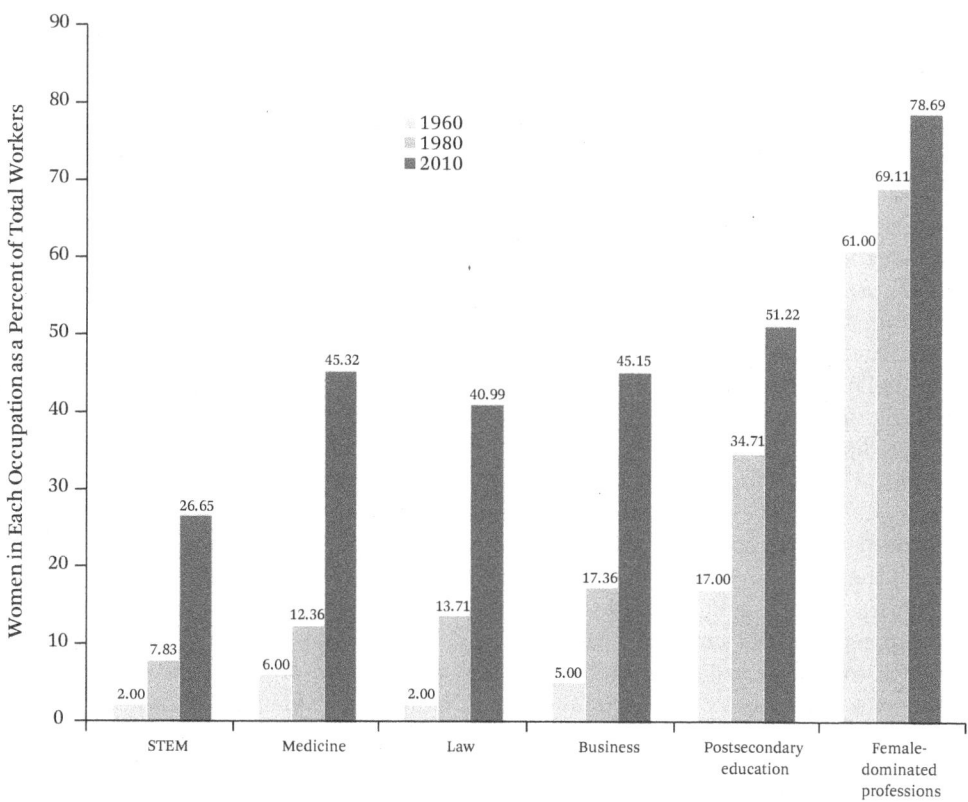

Source: Authors' calculations.

tionally male-dominated professions are often characterized as having higher wages, greater autonomy, and better opportunities for promotion than other occupations (Glass 1990), but they have also typically entailed longer work hours and norms of overwork (Jacobs and Gerson 2004; Cha 2013). Thus it is an open question whether women in traditionally male-dominated professions are advantaged or disadvantaged in their ability to combine work and family, relative to other women.

Women in demanding professions are said to experience "competing devotions" (Blair-Loy 2003) to their careers and their families, both of which are "greedy institutions" (Coser 1974). This may be especially true for women in the United States, which has no publicly provided childcare and no national policy of paid parental leave (Percheski 2008; Gornick and Meyers 2003). One of the most prevalent explanations for occupational sex segregation among supply-side theorists is that women choose jobs that maximize their ability to combine paid work and family responsibilities (Marini and Brinton 1984) and that as a result they enter traditionally female-dominated occupations that offer greater flexibility and fewer work hours (Glass 1990). But the recent rise of women in several traditionally male-dominated professions raises important questions about the degree to which different occupations offer amenities conducive to balancing work and family demands. Are more women entering traditionally male-dominated professions regardless of the work-family challenges they impose and merely conforming to the demands of the professions? Or have some professions changed to offer more workplace flexibility thus enabling greater work-family balance for women?

One indicator of women's challenges in combining work and family is the consistent finding that mothers earn less than childless women. The family wage gap—the differential in wages between women with children and women without children—has been documented across studies using a variety of model specifications and for many industrialized societies (Gough and Noonan 2013; Harkness and Walfogel 2003; Budig and England 2001). A family wage gap exists for women of varying levels of education (Anderson, Binder, and Krause 2002), earnings (Budig and Hodges 2014), race and ethnic status (Budig and England 2001; Glauber 2007), age at childbirth (Taniguchi 1999), and cohort (Avellar and Smock 2003). In contrast, men experience a positive wage differential for fatherhood, in that fathers tend to earn more than childless men (Glauber 2008; Hodges and Budig 2010; Percheski and Wildeman 2008). The differential association between parenthood and men's and women's wages is thought to result from gendered responses to having children, where women reduce work hours to care for children and men increase work hours to provide for their family, as well as employer discrimination against mothers and favoritism toward fathers (Coltrane 1997).

In this paper, we advance the understanding of the family wage gap in three ways. First, we examine the degree to which it has changed among college-educated women in professional and managerial occupations (professional occupations) from 1980 to 2010 with data from the Integrated Public Use Microdata Series (IPUMS) of the U.S. Census and the American Community Survey (ACS). Women's experiences have become more heterogeneous over time in terms of educational attainment and occupational choices, but few studies have explored differences in the association between parenthood and wages over time or have examined such trends beyond the late 1990s (but see Pal and Waldfogel, this volume). We compare women across a range of educational and occupational groups to determine which groups have experienced the largest changes in the family wage gap.

Second, we investigate the family wage gap for highly educated women in professional occupations and examine differences for women in traditionally female-dominated and several male-dominated professions. Because most research has studied the family wage gap for women as a cohesive group, we know little about the degree to which the general finding holds for women in different occupations.

Third, to be as comprehensive as possible, we compare the family wage gap for women with that for men and examine the degree to which the association between parenthood and wages varies by race-ethnicity. Research on the family wage gap tends to focus either on women or men. Comparing their experiences provides a more complete picture of changing inequalities in the family wage gap—between men and women as well as among women and among men. We know from prior research that the negative wage differential for motherhood and the positive wage differential for fatherhood vary by race and ethnicity (Waldfogel 1997; Budig and England 2001; Glauber 2008; Greenman 2011).[1] However, we do not know whether or how they vary by race and ethnicity among highly educated men and women in different professions.

PRIOR RESEARCH

The differential in wages between women with children and women without children is well established in prior research. The reasons for the commonly-found negative association between motherhood and wages are complex (for a review, see Gough and Noonan 2013). Employers may discriminate against mothers in hiring, promotion, and compensation, likely because mothers are perceived as less committed to work (England 2005). Women often take maternity leave and reduce their work hours when they have a child, which results in the loss of work experience—a key determinant of higher wages, promotion, and future productivity (Budig and England 2001; Staff and Mortimer 2012).

In contrast, the positive wage differential

---

1. White women experience a 6 percent, 10 percent, and 7 percent negative wage differential for one, two, and three or more children, whereas black women and Latinas tend to experience smaller ones (Glauber 2007). Black men experience a smaller positive wage differential for fatherhood than whites or Latinos (Glauber 2008).

for fathers is believed to be due to "men's gender-traditional response to the birth of a child, wherein normatively good fathers increase their breadwinning capacity" (Hodges and Budig 2010, 718) by increasing work hours and effort when they have a child, particularly when mothers reduce work hours, thereby maximizing their earnings (Bianchi, Robinson, and Milkie 2006; Lundberg and Rose 2000). Some employers may favor fathers because of their fatherhood and perceived breadwinning status. To the degree that fathers are less involved in childcare than mothers, their earnings are less likely to be affected than those of mothers, even in inflexible jobs. At any rate, the positive wage differential for fatherhood persists even after controlling for a host of other relevant factors that include human capital, work hours, and effort (Glauber 2008; Lundberg and Rose 2000).

How has the family wage gap changed over time for women or men in the United States? Sarah Avellar and Pamela Smock (2003) compare the average wage gap for mothers and nonmothers for two cohorts of women (1975 to 1986 and 1986 to 1998) and find no differences between the two groups. Christine Percheski and Christopher Wildeman (2008) finds rising full-time, year-round employment rates across women born between 1906 and 1975, even for women in traditionally male-dominated professions and among mothers of young children. She also finds that the differences in employment rates between mothers and childless women are shrinking across cohorts (see also Boushey 2005). She does not examine whether the wage gap between mothers and childless women also declined over that period, however. Most recently, Ipshita Pal and Jane Waldfogel (this volume) find a decline in the family gap in wages over time, from about 5 to 6 percent in 1967 and 1968 to about 1 percent in 2011 through 2013, with variations for marital status, education, race-ethnicity, and immigration status.

There are several reasons to expect that the family wage gap declined between 1980 and 2010. Two of the purported mechanisms for the gap, discrimination and the traditional gender division of labor, have declined over the past thirty years. Federal legislation, including Title VII provisions of the Civil Rights Act of 1965 and the Family and Medical Leave Act, barred discrimination against women in the workplace and require employers to provide unpaid maternity leave. Since the middle of the 1970s, Americans have become more supportive of gender equality (Bolzendahl and Myers 2004). Moreover, some evidence indicates that traditional gender roles have eased in recent decades. The gender gap in time spent on housework and childcare has declined, especially among highly educated, dual-earner couples such that, by the late 1990s, the ratio of mothers' to fathers' time spent on housework and childcare decreased to 1.8 and 1.6, respectively (Sayer 2005; see also Hook 2006). Also, men's and women's attitudes toward work and family may be converging. A study by the Families and Work Institute finds that men and women are now equally likely to want jobs with greater responsibility (Galinsky, Aumann, and Bond 2009). These large-scale changes may have resulted in mothers taking less time off for childrearing as well as in employers discriminating less against mothers or reducing the penalty for time off for childrearing, which, coupled with changes in the selection of women into motherhood and into professions, could have led to a decline in the family wage gap. To determine whether the family wage gap declined generally for all women during this period, we examine the degree to which the association between parenthood and wages has changed for women between 1980 and 2010 and compare these changes with those for men over the same period.

GROWING HETEROGENEITY IN THE FAMILY WAGE GAP FOR WOMEN

Although large-scale societal changes may be related to overall changes in the family wage gap, we also expect that the gap has become increasingly heterogeneous for women over time. After all, the declines in inequality between women and men in many realms of society in recent decades have been coupled with increasing inequalities among women in terms of the resources they can bring to bear on managing work and family demands. For example, occupational sex segregation has declined most among those with a college degree, and professional and managerial jobs have become more integrated than clerical and blue-collar jobs have (Cotter, Hermsen, and Vanneman 2004). As a result, today college graduates work in dramatically less sex-segregated contexts than those at other educational levels.

The few studies that examine the heterogeneity of women's experiences find that some women experience smaller negative wage differentials for motherhood than others. For example, highly paid, highly educated women and those who delay childbearing to later ages experience a smaller family wage gap and, in some cases, earn higher wages than childless women (Taniguchi 1999; Anderson, Binder, and Krause 2002; Amuedo-Dorantes and Kimmel 2005). Analyses of the 1979 National Longitudinal Survey of Youth (NLSY79) find variations in the family wage gap across the wage distribution and, depending on estimates, either no gap or even a small positive wage differential for women at the very top of the distribution (Budig and Hodges 2014; Killewald and Bearak 2014). In addition, recent research examines heterogeneity in the association between fatherhood and wages. Alexandra Killewald (2013) finds that the positive wage differential for fatherhood exists only for married, residential, biological fathers.

Beyond considering heterogeneity among individuals with different attributes, there are good reasons to expect that variations across professions impact the family wage gap. If occupations vary in terms of workplace flexibility or penalties for job interruptions, the family wage gap may be smaller for women in some professions than in other professions. Some preliminary evidence supports this idea. Using data from the NLSY, Rebecca Glauber (2011) finds that among working women, mothers earn 5 percent less if they work in gender-integrated jobs and 12 percent less in female-dominated jobs than their counterparts in traditionally male-dominated jobs (including both professional and nonprofessional occupations). Glauber also finds that women in male-dominated and integrated jobs experience no negative wage differential for having one or two children. Using data from 1982 through 1993, Michelle Budig and Paula England find that the family wage gap was smaller for women in male-dominated (less than 35 percent female) professional or managerial occupations than women working in female-dominated occupations. They conclude that "high-level, 'male' jobs penalize women a bit less for having children," but do not speculate about why this is the case (2001, 219).

DATA AND METHODS

We analyze differences in wages for highly educated parents and nonparents working in elite occupations using decennial census data from the 1980 IPUMS 5 percent sample and the 2006–2010 ACS (Ruggles et al. 2010). Throughout the paper, we refer to the ACS data as *2010* or *the most recent period*. We seek to understand how parenthood is associated with wages across professional occupational groups; therefore, we restrict the sample to thirty- to forty-four-year-olds because they have most likely completed their education and established career and family formation trajectories (Hertz 2004). We further restrict the sample to those with a bachelor's degree or higher who are currently employed in professional occupations. This sample includes 17,413 women and 30,772 men in 1980 and 261,380 women and 227,643 men in 2010. Using ordinary least squares (OLS) regression, we analyze the family wage gap measured as logged hourly wages for separate models for each professional group of interest for 1980 and 2010; we create interacted models with the pooled samples from 1980 and 2010 to see whether the family wage gap is different at these two time points. We produce parallel analyses for men and discuss key findings as well as important differences between women and men where they are found.

Research on the wage differentials between mothers and childless women tends to use longitudinal data and individual fixed-effects models to examine changes in women's wages over their life course and control for factors that do not change over time. Budig and England (2001) report a 6.8 percent motherhood penalty from a fixed-effects model and an 8.1 percent motherhood penalty from an OLS model. Deborah Anderson, Melissa Binder, and Kate Krause (2002) report a 3.0 percent penalty from a fixed-effects model and a 5.2 percent penalty from an OLS model. Avellar and Smock (2003) report OLS estimates that are slightly

Table 1. Participation in the Labor Force, Thirty- to Forty-Four-Year-Olds, All

	1960		1980		2010	
	Percent	N	Percent	N	Percent	N
Women						
Nonprofessional, less than bachelor's degree	84.5	51,737	68.5	83,810	49.0	484,924
Nonprofessional, bachelor's degree or higher	2.8	1,682	6.1	7,469	12.8	126,556
Professional, less than bachelor's degree	7.0	4,292	11.2	13,688	11.8	116,460
Professional, bachelor's degree or higher	5.7	3,529	14.2	17,413	26.4	261,380
Total	100	61,240	100	122,380	100	989,320
Men						
Nonprofessional, less than bachelor's degree	78.3	109,488	62.4	108,666	56.7	624,236
Nonprofessional, bachelor's degree or higher	5.5	7,651	10.6	18,458	14.6	161,285
Professional, less than bachelor's degree	8.8	12,271	9.3	16,231	8.0	88,390
Professional, bachelor's degree or higher	7.4	10,459	17.7	30,772	20.7	227,643
Total	100	139,869	100	174,127	100	1,101,554

Source: Authors' calculations.
Note: Data are weighted.

smaller than fixed-effects estimates, but their general conclusions remain the same. Thus, overall, it appears that unobserved heterogeneity accounts for about 20 to 30 percent of the motherhood wage penalty. Because the IPUMS and ACS data we use here are cross-sectional, we are not able to estimate fixed-effects models, so it is possible that our estimates are biased by unobserved heterogeneity. The benefit of using IPUMS and ACS data is that we have appropriate sample sizes to analyze differences in the association between parenthood and wages for men and women across professions and over time. Sample sizes of women in traditionally male-dominated occupations like STEM, medicine, and law are small (see table 1) and therefore are not possible to study using longitudinal datasets like the NLSY.

Highly educated professional women make up only 5 percent of working women in 1960, 14 percent of working women in 1980, and 26 percent of working women in 2010. Highly educated professional men make up 7, 18, and 21 percent of the male labor force in 1960, 1980, and 2010, respectively (see tables 1 and 2). Although we focus on highly educated professional women, we also compare them with all employed women to see how they differ. For this analysis, we break the full sample of employed women into four categories: nonprofessionals with less than a college degree, nonprofessionals with at least a college degree, professionals with less than a college degree, and professionals with at least a college degree. Professional occupations include the six occupational categories discussed in the following section.

Occupational and Education Categories

The occupational classification scheme for the 1990 census offers a consistent, long-term classification of occupations comparable from 1960 to 2010. It contains 389 occupations that fall into seven broad occupational categories, including professional and managerial occupations.[2] We created a six-category occupational

---

2. These occupational categories include managerial and professional; technical, sales, and administrative; service; farming, forestry, and fishing; precision, production, craft, and repairers; operatives and laborers; and nonoccupational responses.

Table 2. Participation in the Labor Force, Thirty- to Forty-Four-Year-Olds, College Graduate Professionals

	1960		1980		2010	
	Percent	N	Percent	N	Percent	N
Women						
STEM	1.6	58	2.7	465	7.0	18,398
Medical professions	1.0	37	1.6	284	4.2	10,987
Law	0.2	7	1.2	213	2.8	7,278
Business	5.7	200	17.5	3,049	35.0	91,505
Postsecondary education	3.1	108	5.1	893	3.7	9,615
Female-dominated professions	88.4	3,119	71.8	12,509	47.3	123,597
Total	100	3,529	100	17,413	100	261,380
Men						
STEM	28.9	3,013	17.8	5,473	22.2	50,643
Medical professions	5.3	554	6.5	2,013	5.8	13,255
Law	3.2	341	4.4	1,341	4.6	10,477
Business	38.3	4,008	47.2	14,514	48.8	111,168
Postsecondary education	5.0	526	5.5	1,680	4.0	9,156
Female-dominated professions	19.3	2,017	18.7	5,751	14.5	32,944
Total	100.0	10,459	100	30,772	100	227,643

Source: Authors' calculations.
Note: Data are weighted.

code representing only professional and managerial occupations: STEM (mathematics, statistics, engineering, computer science, life science, and physical science); medicine (physicians, dentists, veterinarians, optometrists, podiatrists, and pharmacists); law (lawyers and judges); business (including managerial and management-related occupations);[3] postsecondary education; and female-dominated specialties (K–12 teachers; health professionals, excluding medical occupations that require a doctoral degree; librarians; and social workers).[4] See appendix for details. Women made up 69 percent of employees in female-dominated occupations in 1980 and 79 percent in 2010. The census records an individual's educational attainment in categories, the highest two are four years of college and five or more years of college. Our sample consists of individuals with at least four years (a bachelor's degree) or more.[5] Our models include a dummy variable indicating whether an individual completed a graduate or professional degree (five or more years of college, bachelor's degree is the refer-

---

3. Managerial and management-related professions both fall under the broader umbrella of business occupations but are separated because managerial represent higher-level business professions, including chief executives, legislatures, managers, and administrators. Management-related professions include accountants, insurance underwriters, human resource personnel, analysts, and other management support occupations. Both are included in our business category.

4. We exclude individuals working in the following professional occupations due to small sample sizes: archivists and curators, social scientists, recreation workers, clergy and religious workers, and writers-artists-entertainers-athletes.

5. Fewer than 1 percent of the sample either had no data on their years of schooling or responded that they received no schooling. They are excluded from the analysis.

ence category). Although this measure is not ideal because it does not distinguish between type of degree completed, it is the best approximation of advanced degree completion available in the data.

CHANGE IN WOMEN'S PARTICIPATION IN PROFESSIONAL OCCUPATIONS

Tables 1 and 2 show the distribution of women and men with or without a college degree in professional and nonprofessional occupations in 1960, 1980 and 2010. The percentage of women holding at least a bachelor's degree and employed in professional occupations was a very low 6 percent in 1960 and grew to 14 percent by 1980. This figure nearly doubled between 1980 and 2010, from 14 percent to 27 percent, as did the percentage of women with at least a bachelor's degree in nonprofessional occupations (from 7 percent to 14 percent). The percentage of women without a college degree employed in nonprofessional jobs shrank from a high 85 percent in 1960 to less than half of all working women (47 percent) in 2010. These figures underscore the rapid rise of women's college degree receipt and entry into professional occupations over the past several decades (DiPrete and Buchmann 2013). Over the same period, the percentage of men holding at least a bachelor's degree and employed in professional occupations more than doubled between 1960 and 1980 (from 7 to 18 percent) but increased only 4 percentage points (from 18 to 22 percent of male workers) between 1980 and 2010. Women's share of all highly educated professionals increased over time. In 1980, women made up 36 percent of professional workers with at least a college degree. By 2010, the figure was 53 percent (not shown).

Table 2 divides the sample of highly educated professionals into six categories: STEM, medical professions, law, business, postsecondary education, and female-dominated professions. One of the most striking changes over time is the exodus of women from traditionally female-dominated professions. Between 1960 and 2010, the number of professional women working in them declined from 88 percent to 47 percent. At the same time, women have made inroads into other professions, most notably business, where 35 percent of college-educated, professional women work in 2010 (versus 18 percent in 1980 and only 6 percent in 1960), and other traditionally male occupations. Fewer than 3 percent of women worked in STEM occupations in 1980, versus 7 percent in 2010. Between 1980 and 2010 the percentage of women working in medical professions increased from nearly 2 percent to more than 4 percent and in law from 1 percent to nearly 3 percent. Although these changes appear small, it is clear that women have moved into business, STEM, medicine, and law, and that these shifts have occurred mainly at the expense of female-dominated professions. The trends for men are less dramatic. Men's participation in female-dominated professions declined (from 19 percent in 1960 to 15 percent in 2010) and their participation in business rose (from 38 percent to 49 percent); their participation in all other professions remained relatively stable.

Figure 1 displays females as a percentage of total employees and shows that women came to make up a much larger share of workers in all six professional categories between 1960 and 2010. This figure underscores the dramatic rise of women in professional occupations, especially those once dominated by men. In light of these striking changes, it is important to ask how women's experiences in these occupations, in particular how the wages for mothers in these occupations relative to childless women, changed over time as more women entered professional occupations. It is also important to compare the experiences of women with those of men.

Dependent Variable

The dependent variable is the natural logarithm of hourly wages for the current occupation. It is derived from respondents' reported income, measured as total pretax income for the past twelve months, including wages, salaries, commissions, cash bonuses, tips, and other income received from an employer, expressed in constant 2014 dollars. We divide annual income by fifty-two weeks, then by the respondent's reported average number of hours worked in a typical week to arrive at average hourly wages. Following earlier research (such as Budig and England 2001), we bottom and top-code hourly wages at $1 and $200 to eliminate potential outliers.[6]

Independent Variables

To examine how parenthood status is related to wages, the main independent variable is a dummy variable measuring whether the individual has any biological, adopted, or stepchildren living in the home (1) or not (0).[7] Following Budig and England (2001), we control for average hours worked per week, industrial sector, and demographic factors. Wages vary across industrial sectors; for example, wages in the public sector tend to be lower than in the financial sector, so we include dummy variables for the industrial sector in which the respondent works.[8] Demographic controls include any education beyond a bachelor's degree (coded as five or more years of postsecondary education), age, age squared, marital status, and race.[9] Marital status is measured with dummy variables indicating currently married, divorced, or separated, with never married serving as the reference category.[10] Race is measured with a series of dummy variables indicating non-Latino black, Latino, Asian American or Pacific Islander, other (which includes American Indian–Alaskan Natives, biracial or multiracial individuals), and non-Latino white (the reference category). Descriptive statistics for all variables are presented by occupational category for 2010 in tables 3 and 4.

CHARACTERISTICS OF ELITE, PROFESSIONAL WOMEN

How do college-educated professional women compare with all other employed women in terms of their labor market and family characteristics? The descriptive statistics in tables 3 and 4 highlight some important differences. In 2010, employed women earn, on average, $20.83 per hour, whereas college-educated, professional women earn $29.94 per hour. College-educated, professional women also work more hours (40.2 per week on average, versus 38.2) and have fewer children (1.25 on average, versus 1.34) than other employed women. Finally, college-educated professionals are more likely to be married (71 percent) and less likely to be divorced (10 percent) than other employed women (of whom 63 percent are married and 17 percent are divorced).

Differences among women within professional occupations are also important. Women in postsecondary education and female-dominated professions earn the lowest hourly wage ($24.08 and $22.69, respectively). Women in medical professions ($48.28) and law ($45.86) earn more than women in other traditionally male-dominated occupations. Even among

---

6. Payments-in-kind or reimbursements for business expenses are not included. IPUMS recommends that income data are top-coded. Before, top- and bottom-coding hourly wages, we top-coded yearly income data. For 1980, income data are top-coded at $75,000 and for 2006-2010, income data are top-coded at 99.5th percentile of income within each state. The top codes for each state vary from a low of 169,000 to a high of 689,000. We replicated all results without top-coding the IPUMs/ACS data as suggested by IPUMs as well as the additional top- and bottom-coding of hourly wages to eliminate outliers.

7. This measure excludes children not currently living in the household. Because the sample comprises highly educated professional women, few are likely to have had children so young that those children are old enough to be living on their own. Although we would like to compare this measure with a woman's total fertility or the number of children ever born to her, these measures are not available in the data.

8. Industrial sectors include agriculture, forestry, and fisheries; mining; construction; manufacturing; transportation, communications, and public utilities; wholesale trade; retail trade; finance, insurance, and real estate; business and repair services; personal services; entertainment and recreation services; public administration; professional and related services; active duty military; and a category for missing or not applicable. Public administration is the reference category.

9. Models for lawyers and doctors do not include professional or graduate degree measure because all respondents in these occupations have completed a professional degree or graduate degree.

10. Currently divorced includes widowed because too few cases are available to analyze separately.

Table 3. Descriptive Statistics in 2010, All Women

	All Women	Nonprofessional, <BA	Nonprofessional, BA+	Professional, <BA	Professional, BA+
Hourly wages	20.83	14.77	23.66	20.59	29.94
	(11.31)	(7.61)	(12.02)	(9.19)	(13.27)
Number of children	1.34	1.42	1.12	1.51	1.25
	(1.19)	(1.22)	(1.13)	(1.19)	(1.14)
Hours worked	38.23	37.05	37.98	38.70	40.22
	(10.71)	(10.22)	(11.68)	(10.07)	(10.99)
Age	37.40	37.65	36.94	37.85	37.01
	(4.33)	(4.33)	(4.34)	(4.28)	(4.31)
Single	0.19	0.20	0.23	0.15	0.18
Married	0.63	0.58	0.65	0.66	0.71
Divorced	0.17	0.22	0.12	0.19	0.10
White	0.74	0.71	0.73	0.77	0.77
African American	0.12	0.15	0.10	0.12	0.08
Latina	0.06	0.07	0.05	0.05	0.04
Asian	0.06	0.04	0.10	0.03	0.09
Other	0.02	0.03	0.02	0.03	0.02
Graduate degree	0.16	—	0.23	—	0.46

Source: Authors' calculations.
Note: Standard deviation in parentheses, wages are reported in 2014 dollars.

Table 4. Descriptive Statistics in 2010, STEM, Medical, Law, Business

	STEM	Medicine	Law	Business	Postsecondary Education	Female-Dominated Professions
Hourly wages	33.65	48.28	45.86	33.05	24.08	22.69
	(11.95)	(21.51)	(17.93)	(13.54)	(11.19)	(11.17)
Number of children	0.96	1.16	0.97	1.10	1.01	1.49
	(1.04)	(1.13)	(1.06)	(1.09)	(1.10)	(1.18)
Hours worked	40.96	44.95	44.50	42.31	37.37	37.58
	(8.56)	(15.77)	(11.16)	(9.87)	(14.38)	(10.49)
Age	36.67	36.45	36.44	37.20	36.94	37.08
	(4.38)	(4.24)	(4.26)	(4.28)	(4.29)	(4.31)
Single	0.23	0.19	0.25	0.21	0.23	0.16
Married	0.67	0.74	0.66	0.68	0.69	0.71
Divorced	0.10	0.06	0.08	0.11	0.09	0.13
White	0.66	0.62	0.80	0.76	0.76	0.73
African American	0.07	0.07	0.07	0.09	0.06	0.11
Latina	0.04	0.06	0.04	0.04	0.04	0.09
Asian	0.21	0.24	0.07	0.10	0.12	0.05
Other	0.02	0.01	0.02	0.02	0.02	0.02
Graduate degree	0.45	1.00	1.00	0.33	0.84	0.31

Source: Authors' calculations
Note: Standard deviations in parentheses, wages are reported in 2014 dollars.

Figure 2. Average Annual Income, Women

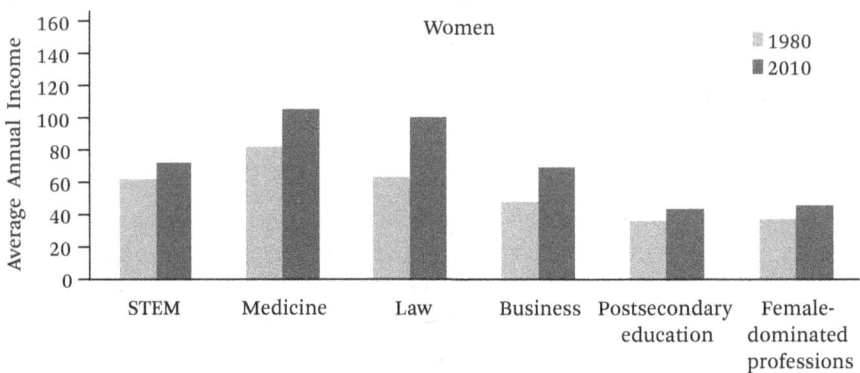

Source: Authors' calculations.

Figure 3. Average Annual Income, Men

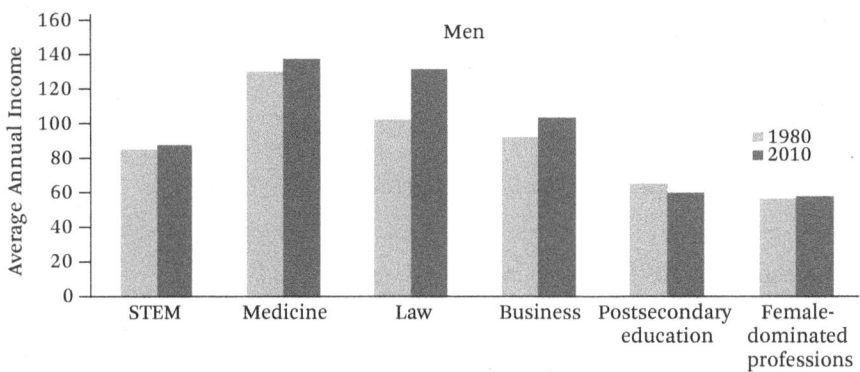

Source: Authors' calculations.

those with a graduate or professional degree, women earn an average hourly wage of $33.65 in STEM and $33.05 in business.

As Tanya Byker (this volume) and Kim Weeden, Youngjoo Cha, and Mauricio Bucca (this volume) explore in detail, hours worked are related to wage differentials between mothers and childless women, especially during the period after childbirth. Here we compare women's work hours across professional occupations. Women in medicine and law work the most hours per week (44.9 and 44.5), followed by women in business and STEM (42.3 and 40.9). Women in postsecondary education and female-dominated professions work fewer than forty hours per week, on average. Women in female-dominated professions also have the highest average number of children (1.49), followed by women in medicine (1.16); women in STEM and law have the fewest (0.96 and 0.97). In sum, women in medical professions stand out in that they earn the highest wages and work more hours but also have higher rates of marriage and more children. Women in law are similar to those in the medical professionals in that they enjoy higher wages and work longer hours, but have lower rates of marriage and fewer children than female medical professionals. Women in STEM professions have equally low marriage rates and number of children as their counterparts in law but earn lower average wages.

Figures 2 and 3 present average annual incomes for highly educated women and men in professional occupations in 1980 and 2010 reported in 2014 dollars. The higher earnings of women in medicine and law in 2010 are striking, as is their income growth between 1980

Table 5. OLS Regression of the Effect of Children on Women's Hourly Wages

	All Women	Professional, BA+	Professional, <BA	Nonprofessional, BA+	Nonprofessional, <BA
Model 1: 1980					
Children	−0.18*	−0.22*	−0.21*	−0.27*	−0.16*
	(0.01)	(0.01)	(0.02)	(0.02)	(0.01)
Constant	2.55**	2.6**	1.59*	4.24**	2.79**
	(0.19)	(0.45)	(0.54)	(0.82)	(0.23)
Adjusted R^2	0.12	0.07	0.06	0.09	0.07
N	122,380	17,413	13,688	7,469	83,810
Model 2: 2010					
Children	−0.03*	−0.02*	−0.08*	−0.02*	−0.03*
	(0.00)	(0.00)	(0.01)	(0.01)	(0.00)
Constant	0.47	0.52	0.65	−0.03	1.04**
	(0.07)	(0.13)	(0.21)	(0.21)	(0.11)
Adjusted R^2	0.23	0.09	0.07	0.11	0.08
N	989,320	261,380	116,460	126,556	484,924

Source: Authors' calculations.
Note: Models control for age, age^2, race, marital status, logged work hours, and industry.
Difference between effect of children for 1980 and 2010 is significant ($p < 0.001$) for all five columns.
*$p < 0.01$; ** $p < 0.001$

and 2010. Women's incomes in STEM, postsecondary education and female-dominated professions changed little, increasing by an average $7,000 over the period. Despite professional women's increasing wages over time, in 2010 they still earn less than men in all occupations.

THE FAMILY WAGE GAP

Before we examine the family wage gap for highly educated women in different professional occupations, we determine how the family wage gap has changed over time. The very low numbers of women in professional occupations precludes analysis of 1960 data, so this analysis is limited to 1980 and 2010. Table 5 presents the OLS regression of logged hourly wages on number of children for women in each professional and education group, after controlling for work hours, industry, and demographic factors. Model 1 presents the results for 1980; model 2, for 2010. Results align with prior research, in that they show a significant negative family wage gap in all professional and education groups in 1980 and 2010.

In another analysis, we pooled the sample of women in 1980 and 2010 and included an interaction between year and the dummy variable for children to see whether the family wage gap differed substantially in the two periods. The size of the family wage gap declined between 1980 and 2010 for all profession-education groups. In 1980, the logged hourly wages of women with children were 19 percent lower than those of childless women, but by 2010 this gap had declined to 3 percent.[11] In contrast, fathers in all professional and educational groups at both time points experienced a positive wage differential relative to nonfathers (not shown). Next we investigate whether the patterns for the family wage gap found in 1980 and 2010 differ for highly educated profession women in traditionally female-dominated and several male-dominated professions.

PARENTHOOD AND THE WAGES OF PROFESSIONAL WOMEN AND MEN

To assess differences in the relationship between parenthood and wages for different pro-

---

11. To calculate the percentage change in logged hourly wages for a 1 unit change in number of children, we exponentiate the coefficient.

Table 6. OLS Regression of the Effect of Children on Wages

	STEM			Medicine			Law		
	Women	Men	W:M	Women	Men	W:M	Women	Men	W:M
Model 1: 1980									
Children	−0.12	0.09**	**	−0.20	0.07		−0.16	0.16	
	(0.06)	(0.02)		(0.12)	(0.06)		(0.13)	(0.07)	
Constant	−1.03	3.88**		−1.51	1.09		−2.89	1.38	
	(2.37)	(0.54)		(4.40)	(1.75)		(5.39)	(2.52)	
Adjusted R²	0.10	0.16		0.13	0.16		0.05	0.08	
N	465	5,473		284	2,013		213	1,341	
Model 2: 2010			W:M			W:M			W:M
Children	0.04*	0.09**	**	0.10**	0.12**	**	0.05	0.11	**
	(0.01)	(0.01)		(0.02)	(0.02)		(0.02)	(0.02)	
Constant	1.47**	2.67**		−0.16	−3.17**		0.92	0.04	
	(0.45)	(0.24)		(0.71)	(0.65)		(0.73)	(0.72)	
Adjusted R²	0.07	0.10		0.13	0.24		0.06	0.07	
N	18,398	50,643		10,987	13,255		7,278	10,477	
Model 3: 1980 and 2010			W:M			W:M			W:M
Children	−0.15*	0.09**	**	−0.08	0.10	*	−0.24	0.14*	**
	(0.05)	(0.02)		(0.10)	(0.04)		(0.11)	(0.05)	
Year (2010)	0.02	0.01		0.16	0.09		0.28**	0.29**	
	(0.03)	(0.01)		(0.08)	(0.04)		(0.06)	(0.05)	
Children x year	0.20**	−0.005		0.18	0.01		0.29	−0.04	
	(0.05)	(0.02)		(0.11)	(0.05)		(0.12)	(0.06)	
Constant	0.86	2.74**		0.46	−1.42		−0.06	0.00	
	(0.47)	(0.25)		(0.56)	(0.82)		(0.62)	(1.03)	
Adjusted R²	0.07	0.12		0.14	0.20		0.10	0.09	
N	18,863	56,116		11,271	15,268		7,491	11,818	

Source: Authors' calculations.
Note: Models control for age, age², graduate degree, race, marital status, logged work hours, and industry.
*p < 0.01; **p < 0.001

fessions, we conduct OLS regressions of logged hourly wages on whether children are in the home for women in each professional category, after controlling for work hours, industry, and demographic factors for 1980 and 2010. Table 5 shows a negative pay differential for motherhood in the full sample of college-educated, professional women; tables 6 and 7 demonstrate different relationships between motherhood and wages for women in different professions. According to model 1 in table 6, in 1980, the presence of children has no significant association with women's wages in STEM, medical professions, law, and postsecondary education. Mothers in business and female-dominated professions experience a negative wage differential relative to nonmothers.

Model 2 of table 6 indicates that in 2010, women within STEM and medical professions actually experience a positive pay differential relative to those without children. For women in STEM, motherhood is associated with a 4.1 percent increase in logged hourly wages. In medicine, the positive wage differential for mothers is even larger: 10.5 percent. Model 2 of table 7 indicates that mothers in female-dominated professions experience a negative wage differential relative to nonmothers. Motherhood is not related to the wages of women in business or postsecondary education.

Table 7. OLS Regression of the Effect of Children on Wages

	Business			Postsecondary Education			Female-Dominated Professions		
	Women	Men	W:M	Women	Men	W:M	Women	Men	W:M
Model 1: 1980									
Children	-0.15**	0.10**	**	-0.12	0.14**	**	-0.25**	0.10**	**
	(0.03)	(0.01)		(0.06)	(0.04)		(0.02)	(0.02)	
Constant	2.86	1.95**		1.58	-0.85		2.71**	2.31**	
	(1.23)	(0.40)		(1.81)	(1.31)		(0.53)	(0.64)	
Adjusted R^2	0.05	0.18		0.05	0.13		0.06	0.19	
N	3,049	14,514		893	1,680		12,509	5,751	
Model 2: 2010			W:M			W:M			W:M
Children	-0.01	0.09**	**	0.04	0.15**	**	-0.04**	0.05**	**
	(0.01)	(0.01)		(0.02)	(0.02)		(0.01)	(0.01)	
Constant	0.40	1.23**		-1.03	-1.34		1.16**	0.84	
	(0.20)	(0.18)		(0.71)	(0.64)		(0.18)	(0.35)	
Adjusted R^2	0.07	0.11		0.07	0.15		0.05	0.08	
N	91,505	111,168		9,615	9,156		123,597	32,944	
Model 3: 1980 and 2010			W:M			W:M			W:M
Children	-0.16**	0.11**	**	-0.10	0.13**	**	-0.23**	0.09**	**
	(0.03)	(0.01)		(0.05)	(0.03)		(0.01)	(0.02)	
Year(2010)	0.23**	0.09**		-0.02	-0.12**		0.02	0.04*	
	(0.02)	(0.01)		(0.04)	(0.03)		(0.01)	(0.02)	
Children x year	0.14**	-0.03		0.14*	0.03		0.19**	-0.04	
	(0.03)	(0.01)		(0.05)	(0.03)		(0.01)	(0.02)	
Constant	0.33	1.08**		-0.41	-1.40		1.26**	1.11*	
	(0.24)	(0.19)		(0.76)	(0.69)		(0.22)	(0.35)	
Adjusted R^2	0.09	0.13		0.06	0.15		0.06	0.12	
N	94,554	125,682		10,508	10,836		136,106	38,695	

Source: Authors' calculations.
Note: Models control for age, age^2, graduate degree, race, marital status, logged work hours, and industry.
*p < 0.01; **p < 0.001

No consensus is evident in prior research on how to construct the independent variable for children. Some studies use a dummy variable (Lundberg and Rose 2000; Pal and Waldfogel this volume; Byker this volume), others use a dummy variable distinguishing between children under and over the age of five, no children being the reference category (Percheski 2008). Some use a categorical variable indicating one child, two children, and three or more children (Petersen, Penner, and Hogsnes 2010). In light of this lack of consensus, we tested a host of model specifications using different measures for children. Generally, the results are robust to variations in model specification with the following exception: in the model using a continuous variable for the number of children, in law (as in medicine and STEM), mothers experience a positive pay differential relative to childless women.[12] When we specify the variable in categories of no children (reference), one child, two children, or three or more

---

12. Also, the association between number of children and logged hourly wages differs significantly across professional occupations. For example, the positive wage differential for women in medicine is significantly larger than for women in STEM.

children (following Petersen and his colleagues), we again find that in medicine, STEM, and law, mothers earn more than nonmothers, regardless of number of children.[13] On the basis of these results, it is reasonable to conclude that women in law are similar to women in medicine and STEM in that mothers earn more than childless women, even though the statistical significance of the association between children and the wages of women in law professions varies depending on how the measure of children is specified.

Model 3 of tables 6 and 7 examines the full sample of women and includes an interaction for children and time period. In STEM, the positive, significant coefficient for the interaction term indicates that a positive wage differential emerged for motherhood between 1980 and 2010. The size of the wage differential for motherhood did not change over time in medical or law professions. In postsecondary education and business, the relationship between children and women's wages changed from being negative in 1980 to having no significant relationship with wages in 2010. Finally, the size of the negative wage differential for mothers relative to childless women significantly declined over time in female-dominated professions. In sum, over the past three decades, a positive wage differential for mothers emerged in STEM, and the negative pay differential for mothers in business and postsecondary education disappeared.

The finding of a positive wage differential for motherhood in medical, STEM, and law occupations (depending on specification) is remarkable given that numerous studies have consistently documented a negative association between motherhood and women's wages across varying levels of education (Anderson, Binder, and Krause 2002), age (Avellar and Smock 2003), and the timing of children (Taniguchi 1999). Women in these three professions represent 14 percent of all highly educated, professional women. Furthermore, mothers in business and postsecondary education experience no wage differential relative to childless women, and the negative pay differential for mothers has declined over time in female-dominated professions.

How do the associations between parenthood and wages for women compare to those for men in professional occupations? Are the positive wage differentials that mothers now experience relative to childless women in medicine, STEM, and (to a lesser degree) law professions similar in size to those for fathers in these professions? We address these questions by comparing the results of women and men and report them in tables 6 and 7. Column 2 shows the relationship between parenthood and the wages of fathers; column 3 indicates whether the relationship between children and men's and women's wages are significantly different. Model 1 indicates that this relationship is significantly different for men and women in all professions in 1980. The association between children and wages is either nonexistent or negative for women though it is positive and significant for men in STEM, business, postsecondary education, and female-dominated professions. In medical professions and law, the association is not significant for men or women, nor is the interaction between gender and children in 1980 significant.

According to model 2, by 2010, both women and men enjoyed a positive pay differential in STEM and medicine, though it is larger for men than women. In business, postsecondary education, and female-dominated professions, the association between parenthood and wages is significantly different for men and women. Fathers experience a positive wage differential in business and postsecondary education and mothers do not, whereas in female-dominated professions, women experience a negative wage differential and men experience a positive one for parenthood.

---

13. In STEM, women with one child or three or more children earn similar wages to women with no children. Yet women with two children earn significantly more than women with no children. For women in business, having one child is not associated with wages, but each additional child is associated with a negative wage differential. For women in female-dominated professions, the association between one child and wages is negative and each subsequent child is associated with a larger negative wage differential.

Figure 4. Effect of Children on Wages, Women

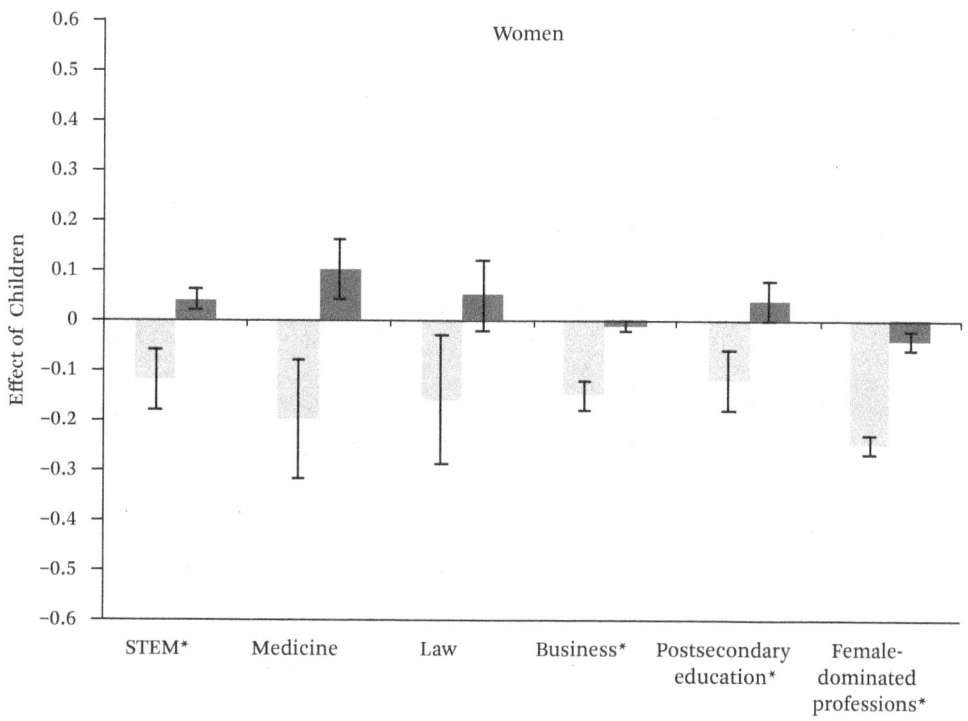

Source: Authors' calculations.
Note: Models control for age, age², graduate degree, race, marital status, logged work hours, and industry.
*= significant difference between effect of children for 1980 and 2010.

Figures 4 and 5 redisplay the coefficients from table 5 and present the association between children and logged hourly wages for women and men in 1980 and 2010 in each professional occupation. For women, it is striking that the size of the negative wage differential has declined in every occupation over time, and has even become positive in some occupations. For men, the positive differential for having children has been remarkably stable over time, showing virtually no difference between 1980 and 2010. The only exception is for female-dominated professions, where the positive wage differential is significantly smaller in 2010. Our results show that by 2010 within some elite professions, most notably STEM, medical professions, law, and postsecondary education, the association between parenthood and wages has become more similar than different for men and women. In female-dominated occupations, the family wage gap continues to be negative for women but does not exist for men.

RACIAL DIFFERENCES IN THE FAMILY WAGE GAP

Research finds that the family wage gap varies by race and ethnicity (Pal and Waldfogel, this volume; Waldfogel 1997; Budig and England 2001; Glauber 2007, 2008; Greenman 2011). Glauber finds that African American and Latina women tend to have smaller negative wage differentials for motherhood than white women (2007) and that African American men experience smaller positive wage differentials for fatherhood than whites or Latinos (2008). Prior research has not examined whether racial differences exist for highly educated men and women in different occupations. Tables 8 and 9 present the results of an OLS regression that

Figure 5. Effect of Children on Wages, Men

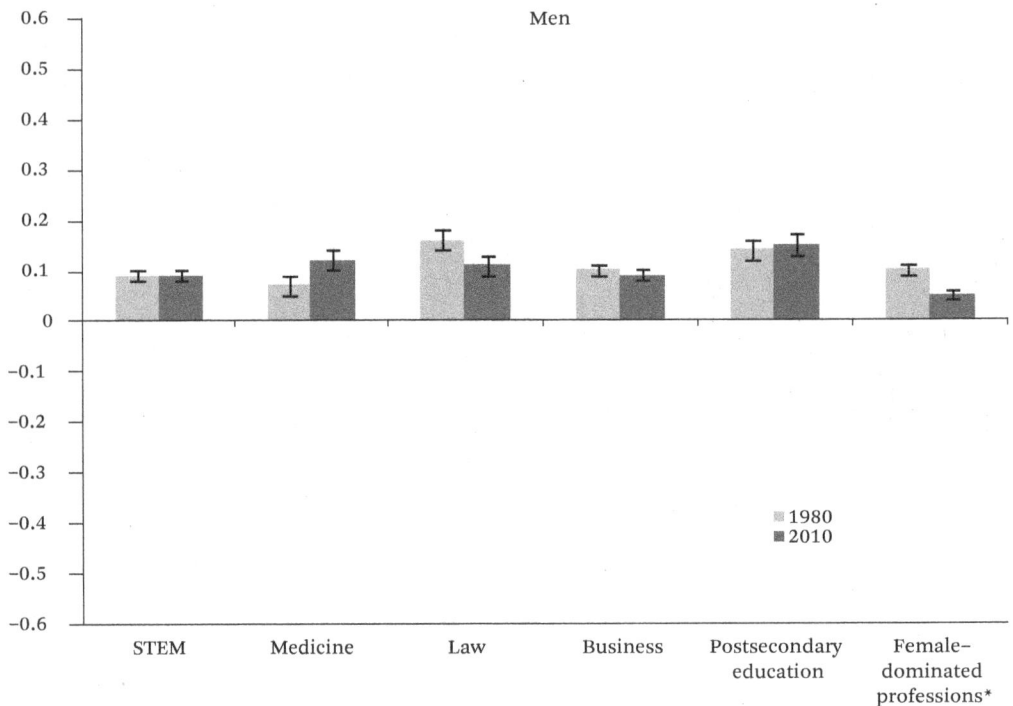

Source: Authors' calculations.
Note: Models control for age, age², graduate degree, race, marital status, logged work hours, and industry.
* = significant difference between effect of children for 1980 and 2010.

includes an interaction term for children and race for logged hourly wages for women and men in 2010.[14] The results show that the family wage gaps hardly vary for women of different races. The association between children and women's wages does not vary by race in any profession with the exception of female-dominated professions, where the interaction terms for blacks and Asians indicate that they experience no family wage gap in contrast to whites, Latinos, and others.

For men, all races enjoy a positive wage differential for fatherhood and this relationship does not vary much by race, except for in business, where black and Asian men experience a smaller positive wage differential for fatherhood than white men. The finding for black men in business compared to white men aligns with Glauber's (2008) finding that positive association between fatherhood and wages is smaller for black men than white men. To the best of our knowledge, prior research has not examined the association between parenthood and wages for Asians in addition to whites, Latinos, and blacks. Moreover, although prior research examines heterogeneity in women's and men's experiences by race and ethnic status, our findings demonstrate that, with the few exceptions noted, the association between parenthood and wages is not substantially different across racial-ethnic groups.

14. Small sample sizes of some highly educated racial groups in professional occupations prevent such an analysis for 1980.

Table 8. OLS Regression of the Effect of Children and Race on Wages, Profession

	STEM			Medicine			Law		
	Women	Men	W:M	Women	Men	W:M	Women	Men	W:M
Children	0.03	0.09**	**	0.10**	0.11**	**	0.05	0.11**	*
	(0.01)	(0.01)		(0.02)	(0.02)		(0.02)	(0.02)	
Race (reference white)									
Black	0.00	−0.11**	*	−0.01	−0.18		−0.06	−0.34	
	(0.03)	(0.02)		(0.06)	(0.09)		(0.05)	(0.23)	
Asian	−0.01	0.01		0.02	−0.04		0.10	0.04	
	(0.02)	(0.01)		(0.03)	(0.03)		(0.04)	(0.05)	
Latino	−0.07	−0.10**		−0.17*	−0.21**		−0.08	−0.11	
	(0.03)	(0.02)		(0.06)	(0.06)		(0.05)	(0.06)	
Other	−0.01	−0.09		−0.11	−0.05		−0.04	0.00	
	(0.04)	(0.04)		(0.09)	(0.08)		(0.07)	(0.07)	
Children x race									
x black	−0.08	−0.01		−0.03	0.14		−0.02	0.08	
	(0.04)	(0.03)		(0.07)	(0.10)		(0.07)	(0.24)	
x Asian	0.05	0.02		−0.05	0.01		−0.01	0.00	
	(0.03)	(0.01)		(0.05)	(0.04)		(0.06)	(0.07)	
x Latino	−0.01	0.02		0.14	0.08		0.02	0.05	
	(0.04)	(0.02)		(0.08)	(0.07)		(0.07)	(0.07)	
x other	−0.01	0.04		0.14	0.07		0.04	−0.01	
	(0.06)	(0.05)		(0.11)	(0.11)		(0.11)	(0.10)	
Constant	1.49*	2.68**		−0.18	−3.16**		0.92	0.04	
	(0.45)	(0.24)		(0.71)	(0.65)		(0.74)	(0.72)	
Adjusted R^2	0.07	0.10		0.13	0.24		0.06	0.07	
N	18,398	50,643		10,987	13,255		7,278	10,477	

Source: Authors' calculations
Note: Models control for age, age^2, graduate degree, race, marital status, logged work hours, and industry.
*$p < 0.01$; **$p < 0.001$.

CONCLUSION

Between 1960 and 2010, women entered traditionally male-dominated professions in greater numbers, and now are close to reaching parity with men in terms of the size of cohorts in business, medical professions, and law. Between 1980 and 2010, women also surpassed men as the majority of workers in postsecondary education. Women have made smaller gains in STEM occupations, and these professions remain male dominated. This study examined how the family wage gap changed for women and men across these professional occupations over time. We find that the gap for women declined in every occupation. It disappeared in business and postsecondary education and a positive wage differential emerged in STEM, medicine, and law. In contrast, for men, the positive association between fatherhood and wages has been remarkably stable over time, declining only for men in female-dominated professions.

Although most research assumes that the family wage gap is negative for all women and positive for all men, some recent work argues that the size for men and women varies by income, race, marital status, or broad professional category (Budig and England 2001; Glauber 2007, 2008, 2011; Killewald 2013). Some of this research provides hints that the experi-

Table 9. OLS Regression of the Effect of Children and Race on Wages, Other

	Business			Postsecondary Education			Female-Dominated Professions		
	Women	Men	W:M	Women	Men	W:M	Women	Men	W:M
Children	-0.01	0.10**	**	0.04	0.16**	**	-0.06**	0.05**	**
	(0.01)	(0.01)		(0.02)	(0.02)		(0.01)	(0.01)	
Race (reference white)									
Black	-0.10**	-0.14**		0.01	0.05		-0.02	-0.04	
	(0.01)	(0.02)		(0.05)	(0.06)		(0.01)	(0.02)	
Asian	0.00	0.01		-0.03	-0.07		0.18**	0.12**	
	(0.01)	(0.01)		(0.04)	(0.03)		(0.02)	(0.03)	
Latino	-0.09**	-0.11**		0.03	-0.01		-0.01	0.02	
	(0.01)	(0.02)		(0.04)	(0.04)		(0.01)	(0.02)	
Other	-0.07	-0.07		-0.06	-0.04		-0.07	-0.05	
	(0.03)	(0.03)		(0.06)	(0.09)		(0.03)	(0.05)	
Children x race									
x black	-0.01	-0.09**	**	0.02	-0.16		0.06**	-0.04	**
	(0.02)	(0.02)		(0.07)	(0.09)		(0.02)	(0.03)	
x Asian	-0.04	-0.05*		0.02	0.03		0.08**	0.08	
	(0.02)	(0.02)		(0.05)	(0.04)		(0.02)	(0.04)	
x Latino	-0.02	-0.01		-0.06	-0.06		0.02	0.00	
	(0.02)	(0.02)		(0.06)	(0.06)		(0.02)	(0.03)	
x other	0.02	-0.04		0.05	-0.04		0.06	-0.04	
	(0.04)	(0.04)		(0.12)	(0.11)		(0.04)	(0.06)	
Constant	0.40	1.22**		-1.02	-1.33		1.16**	0.86	
	(0.20)	(0.18)		(0.71)	(0.64)		(0.18)	(0.35)	
Adjusted R^2	0.07	0.11		0.07	0.15		0.05	0.08	
N	91,505	111,168		9,615	9,156		123,597	32,944	

Source: Authors' calculations

Note: Models control for age, age^2, graduate degree, race, marital status, logged work hours, and industry.
*$p < 0.01$; **$p < 0.001$.

ences of highly educated professional women, especially those at the top of earnings distribution (Budig and Hodges 2014) or in male-dominated occupations (Glauber 2011), are quite different from those of other women. However, prior work has not investigated explicitly the experiences of highly educated, professional women in various occupations. This paper definitively demonstrates substantial heterogeneity in the family wage gap, depending in particular on the professional field in which women are working. Furthermore, by comparing men and women, which prior work fails to do, we find that in some elite occupations, the gap is more similar than different for men and women. This finding accords with Claudia Goldin's argument of "a grand gender convergence" (2014) marked by the narrowing of the economic and social roles of women and men, and especially a convergence in their earnings, over the last century.

The finding of a positive wage differential in STEM, medicine, and law is surprising and raises an important question: why is there a positive association between motherhood and wages in some professions? Research has documented a positive association between fatherhood and wages, but the mechanisms behind the premium remain elusive. Cecilia Ridgeway and Shelly Correll (2004) argue that the "fatherhood wage premium" as well as the "motherhood wage penalty" is due to institutionalized gender inequalities and cultural ideologies about motherhood and fatherhood. Because, on average, fathers take on fewer childcare responsibilities than mothers after the birth of a child (Yavorsky, Kamp Dush, and Schoppe-Sullivan 2015), the inflexibility of many jobs may benefit fathers who not disrupt their work to take care of children. It has also been argued that employers favor fathers over childless men because fathers may be motivated to be more productive at work, or that employers view fathers as breadwinners and reward them with higher wages (Coltrane 1997; Glauber 2008). However, the succession of women in professional occupations may have also changed the continuity of their employment over the life course and in response to family events, thus becoming more productive at work or making career choices to maximize earnings as it is believed fathers do. Because we do not have data on work tenure or continuity, we cannot investigate this possibility. Women are also more likely to be the breadwinners in families than in the past (Wang, Parker, and Taylor 2013), which could increase their motivation to be productive at work. It is possible that when employers recognize women's breadwinner status, they reward it accordingly, just as they have long done for male breadwinners. However, this assumption should be approached with caution because our results also show that the majority of working mothers still experience a negative wage differential for motherhood.

Another possible reason for the positive association between motherhood and wages in some occupations is that those occupations afford workers with greater workplace flexibility and autonomy which benefits both mothers and fathers. Some occupations appear to have changed to offer more workplace flexibility in recent decades (Goldin and Katz 2011). Research finds increasing flexibility, declining work hours, and smaller penalties for part-time work in pharmacy, optometry, and some subspecialties of medicine, which may be related to the increasing share of women in these medical professions (Goldin and Katz 2011, 2012).[15] Other professional occupations have been slower to change. Business carries larger penalties for career interruptions due to childbearing than other elite professions, which is a key contributor to the gender gap in earnings among individuals with an MBA. In fact, among Harvard University graduates, the earnings penalties for job interruptions due to childbearing are the largest for MBAs, followed by JDs and MDs (Goldin and Katz 2011). This finding for a highly select group of women aligns well with our findings for nationally representative data of all college-educated women: in business, the wages of mothers and childless women are not significantly different, but in medicine and law they are.

Future research should address the open question of why women experience a positive wage differential for motherhood in some occupations and a negative one in others. This paper outlines historical trends in motherhood wage differentials but is unable to tease out the mechanisms behind them. No doubt, important differences exist between women who enter each of the occupations studied and how women within occupations respond to having children. For example, higher incomes in some professions, such as medicine, may provide strong incentives to remain employed after the birth of a child, whereas lower paid female-dominated professions may not offer similar incentives. Higher incomes may

---

15. The shift away from small private practices and the rise of regional hospitals and emergency care facilities have led to the increasing ability of doctors in some specialties to schedule set hours and reduce on-call, night, and weekend hours. Likewise, the decline of pharmacists and optometrists in small private practices and the rise of large national pharmacy chain stores and big box retailers offering these services means that many pharmacists and optometrists are employees who "became better substitutes for each other" and thus "decreased the pecuniary penalty for working part-time and part-year" (Goldin and Katz 2012, 9). Notably, Goldin and Katz show that medical specialties with lower weekly hours that do not require regular on-call, emergency or night hours are now dominated by women (2011).

also mean greater financial resources to purchase high quality childcare. Women in elite, male-dominated professions are likely qualitatively different than women in other professions in ways that we cannot measure. Future research should attempt to tease out these differences, but the challenge lies in finding data with appropriate sample sizes to analyze women within these elite professions. At any rate, the experiences of women in these professions will grow in their importance as women continue earning more college and professional degrees and entering professional occupations in greater numbers than any time in history.

APPENDIX
Coding of occupational classification scheme into professional occupations from census variable OCC1990, including numeric code. Note that n.c.e. means not classified elsewhere.

1) STEM
Math and Physical Science
  066 actuary
  067 statistician
  068 mathematician/math scientist
  069 physicist and astronomer
  073 chemist
  074 atmospheric and space scientist
  075 geologist
  076 physical scientist, other
Engineering and Computer Science
  043 architect
  044 aerospace engineer
  045 metallurigical/materials engineer
  047 petroleum, mining and geological engineer
  048 chemical engineer
  053 civil engineer
  055 electrical engineer
  056 industrial engineer
  057 mechanical engineer
  059 other engineer
  064 computer systems analyst/computer scientist
  065 operations and systems researcher and analyst
Life Science
  077 agricultural/food scientist
  078 biological scientist
  079 forester/conservation scientist
  083 medical scientist

2) MEDICAL PROFESSIONS
  084 physician
  085 dentist
  086 veterinarian
  087 optometrist
  088 podiatrist
  089 other health and therapy
  096 pharmacist

3) LAW
  178 lawyer
  179 judge

4) BUSINESS
  003 legislator
  004 chief executive and public admin
  007 financial manager
  008 human resource and labor relations manager
  013 manager in marketing, advertising, and public relations
  014 manager in education and related fields
  015 manager of medicine and health occupations
  016 postmaster and mail superintendent
  017 manager of food-serving/lodging establishments
  018 manager of properties/real estate
  019 funeral director
  021 manager of service organizations
  022 manager and administrator
  023 accountant and auditor
  024 insurance underwriter
  025 other financial specialist
  026 management analyst
  027 personnel, HR, training, and labor relation specialist
  028 purchasing agent/buyer of farm products
  029 buyer, wholesale and retail
  033 purchasing manager, agent, and buyer
  024 business and promotion agent
  035 construction inspector
  036 inspector/compliance officer outside construction
  037 management support occupation

5) POSTSECONDARY EDUCATION
  113/154, teacher, postsecondary

6) FEMALE-DOMINATED PROFSSIONS
Health Professionals
  095 registered nurse
  097 dietitian and nutritionist
  098 respiratory therapist
  099 occupational therapist
  103 physical therapist
  104 speech therapist
  105 therapist, n.e.c.
  106 physician's assistant
K–12 Education
  155/163 teacher, except postsecondary
Other Female-Dominated
Professional Occupations
  164 librarian
  174 social worker

REFERENCES

Amuedo-Dorantes, Catalina, and Jean Kimmel. 2005. "The Motherhood Wage Gap for Women in the United States: The Importance of College Fertility Delay." *Review of Economics of the Household* 3(1): 17–48.

Anderson, Deborah J., Melissa Binder, and Kate Krause. 2002. "The Motherhood Wage Penalty: Which Mothers Pay It and Why?" *American Economic Review* 92(2): 354–58.

Avellar, Sarah, and Pamela J. Smock. 2003. "Has the Price of Motherhood Declined over Time? A Cross-Cohort Comparison of the Motherhood Wage Penalty." *Journal of Marriage and Family* 65(3): 597–607.

Bianchi, Suzanne M., John P. Robinson, and Melissa A. Milkie. 2006. *Changing Rhythms of American Family Life.* New York: Russell Sage Foundation.

Blair-Loy, Mary. 2003. *Competing Devotions: Career and Family Among Women Executives.* Cambridge, Mass.: Harvard University Press.

Bolzendahl, Catherine, and Daniel Myers. 2004. "Feminist Attitudes and Support for Gender Equality: Opinion Change in Women and Men, 1974–1998." *Social Forces* 83(2): 759–89.

Boushey, Heather. 2005. "Are Women Opting Out? Debunking the Myth." Briefing Paper. Washington, D.C.: Center for Economic and Policy Research.

Budig, Michelle J., and Paula England. 2001. "The Wage Penalty for Motherhood." *American Sociological Review* 66(2): 204–25.

Budig, Michelle J., and Melissa J. Hodges. 2014. "Statistical Models and Empirical Evidence for Differences in the Motherhood Penalty Across the Earnings Distribution." *American Sociological Review* 79(2): 358–64.

Cha, Youngjoo. 2013. "Overwork and the Persistence of Gender Segregation in Occupations." *Gender and Society* 27(2): 158–84.

Byker, Tanya. 2016. "The Opt-Out Continuation: Education, Work, and Motherhood from 1984 to 2012." *RSF: The Russell Sage Journal of the Social Sciences* 2(4). doi: 10.7758/RSF.2016.2.4.02.

Chao, Elaine L., and Philip L. Rones. 2007. "Women in the Labor Force: A Databook." Washington, D.C.: Bureau of Labor Statistics. Accessed April 11, 2016. http://www.bls.gov/opub/reports/womens-databook/archive/women-in-the-labor-force-a-databook-2014.pdf.

Coltrane, Scott. 1997. *Family Man: Fatherhood, Housework, and Gender Equity.* New York: Oxford University Press.

Coser, Lewis. 1974. *Greedy Institutions: Patterns of Undivided Commitment.* New York: Free Press.

Cotter, David A., Joan M. Hermsen, and Reeve Vanneman. 2004. *Gender Inequality at Work.* New York: Russell Sage Foundation.

DiPrete, Thomas A., and Claudia Buchmann. 2013. *The Rise of Women: The Female Advantage in Education and What It Means for American Schools.* New York: Russell Sage Foundation.

England, Paula. 2005. "Gender Inequality in Labor Markets: The Role of Motherhood and Segregation." *Social Politics* 12(2): 264–88.

Galinsky, Ellen, Kerstein Aumann, and James T. Bond. 2009. *Times Are Changing: Gender and Generation at Work and Home.* New York: Families and Work Institute.

Glass, Jennifer. 1990. "The Impact of Occupational Segregation on Working Conditions." *Social Forces* 68(3): 779–96.

Glauber, Rebecca. 2007. "Marriage and the Motherhood Wage Penalty Among African Americans, Hispanics, and Whites." *Journal of Marriage and Family* 69(4): 951–61.

———. 2008. "Race and Gender in Families and at Work: The Fatherhood Wage Premium." *Gender and Society* 22(1): 8–30.

———. 2011. "Women's Work and Working Conditions: Are Mothers Compensated for Lost Wages?" *Work and Occupations* 39(2): 115–38.

Goldin, Claudia. 2014. "A Grand Gender Convergence: Its Last Chapter." *American Economic Review* 104(4): 1091–119.

Goldin, Claudia, and Lawrence F. Katz. 2011. "The Cost of Workplace Flexibility for High-Powered

Professionals." *The Annals of the American Academy of Political and Social Science* 638(1): 45–67.

———. 2012. "The Most Egalitarian of All Professions: Pharmacy and the Evolution of a Family Friendly Occupation." *NBER* working paper no. 18410. Cambridge, Mass.: National Bureau of Economic Research.

Gornick, Janet C., and Marcia K. Meyers. 2003. *Families That Work: Policies for Reconciling Parenthood and Employment.* New York: Russell Sage Foundation.

Gough, Margaret, and Mary Noonan. 2013. "A Review of the Motherhood Wage Penalty in the United States." *Sociology Compass* 7(4): 328–42.

Greenman, Emily. 2011. "Asian American-White Differences in the Effect of Motherhood on Career Outcomes." *Work and Occupations* 38(1): 37–67.

Harkness, Susan, and Jane Waldfogel. 2003. "The Family Gap in Pay: Evidence from Seven Industrialized Countries." *Research in Labor Economics* 22: 369–413.

Hertz, Rosanna. 2004. "Book Review Essay: The Contemporary Myth of Choice." *The Annals of the Academy of Political and Social Science* 596 (November): 232–44.

Hodges, Melissa, and Michelle Budig. 2010. "Who Gets the Daddy Bonus? Organizational Hegemonic Masculinity and the Impact of Fatherhood on Earnings." *Gender and Society* 24(6): 717–45.

Hook, Jennifer. 2006. "Care in Context: Men's Unpaid Work in 20 Countries, 1965–2003." *American Sociological Review* 71(4): 639–60.

Jacobs, Jerry A., and Kathleen Gerson. 2004. *The Time Divide: Work, Family, and Gender Inequality.* Cambridge, Mass.: Harvard University Press.

Killewald, Alexandra. 2013. "A Reconsideration of the Fatherhood Premium: Marriage, Coresidence, Biology, and Fathers' Wages." *American Sociological Review* 78(1): 96–116.

Killewald, Alexandra, and Jonathan Bearak. 2014. "Is the Motherhood Penalty Larger for Low-Wage Women? A Comment on Quantile Regression." *American Sociological Review* 79(2): 350–57.

Lundberg, Shelly, and Elaina Rose. 2000. "Parenthood and the Earnings of Married Men and Women." *Labour Economics* 7(6): 689–710.

Marini, Margaret M., and Mary C. Brinton. 1984. "Sex Typing in Occupational Socialization." In *Sex Segregation in the Workplace: Trends, Explanations, Remedies,* edited by Barbara F. Reskin. Washington, D.C.: National Academies Press.

Pal, Ipshita, and Jane Waldfogel. 2016. "The Family Gap in Pay: New Evidence for 1967 to 2013." *RSF: The Russell Sage Journal of the Social Sciences* 2(4). doi: 10.7758/RSF.2016.2.4.04.

Percheski, Christine. 2008. "Opting Out? Cohort Differences in Professional Women's Employment Rates from 1960 to 2005." *American Sociological Review* 73(3): 497–517.

Percheski, Christine, and Christopher Wildeman. 2008. "Becoming a Dad: Employment Trajectories of Married, Cohabiting, and Non-Resident Fathers." *Social Science Quarterly* 89(2): 482–501.

Petersen, Trond, Andrew M. Penner, and Geir Hogsnes. 2010. "The Within-Job Motherhood Wage Penalty in Norway, 1979–1996." *Journal of Marriage and Family* 72(5): 1274–88.

Ridgeway, Cecilia L., and Shelly J. Correll. 2004. "Motherhood as a Status Characteristic." *Journal of Social Issues* 60(45): 683–700.

Ruggles, Steven, J. Trent Alexander, Katie Genadek, Ronald Goeken, Matthew B. Schroeder, and Matthew Sobek. 2010. Integrated Public Use Microdata Series: Version 5.0 [Machine-readable database]. Minneapolis: University of Minnesota.

Sayer, Liana. 2005. "Gender, Time and Inequality: Trends in Women's and Men's Paid Work, Unpaid Work, and Free Time." *Social Forces* 84(1): 285–303.

Staff, Jeremy, and Jeylan T. Mortimer. 2012. "Explaining the Motherhood Wage Penalty During the Early Occupational Career." *Demography* 49(1): 1–21.

Taniguchi, Hiromi. 1999. "The Timing of Childbearing and Women's Wages." *Journal of Marriage and the Family* 61(4): 1008–19.

Weeden, Kim A., Youngjoo Cha, and Mauricio Bucca. 2016. "Long Work Hours, Part-Time Work, and Trends in the Gender Gap in Pay, the Motherhood Wage Penalty, and the Fatherhood Wage Premium." *RSF: The Russell Sage Journal of the Social Sciences* 2(4). doi: 10.7758/RSF.2016.2.4.03.

Waldfogel, Jane. 1997. "The Effect of Children on Women's Wages." *American Sociological Review* 62(2): 209–17.

Wang, Wendy, Kim Parker, and Paul Taylor. 2013. *Breadwinner Moms.* Washington, D.C.: Pew Research Center.

Yavorsky, Jill E., Claire M. Kamp Dush, and Sarah J. Schoppe-Sullivan. 2015. "The Production of Inequality: The Gender Division of Labor Across the Transition to Parenthood." *Journal of Marriage and Family* 77(3): 662–79.

PART III

Women's Work in Nontraditionally Female Occupations and STEM Fields

Gender Differences in the Early Career Outcomes of College Graduates: The Influence of Sex-Type of Degree Field Across Four Cohorts

KIMBERLEE A. SHAUMAN

The presence of baccalaureates who have specialized in fields not traditional for their gender represents the potential momentum each cohort may contribute to labor-force integration and equity. I examine the extent to which this momentum is present and realized among four cohorts of baccalaureates from the late 1970s through the late 2000s. The results show that the potential equalizing effects of increasing gender equity in postsecondary education are not being fully developed or realized. Gender segregation of majors remains significant, and labor-market outcomes continue to be strongly associated with the sex type of a college graduate's degree field. The negative relationship between female representation in a major and both the rate of full-time employment and earnings persisted across the four cohorts, and the negative gradient for earnings intensified. Educational use is slightly depressed among graduates in fields not traditional for their gender, and gender differences in earnings are already sizable within a year of graduation.

Keywords: gender segregation, higher education, labor-market outcomes

Higher education has been a powerful engine of gender equity both in the United States and internationally. Women's increasing participation in postsecondary education and attainment of both baccalaureate and advanced degrees has fueled significant advances toward gender equity in labor-force participation, job achievement, and earnings (Goldin 1990, 2006). College graduates are a driving force behind occupational equality, given that the fastest progress and greatest gender integration and equality has occurred among college-educated workers and in professional occupations (Blau, Brummond, and Liu 2013; Charles and Grusky 2004; England 2006; Jacobs 2003). Yet occupational segregation by gender among the college-educated workforce remains significant despite the growing female advantage in postsecondary graduation and the increasing integration of college majors (DiPrete and Buchmann 2013; Goldin, Katz, and Kuziemko 2006). The entry of new cohorts of college-educated workers and especially of the baccalaureates who have specialized in gender-nontraditional fields—women who earn degrees in traditionally male-dominated fields and men who earn degrees in traditionally female-dominated fields—are the potential momentum each cohort may con-

---

Kimberlee Shauman is professor of sociology at the University of California, Davis.

The author thanks the anonymous reviewers, the editors, and seminar participants at the Russell Sage Foundation conference "Changing Roles and the Status of Women: Effects on Society and the Economy" for their comments on earlier drafts of this paper. A version of this paper was presented at the 2015 meeting of the Population Association of American meetings in San Diego, California. Direct correspondence to: Kimberlee Shauman at kashauman@ucdavis.edu, Department of Sociology, University of California, Davis, One Shields Ave., Davis, CA 95616–8701.

tribute to labor-force integration and equality. That potential is realized only if a large proportion of such graduates can persist in their nontraditional fields in the labor market. This analysis examines the extent to which the potential desegregating momentum college graduates represent is realized among four cohorts of baccalaureates from the late 1970s through the late 2000s.

I use data from the National Longitudinal Study of the High School Class of 1972 (NLS-72) and the Baccalaureate and Beyond Longitudinal Study (B&B) to examine gender differences in the early labor market outcomes of graduates who earned their degrees in 1976–1978, 1993, 2000, and 2008 from U.S. colleges and universities (NLS 1994, 2003, 2004, 2012). The analysis focuses on three outcomes, each measured one year after the graduates earned their bachelor's degrees: labor-force attachment, educational use (that is, employment closely related to the graduate's degree field), and earnings. The sex-type of each baccalaureate's degree field is the focus of this analysis. I examine whether women and men who earn degrees in gender-nontraditional majors are as likely as their peers to use their educational capital by working in their degree field. I also test whether women and men realize the same economic benefits from working in jobs related to their degree field. The gender-specific outcomes are compared across cohorts to test whether disparities in early career outcomes have changed since the mid-1970s.

SCHOOL-TO-WORK TRANSITIONS AND GENDER DIFFERENCES AMONG THE COLLEGE-EDUCATED

Occupational specificity varies widely across college majors (Roksa and Levey 2010; Shauman 2009). Some majors, like engineering and education, provide specific occupational training and have strong connections to a defined set of occupational categories. Others impart less occupationally specific skills, and graduates from such majors have more diffuse occupational outcomes. The likelihood that college graduates use their specific educational investments by working in their degree field will therefore vary across majors, as will the returns to gaining such employment (Heijke, Meng, and Ramaekers 2003; Morgan 2008; Robst 2007; Roksa and Levey 2010). Although within-major variation in earnings is considerable, the earnings associated with college majors fit into a distinct hierarchy. Graduates from engineering, computer science and mathematics, business, and applied health majors have the highest average earnings; those who earn bachelor's degrees in the biological sciences, humanities, arts, education, psychology, and social work have the lowest (Bobbitt-Zeher 2007; Carnevale, Strohl, and Melton 2011; Loury 1997).

Gender differences in educational investments are strongly associated with gender differences in labor-market outcomes. Because the choice of college major to some extent structures the career opportunities available to graduates in the labor market, the gender segregation of college majors tends to deflect men and women onto different and unequally remunerated occupational paths. Gender segregation of college majors, or "horizontal segregation" (Charles and Bradley 2002), is estimated to account for 10 to 30 percent of the wage gap between college-educated men and women (Bobbitt-Zeher 2007; Brown and Corcoran 1997; Joy 2003; Shauman 2006). Some evidence, however, indicates that the impact of gender segregation of majors on the pay gap has declined over time concurrent with between-major differences in pay (Grogger and Eide 1995; Loury 1997). The fact that gender differences in the returns to specific majors also declined during the 1980s (Loury 1997), especially in male-dominated majors (Morgan 2008; Xie and Killewald 2012), highlights the potential for graduates from gender-nontraditional majors to generate greater gender equity in the labor market if they obtain employment that taps their educational investments.

Although it is clear that gender differences in educational investments help perpetuate gender inequality in the labor market, differences in the use of comparable educational investments also contribute to occupational segregation and the gender pay gap. Young men and women who have the same educational experience and credential may use their investments differently in the labor market, such as by entering largely disparate sets of occupations that may be equally related to their major, or by entering occupations that are unrelated to their major at unequal rates. Such disparities reinforce occupational sex segregation and undermine the potential equalizing effect of degree-field integration (Joy 2006; Shauman 2009). Evidence indicates that among graduates from female-dominated college majors, men are significantly less likely to enter a related occupation. Among graduates in male-dominated fields, however, the disparity in educational use disadvantages women (Shauman 2009). Secular trends toward gender equity, the increasing labor-force participation and labor-force attachment of women, and changing gender norms all suggest that gender differences in educational use will have declined over time. These trends have not been measured, though, nor have their consequences for other labor-market outcomes such as occupational prestige and pay.

SEX-TYPE OF MAJOR AND GENDER DIFFERENCES IN LABOR MARKET OUTCOMES

Mechanisms that may link major sex-type to labor market outcomes are identified by social psychological, organizational, social network, and gender role theories. Tokenism theory posits that the relative representation of types of people within groups directly affects intergroup interactions and the success of individuals in group contexts (Kanter 1977a, 1977b). Minority-group members face heightened visibility that increases performance pressure and social isolation that restricts access to networks of information and support (Eagly and Carli 2007; Kanter 1977b). These pressures may negatively affect their performance, how their work is evaluated, and their likelihood of persistence and success (Rogers and Menaghan 1991). Expectation-states theory posits that cultural stereotypes are reinforced by contextual signals, like sex-ratios within classrooms and workplaces, and that these structure inequality by generating implicit bias in evaluation, association preferences that segregate networks, and interpersonal hostility toward individual members of negatively stereotyped groups (Ridgeway 2014). These perspectives imply that graduates who major in fields not traditional for their gender will have less positive labor-market outcomes than their counterparts with gender-normative majors.

These and other sociocultural perspectives, however, imply that both the likelihood of gender nontraditional behavior and its consequences will be asymmetrical by sex. Expectation-states theory proposes that the positions and characteristics associated with higher status social groups will attract participation among members of lower-status groups, and that the reverse is less likely (Ridgeway 2014). Feminine devaluation theory proposes that because our culture devalues women, all social positions, behaviors, and characteristics associated with women are also devalued and therefore relatively unattractive (England 2006; England, Allison, and Wu 2007; England and Li 2006). The choice of nontraditional college majors will therefore be negatively stigmatized for men but not for women, and gender integration across fields of study (and occupations) will be driven predominantly by women entering male-typed fields (England and Li 2006). This prediction accurately describes the dynamics that generated greater integration of college majors during the 1970s and 1980s (England and Li 2006; Jacobs 2003).

The devaluation perspective also implies that the consequences of nontraditional choices will be asymmetrical by gender given that moving into traditionally male-type fields brings the promise of better pay and higher prestige for women; the opposite is the expected experience for men who make nontraditional choices. But expectation-states theory predicts that among those who enter, or attempt to enter, nontraditional fields, women will experience greater interpersonal backlash than men will because members of high-status groups act to defend their valued positions (Ridgeway 2014). Indeed, studies have shown that women in male-dominated fields face biased evaluation of their work (Knobloch-Westerwick, Glynn, and Huge 2013; Moss-Racusin et al. 2012; Reuben, Sapienza, and Zingales 2014), segregated networks that exclude or marginalize their participation (Koput and Gutek 2010; Sheltzer and Smith 2014), and the experience of discrimination and "chilly" climates (Logel et al. 2009; Steele, James, and Barnett 2002), whereas men in female-dominated fields are implicitly advantaged and experience disproportionate upward mobility (Williams 1992). So, although integration of male-dominated fields may be more likely than integration of female-dominated fields, within-field gender disparities in outcomes will likely be greater in male-dominated than in female-dominated fields.

DATA AND METHODS

The cohorts of recent graduates for whom I observe degree field and labor force outcome are drawn from the National Longitudinal Study of the High School Class of 1972 and the Baccalaureate and Beyond Longitudinal Studies of 1993, 2000, and 2008. The NLS-72 is a nationally representative sample of students who were seniors in high school in the spring of 1972. Information about postsecondary education and employment was collected for this cohort through follow-up surveys in 1973, 1974, 1976, 1979, and 1986 (for a subsample) and from a postsecondary transcript study conducted in 1984. I use the transcript data to identify those who earned their first bachelor's degree in 1976, 1977, or 1978 (that is, four to six years after their high school graduation), the field of their degrees, and the institutions from which they graduated. I select graduates from public and private not-for-profit institutions who were not enrolled in higher education one year after earning their degree. I use self-reported survey items to measure their labor-force outcomes.

Each B&B draws an initial cohort from the National Postsecondary Student Aid Study (NPSAS) and is representative of graduating college seniors in the survey year. The first B&B cohort was drawn from the 1993 NPSAS and surveyed in 1994; it provides a sample of baccalaureates from four-year public and private institutions who earned their baccalaureate between July 1992 and June 1993 and reported their labor-force outcomes in the 1994 survey. The B&B:2000 provides a sample of students who earned their baccalaureate between July 1999 and June 2000 and reported their employment status in a 2001 survey. The B&B:2008 sample represents the cohort of baccalaureates who earned their degree between July 2007 and June 2008 and who reported employment status in 2009. Graduates who reported school enrollment in addition to employment at the time of the B&B surveys are excluded from this analysis because the focus is on graduates who have transitioned to the labor force.[1] The analytical samples include, respectively for the 1976–1978, 1993, 2000, and 2008 cohorts, 3,747, 4,317, 4,922, and 5,856, graduates and are 49.7, 55.5, 61.2, and 58.7 percent female. All analyses are weighted to adjust for sampling design.

Degree Field Sex-Type

The sex-type of each degree field is estimated with data from the Integrated Postsecondary Education Data System (IPEDS). The sex-type of each major in a sixty-eight-category (a slightly aggregated version of the four-digit CIP codes) classification of degree field major is measured as the percentage of all degrees in a field that are awarded to women, %FEMALE, and is specific to the graduates' degree-granting institution and year of graduation. For the NLS-72, the value of %FEMALE is estimated with 1980 IPEDS data, which is the earliest available year of the IPEDS. For all of the B&B cohorts, %FEMALE is estimated using IPEDS data pooled across the three years before each B&B cohort's graduation year: the 1990–1992 IPEDS data operationalize %FEMALE for the B&B:93 cohort; 1997–1999 IPEDS operationalize %FEMALE for the B&B:00 cohort; and 2005–2007 IPEDS operationalize %FEMALE for the B&B:08 cohort.[2] I distinguish the quintiles of the distribution of %FEMALE as representing male-dominated (%FEMALE = 0–20), male-majority (%FEMALE =

---

1. Other groups excluded from the analysis are respondents reporting being on active military service or veterans, individuals who are not U.S. citizens, individuals who earned their degree from a for-profit postsecondary institution or who had previously earned another bachelor's or advanced degree, and individuals in the B&B cohorts who were older than thirty when they earned their degree.

2. If institution-specific data are missing, the value of %FEMALE is imputed using the year- and field-specific mean across all institutions.

Figure 1. Distribution of Female Baccalaureates, by Time-Varying Degree Field %FEMALE

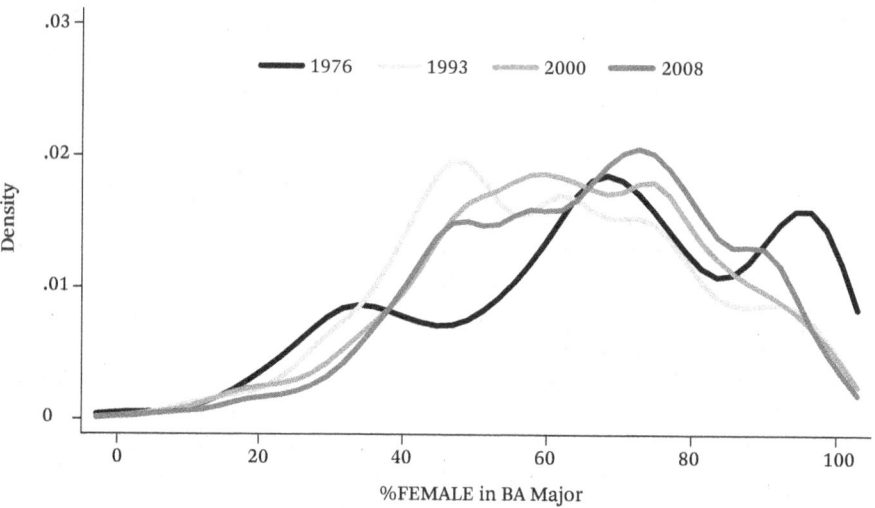

Source: Author's calculations based on data from the IPEDS, NLS-72, B&B:1993, B&B:2000, and B&B:2008 data.
Note: Mean of %FEMALE is weighted by institution size, which is operationalized as the total number of degrees completed as reported in the IPEDS data.

Figure 2. Distribution of Male Baccalaureates, by Time-Varying Degree Field %FEMALE

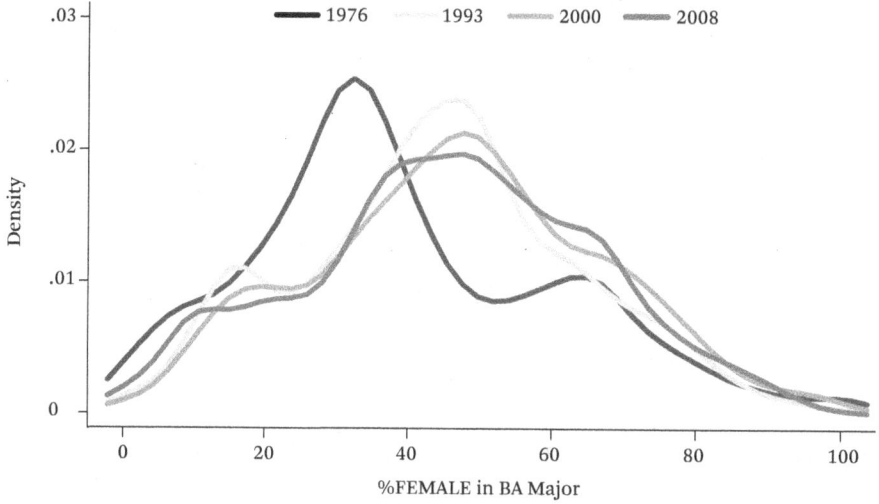

Source: Author's calculations based on data from the IPEDS, NLS-72, B&B:1993, B&B:2000, and B&B:2008 data.
Note: See note to figure 1.

20–40), gender-balanced (%FEMALE = 40–60), female-majority (%FEMALE = 60–80), and female-dominated (%FEMALE = 80–100) majors. Table A1 presents the average percentage female (aggregated across institutions), and the proportion of baccalaureates earning a degree in each field for each cohort of baccalaureates.

Figure 3. Distribution of Female Baccalaureates by 1980 Degree Field %FEMALE

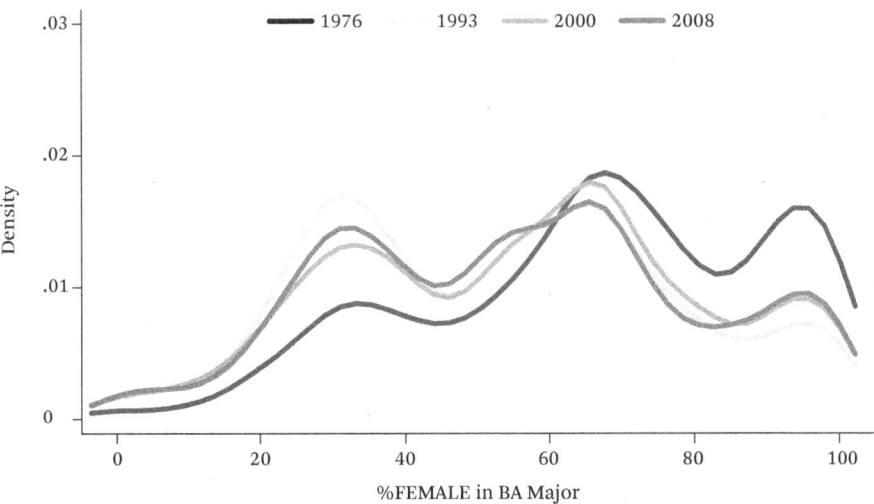

Source: Author's calculations based on data from the IPEDS, NLS-72, B&B:1993, B&B:2000, and B&B:2008 data.
Note: See note to figure 1.

Figure 4. Distribution of Male Baccalaureates by 1980 Degree Field %FEMALE

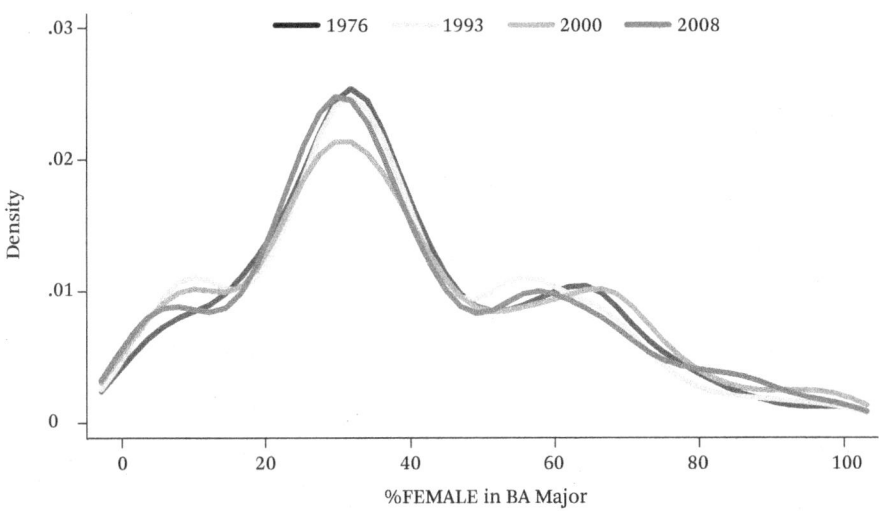

Source: Author's calculations based on data from the IPEDS, NLS-72, B&B:1993, B&B:2000, and B&B:2008 data.
Note: See note to figure 1.

Figures 1 through 4 present the distribution of the 1976–1978, 1993, 2000, and 2008 B&B cohorts of college graduates by %FEMALE in their degree field. Figures 1 and 2 present the distribution of graduates by %FEMALE in their degree field measured at the time of each cohort's graduation. In figure 1, the distribution of the 1976–1978 cohort is the most skewed toward the higher levels of %FEMALE, indicating that women in this cohort of baccalaureates were the most heavily concentrated in female-typed fields; indeed, the vast majority earned degrees in fields where women accounted for 60 to 100 percent of all degree holders. The distribution for the 1993 cohort shifted significantly to the left, representing a wider dispersion of female college-students across a broader range of fields, as represented by %FEMALE, and away from the overwhelming concentration in female-typed fields. The shift illustrates the movement of women into gender-balanced fields (%FEMALE = 40–60), but the density of the distribution in the 20 to 40 range of %FEMALE appears to have decreased across the cohorts and its shape in the 0 to 20 range changed very little. The distribution for each successive cohort after 1993 shifts slightly back to the right, that is, toward more female sex-typed majors. Figure 2 reflects a somewhat contrasting pattern in the cohort-specific distributions of male baccalaureates. The shift of the 1993, 2000, and 2008 distributions to the right of the 1976–1978 distribution indicates that men in the later cohorts were much more likely than the 1976–1978 baccalaureates to earn degrees from gender-balanced and female-majority majors.

Although the distributions presented in figures 1 and 2 represent the relative representation of women the baccalaureates actually experienced in their degree field while they were in college, these figures may not convey a reliable picture of how the field-specific distribution of male and female college graduates has changed across the cohorts. By using time-varying estimates of %FEMALE, figures 1 and 2 conflate potential changes in the degree-field choices of students with changes in the aggregate representation of women in each field. Since the 1960s, women have entered college and completed degrees at increasing rates, and since the 1980s women have earned the majority of four-year degrees (DiPrete and Buchmann 2013). Because women represent an increasing proportion of each successive cohort of students, the %FEMALE in degree fields can increase without any significant changes to the sex-specific distribution of graduates across degree fields (Charles and Bradley 2002, 2009; DiPrete and Buchmann 2013). To test for changes in the degree field preferences among the women and men in these cohorts, I fix the %FEMALE for each degree field at its 1980 level for all of the cohorts. Figures 3 and 4 present the resulting distributions. Figure 3 reveals a notable reallocation of women toward gender-balanced and male-majority fields and even a slight increase in their participation in male-dominated fields between the 1976–1978 and 1993 cohorts, but the distribution changed little across subsequent cohorts. In contrast, the distribution of male baccalaureates (figure 4) was remarkably stable. Successive cohorts remained concentrated in male-majority and male-dominated fields and have not moved into female-majority or female-dominated majors. It even appears that the distribution of male graduates shifted toward male-dominated majors (%FEMALE = 0–20) among recent cohorts as the area in the left tail is slightly greater for the 1993, 2000, and 2008 cohorts than for the 1976–1978 cohort. Any increase in the average %FEMALE in the fields from which male baccalaureates earn their degrees, therefore, is due to the increasing participation of women in the fields from which men have consistently graduated rather than to any notable changes in the distribution of men across fields.

The results presented in figures 1 through 4 illustrate two points. First, they echo previous studies by showing that the increasing representation of women in postsecondary education has not generated significantly greater integration of men and women across fields (DiPrete and Buchmann 2013; England and Li 2006), and that the integration achieved is solely the result of women moving into previously male sex-typed fields (England and Li 2006). These results therefore illustrate the persistent male aversion to entering fields traditionally associated with women (England 2006), the slow movement of women into traditionally male-typed fields, and the resulting resilience of major field segregation that significantly limits the potential for occupational integration among the college educated. Second, the differences between the time-varying and fixed distributions illustrate two aspects of degree field sex-typing that may be independently associated with the labor-market outcomes of graduates: the historical image or character of the field, which can be represented by the %FEMALE at some historical time, and how the gender balance changed over time (England, Allison, and Wu 2007). These components of degree field sex composition are therefore identified separately in the multivariate models used for the analysis reported in this paper.

Figure 5 documents the two components of gender representation for this analysis: the distinct historical sex-typing of the field, which is represented by the %FEMALE in the field in 1980, and the extent to which the gender balance in the field changed between 1980 and 2008 (see also table A1). Panel A of figure 5 presents the mean[3] %FEMALE in each of the sixty-eight detailed major fields separately for the periods 1980, 1990–1993, 1997–2000, and 2005–2008. The list of majors is sorted by the 1980 value of %FEMALE, such that the most male-dominated major fields are at the top of the table and the most female-dominated are at the bottom. Panels B, C, and D present the proportion of all, male, and female NLS-72 and B&B sample members who earned their degree in each field, separately by cohort. Most of the degree fields classified as male-dominated or male-majority experienced significant increases in %FEMALE between 1980 and the late 2000s. The %FEMALE in the physical sciences (chemistry, physics, and so on), for example, increased from 17.7 in 1980 to 41.9 in 2008 and therefore transitioned from a male-dominated to a gender-balanced field. But the statistics represented in panels B and C show that this field has experienced declining enrollments of men and little change in the participation of women across the cohorts of graduates. A few male-dominated and male-majority fields experienced notable declines in %FEMALE. These include computer and information sciences, in which the %FEMALE declined from 30.6 to 17.5 between 1980 and 2008; the proportion of male baccalaureates earning degrees in the field increased consistently across cohorts. Baccalaureates from gender-balanced fields also tended to become increasingly female over the period, whereas most of the female-majority and female-dominated fields experienced a decline in %FEMALE. Some—like psychology, social work, and English—became more female dominated.

The most popular majors across the cohorts of graduates were business-management, communications, English, psychology, and education. The popularity of some majors increased significantly since 1980, most notably business-management, but others, such as protective services, psychology, and nursing, also contributed a growing proportion of all baccalaureates conferred. Others fields—including accounting, biological sciences, and education—accounted for declining shares of all baccalaureates over the three decades.

Labor-Market Outcomes

I examine multiple labor-force outcomes of the graduates one year after graduation: employment (among those in the labor force); full-time employment (thirty-five or more hours); employment in a job related to the graduate's degree field (among those employed full time); and salary (among those employed full time). All are measured with self-reported survey items. Yearly salary for all cohorts is adjusted to constant 2009 dollars and log-transformed to correct for distribution skew. The relationship between a graduate's job and degree field is measured for the B&B cohorts with a survey item that asked the graduates to identify whether their job (at the time of the interview) was closely, somewhat, or not at all related to their degree field. Those responding closely are iden-

---

3. Means are weighted by institution size, which is operationalized as the total number of degrees completed as reported in the IPEDS.

Figure 5. Average Degree Field and %FEMALE Proportion of Graduates in Each Field, NLS-72 and B&B Cohorts

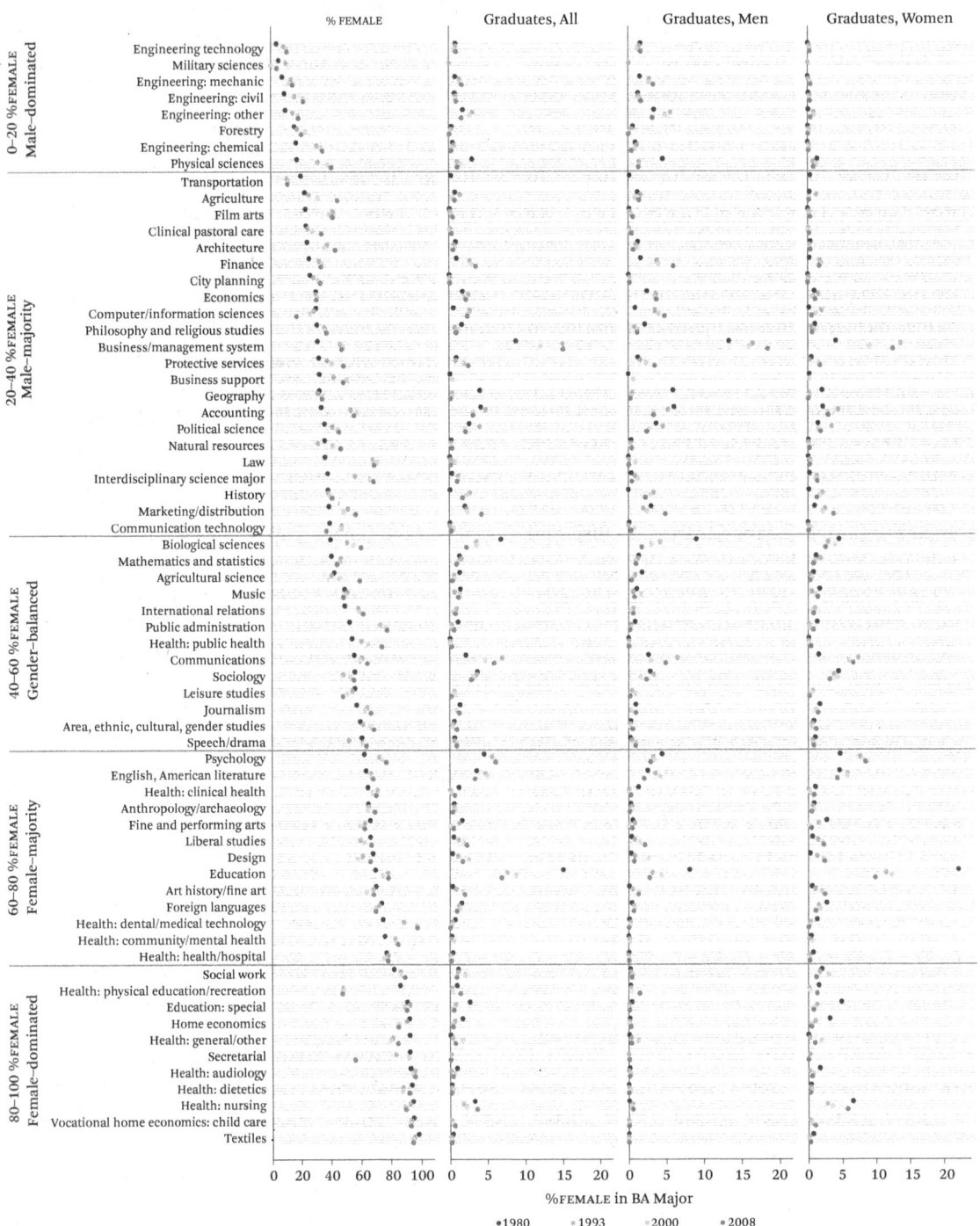

Source: Author's calculations based on data from the IPEDS, NLS-72, B&B:1993, B&B:2000, and B&B:2008 data.

Note: Mean of %FEMALE is weighted by institution size, which is operationalized as the total number of degrees completed as reported in the IPEDS data.

tified as in a job related to their degree field. This survey item is replicated in each B&B survey, so the data are directly comparable across cohorts. The NLS-72 includes a comparable item available only for individuals who earned their degrees in 1976 and 1978 and were working in 1977 and 1979. For these years, I code graduates as in a degree-related job if they respond affirmatively to two series of questions: "Not including on-the-job or employer training, did you receive formal instruction to do this kind of work?" "Where did you receive this training: four-year college or university?" and "What were your experiences while working on this job? . . . . Most of what I did on the job I learned to do in school."

Descriptive statistics for the outcome variables presented in table 1 show that employment rates are high, 89 percent or more, for all cohorts, as are the rates of full-time work among employed graduates. The percentage of full-time employed college graduates reporting that their job is closely related to their degree field ranges between 40 and 55, and average annual salaries from $23,000 to $41,000. These statistics also show that, for every cohort, gender gaps in the labor-market outcomes are already apparent one year after degree completion. Women graduates are less likely than men to be employed and their rates of full-time employment are 3 to 4 percentage points lower. Female baccalaureates earn significantly less than their male peers even when employed full time: the marginal female deficit in yearly earnings ranges from $4,500 among the 1993 cohort to more than $6,800 among the 2008 cohort. Among college graduates employed full time, however, women are more likely than men to report working in a job closely related to their degree field. This female advantage is statistically significant for the 1976–1978, 2000, and 2008 cohorts.

Method

To test for gender differences in the early labor-market outcomes of graduates based on the sex-type of their degree field, I fit regression models for each of the outcome measures separately for each cohort: nonlinear models for the analysis of employment, full-time employment, and whether the job is closely related to degree field; linear models for the log of yearly salary. These models estimate the gender- and cohort-specific associations between degree field sex-type and labor-market outcomes in the presence of controls for individual demographic and achievement characteristics that may influence those associations. The model estimates are used to test for gender differences and to examine whether observed differences have changed over time. Estimation of the causal mechanisms that may drive the observed associations and their variation over time is beyond the scope of this analysis. The basic model is as follows:

$$Y_{ij} = \beta_0 + \beta_1(\%FEMALE_{1980})_{ij} + \beta_2(\Delta\%FEMALE)_{ij} \\ + \beta_3(Female)_{ij} \\ + \beta_4(\%FEMALE_{1980} * \Delta\%FEMALE)_{ij} \\ + \beta_5(\%FEMALE_{1980} * Female)_{ij} \\ + \varphi(X)_{ij} \qquad (1)$$

where Y_{ij} represents the labor force outcome (employment, full-time employment, employment in a job related to the degree field, and salary) for graduate i in cohort j, Female is a dichotomous indicator of the sex of graduate i in cohort j (1=female), %FEMALE is a series of dummy variables indicating the level of %FEMALE (by quintile of the distribution)[4] in the degree field of student i in cohort j, Δ%FEMALE is the change in the value of %FEMALE between 1980 and the graduation year of each cohort. This specification of degree field sex-type allows for the estimation of independent asso-

---

4. Multiple alternative specifications of %FEMALE were tested including dummy variables representing vigintiles (5 percent intervals) and deciles, and multivariable spline specifications with various knot locations. Decile and vigintile specifications suffered from small sample sizes in the tail categories (those representing strongly male- or female-dominated majors). Models with spline specifications did not fit the data better than the models with the dummy-variable quintile specification of %FEMALE.

Table 1. Descriptive Statistics for Measures

	1976–1978 Cohort		1993 Cohort		2000 Cohort		2008 Cohort	
	Men Mean (SD)	Women Mean (SD)	Men Mean (SD)	Women Mean (SD)	Men Mean (SD)	Women Mean (SD)	Men Mean (SD)	Women Mean (SD)
Labor market outcomes (measured one year after graduation)								
Employed	0.933 (0.251)	0.940 (0.251)	0.926 (0.262)	0.923 (0.267)	0.929 (0.257)	0.899*** (0.302)	0.906 (0.291)	0.896 (0.306)
Employed full time (among employed)	0.858 (0.349)	0.831* (0.375)	0.918 (0.275)	0.880*** (0.325)	0.949 (0.221)	0.911*** (0.285)	0.874 (0.332)	0.841*** (0.366)
Job is closely related to BA field (among employed)	0.398 (0.490)	0.487*** (0.500)	0.494 (0.500)	0.512 (0.500)	0.517 (0.500)	0.553* (0.497)	0.445 (0.497)	0.475* (0.499)
ln(Salary) (among full-time employed)	10.250 (0.629)	10.029*** (0.704)	10.363 (0.576)	10.208*** (0.417)	10.612 (0.652)	10.448*** (0.618)	10.505 (0.642)	10.297*** (0.750)
Control variables (measured in year of graduation)								
Underrepresented minority	0.051 (0.219)	0.051*** (0.219)	0.084 (0.278)	0.132*** (0.338)	0.107 (0.310)	0.160*** (0.367)	0.128 (0.334)	0.189*** (0.392)
Age	na	na	22.973 (1.751)	22.600*** (1.724)	23.370 (1.621)	23.194*** (1.724)	22.899 (1.612)	22.650*** (1.601)
Parents' highest level of education								
High school or less	0.239 (0.427)	0.214 (0.410)	0.258 (0.438)	0.281 (0.449)	0.201 (0.401)	0.233** (0.423)	0.154 (0.361)	0.181** (0.385)
Some college	0.169 (0.375)	0.193 (0.395)	0.186 (0.389)	0.191 (0.393)	0.164 (0.370)	0.197** (0.398)	0.207 (0.405)	0.265*** (0.441)
BA degree	0.183 (0.387)	0.162 (0.368)	0.265 (0.442)	0.247 (0.431)	0.256 (0.436)	0.241 (0.428)	0.296 (0.457)	0.270* (0.444)

	1	2	3	4	5	6	7	8
Postgraduate degree	0.147	0.184**	0.247	0.243	0.292	0.255**	0.343	0.284***
	(0.354)	(0.388)	(0.432)	(0.429)	(0.455)	(0.436)	(0.475)	(0.451)
Single, never married	0.758	0.719**	0.797	0.715***	0.798	0.718***	0.791	0.709***
	(0.428)	(0.450)	(0.402)	(0.452)	(0.401)	(0.450)	(0.406)	(0.454)
Have kids	0.062	0.062	0.069	0.095**	0.074	0.112***	0.068	0.094***
	(0.241)	(0.241)	(0.254)	(0.293)	(0.262)	(0.316)	(0.252)	(0.292)
Full-time student when enrolled	na	na	0.463	0.505**	0.506	0.516	0.517	0.528
			(0.499)	(0.500)	(0.500)	(0.500)	(0.500)	(0.499)
Hours worked (among employed)	40.831	37.698***	43.501	40.225***	44.664	41.522***	41.843	39.082***
	(11.481)	(9.648)	(9.748)	(8.811)	(10.150)	(9.336)	(10.413)	(10.008)
GPA in BA field (*100)			318.347	329.630	321.297	334.369	310.616	326.364
			(42.849)	(47.063)	(47.515)	(46.343)	(47.002)	(45.792)
Grades in all coursework, 1974–1976								
Mostly As	0.105	0.175***						
	(0.306)	(0.380)						
Half As and half Bs	0.299	0.364***						
	(0.458)	(0.481)						
Mostly Bs	0.303	0.275						
	(0.459)	(0.446)						
Half Bs and half Cs	0.178	0.106***						
	(0.383)	(0.308)						
Mostly Cs, Ds, or below	0.062	0.024***						
	(0.241)	(0.154)						
Sample size	1886	1861	1921	2396	1908	3014	2421	3435

Source: Author's calculations based on data from the IPEDS, NLS-72, B&B:1993, B&B:2000, and B&B:2008 data.
*p<0.05; **p<0.01; ***p<0.001 for 2-tailed t-test of sex difference in means.

ciations between labor market outcomes and—first—the historical sex-typing of the field, which is represented by the degree field sex type in the year 1980, %FEMALE$_{1980}$, and—second—the change over time in the percentage-female in a degree field, Δ%FEMALE. In the models, Δ%FEMALE is operationalized as two linear spline variables, one capturing increasing and the other capturing decreasing values of %FEMALE, and the inclusion of the %FEMALE$_{1980}$ * Δ%FEMALE interactions allows the estimated association between outcomes and changes in field %FEMALE to vary across the baseline (1980) values of %FEMALE. The coefficients for the %FEMALE$_{1980}$ * *Female* interaction term, β_5, is of primary interest for this analysis because they estimate the magnitude and significance of gender differences in the labor market outcomes of graduates according to the sex-type of their degree field.[5]

The vector of control variables, represented by X_{ij} in equation (1), includes demographic and achievement characteristics of student *i* in cohort *j*. The race-ethnicity of the baccalaureates is measured by a dichotomous indicator of underrepresented minority status, which is coded 1 for graduates who self-identify as African American, Hispanic, or Native American. The graduates' age at degree attainment is included as a control variable for the B&B cohorts because age varies significantly in those samples of graduating college students, but is unnecessary for the NLS-72 cohort of high school seniors. The highest education of either parent of the NLS-72 and B&B sample members is measured with a four-category variable that distinguishes baccalaureates whose parent or parents earned high school or less, some college, bachelor's degree, or postgraduate degree. Dichotomous variables identify the marital (single, never married = 1) and parental status (have children = 1) of the graduates, and the estimated coefficients for these family status variables are allowed to vary by the baccalaureate's gender in all models. The B&B graduates' grade point average in their major field is included in the models as a control for their level of performance and level of specialized skill in their field of study (Joy 2003; Loury 1997). For the NLS-72 cohort, achievement is measured with a categorical variable recording the graduates' "estimated grades in all coursework between October 1974 and October 1976." A dichotomous indicator variable distinguishes recent graduates who were enrolled full time during the year before earning their degree from those who were not (was enrolled full time = 1). Descriptive statistics for all control variables are presented in table 1.

RESULTS

The estimated coefficients for all cohort- and outcome-specific models are presented in tables A2 through A4. Because interpretation of the coefficients is complicated by the inclusion of multiple interaction terms, I use predicted probabilities to present the results relevant to the focal research questions of this analysis. Are women and men who earn degrees in nontraditional majors as likely as their peers to use their educational capital by obtaining employment and working in their degree field? Do men and women realize the same economic rewards from utilizing their educational investments? Have the gender disparities in early career outcomes changed over the past three decades?

Figures 6 through 35 present the predicted labor market outcomes for men and women in each graduating cohort by the sex-type of their degree field, adjusted for the influence of the identified covariates. Figures 6 through 9, 11 through 14, 16 through 19, 21 through 24, 26 through 29, and 31 through 35 show the gender-specific association between degree field %FEMALE and employment outcome. Figures 10, 15, 20, 25, and 30 summarize how the %FEMALE-specific gender gap in each employment outcome changes across the cohorts. These fig-

---

5. All analyses are weighted, and standard errors estimated, to adjust for survey design characteristics using the survey data commands (svy) in Stata.

Figure 6. Probability of Employment by Degree Field %FEMALE, 1976–1978 Cohort

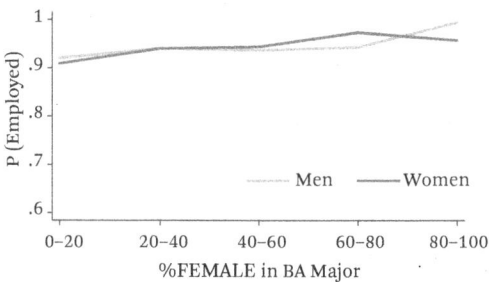

Source: Author's calculations based on data from the NLS-72 survey.
Notes: Predicted values from models that include controls for indicator of underrepresented minority status, age at graduation, parents' highest level of education, marital status, parental status, and whether the graduate was enrolled as a full-time student during the year prior to graduation (models for the 1976 cohort do not include controls for age and full-time enrollment status).

Figure 7. Probability of Employment by Degree Field %FEMALE, 1993 Cohort

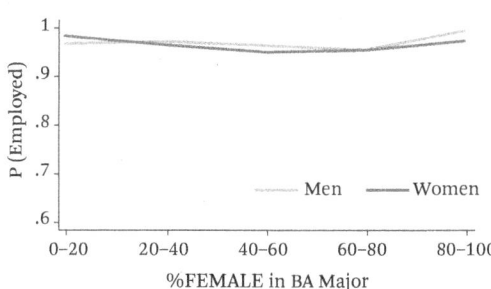

Source: Author's calculations based on data from the B&B:1993 survey.
Note: See notes to figure 6.

Figure 8. Probability of Employment by Degree Field %FEMALE, 2000 Cohort

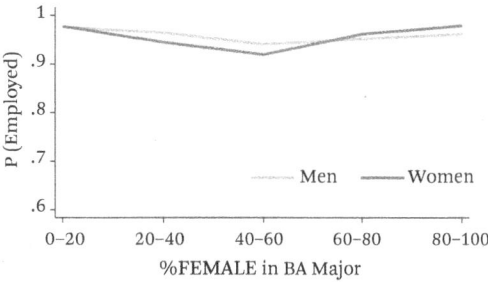

Source: Author's calculations based on data from the B&B:2000 survey.
Note: See notes to figure 6.

Figure 9. Probability of Employment by Degree Field %FEMALE, 2008 Cohort

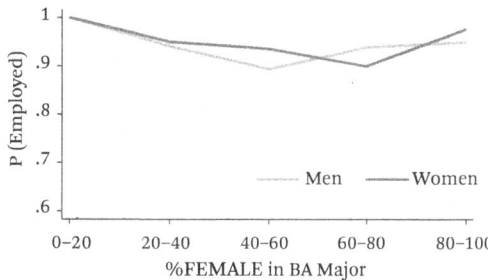

Source: Author's calculations based on data from the B&B:2008 survey.
Note: See notes to figure 6.

ures illustrate the association between degree field sex-type, that is, the degree to which employment outcomes vary across graduates from fields that are male dominated, male majority, and so on, as well as gender differences within type of degree field. The outcomes of gender nontraditional majors are reflected in the tails of the distribution presented in each chart: the outcomes of females in male-dominated and male-majority majors, and the outcomes of males in female-majority and female-dominated majors.

Early Labor-Market Attachment Among Recent Graduates

Figures 6 through 9 show that the predicted probability of employment is high for all cohorts and across all the quintiles of degree field %FEMALE. The likelihood of employment one year after graduation does not vary by degree field sex-type, except for the 1976–1978 and 2008 cohorts. For the 1976–1978 cohort, employment rates for men with degrees in female-

Figure 10. Female-Male Difference in Probability of Employment by Degree Field %FEMALE and Cohort

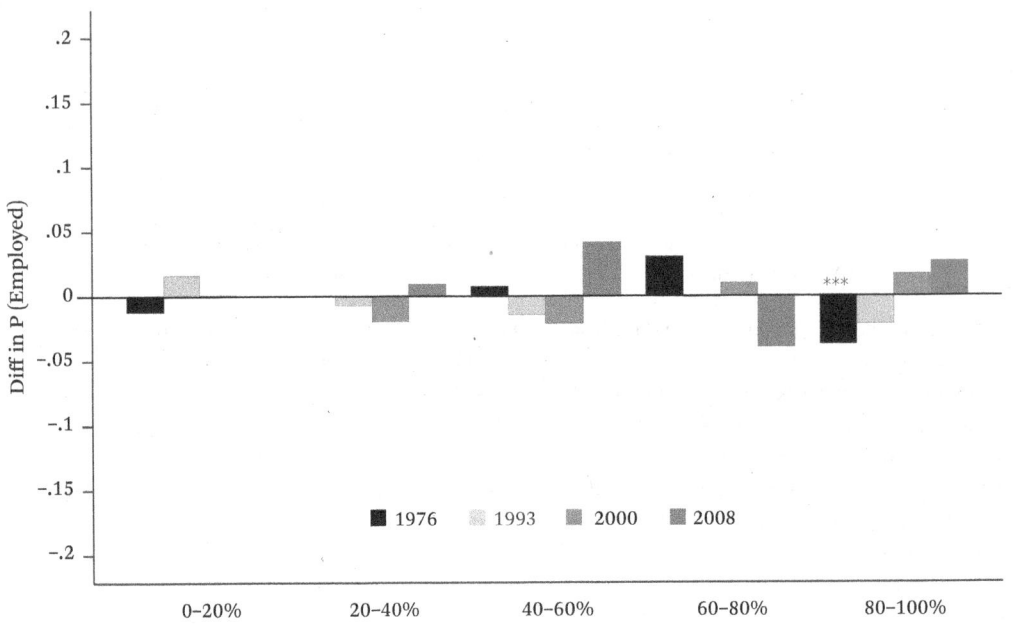

Source: Author's calculations based on data from the NLS-72, B&B:1993, B&B:2000, and B&B:2008 surveys.
Notes: Predicted values from models that include controls for indicator of underrepresented minority status, age at graduation, parents' highest level of education, marital status, parental status, and whether the graduate was enrolled as a full-time student during the year prior to graduation (models for the 1976 cohort do not include controls for age and full-time enrollment status).
† $p < 0.1$; * $p < 0.05$; ** $p < 0.01$; *** $p < 0.001$ for 2-tailed t-test of sex difference in predicted value.

dominated majors exceed those of all other male and female graduates. For the 2008 cohort, the men with degrees in gender-balanced majors are significantly less likely to be employed one year after degree attainment than men with degrees in male-dominated majors are. Figure 10 shows that the gender gap in employment rates is significant only among the 1976–1978 cohort of graduates from female-dominated majors: male graduates are significantly more likely than female graduates from these majors to be employed one year after graduation.

Among the recent graduates who are employed, the probability that they work full time is strongly related with the sex-type of their degree field (see figures 11 through 14). The likelihood of full-time employment is negatively associated with the %FEMALE of their major and is lowest, on average, for graduates from female-majority and female-dominated majors. The probability of working full time also tends to be slightly lower for women. Figure 15 shows that the female deficit is greatest among the earliest cohort of graduates from male-dominated fields. In contrast, nontraditional men, that is, those with degrees from female-dominated fields, are more likely than similarly credentialed women in the 1993 and 2008 cohorts to work full time, though the male advantage is not statistically significant.

Employment in a Job Related to Degree Field

Figures 16 through 19 present the proportion of full-time employed baccalaureates across the range of %FEMALE who report working in

Figure 11. Probability of Full-Time Employment by Degree Field %FEMALE, 1976–1978 Cohort

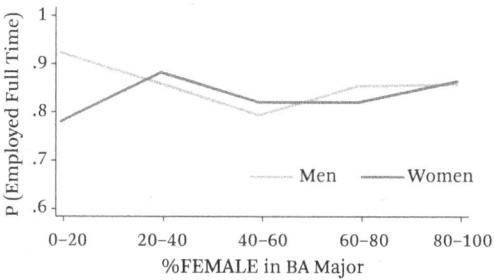

Source: Author's calculations based on data from the NLS-72 survey.
Notes: Predicted values from models that include controls for indicator of underrepresented minority status, age at graduation, parents' highest level of education, marital status, parental status, and whether the graduate was enrolled as a full-time student during the year prior to graduation (models for the 1976 cohort do not include controls for age and full-time enrollment status).

Figure 12. Probability of Full-Time Employment by Degree Field %FEMALE, 1993 Cohort

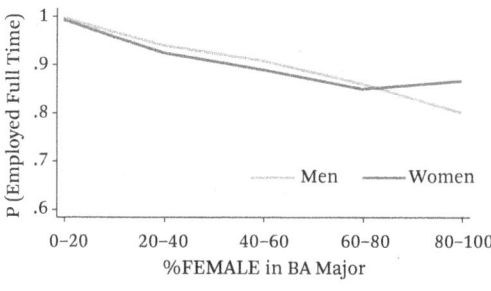

Source: Author's calculations based on data from the B&B:1993 survey.
Notes: See notes to figure 11.

Figure 13. Probability of Full-Time Employment by Degree Field %FEMALE, 2000 Cohort

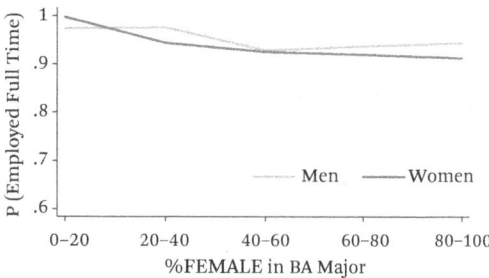

Source: Author's calculations based on data from the B&B:2000 survey.
Notes: See notes to figure 11.

Figure 14. Probability of Full-Time Employment by Degree Field %FEMALE, 2008 Cohort

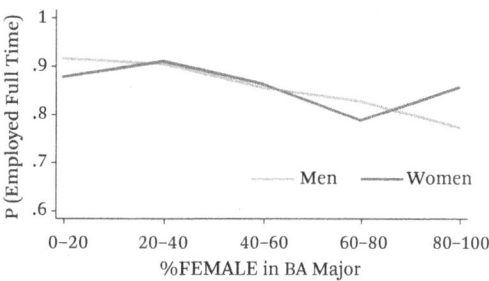

Source: Author's calculations based on data from the B&B:2008 survey.
Notes: See notes to figure 11.

a job closely related to their degree field. Two patterns are notable. First, the likelihood that graduates work in fields they characterize as closely related to their degree tends to be highest among those from the most sex-typed majors, that is, the male- and female-dominated fields. Second, a gendered cross-over pattern is evident in the probability of working in a job related to one's degree: educational use tends to be lower among women than men who graduate from male-dominated and male-majority majors, and, conversely, lower among men than among women who earn degrees from female-majority and female-dominated fields. Although the pattern is consistent across all but the 1993 cohort, figure 20 shows that the gender gaps are significant only for the 1976–1978 and 2008 cohorts.

Salary

Figures 21 through 24 present the average earnings, adjusted to consistent 2009 dollars, among recent college graduates who were working full time. The downward slope of the lines in each of the cohort-specific graphs,

Figure 15. Female-Male Difference in Probability of Full-Time Employment by Degree Field %FEMALE and Cohort

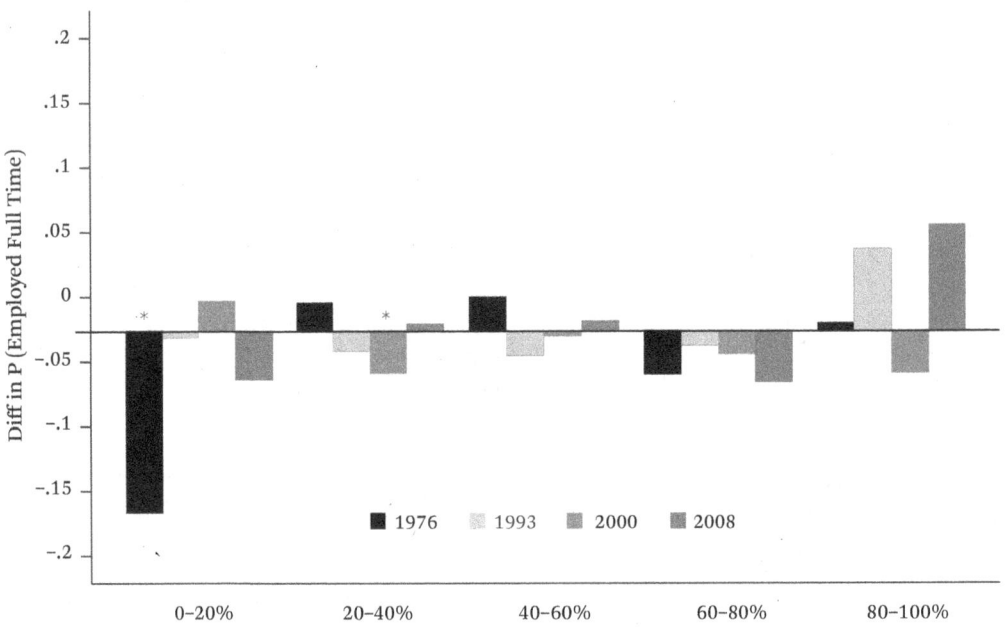

Source: Author's calculations based on data from the NLS-72, B&B:1993, B&B:2000, and B&B:2008 surveys.
Notes: Predicted values from models that include controls for indicator of underrepresented minority status, age at graduation, parents' highest level of education, marital status, parental status, and whether the graduate was enrolled as a full-time student during the year prior to graduation (models for the 1976 cohort do not include controls for age and full-time enrollment status).
† $p < 0.1$; * $p < 0.05$; ** $p < 0.01$; *** $p < 0.001$ for 2-tailed t-test of sex difference in predicted value.

which is statistically significant for all cohorts, reflects the well-known association between degree field sex-type and earnings—that average earnings are greater for graduates from male-dominated than female-dominated fields (England and Li 2006). The magnitude of the negative association between earnings and %FEMALE increased, and the downward slope steepened, such that the 2000 and 2008 cohorts of graduates experienced the greatest disparities in earnings by sex-type of field. The cohort-specific graphs also illustrate the persistence of the gender gap in graduates' earnings across the range of %FEMALE and across cohorts, and this trend is summarized in figure 25. Except for the 2000 and 2008 graduates from female-dominated majors, women tend to earn less than men only a year after graduation in every type of major. The gender gaps in earnings are greatest among the 1976–1978 cohort and especially among those with degrees in male-dominated fields. The nontraditional educational investments made by women in this cohort did not pay off in early earnings: their yearly salaries, among full-time workers, were on average $6,900 less than those of men with degrees from similar fields, and their earnings were not significantly different from those of women who made more gender-traditional educational choices. The relative advantage to women of majoring in traditionally male-dominated and male-majority fields increased over the cohorts as the %FEMALE-salary gradient steepened. Across

Figure 16. Probability of Employment in Degree Field by Degree Field %FEMALE, 1976–1978 Cohort

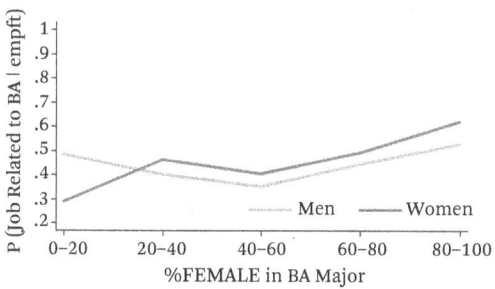

Source: Author's calculations based on data from the NLS-72 survey.
Notes: Predicted values from models that include controls for indicator of underrepresented minority status, age at graduation, parents' highest level of education, marital status, parental status, and whether the graduate was enrolled as a full-time student during the year prior to graduation (models for the 1976 cohort do not include controls for age and full-time enrollment status).

Figure 17. Probability of Employment in Degree Field by Degree Field %FEMALE, 1993 Cohort

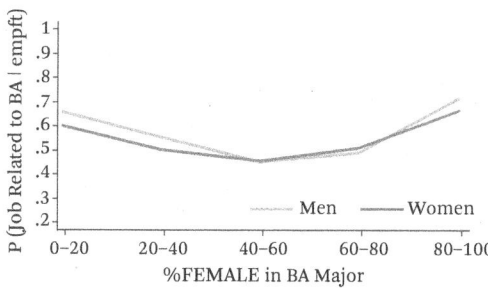

Source: Author's calculations based on data from the B&B:1993 survey.
Notes: See notes to figure 16.

Figure 18. Probability of Employment in Degree Field by Degree Field %FEMALE, 2000 Cohort

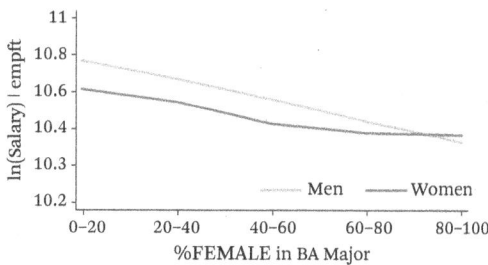

Source: Author's calculations based on data from the B&B:2000 survey.
Notes: See notes to figure 16.

Figure 19. Probability of Employment in Degree Field by Degree Field %FEMALE, 2008 Cohort

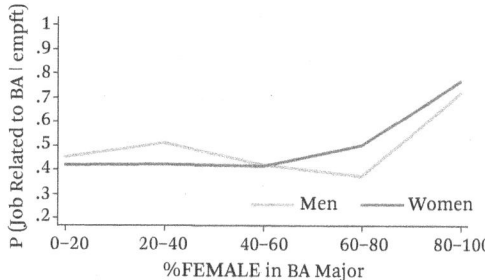

Source: Author's calculations based on data from the B&B:2008 survey.
Notes: See notes to figure 16.

successive cohorts, women who followed non-traditional educational paths continued to experience sizable (and sometimes statistically significant) deficits in earnings relative to male graduates from these fields but earned significantly more than women with degrees in traditionally female-typed fields.

The 1976–1978 and 1993 graduates from female-dominated fields also experienced a significant earnings deficit, indicating that in the early cohorts men suffered less than women did from the negative association between earnings and degree field %FEMALE. That gender gap closed among the 2000 and 2008 cohorts, but this finding cannot be interpreted as evidence of progress toward gender equity in the labor market. For the 2000 cohort, the gap disappeared because the earnings of men with degrees in female-dominated fields declined relative to prior cohorts, so equity was realized because the earnings of male and female graduates in these fields became equally depressed. In contrast, earnings equity among the 2008 cohort resulted from an increase

Figure 20. Female-Male Difference in Probability of Employment in Degree Field, by Degree Field %FEMALE and Cohort

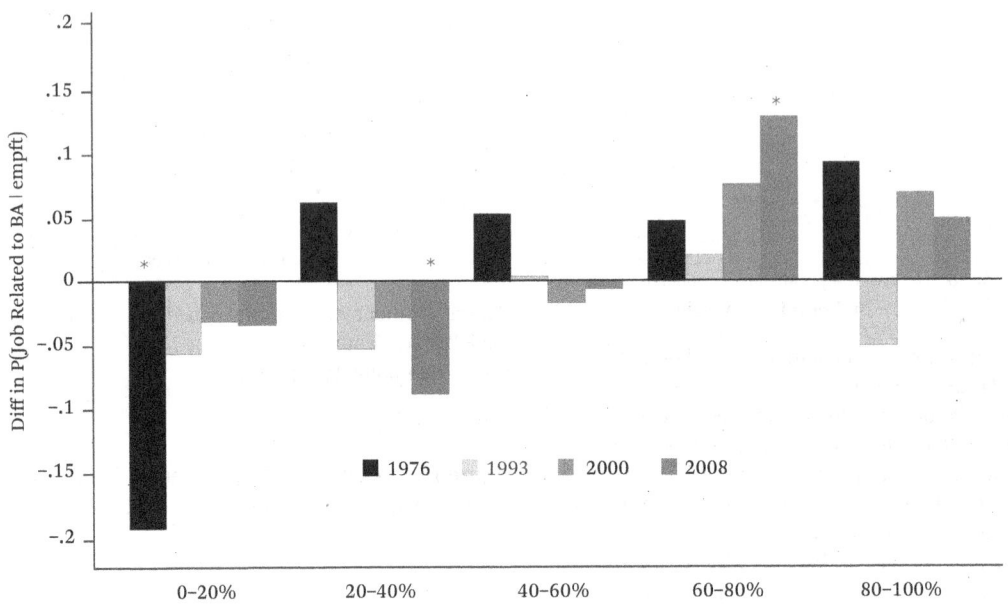

Source: Author's calculations based on data from the NLS-72, B&B:1993, B&B:2000, and B&B:2008 surveys.
Notes: Predicted values from models that include controls for indicator of underrepresented minority status, age at graduation, parents' highest level of education, marital status, parental status, and whether the graduate was enrolled as a full-time student during the year prior to graduation (models for the 1976 cohort do not include controls for age and full-time enrollment status).
† $p < 0.1$; * $p < 0.05$; ** $p < 0.01$; *** $p < 0.001$ for 2-tailed t-test of sex difference in predicted value.

(compared with the 2000 cohort and relative to earnings in female-majority majors) in the average earnings among both male and female graduates in female-dominated majors. But because earnings are relatively low among graduates from female-majority and female-dominated fields and because women continue to vastly outnumber men in these majors, gender equity among graduates from female-typed fields will have little impact on the aggregate-level pay gap among recent college graduates.

To assess whether men and women realize the same benefits from their educational investments, I estimate the predicted earnings among full-time employed college graduates separately for those who report working in a job closely related to their degree field (see figures 26 through 29). Average earnings are higher among graduates whose work is closely related to their degree field, but these results largely mirror those presented in figure 21 for all full-time employed graduates. The negative association between %FEMALE and salary remains significant across all cohorts for graduates who use their education on the job. In addition, figure 30 shows that the female deficit in earnings is sizable for all types of majors and persists across the cohorts, though it tends to be statistically significant only for male-majority and gender-balanced fields. These results are therefore inconsistent with the idea that educational use, especially among women in male sex-typed majors, can minimize gender gaps in earnings. Instead, the results indicate that men and women both ben-

Figure 21. Predicted Salary by Degree Field %FEMALE, 1976–1978 Cohort

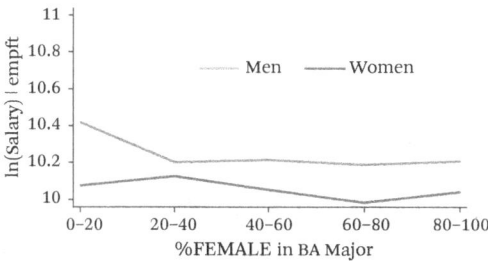

Source: Author's calculations based on data from the NLS-72 survey.
Notes: Predicted values from models that include controls for indicator of underrepresented minority status, age at graduation, parents' highest level of education, marital status, parental status, and whether the graduate was enrolled as a full-time student during the year prior to graduation (models for the 1976 cohort do not include controls for age and full-time enrollment status).

Figure 22. Predicted Salary by Degree Field %FEMALE, 1993 Cohort

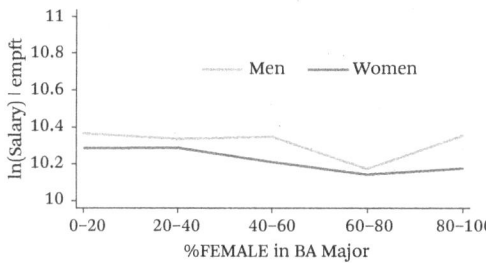

Source: Author's calculations based on data from the B&B:1993 survey.
Notes: See notes to figure 21.

Figure 23. Predicted Salary by Degree Field %FEMALE, 2000 Cohort

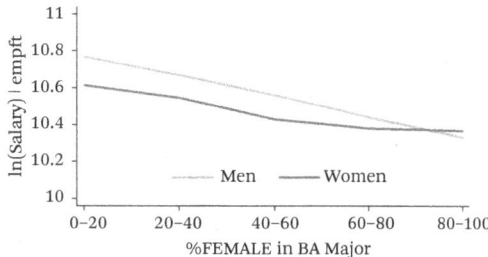

Source: Author's calculations based on data from the B&B:2000 survey.
Notes: See notes to figure 21.

Figure 24. Predicted Salary by Degree Field %FEMALE, 2008 Cohort

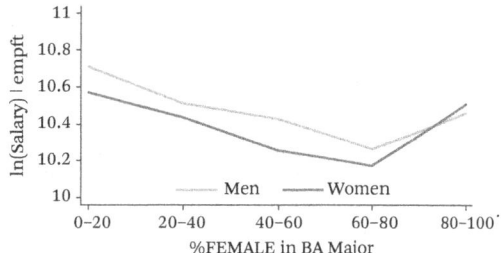

Source: Author's calculations based on data from the B&B:2008 survey.
Notes: See notes to figure 21.

efit from using their education but they do not benefit equally, and the data provide no evidence that this pattern has changed over the three decades covered by the four cohorts of college graduates included in this analysis.

Impact of Changing Gender Distribution Within Majors on Labor-Market Outcomes

According to the IPEDS data for all public and private not-for-profit four-year postsecondary institutions in the United States, the representation of women increased 5.5 percentage points, from 49.9 to 55.4 percent, between 1980 and 2008 (see table A1). As noted and as illustrated in figure 5, the relative representation of women increased 10 to 20 percentage points in many fields, while other fields experienced declines in the %FEMALE. Such changes in field-specific sex composition are linked to labor market outcomes, such as pay within field or occupation, by theories aimed at explaining gender inequality in the labor force. The feminine devaluation perspective (England 1992; England, Allison, and Wu 2007), queuing theory (Reskin and Roos 1990), and crowding theory (Bergmann 1974; Sorensen 1990) all predict a negative association between increasing

Figure 25. Female-Male Difference in Predicted Salary, by Degree Field %FEMALE and Cohort

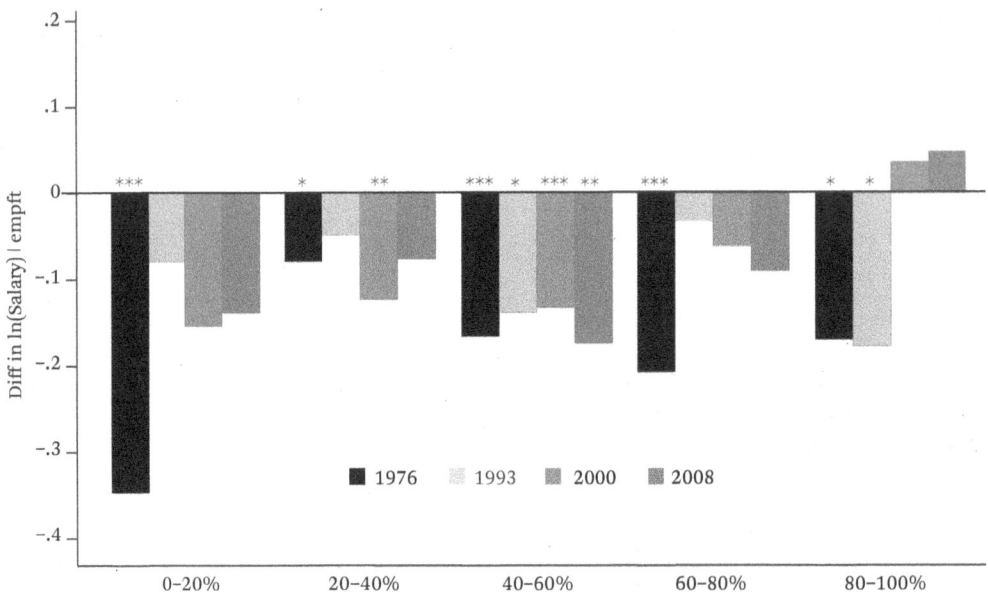

Source: Author's calculations based on data from the NLS-72, B&B:1993, B&B:2000, and B&B:2008 surveys.
Notes: Predicted values from models that include controls for indicator of underrepresented minority status, age at graduation, parents' highest level of education, marital status, parental status, and whether the graduate was enrolled as a full-time student during the year prior to graduation (models for the 1976 cohort do not include controls for age and full-time enrollment status).
† $p < 0.1$; * $p < 0.05$; ** $p < 0.01$; *** $p < 0.001$ for 2-tailed t-test of sex difference in predicted value.

field-specific female representation and pay, though they identify different causal mechanisms. Devaluation theory identifies the cultural devaluation of women as the fundamental mechanism, inferring that the increasing representation of women drives down the value and remuneration in the field simply because it becomes increasingly associated with women (Levanon, England, and Allison 2009). Queuing theory predicts that employer preferences for male workers, coupled with worker preferences for high-paying jobs, will result in a concentration of women in low-paying jobs, that is, that low-paying jobs are the only options for women because employers will not be able to attract male employees for those positions. Crowding theory identifies the association as caused by a supply-demand imbalance that results from employer discrimination against women: women's earnings suffer from artificially high competition for positions in the few fields where employers allow them (Bergmann 1974; Sorensen 1990). These theories do not address the potential for nonlinearities in the association between increasing field-specific female representation and labor-market outcomes, but there is reason to expect the effect of changes in degree field %FEMALE on labor-market outcomes to vary by the sex-type of the field. Extrapolating from tokenism and devaluation theories, initial sex composition of a field may condition the effect of changes in %FEMALE if particular levels of %FEMALE trigger the feminine devaluation effect. For example, a given increase in %FEMALE may be more detrimental to labor-market outcomes for graduates from fields that were already female-majority (because the shift caused a

Figure 26. Predicted Salary Among Those Working Full Time in Employment Related to Degree Field, by Degree Field %FEMALE, 1976–1978

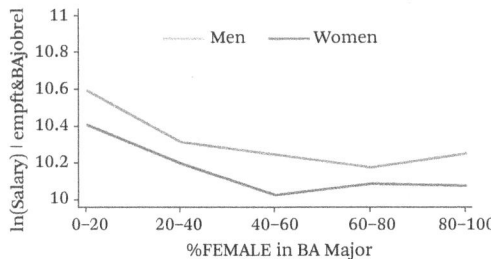

Source: Author's calculations based on data from the NLS-72 survey.
Notes: Predicted values from models that include controls for indicator of underrepresented minority status, age at graduation, parents' highest level of education, marital status, parental status, and whether the graduate was enrolled as a full-time student during the year prior to graduation (models for the 1976 cohort do not include controls for age and full-time enrollment status).

Figure 27. Predicted Salary Among Those Working Full Time in Employment Related to Degree Field, by Degree Field %FEMALE, 1993 Cohort

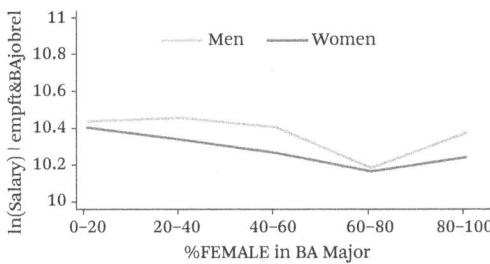

Source: Author's calculations based on data from the B&B:1993 survey.
Notes: See notes to figure 26.

Figure 28. Predicted Salary Among Those Working Full Time in Employment Related to Degree Field, by Degree Field %FEMALE, 2000 Cohort

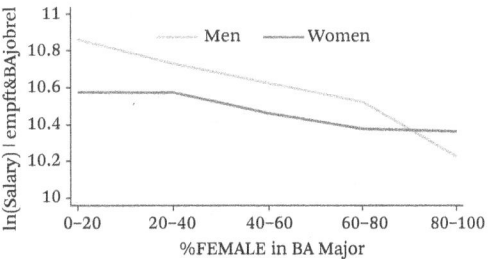

Source: Author's calculations based on data from the B&B:2000 survey.
Notes: See notes to figure 26.

Figure 29. Predicted Salary Among Those Working Full Time in Employment Related to Degree Field, by Degree Field %FEMALE, 2008 Cohort

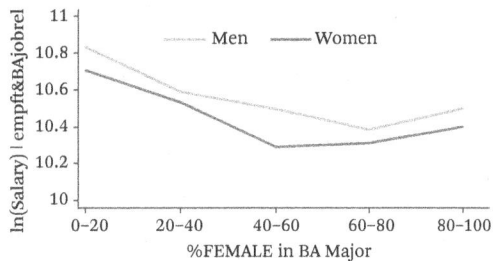

Source: Author's calculations based on data from the B&B:2008 survey.
Notes: See notes to figure 26.

field to become clearly female dominated) than for graduates from previously male-majority fields (because the shift caused a field to become gender-neutral).

The model coefficients for Δ%FEMALE, β_2, and the %FEMALE$_{1980}$ * Δ%FEMALE interaction, β_4, test the association between labor-market outcomes and changes in the representation of women within degree fields, and allow for that association to vary across the sex-type of the field. The estimates for these parameters are presented in tables A2 through A4. To illustrate the results, I calculate predicted probabilities for each of the employment outcomes by values of Δ%FEMALE ranging from 0 to 20 (representing a change of up to 20 percentage points) based on model coefficients estimated using data pooled across the three B&B cohorts. Because I find that declining values of Δ%FEMALE are not associated with any

Figure 30. Female-Male Difference in Predicted Salary Among Those Working Full Time in Employment Related to Degree Field, by Degree Field %FEMALE

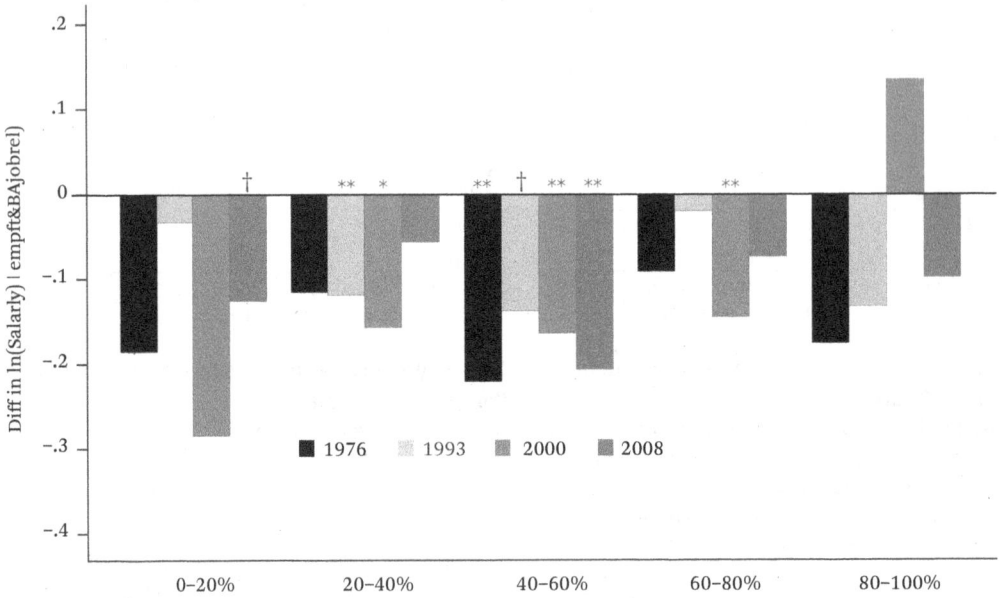

Source: Author's calculations based on data from the NLS-72, B&B:1993, B&B:2000, and B&B:2008 surveys.
Notes: Predicted values from models that include controls for indicator of underrepresented minority status, age at graduation, parents' highest level of education, marital status, parental status, and whether the graduate was enrolled as a full-time student during the year prior to graduation (models for the 1976 cohort do not include controls for age and full-time enrollment status).
† $p < 0.1$; * $p < 0.05$; ** $p < 0.01$; *** $p < 0.001$ for 2-tailed t-test of sex difference in predicted value.

of the labor-market outcomes for any cohort of graduates,[6] I focus on the estimated impact of increasing values of ∆%FEMALE. To test whether the influence of the increasing representation of women within degree fields differs by the sex-type of a degree field, I estimate predicted probabilities separately for degree fields that are male-typed (male-dominated or male-majority) and female-typed (female-dominated or female-majority). The resulting probabilities are presented in figures 31 through 35.

The predicted probabilities illustrate that increasing %FEMALE is significantly associated with all the labor market outcomes examined except the likelihood that recent graduates will be employed a year after earning their degree. More specifically, the estimates show that the increasing representation of women within a degree field is negatively associated with the probability of full-time employment among graduates from that field, their likelihood of securing a job closely related to their degree, and their earnings. Furthermore, the impact of the feminization of degree fields tends to be most negative for graduates with degrees in female-typed than male-typed majors. The

---

6. This conclusion is supported by the fact that that none of the estimated coefficients for Decrease in %FEMALE variable nor its interaction with the %FEMALE indicator variables are statistically significant in any of the cohort-specific models (see tables A2 though A4).

Figure 31. Probability of Employment by Increase in %FEMALE, All Cohorts

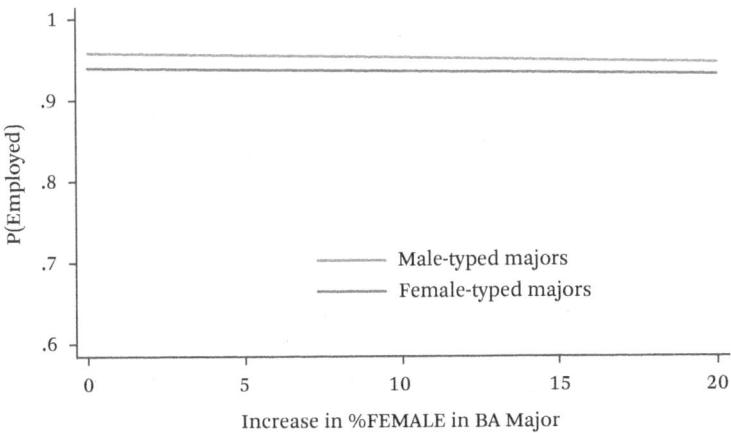

Source: Author's calculations based on data from the NLS-72, B&B:1993, B&B:2000, and B&B:2008 surveys.
Notes: Predicted values from models that include controls for indicator of underrepresented minority status, age at graduation, parents' highest level of education, marital status, parental status, and whether the graduate was enrolled as a full-time student during the year prior to graduation (models for the 1976 cohort do not include controls for age and full-time enrollment status). Male-type majors include those classified as male-dominated (0 to 20 percent female) and male-majority (20 to 40 percent female). Female-type majors include those classified as female-majority (60 to 80 percent female) and female-dominated (80 to 100 percent female).

Figure 32. Probability of Full-Time Employment by Increase in %FEMALE, All Cohorts

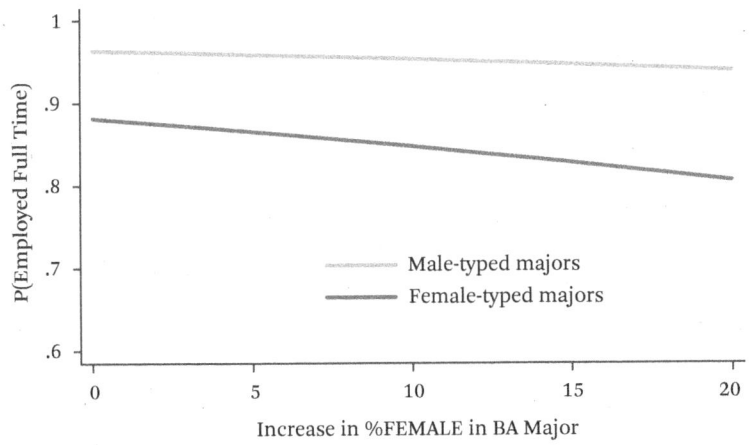

Source: Author's calculations based on data from sample that pools the B&B:1993, B&B:2000, and B&B:2008 surveys.
Notes: See notes to figure 31.

Figure 33. Probability of Employment Closely Related to Degree Field by Increase in %FEMALE, All Cohorts

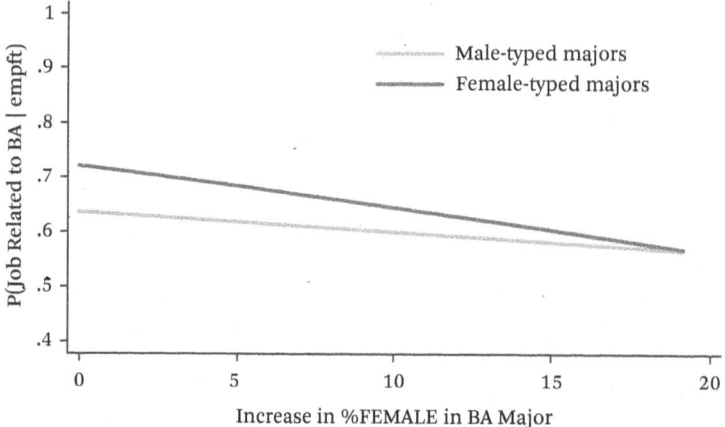

Source: Author's calculations based on data from sample that pools the B&B:1993, B&B:2000, and B&B:2008 surveys.
Notes: Predicted values from models that include controls for indicator of underrepresented minority status, age at graduation, parents' highest level of education, marital status, parental status, and whether the graduate was enrolled as a full-time student during the year prior to graduation (models for the 1976 cohort do not include controls for age and full-time enrollment status). Male-type majors include those classified as male-dominated (0 to 20 percent female) and male-majority (20 to 40 percent female). Female-type majors include those classified as female-majority (60 to 80 percent female) and female-dominated (80 to 100 percent female).

Figure 34. ln(Salary) by Increase in %FEMALE, All Cohorts

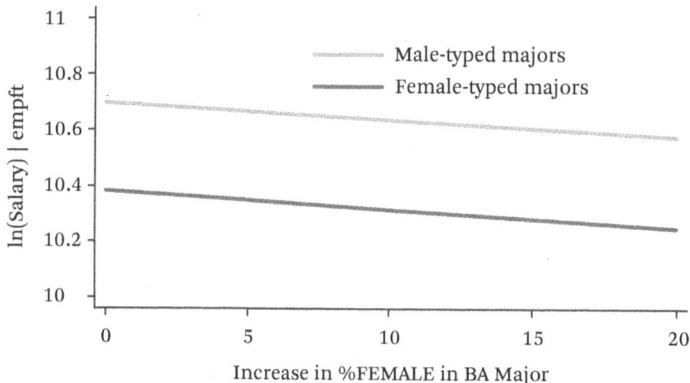

Source: Author's calculations based on data from sample that pools the B&B:1993, B&B:2000, and B&B:2008 surveys.
Notes: Predicted values from models that include controls for indicator of underrepresented minority status, age at graduation, parents' highest level of education, marital status, parental status, whether the graduate was enrolled as a full-time student during the year prior to graduation (models for the 1976 cohort do not include controls for age and full-time enrollment status), and hours worked. Male-type majors include those classified as male-dominated (0 to 20 percent female) and male-majority (20 to 40 percent female). Female-type majors include those classified as female-majority (60 to 80 percent female) and female-dominated (80 to 00 percent female).

Figure 35. ln(Salary) If Employment Related to Degree Field by Increase in %FEMALE, All Cohorts

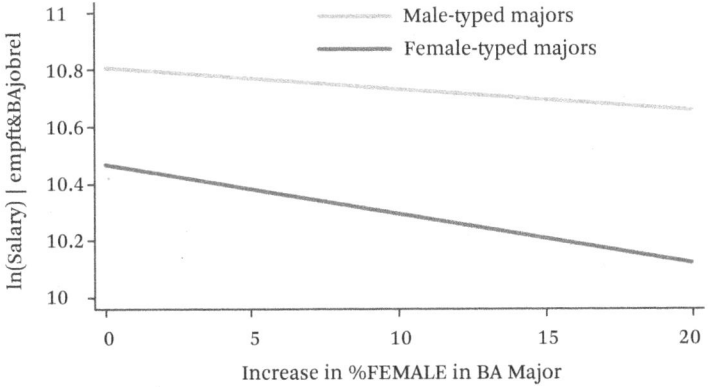

Source: Author's calculations based on data from sample that pools the B&B:1993, B&B:2000, and B&B:2008 surveys.
Note: See notes to figure 34.

estimated interaction is most notable for the probability of full-time employment, educational use, and salary among those who are using their education on the job. These findings imply that existing gaps between graduates from male- and female-typed majors in the probability of full-time employment and in salary have grown as the influx of women into higher education over the past three decades has increased women's representation in all majors. Identifying the potential supply- and demand-side mechanisms that may have generated the increasingly negative labor-market outcomes for graduates from feminizing female-typed majors is beyond the scope of this analysis but warrants attention from scholars of gender inequality in labor market processes.

CONCLUSION

The results of this analysis show that the potential equalizing effects of increasing gender equity in postsecondary education are not being fully developed or realized. Gender segregation of majors remains significant, and the absence of significant movement toward integration between 1993 and 2008 indicates that further progress toward equity is unlikely in the near future. Labor market outcomes continue to be strongly associated with the sex type of a graduate's degree field, so segregation generates labor-market disparities. And graduates from gender nontraditional majors—who represent potential for labor-market integration and equity—account for only a small proportion of all baccalaureates even among the most recent cohorts, and their labor-market outcomes tend to mirror the gender disparities of gender-traditional college graduates.

The sex segregation of college majors changed little across the four cohorts examined in this study. The increasing integration achieved occurred between the 1976–1978 and the 1993 cohorts, and since then the distribution of male and female baccalaureates has changed little. Although the proportionate representation of women among recent cohorts of degree recipients has increased across most fields, women continue to choose majors in historically female-typed fields and men continue to choose majors in male-dominated ones. Furthermore, the integration that has occurred has been asymmetrical: women have moved into male-typed fields but disinclination toward female-typed majors and even gender-neutral fields persists. These findings echo the results of earlier analyses (DiPrete and Buchmann 2013; England, Allison, and Wu 2007; Jacobs 1995) and are consistent with the patterns predicted by the feminine devaluation and expectation-states perspectives. The results also illustrate the inertia built into the cohort replacement process of social change in the labor force: the continued sex segregation of each successive cohort of college graduates reinforces existing patterns of occupational segregation. From the cohort-replacement perspective, that little integration was achieved during dramatic increases in women's participation in higher education (DiPrete and Buchmann 2013) indicates that an opportunity to generate greater gender equity in the U.S. labor force has largely been missed.

The association between degree field sex-type and labor-market outcomes is strong and has persisted across the four cohorts examined here. The representation of women in a major is negatively associated with both full-time employment and earnings among full-time workers. The specific causal relationships that underlie these associations continue to be debated (England, Allison, and Wu 2007; Levanon, England, and Allison 2009). However, in the context of continued degree-field segregation, their consequences are clear: they contribute to significant gender disparities in the labor market. Indeed, the apparent steepening of the negative %FEMALE-earnings gradient has multiple implications for earnings disparities. First, it suggests that the gender gap in earnings among college-educated workers may be widening. Second, it indicates that the utility of gender nontraditional educational paths is increasing for women and that their movement into historically male-dominated fields has and will continue to generate within-gender earnings inequality.

But occupational segregation and between-field disparities in outcomes are not the only dynamics contributing to gender disparities in the labor market. In general, educational use is slightly depressed among gender nontraditional graduates. Among those from male-typed fields, women have been less likely than men to work in their degree field, and among those from female-typed majors, men have been less likely than women to use their education. But even among graduates who do work in their degree field, including those who graduate from gender nontraditional majors, gender differences in earnings are already sizable within only a year of graduation. I also find that increases in the relative representation of women within degree fields, which is common given the increasing predominance of women in postsecondary education, depresses average earnings of all graduates, especially those in female-dominated majors. This finding highlights an additional mechanism that works with sex segregation of college majors to reinforce labor-force gender inequality despite women's increasing advantage in educational attainment.

APPENDIX

Table A1. %FEMALE in Major from IPEDS Data and Percent of All NLS-72 and B&B Graduates in Each Major Degree Field by Cohort

	1976–1978 Cohort		1993 Cohort			2000 Cohort			2008 Cohort			
	1980 IPEDS %FEMALE	NLS-72 Percent of Graduates	1990–1993 IPEDS %FEMALE	1993 B&B:93 Percent of Graduates		1997–2000 IPEDS %FEMALE	B&B:2000 Percent of Graduates		2005–2008 IPEDS %FEMALE	B&B:2008 Percent of Graduates		Change in %FEMALE 1980–2008
Male-dominated majors (%FEMALE = 0–20)												
Engineering technology	3.85	0.83	8.75	0.81		10.69	0.63		11.03	0.89		7.18
Military sciences	5.34	0.00	10.40	0.05		0.00			4.24	0.00		-1.10
Engineering: mechanic	7.74	0.80	13.92	1.37		12.49	1.41		15.00	1.68		7.26
Engineering: civil	9.31	0.74	16.25	0.80		22.16	0.83		22.21	0.94		12.90
Engineering: other	9.99	1.82	15.11	3.09		18.51	2.73		18.80	1.65		8.81
Forestry	16.14	0.36	17.89	0.30		23.81	0.13		20.94	0.06		4.80
Engineering: chemical	17.22	0.49	31.20	0.65		33.89	0.47		35.10	0.28		17.87
Physical Sci.: chemistry/physics/other	17.77	3.03	31.83	1.09		38.59	1.42		41.09	1.09		23.32
Male-majority majors (%FEMALE = 20–40)												
Transportation	20.44	0.27	10.83	0.00		11.94	0.00		11.36	0.00		-9.08
Agriculture	23.04	0.77	25.79	1.44		32.01	0.50		44.97	0.72		21.93
Film arts	23.58	0.06	41.99	0.16		39.37	0.28		41.78	0.49		18.20
Clinical pastoral care	23.94	0.00	25.00	0.10		28.30	0.10		34.26	0.32		10.31
Architecture	24.63	0.85	38.13	0.59		36.21	0.72		43.63	0.51		19.00
Finance	25.91	0.96	32.65	2.70		34.75	2.87		33.87	3.50		7.96
City planning	26.58	0.01	29.00	0.10		32.24	0.08		33.39	0.08		6.81
Economics	30.51	1.75	30.46	2.54		31.54	1.97		30.83	2.21		0.32
Computer/information sciences	30.60	0.55	29.04	2.73		26.38	2.45		17.49	2.38		-13.10
Philosophy and religious studies	31.14	1.65	36.27	0.70		36.82	1.06		37.61	0.89		6.47
Business/mangement system	31.52	8.81	46.53	15.02		48.85	12.09		47.78	15.07		16.26
Protective services	32.37	0.92	38.09	0.86		40.92	1.95		49.01	2.52		16.64
Business support	32.74	0.11	42.48	0.00		51.09	0.42		48.81	0.00		16.07
Geography	32.79	4.05	31.75	0.36		34.36	0.35		34.67	0.18		1.88

(continued)

Table A1. (continued)

	1976–1978 Cohort		1993 Cohort			2000 Cohort			2008 Cohort			
	1980 IPEDS %FEMALE	NLS-72 Percent of Graduates	1990–1993 IPEDS %FEMALE	B&B:93 Percent of Graduates		1997–2000 IPEDS %FEMALE	B&B:2000 Percent of Graduates		2005–2008 IPEDS %FEMALE	B&B:2008 Percent of Graduates		Change in %FEMALE 1980–2008
Political science	36.18	2.61	41.42	4.01		45.08	2.06		45.83	2.14		9.66
Natural resources	36.31	0.24	31.74	0.16		41.76	0.19		47.06	0.35		10.75
Law	36.50	0.03	68.34	0.20		71.20	0.69		69.12	0.17		32.61
Intrdisciplinary: environ/biopsych/other	38.22	0.31	56.47	1.14		66.41	1.22		68.87	1.00		30.65
History	38.42	0.07	38.35	2.70		39.39	2.28		41.34	1.72		2.92
Health: medicine	38.82	0.11	36.00	0.00		0.00	0.00		0.00	0.00		-38.82
Marketing/distribution	39.02	2.02	51.76	2.27		48.91	2.32		56.77	4.23		17.75
Communication technology	39.56	0.05	47.56	0.01		47.24	0.52		37.27	0.20		-2.28
Gender-balanced majors (%FEMALE = 40–60)												
Bio sci: zoology/botany/biophys/other	40.07	6.82	51.12	3.52		55.31	3.54		60.27	2.22		20.21
Mathematics: including statistics	40.64	1.27	46.71	1.53		46.78	1.07		44.43	0.90		3.79
Agricultural science	42.54	1.31	40.60	0.58		46.16	0.59		59.38	0.34		16.84
Music	49.36	1.39	51.08	0.61		50.05	1.35		48.55	1.14		-0.80
International relations	49.43	0.00	58.37	0.87		59.05	0.51		61.64	0.74		12.21
Public administration	52.61	1.09	73.05	0.24		77.11	0.21		77.75	0.53		25.14
Health: public health	54.23	0.04	60.42	0.07		64.89	0.05		74.24	0.27		20.01
Communications	55.63	2.11	60.82	6.95		59.50	4.65		64.42	5.89		8.79
Sociology	55.98	3.64	48.33	3.57		53.08	3.10		55.41	2.84		-0.57
Leisure studies	56.11	0.00	54.51	0.60		51.17	0.68		48.16	0.20		-7.95
Journalism	57.20	1.33	64.15	0.00		62.83	0.80		66.79	1.25		9.59
Area, ethnic, cultural, gender studies	59.67	0.57	61.53	0.41		66.70	0.44		68.91	0.91		9.24

Major							
Female-majority majors (%FEMALE = 60–80)							
Speech/drama	60.62	0.63	52.03	0.56	60.88	0.94	63.73	0.88	3.12
Psychology	62.22	4.54	72.47	5.60	74.45	5.99	77.09	6.10	14.88
English, incl. American lit	63.40	3.54	66.73	4.71	66.85	5.00	68.25	3.32	4.85
Health: clinical health	64.64	1.17	71.05	0.02	67.86	0.18	70.25	0.64	5.61
Anthropology/archaeology	64.87	0.56	65.21	0.57	64.72	0.67	69.29	0.36	4.42
Fine and performing arts	66.21	1.60	62.68	1.19	59.73	0.09	62.50	0.48	-3.71
Liberal studies	66.35	0.49	59.48	1.13	62.24	1.82	67.06	2.22	0.71
Design	68.01	0.31	61.11	1.06	57.60	2.43	66.34	1.67	-1.67
Education: other	69.67	15.03	78.20	7.64	74.59	8.84	78.38	6.87	8.71
Art history/fine art	70.10	0.31	68.21	0.81	63.96	1.74	68.54	1.94	-1.56
Foreign languages	73.87	1.53	72.29	1.18	69.97	1.33	69.90	0.92	-3.97
Health: dental/medical technology	74.83	0.68	88.46	0.30	96.87	0.25	97.41	0.05	22.58
Health: community/mental health	76.03	0.22	82.81	0.13	83.35	0.50	84.80	0.00	8.76
Health: health/hospital	77.17	0.38	78.33	0.06	75.55	0.12	78.21	0.16	1.04
Female-dominated majors (%FEMALE = 80–100)							
Social work	82.26	1.11	86.43	1.05	86.77	1.96	89.30	0.88	7.04
Health: physical education/recreation	86.29	0.90	48.06	0.24	48.14	0.33	47.66	1.39	-38.63
Education: special	90.79	2.62	92.55	0.73	89.13	0.52	90.47	0.51	-0.32
Home economics: all	92.09	1.64	90.41	0.61	85.28	0.30	84.93	0.38	-7.16
Health: general/other	92.33	0.06	81.25	0.32	79.74	1.65	84.65	0.70	-7.68
Secretarial	92.37	0.00	83.40	0.14	91.79	0.00	55.83	0.05	-36.53
Health: audiology	92.78	0.89	95.54	0.09	94.26	0.55	95.70	0.38	2.92
Health: dietetics	93.60	0.19	87.88	0.18	87.68	0.38	92.05	0.17	-1.56
Health: nursing	94.35	3.24	92.39	1.73	89.14	2.13	89.66	3.56	-4.69
Vocational home economics: child care	94.74	0.00	93.16	0.17	92.10	0.33	92.87	0.60	-1.87
Textiles	97.98	0.34	95.30	0.07	94.14	0.08	94.30	0.16	-3.69

Source: Author's calculations based on data from the IPEDS, NLS-72, B&B:1993, B&B:2000, and B&B:2008 data.

Note: Mean of %FEMALE is weighted by institution size, which is operationalized as the total number of degrees completed as reported in the IPEDS data.

Table A2. Estimated Coefficients for Models of Employment and Working Full Time

	Employed				Working Full Time			
	1976–1978	1993	2000	2008	1976–1978	1993	2000	2008
	b se(b)	b se(b)	b se(b)	b se(b)	b se(b)	b se(b)	b se(b)	b se(b)
Female	0.042 (0.620)	0.545 (0.800)	0.005 (0.788)	-1.238* (0.618)	-1.139* (0.475)	-0.768 (0.401)	1.996** (0.695)	-0.360 (0.484)
%FEMALE in degree field (omitted=0–20%)								
20–40%	0.312 (0.275)	0.243 (0.647)	0.066 (0.477)	0.019 (0.441)	-0.659** (0.252)	-0.354 (0.415)	0.236 (0.550)	-1.274** (0.404)
40–60%	0.245 (0.322)	0.206 (0.659)	-0.525 (0.483)	-0.953* (0.420)	-1.118*** (0.264)	-0.932* (0.437)	-1.009 (0.531)	-1.735** (0.445)
60–80%	0.368 (0.359)	-0.208 (0.658)	-0.510 (0.509)	0.001 (0.504)	-0.695* (0.278)	-1.074* (0.431)	-1.491** (0.528)	-1.855*** (0.442)
80–100%	2.764** (1.042)	2.131 (1.086)	-0.801 (0.613)	-1.046* (0.519)	-0.670 (0.452)	-1.414** (0.507)	-0.439 (0.603)	-2.066*** (0.486)
%FEMALE in degree field * Female								
20–40% * Female	0.148 (0.633)	-0.927 (0.934)	-0.450 (0.671)	0.847 (0.585)	1.398** (0.526)	0.570 (0.456)	-2.772*** (0.777)	0.485 (0.524)
40–60% * Female	0.289 (0.651)	-1.039 (0.875)	-0.345 (0.692)	1.212* (0.609)	1.370** (0.522)	0.604 (0.438)	-1.988** (0.769)	0.483 (0.554)
60–80% * Female	0.959 (0.662)	-0.712 (0.848)	0.167 (0.705)	0.120 (0.637)	0.949 (0.516)	0.722 (0.431)	-2.190** (0.775)	0.157 (0.532)
80–100% * Female	-1.955 (1.178)	-2.320 (1.210)	0.398 (0.788)	1.536* (0.664)	1.252* (0.631)	1.282* (0.590)	-2.406** (0.820)	0.977 (0.581)

Increase in %FEMALE		0.016	-0.021	0.000		-(0.002)	-0.036***	-0.037***
		(0.035)	(0.011)	(0.011)			(0.010)	(0.009)
* 20–40 %FEMALE in degree field		-0.012	0.014	-0.018		0.011	0.010	0.021
		(0.041)	(0.020)	(0.016)		(0.014)	(0.016)	(0.013)
* 40–60 %FEMALE in degree field		-0.035	0.019	0.014		0.017	0.029	0.038**
		(0.040)	(0.018)	(0.017)		(0.024)	(0.019)	(0.014)
* 60–80 %FEMALE in degree field		-0.015	0.035	-0.016		0.020	0.077***	0.035
		(0.051)	(0.026)	(0.023)			(0.023)	(0.020)
* 80–100 %FEMALE in degree field		-0.035	0.086	0.098		-(0.009)	-0.001	0.023
		(0.075)	(0.087)	(0.094)		0.025	(0.084)	(0.049)
						(0.016)		
						0.054		
Decrease in %FEMALE		-0.015	0.009	-0.003		0.933	0.062	-0.198
		(0.012)	(0.010)	(0.007)		(0.622)	(0.160)	(0.123)
* 20–40 %FEMALE in degree field						-0.927	-0.073	0.262*
						(0.613)	(0.167)	(0.129)
* 40–60 %FEMALE in degree field						-0.913	-0.080	0.203
						(0.619)	(0.162)	(0.124)
* 60–80 %FEMALE in degree field						-0.926	-0.036	0.190
						(0.623)	(0.160)	(0.124)
* 80–100 %FEMALE in degree field						-0.934	-0.089	0.189
						(0.623)	(0.161)	(0.123)
Black, Hispanic, or Native American	-0.492	-0.776*	-0.036	-0.357	-0.038	-0.355	-0.000	-0.444**
	(0.291)	(0.300)	(0.240)	(0.190)	(0.196)	(0.245)	(0.263)	(0.164)
Parents' highest level of education (omitted = high school or less)								
Some college	-0.201	0.002	0.205	0.062	-0.175	-0.093	-0.006	0.391*
	(0.262)	(0.374)	(0.264)	(0.226)	(0.166)	(0.150)	(0.231)	(0.174)
BA degree	-0.335	0.197	0.268	-0.005	-0.041	0.253	-0.162	0.228
	(0.262)	(0.264)	(0.247)	(0.230)	(0.173)	(0.166)	(0.225)	(0.170)
Postgraduate degree	-0.850***	-0.434	-0.402	-0.148	-0.357*	0.329	-0.094	0.333*
	(0.247)	(0.316)	(0.226)	(0.213)	(0.167)	(0.191)	(0.228)	(0.168)

(continued)

Table A2. (continued)

	Employed				Working Full Time			
	1976–1978	1993	2000	2008	1976–1978	1993	2000	2008
	b se(b)	b se(b)	b se(b)	b se(b)	b se(b)	b se(b)	b se(b)	b se(b)
Single, never married (vs. ever married)	-0.269 (0.261)	-0.417 (0.425)	-0.246 (0.433)	-0.752* (0.360)	-0.121 (0.121)	-0.256 (0.207)	-0.042 (0.205)	-0.217 (0.148)
* Female	0.018 (0.348)	0.265 (0.546)	0.293 (0.516)	0.735 (0.429)				
Have children	1.290 (0.890)	0.751 (0.216)	1.951** (0.717)	-0.072 (0.585)	0.343 (0.355)	-0.163 (0.488)	-0.285 (0.558)	0.345 (0.536)
* Female	-3.357*** (0.937)	-0.616 (0.834)	-2.155** (0.816)	0.143 (0.642)	-0.973* (0.448)	-0.536 (0.527)	-0.708 (0.584)	-0.691 (0.566)
Full-time, full-year student		-0.294 (0.230)	-0.088 (0.171)	-0.114 (0.156)		-(0.076) 0.130	0.131 (0.157)	-0.114 (0.120)
GPA in degree field		0.001 (0.002)	0.001*** (0.001)	0.006*** (0.002)		-0.000 (0.001)	-0.001 (0.001)	0.001 (0.001)

Course grades 1974-1976 (omitted = mostly As)

	(1)	(2)	(3)	(4)	(5)	(6)	(7)	(8)
Half As and half Bs	0.051				0.076			
	(0.208)				(0.155)			
Mostly Bs	1.110***				0.362			
	(0.255)				(0.164)			
Half Bs and half Cs	1.178***				0.526			
	(0.325)				(0.203)			
Mostly Cs, Ds, or below	1.685***				0.740			
	(0.509)				(0.316)			
No grades given	0.180				0.407			
	(0.342)				(0.355)			
Constant	2.309**	5.574**	2.393	2.893*	2.372***	2.650*	2.577	0.403
	(0.416)	(1.877)	(1.612)	(1.338)	(0.280)	(1.085)	(1.589)	(1.080)
Pseudo R^2	0.082	0.038	0.036	0.038	0.024	0.038	0.054	0.046
Sample size (n)	3753	3683	4329	5694	3516	3549	4077	5211

Source: Author's calcuations based on data from the IPEDS, NLS-72, B&B:1993, B&B2000, and B&B 2008 data.

Note: All estimates are weighted to account for sampling design. Models include dummy variable indicators of missing data on GPA in major, course grades, marital status, and parental status.

* $p < 0.05$; ** $p < 0.01$; *** $p < 0.001$

Table A3. Estimated Coefficients for Models of Employment Related to Degree Field and Salary

	Work Closely Related to Degree				Salary			
	1976–1978	1993	2000	2008	1976–1978	1993	2000	2008
	b se(b)	b se(b)	b se(b)	b se(b)	b se(b)	b se(b)	b se(b)	b se(b)
Female	-1.042* (0.509)	-0.389 (0.295)	-0.331 (0.323)	-0.217 (0.366)	-0.335*** (0.093)	-0.104 (0.082)	-0.208 (0.170)	-0.097 (0.078)
%FEMALE in degree field (omitted=0–20%)								
20–40%	-0.330 (0.201)	-0.917*** (0.255)	-0.689* (0.270)	-0.456 (0.306)	-0.217*** (0.037)	-0.217*** (0.064)	-0.151 (0.097)	-0.175* (0.070)
40–60%	-0.542* (0.242)	-1.023*** (0.291)	-1.005*** (0.266)	-0.845* (0.349)	-0.204*** (0.044)	-0.171* (0.072)	-0.233* (0.100)	-0.338*** (0.076)
60–80%	-0.152 (0.251)	-1.222*** (0.306)	-1.073*** (0.295)	-0.974** (0.353)	-0.232*** (0.037)	-0.314*** (0.061)	-0.362*** (0.112)	-0.490*** (0.099)
80–100%	0.180 (0.514)	0.809 (0.491)	0.401 (0.474)	0.304 (0.469)	-0.212*** (0.060)	-0.021 (0.150)	-0.355* (0.140)	-0.346* (0.146)
%FEMALE in degree field * Female								
20–40% * Female	1.084* (0.521)	0.029 (0.364)	0.038 (0.323)	-0.218 (0.369)	0.268** (0.092)	0.031 (0.081)	0.031 (0.183)	0.063 (0.091)
40–60% * Female	1.056 (0.541)	0.256 (0.349)	0.087 (0.328)	0.113 (0.412)	0.181 (0.093)	-0.059 (0.081)	0.022 (0.181)	-0.035 (0.090)
60–80% * Female	1.022 (0.528)	0.323 (0.347)	0.459 (0.310)	0.664 (0.379)	0.140 (0.094)	0.047 (0.081)	0.093 (0.184)	0.048 (0.111)
80–100% * Female	1.213 (0.694)	0.005 (0.452)	0.451 (0.464)	0.401 (0.469)	0.177 (0.117)	-0.098 (0.145)	0.190 (0.205)	0.186 (0.138)

	(1)	(2)	(3)	(4)	(5)	(6)	(7)	(8)
Increase in %FEMALE	−0.021*	−0.017*	−0.008		−0.006***	−0.008**	−0.005*	
	(0.010)	(0.007)	(0.009)		(0.002)	(0.003)	(0.002)	
* 20–40 %FEMALE in degree field	0.051***	0.030**	0.017		0.007*	0.006*	0.000	
	(0.013)	(0.011)	(0.012)		(0.003)	(0.003)	(0.003)	
* 40–60 %FEMALE in degree field	0.026	0.025*	0.016		0.005	0.007*	0.006	
	(0.016)	(0.012)	(0.014)		(0.003)	(0.003)	(0.003)	
* 60–80 %FEMALE in degree field	0.068***	0.042*	0.026		0.002	0.006	0.005	
	(0.020)	(0.018)	(0.018)		(0.003)	(0.006)	(0.008)	
* 80–100 %FEMALE in degree field	−0.042	−0.060	0.040		−0.010	−0.006	0.013	
	(0.046)	(0.055)	(0.065)		(0.009)	(0.009)	(0.013)	
Decrease in %FEMALE	0.027	0.123	−0.142		−0.041*	0.009	0.011	
	(0.109)	(0.110)	(0.096)		(0.017)	(0.014)	(0.011)	
* 20–40 %FEMALE in degree field	0.011	−0.078	0.148		0.047**	−0.003	−0.008	
	(0.117)	(0.112)	(0.098)		(0.018)	(0.015)	(0.012)	
* 40–60 %FEMALE in degree field	−0.020	−0.099	0.162		0.041*	−0.013	−0.003	
	(0.112)	(0.110)	(0.099)		(0.017)	(0.015)	(0.012)	
* 60–80 %FEMALE in degree field	−0.028	−0.127	0.108		0.039*	−0.007	−0.005	
	(0.110)	(0.111)	(0.097)		(0.017)	(0.014)	(0.012)	
* 80–100 %FEMALE in degree field	−0.060	−0.144	0.114		0.037*	−0.009	−0.015	
	(0.111)	(0.110)	(0.096)		(0.017)	(0.014)	(0.011)	
Black, Hispanic, or Native American	−0.684***	0.111	0.125	−0.132	−0.006	0.022	0.038	−0.043
	(0.189)	(0.143)	(0.146)	(0.141)	(0.067)	(0.031)	(0.026)	(0.066)
Parents' highest level of education (omitted = high school or less)								
Some college	−0.121	−0.095	−0.078	0.015	0.001	0.024	−0.031	−0.017
	(0.159)	(0.124)	(0.137)	(0.149)	(0.030)	(0.028)	(0.030)	(0.060)
BA degree	−0.238	−0.179	−0.178	0.054	0.051	0.014	−0.017	0.081
	(0.164)	(0.127)	(0.131)	(0.143)	(0.027)	(0.027)	(0.029)	(0.045)
Postgraduate degree	−0.512**	−0.214	−0.457***	−0.065	−0.043	−0.010	−0.015	0.056
	(0.166)	(0.155)	(0.129)	(0.148)	(0.061)	(0.032)	(0.039)	(0.042)

(continued)

Table A3. (continued)

	Work Closely Related to Degree						Salary							
	1976–1978		1993		2000		2008		1976–1978		1993		2000		2008
	b	se(b)	b	se(b)	b	se(b)	b	se(b)	b	se(b)	b	se(b)	b	se(b)	b	se(b)
Single, never married (vs. ever married)	−0.607***	(0.172)	−0.589**	(0.186)	−0.352	(0.180)	−0.344	(0.202)	−0.056	(0.046)	−0.022	(0.043)	−0.027	(0.040)	−0.032	(0.045)
* Female	0.297	(0.233)	0.177	(0.235)	0.220	(0.224)	0.082	(0.242)	−0.007	(0.057)	0.045	(0.050)	0.063	(0.052)	−0.044	(0.055)
Have children	0.122	(0.290)	−0.078	(0.285)	−0.015	(0.286)	0.086	(0.315)	0.095	(0.058)	0.019	(0.062)	−0.054	(0.066)	0.036	(0.094)
* Female	−0.085	(0.473)	0.188	(0.422)	0.110	(0.344)	0.235	(0.384)	−0.118	(0.073)	−0.125	(0.073)	0.074	(0.073)	−0.128	(0.127)
Full-time, full-year student			−0.048	(0.105)	0.026	(0.092)	−0.002	(0.092)			−0.010	(0.023)	−0.069	(0.024)	−0.006	(0.031)
GPA in degree field			0.003***	(0.001)	0.004***	(0.001)	0.006***	(0.001)			0.001	(0.000)	0.000	(0.000)	0.001	(0.000)

	(1)	(2)	(3)	(4)	(5)	(6)	(7)	(8)
Course grades 1974–1976 (omitted = mostly As)								
Half As and half Bs	-0.184		0.017					
	(0.158)		(0.055)					
Mostly Bs	-0.296		0.035					
	(0.164)		(0.054)					
Half Bs and half Cs	-0.498*		0.012					
	(0.200)		(0.056)					
Mostly Cs, Ds, or below	-0.547		-0.013					
	(0.316)		(0.099)					
No grades given	-0.485		-0.091					
	(0.258)		(0.144)					
Hours worked (among employed)					0.005**	0.018***	0.013***	0.015***
					(0.002)	(0.002)	(0.002)	(0.002)
Constant	0.877***	1.541	1.062	-1.626	10.226***	8.932***	10.054***	9.361***
	(0.259)	(0.921)	(0.818)	(0.974)	(0.085)	(0.273)	(0.215)	(0.392)
Pseudo R^2	0.043	0.050	0.049	0.051	0.052	0.141	0.074	0.088
Sample size (n)	2068	3133	3770	4418	2734	2875	3381	4418

Source: Author's calcuations based on data from the IPEDS, NLS-72, B&B:1993, B&B2000, and B&B 2008 data.

Note: All estimates are weighted to account for sampling design. Models include dummy variable indicators of missing data on GPA in major, course grades, marital status, and parental status.

*$p < 0.05$; **$p < 0.01$; ***$p < 0.001$

Table A4. Estimated Coefficients for Models of Salary for Those Working in Degree Field

	Salary (Among Full-Time Employed and Work Is Closely Related to Degree Field)			
	1976–1978	1993	2000	1976–1978
	b	b	b	b
	se(b)	se(b)	se(b)	se(b)
Female	−0.093	0.009	−0.289	−0.086
	(0.109)	(0.128)	(0.268)	(0.086)
%FEMALE in degree field (omitted=0–20%)				
20–40%	−0.281***	−0.119	−0.217*	−0.275***
	(0.085)	(0.082)	(0.106)	(0.056)
40–60%	−0.347***	−0.124	−0.318**	−0.421***
	(0.064)	(0.117)	(0.112)	(0.063)
60–80%	−0.417***	−0.391***	−0.429***	−0.535***
	(0.063)	(0.093)	(0.110)	(0.084)
80–100%	−0.343*	−0.093	−0.586***	−0.193**
	(0.134)	(0.208)	(0.174)	(0.071)
%FEMALE in degree field * Female				
20–40% * Female	0.070	−0.086	0.128	0.069
	(0.142)	(0.097)	(0.292)	(0.118)
40–60% * Female	−0.036	−0.105	0.121	−0.081
	(0.107)	(0.124)	(0.287)	(0.105)
60–80% * Female	0.094	0.013	0.140	0.052
	(0.130)	(0.098)	(0.275)	(0.099)
80–100% * Female	0.009	−0.100	0.420	0.027
	(0.152)	(0.202)	(0.315)	(0.098)
Increase in %FEMALE		−0.005*	−0.013**	−0.006***
		(0.003)	(0.005)	(0.002)
* 20–40 %FEMALE in degree field		0.004	0.010*	0.000
		(0.003)	(0.004)	(0.004)
* 40–60 %FEMALE in degree field		−0.001	0.014**	0.005
		(0.004)	(0.005)	(0.003)
* 60–80 %FEMALE in degree field		0.005	0.013*	0.007
		(0.004)	(0.006)	(0.005)
* 80–100 %FEMALE in degree field		−0.007	−0.001	−0.011
		(0.010)	(0.013)	(0.008)
Decrease in %FEMALE		−0.039	0.011	−0.001
		(0.031)	(0.017)	(0.014)
* 20–40 %FEMALE in degree field		0.041	−0.002	0.010
		(0.033)	(0.018)	(0.015)
* 40–60 %FEMALE in degree field		0.039	−0.014	0.010
		(0.031)	(0.018)	(0.014)
* 60–80 %FEMALE in degree field		0.039	−0.008	0.001
		(0.031)	(0.017)	(0.014)
* 80–100 %FEMALE in degree field		0.038	−0.009	−0.006
		(0.032)	(0.017)	(0.014)
Black, Hispanic, or Native American	0.202*	0.010	0.004	0.111*
	(0.095)	(0.041)	(0.040)	(0.046)

Table A4. (continued)

	Salary (Among Full-Time Employed and Work Is Closely Related to Degree Field)			
	1976-1978	1993	2000	1976-1978
	b	b	b	b
	se(b)	se(b)	se(b)	se(b)
Parents' highest level of education (omitted = high school or less)				
Some college	-0.043	0.050	-0.038	-0.001
	(0.048)	(0.039)	(0.042)	(0.049)
BA degree	0.051	0.020	0.004	0.043
	(0.041)	(0.040)	(0.033)	(0.047)
Postgraduate degree	-0.071	0.013	-0.020	0.048
	(0.117)	(0.042)	(0.063)	(0.036)
Age at degree attainment		0.020	0.012	0.028**
		(0.009)	(0.007)	(0.009)
Single, never married (vs. ever married)	0.049	0.065	-0.021	0.033
	(0.110)	(0.060)	(0.041)	(0.046)
* Female	-0.135	-0.053	0.005	-0.023
	(0.116)	(0.075)	(0.057)	(0.058)
Have children	0.075	-0.016	-0.022	0.057
	(0.131)	(0.078)	(0.044)	(0.073)
* Female	-0.017	-0.045	0.011	-0.266
	(0.139)	(0.087)	(0.063)	(0.157)
Full-time, full-year student		0.024	-0.056	0.014
		(0.028)	(0.030)	(0.037)
GPA in degree field		0.001*	0.001*	0.001***
		(0.000)	(0.000)	(0.000)
Course grades 1974-1976 (omitted = mostly As)				
Half As and half Bs	-0.040			
	(0.036)			
Mostly Bs	-0.034			
	(0.036)			
Half Bs and half Cs	-0.023			
	(0.050)			
Mostly Cs, Ds, or below	-0.502			
	(0.430)			
No grades given	-0.373			
	(0.395)			
Hours worked (among employed)	0.001	0.012***	0.010***	0.008***
	(0.003)	(0.002)	(0.003)	(0.002)
Constant	10.736***	9.312***	10.033***	9.479***
	0.111	(0.313)	(0.222)	(0.260)
Pseudo R^2	0.086	0.156	0.085	0.110
Sample size (n)	921	1504	1982	2242

Source: Author's calcuations based on data from the IPEDS, NLS-72, B&B:1993, B&B2000, and B&B 2008 data.

Note: All estimates are weighted to account for sampling design. Models include dummy variable indicators of missing data on GPA in major, course grades, marital status, and parental status.

*$p < 0.05$; **$p < 0.01$; ***$p < 0.001$

REFERENCES

Bergmann, Barbara R. 1974. "Occupational Segregation, Wages and Profits When Employers Discriminate by Race or Sex." *Eastern Economic Journal* 1(2): 103–10.

Blau, Francine D., Peter Brummund, and Albert Yung-Hsu Liu. 2013. "Trends in Occupational Segregation by Gender 1970–2009: Adjusting for the Impact of Changes in the Occupational Coding System." *Demography* 50(2): 471–92.

Bobbitt-Zeher, Donna. 2007. "The Gender Income Gap and the Role of Education." *Sociology of Education* 80(1): 1–22.

Brown, Charles, and Mary Corcoran. 1997. "Sex-Based Differences in School Content and the Male-Female Wage Gap." *Journal of Labor Economics* 15(3): 431–65.

Carnevale, Anthony P., Jeff Strohl, and Michelle Melton. 2011. "What's It Worth? The Economic Value of College Majors." Washington, D.C.: Georgetown University Center on Education and the Workforce.

Charles, Maria, and Karen Bradley. 2002. "Equal but Separate? A Cross-National Study of Sex Segregation in Higher Education." *American Sociological Review* 67(4): 573–99.

———. 2009. "Indulging Our Gendered Selves? Sex Segregation by Field of Study in 44 Countries." *American Journal of Sociology* 114(4): 924–76.

Charles, Maria, and David Grusky. 2004. *Occupational Ghettos: The Worldwide Segregation of Women and Men*. Stanford, Calif.: Stanford University Press.

DiPrete, Thomas A., and Claudia Buchmann. 2013. *The Rise of Women: The Growing Gender Gap in Education and What It Means for American Schools*. New York: Russell Sage Foundation.

Eagly, Alice H., and Linda L. Carli. 2007. *Through the Labyrinth: The Truth About How Women Become Leaders*. Boston, Mass.: Harvard Business School Press.

England, Paula. 1992. *Comparable Worth: Theories and Evidence*. New York: Aldine de Gruyter.

———. 2006. "Toward Gender Equality: Progress and Bottlenecks." In *The Declining Significance of Gender?* edited by Francine D. Blau, Mary C. Brinton, and David B. Grusky. New York: Russell Sage Foundation.

England, Paula, Paul Allison, and Yuxiao Wu. 2007. "Does Bad Pay Cause Occupations to Feminize, Does Feminization Reduce Pay, and How Can We Tell with Longitudinal Data?" *Social Science Research* 36: 1237–56.

England, Paula, and Su Li. 2006. "Desegregation Stalled: The Changing Gender Composition of College Majors, 1971–2002." *Gender & Society* 20: 657–677.

Goldin, Claudia. 1990. *Understanding the Gender Gap: An Economic History of American Women*. Oxford: Oxford University Press.

———. 2006. "The Quiet Revolution That Transformed Women's Employment, Education, and Family." *AEA Papers and Proceedings* 96: 1–21.

Goldin, Claudia, Lawrence Katz, and Ilyana Kuziemko. 2006. "The Homecoming of American College Women: The Reversal of the College Gender Gap." *Journal of Economic Perspectives* 20(4): 133–56.

Grogger, Jeff, and Eric Eide. 1995. "Changes in College Skills and the Rise in the College Wage Premium." *Journal of Human Resources* 30(2): 280–310.

Heijke, Hans, Christoph Meng, and Ger Ramaekers. 2003. "An Investigation into the Role of Human Capital Competences and Their Pay-Off." *International Journal of Manpower* 24(7): 750–73.

Jacobs, Jerry A. 1995. "Gender and Academic Specialties: Trends Among Recipients of College Degrees in the 1980s." *Sociology of Education* 68(2): 81–98.

———. 2003. "Detours on the Road to Equality: Women, Work and Higher Education." *Contexts* 2(1): 32–41.

Joy, Lois. 2003. "Salaries of Recent Male and Female College Graduates: Educational and Labor Market Effects." *Industrial and Labor Relations Review* 56(4): 606–21.

———. 2006. "Occupational Differences Between Recent Male and Female College Graduates." *Economics of Education Review* 25(2): 221–31.

Kanter, Rosabeth M. 1977a. *Men and Women of the Corporation*. New York: Basic Books.

———. 1977b. "Some Effects of Proportions on Group Life: Skewed Sex Ratios and Responses to Token Women." *American Journal of Sociology* 82(5): 965–90.

Knobloch-Westerwick, Silvia, Carroll J. Glynn, and Michael Huge. 2013. "The Matilda Effect in Science Communication: An Experiment on Gender Bias in Publication Quality Perceptions and Collaboration Interest." *Science Communication* 35(5): 603–25.

Koput, Kenneth W., and Barbara A. Gutek. 2010. *Gender Stratification in the IT Industry: Sex, Status and Social Capital.* Northampton, Mass.: Edward Elgar.

Levanon, Asaf, Paula England, and Paul Allison. 2009. "Occupational Feminization and Pay: Assessing Causal Dynamics Using 1950-2000 U.S. Census Data." *Social Forces* 88(2): 865-91.

Logel, Christine, Gregory M. Walton, Steven J. Spencer, Emma C. Iserman, William von Hippel, and Amy E. Bell. 2009. "Interacting with Sexist Men Triggers Social Identity Threat Among Female Engineers." *Journal of Personality and Social Psychology* 96(6): 1089-103.

Loury, Linda Datcher. 1997. "The Gender Earnings Gap Among College-Educated Workers." *Industrial & Labor Relations Review* 50(4): 580-93.

Morgan, Laurie A. 2008. "Major Matters: A Comparison of the Within-Major Gender Pay Gap Across College Majors for Early-Career Graduates." *Industrial Relations: A Journal of Economy and Society* 47(4): 625-50.

Moss-Racusin, Corinne A., John F. Dovidio, Victoria L. Brescoll, Mark J. Graham, and Jo Handelsman. 2012. "Science Faculty's Subtle Gender Biases Favor Male Students." *Proceedings of the National Academy of Sciences* 109(41): 16474-79.

National Center for Education Statistics. 1994. NLS-72 National Longitudinal Study of the High School Class of 1972. NCES Publication No. 1994487REV.

———. 2003. Baccalaureate and Beyond Longitudinal Study (B&B:2000/01). {Restricted use data files}.

———. 2004. Baccalaureate and Beyond Longitudinal Study (B&B:93/2003). {Restricted use data files}.

———. 2012. 2008-09 Baccalaureate and Beyond Longitudinal Study: Restricted-Use First Followup Data Files and File Documentation. NCES Publication No. 2012245.

Reskin, Barbara F., and Paula Roos. 1990. *Job Queues, Gender Queues: Explaining Women's Inroads into Male Occupations.* Philadelphia, Pa.: Temple University Press.

Reuben, Ernesto, Paola Sapienza, and Luigi Zingales. 2014. "How Stereotypes Impair Women's Careers in Science." *Proceedings of the National Academy of Sciences* 111(12): 4403-8.

Ridgeway, Cecilia L. 2014. "Why Status Matters for Inequality." *American Sociological Review* 79(1): 1-16.

Robst, John. 2007. "Education and Job Match: The Relatedness of College Major and Work." *Economics of Education Review* 26(4): 397-407.

Rogers, Stacy J., and Elizabeth G. Menaghan. 1991. "Women's Persistence in Undergraduate Majors: The Effects of Gender-Disproportionate Representation." *Gender and Society* 5(4): 549-64.

Roksa, Josipa, and Tania Levey. 2010. "What Can You Do with That Degree? College Major and Occupational Status of College Graduates over Time." *Social Forces* 89(2): 389-415.

Shauman, Kimberlee A. 2006. "Occupational Sex Segregation and the Earnings of Occupations: What Causes the Link Among College-Educated Workers?" *Social Science Research* 35(3): 577-619.

———. 2009. "Are There Sex Differences in the Utilization of Educational Capital Among College-Educated Workers?" *Social Science Research* 38(3): 535-71.

Sheltzer, Jason M., and Joan C. Smith. 2014. "Elite Male Faculty in the Life Sciences Employ Fewer Women." *Proceedings of the National Academy of Sciences* 111(28): 10107-12.

Sorensen, Elaine. 1990. "The Crowding Hypothesis and Comparable Worth." *Journal of Human Resources* 25(1): 55-89.

Steele, Jennifer, Jacquelyn B. James, and Rosalind Chait Barnett. 2002. "Learning in a Man's World: Examining the Perceptions of Undergraduate Women in Male-Dominated Academic Areas." *Psychology of Women Quarterly* 26(1): 46-50.

Williams, Christine L. 1992. "The Glass Escalator: Hidden Advantages for Men in the 'Female' Professions." *Social Problems* 39(3): 253-67.

Xie, Yu, and Alexandra A. Killewald. 2012. *Is American Science in Decline?* Cambridge, Mass.: Harvard University Press.

Explaining the Gender Wage Gap in STEM: Does Field Sex Composition Matter?

KATHERINE MICHELMORE AND SHARON SASSLER

Using the National Science Foundation's SESTAT data, we examine the gender wage gap by race among those working in computer science, life sciences, physical sciences, and engineering. We find that in fields with a greater representation of women (the life and physical sciences), the gender wage gap can largely be explained by differences in observed characteristics between men and women working in those fields. In the fields with the lowest concentration of women (computer science and engineering), gender wage gaps persist even after controlling for observed characteristics. In assessing how this gap changes over time, we find evidence of a narrowing for more recent cohorts of college graduates in the life sciences and engineering. The computer sciences and physical sciences, however, show no clear pattern in the gap across cohorts of graduates.

Keywords: scientists and engineers, gender wage gap, women in STEM

Enormous progress was made in narrowing the gender wage gap in the 1970s and 1980s, but since the 1990s relatively little movement has been made toward wage parity (Blau and Kahn 2006). The gender pay gap has persisted even though women now make up the majority of college graduates and have for a few decades (DiPrete and Buchmann 2013; Goldin, Katz, and Kuziemko 2006). Despite sizable increases in the likelihood that American women graduate with degrees in science, technology, engineering, and math (STEM) fields, women's representation in the STEM workforce lags behind their educational gains (Xie and Shauman 2003). Women who major in STEM fields are less likely than their male counterparts to enter STEM occupations or remain in them (Glass et al. 2013; Ma and Savas 2014; Mann and DiPrete 2013; Sassler et al. 2011). Proponents of diversifying the gender representation of STEM have long argued that having more women in STEM education and employment would help improve retention of women (Committee on Maximizing the Potential of Women 2006; Hill,

Katherine Michelmore is assistant professor in the Department of Public Administration and International Affairs at Syracuse University. **Sharon Sassler** is professor in the Department of Policy Analysis and Management at Cornell University.

This research was supported by Grant no. OSP #68979 from the National Science Foundation (NSF). Katherine Michelmore acknowledges the Institute of Education Sciences, U.S. Department of Education, which provided support through Grant no. R305B110001. The content is solely the responsibility of the authors and does not necessarily represent the official views of the National Science Foundation. The authors wish to thank Martha Bailey and Thomas DiPrete for helpful comments and suggestions. Any remaining errors are the authors'. Direct correspondence to: Katherine Michelmore at kmichelm@umich.edu, 935 S. State St. Ann Arbor, MI 48109; and Sharon Sassler at sharon.sassler@cornell.edu, Department of Policy Analysis and Management, Cornell University, 297 Martha Van Rennselaer Hall, Ithaca, NY 14850.

Corbett, and Rose 2010), which should also narrow the gender wage gap in the labor force overall. To date, however, research on occupations with large increases in the share of female workers has generally failed to find evidence of occupational or economic equality (Kogan and Kalter 2006; Roos and Reskin 1992).

Despite the large literature on the gender wage gap and how it has evolved over time (see, for example, Blau and Kahn 1994, 1997, 2006; Mandel and Semyonov 2014), these studies focus on the labor market as a whole, or broad sectors of the labor market. Two of the most common explanations for the gender pay gap are differences in human capital accumulation and occupational segregation. Such explanations should apply less well to the STEM labor force, given that individuals have already selected occupational concentrations and require the same minimum credentials. Yet findings reveal that the gender pay gap persists, whether among those concentrating in particular fields, or among those with a specific degree (see, for example, Bertrand, Goldin, and Katz 2009; Ginther 2003; Morgan 1998). Such disparities are generally attributed to differences in the working patterns of men and women.

In this paper, we assess the presence of and factors contributing to the gender wage gap in the STEM workforce. Building on previous work, this paper makes several contributions to the literature. First, we present a descriptive portrait of the gap in each of the four main STEM fields by racial-ethnic group. Causality is difficult to determine in this context, because individuals may positively (or negatively) select into STEM majors, and STEM occupations and any analysis based on survey data is likely to suffer from omitted variable bias. We can, however, assess the extent to which observed characteristics can explain the gap by field and racial and ethnic origin. Second, we investigate how a specific factor, change in the sex composition of the field, is associated with wages of all workers in a given field. For this analysis, we rely on within-occupation variation in the share of women working in a given field over time to estimate the relationship between sex composition and the wages of the men and women working in those fields. Although it is difficult to confidently argue that this relationship is causal, the data used in this analysis do allow for a rich set of demographic controls as well as occupation fixed effects to control for time-invariant unobservable characteristics that may affect wages. This is a significant improvement over previous work that relies solely on cross-sectional differences across fields, where omitted variable bias is likely to influence estimates. However, we are unable to control for time-varying unobserved factors specific to an occupation that may influence wages over time. Finally, using repeated cross-sectional data between 1995 and 2008, we estimate how the gender wage gap has evolved across the career span and by college cohort, estimating the extent to which it can be explained by a cohort effect or a glass-ceiling effect.

Results indicate a persistent gender pay gap in the two STEM fields with the smallest female representation—engineering and computer science—which also account for the largest share of STEM workers and have the rosiest growth projections for the future. These differences remain even after accounting for observed characteristics such as disparities in years of potential work experience. In the life sciences and physical sciences, the gender wage gap can be completely explained by observed characteristics for whites, African Americans, and Asians.

In assessing how overall wages change within a field as a function of female representation, we find a positive relationship (at least up to a point) between the lagged sex composition of the field and future wages for those working in computer science, life sciences, and engineering. We find no significant relationship between the share of women working in the physical sciences and wages in that field. In assessing whether the gender wage gap changes over the course of one's career (glass-ceiling effect) or across time (cohort effect), we find evidence of a narrowing across cohorts for women working in the life sciences and engineering, such that the most recent cohorts of women working in STEM earn on par with the men in those fields. In computer science and the physical sciences, we find no significant trend in the gender wage gap over time. Finally, we find some evidence that the gap widens over the careers of women in computer science, but we find no evidence of a glass-ceiling effect in any of the other three STEM fields.

EXPLANATIONS FOR THE PERSISTENT GENDER WAGE GAP

The gender wage gap has received much attention over the last several decades, particularly because progress in narrowing the gap has largely stalled. Gender pay disparities narrowed rapidly in the 1980s, but progress since then has been far more modest (Blau and Kahn 2006). Among the reasons women historically earned less than men are gender differences in occupational concentration, human capital accumulation, work history, and discrimination. Some of these explanations have become less relevant in the twenty-first century as women have increased their participation in the workforce and obtained college and advanced degrees; others, such as differences in the working patterns of men and women, continue to have an impact on earnings differentials (Weeden, Cha, and Bucca, this issue; Blau and Kahn 2006; Mandel and Semyonov 2014).

Women surpassed men in their college attendance and graduation as of the 1980s; by the early 2000s, 60 percent of all college degrees were granted to women (DiPrete and Buchmann 2013; Goldin, Katz, and Kuziemko 2006). The narrowing education gap has been credited with reducing some of the gender pay gap (Mandel and Semyonov 2014). In fact, as of 2012 there was virtually no difference in pay between men and women ages twenty-five to thirty-four working full time (Pew Research 2013). That is not to say that employed women may not experience what is often termed the glass ceiling in terms of earnings. Earnings differentials tend to emerge over the course of careers, given that women are more likely than men to take time out of the labor force, or to reduce the hours they work, to have and raise children (Bertrand, Goldin, and Katz 2009; Budig and England 2001; Byker, this issue; Goldin 2014), although recent studies have found a positive wage differential for some mothers (Buchmann and McDaniel, this issue; Pal and Waldfogel, this issue). This represents a shift in recent years, given that estimates from the late 1980s and early 1990s indicated a negative motherhood wage differential of about 6 percent (Budig and England 2001; Pal and Waldfogel, this issue) that narrowed to about 1 percent as of 2011 (Pal and Waldfogel, this issue). Among certain groups, a positive wage differential has been found in most recent years. Pal and Waldfogel (this issue) find a 2 percent positive wage differential for married mothers versus unmarried childless women in 2011, and Buchmann and McDaniel (this issue) find a similar wage differential for mothers versus nonmothers working in STEM and law in 2010. Recent studies have also shown that a significant share of the gender pay gap can be explained by differences in the number of hours men and women work (Bertrand, Goldin, and Katz 2009; Mandel and Semyonov 2014), as well as the overtime hours of professional workers (Weeden, Cha, and Bucca, this issue).

The presence of older cohorts in the workforce may account for a large portion of the remaining gender wage gap due to differences in working patterns and discrimination; we would expect this to narrow as these cohorts retire. The extent to which discrimination continues to account for the gap is hotly contested. Some assert that variations in employment patterns are the result of preferences (Hakim 2000), though such work has been met with fierce criticism, often focused on the structural barriers women with children face in the labor market (Halrynjo and Lyng 2009; Stähli et al. 2009). Results from Blinder-Oaxaca decompositions of the gap over time indicate that discrimination has diminished as a contributor to the gender earnings gap in the overall labor market between 1970 and 2010 (Mandel and Semyonov 2014).

Nonetheless, although women today may face fewer barriers to employment in challenging professions than they once did, their representation in various fields remains stubbornly low. Tremendous resources have been devoted to increasing women's representation in STEM study across the educational spectrum and into careers (Beede et al. 2011; Committee on Maximizing the Potential of Women 2006).[1] Such efforts are premised on the belief that increasing the presence of women will make women more comfortable pursuing such fields of study, and will also have the long-term effect of diversifying leadership in STEM jobs. Furthermore, an increasing proportion of women working in STEM occupations will signal other women that they can succeed in such positions. The success of such developments rests largely on the accumulation of women across cohorts. But some evidence indicates that when too many women enter into a particular occupation and jobs become feminized, earnings and occupational prestige decline for both women and men (Goldin 2002; Levanon, England, and Allison 2009; Mandel 2013). We test whether this phenomenon applies to the STEM labor force as well.

We expand on prior work analyzing the gender wage gap in STEM occupations. Our analysis uses a broad range of cohorts of college graduates and covers a broader range of STEM professionals than many studies. We pay particular attention to how the presence of women in the field is associated with wages in those fields. Because we have several years of data, we are able to control for time-constant occupation level factors that may affect wages, analyzing how the within-occupation changes in sex composition are associated with wages in the field. There are opposing theoretical views on how the presence of other women in the workplace may affect wages. One argument is that increasing the presence of women may tip the occupation to a predominantly female occupation and subsequently devalue (or pollute) the field, thereby resulting in lower wages for all individuals within the field. Some evidence of this phenomenon is indicated in specific (nonscientific) fields and the overall labor market (Huffman and Velasco 1997; Jacobsen 2007; Mandel 2013). Others have suggested, on the other hand, that increasing the presence of women in the field may increase wages for women specifically, particularly if women have more control over hiring decisions (Cohen and Huffman 2003, 2007; Cotter et al. 1997). The extent to which the presence of women in STEM occupations affects the wages of men and women who work in STEM is an open question.

We begin by illustrating trends in the STEM labor force over time, noting increases in the share of women majoring in, and working in, STEM fields. We next analyze the gender wage gap in each STEM field using ordinary least squares (OLS) regressions of logged wages on observed characteristics, noting how the gap changes with the addition of these controls. We describe differences in pay gaps for racial and ethnic groups and further distinguish between women with children and women without children in some analyses. To test the devaluation theory, we analyze how changes in the sex composition of the field are associated with wages of the men and women who work in those fields. We test our hypotheses regarding the cohort effect and the glass-ceiling effect by analyzing how the gender wage gap has evolved for more recent cohorts of college graduates and whether it grows over the course of the career.

DATA AND MEASUREMENT

Data come from pooling six waves of the National Science Foundation's (NSF) Scientists and Engineers Statistical Data System (SESTAT), covering 1995 through 2008. SESTAT comprises three ongoing surveys designed to create a nationally representative sample of science and engineering college degree holders. The integrated data are from the National Survey of College Graduates Science and Engineering Panel, the National Survey of Recent College Graduates, and the Survey of Doctoral Recipients. SESTAT participants have all received at least a bachelor's degree and have at least one degree in science or engineering, or are individuals holding any college degree who work in a science or engineering occupation. The restricted SESTAT data include detailed in-

---

1. For example, the report produced by David Beede and his colleagues for the U.S. Department of Commerce included the following conclusion: "The findings provide definitive evidence of a need to encourage and support women in STEM with a goal of gender parity" (2011, 8).

formation regarding labor-force participation, occupation categories, educational attainment, and demographic characteristics.

Only those who received their bachelor's degrees between 1970 and 2004 are considered, and only those who majored in STEM and worked in STEM occupations at the time of the interview are included for the analysis. We further restrict our sample to individuals who work at least thirty-five hours per week, although results including part-time workers are quite similar and are available on request. This results in a sample of 61,417 individuals. We then run OLS regressions of the logged hourly wage on gender, adding controls to see whether background characteristics and workforce experience can explain the gender wage gap. Regressions are run separately by racial-ethnic group and for each of the four main STEM occupation categories: computer science and mathematics, life sciences, physical sciences, and engineering. All regressions are weighted by the person weights provided.

Measurement

Our dependent variable of interest is the logged hourly wage for individuals working in STEM occupations. The SESTAT data provide information on annual earnings from the main occupation, as well as average weekly hours spent on the main job, and the number of weeks worked at the main job in the last year. Using these variables, we construct an hourly wage by dividing annual salary by weeks worked per year and by hours worked per week. We then calculate the log of the wage, as is customary in this literature. All wages are converted to year 2014 dollars using the consumer price index.

Our key independent variable of interest is the gender of the respondent. We estimate separate gender wage gaps for whites, blacks, Hispanics, and Asians by running separate regressions for each group. Given the large foreign-born representation in the STEM workforce (Sana 2010), we also include a dummy variable indicating whether respondents were born outside the United States to noncitizen parents.

We also account for a number of other workforce and demographic characteristics that might explain differences in hourly wages between men and women. We include these controls in stages to test the roles of human capital accumulation, family characteristics, and gender composition in contributing to the gender wage gap. Our measures of human capital accumulation include a quadratic specification of potential years of work experience, measured by the number of years since receiving a college degree; college degree cohort, measured in five-year intervals; and graduate school experience, measured by indicators for having a master's degree in a STEM field, a doctorate in a STEM field, or a higher degree in a non-STEM field.[2]

Controls for family characteristics include indicators for respondent's union status and parental status. We construct dummy variables measuring whether the respondent is married or cohabiting with a partner. Our measure of parental status captures whether respondents have any children, and whether respondents have any children under the age of six specifically. We allow the effects of family characteristics to differ for men and women by interacting an indicator for female with each family characteristic.

Finally, to test the devaluation theory that increasing the share of women in a field results in a decline in prestige (and therefore wages) of the field, we analyze how the gender composition of the STEM workforce is associated with wages in those fields. We construct a measure of the lagged share of women working in each specific STEM occupation and model the relationship between the share of women working in STEM on wages of the men and women who work in those fields. This measure is intended to proxy for the gender composition of the work environment, so it is constructed separately for each STEM occupation

---

2. We use potential work experience to avoid issues of endogeneity of labor-force participation, but this also does not account for any time spent out of the labor force. Women are historically more likely to take time out of the labor force for childrearing, so this measure of potential work experience will likely overestimate total years of experience for women.

and varies by survey year. We construct the lag based on the concentration of women working in each specific STEM occupation in the SESTAT wave prior to the current wave. A list of occupations included in each STEM field is presented in table A1. For example, in the 1995 SESTAT, the lagged share of women working in STEM is measured based on the men and women working in each STEM occupation in the 1993 SESTAT survey. This term is updated for each SESTAT wave, such that the gender composition of the field changes with each survey year. Similar to the approach used by Asaf Levanon and his colleagues (2009), in all analyses we include fixed effects for each specific STEM occupation to control for time-invariant differences in unobservable characteristics that might affect wages in each field. Variation in this term is generated by within-occupation changes in the gender composition over time. Although we cannot control for time-varying characteristics within occupations that might be correlated with wages, this strategy does improve upon prior work that relies on cross-sectional variation in sex composition across occupations, which likely suffers from omitted variable bias. To make a causal statement about the relationship between sex composition within an occupation and the gender wage gap with this analysis, we must assume that any unobserved characteristics correlated with wages are time-constant within occupations and can therefore be controlled for with occupation fixed effects.

Scatter plots depicting the variation in the share of women working in each STEM field by SESTAT wave are presented in figures 1 through 4, with separate scatter plots for each of the four main STEM fields. These scatter plots illustrate the variation across occupations as well as within occupations over time. In computer and mathematical sciences, for instance, women make up approximately 40 percent of mathematicians in the 1995 SESTAT wave but only about 25 percent of computer scientists. The share of women working as mathematicians declines substantially over this period to approximately 30 percent of workers in 2008; the proportions were even lower among women in computer science in recent years, at just 20 percent. In many other STEM occupations, women have increased their representation over time, though the extent of this increase varies by occupation. The share of women working as biological scientists increases from about 45 to 55 percent, and that of those in chemical engineering fluctuates between 20 and 25 percent.

We then model the association between logged wages and the lagged share of women working in each field. Because this relationship may not be linear (for instance, wages may rise as the share of women working in STEM increases only up to a threshold, also thought of as a tipping point), we model the share of women working in STEM using a quartile specification. Specifically, we look at the distribution of the concentration of women working in STEM, labeling those with the lowest concentration of women in the bottom quartile and those with the greatest concentration of women working in an occupation in the top quartile. Because variation in the share of women working in an occupation across STEM fields is substantial, we construct these quartiles separately for each of the four broad STEM fields. For instance, the distribution of women working in engineering ranged from 5 to 25 percent. Whereas the mean share of women engineers in the lowest quartile was 7.1 percent, in the highest quartile it was only 18.7 percent—less than the lowest quartile for women in computer science or in the life sciences. Further, because wages might be lower in certain STEM occupations than in others (mathematics versus computer science, for instance) and this is correlated with the share of women working in those fields, we include controls for specific occupations in all models, such that we measure the impact of increasing the share of women within a specific STEM occupation on wages in those fields. This approach enables us to determine, for example, how wages for biological scientists change when the share of female biological scientists increases from 45 to 55 percent.

RESULTS

Figure 5 illustrates the trends in the share of women majoring in and working in STEM for each STEM field by college cohort. The solid lines represent the share of women majoring

Figure 1. Scatter Plots of Women in STEM Occupations, Computer and Mathematical Sciences

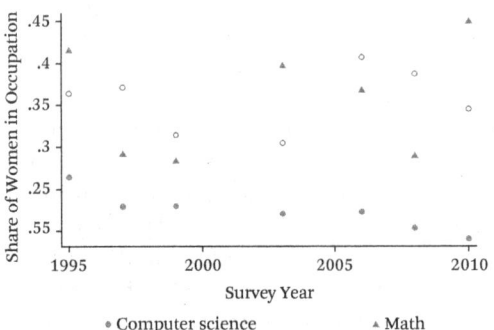

- Computer science
- Math
- Postsecondary professions

Source: Authors' calculations based on data from the National Science Foundation's Scientists and Engineers Statistical Data System (SESTAT) 1995–2008.
Note: All men and women working in STEM.

Figure 2. Scatter Plots of Women in STEM Occupations, Life Sciences

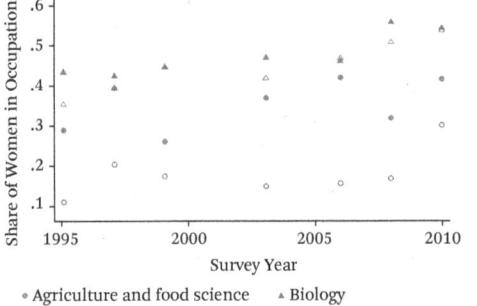

- Agriculture and food science
- Biology
- Environmental science
- Postsecondary professions

Source: Authors' calculations based on data from the National Science Foundation's Scientists and Engineers Statistical Data System (SESTAT) 1995–2008.
Note: All men and women working in STEM.

Figure 3. Scatter Plots of Women in STEM Occupations, Physical Sciences

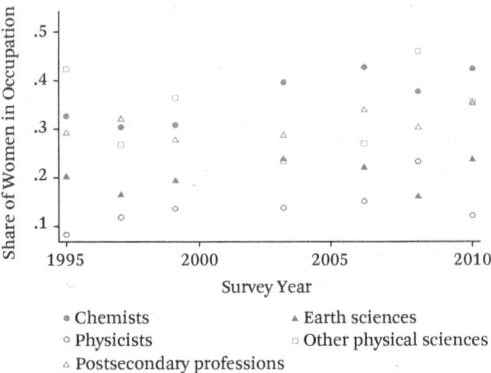

- Chemists
- Earth sciences
- Physicists
- Other physical sciences
- Postsecondary professions

Source: Authors' calculations based on data from the National Science Foundation's Scientists and Engineers Statistical Data System (SESTAT) 1995–2008.
Note: All men and women working in STEM.

Figure 4. Scatter Plots of Women in STEM Occupations, Engineering

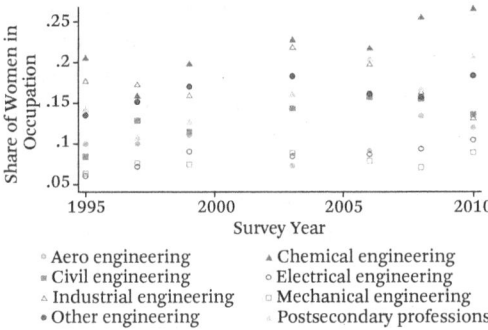

- Aero engineering
- Chemical engineering
- Civil engineering
- Electrical engineering
- Industrial engineering
- Mechanical engineering
- Other engineering
- Postsecondary professions

Source: Authors' calculations based on data from the National Science Foundation's Scientists and Engineers Statistical Data System (SESTAT) 1995–2008.
Note: All men and women working in STEM.

in STEM, and the dotted lines indicate the share of women working in STEM by college cohort. In all fields except for computer science, the increase in the representation of women in STEM majors since the 1960s has been substantial. Whereas women accounted for approximately 30 percent of the 1960 to 1969 cohort of life science majors, they made up more than 60 percent of those graduating between 2000 and 2004. A similar increase occurred in the physical sciences, where the share of women rose from 16 percent to 40 percent over the period. Although still a small proportion, women majoring in engineering increased tenfold between 1960 and 2004, from 2 to 20 percent. In all three of these fields, the share of women majoring in STEM also coincides closely with the share working in STEM.

Figure 5. Female STEM Majors and Workers

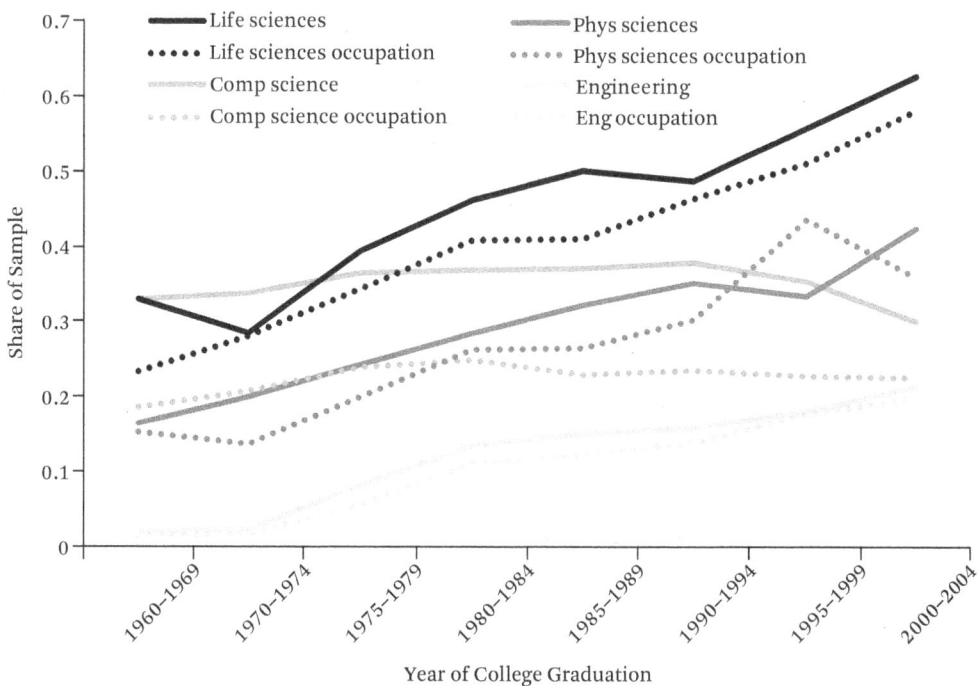

Source: Authors' calculations based on data from the National Science Foundation's Scientists and Engineers Statistical Data System (SESTAT) 1995–2008.
Note: All men and women graduating with a STEM bachelor's degree between 1960 and 2004.

This implies that, conditional on receiving a degree in a STEM field, women appear equally likely to work in STEM as their male counterparts.

Computer science is the exception to the trend of increasing representation of women in STEM. There, women's representation has been stagnant over the last several decades and shown evidence of a decline in computer science majors for the most recent cohorts of college graduates. Women also account for a considerably lower share of the computer science workforce than computer science majors, on the order of 5 to 10 percentage points, indicating that women are less likely to work in computer science than to major in it. For the 1980 to 1984 college cohort, for instance, women made up approximately 30 percent of all computer science majors, but only 20 percent of all computer science workers. This implies that conditional on completing a degree in computer science, women are still less likely to work in the field than men. For more recent graduates, the gap between majoring and working in computer science has converged, but this is primarily due to a decline in the share of women majoring in the field in recent decades. This trend is of particular concern given that computer science accounts for more than 30 percent of the STEM workforce. In fact, the two fields with the fewest women, computer science and engineering, represent approximately 75 percent of STEM workers. So, although women make up more than 50 percent of workers in the life sciences for recent college cohorts, their overall share working in STEM is just 20 percent.

Figures 6 through 9 show descriptive statistics on wages for men and women by STEM occupation, which is our dependent variable. We show wages for all men and women who work in STEM, as well as the women with children who work in STEM to illustrate the wage differential for mothers. For the whole STEM

Figure 6. Average Hourly Wages, Whites

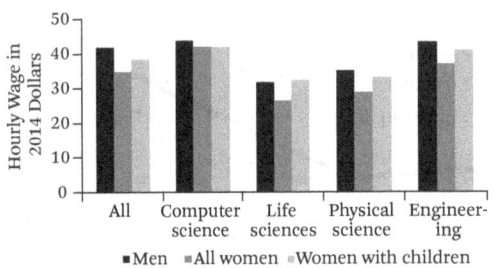

Source: Authors' calculations based on data from the National Science Foundation's Scientists and Engineers Statistical Data System (SESTAT) 1995–2008.
Notes: All men and women graduating with a STEM bachelor's degree between 1970 and 2004, working at least thirty-five hours a week in a STEM occupation. Wages are calculated by dividing annual salary by number of weeks worked.

Figure 7. Average Hourly Wages, Blacks

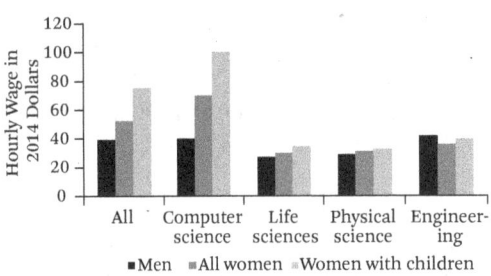

Source: Authors' calculations based on data from the National Science Foundation's Scientists and Engineers Statistical Data System (SESTAT) 1995–2008.
Notes: See notes to figure 6.

Figure 8. Average Hourly Wages, Hispanics

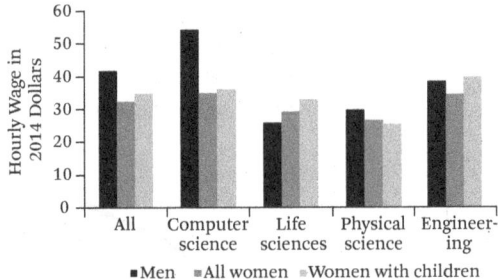

Source: Authors' calculations based on data from the National Science Foundation's Scientists and Engineers Statistical Data System (SESTAT) 1995–2008.
Notes: See notes to figure 6.

Figure 9. Average Hourly Wages, Asians

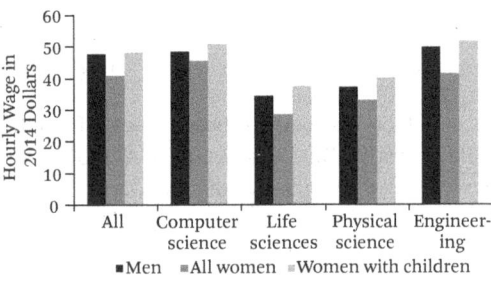

Source: Authors' calculations based on data from the National Science Foundation's Scientists and Engineers Statistical Data System (SESTAT) 1995–2008.
Notes: See notes to figure 6.

workforce, wages are $42 for white men and $35 for white women. That is, white women earn about 84 cents for every dollar that white men earn, slightly higher than the 77 cents in the overall labor force. However, differences across STEM occupations are substantial. The gap is narrowest in computer science, where white women earn 96 cents for every dollar that white men earn. The biggest gap is in the physical sciences, 82 cents for every dollar. Differences are substantial by race as well—Asian women experience similar wage gaps as white women relative to their male peers in all of the STEM occupations. There is evidence of positive selection into the STEM workforce for black women, where black women earn 32 percent higher wages than black men. Figures 6 through 9 also show wages of the women with children under the age of eighteen who work in STEM. Consistent with other work showing that women with children earn higher wages in some professional fields (Buchmann and McDaniel, this issue), we also find higher hourly wages for women with children than among women as a whole in all STEM fields and for most racial groups. This is likely due at least in part to selection factors. Only the women with the highest earning potential may be able to combine motherhood and work in STEM.

Multivariate Results

To what extent do these patterns of wage gaps change upon including controls for human capital characteristics or family measures? Table 1 shows regression results pooling all racial groups and the four main STEM fields. Model 1 includes an indicator for whether the respondent is female, representing the overall male-female wage gap in STEM occupations. Model 2 differentiates the gender wage gap by race and ethnicity, with white men serving as the reference category. Model 3 adds an indicator for whether the respondent is foreign born. Model 4 adds the human capital controls: years of potential experience, college cohort, STEM field, and higher degrees. Model 5 adds measures of family characteristics.

In model 1, which includes no other controls, we estimate an overall male-female gender wage gap of 0.18 log points, indicating that women who work in STEM earn about 18 percent lower hourly wages than men. Differentiating by race (model 2) reveals that all women earn significantly lower wages than white men. Black and Hispanic men also earn significantly lower wages than white men, while Asian men earn 6 percent higher wages than white men. Adding an indicator for whether the respondent is foreign born (model 3) reveals that the Asian male advantage is driven entirely by foreign-born workers. On the other hand, accounting for nativity widens the wage disparity between Asian women and white men, as well as between Hispanic women and men and white men.

The gender wage gap narrows dramatically when including controls for occupation sector and human capital experience (model 4). Including these controls reduces the white male-female wage gap from 0.20 log points to 0.06 log points, which suggests that the women who work in STEM tend to have less potential work experience than the men and are more likely to work in lower-paying sectors of the STEM workforce (such as the life sciences). Those working in computer science and engineering earn the highest hourly wages, whereas those in the life sciences earn significantly less than those in the physical sciences. Not surprisingly, having additional credentials is also associated with higher wages. Individuals with master's degrees in STEM earn approximately 4 percent more, and those with doctorates and non-STEM graduate degrees about 5 to 6 percent more.

Model 5 adds controls for current family characteristics interacted with gender. Of note is that the inclusion of family characteristics shifts the coefficients on race-ethnicity only for women. Our results indicate that being partnered (both married and cohabiting) elevates earnings over being single, which may be important given differences in the experiences of men and women; descriptive results (shown in table A2) reveal that men are considerably more likely to be married than women. Having preschool-age children is associated with higher wages. This effect is concentrated equally between men and women, corroborating evidence from other papers in this volume indicating a positive association between motherhood and wages in recent years (Buchmann and McDaniel, this issue; Pal and Waldfogel, this issue).[3] This positive association between motherhood and wages likely reflects, at least to some extent, selection issues into both motherhood and working in STEM—only those with the highest earning potential are able to balance family life and work life.

We next present results running separate models for each of the four main STEM fields and each of the four main race groups. Figures 10 through 13 show the gender wage gap experienced by women, the dark bars indicating the gap with no other controls in the model (model 1 in table 1), and the light bars indicating the gender wage gap once all controls are included (model 5 in table 1). Italicized coefficients are

---

3. We also examine how the motherhood wage differential has changed over time in table A3, where we interact an indicator for being a woman with a child under the age of eighteen with college cohort.

Table 1. Linear Regressions Predicting Log Hourly Wage

	(1)	(2)	(3)	(4)	(5)
Gender and race					
Female	−0.18***				
White female		−0.20***	−0.20***	−0.06***	−0.04*
Black female		−0.12***	−0.12***	−0.02	−0.01
Hispanic female		−0.26***	−0.28***	−0.10***	−0.08**
Asian female		−0.08***	−0.15***	−0.02	−0.01
White male (reference)					
Black male		−0.09***	−0.10***	−0.06***	−0.06***
Hispanic male		−0.09***	−0.11***	−0.05***	−0.05***
Asian male		0.06***	0.00	0.04***	0.05***
Foreign born			0.08***	0.00	−0.01
Years since degree				0.06***	0.05***
Years since degree squared				0.00***	0.00***
College cohort (reference = 1970–1974)					
1975–1979				0.11***	0.08***
1980–1984				0.20***	0.16***
1985–1989				0.24***	0.19***
1990–1994				0.21***	0.17***
1995–1999				0.22***	0.19***
2000–2004				0.16***	0.14***
STEM occupation (reference = physical sciences)					
Computer and math sciences				0.32***	0.32***
Life sciences				−0.16***	−0.15***
Engineering				0.27***	0.27***
Advanced degrees (reference = bachelor's degree)					
STEM master's				0.03***	0.03***
STEM PhD				0.05***	0.05***
Non-STEM advanced degree				0.06***	0.05***
Marriage and family					
Married					0.06***
Cohabiting					0.01
Has children					0.02*
Has children under six years old					0.04***
Female*married					−0.01
Female*cohabiting					0.09***
Female*has children					−0.01
Female*has children under six years old					0.03
R-squared	0.02	0.02	0.02	0.23	0.23
Number of observations	61,417	61,417	61,417	61,417	61,417

Source: Authors' calculations based on data from the National Science Foundation's Scientists and Engineers Statistical Data System (SESTAT) 1995–2008.
Notes: All men and women graduating with a STEM bachelor's degree between 1970 and 2004, working at least thirty-five hours a week in a STEM occupation. Results from OLS regressions of logged wages on indicator for female and demographic characteristics. Wages are calculated by dividing annual salary by number of weeks worked per year and average number of hours worked per week. Women with children are defined as those who have at least one child under the age of eighteen living in the household. Marriage and cohabitation evaluated at the time of the survey. All wages reported in 2014 dollars. Regressions weighted by person weights.
*** $p < 0.001$; ** $p < 0.01$; * $p < 0.05$

Figure 10. Wage Differentials for Women Relative to Men, Whites

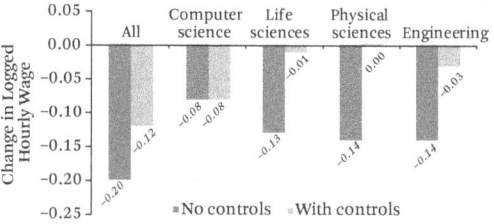

■ No controls   ■ With controls

Source: Authors' calculations based on data from the National Science Foundation's Scientists and Engineers Statistical Data System (SESTAT) 1995–2008.
Notes: All men and women graduating with a STEM bachelor's degree between 1970 and 2004, working at least thirty-five hours a week in a STEM occupation. Results from OLS regressions of logged hourly wages on indicator for female. Dark bar represents coefficient on female in OLS regression with no other controls (model 1 from table 1). Light shaded bar represents coefficient on female in OLS regression with full set of controls (model 5 from table 1). Each bar represents a different regression. Regressions run separately by race and STEM field. Wages are calculated by dividing annual salary by number of weeks worked per year and average number of hours worked per week. All wages reported in 2014 dollars. Regressions weighted by person weights. Italicized terms indicate significantly different from zero at the $p < 0.05$ level.

Figure 11. Wage Differentials for Women Relative to Men, Blacks

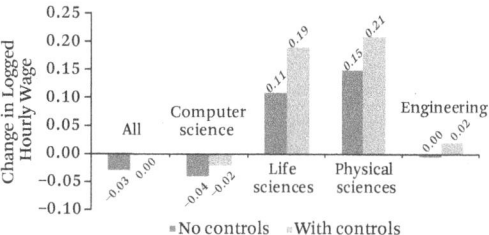

■ No controls   ■ With controls

Source: Authors' calculations based on data from the National Science Foundation's Scientists and Engineers Statistical Data System (SESTAT) 1995–2008.
Notes: See notes to figure 10.

significant at the $p < 0.05$ level. For the life sciences and physical sciences, the gender wage gap for white women is reduced to nearly zero and is insignificant once all controls have been added to the models. Before including controls, white women in the life sciences, physical sciences, and engineering earned about 14 percent lower wages than white men, but differences in wages once controls are included in the model are not significant. These patterns are similar for Asian women and Asian men. Black women exhibit a different pattern, earning higher wages than black men in the life sciences and the physical sciences, and no significantly different wages in computer science or engineering even before controlling for human capital and family characteristics. For all other racial groups, we find persistent wage gaps in computer science, even after controlling for human capital and family characteristics, ranging from 8 to 12 percent lower wages compared to their male counterparts.

We next analyze the extent to which the representation of women in each of the four main STEM fields is associated with wages in these fields. For simplicity, we pool all race groups for this analysis, but models were run separately for each of the four main STEM fields. Results of this exercise are shown in table 2. As discussed, we use a measure for the lagged share of women working in each STEM occupation using the prior SESTAT survey information. The share of women working in STEM are evaluated at the specific occupation level for up to ten occupations within each of the four main STEM fields. We categorize these measures into quartiles separately for each of the four main STEM fields. We regress the logged hourly wages on a full set of controls (model 5 from table 1 along with indicators for each specific STEM occupation), including indicators for the top three quartiles of the lagged share of women working in STEM. The coefficients on these terms indicate the change in the logged hourly wage for all workers in those fields relative to the lowest concentration of women in each STEM field. Variation in this term is generated by changes within each STEM occupation over time.

For the life sciences and engineering, we

Figure 12. Wage Differentials for Women Relative to Men, Hispanics

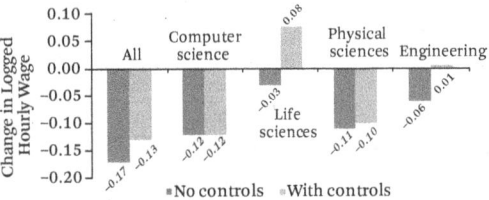

Source: Authors' calculations based on data from the National Science Foundation's Scientists and Engineers Statistical Data System (SESTAT) 1995–2008.
Notes: All men and women graduating with a STEM bachelor's degree between 1970 and 2004, working at least thirty-five hours a week in a STEM occupation. Results from OLS regressions of logged hourly wages on indicator for female. Dark bar represents coefficient on female in OLS regression with no other controls (model 1 from table 1). Light shaded bar represents coefficient on female in OLS regression with full set of controls (model 5 from table 1). Each bar represents a different regression. Regressions run separately by race and STEM field. Wages are calculated by dividing annual salary by number of weeks worked per year and average number of hours worked per week. All wages reported in 2014 dollars. Regressions weighted by person weights. Italicized terms indicate significantly different from zero at the $p < 0.05$ level.

Figure 13. Wage Differentials for Women Relative to Men, Asians

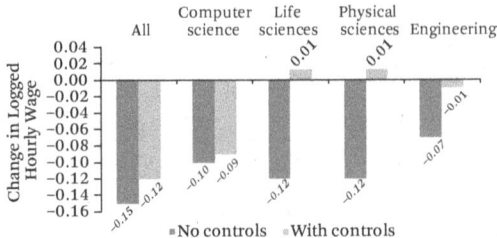

Source: Authors' calculations based on data from the National Science Foundation's Scientists and Engineers Statistical Data System (SESTAT) 1995–2008.
Notes: See notes to figure 12.

find significant increases in wages associated with increasing the concentration of women working in these occupations. Increasing the concentration of women to 51 percent of the life science workforce is associated with 19 percent higher wages for all workers in the field compared with when women made up 33 percent of the that workforce. Similarly for engineering, increasing the concentration of women from 7 percent to 19 percent is associated with 11 percent higher wages for all workers. In these two fields, we find no evidence that increasing the share of women in a field devalues or feminizes the field to the extent that all workers in those fields earn less. In contrast, we find a negative, but not always significant, association between the concentration of women working in the physical sciences and the wages in those fields. We also find evidence of a slight decline in wages in computer science once women make up a significant share of the workforce. In both physical sciences and computer and mathematical sciences, therefore, we find some evidence in support of the devaluation theory that increasing the share of women in the field is associated with lower wages for all workers in those fields, though our estimates are not always significant at conventional levels.

How has the gender wage gap changed over time?

Results from table 1 suggest that one of the biggest contributors to the gender wage gap in STEM is in the human capital accumulation differences between men and women. In most of the STEM fields, the share of women majoring in and working in STEM since the 1970s has increased, which suggests that the women who work in STEM are likely younger and less experienced than the men in the field. This result may portend an optimistic assessment of the future of gender wage equality in the STEM workforce. If women continue to increase their representation in STEM and accumulate similar levels of experience, we would expect to see a continued narrowing of the gender wage gap. On the other hand, we could also see a glass-ceiling effect, where women begin their careers earning wages on par with men, but begin to

Table 2. OLS Regressions of Logged Wages

	Computer Science		Life Sciences		Physical Sciences		Engineering	
	Mean Percent Female	Regression Coefficient	Mean Percent Female	Regression Coefficient	Mean Percent Female	Regression Coefficient	Mean Percent Female	Regression Coefficient
Quartiles								
1st (reference)	20.4	0	33.4	0	14.9	0	7.1	0
2nd	22.2	0.03*	42.5	0.10*	24.8	−0.04*	9.1	0.03***
3rd	24	0.06**	45.2	0.13**	30.9	−0.03	14.3	0.11***
4th	35	−0.04	51.1	0.19***	38.2	−0.04	18.7	0.11***

Source: Authors' calculations based on data from the National Science Foundation's Scientists and Engineers Statistical Data System (SESTAT) 1995–2008.
Note: All men and women graduating with a STEM bachelor's degree between 1970 and 2004, working at least thirty-five hours a week in a STEM occupation. All regressions include controls from model (5) in table 1, weighted by person weights. Each column represents a different regression—regressions run separately for each main STEM field. Wages are calculated by dividing annual salary by number of weeks worked per year and average number of hours worked per week. All wages reported in 2014 dollars. Percent female quartile calculated at the specific occupation level, lagged by one SESTAT survey year. Regressions also include controls for specific occupation so changes in percentage female represent changes within specific occupation over time (such as impact of increasing share of women in electrical engineering over time).
*** $p < 0.001$; ** $p < 0.01$; * $p < 0.05$

fall behind as they progress through their careers. To test this premise, we examine how the gender wage gap has evolved by college cohort, and whether we find evidence that these gaps increase over the career, regardless of cohort. We are able to disentangle this cohort versus glass-ceiling effect because we have multiple years of observation for the same cohorts of college graduates, allowing us to observe wage gaps at several points over the course of the career.

Table 3 shows results of interacting college cohort with gender, and separately, interacting years of potential experience with gender. For the first test, we regress logged wages on an indicator for female and a set of interactions of female with college cohort. In this exercise, women who completed their bachelor's degrees between 1970 and 1974 are the reference category; each interaction of female with subsequent cohorts represents the relative gender wage gap of that cohort compared with the gender wage gap for those who graduated between 1970 and 1974. To estimate the overall gender wage gap for each cohort, we add the coefficient on the female indicator with that on the interaction of the female indicator with college cohort. For instance, the overall gender wage gap for women who graduated in the life sciences between 1975 and 1979 is 0.08 log points (0.18 minus 0.098). The overall gap for those who graduated between 1970 and 1974 is merely the coefficient on the indicator for female in each field. Each column represents a separate regression and all regressions include the full set of controls represented in model 5 of table 1.

In the fields where the share of women increased the most—life sciences and engineering—we also see significant trends in the gender wage gap over time. Despite an overall gap in wages between men and women in these fields (women earn 0.18 and 0.23 log points less than men, respectively), we see positive effects of the interaction of female with degree cohort. This suggests that the wage gap is narrowing among more recent cohorts of college graduates in these fields.

In contrast, we see very little difference in the gap by college cohort for those working in computer science or the physical sciences. In computer science, we find an overall gap of 0.11

Table 3. Trends in Gender Wage Gap

	Computer Science	Life Sciences	Physical Sciences	Engineering
Trends over time				
Female	−0.11	−0.18***	−0.099	−0.225***
Female*1970–1974				
Female*1975–1979	−0.09	0.10	−0.03	0.21**
Female*1980–1984	0.03	0.11*	−0.07	0.15*
Female*1985–1989	0.07	0.06	0.07	0.23**
Female*1990–1994	0.01	0.22***	0.01	0.20**
Female*1995–1999	−0.03	0.16**	0.01	0.20**
Female*2000–2004	0.09	0.09	0.03	0.20**
Trends over career				
Female	−0.069***	−0.035	−0.087	−0.02
Female*years since degree	−0.002*	−0.001	−0.002	−0.002

Source: Authors' calculations based on data from the National Science Foundation's Scientists and Engineers Statistical Data System (SESTAT) 1995–2008.

Notes: All men and women graduating with a STEM bachelor's degree between 1970 and 2004, working at least thirty-five hours a week in a STEM occupation. All regressions include controls from model (5) in table 1, weighted by person weights. Each column represents a different regression—regressions run separately for each main STEM field. Trends over time represents regressions of logged wages on interaction of indicator for female and college cohort, along with full set of controls. Trends over career represents separate regressions of logged wages on interaction of indicator for female and years since college degree, along with full set of controls. Wages are calculated by dividing annual salary by number of weeks worked per year and average number of hours worked per week. All wages reported in 2014 dollars.

*** $p < 0.001$; ** $p < 0.01$; * $p < 0.05$

log points but no indication of a narrowing for more recent cohorts of college graduates. That is, none of the coefficients on the interaction of gender with college cohort are significantly positive. Some are actually negative, indicating that the gender wage gap is wider for some more recent cohorts than for those graduating between 1970 and 1974. In the physical sciences, we find no significant gap for any of the college cohorts.

Although these results imply a somewhat positive story that discrimination against women may be declining for recent cohorts of college graduates (at least in the life sciences and engineering), this trend of a declining gender wage gap for more recent college cohorts could also reflect differences in the gap across the career span. Previous work has shown that gender wage gaps are fairly narrow among workers age twenty-five to thirty-four but tend to emerge over the course of the career. If this were the case in STEM, we should expect to find a widening over time since graduation. Because we have data from 1995 to 2008, we are able to test this hypothesis by observing wage differences at different times for each college cohort. We do so by interacting an indicator for female with the number of years since college graduation, holding college cohort fixed. For computer science, we find some evidence of a widening of the gap over the course of the career. We estimate a 7 percent wage gap overall, and a 0.2 percent increase with each year since graduation. In all other STEM fields, we find no evidence that wage gaps grow over the course of the career, though coefficients are close in magnitude to those observed in computer science but never attain statistical significance at conventional levels. These results further extend the findings of Anastasia Prokos and Irene Padavic (2005) and are consistent with the theory that the gender wage gap in STEM is due to a larger gap among older cohorts of college graduates and that we should expect a narrowing of this gap as older cohorts retire from the labor force.

DISCUSSION

Women have made great strides in closing the gender wage gap over the last several decades but continue to earn less than men. Numerous studies have examined the source of this gap, noting differences in occupation choice, working patterns, and discrimination. Analyzing the gap in STEM occupations alone eliminates some potential factors, such as human capital differences and differences in occupation choice, that contribute to wage disparities. It also enables us to ask whether the STEM labor force exhibits gender wage gaps similar to those in the overall labor force. Increasing the representation of women in STEM has been promoted as one means of reducing the overall earnings disparities between women and men. We use SESTAT data and assess how women's representation in STEM and in particular STEM occupations is associated with wages, whether the gender pay gap narrows among more recent cohorts, and whether an increase in the proportion of women working in fields that remain largely male is associated with higher wages in those fields.

We find sizable and significant gender wage gaps among women working in STEM occupations, though these are smaller than those in the broader labor force. White women in the STEM workforce earn about 84 cents for every dollar their male counterparts earn, which is higher than the 77 cents in the overall labor force. Increasing women's representation in STEM occupations could therefore reduce the overall gender wage gap. Even when women work in STEM occupations, however, they concentrate in lower paid fields, such as the life sciences and physical sciences. These areas also employ smaller shares of the STEM workforce than computer science and engineering do. Although increasing women's representation in STEM occupations can reduce the gender wage gap, narrowing it further would require that women change their concentrations within STEM.

Differences in human capital accumulation accounted for the largest portion of the gender wage gap in many STEM occupations. Women who work in STEM have less potential work experience than the men, because the men who work in STEM tend to be older than their female counterparts. But among more recent cohorts reductions in the gap have been sizable, at least among women in particular fields. Whereas there was never any observed gender wage gap among various cohorts of physical scientists after controlling for observable characteristics, more recent cohorts of women employed as engineers and life scientists have experienced wage increases, and on average women actually outearn men in those fields. Little evidence of a cohort change in the gap, however, is observed among computer scientists, suggesting that women do not experience the same returns to work experience as their male counterparts.

That particular fields of growing importance to the American and global economy continue to manifest gender pay discrepancies requires additional study, and with different types of data than what we use here. Our results document persistent gaps in the wages of men and women in computer science, and these differentials cannot be explained by demographic characteristics alone, or human capital measures such as experience. Many have called attention to the declining proportion of women obtaining college degrees in computer science, and the dearth of women (and minorities) in various high technology corporations. Our results provide some purchase on why women may find computer science an unwelcoming field and highlight the challenges to increasing women's representation there. Not only do they continue to earn less than men, but growing their presence in the field also does not appear to be beneficial. In fact, increasing the share of women working in computer science was associated with lower wages, though in general those working in the field were among the most highly remunerated. Computer science, then, seems most resistant to the increasing presence of women, even though the representation of women is even smaller in engineering. Additional research is required to ascertain how climate factors contribute to the retention of women in some fields and the attrition of women in others.

Our study is not without limitations. We cannot determine, for example, whether the frustration and dissatisfaction women have with the STEM labor force potentially pushes them into other occupations with the current data, or whether this process occurs to any greater extent for women than for men. Despite the increasing presence of women in STEM fields of study, recent research has suggested that these women become dissatisfied with working conditions in STEM; they are significantly less likely to be retained in the STEM labor force than other women with professional degrees, instead exiting the STEM labor force in early or midcareer for non-STEM jobs (Glass et al. 2013). Although we find no evidence of a widening gender wage gap as a function of time since graduation, further research is needed to explore which of these factors is likely driving these differences in potential work experience.

Over the past four decades, progress in closing the gender wage gap has been notable. Our results indicate that disparities in the wages of male and female STEM professionals are smaller than for the overall labor force, and among some fields recent cohorts of women are earning as much as or more than comparable men. Nonetheless, challenges remain. Women remain concentrated in the lower-paying STEM occupations. When they do work in the best-remunerated fields of computer science and engineering, they continue to earn less than comparable men. Additional study into the particular climate welcoming (or repelling) women STEM professionals is needed if we are to better understand the factors that serve to perpetuate the gender wage gap.

APPENDIX

Table A1. Specific Occupations in STEM Fields

Computer science	Computer scientists	**Physical science**	Chemists
	Mathematicians		Earth scientists
	Postsecondary math or computer science teachers		Physicists
Life sciences	Agriculture and food scientists		Other physical scientists
	Biological scientists		Postsecondary physical scientists
	Environmental scientists	**Engineering**	Aerospace engineers
	Postsecondary life science teachers		Chemical engineers
			Civil engineers
			Electrical engineers
			Industrial engineers
			Mechanical engineers
			Other engineers
			Postsecondary engineering teachers

Source: Authors' compilation.

Table A2. Descriptive Statistics for STEM

	Men		Women		All	
	Mean	Std Err	Mean	Std Err	Mean	Std Err
Hourly wage (2014 dollars)	41.57*	0.19	34.78*	0.65	30.22	0.21
Female					0.20	0.00
Race-ethnicity						
White	0.75*	0.00	0.65*	0.00	0.73	0.00
Black	0.03*	0.00	0.07*	0.00	0.04	0.00
Hispanic	0.05	0.01	0.06	0.00	0.05	0.00
Asian	0.17*	0.00	0.22*	0.00	0.18	0.00
Foreign born	0.23*	0.00	0.27*	0.00	0.24	0.00
Years since graduation	14.34*	0.04	12.00*	0.07	13.88	0.03
College cohort						
BA 1970-1974	0.09*	0.00	0.04*	0.00	0.08	0.00
BA 1975-1979	0.11*	0.00	0.08*	0.00	0.10	0.00
BA 1980-1984	0.16*	0.00	0.13*	0.00	0.15	0.00
BA 1985-1989	0.18*	0.00	0.16*	0.00	0.17	0.00
BA 1990-1994	0.19*	0.00	0.20*	0.00	0.19	0.00
BA 1995-1999	0.17*	0.00	0.23*	0.00	0.18	0.00
BA 2000-2004	0.11*	0.00	0.16*	0.00	0.12	0.00
STEM occupation						
Computer and mathematical sciences	0.36*	0.00	0.39*	0.00	0.37	0.00
Life sciences	0.08*	0.00	0.22*	0.00	0.11	0.00
Physical sciences	0.08*	0.00	0.12*	0.00	0.09	0.00
Engineering	0.49*	0.00	0.26*	0.00	0.45	0.00
Undergraduate major						
Computer and mathematical sciences	0.21*	0.00	0.29*	0.00	0.23	0.00
Life sciences	0.10*	0.00	0.27*	0.00	0.14	0.00
Physical sciences	0.12*	0.00	0.15*	0.00	0.12	0.00
Engineering	0.57*	0.00	0.30*	0.00	0.52	0.00
Graduate degrees						
Has master's degree in STEM	0.29	0.00	0.29	0.00	0.29	0.00
Has PhD in STEM	0.08*	0.00	0.09*	0.00	0.08	0.00
Has advanced degree in non-STEM	0.07	0.00	0.07	0.00	0.07	0.00
Family characteristics						
Married	0.71*	0.00	0.59*	0.00	0.69	0.00
Cohabiting	0.02*	0.00	0.03*	0.00	0.02	0.00
Has children < six	0.26*	0.00	0.20*	0.00	0.25	0.00
Has children > six	0.33*	0.00	0.24*	0.00	0.31	0.00
Lagged share of women in STEM occupation	19.80*	0.06	25.69*	0.09	20.99	0.08
Number of observations	46,366		15,051		61,417	

Source: Authors' calculations based on data from the National Science Foundation's Scientists and Engineers Statistical Data System (SESTAT) 1995–2008.

Notes: All men and women graduating with a STEM bachelor's degree between 1970 and 2004, working at least thirty-five hours a week in a STEM occupation. Wages are calculated by dividing annual salary by number of weeks worked per year and average number of hours worked per week. Women with children are defined as those who have at least one child under the age of eighteen living in the household. Marriage and cohabitation evaluated at the time of the survey. All wages reported in 2014 dollars.

* Indicates significant difference between men and women at $p < 0.05$ level.

Table A3. Trends in Motherhood Wage Gap

	Computer Science	Life Sciences	Physical Sciences	Engineering
Trends over time for mothers				
Mother	0.09	0.00	0.06	0.08
Mother*1970–1974				
Mother*1975–1979	−0.24***	−0.04	−0.01	0.02
Mother*1980–1984	−0.08	0.00	0.08	−0.06
Mother*1985–1989	−0.11	0.03	0.05	0.04
Mother*1990–1994	−0.12	0.20*	−0.02	−0.06
Mother*1995–1999	−0.18*	0.13	0.03	0.03
Mother*2000–2004	−0.15	0.09	0.1	0.03

Source: Authors' calculations based on data from the National Science Foundation's Scientists and Engineers Statistical Data System (SESTAT) 1995–2008.

Notes: All men and women graduating with a STEM bachelor's degree between 1970 and 2004, working at least thirty-five hours a week in a STEM occupation. All regressions include controls from model (5) in table 1, weighted by person weights. Each column represents a separate regression—regressions run separately for each of the four main STEM fields. Regressions of logged wages on interaction of indicator for being a mother and college cohort, along with full set of controls. Wages are calculated by dividing annual salary by number of weeks worked per year and average number of hours worked per week. All wages reported in 2014 dollars.

*** $p < 0.001$; ** $p < 0.01$; * $p < 0.05$

REFERENCES

Beede, David N., Tiffany Julian, David Langdon, George McKittrick, Beethika Khan, and Mark Doms. 2011. "Women in STEM: A Gender Gap to Innovation." ESA Issue Brief no. 04-11. Washington: U.S. Department of Commerce, Economics and Statistics Administration.

Bertrand, Marianne, Claudia Goldin, and Lawrence F. Katz. 2009. "Dynamics of the Gender Gap for Young Professionals in the Corporate and Financial Sectors." NBER working paper no. 14681. Cambridge, Mass.: National Bureau of Economic Research.

Blau, Francine D., and Lawrence M. Kahn. 1994. "Rising Wage Inequality and the U.S. Gender Gap." *American Economic Review* 84(2): 23–28.

———. 1997. "Swimming Upstream: Trends in the Gender Wage Differential in the 1980s." *Journal of Labor Economics* 15(1): 1–42.

———. 2006. "The U.S. Gender Pay Gap in the 1990s: Slowing Convergence." *Industrial and Labor Relations Review* 60(1): 45–66.

Buchmann, Claudia, and Anne McDaniel. 2016. "Motherhood and the Wages of Women in Professional Occupations." *RSF: The Russell Sage Journal of the Social Sciences* 2(4). doi: 10.7758/RSF.2016.2.4.05.

Budig, Michelle J., and Paula England. 2001. "The Wage Penalty for Motherhood." *American Sociological Review* 66(2): 204–25.

Byker, Tanya. 2016. "The Opt-Out Continuation: Education, Work, and Motherhood from 1984 to 2008." *RSF: The Russell Sage Journal of the Social Sciences* 2(4). doi: 10.7758/RSF.2016.2.4.02.

Cohen, Philip N., and Matt L. Huffman. 2003. "Individuals, Jobs, and Labor Markets: The Devaluation of Women's Work." *American Sociological Review* 68(3): 443–63.

———. 2007. "Working for the Woman? Female Managers and the Gender Wage Gap." *American Sociological Review* 72(5): 681–704.

Committee on Maximizing the Potential of Women in Academic Science and Engineering and Committee on Science Engineering and Public Policy (Committee on Maximizing the Potential of Women). 2006. *Beyond Bias and Barrier: Fulfilling the Potential of Women in Academic Science and Engineering.* Washington, D.C.: National Academies Press.

Cotter, David A., JoAnn DeFiore, Joan M. Hermsen, Brenda Marsteller Kowalewski, and Reeve Vanneman. 1997. "All Women Benefit: The Macro-Level Effect of Occupational Integration on Gender Earnings Equality." *American Sociological Review* 62(5): 714–34.

DiPrete, Thomas A., and Claudia Buchmann. 2013. *The Rise of Women: The Growing Gender Gap in Education and What It Means for American Schools*. New York: Russell Sage Foundation.

Ginther, Donna K. 2003. "Is MIT an Exception? Gender Pay Differences in Academic Science." *Bulletin of Science, Technology, and Society* 23(1): 21–26.

Glass, Jennifer L., Sharon Sassler, Yael Levitte, and Katherine M. Michelmore. 2013. "What's So Special About STEM? A Comparison of Women's Retention in STEM and Professional Occupations." *Social Forces* 92(2): 723–56.

Goldin, Claudia. 2002. "A Pollution Theory of Discrimination: Male and Female Differences in Occupations and Earnings." *NBER* working paper no. 8985. Cambridge, Mass.: National Bureau of Economic Research.

———. 2014. "A Grand Gender Convergence: Its Last Chapter." *American Economic Review* 104(4): 1091–119.

Goldin, Claudia, Lawrence F. Katz, and Ilyana Kuziemko. 2006. "The Homecoming of American College Women: The Reversal of the Gender Gap in College." *Journal of Economic Perspectives* 20(4): 133–56.

Hakim, Catherine. 2000. *Work-Lifestyle Choices in the 21st Century: Preference Theory*. Oxford: Oxford University Press.

Halrynjo, Sigtona, and Selma Therese Lyng. 2009. "Preferences, Constraints or Schemas of Devotion? Exploring Norwegian Mothers' Withdrawals from High Commitment Careers." *British Journal of Sociology* 60(2): 321–43.

Hill, Catherine, Christianne Corbett, and Andresse St. Rose. 2010. *Why So Few? Women in Science, Technology, Engineering, and Mathematics*. Washington, D.C.: American Association of University Women. Accessed April 6, 2016. https://www.aauw.org/files/2013/02/Why-So-Few-Women-in-Science-Technology-Engineering-and-Mathematics.pdf.

Huffman, Matt L., and Steven C. Velasco. 1997. "When More Is Less: Sex Composition, Organizations, and Earnings in U.S. Firms." *Work and Occupations* 24(2): 214–44.

Jacobsen, Joyce P. 2007. "Occupational Segregation and the Tipping Phenomenon: The Contrary Case of Court Reporting in the USA." *Gender, Work, and Organization* 14(2): 130–61.

Kogan, Irena, and Frank Kalter. 2006. "The Effects of Relative Group Size on Occupational Outcomes: Turks and Ex-Yugoslavs in Austria." *European Sociological Review* 22(1): 35–48.

Levanon, Asaf, Paula England, and Paul Allison. 2009. "Occupational Feminization and Pay: Assessing Causal Dynamics Using 1950–2000 U.S. Census Data." *Social Forces* 88(2): 865–92.

Ma, Yingyi, and Gokhan Savas. 2014. "Which Is More Consequential: Field of Study or Institutional Selectivity?" *Review of Higher Education* 37(2): 221–47.

Mandel, Hadas. 2013. "Up the Down Staircase: Women's Upward Mobility and the Wage Penalty for Occupational Feminization, 1970–2007." *Social Forces* 91(4): 1183–207.

Mandel, Hadas, and Moshe Semyonov. 2014. "Gender Pay Gap and Employment Sector: Sources of Earnings Disparities in the United States, 1970–2010." *Demography* 51(5): 1597–618.

Mann, Allison, and Thomas A. DiPrete. 2013. "Trends in Gender Segregation in the Choice of Science and Engineering Majors." *Social Science Research* 42(6): 1519–41.

Morgan, Laurie A. 1998. "Glass-Ceiling Effect or Cohort Effect? A Longitudinal Study of the Gender Earnings Gap for Engineers, 1982 to 1989." *American Sociological Review* 63(4): 479–93.

Pal, Ipshita, and Jane Waldfogel. 2015. "The Family Gap in Pay: New Evidence for 1967 to 2013." *RSF: The Russell Sage Journal of the Social Sciences* 2(4). doi: 10.7758/RSF.2016.2.4.04.

Pew Research Center. 2013. "On Pay Gap, Millennial Women Near Parity—For Now." Washington, D.C.: Social & Demographic Trends Project. Accessed April 6, 2016. http://www.pewsocialtrends.org/2013/12/11/on-pay-gap-millennial-women-near-parity-for-now/.

Prokos, Anastasia, and Irene Padavic. 2005. "An Examination of Competing Explanations for the Pay Gap Among Scientists and Engineers." *Gender and Society* 19(4): 523–43.

Roos, Patricia A., and Barbara F. Reskin. 1992. "Occupational Desegregation in the 1970s: Integration and Economic Equity?" *Sociological Perspectives* 35(1): 69–91.

Sana, Mariano. 2010. "Immigrants and Natives in U.S. Science and Engineering Occupations, 1994–2006." *Demography* 47(3): 801–20.

Sassler, Sharon, Jennifer L. Glass, Yael Levitte, and Katherine M. Michelmore. 2011. "The Missing Women in STEM? Accounting for Gender Differences in Entrance into Science, Technology, Engineering, and Math Occupations." Presented at the 2012 Population Association of America annual meeting, Washington, D.C. (September 19, 2011).

Stähli, Michèle Ernst, Jean-Marie Le Goff, René Levy, and Eric Widmer. 2009. "Wishes or Constraints? Mothers Labour Force Participation and Its Motivation in Switzerland." *European Sociological Review* 25(3): 333–48.

Weeden, Kim A., Youngjoo Cha, and Mauricio Bucca. 2016. "Long Work Hours, Part-Time Work, and Trends in the Gender Gap in Pay, the Motherhood Wage Penalty, and the Fatherhood Wage Premium." *RSF: The Russell Sage Journal of the Social Sciences* 2(4). doi: 10.7758/RSF.2016.2.4.03.

Xie, Yu, and Kimberlee A. Shauman. 2003. *Women in Science: Career Processes and Outcomes.* Cambridge, Mass.: Harvard University Press.

PART IV

Marriage, Divorce, and Women's Earnings

Trends in Relative Earnings and Marital Dissolution: Are Wives Who Outearn Their Husbands Still More Likely to Divorce?

CHRISTINE R. SCHWARTZ AND PILAR GONALONS-PONS

As women's labor-force participation and earnings have grown, so has the likelihood that wives outearn their husbands. A common concern is that these couples may be at heightened risk of divorce. Yet with the rise of egalitarian marriage, wives' relative earnings may be more weakly associated with divorce than in the past. We examine trends in the association between wives' relative earnings and marital dissolution using data from the 1968-2009 Panel Study of Income Dynamics. We find that wives' relative earnings were positively associated with the risk of divorce among couples married in the late 1960s and 1970s, and that this was especially true for wives who outearned their husbands, but this was no longer the case for couples married in the 1990s. Change was concentrated among middle-earning husbands and those without college degrees, a finding consistent with the economic squeeze of the middle class over this period.

Keywords: divorce, earnings, gender, social change

Women have made large gains in closing the gender pay gap over the past several decades. Although full-time working women earned only 77 percent of what men did in 2012, this figure is up from 61 percent in 1960 (DeNavas-Walt, Proctor, and Smith 2013). As women's earnings have risen, so has the likelihood that wives outearn their husbands. In 2007, 22 percent of wives outearned their husbands versus only 4 percent in 1970 (Fry and Cohn 2010). Marriages in which wives outearn their husband have received special attention among academics and the press given concern that this arrangement may threaten men's gender identity as breadwinners and thereby increase marital conflict and divorce (Tichenor 1999, 2005; Tierney 2006). These concerns have a long history, and public anxiety about women's economic success flared again recently in connection with a Pew Research Center report showing growing numbers of wives outearning their husbands (Fry and Cohn 2010; Ludden 2010; Roberts 2010). Yet, given that Americans have increasingly embraced egalitarian marriage (Cotter, Hermsen, and Vanneman 2014; Gerson 2010), we might expect that wives' earn-

Christine R. Schwartz is professor of sociology at the University of Wisconsin-Madison. **Pilar Gonalons-Pons** is postdoctoral fellow at Goethe University Frankfurt am Main.

This research was carried out using the facilities of the Center for Demography and Ecology at the University of Wisconsin-Madison (R24 HD047873). The collection of data used in this study was partly supported by the National Institutes of Health (R01 HD06909) and the National Science Foundation (1157698). A previous version of this paper was presented at the 2015 Population Association of America in San Diego, CA. We are grateful to Martha Bailey, Tom DiPrete, Kei Nomaguchi, Christopher McKelvey, and the participants of the Russell Sage Foundation conference "Changing Roles and the Status of Women" for helpful comments and advice. Direct correspondence to: Christine R. Schwartz at cschwart@ssc.wisc.edu, Department of Sociology, University of Wisconsin-Madison, 1180 Observatory Drive, Madison, WI 53706; and Pilar Gonalons-Pons at pgonalons@soz.uni-frankfurt.de, School of Social Sciences (FB03), Goethe University Frankfurt am Main, Theodor W. Adorno Platz 6, 60629 Frankfurt am Main, Germany.

ings advantage is more weakly associated with divorce today than in the past.

In many cases, the academic literature on divorce confirms the popular perception that wives who outearn their husbands are more likely to divorce, though the evidence is far from uniform (for a review, see Sayer and Bianchi 2000). A notable limitation of nearly all research on this topic, however, is that it has examined single cohorts of marriages from the relatively distant past or wide cross-sections of marriages. Only two studies to our knowledge have examined changes in the association between wives' economic characteristics and divorce. One focused on the changing relationship between wives' employment and divorce using data through 1993, now more than twenty years old (South 2001). The other examined how the risk of divorce varies by spouses' employment, housework, relative earnings, and other characteristics using data through 2013, but focused on changes among couples marrying before and after 1975 (Killewald, forthcoming). Given the continued changes in wives' labor-force participation and marriage since the mid-1970s, we might expect to see change among couples married in more recent decades. Indeed, previous research on the relationship between spouses' relative education and divorce found that change was relatively slow until the mid-1980s (Schwartz and Han 2014).

This paper provides a detailed description of changes in the association between spouses' relative earnings and marital dissolution across successive decades. We use data from the 1968–2009 Panel Study of Income Dynamics (PSID) to examine change among couples married between 1968 and 2004. In addition to examining change over more finely grained intervals than past research, we provide a closer look at how the risk of divorce varies across the distribution of spouses' relative earnings. For instance, Marianne Bertrand, Emir Kamenica, and Jessica Pan examine differences in whether wives outearn their husbands (2015), but this approach may obscure important variation in the risk of divorce at different points in the relative earnings distribution, as we demonstrate in the next section. In addition, we consider whether changes in the relationship between spouses' relative earnings and divorce are concentrated among more or less advantaged couples. The subgroup analysis gives us clues about the potential mechanisms behind the changes we observe. Some studies have considered variation in these relationships by socioeconomic status (Brines and Joyner 1999; Rogers 2004), but none have examined whether changes have disproportionately occurred for particular groups. Finally, we consider the extent to which our results are robust to alternative measures of spouses' relative earnings and comment on implications for future research.

THEORETICAL PERSPECTIVES

The literature on the relationship between wives' earnings and divorce is considerable. Much of it focuses on the *economic independence hypothesis*, which states that the gains to marriage decline as women become more economically independent, thereby increasing the risk of divorce (Becker 1981; Oppenheimer 1997). Support for the economic independence hypothesis is mixed, with some studies finding that wives' economic contributions destabilize marriage, others finding the opposite, and still others finding no effect or nonlinear effects (for reviews, see Özcan and Breen 2012; Sayer and Bianchi 2000). At least part of the discrepancies between studies are doubtlessly due to the variety of ways that the concept of economic independence has been operationalized and to differences in data sources and methods.

One of the main limitations of the economic independence hypothesis as it was originally formulated is that it is a static theory with no engine of change. For instance, the theory is silent about why an additional dollar of wives' earnings would be more or less associated with divorce today than in the past. Thus, tests of this hypothesis have often centered on whether and under what conditions women's economic independence is associated with divorce, and on distinguishing these effects from other potentially confounding factors such as men's low earnings, total family resources, and reverse causality, rather than on variation over time.

A productive way to move the literature forward is to view change in the relationship be-

Figure 1. Predicted Change in Relationship Between Spouses' Relative Earnings and Marital Dissolution, Specialization with Gender Identity Threat

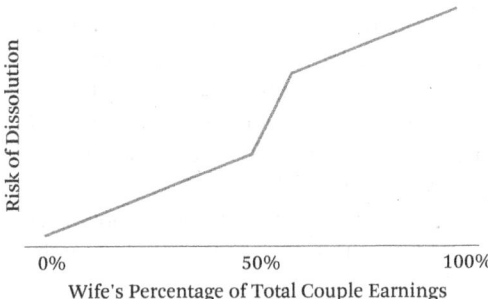

Source: Authors' compilation.

Figure 2. Predicted Change in Relationship Between Spouses' Relative Earnings and Marital Dissolution, Asymmetric Egalitarianism

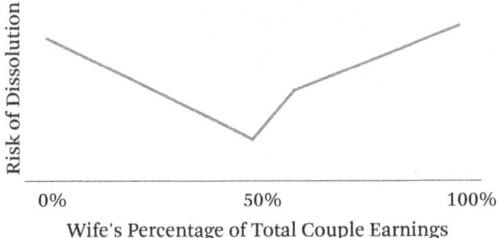

Source: Authors' compilation.

tween relative earnings and divorce through a *gendered institutional change* lens, which sees heterosexual marriage as an institution centrally governed by gender relations and expectations that change over time. Couples "do" gender through their actions, and gender is an accomplishment that individuals are held accountable for (West and Zimmerman 1987). Marriages in which wives outearn their husbands are hypothesized to have negative marital outcomes because of the non-normative power relations this arrangement symbolizes and the threat to men's gender identity as breadwinners it poses (Kaukinen 2004; Tichenor 1999, 2005). These non-normative configurations could come about via a number of scenarios; for example, wives could increase their earnings above the 50 percent mark, husbands' earnings could fall below it, or couples could enter marriage with this arrangement. Regardless of the mechanism, this perspective predicts that couples in which wives outearn their husbands should be at higher risk of divorce given that they violate the conventional marriage contract. Nevertheless, because gender is constructed in performance, individuals may attempt to compensate for non-normative arrangements in one realm by increasing their gender traditionalism in other realms, such as deferring more to their husband's authority or doing more housework (Ridgeway 2011; Tichenor 2005). This may or may not be enough to offset the increased risk of divorce.

As the gendered expectations associated with heterosexual marriage have changed, so may have the association between outearning one's husband and marital dissolution. A common theme among family scholars is that the institution of marriage has shifted away from rigid gender specialization toward more flexible, egalitarian partnerships (see, for example, Cherlin 2004; Goldscheider and Waite 1991; Juhn and McCue, this issue; Nock 2001; Oppenheimer 1997). Thus, the gendered institutional change perspective predicts that when specialization dominated American family life, any increase in wives' share of earnings should have been associated with an increased risk of divorce, and this should have been especially true if men's gender identity as breadwinners was threatened. This hypothesis is illustrated in figure 1 and can be termed the *specialization with gender identity threat* hypothesis. But as Americans have increasingly embraced egalitarian marriage and as their mate selection preferences have become more gender symmetric (Buss et al. 2001; Gerson 2010), we would expect equality of earnings to be increasingly associated with marital stability. Nevertheless, if it remains non-normative for wives to outearn their husbands, then the risk of divorce should still be elevated under these circumstances. The pattern shown in figure 2 may be termed the *asymmetric egalitarianism* hypothesis given that it predicts that equal earnings promote marital stability, but the risk of divorce is still disproportionately high when wives outearn their husbands.

Given recent research on men's and women's preferences for mates from speed and internet dating studies (Fisman et al. 2006; Hitsch, Hortaçsu, and Ariely 2010), it would not be surprising if divorce remains more likely for couples in which wives outearn their husbands. This research shows that young people prefer status-equal partners, but that both men and women tend to avoid pairings in which women have higher status than men. Beyond preferences about dating, experimental evidence shows that within existing romantic relationships, when men are outperformed by their female partners their self-esteem is negatively affected but the reverse is not true for women (Ratliff and Oishi 2013). Other evidence suggests that the extent to which men are bothered by relationships in which women outearn them has declined over time (Willinger 1993) and that the risk of divorce for wives who have more education than their husbands has declined in turn (Schwartz and Han 2014). Thus, outearning one's husband may still be associated with a greater risk of divorce, but perhaps to a lesser extent than in the past. The smaller increase in the risk of divorce at the 50 percent mark shown in figure 2 compared with figure 1 illustrates this expectation.

The hypotheses outlined in figures 1 and 2 build on Brines and Joyner's (1999) influential research on the "ties that bind" couples together in cohabiting and marital unions. They argue that marriages are stabilized by gendered specialization, whereas cohabiting couples, who tend to hold more egalitarian attitudes and do not enjoy the institutional protections of marriage, are stabilized by equality. They find support for gender specialization in marriage and an asymmetric association between relative earnings and dissolution for cohabitors similar to that shown in figure 2. Extending these hypotheses to variation over time, we might expect that as marriages have become more egalitarian, the relationship between relative earnings and divorce for married couples may look increasingly like the relationship among cohabitors of the past. Given that the marriages and cohabiting unions studied by Brines and Joyner were formed in the mid-1970s to mid-1980s, there is substantial room for change in the patterns they observe. Past studies have extended Brines and Joyner's argument to other countries and to same-sex couples (Kalmijn, Loeve, and Manting 2007), but not to change over time.

It would also be possible to overlay other hypotheses onto figure 1. For example, the *mutual dependence* hypothesis predicts that couples will be less likely to divorce not only when wives are economically dependent on their husbands but also when husbands are economically dependent on their wives (Heckert, Nowak, and Snyder 1998; Nock 2001; Rogers 2004). If economic dependency reduces the risk of divorce, we would expect to see a downturn in the probability of divorce at both ends of the relative earnings spectrum.

A related hypothesis predicts that the association between spouses' relative earnings and divorce may have increased because of the growing financial need for two paychecks. As men's earnings have stagnated, inequality widened, childcare and education costs soared, and the standard of living deemed acceptable for marriage increased, families may be increasingly dependent on both spouses' earnings regardless of where they fall on the relative earnings distribution (Cherlin 2004; Oppenheimer 1997; Sweeney 2002). Thus, an *economic necessity* hypothesis would predict a downward shift in the risk of divorce by spouses' relative earnings as wives' contributions become more valuable. It also predicts that declines in the association between wives' relative earnings and divorce should be most pronounced for socioeconomic groups that have experienced larger relative economic losses across the decades. We test this idea by examining shifts in the relationship between relative earnings and divorce by husbands' earnings and wife's education. Change concentrated among couples falling behind economically relative to other couples would support the notion that changes in the gendered relations of family life are more likely when they align with economic incentives (England 2010).

We recognize that each of these mechanisms may combine to produce observed patterns. Unlike past research, which often imposes a functional form on the data to adjudicate between mechanisms, we let the data speak for themselves and begin with a flexible specification of spouses' relative earnings. This allows us to describe observed changes in the association between relative earnings and divorce and subsequently test hypotheses about change based on the relationships we observe.

ANTICIPATORY EFFECTS OF DIVORCE ON WIVES' EARNINGS

A persistent concern in the earnings-divorce literature is that women may increase their labor supply in anticipation of divorce (Johnson and Skinner 1986; Özcan and Breen 2012; Poortman 2005; Teachman 2010). Thus, any study that does not account for reverse causality risks conflating the effects of wives' relative earnings on divorce with the effects of the *anticipation* of divorce on wives' relative earnings. To address this issue, scholars have often advocated using spouses' economic potential rather than their current earnings (Killewald, forthcoming; Özcan and Breen 2012; Xie et al. 2003). Anticipated or potential earnings outside marriage is conceptually appropriate for testing this hypothesis because it argues that women assess their financial ability to divorce based on what they could earn if they divorced (Dechter 1992; Killewald, forthcoming; Özcan and Breen 2012).

By contrast, a "doing" gender perspective emphasizes actual earnings. The argument that wives may neutralize their gender deviant behavior if they outearn their husbands by compensating for it in other realms suggests that it is not potential earnings that matter most for divorce but actual earnings. Indeed, the evidence is compelling that wives cut back on their labor-force participation to avoid outearning their husbands (Bertrand, Kamenica, and Pan 2015). Nevertheless, it is possible that predicted earnings gets at more than just women's economic independence. For instance, men may not feel threatened by wives who currently outearn them as long as their earnings potential exceeds their wives'. But examining spouses' relative earnings potential may be more useful for assessing a selection argument—that the types of wives who are likely to outearn their husbands (have high earnings potential) are more likely to divorce regardless of their realized earnings. The gendered institutional change perspective predicts that unconventional gender behaviors destabilize marriage and thus that spouses' relative earnings potential should only be associated with divorce to the extent that it is associated with realized earnings.

To consider these possibilities, we use three measures of spouses' relative earnings: relative earnings in the previous calendar year, relative earnings lagged by four years, and long-run relative earnings potential at the time of marriage. Following the vast majority of previous studies, we begin by using spouses' relative earnings in the calendar year prior to the year in which a marital dissolution (separation or divorce) occurred. To assess reverse causality concerns, we also examine the association using relative earnings with a four-year lag. A four-year lag is appropriate given past research showing that wives began ramping up their labor-force participation about three years prior to divorce (Johnson and Skinner 1986). Additionally, we examine spouses' relative earnings potential to assess the extent to which the relationships we observe may be due to preexisting differences in the likelihood of divorce for wives who are likely to outearn their husbands.

DATA, MEASURES, AND METHODS

Our main source of data is the 1968–2009 Panel of Income Dynamics. The PSID is a longitudinal survey of American households that began in 1968. All persons living in PSID families in 1968 were interviewed yearly through 1997 and every other year since then. The PSID also follows those born into or adopted by a PSID family even after they moved out of the original household. Those who married into PSID families were followed for as long as they lived with a member of the PSID sample. Our sample is composed of couples married in 1968 or later in which one spouse is the household head and in which wives married between sixteen and forty years of age. The PSID contains couples married before 1968 and thus it would be possible to extend the time series backward, but we do not do this to avoid left censoring marital histories. We exclude the Latino oversample because those respondents were interviewed only from 1990 to 1995 (Gouskova et al. 2008). The representativeness of the PSID is a concern given that it was representative of a cross-section of the population in 1968 and that the population of the United States has changed substantially since then. Nevertheless, previous studies show that use of weights or controls produces estimates of marriage formation and dissolution consistent with other sources (Lillard and Panis 1998). Thus, all of our analyses are weighted using PSID family weights.

The primary goal of our study is to describe, with a special focus on wives who outearn their husbands, how the association between spouses' relative earnings and divorce has changed across marriage cohorts. We use proportional hazard models and a flexible specification of relative earnings, beginning with a nine-category dummy variable corresponding to wives' share of couples' earnings (that is, <10 percent, 10 to 19 percent, ..., 70 to 79 percent, 80 to 100 percent). Nonworking wives are included in our analysis and fall into the lowest relative earnings category. We examine change across marriages formed roughly by decades: 1968 to 1979, 1980 to 1989, 1990 to 1999, and 2000 to 2004. We end the time series with marriages formed in the early 2000s to avoid truncation at very short marital durations.

Spouses' relative earnings are defined as the percentage of total couple earnings earned by the wife in the calendar year prior to the interview. For some analyses, we use the same measure, but lagged by four years. Our measure of spouses' relative earnings potential uses long-term predictions of husbands' and wives' earnings at the time of marriage for married full-time, full-year workers (defined as those working more than thirty-four hours per week for at least fifty weeks per year). To calculate earnings potential, we use IPUMS data from the 1970 to 2000 U.S. decennial censuses and the 2001–2009 American Community Survey (ACS) (Ruggles et al. 2010) to predict individuals' earnings at the time of marriage thirty years into the future or until age sixty-five. Our method for predicting earnings roughly follows the method outlined by Yu Xie and colleagues (2003). First, we predict annual earnings by sex and survey year as a linear function of age, age squared, education, race, and parental status.[1] We use these regressions to predict earnings for all combinations of independent variables, amounting to 8,640 cells per survey year. We linearly interpolate predicted values in years without data (1971 to 1979, 1981 to 1989, and 1991 to 1999) and set predicted earnings for 1968 and 1969 to their 1970 values.

Our predicted earnings measure is the sum of full-time, full-year predicted earnings in the first year of marriage and for the subsequent thirty years or until age sixty-five for each profile (8,640 cells) and year. For instance, the long-run thirty-year earnings potential of a twenty-year-old newlywed husband in 1970 is the sum of predicted earnings for men with his educational attainment and of the same race-ethnicity in 1970 from age twenty to age fifty. This measure assumes that individuals predict future earnings based on the age distributions of earnings they observe in a given year (for example, 1970), and that they do not consider how earnings trajectories may change in future years—the fundamental assumption of any synthetic cohort design. We merge spouses' relative earnings potential to the PSID data using the variables in the census and ACS earnings equation. Conceptually, this measure is attractive because it is estimated based on characteristics at the time of marriage and thus avoids issues of reverse causality and endogeneity between marital quality and subsequent changes in spouses' characteristics, for example, couples at higher risk of divorce may be less likely to have children, which in turn would affect contemporaneous measures of predicted earnings.

For each of our three relative earnings variables, we estimate separate Cox proportional hazard models of the risk of marital dissolu-

---

1. In our prediction equation, education is measured using dummy variables for the following categories: 1 = up to grade four; 2 = grades five, six, seven, or eight; 3 = grade nine; 4 = grade ten; 5 = grade eleven; 6 = grade twelve; 7 = first year of college; 8 = two or three years of college; 9 = four years of college; and 10 = five or more years of college. Race is measured with dummy variables for black and Hispanic. Parental status is measured using a dummy variable identifying individuals without children under eighteen in the household. Age is measured using age and age squared and ranges from sixteen to seventy.

Figure 3. Wives Outearning Husbands

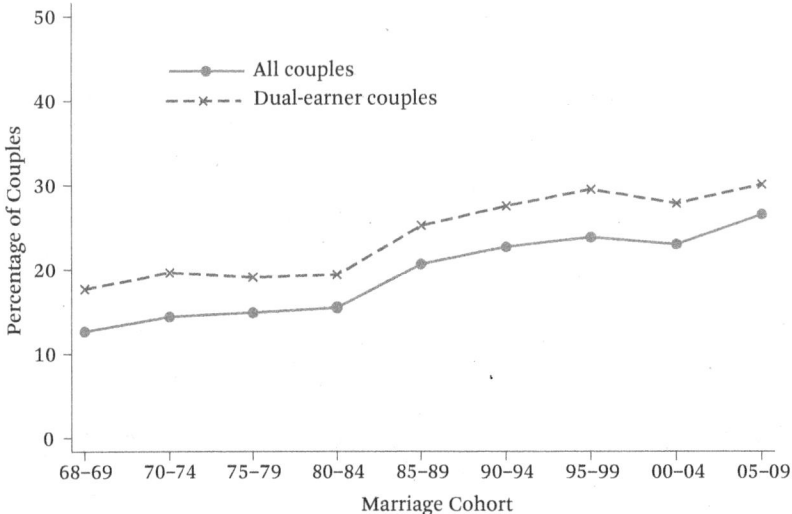

Source: Authors' compilation based on 1968–2009 Panel Study of Income Dynamics.
Notes: Data are weighted using family-level weights. The sample includes couples married in 1968 or later in which one spouse is the household head and in which wives married between sixteen and forty years of age. The Latino oversample is excluded.

tion, in which time is defined as years from marriage to separation, divorce, or censoring, whichever occurred first. Censored observations occur when respondents dropped out of the survey, reached the final interview without a marital dissolution, or were widowed. We estimate change in the relationship between spouses' relative earnings and marital dissolution by including interaction terms between our measures of relative earnings and dummy variables for marriage cohort.[2] We include controls for total couple earnings, total couple earnings squared, wives' employment (all in the previous calendar year), husbands' and wives' age at marriage and age at marriage squared, wives' race-ethnicity, both spouses' educational attainment, their relative educational attainment, and marriage parity.[3] These variables are coded as shown in table 1 and discussed in the following section.

RESULTS

Figure 3 shows trends in the percentage of couples in which wives outearn their husbands for all couples and for those in which both the husband and wife had nonzero earnings in the previous calendar year (dual-earner couples). It shows that the share of wives who outearn their husbands has grown. Among all couples married in 1968 and 1969, just 13 percent of wives outearned their husbands, versus 27 percent among those married in 2005 through 2009, a more than 100 percent increase. For dual-earner couples, the trend is parallel but levels of outearning one's husband are somewhat higher such that by 2005 through 2009,

2. We also estimate models in which each of the control variables are interacted with dummy variables for marriage cohort. Results from these models are very similar but less precise than those shown here.

3. Control variables for the equation using spouses' relative earnings with a four-year lag are the same except total couple earnings, total couple earnings squared, and employment are measured with a four-year lag rather than in the previous calendar year. The equation that includes spouses' relative earnings potential includes total couple earnings potential and total couple earnings potential squared in addition to total couple earnings, total couple earnings squared, wives' employment (all in the previous calendar year), and demographic controls as included in other models.

30 percent of wives in dual-earner couples outearned their husbands. Thus, wives who outearn their husbands are still in the minority, but their ranks are not small and are growing rapidly.

Table 1 compares the characteristics of couples married between 1968 and 1979 (the first marriage cohort in our hazard model analysis) to those married between 2000 and 2004 (the last). First, it shows trends in the extent to which wives outearn their husbands. Focusing on wives in dual-earner couples (both spouses have nonzero annual earnings in the prior calendar year), table 1 shows that wives who outearn their husbands do not outearn them by large amounts and that this percentage has changed very little across the past four decades, declining from 64 percent of total couple earnings to 63 percent. The decline in the extent to which wives outearn their husbands among all couples is somewhat larger (72 to 68 percent of total couple earnings), which is not surprising given that men's employment declined over this period, but the decline is still not large. By contrast, the increase in wives' contribution for dual-earner couples in which wives do not outearn their husbands is somewhat larger, growing from 26 percent to 32 percent of total couple earnings. Thus, even among couples married in the early 2000s, these results suggest that most wives who earn the same or less than their husbands were not verging on becoming the main breadwinners of their families and that wives in dual-earner couples who were outearning their husbands were generally not doing so by large margins.

Table 1 also shows that, consistent with their greater earnings, wives who outearn their husbands are more advantaged than those who earn the same or less in terms of their individual educational attainment and economic status. Wives who earn more than their husbands are more likely to be college graduates and earn more than their counterparts who do not outearn their husbands. They are also more likely to have more education than their husbands, to marry somewhat older men at slightly older ages, and to be African American.

Despite their individual educational and economic advantages, wives who outearned their husbands in the earlier cohort had lower total couple earnings than wives who earned the same or less than their husbands. This is consistent with Sanjiv Gupta's (2007) finding that families in which wives outearn their husbands tend to be more economically disadvantaged. However, this situation has reversed in more recent marriage cohorts. Rather than being more economically disadvantaged, couples married in the early 2000s in which wives outearned their husbands had higher total couple earnings than other couples. This shift occurred because both husbands and wives in marriages in which wives outearned their husbands increased their earnings disproportionately quickly compared with husbands and wives in marriages in which wives did not outearn their husbands. Looking at the full time series reveals that this reversal occurred beginning among couples married in the late 1990s (not shown). Thus, although Gupta's finding that wives who outearn their husbands tend to have lower total couple earnings than other couples was true for couples married before the mid-1990s, it no longer is.

Another notable finding from table 1 is that total couple earnings for wives who earn the same or less than their husbands barely budged between the 1968 to 1979 and 2000 to 2004 marriage cohorts. By contrast, total couple earnings for those in which wives outearn their husbands increased by more than 30 percent. This finding starkly illustrates the stagnating economic standing of the male breadwinner family and the growing importance of women's earnings to couples' economic well-being.

Spouses' Earnings in the Previous Calendar Year

Figure 4 shows trends in the relative risk of divorce by spouses' relative earnings in the previous calendar year and marriage cohort estimated from Cox proportional hazard models. More specifically, it shows the hazard of marital dissolution for roughly each decile of spouses' relative earnings compared with the first decile (wives earn 0 to 9 percent of total couple earnings), which is the reference category. We omit the 2000 to 2004 marriage cohort because the pattern for it is quite variable given its smaller sample size and thus obscures the

Table 1. Characteristics of Couples

	1968 to 1979		2000 to 2004	
Characteristic	W≤H	W>H	W≤H	W>H
Percentage of couple-years	85.7	14.3	77.0	23.0
Wife's percentage of total couple earnings				
All couples	18.1	72.1	24.8	67.6
	(16.9)	(19.1)	(18.0)	(16.8)
Dual-earner couples[a]	25.6	63.6	32.0	62.5
	(14.6)	(12.7)	(13.7)	(11.5)
Wife's years of schooling (%)				
Less than twelve	11.5	7.5	5.6	4.0
Twelve	47.0	41.7	28.8	19.3
Thirteen through fifteen	19.5	19.1	34.1	32.0
Sixteen or more	21.9	31.7	31.5	44.6
Husband's years of schooling (%)				
Less than twelve	11.0	12.2	7.1	6.2
Twelve	37.6	34.0	32.0	30.6
Thirteen through fifteen	22.1	23.0	29.9	37.4
Sixteen or more	29.4	30.9	31.0	25.8
Annual earnings (previous calendar year) (thousands of 2014 dollars)				
Wife	17.0	46.2	24.3	59.4
	(20.4)	(31.1)	(26.0)	(41.7)
Husband	68.0	23.8	63.5	32.6
	(61.1)	(25.0)	(54.9)	(27.3)
Total couple	85.1	70.0	87.8	92.0
	(67.7)	(50.6)	(68.6)	(62.3)
Wife had nonzero annual earnings (previous calendar year) (%)	70.8	100.0	77.5	100.0
Spouse's relative education (%)[b]				
Husband > wife	29.7	21.9	20.7	12.0
Husband = wife	53.5	55.6	53.3	48.1
Husband < wife	16.8	22.5	25.9	40.0
Wife's age at marriage	22.0	22.8	26.2	27.6
	(4.7)	(5.3)	(5.7)	(5.7)
Husband's age at marriage	24.4	25.6	28.4	29.7
	(6.2)	(7.8)	(6.8)	(7.4)
Wife African American (%)	6.5	7.6	6.8	12.0
Remarriage (wife) (%)	17.1	16.0	20.0	16.8
Sample size (couple-years)	30,951	5,355	1,818	550

Source: Authors' compilation based on 1968–2009 Panel Study of Income Dynamics.
Notes: W=wife's earnings in previous calendar year; H=husband's earnings in previous calendar year. Data are weighted using family-level weights. The sample includes couples married in 1968 or later in which one spouse is the household head and in which wives married between sixteen and forty years of age. The Latino oversample is excluded.
[a]Sample size differs from the full sample. 1968 to 1979 n = 25,684; 2000 to 2004 n = 1,895.
[b]Based on husband's and wife's years of schooling categories (<twelve, twelve, thirteen through fifteen, sixteen or more).

Figure 4. Hazard Ratios of Marital Dissolution

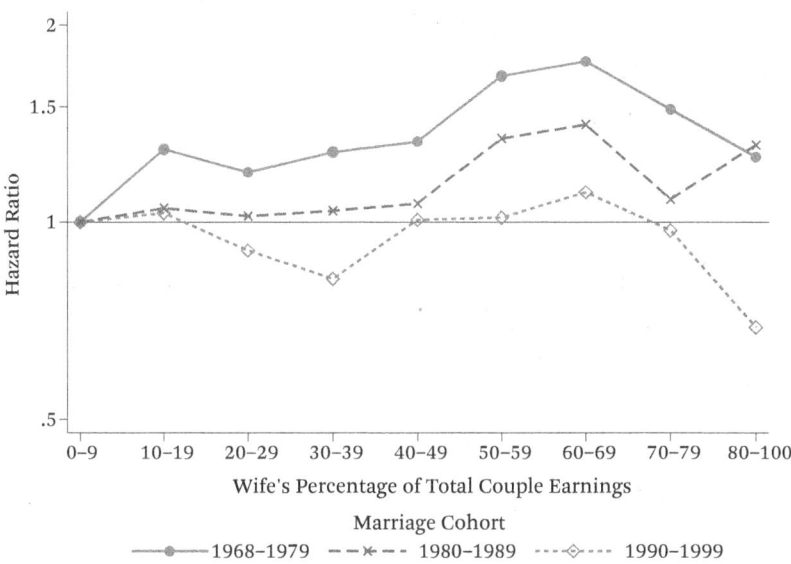

Source: Authors' compilation based on 1968–2009 Panel Study of Income Dynamics.
Notes: Data are weighted using family-level weights. The sample includes couples married in 1968 or later in which one spouse is the household head and in which wives married between sixteen and forty years of age. The Latino oversample is excluded. Change in the association between spouses' relative earnings and marital dissolution is estimated using interaction terms between dummy variables for relative earnings and marriage cohort. Control variables are total couple earnings, total couple earnings squared, a dummy variable indicating wives' nonzero earnings (all in previous calendar year), husbands' and wives' age at marriage and age at marriage squared, wives' race-ethnicity, both spouses' educational attainment, their relative educational attainment, and marriage parity.

pattern of change evident in the first three marriage cohorts. We show results for this cohort in table 2.

Across these three marriage cohorts, the risk of divorce appears to have become successively more weakly associated with wives' relative earnings. Within this general pattern of change are several notable features. First, the association between wives' relative earnings and marital dissolution among couples in which wives earn less than their husbands has declined. For those married between 1968 and 1979, virtually any increase in wives' economic contribution was positively associated with divorce. By contrast, for those marrying in the 1980s, the association between relative earnings and divorce for wives earning less than half of total couple earnings had disappeared. Interestingly, for those married in the 1990s, the association between wives' relative earnings and divorce reversed for wives earning less than half of total couple earnings. The point estimates indicate that couples in which wives earned 20 to 39 percent of total couple earnings were less likely to divorce than couples in which wives earn very little compared with their husbands. These shifts are consistent with the growing expectation that women contribute economically to the household (Gerson 2010).

It is also evident that the situation differs for couples in which wives earn half or more of total couple earnings. Consistent with the notion that the 50 percent mark represents a

Table 2. Hazard Ratios of Marital Dissolution

Relative Earnings Measure and Contrast	Marriage Cohort				Cohort Change[a]
	1968-1979 (1)	1980-1989 (2)	1990-1999 (3)	2000-2004 (4)	
Wife's percentage of total couple earnings (previous calendar year)					
10-49 percent versus 0-9 percent	1.27*	1.04	0.93	1.39	1,3 [†]
	(2.17)	(0.34)	(0.45)	(1.13)	
50-69 percent versus 0-9 percent	1.70**[b]	1.36[†b]	1.04	1.05	1,3*
	(3.57)	(1.92)	(0.19)	(0.13)	
≥ 70 percent versus 0-9 percent	1.31	1.27	0.75	0.86	1,3[†]
	(1.46)	(1.21)	(1.17)	(0.32)	
Wife's percentage of total couple earnings (four-year lag)[c]					
10-49 percent versus 0-9 percent	0.90	1.03	0.91	—	
	(0.82)	(0.18)	(0.41)		
50-69 percent versus 0-9 percent	0.99	1.23	0.82	—	
	(0.05)	(0.93)	(0.60)		
≥ 70 percent versus 0-9 percent	1.26	1.04	0.59	—	1,3[†]
	(0.25)	(0.14)	(1.54)		
Wife's percentage of total couple earnings potential					
≥ 50 percent versus < 50 percent	1.05	0.98	0.72*	0.58[†]	1,3[†]
	(0.32)	(0.12)	(2.10)	(1.84)	1,4[†]

Sources: Authors' compilation based on 1968-2009 Panel Study of Income Dynamics and 1970-2000 U.S. decennial census and 2001-2009 American Community Survey (Ruggles et al. 2010).
Notes: Hazard ratios are given with |z| statistics in parentheses. Data are weighted using family-level weights. The sample includes couples married in 1968 or later in which one spouse is the household head and in which wives married between sixteen and forty years of age. The Latino oversample is excluded. Change in the association between spouses' relative earnings and marital dissolution is estimated using interaction terms between dummy variables for relative earnings and marriage cohort. Control variables are total couple earnings, total couple earnings squared, a dummy variable indicating wives' nonzero earnings (all in previous calendar year), husbands' and wives' age at marriage and age at marriage squared, wives' race-ethnicity, both spouses' educational attainment, their relative educational attainment, and marriage parity. Variables are coded as shown in table 1. The equation using spouses' relative earnings with a four-year lag is the same except total couple earnings, total couple earnings squared, and wives' nonzero earnings are measured with a four-year lag. The equation that includes spouses' relative earnings potential includes total couple earnings potential and total couple earnings potential squared in addition to total couple earnings, total couple earnings squared, a dummy variable for wives' nonzero earnings (all in previous calendar year), and demographic controls as included in other models.
[a]Cohort pairs are shown when two-tailed z-tests for differences between cohort 1 and subsequent cohorts are significant ([†]$p < 0.10$; *$p < 0.05$; **$p < 0.01$).
[b]Two-tailed z-tests for the hypothesis of no difference between wives who earn between 50 and 69 percent versus 10 to 49 percent of total couple earnings are significant at $p < 0.05$.
[c]Couples married between 2000 and 2004 are not included in the four-year lagged earnings equation due to the short follow-up time for these couples using this measure.
Two-tailed z-tests where [†]$p < 0.10$; *$p < 0.05$; **$p < 0.01$.

threat point to the conventional breadwinner-homemaker marriage contract, the risk of divorce increases at 50 percent, at least for the first two marriage cohorts.[4] As was true for couples in which wives earn less than half of total earnings, the relative risk of divorce declines across each successive marriage cohort.

Results from figure 4 support the notion of mutual dependency. That is, the risk of divorce is lower when husbands depend economically on their wives as well as vice versa. Although the results are not uniform, the risk of divorce declines somewhat when wives contribute 70 percent or more of total earnings. These results are similar to those using earlier data (Heckert, Nowak, and Snyder 1998; Rogers 2004). It may be that disability or temporary unemployment spells are partially responsible for these patterns (Charles and Stephens 2004; Doiron and Mendolia 2012).

Table 2 tests the significance of the descriptive trends shown in figure 4. It confirms that for the early marriage cohort wives who earned between 10 and 49 percent of total couple earnings were at higher risk of divorce than those earning between 0 and 9 percent. The decline in this association between the 1968 to 1979 and 1990 to 1999 cohorts is marginally statistically significant ($p = 0.059$). Turning to wives who earn between 50 and 69 percent of total couple earnings, the relative risk of divorce is very high in the earliest cohort (70 percent higher than for couples in the 0 to 9 percent range) and significantly higher than for wives who earn 10 to 49 percent of total couple earnings ($p = 0.021$). The risk for this group declined across cohorts, however, and the magnitude of this change was statistically significant between 1968 to 1979 and 1990 to 1999 ($p = 0.032$). Finally, the risk of divorce for couples in which wives earn 70 percent or more of total earnings is elevated among cohorts married in the late 1960s through the 1980s but is lower than the risk among those earning 50 to 69 percent (though these differences are not statistically significant). The large drop in the relative risk of divorce for wives earning 70 percent or more of total couple earnings between the 1968 to 1979 and 1990 to 1999 marriage cohorts is marginally significant ($p = 0.054$).

Thus far, our results are consistent with a shift away from the breadwinner-homemaker model of marriage to a more egalitarian form, but are these results consistent across the socioeconomic spectrum? Given that economic incentives for two paychecks have grown, we might expect to see changes concentrated among couples who have experienced especially challenging economic times. Table 3 tests this idea by showing changes in the risk of dissolution by husband's earnings tercile and wife's education. Because these analyses involve three-way interactions between spouses' relative earnings, marriage cohort, and husband's earnings tercile or wife's education, we collapse across the first two and last two marriage cohorts due to sample size constraints. The 1990s are a natural cut point for the comparison given that many of associations found in earlier cohorts had disappeared by then. Also because of small sample sizes, we do not examine relative earnings separately for wives earning 50 to 69 and 70 percent of total couple earnings, but instead collapse these into a single indicator variable for 50 percent or more.

The results shown in table 3 are consistent with the economic necessity hypothesis. First, they show that wives' relative earnings among couples in which husbands are in the bottom third of the earnings distribution are not positively associated with marital dissolution for either cohort. Thus, for couples in which wives' earnings are the most economically necessary, we see no negative association with marital stability across the entire period. These findings hold when we exclude men with zero annual earnings (not shown), which demonstrates that the results are not driven by the economic dependency of zero-earner husbands. By contrast, wives' relative earnings were strongly associated with the risk of divorce for middle-

---

4. We experimented with a slightly different categorization of relative earnings corresponding more closely to the notion of outearning one's husband (0 to 10 percent, 11 to 20 percent, ... 51 to 60 percent, ...) but the risk of divorce appears to rise at 50 percent rather than at 51 percent. This is obscured when those earning 50 percent are categorized into a 41 to 50 percent group.

Table 3. Hazard Ratios of Marital Dissolution by Husband's Earnings and Wife's Education

Wife's Percentage of Total Couple Earnings Contrast (Previous Calendar Year)	Marriage Cohort 1968–1989	Marriage Cohort 1990–2004	Cohort Change[a]
By husband's earnings tercile			
Bottom third			
10–49 percent versus 0–9 percent	0.77†	0.85	
	(1.87)	(0.77)	
≥ 50 versus 0–9 percent	1.06[b]	0.67†	*
	(0.43)	(1.83)	
Middle third			
10–49 percent versus 0–9 percent	1.39*	1.02	
	(2.43)	(0.08)	
≥ 50 versus 0–9 percent	1.82**	0.73	**
	(3.07)	(1.02)	
Top third			
10–49 percent versus 0–9 percent	1.28†	1.04	
	(1.83)	(0.13)	
≥ 50 versus 0–9 percent	1.05	1.39	
	(0.14)	(0.69)	
By wife's education			
High school or less			
10–49 percent versus 0–9 percent	1.08	1.00	
	(0.72)	(0.00)	
≥ 50 versus 0–9 percent	1.43**[b]	0.96	†
	(2.85)	(0.20)	
Some college			
10–49 percent versus 0–9 percent	1.29	0.94	
	(1.55)	(0.28)	
≥ 50 versus 0–9 percent	1.39	0.78	†
	(1.64)	(0.88)	
College or more			
10–49 percent versus 0–9 percent	1.39	1.67	
	(1.33)	(1.15)	
≥ 50 versus 0–9 percent	1.73*	1.75	
	(2.13)	(1.19)	

Source: Authors' compilation based on 1968–2009 Panel Study of Income Dynamics.

Notes: Hazard ratios are given with |z| statistics in parentheses. Data are weighted using family-level weights. The sample includes couples married in 1968 or later in which one spouse is the household head and in which wives married between sixteen and forty years of age. The Latino oversample is excluded. Changes in the association between spouses' relative earnings and marital dissolution by husband's earnings tercile and wife's education are estimated using three-way interaction terms between dummy variables for relative earnings, marriage cohort, and husband's earnings tercile or wife's education. Control variables are total couple earnings, total couple earnings squared, a dummy variable indicating wives' nonzero earnings (all in previous calendar year), husbands' and wives' age at marriage and age at marriage squared, wives' race-ethnicity, both spouses' educational attainment, their relative educational attainment, and marriage parity. Variables are coded as shown in table 1.

[a]Cohort pairs are shown when two-tailed z-tests for differences between cohort 1 and subsequent cohorts are significant (†$p < 0.10$; *$p < 0.05$; **$p < 0.01$).

[b]Two-tailed z-tests for the hypothesis of no difference between wives who earn between 50 and 69 percent versus 10 to 49 percent of total couple earnings are significant at $p < 0.05$.

Two-tailed z-tests where †$p < 0.10$; *$p < 0.05$; **$p < 0.01$.

earning husbands in the early marriage cohort, but not for couples married more recently. Evidence of change is weaker for couples in which husbands are in the top third of the earnings distribution, especially for wives who outearn their husbands. Thus, much of the change in the association between relative earnings and divorce shown in the full sample is the result of change among couples with middle-earning husbands.

The results by wife's education are similar. They show that changes in the association between spouses' relative earnings and divorce were concentrated among wives with some college or less education and appear to be more persistent for wives with a college degree. Patterns by husbands' education are very similar to those by wives' education (not shown). Thus, change in these relationships was concentrated among those without college degrees, who have increasingly fallen behind on indicators of economic well-being since the 1970s (Autor 2014).[5]

Lagged Spouses' Relative Earnings

One way of addressing the concern that wives increase their earnings in anticipation of divorce is to examine trends using a four-year lagged measure of spouses' relative earnings. We do not include the most recent marriage cohort in these models given the short follow-up when implementing the four-year lag. Table 2 shows that the relationship between relative earnings and divorce is much weaker using the four-year lagged measure than when using earnings in the previous calendar year, a pattern consistent with research focusing on the association between wives' employment and divorce (Killewald, forthcoming). The increased risk of divorce for those earning from 10 to 49 and from 50 to 69 percent of total couple earnings evident in the previous results is wiped out. The only hint of a relationship that remains is an elevated risk of divorce for couples in which wives earn 70 percent or more of total couple earnings for the earliest cohort, but even this is not statistically significant.[6]

What implications do these findings have for our estimates using earnings in the previous calendar year? The first interpretation of the four-year lagged results is that the associations using earnings from the previous year are the result of the anticipatory effects of divorce on women's labor-force participation. For this to explain the declining association between relative earnings and divorce across marriage cohorts, it would also need to be the case that the extent to which women increase their labor-force participation in anticipation of divorce has declined across cohorts. This scenario is not implausible given that wives work more today than in the past and thus perhaps do not need to increase their labor-force participation in anticipation of divorce as much as they once did (Sen 2000). It is less plausible that reverse causality explains the uptick in the risk of divorce at the 50 percent mark shown in figure 4. For reverse causality to explain this increase, one would need to believe that women specifically target earning more than their husbands before they are willing to separate, or that women who are likely to outearn their husbands disproportionately increase their labor-force participation prior to divorce. This is not something that scholars of the anticipatory effects of divorce have generally assumed. Instead, scholars have operationalized the anticipation hypothesis as occurring uniformly across the income spectrum (Johnson and Skinner 1986; Poortman 2005).

Second, it is possible that outearning one's husband has mainly short-term impacts. Given

---

5. Comparable results by race show that the association between wives' relative earnings and divorce was similar for black and white wives married between 1968 and 1989, but that declines in the association have been concentrated among white wives. It is unclear whether an increased economic need for two paychecks among white couples can explain this difference because, if anything, median incomes among black households lagged behind white households over this period (DeNavas-Walt and Proctor 2014). Explanations for differences in trends by race deserve further exploration, but this is outside the scope of this article.

6. Results using a two-year lag are similar to those using earnings in the previous year and show evidence of a decline in the association between spouses' relative earnings and divorce across cohorts, but like the four-year lag, the associations between wives' relative earnings and divorce are generally weaker.

that outearning one's husband is often transitory (Winkler, McBride, and Andrews 2005), a wife may outearn her husband in one year, but her doing so may not matter for divorce four years later if she is no longer outearning him. Even if a wife's higher earnings are permanent, that she outearns her husband may only matter in the short term if husbands and wives either split up or are able to renegotiate the marital contract in a year or two after the earnings shift. Future studies should use exogenous variation in men's or women's earnings to examine the extent to which spouses' relative earnings have short-term, long-term, or no effects on marital dissolution. The bottom line for the current study is that the four-year lagged measures of earnings show no evidence of an association between relative earnings and divorce for any of the marriage cohorts we examine. Nevertheless, there are also good reasons to believe that this measure may not be ideal for capturing the effects of spouses' relative earnings on divorce.

Spouses' Relative Earnings Potential at Marriage

Table 2 also shows cohort trends in the association between spouses' relative earnings potential measured at the time of marriage. The main purpose of this analysis is to estimate the extent to which a particular kind of selection may explain our results—that is, wives who are likely to outearn their husbands could be more divorce prone going into marriage. It may be that the correlation between their earnings potential and their realized earnings explains the associations we observe using earnings in the previous year. To test this, we estimate a model for spouses' relative earnings potential similar to previous models but add the previous year earnings measures (dummy variables for deciles of spouses' relative earnings, total couple earnings, total couple earnings squared, and wives' nonzero earnings) as control variables. Because few wives' full-time, full-year earnings potential exceeds their husbands' and because few wives' full-time, full-year earnings potential is only a small fraction of their husbands' (0 to 20 percent), we present the results with less detail here than for the other measures, showing only the contrast between wives earning half or more of total couple earnings potential and those earning less than half.

For the earliest cohorts, as table 2 shows, the positive association between spouses' relative earnings and divorce evident using the previous year relative earnings variable has disappeared. Interestingly, we do see some evidence that wives with the same or higher earnings potential than their husbands are increasingly stable compared with those whose earnings potential is lower. This shift is consistent with the growing economic advantage of couples in which wives outearn their husbands. Although in this model we control for total couple earnings, total couple earnings squared, and both couples' educational attainment (in addition to other factors), it is possible that these couples are also becoming more advantaged in ways we have not captured. Regardless, these results are inconsistent with a selection story in which women who are the most likely to outearn their husbands at the outset of their marriages are more divorce prone (see also Weiss and Willis 1997). If anything, these women are becoming less divorce prone in recent marriage cohorts.

DISCUSSION

Our results show that if there ever was a positive association between outearning one's husband and marital dissolution, it has diminished across cohorts and is now small and statistically insignificant. Among couples married in the late 1960s and 1970s, virtually any increase in wives' relative earnings was associated with an increased risk of divorce, especially among wives who outearned their husbands. But the association between spouses' relative earnings and divorce has declined markedly. Among couples married in the 1990s, increases in wives' relative earnings were no longer associated with an increased risk of divorce and the risk of divorce for wives who outearned their husbands was not significantly different from that of other wives. These findings are consistent with changes in marriage as a gendered institution. When the breadwinner-homemaker model of marriage dominated American family life, deviations from this ideal were associated with a heightened risk of divorce, especially for wives who outearned their husbands. As Americans have increasingly embraced egalitarian marriage and as flexibility about the breadwinner role has grown, these associations have weakened and become statistically insignificant.

But change has not been uniform across all groups. The biggest changes have occurred among middle-earning husbands and those without baccalaureates, coinciding with the economic squeeze of the middle and working classes over this period. Beginning in the late 1970s, inequality in the United States grew sharply. College graduates and top-earners faired substantially better than the rest of the nation. Middle- and working-class men's stagnating incomes combined with rising education, childcare, and housing costs have substantially increased the economic incentive for two paychecks (Sweeney 2002). Thus, the economic squeeze of the middle and working classes over this period may have been an incentive to renegotiate the marital bargain toward greater flexibility about the breadwinner role. Also consistent with the argument that changes in gendered relationships are most pronounced when they align with economic incentives (England 2010) is the relative lack of change among more advantaged couples. Although our estimates for these couples are less precise, we find little evidence of a decline in the negative association between outearning one's husband and marital stability among college graduates and those with high-earning husbands. Future research should test whether these patterns hold using data from other sources.

One explanation for our subgroup findings is that wives' relative earnings are more threatening to the male breadwinner identity when their employment is seen as more of a choice than a necessity (Usdansky 2011). Another explanation points to the structural constraints of professional versus working-class occupations. Outearning one's husband may be more disruptive of marital life among professionals because of the time pressures it creates. Many professional occupations require long hours, and workers in these jobs are not easy substitutes for one another (Goldin 2014). When professional husbands work long hours, it is likely that their wives must also work long hours to outearn them. From a household perspective, the expansion of paid work hours for both partners squeezes the time for domestic pursuits ever smaller, resulting in a time bind that is especially pronounced for those with the most prestigious occupations (Jacobs and Gerson 2001). Indeed, when husbands hold jobs with long inflexible hours, their wives are more likely to drop out of the labor force, thus converting formerly dual-earner households to breadwinner-homemaker ones (Cha 2010). By contrast, working-class families are more likely to be employed in jobs with nonstandard schedules or hold part-time jobs, which allow them to alternate shifts, sharing both the economic provider and childcare roles (Deutsch 1999; Shows and Gerstel 2009).

Variation in beliefs about parenthood may also reinforce class differences in work-family life. Highly educated mothers are under significant pressure to conform to an "intensive mothering" ideal, which requires constant availability and huge energy investments in the management of children's daily lives (Hays 1998). By contrast, working-class parents are more likely to subscribe to a philosophy of "natural growth," in which children's leisure activities are more informal and less adult-directed (Lareau 2003). Thus, differences in the economic incentives, employment conditions, and cultural ideals surrounding parenthood may make it especially difficult for the wives of professional men to hold full-time jobs, jobs that would increase their likelihood of outearning their husbands (Cha 2010; Usdansky 2011).

Although our results are consistent with the idea that spouses' relative earnings are less consequential for marriage outcomes today than in the past (albeit more so for some than others), it is possible that they reflect changes in how women adjust their earnings in anticipation of divorce rather than changes in the effects of relative earnings on divorce. To address this issue, we include additional measures of spouses' relative earnings: lagged spouses' relative earnings and spouses' relative earnings potential. These sensitivity tests suggest that our findings could be the result of changes in the extent to which women anticipate divorce by increasing their earnings but could also indicate that the effects of outearning one's husband are short lived and that couples either split up or satisfactorily renegotiate the marriage contract relatively quickly. Future research should investigate these possibilities by using exogenous variation to identify causal effects or by examining the extent to which the effects of changes in spouses' relative earnings on divorce are concentrated in the short term.

Even if our findings are entirely due to a reduction in wives' anticipation of divorce with increased labor force participation, our results still point to a major shift away from the breadwinner-homemaker model of marriage and the growing prevalence of a relatively new form of marriage—the dual-earner couple (Ruggles 2014; Stanfors and Goldscheider 2015). Change has not been uniform across social groups and more work should be done to investigate the reasons behind these differences. Overall, though, our results point to substantial shifts away from rigid gender specialization to increased egalitarianism and flexibility about husbands' and wives' economic roles in marriage.

REFERENCES

Autor, David H. 2014. "Skills, Education, and the Rise of Earnings Inequality Among the 'Other 99 Percent.'" *Science* 344(6186): 843–51.

Becker, Gary S. 1981. *A Treatise on the Family*. Cambridge, Mass.: Harvard University Press.

Bertrand, Marianne, Emir Kamenica, and Jessica Pan. 2015. "Gender Identity and Relative Income within Households." *Quarterly Journal of Economics* 130(2): 571-614.

Brines, Julie, and Kara Joyner. 1999. "The Ties That Bind: Principles of Cohesion in Cohabitation and Marriage." *American Sociological Review* 64(3): 333-55.

Buss, David M., Todd K. Shackelford, Lee A. Kirkpatrick, and Randy J. Larsen. 2001. "A Half Century of Mate Preferences: The Cultural Evolution of Values." *Journal of Marriage and Family* 63(2): 491-503.

Cha, Youngjoo. 2010. "Reinforcing Separate Spheres: The Effect of Spousal Overwork on Men's and Women's Employment in Dual-Earner Households." *American Sociological Review* 75(2): 303-29.

Charles, Kerwin Kofi, and Melvin Stephens. 2004. "Disability, Job Displacement, and Divorce." *Journal of Labor Economics* 22(2): 489-522.

Cherlin, Andrew J. 2004. "The Deinstitutionalization of American Marriage." *Journal of Marriage and Family* 66(4): 848-61.

Cotter, David A., Joan M. Hermsen, and Reeve Vanneman. 2014. "Back on Track? The Stall and Rebound in Support for Women's New Roles in Work and Politics, 1977-2012." New York: Council on Contemporary Families.

Dechter, Aimée R. 1992. "The Effect of Women's Economic Independence on Union Dissolution." *CDE* working paper no. 92-28. Madison: University of Wisconsin–Madison.

DeNavas-Walt, Carmen, and Bernadette D. Proctor. 2014. "Income and Poverty in the United States: 2013." *Current Population Reports*, series P60, no. 249. Washington: U.S. Government Printing Office for U.S. Census Bureau.

DeNavas-Walt, Carmen, Bernadette D. Proctor, and Jessica C. Smith. 2013. "Income, Poverty, and Health Insurance Coverage in the United States: 2012." *Current Population Reports*, series P60, no. 245. Washington: U.S. Government Printing Office for U.S. Census Bureau.

Deutsch, Francine. 1999. *Halving It All: How Equally Shared Parenting Works*. Cambridge, Mass.: Harvard University Press.

Doiron, Denise, and Silvia Mendolia. 2012. "The Impact of Job Loss on Family Dissolution." *Journal of Population Economics* 25(1): 367-98.

England, Paula. 2010. "The Gender Revolution: Uneven and Stalled." *Gender & Society* 24(2): 149-66.

Fisman, Raymond, Sheena S. Iyengar, Emir Kamenica, and Itamar Simonson. 2006. "Gender Differences in Mate Selection: Evidence from a Speed Dating Experiment." *Quarterly Journal of Economics* 121(2): 673-97.

Fry, Richard, and D'Vera Cohn. 2010. "Women, Men, and the New Economics of Marriage." Washington, D.C.: Pew Research Center. Accessed April 6, 2016. http://www.pewsocialtrends.org/files/2010/11/new-economics-of-marriage.pdf.

Gerson, Kathleen. 2010. *The Unfinished Revolution: How a New Generation Is Reshaping Family, Work, and Gender in America*. Oxford: Oxford University Press.

Goldin, Claudia. 2014. "A Grand Gender Convergence: Its Last Chapter." *American Economic Review* 104(4): 1091-119.

Goldscheider, Frances K., and Linda J. Waite. 1991. *New Families, No Families? The Transformation of the American Home.* Berkeley: University of California Press.

Gouskova, Elena, Steven G. Herringa, Katherine McGonagle, and Robert F. Schoeni. 2008. "Panel Study of Income Dynamics, Revised Longitudinal Weights, 1993-2005." Ann Arbor: University of Michigan.

Gupta, Sanjiv. 2007. "Autonomy, Dependence, or Display? The Relationship Between Married Women's Earnings and Housework." *Journal of Marriage and the Family* 69(2): 399-417.

Hays, Sharon. 1998. *The Cultural Contradictions of Motherhood.* New Haven, Conn.: Yale University Press.

Heckert, D. Alex, Thomas C. Nowak, and Kay A. Snyder. 1998. "The Impact of Husbands' and Wives' Relative Earnings on Marital Disruption." *Journal of Marriage and the Family* 60(3): 690-703.

Hitsch, Günter J., Ali Hortaçsu, and Dan Ariely. 2010. "Matching and Sorting in Online Dating." *American Economic Review* 100(1): 130-63.

Jacobs, Jerry A., and Kathleen Gerson. 2001. "Overworked Individuals or Overworked Families? Explaining Trends in Work, Leisure, and Family Time." *Work and Occupations* 28(1): 40-63.

Johnson, William R. and Jonathan Skinner. 1986. "Labor Supply and Marital Separation." *American Economic Review* 76(3): 455-69.

Juhn, Chinhui, and Kristin McCue. 2016. "Selection and Specialization in the Evolution of Marriage Earnings Gaps." *RSF* 2(4). doi: 10.7758/RSF.2016.2.4.09.

Kalmijn, Matthijs, Anneke Loeve, and Dorien Manting. 2007. "Income Dynamics in Couples and the Dissolution of Marriage and Cohabitation." *Demography* 44(1): 159-79.

Kaukinen, Catherine. 2004. "Status Compatibility, Physical Violence, and Emotional Abuse in Intimate Relationships." *Journal of Marriage and Family* 66(2): 452-71.

Killewald, Alexandra. Forthcoming. "Money, Work, and Marital Stability: Assessing Change in the Determinants of Divorce." *American Sociological Review.*

Lareau, Annette. 2003. *Unequal Childhoods: Class, Race, and Family Life.* Berkeley: University of California Press.

Lillard, Lee A., and Constantijn W. A. Panis. 1998. "Panel Attrition from the Panel Study of Income Dynamics: Household Income, Marital Status, and Mortality." *Journal of Human Resources* 33(2): 437-57.

Ludden, Jennifer. 2010. "Modern Marriages: The Rise of the Sugar Mama." *National Public Radio: Morning Edition,* January 19. Accessed April 6, 2016. http://www.npr.org/templates/story/story.php?storyId=122612096.

Nock, Steven L. 2001. "The Marriages of Equally Dependent Spouses." *Journal of Family Issues* 22(6): 755-75.

Oppenheimer, Valerie Kincade. 1997. "Women's Employment and the Gain to Marriage: The Specialization and Trading Model." *Annual Review of Sociology* 23: 431-53.

Özcan, Berkay, and Richard Breen. 2012. "Marital Instability and Female Labor Supply." *Annual Review of Sociology* 38: 463-81.

Panel Study of Income Dynamics, public use dataset. 2012. Produced and distributed by the Survey Research Center, Institute for Social Research, University of Michigan. Ann Arbor.

Poortman, Anne-Rigt. 2005. "Women's Work and Divorce: A Matter of Anticipation? A Research Note." *European Sociological Review* 21(3): 301-9.

Ratliff, Kate A., and Shigehiro Oishi. 2013. "Gender Differences in Implicit Self-Esteem Following a Romantic Partner's Success or Failure." *Journal of Personality and Social Psychology* 105(4): 688-702.

Ridgeway, Cecilia L. 2011. *Framed by Gender: How Gender Inequality Persists in the Modern World.* New York: Oxford University Press.

Roberts, Sam. 2010. "More Men Marrying Wealthier Women." *New York Times,* January 19.

Rogers, Stacey J. 2004. "Dollars, Dependency, and Divorce: Four Perspectives on the Role of Wives' Income." *Journal of Marriage and Family* 66(1): 59-74.

Ruggles, Steven. 2014. "Marriage, Family Systems, and Economic Opportunity in the United States Since 1850." *Minnesota Population Center* working paper no. 2014-11. Minneapolis: University of Minnesota. Accessed April 6, 2016. http://www.hist.umn.edu/~ruggles/Articles/Ruggles_Marriage_2014.pdf.

Ruggles, Steven, J. Trent Alexander, Katie Genadek, Ronald Goeken, Matthew B. Schroeder, and Matthew Sobek. 2010. Integrated Public Use Microdata Series: Version 5.0. [Machine-readable database]. Minneapolis: University of Minnesota.

Sayer, Liana C., and Suzanne M. Bianchi. 2000. "Women's Economic Independence and the Probability of Divorce: A Review and Reexamination." *Journal of Family Issues* 21(7): 906–43.

Schwartz, Christine R., and Hongyun Han. 2014. "The Reversal of the Gender Gap in Education and Trends in Marital Dissolution." *American Sociological Review* 79(4): 605–29.

Sen, Bisakha. 2000. "How Important Is Anticipation of Divorce in Married Women's Labor Supply Decisions? An Intercohort Comparison Using NLS Data." *Economics Letters* 67(2): 209–16.

Shows, Carla, and Naomi Gerstel. 2009. "Fathering, Class, and Gender: A Comparison of Physicians and Emergency Medical Technicians." *Gender & Society* 23(2): 161–87.

South, Scott J. 2001. "Time-Dependent Effects of Wives' Employment on Marital Dissolution." *American Sociological Review* 66(2): 226–45.

Stanfors, Maria A., and Frances K. Goldscheider. 2015. "The Forest and the Trees: Industrialization, Demographic Change, and the Ongoing Gender Revolution in the United States and Sweden, 1870–2010." Stockholm Research Reports in Demography 2015: 18. Stockholm: Stockholm University.

Sweeney, Megan M. 2002. "Two Decades of Family Change: The Shifting Economic Foundations of Marriage." *American Sociological Review* 67(1): 132–47.

Teachman, Jay D. 2010. "Wives' Economic Resources and Risk of Divorce." *Journal of Family Issues* 31(10): 1305–23.

Tichenor, Veronica Jaris. 1999. "Status and Income as Gendered Resources: The Case of Marital Power." *Journal of Marriage and the Family* 61(3): 638–50.

———. 2005. "Maintaining Men's Dominance: Negotiating Identity and Power When She Earns More." *Sex Roles* 53(3–4): 191–205.

Tierney, John. 2006. "Male Pride and Female Prejudice." *New York Times*, January 3. Accessed April 26, 2016. http://query.nytimes.com/gst/fullpage.html?res=9902EFDF1130F930A35752C0A9609C8B63.

Usdansky, Margaret L. 2011. "The Gender-Equality Paradox: Class and Incongruity Between Work-Family Attitudes and Behaviors." *Journal of Family Theory & Review* 3(3): 163–78.

Weiss, Yoram, and Robert J. Willis. 1997. "Match Quality, New Information, and Marital Dissolution." *Journal of Labor Economics* 15(1): S293–329.

West, Candace, and Don H Zimmerman. 1987. "Doing Gender." *Gender & Society* 1(2): 125–51.

Willinger, Beth. 1993. "Resistance and Change: College Men's Attitudes Toward Family and Work in the 1980s." In *Men, Work, and Family*, edited by Jane C. Hood. Newbury Park, Calif.: Sage Publications.

Winkler, Anne E., Timothy D. McBride, and Courtney Andrews. 2005. "Wives Who Outearn Their Husbands: A Transitory or Persistent Phenomenon for Couples?" *Demography* 42(3): 523–35.

Xie, Yu, James M Raymo, Kimberly Goyette, and Arland Thornton. 2003. "Economic Potential and Entry into Marriage and Cohabitation." *Demography* 40(2): 351–67.

Selection and Specialization in the Evolution of Marriage Earnings Gaps

CHINHUI JUHN AND KRISTIN McCUE

We examine changes in marriage and earnings patterns across four cohorts born between 1936 and 1975 using data from Survey of Income and Program Participation panels linked to administrative data on earnings. We find that, for both men and women, marriage has become increasingly positively associated with education and earnings potential. We compare ordinary least squares and fixed-effect estimates of the earnings differential associated with marriage. We find that the marriage earnings gap fell for women in fixed-effect estimates, implying that the impact of specialization has diminished over time. We also find that increasingly positive selection into marriage overstates the reduction in the marriage earnings gap. Although marriage is no longer associated with lower earnings among women in our most recent cohort, the motherhood gap remains large. Among men, we find that the marriage premium actually increases for more recent birth cohorts in fixed-effects regressions.

Keywords: marriage, motherhood, earnings

Differences in work behavior and earnings associated with marital status and the presence of children are well documented. In the cross-section, wage regressions typically find that married men earn from 10 percent to 40 percent more than single men (see, for example, Korenman and Neumark 1991; Antonovics and Town 2004). In contrast, married women earn significantly less than unmarried women with similar human capital characteristics, especially those with children (see, for example, Waldfogel 1997, 1998).[1] Evidence indicates that

Chinhui Juhn is Henry Graham Professor of Economics at the University of Houston and research associate of the National Bureau of Economic Research. **Kristin McCue** is principal economist at the Center for Economic Studies at the U.S. Census Bureau.

Any opinions and conclusions are those of the authors and do not necessarily represent the views of the U.S. Census Bureau, the SSA, the NBER, or any other agency of the federal government. All results have been reviewed to ensure that no confidential information is disclosed. This research was supported by the U.S. Social Security Administration through Grant #NB10-10 to the National Bureau of Economic Research (NBER) as part of the SSA Retirement Research Consortium. We would like to thank Martha Bailey, Thomas DiPrete, and other participants of the Russell Sage conference "Changing Roles and the Status of Women," and Martha Stinson for helpful comments. We also thank Gary Benedetto and Martha Stinson for help in using the data. Direct correspondence to: Chinhui Juhn at cjuhn@uh.edu, University of Houston, Department of Economics, 3623 Cullen Boulevard, Room 204, Houston, TX 77204-5019; and Kristin McCue at kristin.mccue@census.gov, U.S. Census Bureau, CES/2K130E, 4600 Silver Hill Rd., Washington, D.C. 20233-6300.

1. Fixed-effects models using data from the National Longitudinal Survey of Youth (NLSY79) find that for women, marriage, absent children, is positively associated with wages (Budig and England 2001; Killewald and Gough 2013). These results are consistent with what we find for the most recent birth cohort.

Figure 1. Marriage Earnings Differentials

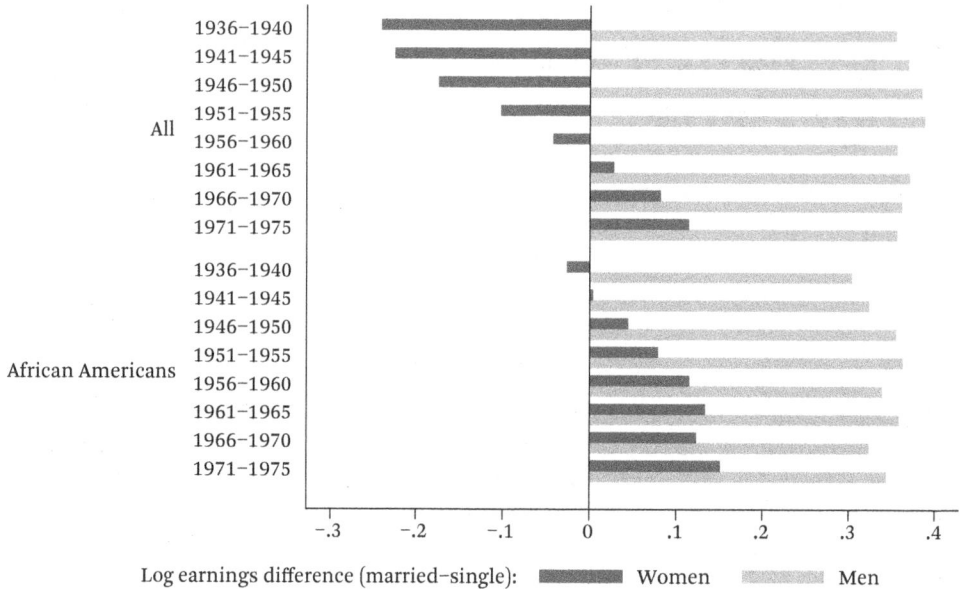

Source: Authors' compilation based on Integrated Public Use Microdata Series (IPUMS) versions of 1960–2000 decennial census and 2010 American Community Survey public use data.
Note: OLS estimates based on population census and ACS public-use data.

two patterns contribute to these differentials: first, selection, by which we mean that characteristics related to earnings differ between those who are married and those who are not; and, second, specialization, in which spouses increase total family consumption when one spouse invests more heavily in skills rewarded in the labor market and the other takes a primary role in home production. We expect specialization to lead to faster wage growth relative to single peers for one spouse, but a decline relative to peers for the other. For example, Sanders Korenman and David Neumark (1991) find evidence of positive selection of men into marriage based on earnings—that is, men with higher earnings are more likely to marry. But they also find that much of the marriage premium accrues from faster wage growth for men after marriage, which is consistent with marriage allowing men to shift toward more market work and less home production.[2] Comparing married and cohabitating couples in Sweden, Donna Ginther, Marianne Sundstrom, and Anders Bjorklund (2008) find that most of the marriage premium among men can be attributed to positive selection while increased specialization after marriage accounts for the marriage penalty for women.[3] How have earnings differentials associated with marriage—which we refer to as marriage gaps—

---

2. Christopher Dougherty (2006) finds that among men in the NLSY79, wages rise at least five years prior to marriage. This is still consistent with specialization if men invest in steady work and higher paying jobs in anticipation of marriage. On the other hand, it could also be consistent with selection into marriage based on time-varying shocks rather than persistent earnings differences. A simple fixed-effects model would not be able to disentangle the two channels in this case.

3. Another important explanation which we do not address in our paper is discrimination by employers. Conducting a laboratory study, Shelley Correll, Stephen Bernard, and In Paik (2007) find that subjects penalize mothers in terms of perceived competence and recommended starting salary. Part of what we attribute to specialization may be due to statistical discrimination as employers infer actions of individual men and women based on group characteristics.

evolved over time? Figure 1 presents estimates of these gaps for cohorts born between 1936 and 1975 based on a series of cross-sectional surveys.[4] In the cross-section, married men enjoy a substantially positive earnings gap, on the order of 30 to 35 log points, that has remained fairly stable across these cohorts. Married women, on the other hand, began with a substantially negative earnings gap (-24 log points for the 1936 to 1940 cohort) but across cohorts have steadily gained relative to their single counterparts. In the most recent birth cohort (1971 to 1975), married women enjoy a positive earnings gap of 11 log points. The trend among black women is similar but the change is not as dramatic, the gap changing from roughly -3 log points for the 1936 to 1940 cohort to positive 15 log points for the most recent cohort.

Betsey Stevenson and Justin Wolfers (2007) hypothesize that the returns to marriage based on production complementarities have diminished over time. The introduction of technology in household production, such as washing machines, vacuum cleaners, and microwave ovens has reduced incentives to marry based on household specialization (Greenwood and Guner 2008). Women's market opportunities increased for a variety of reasons, making it more costly for women to stay home. In addition, unilateral divorce laws also increased the risk associated with specializing in the household sector for women (Stevenson 2007). Although the returns to specialization may have declined, the benefits of marriage based on consumption and leisure complementarities may have increased with increased longevity and leisure (Aguiar and Hurst 2007). Based on these developments, we would expect to find that the marriage gaps for both men and women have narrowed over time.[5]

The factors that led to declining marriage rates, however, did not affect all men and women equally. Although wages of women in general rose relative to those of men, the gains were larger at the bottom of the skill distribution than at the top (Blau and Kahn 1997). Among less-educated couples especially, the incentive to marry based on household specialization fell as male earnings prospects fell. Evidence is considerable that these changes resulted in shifts in selection into marriage as well. Among women, the cross-sectional correlation between marriage and education has reversed sign. In earlier cohorts, marriage rates were lowest among the most-educated women, whereas now the most-educated women are the most likely to be married (Isen and Stevenson 2010; Goldstein and Kenney 2001). Among men as well, marriage rates have fallen most dramatically for the less educated, reinforcing the positive relationship between marriage and earnings potential in earlier cohorts.

In this study, we examine how these shifts have affected the evolution of earnings differentials associated with marriage and the importance of selection versus specialization in understanding these changes. Our basic empirical strategy is to estimate marriage gaps in earnings using both ordinary least squares (OLS) and fixed-effects (FE) models. OLS estimates combine the effects of changes in earnings associated with a change in marital status (specialization) with any persistent existing differences in mean earnings between those who are married and those who are not (selection effects). When we include fixed effects, the coefficient on marriage isolates changes in earnings associated with a change in marital status. Our specifications include controls for age, so where our FE estimates show negative marriage gaps for women, this reflects slower wage growth for women relative to their peers during periods when they are married. The difference

---

4. The figure is based on 1960 through 2000 decennial census and 2010 American Community Survey's Integrated Public Use Microdata Series (IPUMS) data. The figure reports coefficients on five-year birth cohort dummies interacted with a currently married dummy from a regression of log annual wage and salary earnings on year dummies, a quartic in age, education dummies, number of children, and presence of children younger than five. The sample consists of men and women who have one to thirty-five years of potential work experience.

5. Some evidence indicates that the male marriage premium narrowed in the 1970s and 1980s (Gray 1997; Blackburn and Korenman 1994). Jeffrey Gray (1997) finds that the marriage premium fell, particularly for men whose wives work.

between the two estimates then provides us with the net effect of selection into marriage. We use data from Survey of Income and Program Participation (SIPP) panels matched to Social Security Administration (SSA) earnings records from 1954 to 2011. These data have many advantages for our purposes: they provide detailed earnings histories that allow us to estimate both OLS and fixed-effect models of the marriage premium; the samples of individuals from the pooled SIPP panels are considerably larger than those available from other long panels such as the University of Michigan's Panel Study of Income Dynamics (PSID) or the National Longitudinal Survey of Youth 1979 (NLSY79); and the earnings data span enough time to allow us to meaningfully compare across birth cohorts. Sarah Avellar and Pamela Smock (2003) conduct fixed-effects analysis to compare changes in the motherhood wage gap for two birth cohorts—NLS Young Women and the NLSY. Our paper examines both marriage and motherhood gaps and to the best of our knowledge, our paper is the first to compare OLS and FE models for birth cohorts spanning four decades. An important caveat is that we observe annual earnings but not hours worked in our data, and therefore we cannot separately examine the relative contributions of wages and hours. We do, however, examine the extent to which the earnings changes for women are driven by women leaving the labor force and having zero earnings.

To preview our findings, we find that selection into marriage has become increasingly positive: that is, higher levels of education and earnings potential are both associated with a greater likelihood of being married. Like Adam Isen and Betsey Stevenson (2010), we find that the most-educated women are the most likely to marry among the most recent birth cohorts. Pooling our sample of women born between 1936 and 1975, we find an average earnings gap of approximately -26 percent associated with marriage. The marriage gap is roughly half as large (-12 percent) when we control for the number of children and the presence of young children. Our estimates are somewhat more negative in fixed-effect specifications (-29 percent), indicating that positive selection into marriage leads to some understatement of the average marriage gap for women in our sample.

Comparing across cohorts, we find that the marriage earnings gap became less negative for women in both OLS and FE estimates. In both sets, married women who remain childless actually enjoy an earnings premium in the most recent birth cohort (born between 1966 and 1975). Among women with children, the difference between the earnings of married and single women also narrows. Comparing OLS and FE estimates, we find that increasingly positive selection into marriage contributes to the reduction in the marriage earnings gap in cross-sectional data. Our findings imply that marriage is no longer associated with lower earnings among women in the most recent cohort, but we find that the motherhood gap remains large.

We find quite different results for men. Although educated men with the highest earnings potential have always been the most likely to marry, the relationship has become more pronounced among recent birth cohorts. Pooling across all cohorts of men, we find a positive OLS estimate of the marriage earnings gap of approximately 34 percent. In FE specifications, however, the estimate is reduced by more than half, to about 14 percent, suggesting that selection plays an important role in accounting for the marriage premium for men. When we allow the premium to vary across cohorts, we find successively larger positive marriage gaps in the fixed-effect regressions. This would suggest an increase in specialization across successive birth cohorts. Such an interpretation, however, assumes no selection into marriage on wage growth. We suspect that this empirical regularity instead represents either selection on individual-specific earnings growth rates or an interaction between changes in age-earnings profiles and changes in patterns of selection into marriage. We have begun to investigate these possibilities but have not yet resolved this puzzle.

DATA

Our sample of individuals is drawn from respondents in the 1984, 1990 to 1993, 1996, 2001, 2004, and 2008 SIPP panels who provided the information needed to validate matches to Social Security Administration earnings records.[6] Individuals had to be at least fifteen years old at the time of their second SIPP interview to be eligible for inclusion in the matched data.[7] For matched individuals, we use annual earnings for 1954 through 2011 based on annual summaries of earnings on jobs recorded in the SSA Master Earnings File. The primary source of the earnings information is W-2 records, but self-employment earnings are also included. We include employees' contributions to deferred compensation plans as part of our earnings measure. For the years prior to 1978, earnings measures are truncated at the maximum earnings subject to FICA (Federal Insurance Contributions Act) taxes. A significant number of men in our sample have earnings that exceed the taxable maximum, and so are understated in our data.[8] But the cap affects only a small share of women in our sample, in part because our sample is young in those years, for example, age at most twenty-nine in 1965, the year in which the share of all covered workers who had earnings that exceeded the taxable max reached its peak of 36 percent.[9] For both men and women, we use the full distribution of earnings for 1978 through 1990 to estimate the appropriate adjustment to log earnings based on the assumption that the upper tail of the earnings distribution resembles a Pareto distribution, and then use the parameter estimate to make a mean adjustment to log earnings for those affected by the cap.[10] The small adjustment to earnings for women made little difference for any of our estimates, so we present those with the adjustment here. As expected, the adjustment had more important

---

6. The results presented here are based on confidential data from version 6.0 of the SIPP Gold Standard File. External researchers can access related data through the public-use SIPP Synthetic Beta (SSB) files, and census staff will validate results obtained from the SSB on the internal, confidential version of these data (the Completed Gold Standard Files). For more information visit https://www.census.gov/programs-surveys/sipp/guidance/sipp-synthetic-beta-data-product.html.The U.S. Census Bureau also supports external researchers use of some of these data through the Research Data Center network (http://www.census.gov/ces/rdcresearch).

7. The SIPP is a series of short panel surveys in which respondents are surveyed every four months to collect detailed information on household members' income, employment, and program participation over the previous months (for an overview, see http://www.census.gov/hhes/www/sippdesc.html). The surveys also periodically collect detailed information on the demographic characteristics and relationships of household members. Panels have ranged in length from about two to four years. Because our sample pools data from several SIPP panel samples, we do not use SIPP survey weights in our analysis, so the results cannot be assumed to be nationally representative.

8. In the late 1950s and early 1960s, more than 25 percent of covered workers had earnings that exceeded the taxable maximum in several years (see Whitman and Shoffner 2011).

9. Women may be more affected by the pre-1978 absence of earnings records in these data for workers who were not subject to FICA taxes, given that the excluded group included many public school employees. This will bias our estimates for the earliest cohorts if the relationship between earnings and marital status for this group differs from that among the women we do observe.

10. We estimate separate parameters for men and women, by year and by education group (high school diploma or less than high school versus college degree or some college). For women, the estimates are similar across education groups, so we use an adjustment on estimates that pooled the two groups. For men, the implied adjustment for the more educated group was substantially larger, so we apply it separately by education group. For both men and women, the estimated adjustment parameter does not vary much across years. Marriage premium estimates based on the 1954 through 2011 time series, using the capped data as is, yields somewhat smaller estimates of the marriage premium for men, but a larger increase across cohorts. This simply reflects that married men are more likely to have earnings that exceed the cap, so ignoring the truncation understates the marriage premium in early cohorts. Using the mean adjustment based on the Pareto distribution results in noisier fixed-effect estimates.

effects on the results for men, particularly for estimates of changes across cohorts, given that the earliest cohort was much more affected than later ones. So for men, the regression results we present here are based only on 1978 through 2011 earnings. Marital histories, educational attainment, and women's fertility histories are based on data collected in the SIPP. Age is based on SSA sources.

We use these data to look at cohorts born between 1936 and 1975, following their earnings over years in which we have earnings data, and the individual had one to thirty-five years of potential experience.[11] To determine marital status at a given time, we use the marital history information collected in the relevant SIPP panel with some additional updates from changes in later waves of that panel. This largely gives us the information we need for years leading up to or during the SIPP panel, but not for the years after the panel is over. For this reason, we drop any earnings records from years after the individual is last observed in the panel. Because our focus is on marital status, we further restrict the sample to men and women who are interviewed at age thirty-five or older, so that at a minimum we know marital status through age thirty-five for everyone in the sample. Thus, for a fifty-year-old woman interviewed in the 1990 SIPP panel who did not start college, we use earnings for 1958 to 1992 (ages eighteen through fifty-two); and for a thirty-five-year-old college graduate interviewed in the 1996 panel, we use earnings for 1984 to 1999 (ages twenty-five through thirty-eight).

Table 1 presents descriptive statistics by birth cohort for the men and women in our sample. The first pair of panels (person-weighted) consists of variables that do not vary year by year, so each individual contributes a single observation. The second pair of panels is based on the full set of person-year observations we use in our regressions, so individuals who we follow for more years contribute more observations to the sample means.[12] In general, the differences across cohorts in the top panels reflect well-established trends in the population: for example, the earliest cohort has less education and more children. We can, though, follow members of the older cohorts to later ages. This is why the sample mean of age is larger for the older cohorts. On the other hand, despite their higher fertility, women in the first cohort have lower means for time-varying child variables, such as having a child younger than six in the current year, as shown in the bottom panel.

TRENDS IN MARRIAGE RATES

We first examine who is married among men and women. In particular, we are interested in whether those with relatively high stocks of human capital are more or less likely to marry than the average person. A pattern of positive selection into marriage based on labor-market characteristics will tend to widen the gap in earnings of married couples relative to singles. We characterize labor-market skill in two ways—using education levels and using estimated potential earnings. Although education level is a relatively simple, clean measure, its distribution has shifted significantly over time and in different ways for men and women, making it more complicated to parcel out what represents a change in selection patterns and what is simply the result of shifting education distributions.

We construct a measure of potential earnings based on predicted earnings from a fixed-effect regression of log earnings on year dummies, main effects for education, a quartic in age, interactions between the age terms and education dummies, marital status, and for

---

11. Specifically, for those who finished high school or less, the age range is eighteen to fifty-three. For those with some college, the range is twenty-one to fifty-six. For college graduates, the range is twenty-three to fifty-eight. For those with postcollege education, it is twenty-five to sixty. We drop the very small share of men for whom we never observe positive earnings but keep women with no earnings because we estimate participation regressions for women but not men.

12. Sample counts are rounded to the nearest hundred here to help maintain respondent confidentiality. Person-year counts include all years in the window over which we have data for the individual, whether or not earnings are observed in a particular year.

Table 1. Sample Means

Birth Cohorts	1936–1945	1946–1955	1956–1965	1966–1975
	Averages Across Individuals			
Women				
Ever married	0.942	0.909	0.868	0.833
Any children	0.864	0.824	0.821	0.828
Number of children ever born	2.5	2.0	1.9	2.0
Number of years with earnings	19.1	19.5	17.0	14.1
Number of years in sample	33.5	28.4	23.6	18.8
<=High school graduate	0.555	0.421	0.386	0.285
Some college	0.256	0.320	0.352	0.374
College graduate	0.189	0.259	0.262	0.341
N (rounded)	19,300	35,700	28,300	10,800
Men				
Ever married	0.946	0.906	0.849	0.818
Number of years with earnings	31.3	27.1	23.3	19.0
Number of years in sample	33.7	28.2	23.6	19.0
<=High school graduate	0.472	0.371	0.409	0.331
Some college	0.253	0.313	0.319	0.347
College graduate	0.275	0.316	0.272	0.322
N (rounded)	21,000	32,100	25,200	9,700
	Averages Across Person-Years			
Women				
Log earnings, 2014 dollars, adjusted for cap in years<1978	9.685	9.820	9.799	9.772
Has positive earnings in current year	0.611	0.719	0.761	0.789
Age	36.3	34.8	32.5	30.1
Married	0.716	0.648	0.578	0.525
Number of children < eighteen	1.396	1.281	1.306	1.336
Has child who is < six	0.149	0.166	0.193	0.228
N (rounded)	646,800	1,014,900	666,700	202,800
Men				
Log earnings, 2014 dollars, adjusted for cap in years<1978	10.590	10.515	10.363	10.272
Has positive earnings in current year	0.887	0.893	0.887	0.895
Age	36.9	35.0	32.4	30.0
Married	0.710	0.633	0.530	0.468
N (rounded)	708,500	905,200	595,500	183,500

Source: Authors' compilation based on data from SIPP panels matched to Social Security Administration earnings records.

women, age and presence of children. We use the results to predict earnings for a single, childless person at age forty, and then add the estimated person-specific fixed effect to that prediction to get potential earnings.[13] For the small portion of women in the sample who matched to the SSA earnings database but had zero earnings in all the years they were in the

13. This measure is essentially based on average earnings that have been adjusted for differences in age, calendar years observed, marital status, and for women, presence and age of children using the regression coefficients.

Table 2. Marriage Rates, Age Thirty-Five

Birth Cohort	<=HS	Some College	College Grads	Overall
Women				
1936–1945	0.796	0.790	0.783	0.792
1946–1955	0.703	0.711	0.716	0.709
1956–1965	0.671	0.667	0.721	0.683
1966–1975	0.628	0.643	0.751	0.676
Men				
1936–1945	0.799	0.804	0.825	0.807
1946–1955	0.706	0.722	0.750	0.725
1956–1965	0.653	0.677	0.724	0.680
1966–1975	0.636	0.672	0.761	0.688

Source: Authors' compilation based on data from SIPP panels matched to Social Security Administration earnings records.
Notes: N= 94,100 women and 88,000 men.

sample, we assign a random draw from the distribution of this measure. The random draw is taken from among other members of their birth cohort with the same education level who had relatively large numbers of years with zero earnings. We then assign each person to a potential earnings quartile based on their ranking among those of the same gender in their ten-year birth cohort. Although this measure will capture potential earnings imperfectly, it incorporates information drawn from the earnings data in addition to education level, and also has the advantage that we can use it to divide men and women into equal size groups over time.

Table 2 presents the share of men and women who are married at age thirty-five by level of education and by ten-year birth cohort. Overall, the probability of marriage fell between the 1936 to 1945 and 1956 to 1965 cohorts for all education groups, and for both men and women. Some evidence indicates a rise in the share married at thirty-five for the last birth cohort among college graduates, but the share married among those with less schooling continued to fall. Among men, the general pattern is that, with few exceptions, being married is positively associated with higher levels of education. Over time, however, marriage rates dropped more among the less educated, widening the gap across education groups. For women, marriage was modestly negatively associated with education in the first birth cohort, but a larger drop in marriage rates for the less educated resulted in a substantially positive relationship in the most recent birth cohort.

These changes in the relationship between the probability of marriage and education level resulted in a substantial decline in the education levels of single relative to married people, particularly for women. Reconfiguring the information in table 2, in the 1936 to 1945 birth cohort, single women were slightly more likely to be college graduates than married women (20 percent versus 19 percent), but by the 1966 to 1975 cohort, that pattern had reversed. Approximately 38 percent of married women were college graduates, but only 26 percent of single women were. For men, the change is less dramatic but still substantial: the share of college graduates grew 8 percentage points among married men but not at all among single men.[14]

This pattern of a shift toward those who are married being those with greater labor-market skills also appears in the statistics on marriage

---

14. For men, the share of college graduates does not consistently grow across each of these birth cohorts. The sharp increase and then decline over the first three cohorts of men likely reflects the effect of Vietnam-era draft deferrals on men's college attendance documented in David Card and Thomas Lemieux (2000), which was

Table 3. Marriage Rates at Age Thirty-Five, Potential Earnings Distribution

Birth Cohort	(1)	(2)	(3)	(4)	Total
Women					
1936–1945	0.795	0.811	0.795	0.767	0.792
1946–1955	0.700	0.723	0.692	0.722	0.709
1956–1965	0.623	0.677	0.679	0.751	0.683
1966–1975	0.604	0.654	0.666	0.779	0.676
Men					
1936–1945	0.712	0.810	0.844	0.863	0.807
1946–1955	0.590	0.736	0.776	0.799	0.725
1956–1965	0.536	0.680	0.726	0.778	0.680
1966–1975	0.548	0.682	0.725	0.799	0.688

Source: Authors' compilation based on data from SIPP panels matched to Social Security Administration earnings records.
Notes: N= 94,100 women and 88,000 men.

rates by quartiles of the potential earnings distribution, as illustrated in table 3. Again, overall the share of men and of women who are married at age thirty-five drops, but the decline in marriage is particularly large among those in the bottom part of the distribution. Comparing across the 1936 to 1945 and 1966 to 1975 birth cohorts of women, the share married increased slightly in the top quartile but fell 20 percentage points, from 0.80 to 0.60, in the bottom quartile. For men, the marriage rate in the top quartile declined 6 percentage points but 16 points in the bottom quartile. It is striking that in the most recent cohort only 55 percent of the men in the lowest earnings category are married at age thirty-five. Because the overall shares in these quartiles are fixed over time, these changes imply that marriage is becoming increasingly associated with better labor-market prospects. For men, this is a change in degree—married men are more educated and more likely to be in the upper part of the earnings distribution even in our earliest birth cohort, but the gap between married and single men increases over time. For women, negative selection into marriage on labor-market prospects was modest in the earliest cohort, but in our two most recent birth cohorts positive. Isen and Stevenson (2010) report similar changes in marriage patterns by education. Our analysis here using earnings percentiles confirm that the patterns reflect real changes in the selection into marriage, rather than shifting composition of education groups.

RELATIONSHIP BETWEEN MARRIAGE AND EARNINGS

Comparison of OLS earnings regressions with FE models is the basis of much of our regression analysis. To fix ideas, we start with the following stylized statistical model of earnings:

$$\ln Y^j_{it} = \beta^{jC} X^j_{it} + \gamma^{jC} M_{it} + \pi^{jC} K_{it} + \varepsilon^{jC}_{it},$$
$$\varepsilon^{jC}_{it} + \alpha^{jC}_i + \nu^{jC}_{it}$$

where i indexes an individual, C indexes birth cohort, $j = m$ (male) or f (female), and X = observable characteristics such as education and age, M = marital status indicators, and K = indicators for the presence and age of children. In this specification, $E(\varepsilon^{jC}_i) + E(\nu^{jC}_{it}) = 0$, α^{jC}_i = permanent (unobserved) skill component of earnings and ν^{jC}_{it} = transitory shocks. Adding interaction terms between M and characteristics of the individual allows us to examine how

---

greatest for men born in the late 1940s. We focus on the increase from the first to the last cohort as reflecting the longer-term trend increase in college attendance.

the marriage gap varies with these characteristics. We also include analogous interactions between K and individual characteristics in this part of the analysis.

Our first step is to examine changes in average differences in earnings associated with marital status, which are measured by γ^{jC}. We run the regressions for men and women allowing for differences across birth cohorts. We first estimate the earnings regressions via ordinary least squares, in which case the marital status and parenthood coefficients include selection effects—that is, they confound changes in earnings with marriage-children with average differences in the permanent skill component (α^{jC}_i) associated with marriage and children. We then estimate the regressions using fixed person effects in an attempt to remove effects of selection on earnings levels.[15] The FE marriage earnings gap captures the average difference in an individual's earnings between periods in which they are married and those in which they are not, relative to the average age-earnings profile. These are our estimates of the effects of specialization, by which we mean changes in earnings that arise from changes in work behavior that result from marriage. The difference between the OLS and FE estimates provides us with an estimate of the net effects of selection on these differentials. That is, the difference gives us an estimate of the extent to which the earnings of those who are currently married are persistently different from the earnings of those who are currently single.[16]

MARRIAGE AND WOMEN'S EARNINGS

Table 4 presents coefficient estimates from the earnings regressions for women. In column (1) we report the coefficient on the "married" dummy without controlling for children and in column (2) we control for the number of children and whether any of those children are younger than six.[17] In column (3), we interact both married and children dummies with birth cohort to estimate the evolution of marriage and child effects on earnings. Finally, in column (4), we additionally interact the married and children variables with each other and with birth cohort dummies, thereby allowing the impact of children on earnings to differ between married and single women, and for that interaction effect to vary across cohorts.

We find a substantial negative earnings differential for married women in the first specification for both OLS and FE estimates. The larger absolute size of the fixed-effect estimate implies that, for this set of cohorts overall, positive selection into marriage offsets a modest share of the differential. That is, pooling all of our data, the negative changes in earnings

---

15. This method interprets steeper wage growth among married men as an effect of marriage, but it is difficult to entirely rule out selection because men with higher expected wage growth may be more likely to marry.

16. Our specifications implicitly assume that divorce is associated with the same absolute change in earnings as marriage, but with the opposite sign. We examine specifications that allowed these effects to differ but find that this simplification is a reasonably good description of the patterns in our data.

17. In our specification, we cap the number of children at three because in specifications in which we use a series of dummy variables to control for children, additions beyond three had little additional effect on our estimates. The count of children younger than eighteen includes those younger than six, so the coefficient on the count of children younger than eighteen represents the effect of one school-age child and that on the dummy for having a child younger than six gives the additional effect of having that child be preschool age. We use information from fertility histories to measure the number and ages of children. These questions apply only to biological children, and we know the year of birth for only the oldest and youngest children. We therefore miss the presence of all step- and adopted children. To create controls for children, if there are one or two biological children, we assume that both live with their mother between birth and the year they turn eighteen and set the control for the presence of young children based on the years in which one or both children were younger than six. For mothers with three or more children, we assume that a child younger than six was present between the sixth birthday of the first child and the birth of the last child. We count the number of children present between the birth of the first and of the last by assuming that the intervening child or children are evenly spaced. These measures are clearly approximations with errors in both directions—not all children are counted, but some of those who are counted do not live at home.

Table 4. Log Earnings Regressions, Women

Controls	OLS Coefficient Estimates				Fixed-Effect Coefficient Estimates			
	1	2	3	4	1	2	3	4
Married	-0.256***	-0.118***	-0.266***	-0.237***	-0.292***	-0.197***	-0.312***	-0.277***
Married*cohort 1946–1955			0.116***	0.115***			0.101***	0.117***
Married*cohort 1956–1965			0.245***	0.203***			0.166***	0.179***
Married*cohort 1966–1975			0.331***	0.314***			0.277***	0.330***
Number of children < eighteen		-0.177***	-0.149***	-0.133***		-0.167***	-0.145***	-0.128***
# children*cohort 1946–1955			-0.025***	-0.024**			-0.022***	-0.012**
# children*cohort 1956–1965			-0.048***	-0.067***			-0.046***	-0.039***
# children*cohort 1966–1975			-0.054***	-0.061***			-0.029***	-0.010
Child < six years old		-0.167***	-0.257***	-0.223***		-0.250***	-0.344***	-0.271***
Child < six*cohort 1946–1955			0.076***	0.054*			0.073***	0.077***
Child < six*cohort 1956–1965			0.126***	0.053*			0.139***	0.098***
Child < six*cohort 1966–1975			0.138***	0.067*			0.160***	0.133***
Married*# children				-0.024***				-0.025***
Married*# children*cohort 1946–1955				-0.003				-0.014***
Married*# children*cohort 1956–1965				0.029**				-0.013**
Married*# children*cohort 1966–1975				0.007				-0.039***
Married*child < six				-0.041				-0.088***
Married*child < six*cohort 1946–1955				0.027				-0.009
Married*child < six*cohort 1956–1965				0.093**				0.047**
Married*child < six*cohort 1966–1975				0.096**				0.026

Source: Authors' compilation based on data from SIPP panels matched to Social Security Administration earnings records.

Notes: N=1,696,700 (to nearest 100). Dependent variable is log annual earnings from SSA records. Regressions also include controls for year, education, dummies indicating if race is African American, and indicating if ethnicity is Hispanic, main effects for birth cohort, and a quartic in age. Standard errors for each cell appear in table A5.

Figure 2. Earnings Relative to Single, Childless Women (OLS)

Source: Authors' compilation based on data from SIPP panels matched to Social Security Administration earnings records.

profiles associated with marriage are slightly larger than the average difference in earnings between married and single women because women with higher earnings are slightly more likely to be married. Consistent with others' findings, adding controls for children in column (2) reduces the marriage differential substantially. In the OLS regression, the marriage earnings differential falls by more than half, from –0.256 to –0.118. In the FE regression, the coefficient falls by about one-third, from –0.292 to –0.197.

In column (3), we add interactions between the married and children variables and ten-year birth cohort dummies to examine changes in these earnings differentials across these cohorts of women. In both the OLS and FE regressions, the earnings differential associated with marriage becomes less negative across birth cohorts. The decline in the earnings differential in fixed-effect estimates suggests a much reduced role for specialization. Comparing the OLS and FE estimates, we find a larger increase between the earliest and the most recent birth cohorts in the OLS estimate (0.331) than in the FE (0.277). This implies that selection into marriage based on potential earnings became increasingly positive across these cohorts—that is, women with higher potential earnings became more likely to marry. The finding of positive selection into marriage on earnings characteristics is quite consistent with the evidence we present in table 2, and also with the findings of Isen and Stevenson (2010) on selection based on education. In contrast to the consistent shrinkage of the marriage differential across these cohorts, the coefficients on the children-cohort interaction terms do not show a notable decline in the earnings differentials associated with children. The differential associated with young children has declined across cohorts but the differential associated with school-age children has actually increased.

In the final specification in (4), we also include three-way interactions that allow the earnings differentials associated with children to differ between married and single women, and for that to vary across cohorts as well. The three-way interactions make it much more difficult to interpret individual coefficients, so we present a series of earnings differentials in figures 2 and 3 that describe the patterns of interest: figure 2 based on the OLS results, and fig-

Figure 3. Earnings Relative to Single, Childless Women (FE)

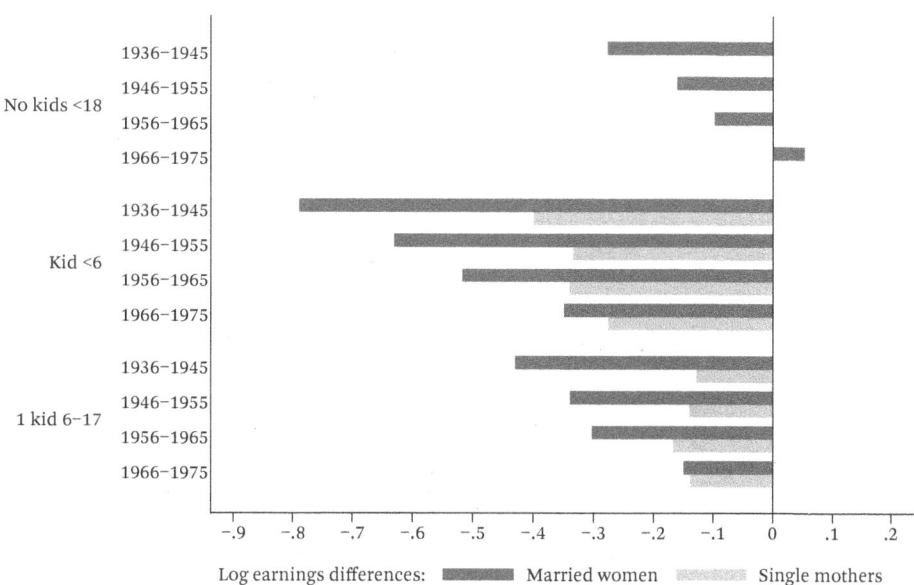

Source: Authors' compilation based on data from SIPP panels matched to Social Security Administration earnings records.

ure 3 on our FE estimates. Each estimate in the figures gives an earnings differential for a particular group based on specification (4) relative to single, childless women in the same cohort. To illustrate how changes across cohorts in the marriage differential differ between women with children and those without, we include implied differentials for two child scenarios—having one school-age and having one preschool-age child.

The more heavily shaded bars in the graphs represent differentials for married women, and the lighter ones indicate those for single women. The top panel gives the marriage differential for women without children, and in both figures this differential is positive for the most recent cohort. In other words, among the most recent birth cohort of women who remain childless, marriage actually increases earnings relative to single women without children.[18] The second and third panels give estimated differentials for married and single women with one preschool aged child and one school-age child respectively. In both the OLS and FE results, we see little change in the earnings of single mothers relative to single, childless women, but large decreases relative to that group for married women with children.

The marriage differential in these figures, conditional on children, is given by the difference between the married and single bars and we present this differential in figures 4 and 5. Both the OLS and FE estimates imply that the gap in earnings between married and single women with children has declined dramatically. The OLS results (figure 4) suggest that married women with children now earn more than single women with children, but compar-

---

18. That this is also true for the fixed-effect estimates suggests that this is not due to selection on earnings levels. Both Alexandra Killewald and Margaret Gough (2013) and Michelle Budig and Paula England (2001) report similar results using the National Longitudinal Survey of Youth (NLSY79). One possibility is that women are increasingly likely to marry upon finishing college so that we observe their earnings rise along with change in marital status. When we disaggregate by education group, we find that the marriage premium for women without children among the recent birth cohort is due to women with a college degree.

Figure 4. Marriage Earnings Gap, Women (OLS)

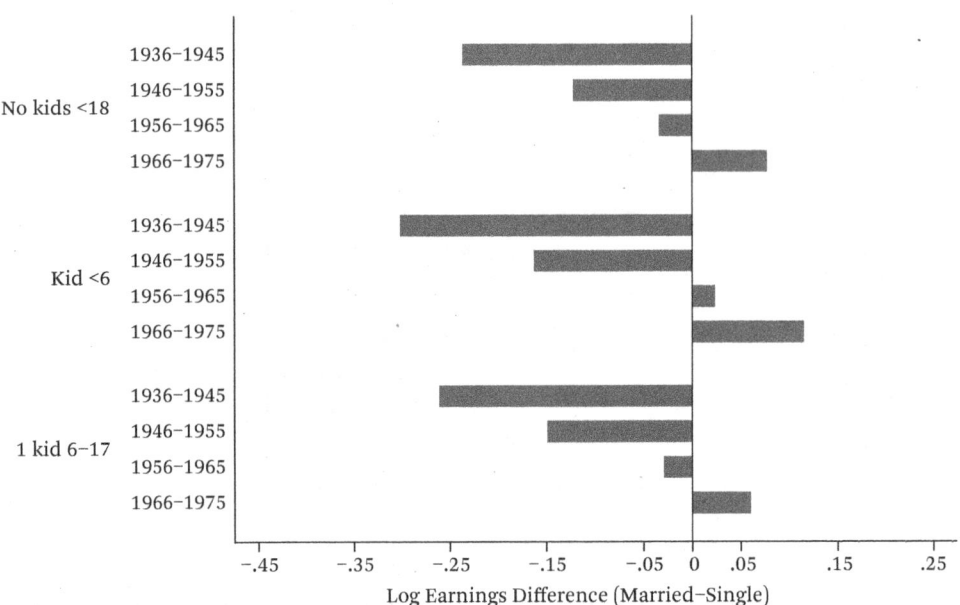

Source: Authors' compilation based on data from SIPP panels matched to Social Security Administration earnings records.

Figure 5. Marriage Earnings Gap, Women (FE)

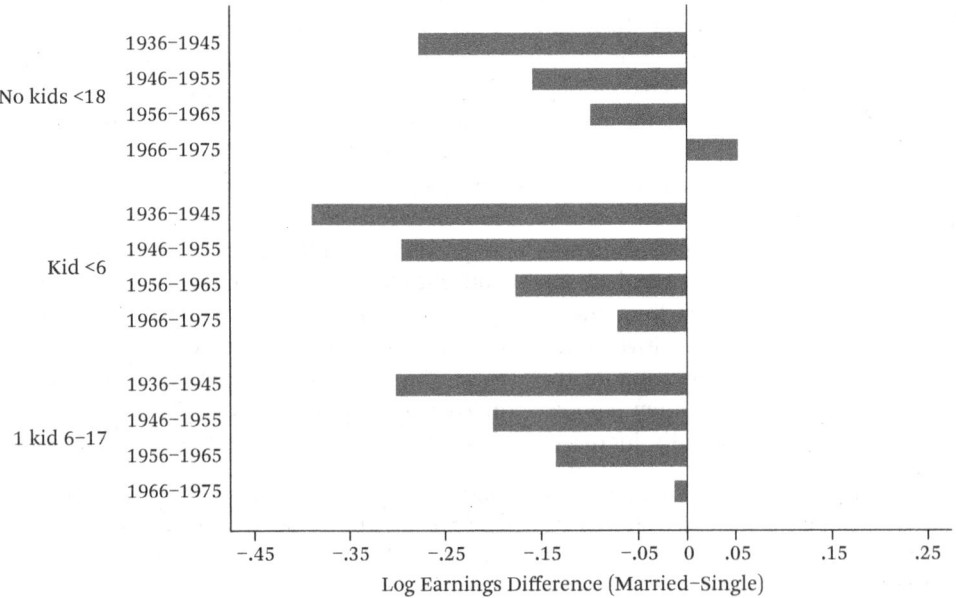

Source: Authors' compilation based on data from SIPP panels matched to Social Security Administration earnings records.

ison with the FE results (figure 5) suggests that this is due to married women with children being increasingly positively selected relative to single women with children. In FE estimates shown in figure 5, we find that the motherhood wage gap is larger for married women than single women. Michelle Budig and Paula England (2001) and Alexandra Killewald and Margaret Gough (2013) find similar results using the NLSY79 data. They interpret these results as being consistent with the motherhood wage gap being augmented by specialization between married parents.

Although our findings imply that marriage is no longer associated with lower earnings among women in the most recent cohort (with the exception of married women with young children who are still slightly behind their single counterparts), it is important to keep in mind that the motherhood gap (as shown in figure 3) remains substantial. Even among the most recent birth cohort, married women with preschool-age children have approximately 35 percent lower earnings than married women without children and that married women with school-age children have approximately 15 percent lower earnings. These findings are broadly consistent with Avellar and Smock (2003), who find that in fixed-effects regressions the motherhood wage gap had not diminished across two recent cohorts—NLS Young Women and the NLSY.

MARRIAGE AND WOMEN'S PARTICIPATION

These log earnings results condition on having positive earnings. We cannot separately examine wages and hours worked in our data, but we can examine changes in women's entering or leaving the labor force and having positive versus zero earnings. To look at this extensive margin, we estimate specifications similar to (1) but with an indicator for having positive earnings in a calendar year as the dependent variable.[19]

The results of the regressions are reported in table A1 but we illustrate changes in the participation gap associated with marriage and motherhood in figures 6 and 7 (showing OLS and FE estimates respectively). Like figures 4 and 5, these are based on specifications in which we allow for interactions between marriage and children that change across cohorts. In both figures, we see that the participation differential between married women without children and single women without children declined so that married women are in fact slightly more likely to participate than single women among the most recent birth cohort. In contrast, the participation differential between married mothers and single mothers remains negative and shows no clear pattern of decline. Mothers with young children in particular continue to participate substantially less than single and married women without children. Our results on the participation effect of young children are broadly consistent with Byker (this volume) who also does not find much trend across cohorts in changes in mother's labor force participation around the time of birth.

MARRIAGE AND WOMEN'S EARNINGS BY EDUCATION AND RACE

Finally we explore the effect of marriage on women's earnings by education groups and also separately for African American women. We report the regression results in table A2 but highlight the trends associated with the fully interacted model in figures 8 through 11 and 12 though 15. We find patterns similar to those in the overall changes when we disaggregate by education group and race, with the exception of college educated women. Looking first at the OLS estimates shown in figures 8 through 11, we find that the earnings differential associated with marriage becomes less negative. These changes are larger in the OLS estimates than the corresponding FE estimates shown for women without a college degree (figure 12) and for black women (figure 15). It appears that among these groups, women with higher earnings potential were increasingly more likely to marry, suggesting that selection plays an important role. Changing selection is less evident among female college graduates. For example,

---

19. Note that the estimates for the first two cohorts are likely to be affected by the exclusion of those not subject to FICA taxes in years prior to 1978.

Figure 6. Participation Relative to Single, Childless Women (OLS)

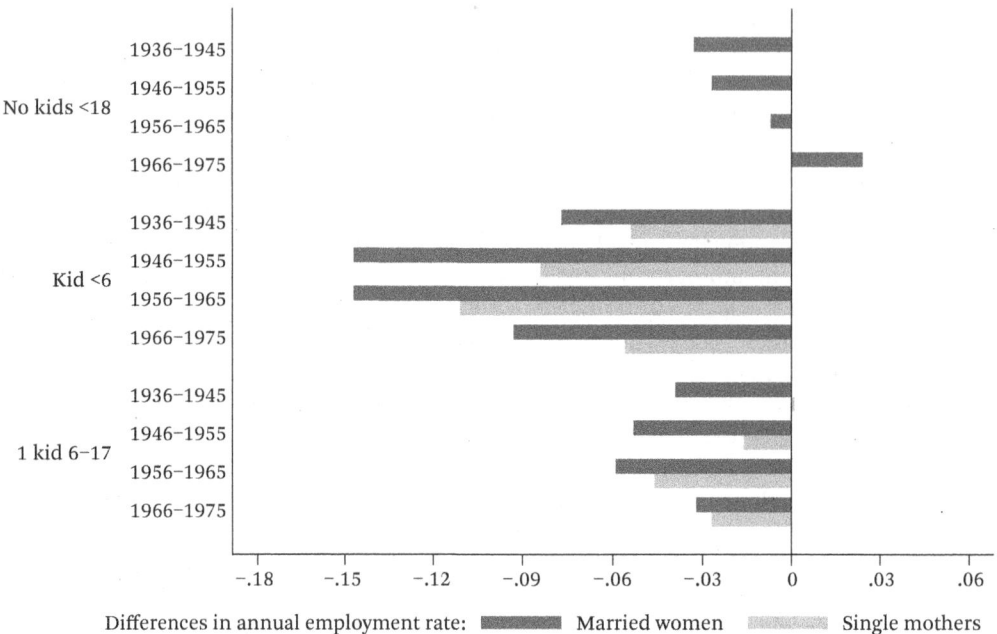

Source: Authors' compilation based on data from SIPP panels matched to Social Security Administration earnings records.

Figure 7. Participation Relative to Single, Childless Women (FE)

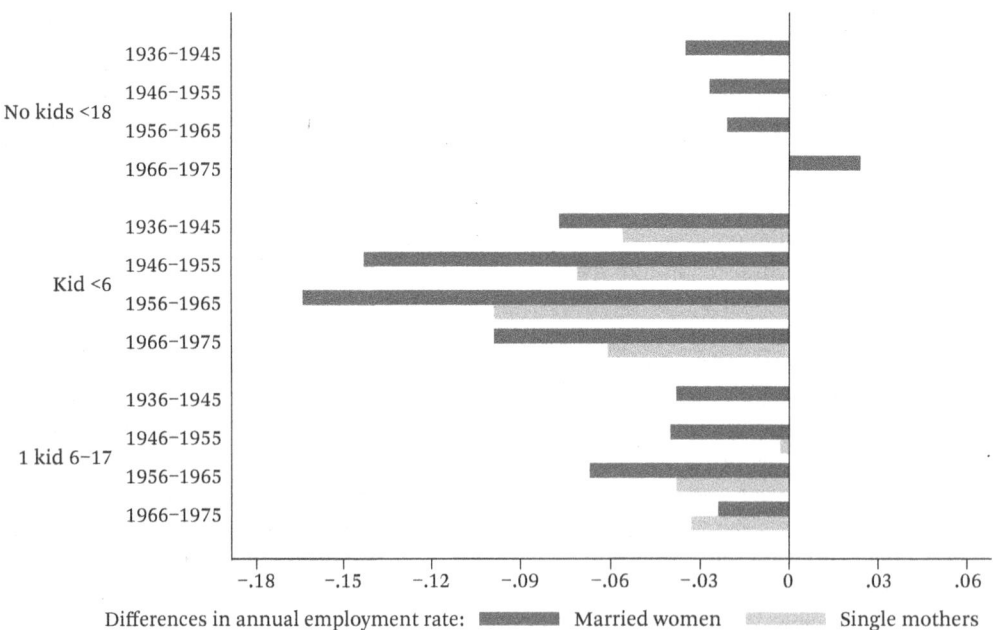

Source: Authors' compilation based on data from SIPP panels matched to Social Security Administration earnings records.

Figure 8. Earnings Relative to Single, Childless Women (OLS), High School or Less

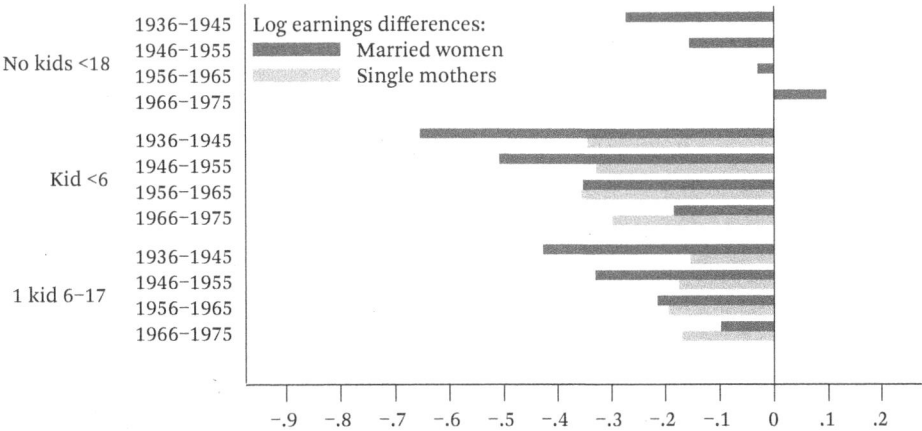

Source: Authors' compilation based on data from SIPP panels matched to Social Security Administration earnings records.

Figure 9. Earnings Relative to Single, Childless Women (OLS), Some College

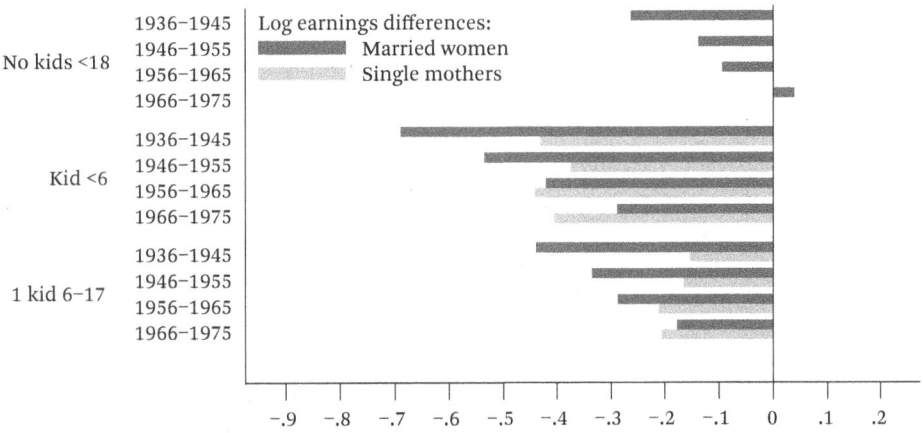

Source: Authors' compilation based on data from SIPP panels matched to Social Security Administration earnings records.

among women without children, the 1966 to 1975 cohort of married women have higher earnings relative to single women in OLS estimates. For less-educated women, this positive earnings differential disappears in FE estimates, suggesting that positive selection played a role. Among college graduate women, however, the positive earnings differential remains even in FE estimates.

MARRIAGE AND MEN'S EARNINGS

Table 5 presents estimates of the marriage premium for men based on the same log earnings regressions we estimated for women except that we do not control for children.[20] We find a very large positive marriage premium for men in the pooled regressions, but the fixed-effect estimates are much smaller. This is consistent with our findings in tables 2 and 3 that

20. We omit controls for children mostly because in the fertility history SIPP only collects a count of total number of biological children for men. Although we could put together information on the age and presence of children during the SIPP panel, doing so would miss the grown children of older respondents.

Figure 10. Earnings Relative to Single, Childless Women (OLS), College Graduate

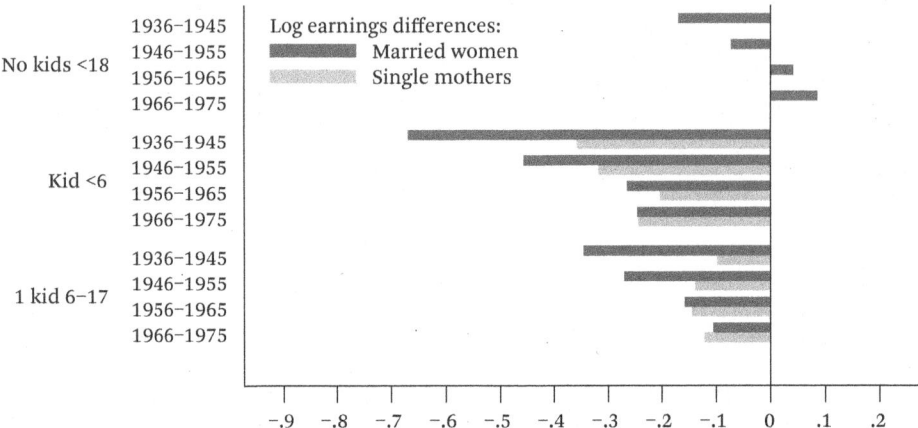

Source: Authors' compilation based on data from SIPP panels matched to Social Security Administration earnings records.

Figure 11. Earnings Relative to Single, Childless Women (OLS), African American

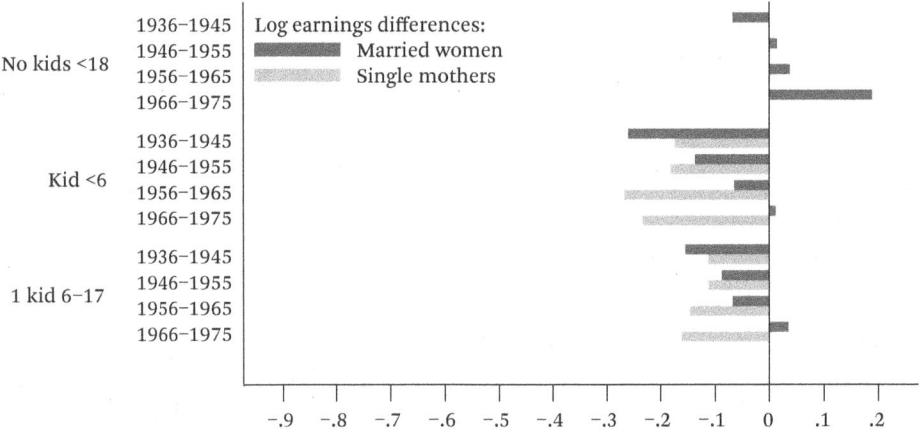

Source: Authors' compilation based on data from SIPP panels matched to Social Security Administration earnings records.

selection on labor-market skills into marriage is quite positive for men. The estimated interaction effects with birth cohort dummies are somewhat puzzling. They indicate that the FE marriage premium has risen steadily across cohorts. The OLS estimates have risen as well, but have done so more slowly and less consistently. The large increase in the marriage premium over time in the FE results suggests that selection into marriage has declined somewhat in importance, and that the effects of specialization after marriage have increased. That seems inconsistent with both the increase in the selectivity of marriage for men—documented in tables 2 and 3—and with evidence of increased labor-market skills and work among married women across these cohorts. When we allow the marriage premium to vary with education level (table A4), the OLS and FE results similarly imply a reduction in selection but growth in specialization for each group of men we examine.

One possibility is that the fixed-effect estimates for early cohorts of men are downward

Figure 12. Earnings Relative to Single, Childless Women (FE), High School or Less

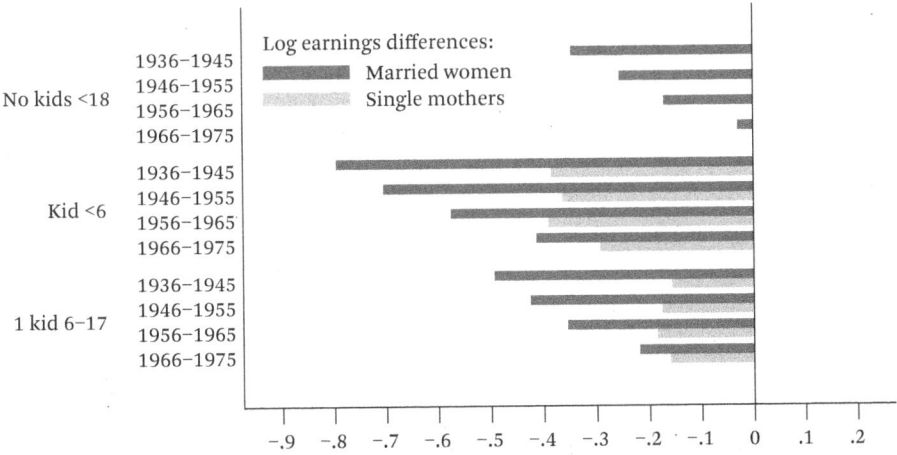

Source: Authors' compilation based on data from SIPP panels matched to Social Security Administration earnings records.

Figure 13. Earnings Relative to Single, Childless Women (FE), Some College

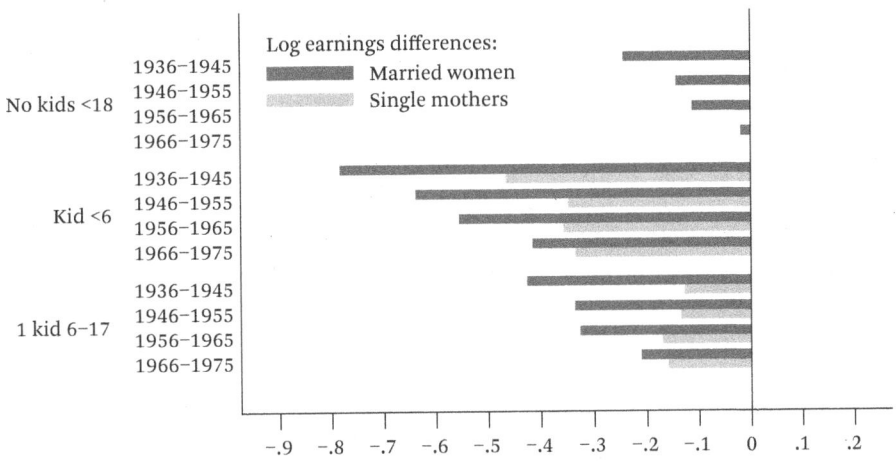

Source: Authors' compilation based on data from SIPP panels matched to Social Security Administration earnings records.

biased because we have earnings for them only at older ages. For example, for those born in 1936, we observe earnings beginning at age forty-two, long after most would have married. Thus changes in marital status for this group are likely to involve primarily divorce and remarriage which might have smaller effects on earnings than first marriages. But our OLS estimates for men based on public-use data in figure 1 also show an inconsistent rise in the marriage gap for men. It is also possible that our implicit assumption of constant returns to experience over time is leading to a rising estimate of the marriage premium in both the fixed-effect and pooled results because married men on average have greater experience than unmarried men. However, examination of alternative specifications in which we allow returns to experience and education to change over time leads to essentially the same pattern as in the results presented here. A third possibility is that some selection into marriage is

Figure 14. Earnings Relative to Single, Childless Women (FE), College Graduate

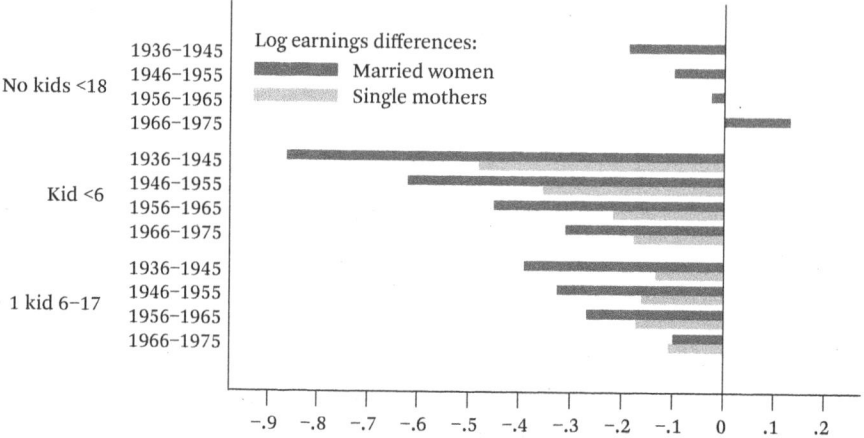

Source: Authors' compilation based on data from SIPP panels matched to Social Security Administration earnings records.

Figure 15. Earnings Relative to Single, Childless Women (FE), African American

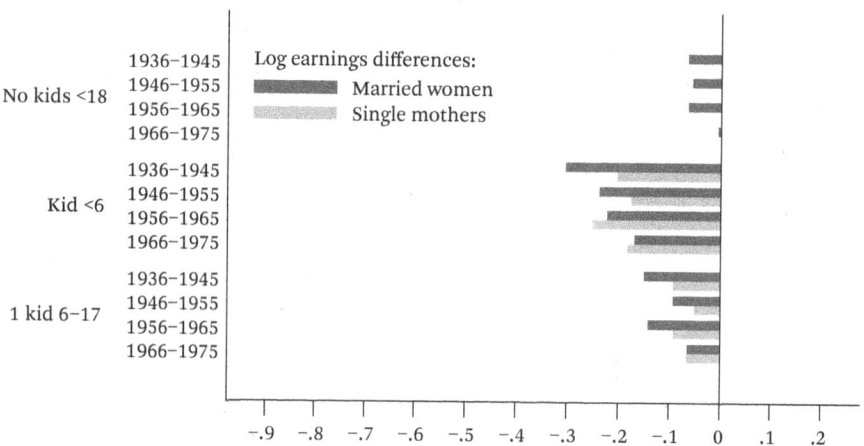

Source: Authors' compilation based on data from SIPP panels matched to Social Security Administration earnings records.

based on individual-specific earnings growth, in which case the fixed-effect estimates are also subject to bias from selection. Given such a misspecification, changes in the distribution of the individual-specific growth component, or in selection based on that component, could result in the pattern we find here.

CONCLUSION

We find that those who are married have become increasingly positively selected from the population at large in terms of both education and earnings potential. Consistent with other studies, we find that the most-educated women are the most likely to be married among recent birth cohorts. Although educated men with the highest earnings potential have always been the most likely to be married, the relationship has become more pronounced across birth cohorts spanning 1936 to 1975.

How has this increased selection affected male and female marriage gaps? Among women born between 1936 and 1975, we find an average earnings gap of approximately 26 percent

Table 5. Log Earnings Regressions, Men

Controls	OLS Coefficient Estimates		Fixed-Effect Coefficient Estimates	
	1	2	1	2
Married	0.339***	0.287***	0.139***	0.042***
	(0.004)	(0.011)	(0.002)	(0.005)
Married*cohort 1946–1955		0.067***		0.089***
		(0.014)		(0.006)
Married*cohort 1956–1965		0.053***		0.110***
		(0.013)		(0.006)
Married*cohort 1966–1975		0.075***		0.163***
		(0.016)		(0.007)

Source: Authors' compilation based on data from SIPP panels matched to Social Security Administration earnings records.
Notes: N=1,617,700 (to nearest 100). Dependent variable is log annual earnings from SSA records for years 1978 to 2011. Regressions also include controls for year, education, dummies indicating if race is African American, and indicating if ethnicity is Hispanic, main effects for birth cohort, and a quartic in age.

associated with marriage that falls to 12 percent when we control for children. Our fixed-effect estimates are somewhat larger, at 29 percent, indicating a slight positive selection into marriage overall. Comparing across cohorts, we find that the marriage earnings gap fell for women both in the cross-section and in fixed-effect estimates. In both the OLS and FE estimates, married women who remain childless actually enjoy an earnings premium in the most recent birth cohort—women born between 1966 and 1975. Among women with children, the difference between the earnings of married and single women also narrows. Our findings imply that marriage is no longer associated with lower earnings among women in our most recent cohort, but the motherhood gap remains large. In contrast to the consistent shrinkage of the marriage differential across these cohorts, the coefficients on the children-cohort interaction terms do not show a notable decline in the earnings differentials associated with children.

Our results are somewhat at odds with Pal and Waldfogel (this volume), who find a decline in the overall motherhood wage gap in the more recent period, from 1993 to 2013. One potential explanation for the differences in our findings is that they focus on hourly wages rather than annual earnings. They also include more recent birth cohorts at younger ages, which may put more weight on the motherhood gap associated with having young children. We also find that the motherhood gap associated with young children has decreased.

Comparing OLS and fixed-effect estimates, we find that increasingly positive selection into marriage contributes to the reduction in the marriage earnings gap measured in cross-sectional data. Particularly for mothers of preschool-age children, OLS estimates are somewhat misleading in that marriage continues to be associated with a reduction in earnings growth relative to peers that we associate with household specialization.

We find quite different results for men. We find an OLS estimate of the marriage earnings premium equaling 34 percent for men. In FE results, however, the estimate is reduced to less than 14 percent, suggesting that selection plays a much more important role in accounting for the positive marriage gap for men. In specifications that allow marriage to affect only the level of male earnings, we find successively larger marriage premiums in the FE regressions. Taken literally, this would suggest an increase in specialization across successive birth cohorts. We suspect that instead this represents some form of misspecification. We have begun to investigate these possibilities but have not yet resolved the puzzle.

APPENDIX

Table A1. Participation Regressions, Women

Controls	OLS Coefficient Estimates				Fixed-Effect Coefficient Estimates			
	1	2	3	4	1	2	3	4
Married	-0.063***	-.0034***	-0.039***	-0.033***	-0.057***	-0.038***	-0.037***	-0.035***
Married*cohort 1946-1955			-0.002	0.006			-0.006***	0.008***
Married*cohort 1956-1965			0.021***	0.026***			0.002	0.014***
Married*cohort 1966-1975			0.017***	0.057***			0.034***	0.059***
Number of children < eighteen		-0.025***	-0.003***	0.001		-0.016***	-0.002***	0.000
# children*cohort 1946-1955			-0.018***	-0.017***			-0.008***	-0.003***
# children*cohort 1956-1965			-0.045***	-0.047***			-0.040***	-0.038***
# children*cohort 1966-1975			-0.036***	-0.028***			-0.039***	-0.033***
Child < six years old		-0.076***	-0.041***	-0.055***		-0.080***	-0.041***	-0.056***
Child < six*cohort 1946-1955			-0.049***	-0.013*			-0.055***	-0.012**
Child < six*cohort 1956-1965			-0.041***	-0.010			-0.047***	-0.005
Child < six*cohort 1966-1975			-0.011**	0.026***			-0.021***	0.028***
Married*# children				-0.007***				-0.003***
Married*# children*cohort 1946-1955				-0.003				-0.007***
Married*# children*cohort 1956-1965				0.001				-.0005***
Married*# children*cohort 1966-1975				-0.022***				-0.012***
Married*child < six				0.017***				0.017***
Married*child < six*cohort 1946-1955				-0.043***				-0.052***
Married*child < six*cohort 1956-1965				-0.040***				-0.053***
Married*child < six*cohort 1966-1975				-0.049***				-0.064***

Source: Authors' compilation based on data from SIPP panels matched to Social Security Administration earnings records.

Notes: N=2,382,700 (to nearest 100). Dependent variable =1 if the individual has any SSA earnings in the current year, 0 otherwise. Regressions also include controls for year, education, dummies indicating if race is African American, and indicating if ethnicity is Hispanic, main effects for birth cohort, and a quartic in age. Standard errors for each cell appear in table A6.

Table A2. Log Earnings Regressions, Women

Controls	<=High School OLS	<=High School FE	Some College OLS	Some College FE	College Graduates OLS	College Graduates FE	African Americans OLS	African Americans FE
Married	-0.273**	-0.345**	-0.263**	-0.243**	-0.170**	-0.188**	-0.067	-0.066**
Married*1946–1955 cohort	0.118**	0.090**	0.126**	0.101**	0.097**	0.089**	0.081	0.009
Married*1956–1965 cohort	0.242**	0.175**	0.169**	0.132**	0.211**	0.162**	0.104*	0.001
Married*1966–1975 cohort	0.369**	0.315**	0.302**	0.224**	0.255**	0.319**	0.255**	0.060
Number of children < eighteen	-0.153**	-0.156**	-0.153**	-0.127**	-0.098**	-0.133**	-0.112**	-0.093**
# children * 1946–1955 cohort	-0.022*	-0.019**	-0.012	-0.007	-0.041*	-0.028**	-0.000	0.042**
# children * 1956–1965 cohort	-0.041**	-0.029**	-0.059**	-0.043**	-0.047**	-0.039**	-0.034	0.001
# children * 1966–1975 cohort	-0.016	-0.004	-0.053**	-0.032**	-0.024	0.025	-0.050*	0.027
Has child < six years old	-0.191**	-0.228**	-0.278**	-0.338**	-0.260**	-0.348**	-0.062	-0.110**
Child < six * 1946–1955 cohort	0.038	0.040	0.069	0.125**	0.081	0.155**	-0.008	-0.015
Child < six * 1956–1965 cohort	0.030	0.023	0.048	0.152**	0.201**	0.303**	-0.059	-0.050
Child < six * 1966–1975 cohort	0.061	0.095**	0.079	0.163**	0.138	0.280**	-0.009	-0.007
Married * number of children < eighteen	-0.001	0.008	-0.023	-0.056**	-0.078**	-0.069**	0.024	0.009
Married * # children * 1946–1965 cohort	0.001	-0.003	-0.010	-0.003	0.020	0.004	-0.013	0.006
Married * # children * 1956–1965 cohort	0.011	-0.007	0.041*	0.011	0.024	-0.001	0.018	0.006
Married * # children * 1966–1975 cohort	-0.024	-0.037**	0.013	0.023*	0.009	-0.053**	-0.016	-0.002
Married*child < six	-0.036	-0.074**	0.028	-0.019	-0.063	-0.125**	-0.043	-0.044
Married * child < six * 1946–1955 cohort	0.011	-0.018	-0.019	-0.071*	0.056	0.023	0.063	0.024
Married * child < six * 1956–1965 cohort	0.060	0.058*	0.069	-0.023	0.015	-0.013	0.167**	0.123**
Married * child < six * 1966–1975 cohort	0.080	0.013	0.059	-0.010	0.045	-0.018	0.092	0.057
N (rounded)	670,300	670,300	584,000	584,000	442,400	442,400	210,900	210,900

Source: Authors' compilation based on data from SIPP panels matched to Social Security Administration earnings records.

Notes: Dependent variable is log annual earnings from SSA records. Regressions also include controls for year, education (except in columns 3/4 where no additional detail is available), dummies indicating if race is African American (in regressions for education groups), and indicating that ethnicity is Hispanic, main effects for birth cohort, and a quartic in age. Standard errors for each cell appear in table A7.

Table A3. Participation Regressions, Women

Controls	<=High School		Some College		College Graduates		African Americans	
	OLS	FE	OLS	FE	OLS	FE	OLS	FE
Married	-0.034**	-0.031**	-0.033**	-0.035**	-0.034**	-0.042**	-0.010	0.004
Married*1946–1955 cohort	0.012*	0.001	0.009	0.005	0.003	0.021**	-0.003	-0.013*
Married*1956–1965 cohort	0.036**	0.004	0.020*	0.005	0.032**	0.037**	0.063**	0.008
Married*1966–1975 cohort	0.076**	0.043**	0.054**	0.046**	0.044**	0.074**	0.043	0.016
Number of children < eighteen	-0.004*	-0.006**	0.000	0.001	0.003	-0.004	-0.008*	-0.010**
# children * 1946–1955 cohort	-0.011**	0.006**	-0.012**	-0.006**	-0.022**	-0.014**	-0.015**	0.013**
# children * 1956–1965 cohort	-0.044**	-0.026**	-0.036**	-0.040**	-0.033**	-0.040**	-0.020**	-0.000
# children * 1966–1975 cohort	-0.020**	-0.022**	-0.020**	-0.039**	-0.019**	-0.034**	0.002	0.006
Has child < six years old	-0.055**	-0.049**	-0.062**	-0.073**	-0.055**	-0.058**	-0.022**	-0.022**
Child < six * 1946–1955 cohort	-0.009	-0.019**	-0.016	0.002	-0.006	0.006	-0.018	-0.026**
Child < six * 1956–1965 cohort	-0.004	-0.013*	-0.016	0.010	0.013	0.019	-0.030**	-0.037**
Child < six * 1966–1975 cohort	0.035**	0.027**	0.014	0.029**	0.043*	0.054**	0.030*	0.014
Married * number of children < eighteen	-0.004*	-0.000	-0.010**	-0.009**	-0.012**	-0.006**	0.004	0.001
Married * # children * 1946–1955 cohort	-0.001	-0.006**	-0.007	-0.003	-0.004	-0.009**	0.012*	0.004
Married * # children * 1956–1965 cohort	0.003	0.002	-0.006	-0.003	-0.010	-0.013**	-0.004	0.010**
Married * # children * 1966–1975 cohort	-0.026**	-0.005	-0.022**	-0.005	-0.029**	-0.017**	-0.018	0.003
Married*child < six	0.021**	0.016**	0.029**	0.037**	0.013	0.014	-0.015	-0.012
Married * child < six * 1946–1955 cohort	-0.048**	-0.044**	-0.047**	-0.073**	-0.051**	-0.064**	0.025*	0.018*
Married * child < six * 1956–1965 cohort	-0.046**	-0.047**	-0.038**	-0.069**	-0.062**	-0.064**	0.055**	0.042**
Married * child < six * 1966–1975 cohort	-0.057**	-0.061**	-0.037**	-0.064**	-0.070**	-0.086**	-0.008	-0.011
N (rounded)	1,070,500	1,070,500	761,700	761,700	550,600	550,600	290,000	290,000

Source: Authors' compilation based on data from SIPP panels matched to Social Security Administration earnings records.

Notes: Dependent variable is =1 if the individual has any SSA earnings in the current year, 0 otherwise. Regressions also include controls for year, education (except in columns 3/4 where no additional detail is available), dummies indicating if race is African American (in regressions for education groups), and indicating that ethnicity is Hispanic, main effects for birth cohort, and a quartic in age. Standard errors for each cell appear in table A8.

Table A4. Log Earnings Regressions, Men

Controls	<=High School		Some College		College Graduates		African Americans	
	OLS	FE	OLS	FE	OLS	FE	OLS	FE
Married	0.290***	0.034***	0.262***	0.043***	0.303***	0.045***	0.344***	0.088***
	(0.007)	(0.009)	(0.008)	(0.010)	(0.008)	(0.009)	(0.036)	(0.020)
Married*1946–1955 cohort	0.063***	0.064***	0.080***	0.065***	0.030***	0.059***	0.042	0.049*
	(0.008)	(0.011)	(0.009)	(0.011)	(0.009)	(0.010)	(0.044)	(0.023)
Married*1956–1965 cohort	0.060***	0.084***	0.050***	0.092***	0.014	0.081***	0.012	0.059*
	(0.008)	(0.010)	(0.009)	(0.011)	(0.009)	(0.011)	(0.044)	(0.023)
Married*1966–1975 cohort	0.098***	0.118***	0.043***	0.103***	0.004	0.128***	0.051	0.145***
	(0.011)	(0.012)	(0.011)	(0.012)	(0.012)	(0.013)	(0.053)	(0.028)
N (rounded)	609,400	609,400	519,000	519,000	489,300	489,300	142,900	142,900

Source: Authors' compilation based on data from SIPP panels matched to Social Security Administration earnings records.

Notes: Dependent variable is log annual earnings. Regressions also include controls for year, education (except in columns 3/4 where no additional detail is available), dummies indicating if race is African American (in regressions for education groups), and indicating that ethnicity is Hispanic, main effects for birth cohort, and a quartic in age.

Table A5. Standard Errors for Table 4

Controls	OLS Coefficient Estimates				Fixed-Effect Coefficient Estimates			
	1	2	3	4	1	2	3	4
Married	(0.004)	(0.004)	(0.010)	(0.012)	(0.002)	(0.002)	(0.005)	(0.006)
Married*cohort 1946–1955			(0.012)	(0.015)			(0.006)	(0.007)
Married*cohort 1956–1965			(0.013)	(0.016)			(0.006)	(0.008)
Married*cohort 1966–1975			(0.016)	(0.020)			(0.009)	(0.012)
Number of children < eighteen		(0.002)	(0.004)	(0.006)		(0.001)	(0.002)	(0.003)
# children*cohort 1946–1955			(0.005)	(0.007)			(0.002)	(0.004)
# children*cohort 1956–1965			(0.005)	(0.008)			(0.003)	(0.004)
# children*cohort 1966–1975			(0.007)	(0.010)			(0.004)	(0.006)
Child < six years old		(0.004)	(0.011)	(0.023)		(0.002)	(0.006)	(0.013)
Child < six*cohort 1946–1955			(0.012)	(0.026)			(0.007)	(0.015)
Child < six*cohort 1956–1965			(0.013)	(0.027)			(0.007)	(0.015)
Child < six*cohort 1966–1975			(0.015)	(0.030)			(0.009)	(0.018)
Married*# children				(0.007)				(0.003)
Married*# children*cohort 1946–1955				(0.009)				(0.004)
Married*# children*cohort 1956–1965				(0.009)				(0.005)
Married*# children*cohort 1966–1975				(0.012)				(0.007)
Married*child < six				(0.026)				(0.015)
Married*child < six*cohort 1946–1955				(0.030)				(0.017)
Married*child < six*cohort 1956–1965				(0.031)				(0.017)
Married*child < six*cohort 1966–1975				(0.035)				(0.021)
N (rounded)	1,696,700	1,696,700	1,696,700	1,696,700	1,696,700	1,696,700	1,696,700	1,696,700

Source: Authors' compilation based on data from SIPP panels matched to Social Security Administration earnings records.

Notes: Log earnings regressions, women. N=1,696,700 (to nearest 100). Dependent variable is log annual earnings from SSA records. Regressions also include controls for year, education, dummies indicating if race is African American, and indicating if ethnicity is Hispanic, main effects for birth cohort, and a quartic in age. Standard errors for each cell appear in table A5.

Table A6. Standard Errors for Table A1

Controls	OLS Coefficient Estimates				Fixed-Effect Coefficient Estimates			
	1	2	3	4	1	2	3	4
Married	(0.001)	(0.001)	(0.002)	(0.003)	(0.001)	(0.001)	(0.001)	(0.002)
Married*cohort 1946–1955			(0.003)	(0.004)			(0.002)	(0.002)
Married*cohort 1956–1965			(0.004)	(0.005)			(0.002)	(0.002)
Married*cohort 1966–1975			(0.005)	(0.006)			(0.002)	(0.003)
Number of children < eighteen		(0.001)	(0.001)	(0.001)		(0.000)	(0.000)	(0.001)
# children*cohort 1946–1955			(0.001)	(0.002)			(0.001)	(0.001)
# children*cohort 1956–1965			(0.001)	(0.002)			(0.001)	(0.001)
# children*cohort 1966–1975			(0.002)	(0.003)			(0.001)	(0.002)
Child < six years old	(0.001)		(0.002)	(0.004)		(0.001)	(0.001)	(0.003)
Child < six*cohort 1946–1955			(0.002)	(0.005)			(0.001)	(0.004)
Child < six*cohort 1956–1965			(0.003)	(0.006)			(0.002)	(0.004)
Child < six*cohort 1966–1975			(0.004)	(0.008)			(0.002)	(0.005)
Married*# children				(0.002)				(0.001)
Married*# children*cohort 1946–1955				(0.002)				(0.001)
Married*# children*cohort 1956–1965				(0.003)				(0.001)
Married*# children*cohort 1966–1975				(0.004)				(0.002)
Married*child < six				(0.004)				(0.003)
Married < six*cohort 1946–1955				(0.006)				(0.004)
Married*child < six*cohort 1956–1965				(0.007)				(0.004)
Married*child < six*cohort 1966–1975				(0.009)				(0.005)

Source: Authors' compilation based on data from SIPP panels matched to Social Security Administration earnings records.
Note: Participation regressions, women.

Table A7. Standard Errors for Table A2

Controls	<=High School		Some College		College Graduates		African Americans	
	OLS	FE	OLS	FE	OLS	FE	OLS	FE
Married	(0.017)	(0.009)	(0.022)	(0.011)	(0.027)	(0.013)	(0.035)	(0.018)
Married*1946–1955 cohort	(0.022)	(0.011)	(0.026)	(0.013)	(0.031)	(0.015)	(0.044)	(0.022)
Married*1956–1965 cohort	(0.025)	(0.013)	(0.028)	(0.014)	(0.032)	(0.016)	(0.049)	(0.025)
Married*1966–1975 cohort	(0.042)	(0.024)	(0.035)	(0.020)	(0.035)	(0.019)	(0.066)	(0.041)
Number of children < eighteen	(0.008)	(0.004)	(0.011)	(0.005)	(0.016)	(0.008)	(0.014)	(0.007)
# children * 1946–1955 cohort	(0.010)	(0.006)	(0.013)	(0.007)	(0.020)	(0.010)	(0.018)	(0.009)
# children * 1956–1965 cohort	(0.012)	(0.006)	(0.014)	(0.007)	(0.021)	(0.011)	(0.018)	(0.010)
# children * 1966–1975 cohort	(0.016)	(0.010)	(0.017)	(0.010)	(0.025)	(0.014)	(0.023)	(0.015)
Has child < six years old	(0.029)	(0.018)	(0.041)	(0.024)	(0.067)	(0.035)	(0.039)	(0.024)
Child < six * 1946–1955 cohort	(0.036)	(0.022)	(0.046)	(0.027)	(0.075)	(0.039)	(0.047)	(0.028)
Child < six * 1956–1965 cohort	(0.037)	(0.022)	(0.046)	(0.027)	(0.076)	(0.041)	(0.048)	(0.028)
Child < six * 1966–1975 cohort	(0.044)	(0.027)	(0.051)	(0.029)	(0.083)	(0.047)	(0.052)	(0.032)
Married * number of children < eighteen	(0.009)	(0.005)	(0.013)	(0.006)	(0.018)	(0.008)	(0.017)	(0.008)
Married * # children * 1946–1965 cohort	(0.012)	(0.006)	(0.015)	(0.007)	(0.022)	(0.010)	(0.022)	(0.011)
Married * # children * 1956–1965 cohort	(0.014)	(0.007)	(0.016)	(0.008)	(0.024)	(0.011)	(0.024)	(0.012)
Married * # children * 1966–1975 cohort	(0.021)	(0.012)	(0.021)	(0.011)	(0.028)	(0.015)	(0.034)	(0.019)
Married*child < six	(0.033)	(0.020)	(0.047)	(0.026)	(0.074)	(0.037)	(0.049)	(0.029)
Married * child < six * 1946–1955 cohort	(0.041)	(0.025)	(0.053)	(0.030)	(0.082)	(0.042)	(0.059)	(0.035)
Married * child < six * 1956–1965 cohort	(0.043)	(0.025)	(0.053)	(0.030)	(0.083)	(0.044)	(0.061)	(0.036)
Married * child < six * 1966–1975 cohort	(0.054)	(0.033)	(0.059)	(0.034)	(0.091)	(0.050)	(0.070)	(0.045)

Source: Authors' compilation based on data from SIPP panels matched to Social Security Administration earnings records.

Note: Log earnings regressions for women, by education and race.

Figure A1. Participation Relative to Single, Childless Women (OLS), High School or Less

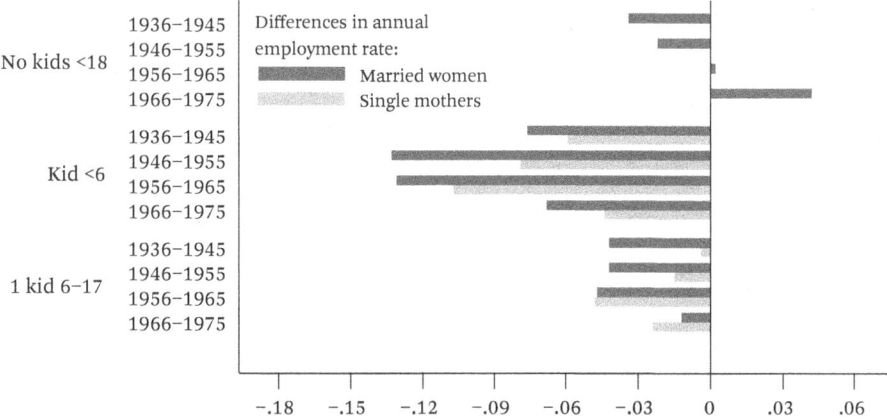

Source: Authors' compilation based on data from SIPP panels matched to Social Security Administration earnings records.

Figure A2. Participation Relative to Single, Childless Women (OLS), Some College

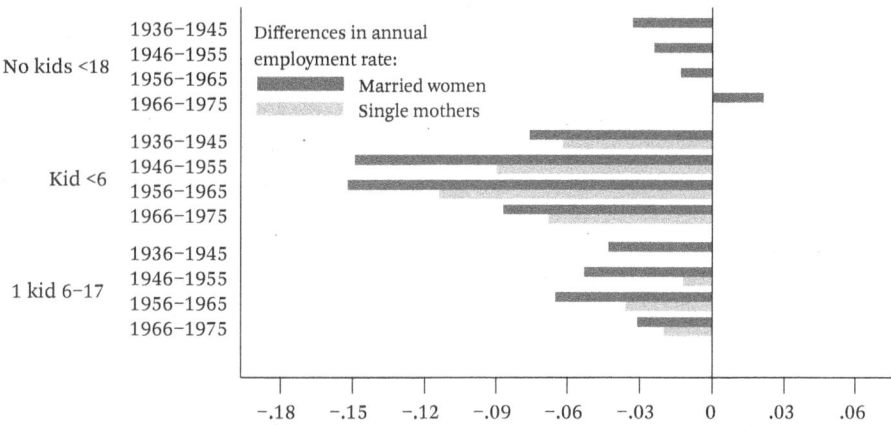

Source: Authors' compilation based on data from SIPP panels matched to Social Security Administration earnings records.

Figure A3. Participation Relative to Single, Childless Women (OLS), College Graduate

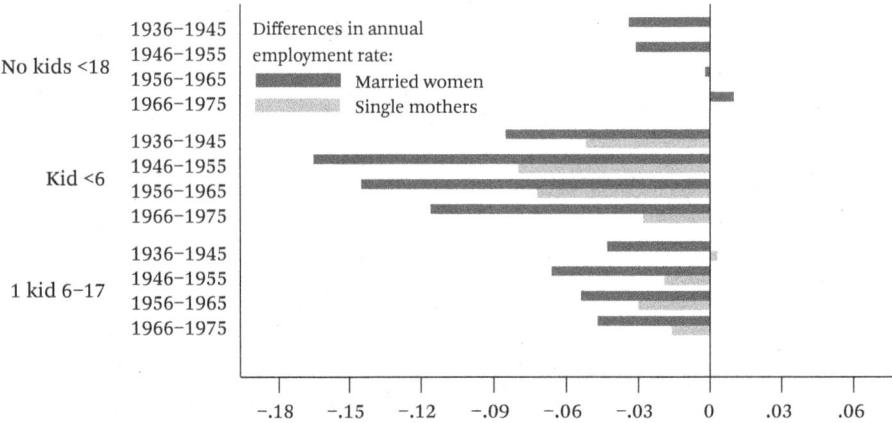

Source: Authors' compilation based on data from SIPP panels matched to Social Security Administration earnings records.

Figure A4. Participation Relative to Single, Childless Women (OLS), African American

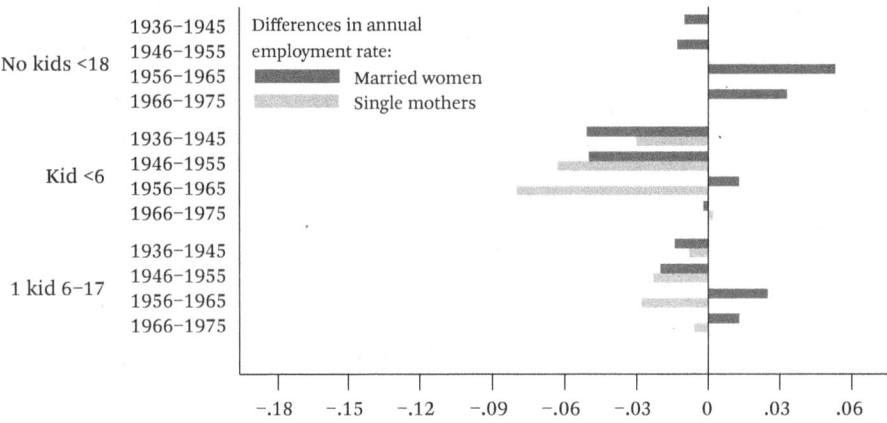

Source: Authors' compilation based on data from SIPP panels matched to Social Security Administration earnings records.

Figure A5. Participation Relative to Single, Childless Women (FE), High School or Less

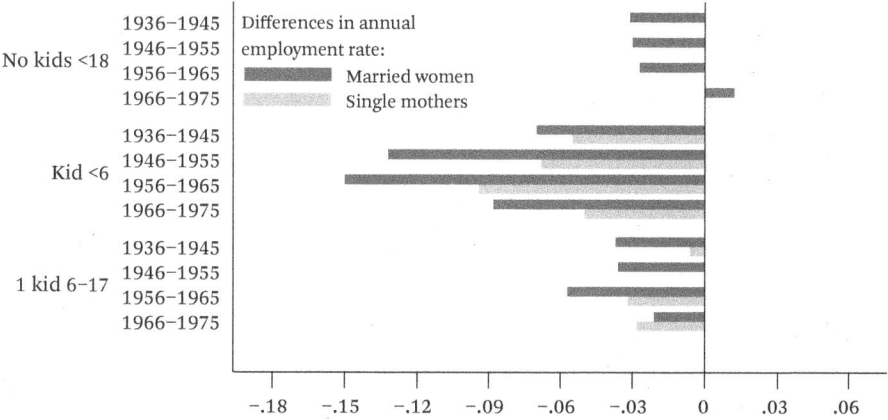

Source: Authors' compilation based on data from SIPP panels matched to Social Security Administration earnings records.

Figure A6. Participation Relative to Single, Childless Women (FE), Some College

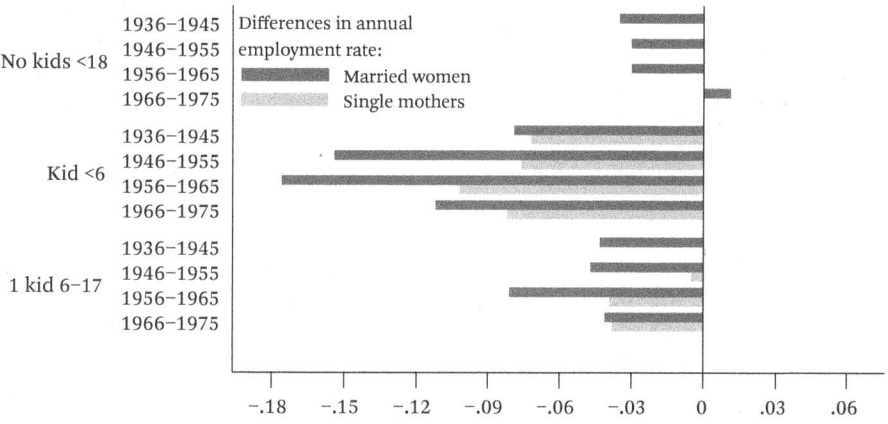

Source: Authors' compilation based on data from SIPP panels matched to Social Security Administration earnings records.

Figure A7. Participation Relative to Single, Childless Women (FE), College Graduate

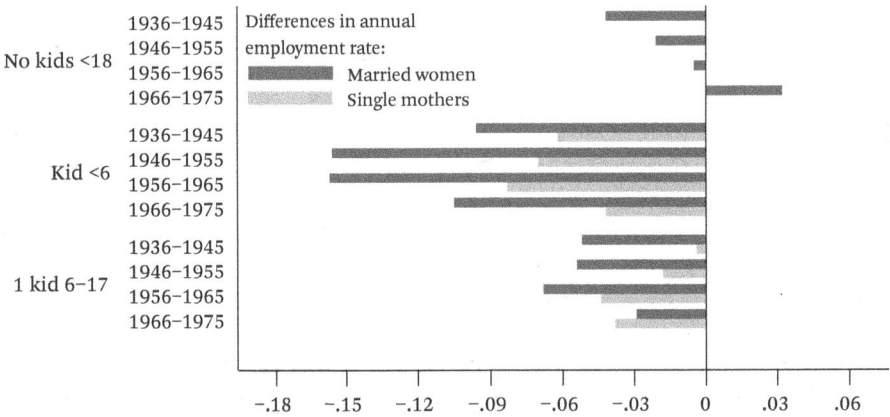

Source: Authors' compilation based on data from SIPP panels matched to Social Security Administration earnings records.

Figure A8. Participation Relative to Single, Childless Women (FE), African American

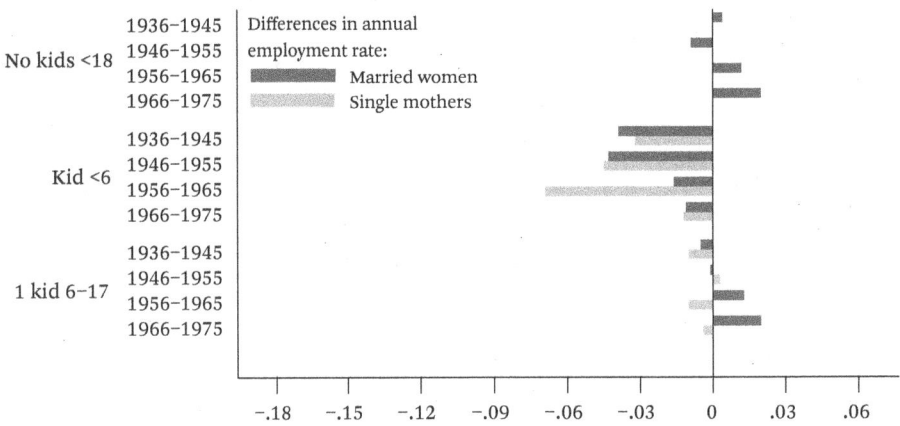

Source: Authors' compilation based on data from SIPP panels matched to Social Security Administration earnings records.

REFERENCES

Aguiar, Mark, and Erik Hurst. 2007. "Measuring Trends in Leisure: The Allocation of Time over Five Decades." *Quarterly Journal of Economics* 122(3): 969–1006.

Antonovics, Kate, and Robert Town. 2004. "Are All the Good Men Married? Uncovering the Sources of the Marital Wage Premium." *American Economics Review* 94(2): 317–21.

Avellar, Sarah, and Pamela J. Smock. 2003. "Has the Price of Motherhood Declined Over Time? A Cross-Cohort Comparison of the Motherhood Wage Penalty." *Journal of Marriage and Family* 65(3): 597–607.

Blackburn, McKinley, and Sanders Korenman. 1994. "The Declining Marital-Status Earnings Differential." *Journal of Population Economics* 7(3): 247–70.

Blau, Francine, and Lawrence Kahn. 1997. "Swimming Upstream: Trends in the Gender Wage Differential in the 1980s." *Journal of Labor Economics* 15(1): 1–42.

Budig, Michelle J., and Paula England. 2001. "The Wage Penalty for Motherhood." *American Sociological Review* 66(2): 204–25.

Byker, Tanya. 2011. "The Opt-Out Continuation: Education, Work and Motherhood from 1984–2008." Working paper. Ann Arbor: University of Michigan.

———. 2016. "The Opt-Out Continuation: Education, Work, and Motherhood from 1984 to 2012." *RSF: The Russell Sage Journal of the Social Sciences* 2(4). doi: 10.7758/RSF.2016.2.4.02.

Card, David, and Thomas Lemieux. 2001. "Going to College to Avoid the Draft: The Unintended Legacy of the Vietnam War." *American Economic Review* 91(2): 97–102.

Correll, Shelley J., Stephen Bernard, and In Paik. 2007. "Getting a Job: Is There a Motherhood Penalty?" *American Journal of Sociology* 112(5): 1297–339.

Dougherty, Christopher. 2006. "The Marriage Earnings Premium as a Distributed Fixed Effect." *Journal of Human Resources* 42(2): 433–43.

Ginther, Donna, Marianne Sundstrom, and Anders Bjorklund. 2008. "Does Marriage Lead to Specialization in Sweden? An Evaluation of Trends in Adult Earnings Before and After Marriage." Working paper. Lawrence: University of Kansas. Accessed April 9, 2016. http://paa2008.princeton.edu/papers/80816.

Goldstein, Joshua, and Catherine T. Kenney. 2001. "Marriage Delayed or Marriage Forgone? New Cohort Forecasts of First Marriage for U.S. Women." *American Sociological Review* 66(4): 506–19.

Gray, Jeffrey. 1997. "The Fall in Men's Return to Marriage." *Journal of Human Resources* 32(3): 481–504.

Greenwood, Jeremy, and Nizah Guner. 2008. "Marriage and Divorce since World War II: Analyzing the Role of Technological Progress on the Formation of Households." NBER working paper no. 10772. Cambridge, Mass.: National Bureau of Economic Research. Accessed April 9, 2016. http://www.nber.org/papers/w10772.

Isen, Adam, and Betsey Stevenson. 2010. "Women's Education and Family Behavior: Trends in Marriage, Divorce and Fertility." NBER working paper no. 15725. Cambridge, Mass.: National Bureau of Economic Research.

Killewald, Alexandra, and Margaret Gough. 2013. "Does Specialization Explain Marriage Penalties and Premiums?" *American Sociological Review* 78(3): 477–502.

Korenman, Sanders, and David Neumark. 1991. "Does Marriage Really Make Men More Productive?" *Journal of Human Resources* 26(2): 282–307.

Pal, Ipshita, and Jane Waldfogel. 2016. "The Family Gap in Pay: New Evidence for 1967 to 2013." *RSF: The Russell Sage Journal of the Social Sciences* 2(4). doi: 10.7758/RSF.2016.2.4.04.

Stevenson, Betsey. 2007. "The Impact of Divorce Laws on Marriage-Specific Capital." *Journal of Labor Economics* 25(1): 75–94.

Stevenson, Betsey, and Justin Wolfers. 2007. "Marriage and Divorce: Changes and their Driving Forces." *Journal of Economic Perspectives* 21(2): 27–52.

Waldfogel, Jane. 1997. "The Effect of Children on Women's Wages." *American Sociological Review* 62(2): 209–17.

———. 1998. "Understanding the 'Family Gap' in Pay for Women with Children." *Journal of Economic Perspectives* 12(1): 137–56.

Whitman, Kevin, and David Shoffner. 2011. "The Evolution of Social Security's Taxable Maximum." Policy Brief no. 2011-02. Washington, D.C.: Social Security Administration. Accessed April 9, 2016. https://www.ssa.gov/policy/docs/policybriefs/pb2011-02.html.

PART V
Education, Work, and Political Participation

Advances and Ambivalence: The Consequences of Women's Educational and Workforce Changes for Women's Political Participation in the United States, 1952 to 2012

ASHLEY JARDINA AND NANCY BURNS

Over the last forty years, the gap between men and women with respect to labor-market outcomes, paid hours of work, hours working at home, occupations, college majors, and education levels in the United States has narrowed or disappeared. We ask whether these substantial changes in women's lives—changes in precisely the variables that have seemed to matter so much to our understanding of political participation—have enabled women's political action in the United States. We find that they have not, and we suggest that the brakes on the translation of education and occupation into political participation come from continuing ambivalence about jobs and careers. Of course, these ambivalent attitudes may very well reflect a reality about the complications of workforce participation in a world with unequal and limited access to childcare, parental leave, high-paying jobs, and opportunities for career advancement.

Keywords: political participation, ambivalence, education, occupation, gender roles

Over the last forty years, what was once nearly impossible for many women in the United States—a career with promotion opportunities—became possible and even ordinary. At the same time, the gap between men and women with respect to labor-market outcomes, paid hours of work, hours working at home, occupations, college majors, and education levels in the United States has narrowed or disappeared. As Marth Bailey, Melanie Guldi, and Brad Hershbein put it, "younger women delayed their marriages, increased their educational attainment, and pursued previously male-dominated careers" (2014, 304). These changes were, in part, likely due to the availability of the birth control pill (Goldin and Katz 2002; Bailey 2010). They were also likely enabled by the Kennedy government's contracting policies in the early 1960s, which called for equal hiring and promotion practices within companies (Dobbin 2009). Furthermore, efforts of the civil rights movement and the women's movement to make employment opportunities a right also contributed to these major shifts in women's career opportunities. Along with these changes came a substantial increase in women's educational outcomes.

Many of these shifts in opportunities and

Ashley Jardina is assistant professor of political science in the Department of Political Science at Duke University. **Nancy Burns** is Warren E. Miller Collegiate Professor and chair in the Department of Political Science at the University of Michigan.

Direct correspondence to: Ashley Jardina at ashley.jardina@duke.edu, Duke University Department of Political Science, 140 Science Drive, 208 Gross Hall, Campus Box 90204, Durham, NC 27708; and Nancy Burns at nburns@umich.edu, The University of Michigan Department of Political Science, 5700 Haven Hall, 505 South State Street, Ann Arbor, MI 48109.

expectations for women were ushered in over a single decade; in the early 1960s, a substantial majority of young women imagined their adult lives without jobs and careers. By the late 1960s, only a minority of young women envisioned their adult lives without jobs and careers (Goldin and Katz 2000; Goldin 2004). The effects of this transformation were carried into the next five decades as an increasing number of women went to college and entered the labor market. In this article, we ask whether these changes have shaped individual-level political participation in the United States. As we explain, decades of scholarship have made clear that education and jobs with skill-providing opportunities are strongly related to individual-level political participation. We ask whether these substantial changes in women's lives—changes in precisely the variables that have seemed to matter so much to our understanding of political participation—have enabled women's political action in the United States.

We begin by providing a portrait of these substantial changes with respect to jobs and education. These changes are well known in sociology and economics, but less so in political science, and so have not been taken up in the literatures there. We then turn to accounts of political participation, making clear both what we mean by political participation and how education and jobs play a central role in accounts of political participation. This section sets the stage for the expectation that these fairly dramatic changes in women's education and employment status should translate into fairly dramatic changes in women's political participation. We consider the place of jobs and education separately and ask whether these changes have in fact materialized. We find, quite surprisingly, that some have and some have not. We argue that a range of attitudinal factors—especially attitudes about the roles women should take on—may have dampened the potential impacts of these changes.

A BRIEF PORTRAIT OF THE CHANGE

We begin by outlining the dramatic changes in the employment expectations and education levels of young women in the United States over the latter half of the twentieth century. Beginning in the 1960s, women made an almost complete shift in expectations about their future employment; before this period, most women expected to be at home, working as caretakers and mothers by their mid-thirties. But between the 1960s and 1980s, an increasing proportion of women expected instead to be employed at age thirty-five (Goldin 2006).[1]

Over this same period, women made enormous gains in educational attainment, helping boost their ability to achieve their new employment expectations. In 1952, a vanishingly small percentage of women had a college degree, and women were some 10 points less likely to complete college than men. By the late 1980s and early 1990s, their rates of college completion equaled men's. In the 2000s, they exceeded them, and by 2010, women were almost 10 points more likely to complete college than men. Today, nearly half of all women have a college degree (U.S. Census Bureau 2011).

As women sought college degrees, and as more jobs became available to women, the kinds of jobs they held changed markedly. In 1952, the overwhelming majority of women reported themselves to be homemakers. Over the past several decades, however, the number of women whose primary job is in the home decreased, and today, only about 20 percent of women report being homemakers. A steadily increasing percentage of women have moved into jobs in the clerical, skilled, and semi-skilled service sectors. Women have also moved more into professional and managerial jobs. Although men's occupations have changed over this time as well, with the important exception of agricultural employment, the overall picture men's occupations present is of tremendous stability (ANES 2012; see also Blau and Kahn 2005).

Not all women have had access to these in-

---

1. We have some insight from existing work about the impetus for these changes; Kathleen Gerson (2011), for example, in her interviews with young women, makes clear that some of this change in expectations is likely about the opportunities available. More recently, however, if Gerson's interviews are any guide, some of the expectations are about women's desire for independence and long-run financial security.

creased levels of education and the ability to move into occupations with more elaborate career ladders. Of course, women today are far less constrained than they were in the 1950s and early 1960s, when fewer than 8 percent had completed four years of college. But even today, stratification among women by education is considerable. In 2014, 11 percent of women over twenty-five did not have a high school diploma; 29 percent terminated their education with only that; 28 percent received some college or an associate's degree; and 20.4 percent received a bachelor's degree (U.S. Census Bureau 2014). As Sara McLanahan makes clear, this stratification by education has made economic inequality between women more severe—partly because, unlike their counterparts, women with more education tend to be married and employed and to delay childbirth (2004).

Our question is whether these large and uneven changes in education and jobs have consequences for political participation. Our answer draws on the frameworks that scholars—political scientists, especially—have used to understand political participation. To help answer the question, we embed the changes we just described in the literature on resources and political participation. From there, we turn to explaining why these impressive structural changes have not translated into higher levels of political participation. We argue that the ambivalence women express about their work and family roles powerfully hampers their willingness and ability to leverage jobs and higher levels of education into political participation.

MODELS OF POLITICAL PARTICIPATION

Whether an individual participates in politics depends on the costs and benefits of participation. We describe the ingredients of a model of participation with this cost-benefit framework in mind. Scholars have found, over and over, that individual-level resources, and especially education and income, are correlated with political participation (Verba, Schlozman, and Brady 1995; Rosenstone and Hansen 1993). Education enables people to be more knowledgeable about politics. Education fosters interest in politics. Education puts people in social networks, gives them cognitive tools, and opens up occupations. It also provides opportunities for increased incomes, making people visible to political mobilizers. Of course, money and education also make it less costly for individuals to participate in politics by opening mobilization opportunities and making potential outcomes more comprehensible.

Political participation is enabled by resources like education. It is also facilitated by a second set of resources—the practical tools people acquire on the job and in religious institutions, through the opportunities to organize meetings, give speeches, participate in meetings, and the like—activities that offer skill-building opportunities. Scholars call this second set of resources civic skills (Verba, Schlozman, and Brady 1995). These also lower the cost of participation by making politics easier to engage in.

These factors—education and civic skills—are the central players in any account of political action. They affect people's sense of being able to do the work of politics and their engagement in the political process. They cumulate inequality in participation, making it ever easier for some to participate in politics and affecting the voices that get spoken and heard in the political arena. They also, therefore, create the tremendous stratification in political participation. Some 70 percent of those in the top quintile of education and income participate in politics; by contrast, only 33 percent of those in the bottom quintile participate (Schlozman, Verba, and Brady 2013, 124).

What do we mean by political participation? We mean activities aimed at speaking to and influencing government in terms of policy or in terms of practice and implementation. Scholars outside political science often focus on two ways of participating in politics: voting and donating money. Political scientists, by contrast, tend to focus on a broad array of activities. In figures 1 through 4, we report participation levels (in this case, the proportion of women who report participating and the average level of participation, where appropriate) using both a broad array of participatory activities and questions asked in comparable ways over time using data from the American National Election Studies

Figure 1. Women's Political Participation, Voting Turnout

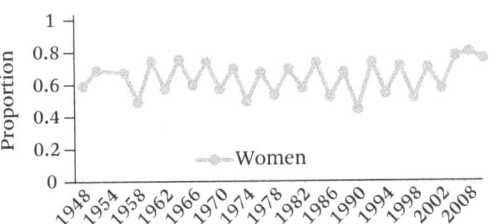

Source: Authors' compilation based on ANES Cumulative Data File 2012.
Note: Data are weighted. Number of cases available in table A1.

Figure 2. Women's Political Participation, Contribute to a Candidate or Campaign

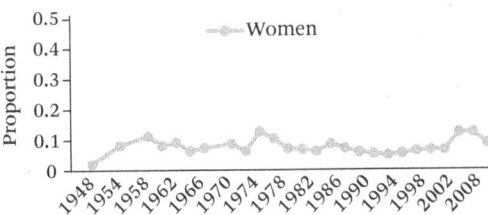

Source: Authors' compilation based on ANES Cumulative Data File 2012.
Note: Data are weighted. Number of cases available in table A2.

Figure 3. Women's Political Participation, Interest in Political Campaigns

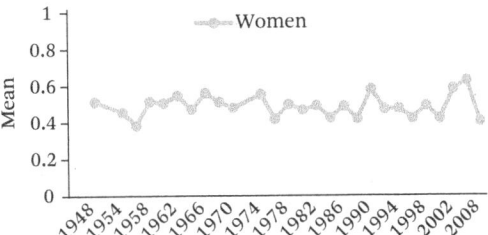

Source: Authors' compilation based on ANES Cumulative Data File 2012.
Note: Data are weighted. Number of cases available in table A3. Values coded to range from zero to one.

Figure 4. Women's Political Participation, Events and Volunteering

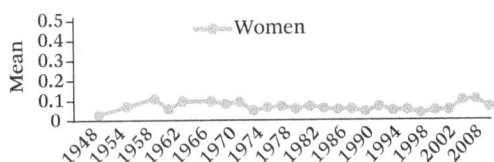

Source: Authors' compilation based on ANES Cumulative Data File 2012.
Note: Data are weighted. Number of cases available in table A4. Values coded to range from zero to one.

(ANES).[2] The ANES provides impressive continuity in the study of American national elections. In every presidential year since 1952, the ANES has been made up of a national random sample of U.S. adult citizens surveyed, in-person, by professional interviewers, before and after each election.

Our broad array of participatory activities includes voting, contributing to a political candidate or campaign, expressing interest in politics, and an index measure of several types of participatory behavior (such as attending a political event, working for a candidate, or wearing a campaign button). We have just described how factors like education and civic skills acquired in the workplace boost political partic-

ipation, but in figures 1 through 4, where we have clustered women together regardless of education or occupation status, we see little change over time. In other words, although we might expect women's political participation levels to have risen markedly in correspondence with the large shifts in education achievement and labor-market participation women have experienced over the past fifty or so years, the data presented in figures 1 through 4 do not immediately corroborate such a story. To be sure, changes in levels of women's participation over time are certainly not entirely undetectable, but they are far from dramatic. Herein, we argue, lies a puzzle. Why have wom-

---

2. We combine both blacks and whites in this analysis and the others throughout this chapter. Although participation among blacks is somewhat more depressed than it is for whites, the overall trends described here hold true across racial groups.

Figure 5. Women's Political Participation, Education, Voting Turnout

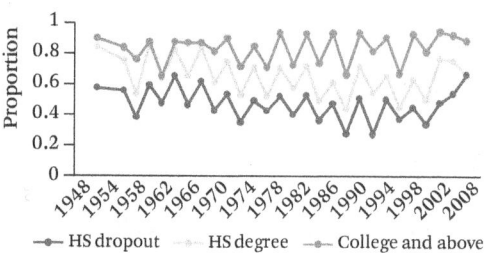

Source: Authors' compilation based on ANES Cumulative Data File 2012.
Note: Data are weighted. Number of cases available in table A1.

Figure 6. Women's Political Participation, Education, Contribute to a Candidate or Campaign

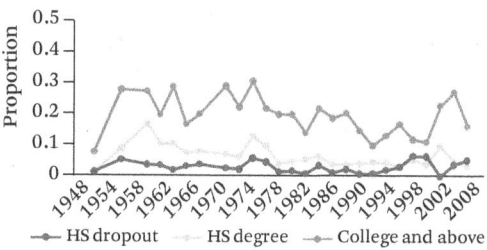

Source: Authors' compilation based on ANES Cumulative Data File 2012.
Note: Data are weighted. Number of cases available in table A2.

Figure 7. Women's Political Participation, Education, Interest in Political Campaigns

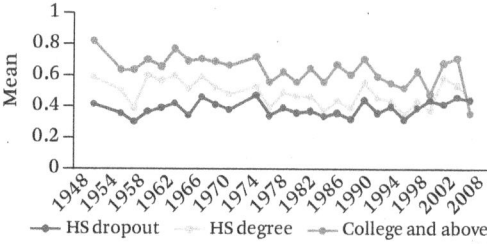

Source: Authors' compilation based on ANES Cumulative Data File 2012.
Note: Data are weighted. Number of cases available in table A3. Values coded to range from zero to one.

Figure 8. Women's Political Participation, Education, Events and Volunteering

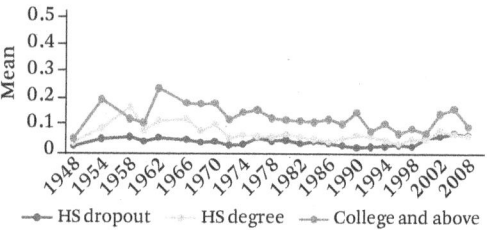

Source: Authors' compilation based on ANES Cumulative Data File 2012.
Note: Data are weighted. Number of cases available in table A4. Values coded to range from zero to one.

en's levels of participation over time appeared not to have mirrored large shifts in the factors that drive participation?

STRATIFICATION BY EDUCATION AND OCCUPATION

One expectation might be that stratification by education and occupation explains why we do not observe larger shifts in participation over time. As we described, not all women have made the gains that would lead to higher levels of political participation. To more fully unpack trends in political participation among women over time, we use the ANES time series—comparing rates of participation in a number of domains among women without high school diplomas, those who graduated high school, and those who obtained at least a college degree. We might expect that, as norms and expectations about women's college and career options changed over time, women with more education would increasingly diverge in their rates of political participation compared with women with less education.

We present results of this overtime analysis in figures 5 through 8. When we consider the proportion of women who have contributed to campaigns or who have voted, for instance, we find a consistent and somewhat surprising trend. It is true that today women with more education participate in these activities more often than those with less. Yet panning over the time series, we can see that both the slope of these lines and the distance between them

Figure 9. Women's Political Participation, Educational Quartiles, Voting Turnout

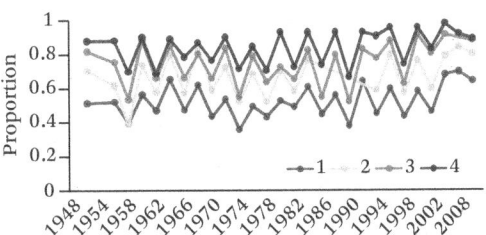

Source: Authors' compilation based on ANES Cumulative Data File 2012.
Note: Data are weighted. Number of cases available in table A5.

Figure 10. Women's Political Participation Educational Quartiles, Contribution to a Candidate or Campaign

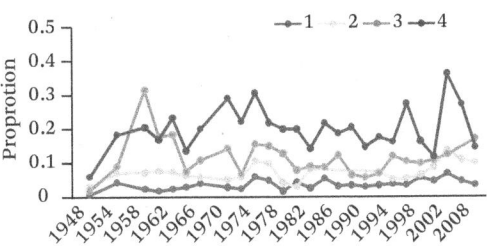

Source: Authors' compilation based on ANES Cumulative Data File 2012.
Note: Data are weighted. Number of cases available in table A6.

Figure 11. Women's Political Participation, Educational Quartiles, Interest in Political Campaigns

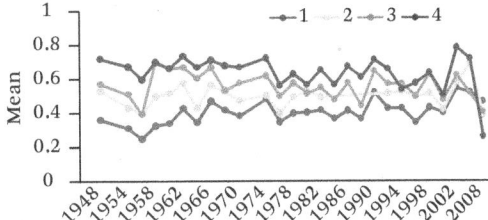

Source: Authors' compilation based on ANES Cumulative Data File 2012.
Note: Data are weighted. Number of cases available in table A7. Values coded to range from zero to one.

Figure 12. Women's Political Participation, Educational Quartiles, Events and Volunteering

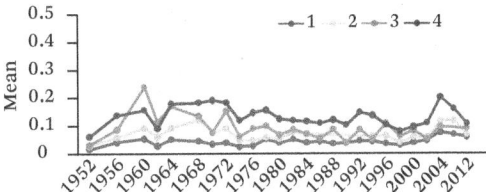

Source: Authors' compilation based on ANES Cumulative Data File 2012.
Note: Data are weighted. Number of cases available in table A8. Values coded to range from zero to one.

has remained relatively stable. In other words, in terms of political participation, the women with the most education have always looked different than women with less. No dramatic shift is evident in the rates with which women at each level of education engaged in political activities over the period of large changes.

Of course, the graphs take education as an absolute; they treat the credential as the key variable of interest. We could, instead, treat education as a relative variable, in comparison with the educational level of others in the society. In other words, perhaps a college degree has a different meaning and value depending on whether a college degree is a rare achievement or a more common achievement in society. We explore this possibility by looking again at the same data, this time using education in quartiles in figures 9 through 12. What we see is that the stratification is not so much about relative education as it is about absolute education. Although those at the top participate more than those at the bottom, the quartile approach obscures the work the credentials do to stratify the population.

That college degrees matter in roughly the same way now as they did in years past is perhaps surprising, and especially so in the face of the increasing heterogeneity of women who receive a college degree. College completion stratifies the population as crisply now, when nearly half of all women have the degree, as it did when only a tiny percentage did, and this continuity is in many ways startling.

Figure 13. Women's Political Participation, Professional Status, Voting

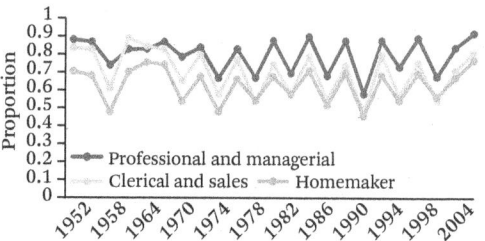

Source: Authors' compilation based on ANES Cumulative Data File 2012.
Note: Data are weighted. Number of cases available in table A9.

Figure 14. Women's Political Participation, Professional Status, Contribution to a Candidate or Campaign

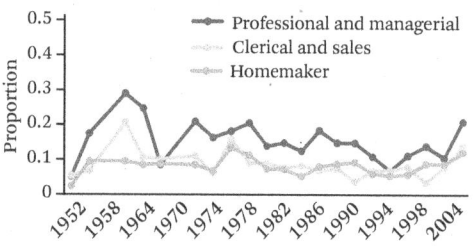

Source: Authors' compilation based on ANES Cumulative Data File 2012.
Note: Data are weighted. Number of cases available in table A10.

Figure 15. Women's Political Participation, Professional Status, Interest in Political Campaigns

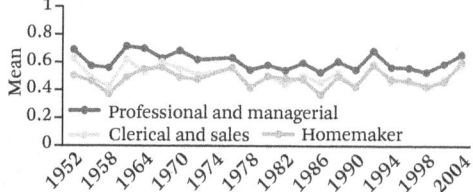

Source: Authors' compilation based on ANES Cumulative Data File 2012.
Note: Data are weighted. Number of cases available in table A11. Values coded to range from zero to one.

Figure 16. Women's Political Participation, Professional Status, Events and Volunteering

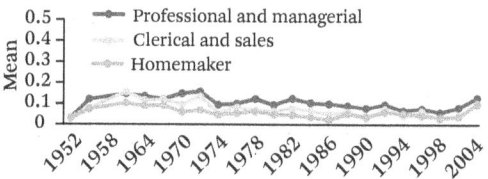

Source: Authors' compilation based on ANES Cumulative Data File 2012.
Note: Data are weighted. Number of cases available in table A12. Values coded to range from zero to one.

Of course, education is only one part of the large change of the past decades, only one component of the way women have made good on their expectations. The second way they have made good is in terms of jobs and careers. As women have moved into jobs with skill-giving opportunities and as employment has become normative in adult women's lives, have jobs and employment come to stratify differently now than they did in the past? We face some data limitations with respect to women and full-time jobs, and so we focus here (in figures 13 through 16) on differentiating participation over time by three kinds of job classifications—professional and managerial jobs, clerical and sales jobs, and homemakers.

The story here is remarkably similar to the story for education. Women in professional and managerial jobs—jobs that provide precisely the kind of civic skills that enable political action—have always participated more than have women in clerical and sales jobs and women at home. This continues for the entire fifty-year series, despite the tremendous change in access to these jobs for women. In other words, no change over time is evident in the relationship between education or occupation and political participation.

To view this another way, we pool data from the ANES over the entire time series from 1970 to the present and estimate political participation among women as a function of education, occupation, and the interaction between these factors and year indicator variables. We also control for age, income, church attendance,

Figure 17. Education, Occupation, and Women's Political Participation

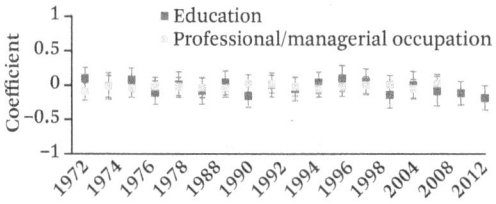

Source: Authors' compilation based on ANES Cumulative Data File 2012.
Note: Data are weighted. OLS regression model results available in table A13. Occupation categories were not available on the 2008 and 2012 ANES. Boxes represent coefficient values. Error bars represent 95 percent confidence intervals.

employment status, and marital status. In figure 17, we plot the coefficients with their respective standard errors for both the interaction between year and education and year and professional occupation. The results tell a consistent story. The relationship between education and professional occupation is not moderated by year. Instead, the relationship between these variables and political participation is quite consistent over time.

Again, we find this continuity in the face of the tremendous changes in selection into these jobs over time to be surprising. As with education, the association appears to come from the experience, not from the process of selection. This relationship seems, again somewhat unexpectedly, not to be muddied by the changes in the heterogeneity within these categories.

ATTITUDES ABOUT THE ROLE OF WOMEN IN THE WORKPLACE

We turn now to the third way women could make good on the dramatic changes in their early expectations about labor-force attachment, with respect to attitudes about the role of women in the workplace. Women are of course in the workforce in great numbers, and increasingly in professional and managerial occupations. Yet men's presence in the workforce is seen as natural, and the question of staying or leaving the workplace is not ever-present. We ask, then, whether women—or at least some women—come to see their presence in the workplace as normative and unproblematic.

Although we do not have measures of women's satisfaction with their jobs and their levels of commitment to the workplace, we do have measures over time of whether women and men view women's presence in the workplace as normative and unproblematic. Have women made good on this third outcome, their views about whether women are comfortably in the workplace? To what extent have women's views about women's workforce involvement remained ambivalent?

Given the tremendous attention paid to discussions of opting out (Belkin 2003; Stone 2007) and to what Betsey Stevenson and Justin Wolfers call the "paradox of declining female happiness" (2009), and given the emerging literature on gender identity within labor-force economics (Bertrand 2011; Fortin 2015), we have reasons to expect that women in the United States have not lost their ambivalence.

In the United States, debates about gender have centered largely on whether women should be relegated to the private sphere, at home, with their family. In the midst of the women's rights movement in the early 1970s, when significant attention was paid to gender equality issues, scholars developed survey measures to gauge the extent to which individuals subscribed to the traditional belief that the role of women was in the home, or whether they adopted more egalitarian views about women's place (Spence and Helmreich 1972). We might expect that over the past several decades, as women have increasingly left the home, earned college degrees, and entered the labor market en masse, attitudes about women's roles would shift dramatically toward a more egalitarian position.

Alternatively, and consistent with the opting-out literature, we might anticipate less change in attitudes than the enormous shift in women's behaviors might suggest. In part, changes in attitudes about women's proper roles might be modest because the characteristics we attribute to men and women are largely seen as immutable and essential. In other words, particular qualities people generally ascribe to women—that they are inherently caretakers, nurturers, and meant to be at home raising children—are not attitudes that have necessarily been abandoned (Goffman 1977). We suspect that such traditional beliefs may very well be hampering the extent to which women's increased resources boosted political engagement.

We can observe whether such attitudinal shifts have occurred by examining responses to survey questions often employed to gauge attitudes about women's roles. We examine average responses to such questions over time among both men and women, for good reason. Women's decisions about whether to work, to participate in politics, to pursue careers, and more are inextricably linked to the attitudes possessed by men—both men they encounter in their daily lives, and men who influence the policies and practices that give women options and opportunities to pursue such activities. Thus, to examine attitudes over time, we turn to the General Social Survey (GSS), a nationally representative survey that has featured questions about women's roles routinely since 1977 (Thornton, Alwin, and Camburn 1983; see also Fortin 2015). We center our attention not on all questions the surveys have asked about women's roles, but rather those that focus most intensively on acceptance and ambivalence about women's workforce participation.

We begin with the most pointed question in the battery, the question about the extent to which individuals agree or disagree that a working mother can establish just as warm and secure a relationship with her children as a mother who does not work. In figure 18, we plot the mean response to this question on a scale recoded such that values range from zero to one, with higher values representing a more traditional view.

The results are striking. We can see that despite a discernible drop toward the end of the 1970s and into the 1980s, such that both men and women are somewhat more supportive of women's employment, the slope of the lines remains markedly unchanged. There is also a noteworthy gender gap between men and women, with women more likely to endorse egalitarian gender roles. On average, however beliefs about the role of women as caretakers have persisted among both men and women. Furthermore, such attitudes seem largely un-

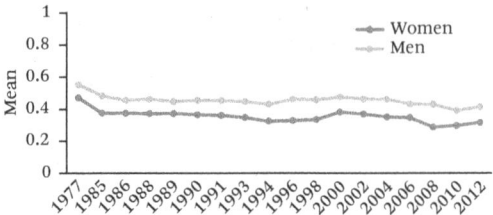

Figure 18. Attitudes About Working Mothers

Source: Authors' compilation based on GSS cumulative file (Smith et al. 2015).
Note: Data are weighted. Question wording: "A working mother can establish just as warm and secure a relationship with her children as a mother who does not work." (Agree/Disagree). Number of cases available in table A14. Values coded to range from zero to one.

moved by the overwhelming gains women have made in terms of educational attainment and labor-market participation. Even in 2012, a sizable portion of both men and women maintained that working mothers cannot establish the same relationships with their children as mothers who do not work.

A similar trend emerges when we look at other questions gauging attitudes about women's roles. When asked whether it is more important for a wife to help her husband's career than to have one herself, we do see a slight drop in endorsement of this notion over the course of the time series (figure 19), but not nearly as dramatic of a change as we might expect given the huge shift in women's work lives.

The same trend is present when asked whether children suffer when a mother works (figure 20), and whether it is better for a man to be the achiever outside the home and for the woman to take care of the family (figure 21). In both instances, we see slight movement away from the more traditional perspective in the late 1970s, and then attitudes are mostly stable.

Perhaps most surprisingly, when we look at these same attitudes by level of education in figures 22 through 25, it is clear that what changes there have been toward less ambivalence about women's employment have come to women at all levels of education in fairly

Figure 19. Attitudes About Women Supporting Husband's Career

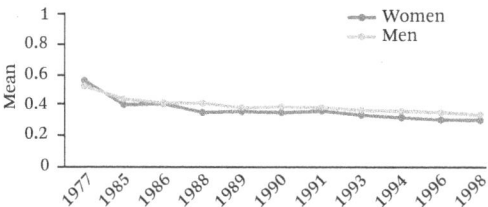

Source: Authors' compilation based on GSS cumulative file (Smith et al. 2015).
Note: Data are weighted. Question wording: "It is more important for a wife to help her husband's career than to have one herself." (Agree/Disagree). Number of cases available in table A15. Values coded to range from zero to one.

Figure 20. Attitudes About Children if Mother Works

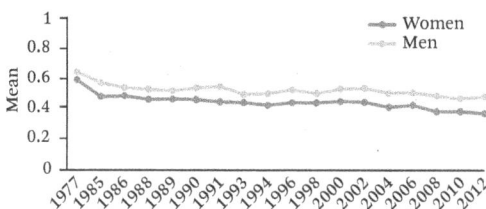

Source: Authors' compilation based on GSS cumulative file (Smith et al. 2015).
Note: Data are weighted. Question wording: "A preschool child is likely to suffer if his or her mother works." (Agree/Disagree). Number of cases available in table A16. Values coded to range from zero to one.

Figure 21. Attitudes About Men Working and Women Staying Home

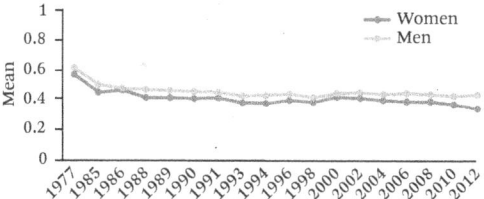

Source: Authors' compilation based on GSS cumulative file (Smith et al. 2015).
Note: Data are weighted. Question wording: "It is much better for everyone involved if the man is the achiever outside the home and the woman takes care of the home and family" (Agree/Disagree). Number of cases available in table A17. Values coded to range from zero to one.

even measure. For women at each of the three levels of education, attitudes changed most markedly between 1977 and 1988, and then leveled off. Although it is true throughout the series that college-educated women are more supportive of women's labor-force participation, no group changed especially dramatically. It is also true that a large proportion of all of these groups believe that children suffer when their mother works.

For the most part, then, women and men have not become significantly more comfortable and less conflicted about women's employment. A sizable subset of both men and women in the United States still hold more traditional views about women's place, or remain at least ambivalent about whether women are better suited for the private sphere than the public. This ambivalence translates, we suspect, into workforce outcomes, outcomes that, in our framework, shape the opportunities women have to develop politically relevant skills on the job.

This ambivalence about the workplace is fairly widespread, but it also stratifies workforce outcomes, and stratifies those outcomes over and above the stratification from education. The following charts reinforce what we already know about the way that education stratifies presence in the workforce. College-educated women are notably more likely to be working full time than high school graduates or women with less than a high school diploma. The other side of the story is also true: college-educated women are notably less likely to be homemakers than women with less education. Views on women's place stratify these outcomes even more. Women with college degrees who believe that women are appropriately in the workforce are some 30 points more likely to be in the workforce full time than their counterparts who believe differently. Those who are ambivalent are in between but are a bit closer to conservative than liberal women here.

Figure 22. Women's Attitudes About Roles, by Working Mothers

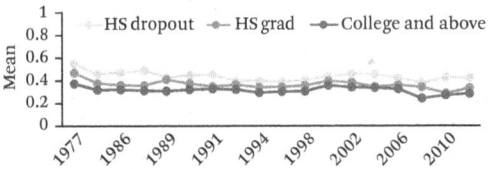

Source: Authors' compilation based on GSS cumulative file (Smith et al. 2015).
Note: Data are weighted. Number of cases available in table A18. Values coded to range from zero to one.

Figure 23. Women's Attitudes About Roles, Children

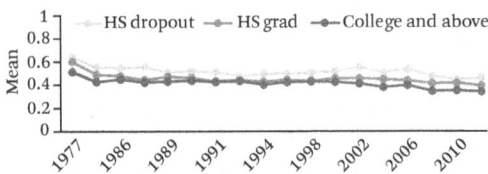

Source: Authors' compilation based on GSS cumulative file (Smith et al. 2015).
Note: Data are weighted. Number of cases available in table A19. Values coded to range from zero to one.

Figure 24. Women's Attitudes About Roles, Staying Home

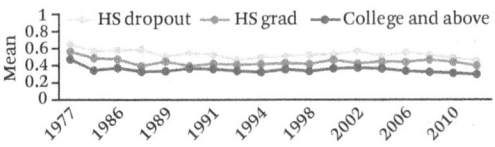

Source: Authors' compilation based on GSS cumulative file (Smith et al. 2015).
Note: Data are weighted. Number of cases available in table A21. Values coded to range from zero to one.

Figure 25. Women's Attitudes About Roles, Husband's Career

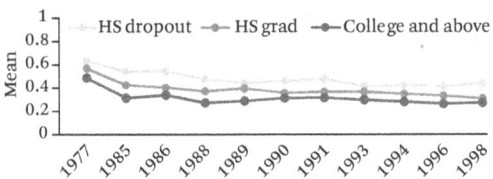

Source: Authors' compilation based on GSS cumulative file (Smith et al. 2015).
Note: Data are weighted. Number of cases available in table A20. Values coded to range from zero to one.

This ambivalence about women's place makes some trouble for the full realization of young women's expectations. We explored these relationships by collecting data on both men's and women's attitudes and expectations using the 2014 Cooperative Congressional Election Survey (CCES). Our data were drawn from a nationally representative sample of 431 men and 569 women, who were asked questions about gender, expectations, attitudes, employment, and political preferences. The preelection survey was fielded in September and October 2014. We returned to reinterview this sample in a postelection study, which was fielded in November and December 2014.

These data make clear that women who at age eighteen expected to be in the workforce full time acquired more education than those women who did not expect to be in the workforce full time. They made good on the first part of their expectations. The next two charts illustrate this point. First, in figure 26, we see that, as in the Goldin data (2005), most women report that they expected to be in the workforce. In figure 27, we see that women who expected to be in the workforce full time acquired more education than did women who did not. In figure 28, we see that women who expected to be in the workforce full time achieved jobs that were more likely to provide the kind of on-the-job training that can make participation less costly. That is, they were more likely to work at a job where they gained the sort of civic skills—like serving on committees, organizing meetings, or giving presentations—that they can carry into the political world.

However, these women had more trouble making good on their expectations about employment. When we look at the difference be-

Figure 26. Gender Differences in Career Expectations

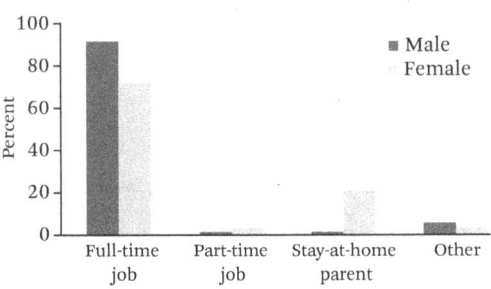

Source: Authors' compilation based on CCES 2014 (Schaffner and Ansolabehere 2015).
Note: Data are weighted. Number of cases: Women=518; Men=482.

Figure 27. Women's Education Today by Work Expectations

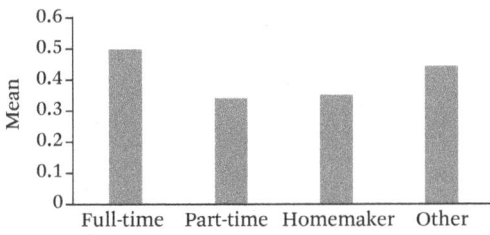

Source: Authors' compilation based on CCES 2014 (Schaffner and Ansolabehere 2015).
Note: Data are weighted. All variables rescaled to range from zero to one. Number of cases=518. Values coded to range from zero to one.

Figure 28. Women's Civic-Related Job Skills by Expectation

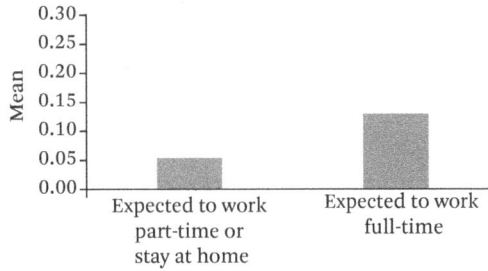

Source: Authors' compilation based on CCES 2014 (Schaffner and Ansolabehere 2015).
Note: Data are weighted. All variables rescaled to range from zero to one. Civic skills is average number of three possible activities individual could report partaking in at workplace over the past six months: serving on committees, given time for special projects, or helping organizing meetings; planning or chairing a meeting; giving a presentation or speech. Number of cases=537.

Figure 29. Women's Career Expectations Versus Later Employment

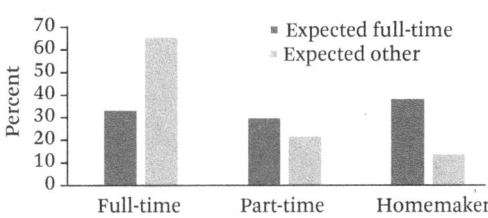

Source: Authors' compilation based on CCES 2014 (Schaffner and Ansolabehere 2015).
Note: Data are weighted. Number of cases: Women=534.

Figure 30. Women's Decisions to Cut Back on Work to Care for Family

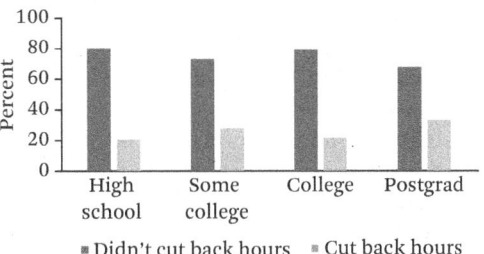

Source: Authors' compilation based on CCES 2014 (Schaffner and Ansolabehere 2015).
Note: Data are weighted. Number of cases=537.

tween women's employment expectations at eighteen and their employment today in these 2014 data (figure 29), it is clear that just under 40 percent of the women who expected to be full time are full time. Furthermore, across the range of education, a sizable proportion of women cut their work hours back to care for their families; this is a long-time standard result (figure 30) (see Pleck 1977). Although a good deal of women's ability to make good on their expectations about their employment varies very little across the dimensions of stratification we examine here, one dimension does seem to condition their ability to follow through on their expectations—their views about women in the workplace. Women who are less

Figure 31. Women's Workforce Participation, Conservative About Gender Roles

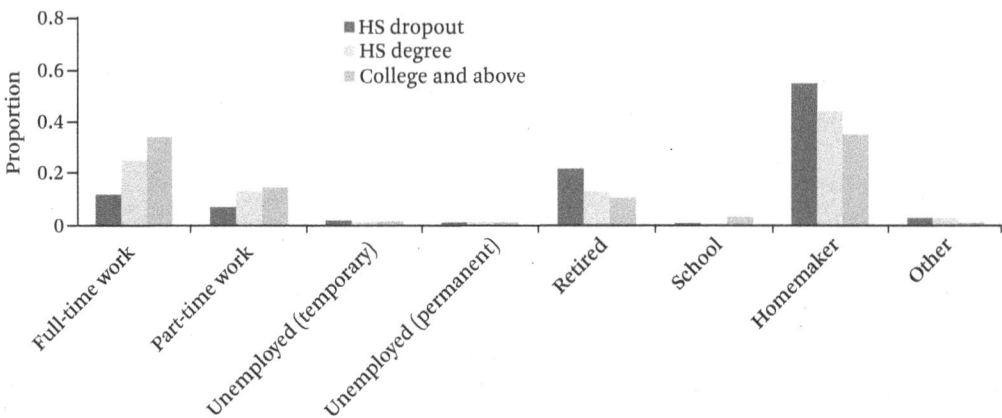

Source: Authors' compilation based on GSS cumulative file (Smith et al. 2015).
Note: Data are weighted. Years 1977 through 2010 combined. Number of cases available in table A22.

Figure 32. Women's Workforce Participation, Ambivalent About Gender Roles

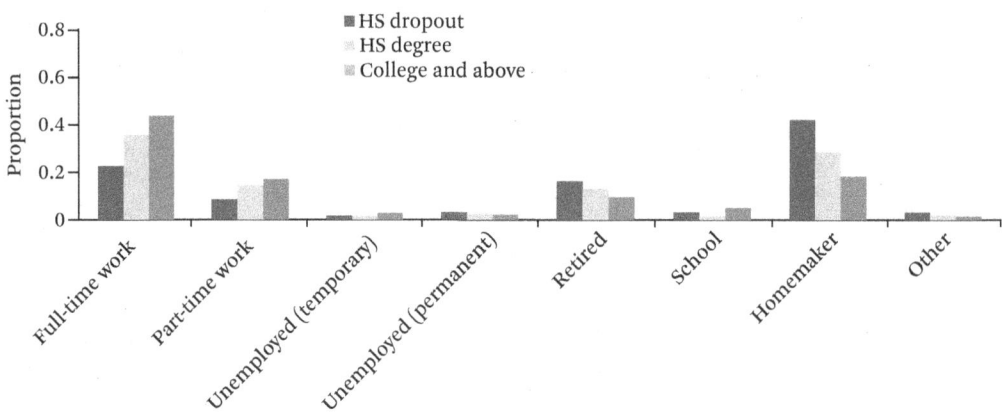

Source: Authors' compilation based on GSS cumulative file (Smith et al. 2015).
Note: Data are weighted. Years 1977 through 2010 combined. Number of cases available in table A22.

conflicted on the issue are notably more likely to work full time (figures 31 through 33) (see also Correll 2004; Farre and Vella 2013).

We suspect that this ambivalence, or this sense that women's workforce participation is problematic for families and children and, in fact, workplaces—a worry that is centrally focused on the sense that children's lives are best when mothers are home—has consequences that reach beyond whether individual women achieve their expectations. This ambivalence also ought to undermine support for policies that might play a role in translating education into jobs—policies that might make it easier for women to keep, hold, and advance in their positions. We focus here on four policies. We ask about the relationship between women's views on women's employment and their support for federally provided childcare, parental leave, equal pay for equal work, and federal efforts to prevent job discrimination against women.

Using our 2014 CCES data, we examine the relationship between beliefs about women's proper place and support for these policies. We measure attitudes toward women by scaling

Figure 33. Women's Workforce Participation, Liberal About Gender Roles

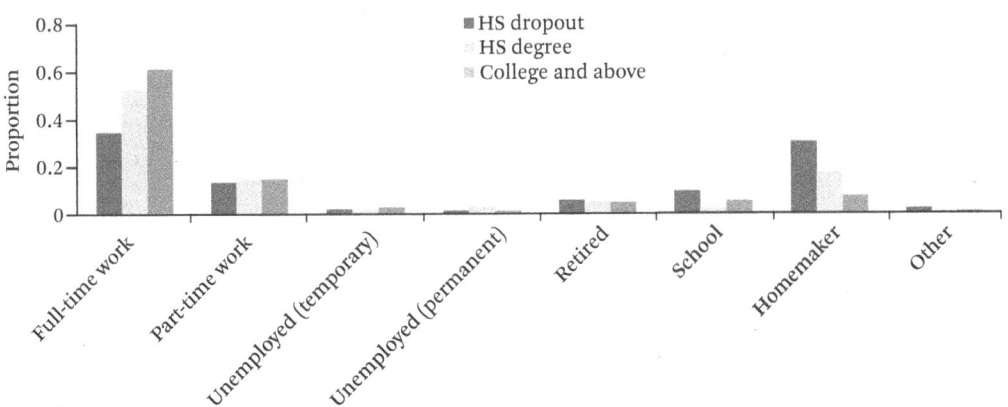

Source: Authors' compilation based on GSS cumulative file (Smith et al. 2015).
Note: Data are weighted. Years 1977 through 2010 combined. Number of cases available in table A22.

together items designed to assess beliefs about women's proper place. Survey respondents were asked the extent to which they agree or disagree with the following three statements:

1. A working mother can establish just as warm and secure a relationship with her children as a mother who does not work.
2. Men should not be expected to spend the same amount of time on household chores as women.
3. I would be equally comfortable having a woman as a boss as I would a man.

We estimate the extent to which support for policies aimed at easing women's path into and presence within the workforce is a function of these attitudes about women's place, controlling for a number of factors including employment status, age, education, marital status, income, conservative church membership (respondent identifies as Catholic, Baptist, or Mormon), solidarity with other women, and party identification. All variables in our models are coded to range from zero to one.

Table 1 provides the results of our ordinary least squares regression estimations, with our policy items regressed on the variables described. With the exception of support for federal spending for childcare (though results are in the expected direction), the results are quite consistent; in each case, more conservative views about women's place significantly decrease support for our workplace-related policies. Furthermore, the associations are powerful, reducing support by approximately 20 percent on the zero to one scale in each case.

In short, these results provide further evidence for the powerful role attitudes about the proper place of women have in terms of depressing what otherwise might be more sweeping consequences of gains in education and jobs. The persistence of these more traditional attitudes undermines support for policies that make it easier for women to enter into and remain in the workforce.

CONCLUSION

Our analyses suggest that women's changing expectations—and especially the ways they translated into more women with college degrees and more women with professional and managerial jobs—mattered a lot for women's political participation. They helped enable higher levels of education and more professional occupations, both of which provide skills that enable political participation. Nevertheless, what is also clear is that attitudes about women's place have put brakes on the translation of these opportunities into participation-relevant resources for women. Our data suggest that some of these brakes come from the tradeoffs women make to care for their fami-

Table 1. Attitudes toward Promoting Women's Workforce Participation

	Support for Childcare Spending	Support for Parental Leave Spending	Support for Equal Pay for Equal Work	Support for Fighting Job Discrimination
Women's roles (conservative)	−0.120	−0.197**	−0.229**	−0.236**
	(0.096)	(0.085)	(0.093)	(0.098)
Observations	408	408	406	409
R^2	0.248	0.223	0.345	0.368

Source: Authors' compilation based on 2014 CCES (Schaffner and Ansolabehere 2015).
Note: Data are weighted. All variables coded to range from zero to one. Model controls for employment status, age, education, marital status, income, membership in a conservative church, gender solidarity, and party identity. Full model specification and results are available in table A23.
Standard errors in parentheses
*** $p < 0.01$; ** $p < 0.05$; * $p < 0.1$

lies, and from ideas about women's place that foster ambivalence when it comes to embracing jobs and careers.

Taken together, these results offer a valuable portrait of the changes in women's participation-relevant skills and resources over the last fifty years. They do a second thing, as well. They offer some evidence in favor of a treatment as opposed to selection view of education as a resource for political action. Despite the large changes in access to education and in relative education levels in the United States for women and for men, education stratifies participation today roughly as it did fifty years ago. Previous literature, literature not focused on the changes in women's lives, has reached conflicting conclusions on whether education's consequences are a product of selection processes. Some have found that education, especially attending college, works as a treatment, boosting political participation (Sondheimer and Green 2010; Card 1993; Acemoğlu and Angrist 2001; Dee 2004; Hillygus 2005). Others, however, argue that education's effects are about selection, that education is a proxy for other attitudes and socialization experiences that more directly affect political participation and engagement (Kam and Palmer 2008; Tenn 2007; Berinsky and Lenz 2010; Jennings and Niemi 1981). Our results offer suggestive evidence for the education-as-treatment side of the argument, and they offer hints about a potential strategy for using these changes in women's lives to investigate this question, yet again.

These data also make clear the value of pursuing the question of attitudinal brakes on women's workforce participation. Scholars have argued that gender is especially essentialized; that gender hierarchy is so structurally and attitudinally embedded that it is not disappearing any time soon (Haslanger 2000). We see in our data some confirmation of this attitudinal embedding; many women endorse more traditional roles for women and express ambivalence about entering and remaining in the workforce, ultimately making them less likely to obtain the skills and interests that promote political engagement.

Our data provide further clues that, for many women, commitment to the workforce is tenuous. We asked women in our 2014 CCES sample whether they had ever considered cutting back on employment, and the results of our open-ended question offer a portrait of women's attitudes about both work and family. Many women at even the highest levels of education expressed a desire to stay at home with their children. Those who remained in the workforce claimed to do so because they felt economic pressure to continue working. One college-educated woman wrote, for instance, "I decided to continue working because I can't afford to stay at home with my son." Another said she "considered it but could not afford to do it." Even many women who did drop out of the workforce couched their explanation in economic terms, as one women explained, "I took nine years off; however, I was able to do so because my husband had an excellent job."

In this way, the women at the top of the education stratum look strikingly like those with the least education. Many of the women who did not graduate high school or received only their high school diploma echoed these sentiments, providing comments such as "I would have considered it if we could have afforded it." And across the education spectrum, many women reported staying at home simply because they believed it was most beneficial to their children. They made comments such as one woman who had attended some college explained, "I did not work after I had my children. I would not have had children if I had to work. My children were my job." One high school graduate said, "When my children were born I stayed at home. My mother always said that if you were going to have kids they deserved at least one full-time parent. She was right, they did." A woman with a postgraduate degree stated, "I quit my job to stay at home with my kids because it was in their best interests." Even a sizable portion of the women who continued to work for financial reasons still emphasized the importance of being at home:

> If I could afford it, I would have (and still would) gone part-time to help juggle my parenting with my career, but we need my full income. Also, I've taken PTO frequently over the years to help my terminally ill parents (now both deceased) and it would have been better to be able to take leave without worrying about money to devote more time there. It's all about the money.

To us, these responses read like the attitudinal residues of ambivalence. They show the significant pull women feel toward the private sphere, into family life as primary caregivers. What stands out, however, is how rarely our respondents seemed to be similarly compelled by their jobs or careers; very few expressed a desire to stay in the workforce for reasons beyond economic necessity. The respondent who said, "I considered being a stay-at-home mom once we had children ... I decided I wanted to continue working because I find joy in doing my job and would miss it" was an outlier in our data.[3]

We see the conflict expressed by many women in our data as another illustration of a brake on women's workforce participation. What our findings suggest, then, is that regardless of women's expectations, their levels of education, and their labor-market participation, attitudes about women's place and a strong desire to assume the role of caretakers—coupled with a lack of enthusiasm for jobs or careers—likely dampen the more sweeping changes in political behavior we might expect to have observed over the past sixty years. Of course, these attitudes may very well reflect a reality about the complications of workforce participation in a world with unequal and limited access to childcare, parental leave, high paying jobs, and opportunities for career advancement.

---

3. Interestingly, few men expressed such sentiments either. Yet the men in our sample also described juggling work with family or needing to care for family far less frequently than the women. These responses suggest that while individuals, regardless of gender, are not, perhaps, overwhelmingly or routinely attached to their jobs, attitudes about the proper role of men and women provide an enduring framework for how individuals talk about their responsibilities.

APPENDIX

Table A1. Weighted Sample Size for "Voted" Variable

	High School Dropout	High School Degree	College
1952	501	254	39
1956	490	327	61
1958	455	329	71
1960	448	311	102
1962	325	234	72
1964	364	277	73
1966	308	272	54
1968	326	265	85
1970	335	324	85
1972	510	463	151
1974	490	543	172
1976	438	545	178
1978	364	511	157
1980	196	322	116
1982	168	288	121
1984	236	438	169
1986	265	451	211
1988	227	360	162
1990	273	418	167
1992	256	437	217
1994	191	326	153
1996	149	271	160
1998	105	256	146
2000	126	310	184
2002	98	266	159
2004	73	169	132
2008	130	349	327
2012	99	369	266

Source: Authors' compilation based on ANES Cumulative Data File 2012.
Note: Data are weighted.

Table A2. Weighted Sample Size by Category for "Contribute" Variable

	High School Dropout	High School Degree	College
1952	499	253	39
1956	490	327	61
1960	448	308	102
1962	325	231	71
1964	362	275	73
1966	301	270	54
1968	310	249	80
1972	487	443	141
1974	493	544	171
1976	436	540	178
1978	363	510	156
1980	195	322	116
1982	167	288	121
1984	224	429	164
1986	263	448	208
1988	228	360	161
1990	270	418	167
1992	255	437	218
1994	191	323	153
1996	149	271	160
1998	105	256	146
2000	126	312	184
2002	98	266	160
2004	73	169	132
2008	130	349	327
2012	100	371	266

Source: Authors' compilation based on ANES Cumulative Data File 2012.
Note: Data are weighted.

Table A3. Weighted Sample Size by Category for "Electoral Interest" Variable

	High School Dropout	High School Degree	College
1952	554	280	42
1956	489	325	61
1958	456	329	72
1960	477	327	108
1962	326	234	72
1964	387	295	79
1966	298	271	54
1968	360	307	88
1970	340	328	85
1972	602	558	168
1976	534	621	206
1978	362	514	156
1980	231	376	115
1982	171	290	121
1984	282	493	176
1986	264	452	209
1988	272	427	178
1990	273	417	167
1992	274	474	243
1994	189	320	149
1996	178	311	172
1998	105	258	146
2000	139	369	208
2002	111	298	179
2004	80	203	152
2008	75	197	188
2012	109	395	280

Source: Authors' compilation based on ANES Cumulative Data File 2012.
Note: Data are weighted.

Table A4. Weighted Sample Size by Category for "Index: Attending Political Events, Working for a Candidate, or Wearing a Button" Variable

	High School Dropout	High School Degree	College
1952	499	253	39
1956			
1960	490	327	61
1964			
1966	448	311	102
1968	325	231	71
1970	363	276	73
1972			
1974	320	252	82
1976	340	328	85
1978	487	443	141
1980	493	544	172
1982	438	542	178
1984	363	510	156
1988	197	322	116
1990	167	288	121
1992	224	429	164
1994	265	452	211
1996	228	360	162
1998	271	418	167
2000	256	437	218
2002	191	325	153
2004	149	271	160
2008	105	258	146
2012	126	312	184

Source: Authors' compilation based on ANES Cumulative Data File 2012.
Note: Data are weighted.

Table A5. Weighted Sample Size by Category for "Voted" Variable by Education Quartiles

	1	2	3	4
1952	332	169	165	207
1956				
1958	288	202	327	153
1960	272	183	329	166
1962	261	384	114	231
1964	186	320	53	150
1966	364	194	83	163
1968	183	302	95	135
1970	326	167	204	85
1972	335	212	112	188
1974	510	312	334	151
1976	490	334	456	172
1978	438	340	453	178
1980	364	511	242	157
1982	196	322	158	116
1984	350	106	196	121
1986	484	190	267	169
1988	716		282	211
1990	587		241	162
1992	691		207	167
1994	693		279	217
1996	517	248	106	46
1998	421	241	107	54
2000	361	181	90	55
2002	436	254	127	58
2004	364	212	114	45
2008	242	165	75	57
2012	480	352		327

Source: Authors' compilation based on ANES Cumulative Data File 2012.
Note: Data are weighted.

Table A6. Weighted Sample Size by Category for "Contribute" Variable by Education Quartiles

	1	2	3	4
1952	330	169	165	206
1956				
1960	288	202	327	153
1962				
1964	261	381	114	231
1966	185	320	51	149
1968	362	193	82	163
1972	179	297	95	134
1974	310	158	196	80
1976				
1978	487	299	324	141
1980	493	334	453	171
1982	436	336	451	178
1984	363	510	242	156
1986	195	322	158	116
1988	349	106	196	121
1990	466	187	259	164
1992	711		282	208
1994	588		240	161
1996	688		208	167
1998	692		279	218
2000	514	246	106	46
2002	421	241	107	54
2004	361	181	90	55
2008	438	254	127	58
2012	365	212	114	46

Source: Authors' compilation based on ANES Cumulative Data File 2012.
Note: Data are weighted.

Table A7. Weighted Sample Size by Category for "Electoral Interest" Variable by Education Quartiles

	1	2	3	4
1952	366	188	177	228
1956				
1958	287	202	325	152
1960	273	183	329	167
1962	279	413	112	246
1964	186	321	53	150
1966	387	206	89	179
1968	179	296	94	132
1970	360	199	219	88
1972	340	213	115	188
1976	602	382	381	168
1978				
1980	534	391	516	206
1982	362	514	243	156
1984	231	376	168	115
1986	354	107	196	121
1988	562	213	304	176
1990	716		282	209
1992	699		267	178
1994	690		207	167
1996	748		305	243
1998	509	247	103	46
2000	489	270	115	56
2002	363	181	90	55
2004	508	295	145	63
2008	409	244	125	54
2012	282	189	91	61

Source: Authors' compilation based on ANES Cumulative Data File 2012.
Note: Data are weighted.

Table A8. Weighted Sample Size by Category for "Index: Attending Political Events, Working for a Candidate, or Wearing a Button" Variable by Education Quartiles

	1	2	3	4
1952	330	169	165	206
1956				
1960	288	202	327	153
1964	0	0	0	0
1966	261	384	114	231
1968	185	320	51	149
1970	363	194	82	163
1972				
1974	320	159	198	82
1976	340	213	115	188
1978	487	299	324	141
1980	493	334	457	172
1982	438	337	453	178
1984	363	510	242	156
1988	197	322	158	116
1990	349	106	196	121
1992	466	187	260	164
1994	717		282	211
1996	588		241	162
1998	689		208	167
2000	693		279	218
2002	516	246	106	46
2004	421	241	107	54
2008	363	181	90	55
2012	438	254	127	58

Source: Authors' compilation based on ANES Cumulative Data File 2012.
Note: Data are weighted.

Table A9. Weighted Sample Size by Category for "Voted" Variable

	Professional and Managerial	Clerical and Sales	Homemaker
1952	62	102	568
1956	71	110	627
1958	71	118	598
1960	99	160	542
1962	83	109	444
1964	92	126	394
1966	107	146	418
1968	158	228	609
1970	215	277	566
1972	203	300	531
1974	231	258	437
1976	149	188	216
1978	140	194	221
1980	233	311	254
1982	272	328	265
1984	230	254	202
1986	223	267	229
1988	281	319	233
1990	194	268	173
1992	201	222	123
1994	170	177	148
1996	261	248	134
1998	145	175	88
2000	62	102	568
2002	71	110	627
2004	71	118	598
2008	99	160	542
2012	83	109	444

Source: Authors' compilation based on ANES Cumulative Data File 2012.
Note: Data are weighted.

Table A10. Weighted Sample Size by Category for "Contribute" Variable

	Professional and Managerial	Clerical and Sales	Homemaker
1952	62	101	568
1956	71	110	627
1960			
1962	99	160	541
1964	83	108	442
1966	86	124	369
1968			
1972	153	216	583
1974	215	276	566
1976	202	299	529
1978	231	257	436
1980	149	188	215
1982	140	193	221
1984	225	305	247
1986	270	325	264
1988	230	253	202
1990	224	267	228
1992	281	320	232
1994	195	266	171
1996	201	222	123
1998	170	177	148
2000	261	248	134
2002	145	175	88
2004	62	101	568
2008	71	110	627
2012			

Source: Authors' compilation based on ANES Cumulative Data File 2012.
Note: Data are weighted.

Table A11. Weighted Sample Size by Category for "Electoral Interest" Variable

	Professional and Managerial	Clerical and Sales	Homemaker
1952	72	109	626
1956	71	110	625
1958	70	118	598
1960	103	171	581
1962	89	118	475
1964	95	142	441
1966	107	147	419
1968	179	277	715
1970			
1972	248	348	608
1976	232	258	435
1978	160	215	247
1980	140	194	223
1982	251	354	287
1984	270	328	265
1986	251	298	231
1988	223	267	229
1990	314	349	250
1992	191	262	172
1994	221	252	138
1996	170	179	148
1998	299	291	146
2000	174	199	95
2002	72	109	626
2004	71	110	625
2008	70	118	598
2012	103	171	581

Source: Authors' compilation based on ANES Cumulative Data File 2012.
Note: Data are weighted.

Table A12. Weighted Sample Size by Category for "Index: Attending Political Events, Working for a Candidate, or Wearing a Button" Variable

	Professional and Managerial	Clerical and Sales	Homemaker
1952	62	101	568
1956	71	110	627
1960			
1964	99	160	542
1966	83	108	443
1968	87	124	381
1970	107	147	419
1972	153	216	583
1974	215	278	566
1976	203	299	529
1978	231	257	436
1980	149	188	216
1982	140	193	221
1984	225	306	247
1988	272	328	266
1990	230	254	202
1992	224	267	228
1994	281	320	233
1996	195	266	172
1998	201	222	123
2000	170	179	148
2002	261	248	134
2004	145	175	88
2008	62	101	568
2012	71	110	627

Source: Authors' compilation based on ANES Cumulative Data File 2012.
Note: Data are weighted.

Table A13. The Interactive Effect of Year with Education and Professional Occupation Among Women

Age	0.647***	1986	−0.020	1978*education	−0.112
	(0.023)		(0.039)		(0.088)
Education	0.429***	1988	0.055	1980*education	0.004
	(0.066)		(0.041)		(0.094)
Married	0.043***	1990	−0.122***	1982*education	−0.088
	(0.009)		(0.038)		(0.098)
Income	0.208***	1992	0.120***	1984*education	0.032
	(0.016)		(0.038)		(0.087)
Church attendance	0.153***	1994	−0.122***	1986*education	−0.159*
	(0.010)		(0.044)		(0.087)
Employed	0.039***	1996	0.060	1988*education	0.003
	(0.008)		(0.048)		(0.088)
Professional occupation	0.036	1998	−0.061	1990*education	−0.056
	(0.053)		(0.049)		(0.089)
1972	0.102***	2000	0.073	1992*education	0.033
	(0.035)		(0.053)		(0.079)
1974	−0.074*	2004	0.155**	1994*education	0.096
	(0.042)		(0.064)		(0.095)
1976	0.058	2008	0.210***	1996*education	0.046
	(0.040)		(0.048)		(0.095)
1978	−0.003	2012	0.196***	1998*education	−0.143
	(0.039)		(0.052)		(0.100)
1980	0.084*	1972*education	0.093	2000*education	−0.003
	(0.045)		(0.080)		(0.101)
1982	0.017	1974*education	−0.016	2004*education	−0.090
	(0.047)		(0.099)		(0.111)
1984	0.109***	1976*education	0.074	2008*education	−0.121
	(0.041)		(0.088)		(0.089)
Observations	43,284				
R^2	0.203				

Source: Authors' compilation based on ANES Cumulative Data File 2012.
Note: Data are weighted. Standard errors in parentheses.
*** $p < 0.01$, ** $p < 0.05$, * $p < 0.1$

2012*education	−0.187**	1998*professional occupation	−0.002
	(0.091)		(0.072)
1972*professional occupation	−0.097	2000*professional occupation	−0.056
	(0.065)		(0.068)
1974*professional occupation	−0.024	2004*professional occupation	0.022
	(0.081)		(0.067)
1976*professional occupation	−0.044	Constant	−0.094***
	(0.067)		(0.030)
1978*professional occupation	−0.019		
	(0.067)		
1980*professional occupation	−0.021		
	(0.068)		
1982*professional occupation	−0.039		
	(0.074)		
1984*professional occupation	−0.052		
	(0.062)		
1986*professional occupation	0.022		
	(0.065)		
1988*professional occupation	0.013		
	(0.064)		
1990*professional occupation	−0.023		
	(0.068)		
1992*professional occupation	−0.055		
	(0.061)		
1994*professional occupation	−0.023		
	(0.070)		
1996*professional occupation	−0.002		
	(0.064)		

Table A14. Weighted Sample Size by Gender for Attitudes About Working Moms

	Men	Women
1977	701	804
1985	713	804
1986	640	819
1988	451	523
1989	457	546
1990	422	515
1991	431	569
1993	489	580
1994	837	1100
1996	1136	1279
1998	831	1025
2000	812	1034
2002	404	491
2004	419	473
2006	889	1085
2008	639	691
2010	624	804
2012	610	694

Source: Authors' compilation based on GSS cumulative file (Smith et al. 2015).
Note: Data are weighted.

Table A16. Weighted Sample Size by Gender for Belief That Kids Suffer if Mother Works

	Men	Women
1977	696	800
1985	704	793
1986	635	810
1988	442	520
1989	449	541
1990	411	502
1991	426	564
1993	483	568
1994	826	1100
1996	1103	1257
1998	816	1012
2000	794	1014
2002	405	490
2004	414	472
2006	884	1085
2008	631	685
2010	617	797
2012	605	691

Source: Authors' compilation based on GSS cumulative file (Smith et al. 2015).
Note: Data are weighted.

Table A15. Weighted Sample Size by Gender for Belief That Wife Should Help Man's Career

	Men	Women
1977	677	793
1985	689	778
1986	625	809
1988	448	517
1989	438	536
1990	414	502
1991	426	563
1993	479	571
1994	813	1079
1996	1111	1255
1998	806	1015

Source: Authors' compilation based on GSS cumulative file (Smith et al. 2015).
Note: Data are weighted.

Table A17. Weighted Sample Size by Gender for Belief That Man Should Work, Woman Should Stay Home

	Men	Women
1977	698	805
1985	703	799
1986	632	811
1988	440	521
1989	450	537
1990	409	506
1991	426	559
1993	487	572
1994	817	1090
1996	1111	1261
1998	814	1019
2000	799	1006
2002	407	485
2004	416	469
2006	887	1083
2008	636	680
2010	623	798
2012	606	692

Source: Authors' compilation based on GSS cumulative file (Smith et al. 2015).
Note: Data are weighted.

Table A18. Weighted Sample Size by Category for Women's Attitudes About Working Moms, by Educational Attainment

	High School Dropout	High School Degree	College
1977	284	313	208
1985	207	294	303
1986	223	315	281
1988	140	166	217
1989	137	198	210
1990	108	181	227
1991	129	184	255
1993	104	192	284
1994	182	364	554
1996	217	392	669
1998	157	320	548
2000	189	300	545
2002	67	167	257
2004	54	135	285
2006	154	282	649
2008	103	187	401
2010	125	235	444
2012	100	192	403

Source: Authors' compilation based on GSS cumulative file (Smith et al. 2015).
Note: Data are weighted. Women only.

Table A19. Weighted Sample Size by Category for Women's Attitudes About Kids Suffer if Mother Works by Educational Attainment

	High School Dropout	High School Degree	College
1977	284	312	205
1985	201	294	298
1986	217	315	278
1988	139	167	214
1989	138	194	209
1990	105	171	226
1991	128	185	251
1993	99	190	279
1994	185	363	552
1996	208	386	664
1998	153	316	543
2000	183	289	541
2002	66	166	257
2004	54	134	284
2006	151	284	650
2008	103	186	395
2010	125	234	439
2012	98	193	400

Source: Authors' compilation based on GSS cumulative file (Smith et al. 2015).
Note: Data are weighted. Women only.

Table A21. Weighted Sample Size by Category for Women's Attitudes About Better for Man to Work by Educational Attainment

	High School Dropout	High School Degree	College
1977	286	312	207
1985	204	294	301
1986	221	311	279
1988	138	167	216
1989	133	193	211
1990	105	175	226
1991	128	182	249
1993	101	190	280
1994	182	357	551
1996	213	386	662
1998	156	323	541
2000	179	292	536
2002	65	165	255
2004	54	133	283
2006	153	279	652
2008	102	187	391
2010	122	235	441
2012	99	191	401

Source: Authors' compilation based on GSS cumulative file (Smith et al. 2015).
Note: Data are weighted. Women only.

Table A20. Weighted Sample Size by Category for Women's Attitudes About Wife Should Help Husband's Career by Educational Attainment

	High School Dropout	High School Degree	College
1977	278	307	208
1985	196	284	297
1986	219	312	278
1988	139	164	214
1989	136	191	209
1990	104	172	226
1991	130	181	252
1993	101	192	278
1994	178	352	550
1996	214	383	658
1998	153	317	544

Source: Authors' compilation based on GSS cumulative file (Smith et al. 2015).
Note: Data are weighted. Women only.

Table A22. Weighted Sample Size by Education for Women's Workforce Participation Stratified by Education and Attitudes About Gender Roles

	Conservative About Gender Roles	Ambivalent About Gender Roles	Liberal About Gender Roles
High school dropout	418	1765	425
High school degree	393	2737	1124
College and above	334	3543	2499

Source: Authors' compilation based on GSS cumulative file (Smith et al. 2015).
Note: Data are weighted. Women only.

Table A23. Attitudes Toward Promoting Women's Workforce Participation

	Support for Childcare Spending	Support for Parental Leave Spending	Support for Equal Pay for Equal Work	Support for Fighting Job Discrimination
Women's roles (conservative)	−0.120	−0.197**	−0.229**	−0.236**
	(0.096)	(0.085)	(0.093)	(0.098)
Employment	0.028	0.022	0.034	0.017
	(0.038)	(0.038)	(0.037)	(0.038)
Age	0.030	−0.132	0.166***	0.087
	(0.079)	(0.082)	(0.064)	(0.073)
Education	0.020	0.077	−0.180***	−0.199***
	(0.067)	(0.067)	(0.062)	(0.064)
Married	−0.051	−0.002	−0.038	−0.062
	(0.036)	(0.035)	(0.039)	(0.039)
Income	−0.101	−0.035	−0.089	−0.034
	(0.079)	(0.078)	(0.081)	(0.081)
Conservative church member	0.048	0.038	0.031	0.047
	(0.038)	(0.040)	(0.037)	(0.038)
Gender solidarity	0.225***	0.199***	0.212***	0.242***
	(0.064)	(0.062)	(0.056)	(0.059)
Party ID (Republican)	−0.255***	−0.198***	−0.388***	−0.398***
	(0.048)	(0.051)	(0.058)	(0.056)
Constant	0.675***	0.692***	0.885***	0.849***
	(0.072)	(0.067)	(0.067)	(0.075)
Observations	408	408	406	409
R^2	0.248	0.223	0.345	0.368

Source: Authors' compilation based on 2014 CCES (Schaffner and Ansolabehere 2015).
Note: Data are weighted. All variables coded to range from zero to one.
Standard errors in parentheses.
*** $p < 0.01$; ** $p < 0.05$; * $p < 0.1$

REFERENCES

Acemoğlu, Daron, and Joshua Angrist. 2001. "How Large Are Human-Capital Externalities? Evidence from Compulsory-Schooling Laws." *NBER Macroeconomics Annual 2000* 15 (January): 9–74.

American National Election Studies (ANES). Time Series Cumulative Data File [dataset]. 2012. Stanford University and the University of Michigan [producers and distributors]. Accessed April 9, 2016. http://www.electionstudies.org/study pages/anes_timeseries_cdf/anes_timeseries_cdf.htm.

Bailey, Martha J. 2010. "'Momma's Got The Pill': How Anthony Comstock and Griswold v. Connecticut Shaped US Childbearing." *American Economic Review* 100(1): 98–129. doi:10.1257/aer.100.1.98.

Bailey, Martha J., Melanie Guldi, and Brad J. Hershbein. 2014. "Is There a Case for a 'Second Demographic Transition?' Three Distinctive Features of the Post-1960 US Fertility Decline." In *Human Capital in History: The American Record*, edited by Leah Platt Boustan, Carola Frydman, and Robert A. Margo. Chicago: University of Chicago Press.

Belkin, Lisa. 2003. "The Opt-Out Revolution." *New York Times Magazine*, October 26. doi:10.1002/mde.1290. Accessed April 9, 2016. http://www.nytimes.com/2003/10/26/magazine/26WOMEN.html?pagewanted=all.

Berinsky, Adam J., and Gabriel S. Lenz. 2010. "Education and Political Participation: Exploring the Causal Link." *Political Behavior* 33(3)(August 19): 357–73. doi:10.1007/s11109-010-9134-9.

Bertrand, Marianne. 2011. "New Perspectives on Gender." In *Handbook of Labor Economics*, vol. 4b, edited by David Card and Orley Ashenfelter. San Diego: Elsevier Science. doi:10.1016/S0169-7218(11)02415-4.

Blau, Francine D., and Lawrence M. Kahn. 2005. "Changes in the Labor Supply Behavior of Married Women: 1980–2000." *NBER* working paper no. 11230. Cambridge, Mass.: National Bureau of Economic Research.

Card, David. 1993. "Using Geographic Variation in College Proximity to Estimate the Return to Schooling." *NBER* working paper no. 4483. Cambridge, Mass.: National Bureau of Economic Research.

Correll, Shelley J. 2004. "Constraints into Preferences: Gender, Status, and Emerging Career Aspirations." *American Sociological Review* 69(1): 93–113.

Dee, Thomas S. 2004. "Are There Civic Returns to Education?" *Journal of Public Economics* 88(9-10): 1697–720.

Dobbin, Frank. 2009. *Inventing Equal Opportunity*. Princeton, N.J.: Princeton University Press.

Farre, Lidia, and Francis Vella. 2013. "The Intergenerational Transmission of Gender Role Attitudes and Its Implications for Female Labour Force Participation." *Economica* 80(318): 219–47.

Fortin, Nicole M. 2015. "Gender Role Attitudes and Women's Labor Market Participation: Opting-Out, AIDS, and the Persistent Appeal of Housewifery." *Annals of Economics and Statistics* 117/118: 379–401.

Gerson, Kathleen. 2011. *The Unfinished Revolution: Coming of Age in a New Era of Gender, Work, and Family*. New York: Oxford University Press.

Goffman, Erving. 1977. "The Arrangement Between the Sexes." *Theory and Society* 4(3): 301–31.

Goldin, Claudia. 2004. "The Long Road to the Fast Track: Career and Family." *Annals of the American Academy of Political and Social Science* 596(1): 20–35. doi:10.1177/0002716204267959.

———. 2006. "The Quiet Revolution That Transformed Women's Employment, Education, and Family." *NBER* working paper no. 11953. Cambridge, Mass.: National Bureau of Economic Research.

Goldin, Claudia, and Lawrence F. Katz. 2000. "Career and Marriage in the Age of the Pill." *The American Economic Review* 90(2): 461–65.

———. 2002. "The Power of the Pill: Oral Contraceptives and Women's Career and Marriage Decisions." *Journal of Political Economy* 110(4): 730–70. doi:10.1086/340778.

Haslanger, Sally. 2000. "Gender and Race: (What) Are They? (What) Do We Want Them To Be?" *Nous* 34(1): 31–55.

Hillygus, D. Sunshine. 2005. "The Missing Link: Exploring the Relationship Between Higher Education and Political Engagement." *Political Behavior* 27(1): 25–47. doi:10.1007/s11109-005-3075-8.

Jennings, M. Kent, and Richard G. Niemi. 1981. *Generations and Politics: A Panel Study of Young Adults and Their Parents*. Princeton, N.J.: Princeton University Press.

Kam, Cindy D., and Carl L. Palmer. 2008. "Reconsidering the Effects of Education on Political Participation." *Journal of Politics* 70(3): 612–31. doi:10.1017/S0022381608080651.

McLanahan, Sara. 2004. "Diverging Destinies: How Children Are Faring Under the Second Demographic Transition." *Demography* 41(4): 607–27. doi:10.1353/dem.2004.0033.

Pleck, Joseph H. 1977. "The Work-Family Role System." *Social Problems* 24(4): 417–27. doi:10.1525/sp.1977.24.4.03a00040.

Rosenstone, Steven J., and John M. Hansen. 1993. *Mobilization, Participation, and Democracy in America*. New York: Macmillan.

Schaffner, Brian, and Stephen Ansolabehere. 2015. CCES Common Content, 2014. Harvard Dataverse, V2. doi:10.7910/DVN/XFXJVY.

Schlozman, Kay Lehman, Sidney Verba, and Henry E. Brady. 2013. *The Unheavenly Chorus: Unequal Political Voice and the Broken Promise of American Democracy*. Princeton, N.J.: Princeton University Press.

Smith, Aaron. 2013. "Civic Engagement in the Digital Age." Washington, D.C.: Pew Research Center. Accessed March 31, 2016. http://www.pewinternet.org/2013/04/25/civic-engagement-in-the-digital-age-2/.

Smith, Aaron, Kay Lehman Schlozman, Sidney Verba, and Henry Brady. 2009. "The Internet and Civic Engagement." Washington, D.C.: Pew Research Center. Accessed March 31, 2016. http://www.pewinternet.org/2009/09/01/the-internet-and-civic-engagement/.

Smith, Tom W., Peter Marsden, Michael Hout, and Jibum Kim. 2015. General Social Surveys, 1972-2014. Chicago: NORC at the University of Chicago; Storrs, Conn.: The Roper Center for Public Opinion Research, University of Connecticut.

Sondheimer, Rachel M., and Donald P. Green. 2010. "Using Experiments to Estimate the Effects of Education on Voter Turnout." *American Journal of Political Science* 54(1): 174–89.

Spence, Janet T., and Robert Helmreich. 1972. "The Attitudes Toward Women Scale: An Objective Instrument to Measure Attitudes Toward the Rights and Roles of Women in Contemporary Society." *JSAS Catalog of Selected Documents in Psychology* 2(66).

Stevenson, Betsey, and Justin Wolfers. 2009. "The Paradox of Declining Female Happiness." *NBER* working paper no. 14969. Cambridge, Mass.: National Bureau of Economic Research.

Stone, Pamela. 2007. *Opting Out?: Why Women Really Quit Careers and Head Home*. Berkeley: University of California Press.

Tenn, Steven. 2007. "The Effect of Education on Voter Turnout." *Political Analysis* 15(4)(April 2): 446–64. doi:10.1093/pan/mpm012.

Thornton, Arland, Duane F. Alwin, and Donald Camburn. 1983. "Causes and Consequences of Sex-Role Attitudes and Attitude Change." *American Sociological Review* 48(2): 211–27.

U.S. Census Bureau. 2011. "More Working Women Than Men Have College Degrees, Census Bureau Reports." News Release CB11-72. Washington: U.S. Department of Commerce. Accessed April 0, 2016. https://www.census.gov/newsroom/releases/archives/education/cb11-72.html.

———. 2014. "Annual Social and Economic Supplement of the Current Population Survey." Washington: U.S. Department of Commerce. Accessed April 9, 2016. https://www.census.gov/did/www/saipe/data/model/info/cpsasec.html.

Verba, Sidney, Kay Lehman Schlozman, and Henry E. Brady. 1995. *Voice and Equality: Civic Voluntarism in American Politics*. Cambridge, Mass.: Harvard University Press.

Verba, Sidney, Kay Lehman Schlozman, Henry E. Brady, and Norman Nie. 1995. American Citizen Participation Study, 1990. ICPSR06635-v1. Ann Arbor, Mich.: Inter-university Consortium for Political and Social Research. doi:10.3886/ICPSR06635.v1.